A textbook of economic theory

By the same authors:

The essentials of economics

A textbook of economic theory

Fourth edition

Alfred W. Stonier
Formerly Professor of Economic Theory,
Makerere University College,
Kampala, Uganda.

Douglas C. Hague
Professor of Managerial Economics,
Manchester Business School,
University of Manchester.

Longman

Longman Group Limited
London

*Associated companies, branches and representatives
throughout the world*

© Alfred W. Stonier and Douglas C. Hague 1964, 1972

First published 1953

Fourth edition 1972

ISBN 0582 44854 9 cased
       44855 7 paper

Printed photolitho in Great Britain by
Ebenezer Baylis and Son Limited
The Trinity Press, Worcester, and London

Acknowledgements

The authors have pleasure in thanking Messrs. Macmillan & Co. Ltd. for giving permission to quote from Alfred Marshall's *Principles of Economics;* Messrs. Routledge and Kegan Paul for quotations from P. H. Wicksteed's *Commonsense of Political Economy;* Professor J. R. Hicks for permission to reproduce the proof of the 'Adding-up Problem' from his *Theory of Wages;* and the Editorial Board of *Economica* who gave permission to summarise Professor Oscar Lange's article 'The Rate of Interest and the Optimum Propensity to Consume'. We also thank Professor Hicks for permission to quote the final paragraph of his article 'Thoughts on the Theory of Capital— the Corfu Conference'. We thank Messrs. George Allen & Unwin for permission to quote from *Capitalism, Socialism and Democracy* by J. A. Schumpeter.

Contents

Preface to the fourth edition

This book is designed for students with no previous knowledge of economic theory who wish to study the elements of the subject systematically. It is hoped that some parts of the book will also be useful to more-advanced students. The book provides a general introduction to economic theory, but does not deal with the special problems of international trade, public finance and welfare economics.

The first two editions did not cover the theory of economic growth. In the third edition, we attempted to provide a comprehensive discussion of the theory of economic growth which by that time (1963) had reached a state where a body of doctrine was emerging. We did our best to summarise that part of growth theory on which there then appeared to be agreement, and hoped that the third edition would leave readers in a position to understand and to reach their own conclusions about current controversies in growth theory.

The fourth edition makes major changes. While the book is still aimed at anyone wishing to obtain a thorough grounding in economic theory, it has been substantially re-written. In Part One, Chapter 4 now provides an introduction to Revealed Preference. We hope that an extended discussion of Marshallian economics of the firm and industry in Chapter 7 is now more faithful to Marshall's original treatment. The discussion of costs in Chapter 5 has been expanded, as has the discussion of oligopoly in Chapter 9. An introduction to discounted cash flow analysis has been added to Chapter 14, and a summary of general-equilibrium analysis, which is in the European rather than the Anglo-Saxon tradition, has been added to Chapter 16. The remainder of Part One has been brought up to date.

Part Two, on Macro-Economic Theory, has been so radically re-written as to be almost new. While continuing to give an introduction to Keynesian macro-economics, Part Two also covers the main changes that later writers have made to the original Keynesian model.

There have also been considerable changes in Part Three. While the broad outline of our introduction to the theory of economic growth remains the same, we have brought Part Three up to date. As in the third edition, we have tried to summarise those parts of the theory of economic growth which now appear to be sufficiently widely accepted to have become received doctrine.

May 1972   ALFRED W. STONIER

DOUGLAS C. HAGUE

Introduction

Economics can be divided into three parts. These are descriptive economics, economic theory and applied economics. In descriptive economics one collects together all the relevant facts about particular topics; for example, the agricultural system of Tanzania, or the British textile industry. Economic theory, or economic analysis, gives a simplified explanation of the way in which an economic system works and the important features of such a system. Applied economics takes the framework of analysis provided by economic theory. It tries either to use this analysis to explain the causes and significance of events reported by descriptive economists; or it tries to 'test' economic theory, discovering whether particular theories appear to be supported by statistical and other evidence about the real world.

This book is about economic theory and gives an outline of the way in which economic systems operate. Without such theories to test or apply, applied economists could not work. In introducing our readers to economic theory, we shall be forced to discuss our subject in abstract and over-simplified terms. The real world is very complex, and to create a theory of economics which tried to take account of all, or even most, of that complexity would be beyond the capacity of any human brain. It would not increase our understanding, but would confuse us. We shall therefore confine ourselves to considering only the most important features of modern economies. While inevitably abstract and a little unreal, such a theory has the virtue of being simple and easily intelligible.

In order to construct a theory of economics one has to undertake two tasks. First, one must make assumptions about conditions in the economy one wishes to analyse. These assumptions, or hypotheses, will be of a broad and general kind. They will be about such things as the way human beings act, their physical environment and their social and economic institutions. Second, one must draw inferences or deductions from such assumptions.

This is how economic theories are constructed. It will help readers if, even at this early stage, we consider these assumptions, and the way economic theorists derive conclusions from them, in greater detail.

We begin by considering the three broad categories of assumptions, which we have just mentioned. First there are assumptions about the behaviour of individual human beings. Economists are most usually concerned with people in two capacities, as consumers and as businessmen running their own firms—or *entrepreneurs* as economists often call them. When economists discuss the actions of consumers they assume that consumers behave 'rationally'. For example, they assume that when a consumer goes into a shop and asks for a newspaper, he does not want a box of chocolates. Economists also assume that consumers tastes remain fairly constant and that people do not, for instance, frequently change from being meat eaters to being vegetarians and back again. Economists also assume that consumers always try to get the greatest possible value for their money and that they balance the satisfactions they derive from spending money in one way against the satisfactions they would derive if they were to spend the same money in a different way.

Similarly, when economic theorists consider the actions of businessmen, they assume that the main aim of every entrepreneur is to make as much money as possible. The assumption that consumers seek the greatest satisfaction from spending their money and that entrepreneurs seek maximum money profits, is often referred to as the assumption of 'economic rationality'. So far as consumers are concerned it seems a very reasonable assumption. In the case of businessmen it may sound a little less plausible. Nevertheless, even there the assumption of economic rationality is probably the most useful one to make. It would certainly be unreasonable to suppose that all businessmen try to *lose* as much money as possible; so we assume that businessmen go into business to make money. It may be objected that what businessmen are really trying to do is something more complicated than simply seeking maximum profits. But to introduce a more realistic assumption would make economic theory very difficult, while no-one is at all certain what the best alternative assumption would be.

The big attraction of the assumption that entrepreneurs seek maximum profits is that it enables us to construct a fairly simple theory of the firm and the industry. It would, of course, be perfectly possible to construct a theory on any other conceivable hypothesis. One could, if one thought fit, construct a theory of business behaviour on the assumption that every businessman tries to make profits equal to the square root of his wife's age, multiplied by £1 000, £10 000, or, indeed, £1 000 000, as appropriate. Such a theory would be extremely intricate both to construct and to use. Since it would also be unrealistic, it seems much more sensible to begin by basing the theory of both consumers' and producers' behaviour on a simple and yet plausible hypothesis. The assumption that both seek the greatest possible benefit for themselves seems the best starting point, though there will be occasions when we shall want to relax it.

The second broad group of assumptions underlying economic theory is about the physical structure of the world. These assumptions are about geography, biology and climate. Such assumptions are usually implicit rather than explicit, but an attempt is made to ensure that economic theory asks nothing which is physically impossible. For example, when economic theorists discuss agricultural problems they acknowledge that harvest time is determined by nature. The economist has to accept this as a fact. Again, no reputable economist would put forward a theory based on the assumption that bananas and grapes grow in profusion in Scotland. Similarly, economic analysis accepts the fact that industrial workers need some rest each day and that technical factors prevent industrial output from being unlimited in amount.

This leads to the basic assumption which economic analysis makes about the physical world. It is assumed that the fundamental feature of the economic world, the feature which gives rise to economic problems at all, is that goods are *scarce*. Very few things in the world, with the exception of air, water and (in some countries) sunshine, are available in unlimited amounts. It is because of scarcity that goods have to be shared out among individuals. If scarcity did not exist, there would be no economic system and no economics.

Dealing with economic problems—with the problems of scarcity— is the function of the price system. In any country using a price system, individuals in that country are provided with money incomes, whether in exchange for working or owning property, in the form of pensions after retirement, or in some other way. Everyone is then free to spend the money he has in whatever way he wishes at current prices. The general level of prices has to be the one required to ensure that neither gluts nor shortages develop. Money is the rationing device by which goods and services are rationed out between members of the community. Individual prices show which goods are more plentiful (and cheaper) or scarcer (and more expensive). They divert spending away from expensive goods, using a lot of resources to ones using fewer resources.

Of course, at some times in all economies, for example during wars, shortages of some or all goods and services develop. It may then be necessary to supplement money as a rationing device either by allowing queues and shortages to grow or by introducing ration tickets which have to be given up (as well as money) when the scarcer goods are bought. Money can be looked on as a 'generalised' ration ticket. It allows each of us to buy our 'ration' of goods and services in general.

These are particular ways in which the problems of scarcity are dealt with. They emphasise the fact that the basic task of an economy is to divide out the available goods and services in some way or other. Whether a price mechanism or some more direct way of rationing goods is used, the task of every economy is to allocate goods to consumers.

The third broad group of assumptions on which economic theory is based relate to social and economic institutions. Two examples of such assumptions used in this book will suffice. We shall assume on the one hand that the analysis relates to a country with a relatively stable political system. For instance, we shall assume that consumers and producers earn their living by exchanging money for goods, and work for wages, in a law-abiding fashion. We shall rule out the possibility that many people might live on the proceeds of smash-and-grab raids or highway robberies.

On the other hand we shall make considerable reference to the market—an economic institution. By a market, economists mean any organisation whereby the buyers and sellers of a particular commodity are kept in close touch with each other and so are able to fix its price. Those dealing in any market need not be physically close to each other—they may keep in touch by telephone. All that is required for there to be a market is that all consumers must be well informed about what is going on, so that a single price can rule throughout the market. Much of the analysis in this book will be based on the assumption that there are numerous 'markets' where the prices of the various goods are determined.

So much for the assumptions which we, in common with other economic theorists, shall make. We must now say something about the process of reasoning whereby economic theories, or 'economic laws' as they are sometimes called, are deduced from assumptions of the kind we have just been discussing. Unfortunately, it is not easy to illustrate shortly the way in which this is done, but perhaps a simple instance will suffice.

When economists discuss the determination of the price of a good in a market, they deduce that one can legitimately expect the price of the commodity traded to tend to a single uniform price throughout the market. For example, economists deduce that if the same kind of fruit is dearer on some stalls in a market than on others, buyers acting 'rationally' will buy the cheaper fruit, so that the sellers of the dearer fruit will have to lower their prices in order to dispose of their stocks. For, since an essential characteristic of the market is that all buyers and sellers in the market are in close touch with each other, everyone will have a shrewd idea what everyone else is doing and thinking. It is only reasonable to conclude that all buyers and sellers will know all the time what the price of the good traded is.

We have explained that applied economists are often concerned to 'test' theory, studying statistical and other evidence to discover whether it appears to support particular economic theories. The branch of economics that has developed most rapidly in recent years is known as econometrics, and econometricians have been developing ways of using statistical methods to test the validity of economic theory. Since econometrics is likely to be of growing importance, we shall look briefly at one example of the way in which econometricians work.

We shall see later that an important concept in contemporary economic theory is that of the 'consumption function'. Economic theorists hold that there is a reasonably stable relationship between a country's total national income and its total expenditure on the consumption of goods and services.

If an econometrician were testing this notion he might take statistics relating, for a number of quarters, total expenditure on consumption to total national income. For example, he might collect the data given in Fig. o.1a. Here, we show total national income

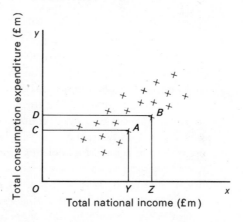

Fig. o.1a

along the horizontal, x-axis. We show total consumption up the vertical, y-axis. So, for example, if the econometrician took data for twenty quarters, he would obtain the twenty crosses shown in Fig. o.1a. He might discover that, in the quarter represented by point A, national income was £OYmillion, while consumption was £OC million. In the quarter represented by point B, national income was £OZmillion and consumption £ODmillion.

Using statistical techniques, the econometrician would then discover which line best represented the general relationship between consumption and income shown by the crosses in Fig. o.1a. If this were the line OC, as shown in Fig. o.1b, the econometrician would then say that this line represented the consumption function. It would show the relationship between total consumption and total income. The evidence would be taken as suggesting that there was a definite functional relationship between income and consumption of the kind that the idea of a consumption function suggested, and that its shape was *OC*. While few (or indeed none) of the points in Fig. 0.1a might lie on the line *OC*, this line would be accepted by the statisticians as giving the best 'fit' that econometric methods could provide between the points in Fig. 0.1a and any single line, like *OC*.

Fig. 0.1b

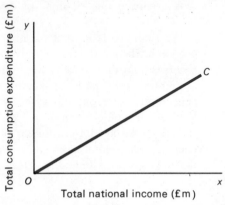

This evidence would also be taken as showing that the consumption function was linear (a straight-line), with the slope of *OC* in Fig. 0.1b. The 'test' would have shown that there *was* a consumption function, and that currently its shape was *OC*.

Like all econometric work, this is an example of what is known as 'positive' economics. One is concerned with observing the world as it is, not with advocating what the best possible world might be. A great deal of economics is of this kind. Positive economics attempts to describe and analyse the existing situation, rather than suggesting how to change it. It is with positive economics of this kind that we shall be entirely concerned in this book.

However, economists do often make 'normative' statements. Instead of explaining how the economy actually operates, they suggest how it *should* operate. Especially where problems of the national economy are concerned, economists abandon the objectivity of 'positive' economics and make 'normative' statements. Indeed many of us do this, whether we are economists or not. If only in discussing economic problems with our friends, we suggest what the government's economic policy ought to be; how government should act to increase the level of employment; to change the tax system, and so on. We say what ought to be rather than what is; we make normative rather than positive statements.

The reason why this book excludes normative economics is *not* that we regard it as unimportant. It is that we simply do not have the space that would be required to consider 'normative' economics sufficiently thoroughly, as well as providing a grounding in economic theory.

We have now explained in general terms what economic theory is about. It remains to say a little more explicitly what we shall do in this book. We have seen that one of the economic analyst's interests is in prices; and rightly so. Everyone is affected when prices rise or fall. The housewife going shopping is seriously interested in whether goods in the shops she visits are dear or cheap. Similarly, every entrepreneur is anxious to find out whether the prices of his products, and of any factors of production he uses, are high or low. Prices are important to everyone. The economist must therefore explain how prices are determined and why they are high when they are high or low when they are low. However, we shall not call Part One of this book 'price theory'. Another important distinction in economics is between micro-economics and macro-economics.

Micro-economics looks at what happens in particular parts of the economy. It looks, say, at what determines the price of apples or the wages of computer programmers. Macro-economics looks at the economy as a whole.

Part One is concerned with micro-economic problems. It is concerned with what determines the prices of individual goods. It also considers what determines the incomes of particular factors of production. We therefore give it the title *Micro-Economic Theory*. We explain the way in which prices, whether of goods or factors of production, are determined.

Although prices are important in the real world, they are not the only things which matter. In particular, no economist can overlook the importance of knowing what determines the level of employment and activity. For conditions both of depression and unemployment and of high activity and inflation cause social unrest. The second part of this book therefore deals with *Macro-Economic Theory*. It looks at the total economy, instead of at small parts of it. It shows what are the causes of high and low levels of unemployment and activity.

Finally, most of us are keenly interested in raising our own and other peoples' standards of living. The third part of the book therefore turns to the *Theory of Growth*. It considers the factors which lie behind rising living standards and studies what it is that determines whether economic growth is slow or rapid.

We turn now to our first topic; the explanation of how prices are determined.

Part 1

Micro-economic theory

1

Demand and supply

1. Price
The price of anything is the rate at which it can be exchanged for anything else. As we saw in the Introduction, one of the main tasks of economic theory is to explain why goods have prices and why some goods are expensive and others cheap. Economic theorists have built up a generalised theory of prices which can be used to analyse the whole range of pricing problems. For all these problems, such as the determination of prices of consumer goods, wage rates, rates of foreign exchange, stock exchange prices and the like, exemplify the general principles by which prices are determined.

The fundamental question which price theory sets out to answer is: 'Why is it that goods and factors of production have prices?' Put baldly, the answer is that they have prices because, on the one hand, they are useful and, on the other hand, they are scarce in relation to the uses to which people want to put them. For example, meat could never command a price in an economy composed entirely of vegetarians. However many or few cows or sheep there were it would not be useful and could not have a price. In addition to being useful, goods must be scarce in relation to the uses to which people want to put them, if they are to be priced. For instance, whilst air is clearly useful to any and every human being, the fact that it is freely available in unlimited amounts ensures that it cannot command a price. It is useful but it is not scarce. Goods like air, which are the gifts of nature and are useful but not scarce, are known as 'free' goods and do not bear a price. By contrast, economic goods are scarce and do bear a price.

Goods can be divided into commodities, for example, oranges, shirts or sideboards, and services, like haircuts, insurance or the services of actors or musicians. In order that such goods may be priced, they must be both useful and scarce.

We have now explained in very broad outline why economic goods have prices. It is only because economic goods, whether commodities or services, are useful that they are demanded by buyers, and only because they are scarce that sellers cannot supply them in unlimited

B

quantities. But usefulness and scarcity are only the underlying forces which cause prices to exist. When the price of any good is determined in the market for that good, it is because usefulness and scarcity express themselves concretely in the form of the demand of buyers on the one hand and supply by sellers on the other. This, then, is the first major step in our argument.

2. The Market

We now know that prices are determined by demand and supply. The next step is to consider the way demand and supply interact in the market. The easiest way to do this will be by building up a simplified hypothetical model of a market for a commodity. Before doing so, however, it will be useful to say more about what economic theorists mean by a 'market'. Briefly, they mean any organisation whereby the buyers and sellers of a good are kept in close touch with each other. It is important to realise that there is no need for a market to be in a single building as happens, for example, with the Smithfield meat market in London or a Stock Exchange. It will be just as much a market if buyers and sellers sit beside batteries of telephones, as happens in a foreign exchange market. The essential feature of a market is that all buyers and sellers should be able to get in touch with each other whenever the market is open, either because they are in the same building or because they are able to talk by telephone at a moment's notice.

Let us now build up a model of a hypothetical market for a commodity. We shall call it a cotton market, though it is unlikely that any actual cotton market will correspond to this simple model. We shall make several simplifying assumptions about conditions in this 'cotton market', and it is important to state them explicitly at the outset. First, we shall assume that every bale of cotton offered for sale is of the same quality, so that there can be no price difference because some bales of cotton are better or worse in quality than others. Second, we shall assume that all the cotton can be bought in either small or large amounts at the same price per bale. This is a reasonable assumption in the case of cotton, but would not be so reasonable when dealing, for example, with automobiles. One could hardly sell them in halves, quarters or eighths. This assumption implies that there are no rebates of the 'five pence each, six for twenty pence' variety and that, when price changes it can change by very small steps. Third, we shall assume there are large numbers of buyers and sellers in the market. Fourth, we shall assume that the market, while not necessarily in a single building, is one where information is easily exchanged and where there are no transport costs between the various parts. Because of this, we can assume that every buyer and seller in the market knows what every other buyer and seller is doing, and that the same price will rule throughout the market. If price changes in one part of the market, it must change similarly in all parts.

These four assumptions are often made by economists and technical terms have been coined to describe them. In technical language the assumptions are: 1. Homogeneity; 2. Divisibility; 3. Pure competition; and 4. A perfect market. In a word, we are assuming 'competitive' conditions.

Having made these assumptions about conditions in a competitive market, we must now make some assumptions about the nature of the forces at work in that market—demand and supply. So far as demand by buyers is concerned, it seems reasonable to think that there will be some very high prices at which no buyer will purchase anything, and some very low prices at which all buyers will buy large quantities of cotton. Between these limits, the lower the price is the more cotton will be bought. For buyers who were previously unable to afford any cotton will be able to do so when its price falls and vice versa. Similarly, it is reasonable to assume that when prices are very high sellers will be only too keen to sell as much cotton as they can, while conditions remain good. Again, when prices are low, sellers will tend to hold back their supplies in the hope that prices will rise. At intermediate prices, varying amounts of cotton will be sold. The higher the price is, the greater the amount of cotton offered by sellers is likely to be. For, the higher the price, the more anxious sellers will be to dispose of their supplies while prices remain high.

We shall therefore assume that the amounts of cotton supplied and demanded at various hypothetical prices are as shown in Table 1.1.

Table 1.1

Demand and supply schedules

Price per bale	Demand schedule (at this price buyers will take (bales))	Supply schedule (at this price sellers will offer (bales))
£6·50	–	120 000
£5·50	20 000	100 000
£4·50	40 000	80 000
£3·50	60 000	60 000
£2·50	80 000	40 000
£1·50	100 000	20 000
£0·50	120 000	–

Assuming that the demand and supply schedules are as shown in Table 1.1, our assumption that competition is keen means that a price of £3·50 per bale will be reached before the market closes. For this is the only price at which the amount demanded is equal to the amount supplied. Only at this price can *all* those wishing to sell and to buy *at any one price* be satisfied.

If the market price is above £3·50, more cotton will be offered by sellers than is demanded by buyers and the tendency will be for the price to fall. Those sellers who are unable to dispose of their supplies at the existing price will begin to make price reductions in the hope of attracting custom. As the price falls, amount demanded will increase and amount supplied will decline in the way shown in Table 1.1 until, at the price of £3·50, all the sellers who are willing to sell will be able to find purchasers for their cotton. Similarly, if the price is below £3·50 a bale, the amount of cotton demanded will exceed the amount supplied and the price of cotton will tend to rise. For there will be many unsatisfied buyers at any price below £3·50. While they would be only too glad to buy at a lower price if possible, they will be prepared to see the price rise rather than go away empty-handed. When the price has risen to £3·50, all the buyers who are prepared to buy at that price will be satisfied.

Only at a price of £3·50 a bale will there be no tendency for the price to change. Only at this price will there be no unsatisfied buyers or sellers who are prepared to see prices alter rather than go away without having bought or sold any cotton. Consequently, it is only when the price is £3·50 a bale that the price will remain stable at a given level. This price at which the amounts demanded and supplied are equal is known in technical language as the *equilibrium price*. At this price the forces of demand and supply are balanced, or in equilibrium. It is called an equilibrium price because price settles down, or comes to rest, at this level as the result of the balancing of the opposing forces of demand and supply.

This diagrammatic demonstration of the fact that a market is in equilibrium when the amount demanded equals the amount supplied could, equally easily, be carried out using simultaneous equations. If we denote amount demanded by q_d and price by p, the demand schedule in Table 1.1 simply represents the same information as the demand equation:

$$q_d = (6·50 - p)\ 20\ 000$$

We can check this by taking, say, the price of £5·50, and substituting into the demand equation. We then have the quantity demanded (20 000 bales) shown in Table 1.1:

$$q_d = (6·50 - 5·50)\ 20\ 000$$
$$= 20\ 000.$$

If q_s equals amount supplied and p still equals price, the supply equation (representing the same information as the supply schedule in Table 1.1) is:

$$q_s = (p - 0 \cdot 50) \ 20\ 000$$

For equilibrium, we know that amount demanded (q_d) must equal amount supplied (q_s). This will happen when the right-hand sides of the two equations are equal. We then have:

$(6 \cdot 50 - p) \ 20\ 000 = (p - 0 \cdot 50) \ 20\ 000$
$\therefore 130\ 000 - 20\ 000\ p = 20\ 000\ p - 10\ 000$
$\therefore -40\ 000\ p = -140\ 000$
$\therefore p = 3 \cdot 5$

The equilibrium price is £3·50. This again agrees with Table 1.1. If we know that the equilibrium price is £3·50, we can at once deduce from the demand equation (*or* the supply equation) that the equilibrium quantities demanded and supplied are:

$(6 \cdot 50 - 3 \cdot 50) \ 20000$
$= 3 \times 20\ 000$
$= 60\ 000$

The equilibrium position for *any* market can be calculated if one knows the equations for the demand and supply schedules, whether these are independently given or derived from data like that in Table 1.1. Consider the following hypothetical demand and supply equations, where q_d is again quantity demanded, q_s is again quantity supplied and p is again price:

$q_d = 50\ 000 - 2\ 000\ p$
and $q_s = 10\ 000 + 3\ 000\ p$.

Equilibrium then occurs where:

$50\ 000 - 2000\ p = 10\ 000 + 3\ 000\ p;$
or $-5\ 000\ p = -40\ 000;$
or $p = 8$

The equilibrium price is 8. Substitution in the demand *or* supply equation shows that the equilibrium amount demanded and supplied is 34 000 units. While we shall concentrate on diagrams in this book, much of the analysis could be easily translated into algebra in this way if one wished.

One conclusion from this type of analysis is that demand and supply determine price. It is also often said that price determines demand and supply. These are important generalisations about the relationship between demand, supply and market price, but they are not precise and are at first sight contradictory. The reason why it is difficult to make sense of them is that we have not, so far, made one very important distinction. It is essential in economics to distinguish between the quantity of a good which is demanded or supplied at a particular price, and the general conditions of demand and supply. These can be depicted by schedules showing the various quantities of the commodity which would be demanded or supplied at many different prices. Only one of these prices can be the actual market price, in our example £3·50. It is this market price which determines the amount actually exchanged in the market, in our case 60 000 bales, but this price is itself determined by the interaction of the demand schedule with the supply schedule. It is quite possible that a change in the price at which the market is in equilibrium may occur and that such a change will alter the amount demanded and supplied. Such a change in the equilibrium price must itself have been brought about by a change in the demand schedule, the supply schedule, or both. This distinction between the general demand and supply conditions shown in schedules like those in Table 1.1 and the actual amounts demanded or supplied at one particular price is important and should always be borne in mind.

Two other important points about an analysis like this must be mentioned here. First, it should be obvious that since demand and supply are the two forces which determine price, the analysis of a market will hold only if demand and supply really are independent of each other. That is to say, one must make the simplifying assumption that buyers do not also appear as sellers and vice versa. Since we are concerned here with a cotton market, it is reasonable to assume that suppliers are not likely to buy their own goods, and that even if they occasionally do, they buy only in negligible quantities. If we were dealing with a chocolate manufacturer, we should be entitled to assume that even if he did sometimes eat chocolates, he would never eat a significant proportion of the output of his own factory. We shall assume that, as a rule, buyers and sellers are quite different people, so that demand and supply are independent.

Second, it is important not to overlook the relationship between prices in different markets. We have seen that in competitive conditions the same price will rule throughout the market for a single good. Naturally there will be less tendency for prices in different markets to bear any particular relationship to each other. There will be less connection *between* markets because each market is concerned with a different commodity. Nevertheless, there will be some connections even here. For example, if prices in the meat market rise there is likely to be some rise in prices in the fish market. People will tend to eat more fish and less meat if meat becomes more expensive. The demand for fish will increase and its price will rise. Similarly, a change in the price of cotton may affect the price of wool, since both are used in clothing.

Some markets will be very much less closely related. It is unlikely, for example, that a rise in the price of mustard or of pepper will alter the price of hats. Yet it may have a slight effect. If people spend more money on mustard, they will have less money to spend on other things and they may conceivably decide to wear their hats just a little longer. Thus, while each market is primarily concerned with determining the price of a single good every market is related in some degree, sometimes quite great, sometimes very small indeed, to all the other separate markets.

In view of this, it is clear that if we were to try to take account of all the repercussions of a change in the price of, say, cotton, on the prices of other goods, we should be faced with a very complicated problem. We are concerned at this stage to make our analysis as simple as possible. We shall therefore confine our attention to analysing only one market at a time, and rule out the possibility that disturbances from other markets can upset this analysis. Such an analysis is often used by economists and is known as *particular equilibrium* analysis, since it seeks to explain what happens in one particular market and ignores what is happening in others. Alternatively, it is known as *partial equilibrium* analysis because it seeks to analyse only a part of the economic system. This is in distinction to *general equilibrium* analysis, which we shall use later in the book, where we analyse the effects of changes in one market on conditions in others.

What we do in particular equilibrium analysis is to confine our attention to changes in a single market by taking it for granted, either that demand and supply in the market isolated for special study is independent of price changes in other markets, or alternatively that such price changes do not occur. It is also important to realise that the demand schedule is constructed on the assumption that consumers have given, constant money incomes. Any changes in these incomes would alter the demand schedule. The amount demanded at each price would be different.

We therefore assume in particular equilibrium analysis that all prices are given, except the one in which we are interested, and that consumers have money incomes of given size to spend. We also assume, as already noted, that demand and supply schedules are completely independent of each other. Obviously, with such an analytical framework we can give only a partial or incomplete picture of the economic system. The fact that occasionally changes in one market affect price in another is explicitly ruled out. Nevertheless, this will make our task much simpler, while enabling us to give a quite accurate picture of the way in which prices are determined. We can then introduce the complications of general equilibrium when the building of our theoretical system is sufficiently advanced.

3. Demand

3.1 Effective demand

We have shown how the price of any commodity or economic service is determined by the interaction of demand and supply. It is now necessary to see more precisely what demand and supply are. First, let us consider demand. What do we mean when we speak of demand? We have seen that goods are demanded because they are useful, and it might be thought that each good is demanded by everyone who thinks that it is useful—by everyone who wants it. In fact, not every want on the part of a consumer expresses itself as a demand in the market. A consumer's desire to buy a good will affect the market price of that good only if this desire can be translated into a money demand for the good in question. Demand in economics means demand backed up by enough money to pay for the good demanded. For example, while every Englishman is supposed to want a country house, very few are able to afford one. Only the demand of those who have enough money to buy country houses affects their price. We are concerned in this book only with demand which is effectively backed up by an adequate supply of purchasing power—with 'effective demand'.

3.2 A demand curve

We have so far considered the demand for cotton in a hypothetical cotton market. We did so by drawing up a schedule showing the amounts of cotton demanded at various prices, in Table 1.1. But, while economists do use arithmetical demand schedules, the demand schedule for a good is more usually shown graphically by drawing what is called a demand curve for the good in question. A demand curve shows in visual form the state of affairs on the demand side of the market for a commodity at a given time. We make the usual assumptions of *particular equilibrium analysis*, namely, that all prices are constant except that of the good in which we are interested, and

Fig. 1.1

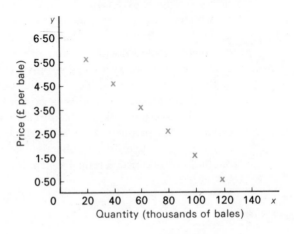

that consumers have fixed money incomes. On these assumptions we can draw a curve showing how much of the given commodity will be bought at various prices. In the following diagrams we shall show, in stages, how a demand curve is drawn up.

The first stage is shown in Fig. 1.1. Up the vertical axis, the y-axis, we measure various hypothetical market prices with which we assume consumers to be faced. In fact, what we have done is to take the prices from Table 1.1. Prices are therefore measured in pounds per bale. Along the horizontal axis, the x-axis, is measured from left to right the increasing total quantity of the good, in this case thousands of bales of cotton, which consumers are assumed to buy at these prices. We can then plot the demand schedule from Table 1.1 as a series of points. Each point represents the amount of cotton which would be bought at a particular price. We have exactly the same information in Fig. 1.1 as in Table 1.1, but we have it in a different form.

In Fig. 1.2, perpendiculars are drawn from each of same points as are shown in Fig. 1.1 to the two axes, forming rectangles. This provides us with more information because the area of each rectangle represents consumers' total money outlay at the price in question, namely the price per bale multiplied by the number of bales bought.

In Fig. 1.3 we assume that there is complete divisibility, so that price and amount demanded can both change by infinitely small steps. This enables us to draw a demand curve, joining the points shown in Fig. 1.1 by a continuous line—*DD*. We also assume that

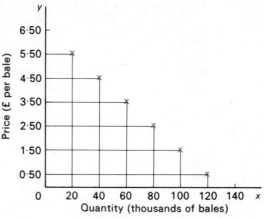

Fig. 1.2

there are no irregularities in demand conditions anywhere between the particular points we have shown in our demand schedule in Fig. 1.1. This makes the demand curve smooth and regular. Finally we assume, for the sake of simplicity, that in this particular instance the amount of cotton demanded increases by 1 000 bales for every fall of 5p in price. This enables us to draw the demand curve in

Fig. 1.3 as a straight line. It follows that a demand curve is a curve showing for each price how much of the good in question consumers would buy at that price. It represents a *functional relationship* between price and amount demanded. The function is $q_d = f(p)$, where p is price, q_d is quantity demanded and the term f simply means 'is a function of'. We used a more specific demand function earlier $q_d = (6 \cdot 50 - p)\, 20\,000$.

We have drawn the demand curve in Fig. 1.3 sloping downwards from left to right. This is the assumption about the general nature of

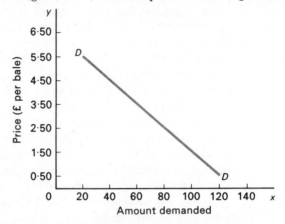

Fig. 1.3

demand curves which economists normally make. One reason why they assume that demand curves slope downwards from left to right is, as we have seen, that as the price of a good falls people who were previously unable to buy it will enter the market, and the amount of the good demanded will rise. There are other reasons. Now that the price of the good has fallen, some people will buy it in preference to other goods, which they bought before, but which are now relatively more expensive. Again, some people who bought some of the good

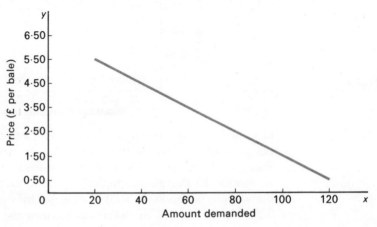

Fig. 1.4a

before its price fell may buy more now that it is cheaper. For these reasons economists assume that demand curves slope downwards to the right.

One fact about demand curves which is worth noting is that their slope depends on the scale used. In Fig. 1.4a and 1.4b the two demand

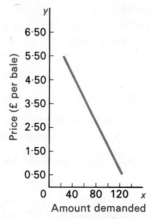

Fig. 1.4b

curves represent exactly the same information as in Fig. 1.3. But in Fig. 1.4a the units on the x-axis are larger than in Fig. 1.3, and in Fig. 1.4b they are smaller. Similarly, one could alter the units on the y-axis. It is therefore always important to be certain about the scale when drawing or interpreting demand curves.

Finally, it is sometimes useful to show the same information as in Fig. 1.3 on a different type of curve. Instead of showing the amount of the good demanded at each price, we show the total amount of money which consumers are prepared to spend on various hypothetical amounts of the good. This has been done in Fig. 1.5 where we have drawn a *total outlay curve* or *total expenditure curve*. Along the x-axis we measure thousands of bales of cotton. Up the y-axis, we

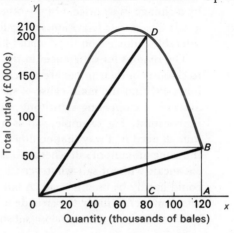

Fig. 1.5

measure total outlay in pounds, as in the rectangles in Fig. 1.2. Thus the line AB shows that consumers are willing to spend £60 000 on cotton when they buy 120 000 bales. The size of total outlay when a given quantity of cotton is being bought can therefore be shown either by the height of a total expenditure curve, as in Fig. 1.5, or by the size of an outlay rectangle as in Fig. 1.2. The total outlay curve expresses another functional relationship. This time, it is between total expenditure on a good and the amount bought.

It is important to realise that although price is not measured on either axis in Fig. 1.5 it can be discovered from this diagram. For example, in Fig. 1.5 the slope of the straight line OB, i.e. $\frac{AB}{OA}$, repre-

sents the price buyers will pay for cotton (£0·50 per bale) if OA bales (120 000) are demanded and total expenditure is £AB (£60 000). Similarly, the slope of the line OD, i.e. $\frac{CD}{OC}$, represents the price paid

for cotton (£2·50 per bale) if OC bales are demanded, so that outlay is £CD. The fact that the slope of the line OB is flatter than the line OD shows that price is lower if OA bales are demanded then if OC are being bought.

4. Elasticity of demand

We have seen that there is a very good case for thinking that demand curves slope downwards from left to right. This means that the amount of a good which is demanded increases as its price falls. Alternatively, we may say that the demand for the good is 'responsive' to a fall in its price. Although the demand for a good usually responds to a fall in its price in this way, there will be differences in the degree of responsiveness of different goods to price changes. It is usually agreed that the demand for a good like salt is not very much affected by a change in its price. On the other hand, changes in the prices of goods like colour television sets or foreign holidays do exert a considerable influence on the demand for them.

The reasons for differences in the responsiveness of various goods to changes in their prices are not easy to discover. It is broadly true, however, that the main cause of such differences is the presence or absence of competing substitutes, all of whose prices we assume to be constant. For example, salt is a necessity which fulfils a basic human need in a way that no other good will. We have to use much the same amount of salt whether it is dear or cheap. Few people will eat meals without salt whatever its price, and pepper and mustard could hardly be used instead. A fall in the price of colour television sets, however, is likely to persuade more people to buy them because black and white sets are close substitutes, as also are, for example, record players, cinemas and theatres. Similarly, a fall in the price of rail travel, with the price of road and air travel constant, would attract travellers from road and air. The demand for travel by rail is therefore likely to be responsive to a change in its price. The main cause of differences in the responsiveness of the demand for goods to changes in their prices lies in the fact that there are more competing substitutes for some than for others.

Economic theory finds it useful to distinguish between those goods which are more responsive to price changes and those which are less responsive. In technical jargon, economists say that the former goods have a demand which is *more elastic* than that for the latter, or that their *elasticity of demand* is greater. *Elasticity of demand is therefore a technical term used by economists to describe the degree of responsiveness in the demand for a good to a fall in its price.*[1] Alfred Marshall, the great Cambridge economist of the late nineteenth and early twentieth centuries, introduced the concept of elasticity of demand into economic theory. He said that 'the *elasticity* (or *responsiveness*) *of demand* in a market is great or small according as the amount demanded increases much or little for a given fall in price, and diminishes much or little for a given rise in price'.[2] We shall find that differences in elasticity of demand between goods are very important in economic theory and that merely to say that the demand for one good is more or less elastic than the demand for another, is often not sufficiently precise. We need a more accurate method of comparing the elasticities of demand for different products.

This can easily be done and there are two commonly-used measures of elasticity of demand. First, we can measure it at a point on a demand curve. Consider Fig. 1.6. Suppose we want to know what is elasticity of demand at point R on this demand curve. The formula for calculating what is known as 'point elasticity of demand' is as follows:

Elasticity of demand

$$= \frac{\text{proportionate change in amount demanded}}{\text{proportionate change in price}}$$

$$= \frac{\text{change in amount demanded}}{\text{amount demanded}} \div \frac{\text{change in price}}{\text{price}}$$

In Fig. 1.6, this gives us point elasticity of demand equal to:

$$\frac{qq_1}{oq} \div \frac{pp_1}{op}$$

[1]Strictly speaking, elasticity of demand refers to the way in which the demand for a good responds to a *change* in its price; whether a rise or a fall. We talk in this section of responsiveness to a *fall* in price, purely for the sake of convenience. The argument applies equally to the case of a *rise* in price.

[2]Alfred Marshall, *Principles of Economics,* 1920, (8th Edition), p. 102.

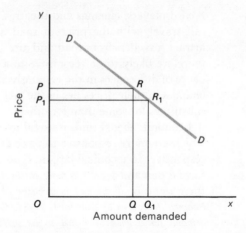

Fig. 1.6

It must be remembered that it is usual to take the original price and the original quantity demanded as the denominators in these fractions. Strictly, because we are interested in elasticity of demand at a point on a demand curve, we should use calculus to work out the effect on the quantity demanded of an infinitesimally small change in price. If p=price and q=quantity demanded, the formula is:

$$\text{elasticity of demand} = \frac{dq}{q} \div \frac{dp}{p}$$

For most practical purposes, provided that the percentage change in price is not large (e.g. 1 or 2 per cent) the answer we get will be good enough. The fact is that in using the formula $\frac{qq_1}{oq} \div \frac{pp_1}{op}$ we are not really measuring elasticity at point R. We are concerned with a small range of the demand curve—here from R to R_1.

Let us look at an example. Suppose that a fall in price from 100 to 98 leads to an increase in quantity demanded from 100 to 104. The formula $\frac{qq_1}{oq} \div \frac{pp_1}{op}$ then becomes $\frac{4}{100} \div \frac{2}{100} = \frac{4}{100} \times \frac{100}{2} = 2$.

It will be noted that, strictly, elasticity of demand should be represented by a negative number. Because demand curves slope downwards, changes in price and amount demanded will be in opposite directions. What we have just written as elasticity equals 2 should strictly be elasticity equals -2. However, for convenience, we shall denote elasticities by positive numbers.

The concept of elasticity of demand is essentially a simple one, but there are one or two important points about it which should be borne in mind. First, it is tempting to imagine that a flat demand curve indicates that the demand for the good to which it relates has a greater elasticity than the demand for a good whose demand curve is steep. It is natural to think that where the slope of a demand curve is relatively small the demand for the good is increasing much more rapidly, as price falls, than with a very steep curve. But this is to oversimplify. If we look again at Fig. 1.4a and 1.4b, it seems likely that, on this argument, the elasticity of the demand curve in Fig. 1.4b will be less than that of the curve in Fig. 1.4a. Yet we have already seen that the two curves represent precisely the same demand conditions. The only difference between them is that the scales along the x-axes are different. It is therefore clearly dangerous to make any assertions about the relative elasticities of any two demand curves if they are not drawn to the same scale.

If two demand curves are drawn on the same scale and one is steeper than the other, it is true that they do represent different demand schedules. But it is still dangerous to make assertions about their respective elasticities of demand. One can, however, say something. Figure 1.7 shows two demand curves, *AA* and *BB,* relating to two entirely separate, hypothetical markets for the same good (markets *A* and *B*), perhaps in different countries. If the price in both markets falls over exactly the same range, for example from

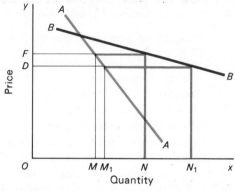

Fig. 1.7

OF to *OD,* the responsiveness of demand in the market with demand curve *BB* is greater than in the market with demand curve *AA.* Demand increases by NN_1 in market *B* but only by MM_1 in market *A.* So long as one is concerned with a fall in price *over exactly the same price range* in each market, it is possible to say that a flatter curve represents a more elastic demand than a steeper curve if both are drawn to the same scale—provided that the initial amounts demanded in each market are much the same. But one can say no more. One cannot say anything, merely by looking at the slopes of two curves, about elasticities over *different* price ranges on each curve, even if there is the same *absolute* change in price in each market. For example, one could not infer anything about elasticity of demand, merely from looking at the slopes of the two curves, if price in market *A* were to fall by 5p from *OF*p and price in market *B* were to fall also by 5p from *OD*p. This can be seen by studying a single demand curve.

In Fig. 1.8 the slope of the demand curve *DD* is constant. If elasticity and slope were closely related, one would naturally expect elasticity to be constant as well. But when price falls by five pence,

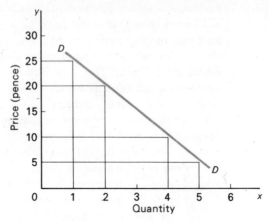

Fig. 1.8

from 25p to 20p, the amount demanded rises from one unit to two. Price has fallen by a fifth and the amount demanded has doubled. Elasticity of demand is five (i.e. $\frac{1}{1} \div \frac{5}{25}$). Yet when price falls from 10p to 5p, the amount demanded only rises by one unit, from 4 to 5. It is clearly unreasonable to regard the responsiveness of demand to changing price as the same in both cases; yet the slope of the demand curve is constant, and one might well expect elasticity to be constant as well. If one cannot tell what is the elasticity of demand on a single demand curve without some calculation, it is clearly dangerous to make assertions about demand on two different curves, except over the same price range in each case.

It follows from this that even a straight line demand curve, like that in Fig. 1.8 will have no such thing as *an* elasticity of demand. A little calculation will show that numerical elasticity of demand is high towards the left-hand end of the curve and low towards the right-hand end of it. Elasticity falls steadily as one moves from left

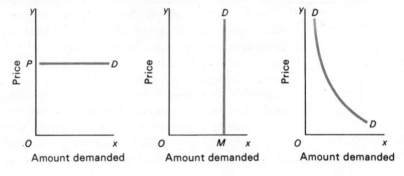

Fig. 1.9 a|b|c

to right down the curve. This is the usual situation, though some demand curves do have a single elasticity throughout their length.

One example is shown in Fig. 1.9a, where the demand curve is a horizontal straight line. Numerical elasticity of demand is therefore infinite. A small fall in price below OP gives rise to an indefinitely large increase in amount demanded. Again, where the demand curve is a vertical straight line, as in Fig. 1.9b, numerical elasticity of demand is zero. Whatever the original price is, a reduction in that price will lead to no increase at all in the amount demanded. It will remain at OM throughout. Similarly, although it is not obvious at a glance, the demand curve shown in Fig. 1.9c also has one elasticity throughout its length. Here elasticity of demand is equal to 1. Indeed, Fig. 1.10a and 1.10b both also show demand curves with elasticities equal to 1. To emphasise the point about the appearance of demand curves being deceptive where elasticity is concerned, these curves both show the same information but are drawn to different scales:

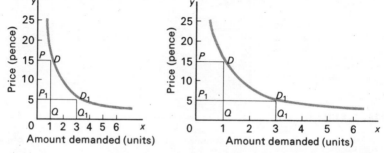

Fig. 1.10 a b

In Fig. 1.10a, let us consider the two points D and D_1. At each point, total outlay is the same. Whether price is 15p as at D, or 5p as at D_1, total outlay is still 15p. The same situation is shown in Fig. 1.10b, but the scale on the x-axis is larger. In both diagrams, a fall in price from 15p to 5p, leads to an increase in amount demanded from 1 to 3 units. Elasticity of demand is therefore $\frac{1}{3} \div \frac{5}{15} = 1$. Readers with mathematical training will realise that the demand curves in both Fig. 1.10a and 1.10b are rectangular hyperbolae.[1] This means that every rectangle which we inscribe under these demand curves—like $OPDQ$ and $OP_1D_1Q_1$—is of exactly the same area. This is true wherever one draws the inscribed rectangle.

We must now look at the economic significance of these rectangles. It is that the area of such a rectangle shows total expenditure, or total outlay, on the commodity at the price in question. Multiplying the price by quantity, which is what one does when one draws the

[1] Because each curve is a rectangular hyperbola it is asymptotic to (i.e. approaches but never touches) the x- and y-axes. If it did touch them, the inscribed rectangles would vanish.

rectangle, gives one total outlay, or total expenditure, on the commodity. If one thinks about it, it is obvious that elasticity of demand equal to one, on a curve like that in Fig. 1.10a, means that the percentage change in quantity demanded is just equal to the percentage change in price which gives rise to it. Otherwise, elasticity would not be one. It is because each inscribed rectangle is of exactly the same size that total outlay on the product is exactly the same whatever price is. This is a general characteristic of demand curves with elasticity equal to one.

If one studies those demand curves which are very elastic and those which are inelastic, it is not long before one notices an important fact. This emerges clearly from Figs. 1.11a and 1.11b. With the

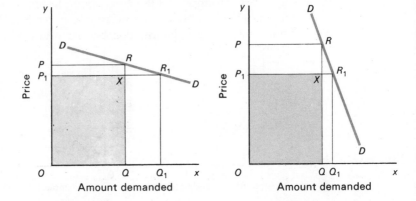

Fig. 1.11 a | b

demand curve in Fig. 1.11a a fall in price from OP to OP_1 leads to a large increase in quantity demanded from OQ to OQ_1. The result is that total outlay on the product rises considerably, from $OPRQ$ to $OP_1R_1Q_1$. In other words, what we are saying is that the amount of total outlay shown by the shaded rectangle OP_1XQ continues to be spent in the new situation. The amount of expenditure shown by rectangle $PRXP_1$ is lost when price falls, but is replaced by the much larger amount of expenditure shown by the rectangle QXR_1Q_1. Total outlay therefore rises sharply as price falls.

With the demand curve shown in Fig. 1.11b, exactly the opposite happens. When price falls from OP to OP_1, total outlay falls very considerably. Once again, the total amount of revenue represented by the shaded rectangle OP_1XQ is received both with the original and the new price. Now, however, the amount of revenue lost after the cut in price is shown by the large rectangle $PRXP_1$. This is far from being made up for by the additional revenue QXR_1Q_1 that replaces it.

A little reflection will show that while the demand curve in Fig.

1.11a is not horizontal, so that elasticity of demand is not infinite, it is very nearly horizontal. Similarly, while the demand curve in Fig. 1.11b is not a vertical line with zero elasticity, it is close to being vertical. This naturally leads one to wonder whether there is some link between elasticity of demand for a product and the way in which the total outlay on that product alters when its price is changed. It turns out that there is such a relationship and that it can be stated precisely.

The relationship is this. Whenever numerical elasticity of demand for a product is greater than one, a reduction in its price will increase total expenditure (outlay) on that product. Whenever numerical elasticity of demand for a product is less than one, a reduction in its price will reduce total outlay on it. And, whenever numerical elasticity of demand for a product is exactly equal to one, a reduction in its price will leave total outlay completely unchanged, in the way we have just seen. It follows at once that similar relationships will hold for increases in price. If the price of a product is increased, then total expenditure on it will fall if elasticity of demand is greater than one, but will rise if elasticity is less than one. Again, total outlay will remain unchanged if elasticity of demand is just one.

This explains why so much emphasis has been put on elasticity of demand equal to one in this Chapter; what is sometimes known as unitary elasticity of demand. It represents an important dividing line. On one side of it are all those numerical elasticities less than 1 (e.g. $\frac{1}{2}$, $\frac{1}{4}$ or a $\frac{1}{16}$). With all numerical elasticities less than one, we say that demand is inelastic. Demand increases less than proportionately as price falls. It is not very responsive to price reductions. Similarly, outlay falls as price falls. Any demand with numerical elasticity less than one can thus be called inelastic.

On the other side of elasticity of demand equals one, numerical elasticity is greater than one, e.g. 2, 5, 7 or 16. There, demand is elastic. Demand increases more than in proportion to any fall in price and total outlay rises as prices fall. One can classify any demand with numerical elasticity greater than one as elastic. Numerical elasticity shows at sight whether demand is elastic or inelastic.

We can now see why elasticity equals one is so important. It represents the dividing line between elastic and inelastic demands. Whenever numerical elasticity of demand is greater than one, demand for the product is elastic and a reduction in price will increase total expenditure on the product while an increase in price will reduce it. Wherever numerical elasticity of demand for the product is less than one, we know that demand for that product is inelastic. A fall in its price will reduce total outlay on it and an increase in its price will increase it. Finally, there is the dividing line of elasticity equals one where, if price changes, the demand for the product changes in exact proportion and there is no increase in total expenditure on the product.

The reason why these relationships hold should be intuitively obvious to the reader by now. If elasticity of demand equals one, the percentage change in price is exactly equal to the percentage change in quantity demanded. If price is reduced, the tendency for an increase in quantity demanded to raise total outlay will be just cancelled out by the tendency for the reduction in price to reduce it. Total outlay therefore remains unchanged.

If elasticity of demand is greater than one, the change in price and quantity demanded no longer just cancel out. A given fall in price now leads to a more than proportionate response from quantity demanded, so that total expenditure increases. This is effectively what we were showing when we saw in Fig. 1.11a that the loss in outlay given by rectangle $PRXP_1$ was more than offset by the gain of outlay shown by rectangle QXR_1Q_1. The opposite situation exists if demand is inelastic. Here, a given percentage fall in price leads to a less than proportionate response from quantity demanded. The loss of outlay caused by the fall in price is not made up by the increase in quantity demanded. The total outlay therefore falls. Again, this is what we were showing when we explained in Fig. 1.11b that the rectangle $PRXP_1$, representing lost expenditure, was bigger than the rectangle QXR_1Q_1, representing expenditure gained.

We can show this relationship between the elasticity of demand and total outlay in Fig. 1.12. Here, instead of drawing an ordinary demand curve as we have through most of this chapter, we have plotted total outlay on the y-axis against quantity demanded shown on the x-axis. (We could have shown price on the x-axis instead. Obviously, one cannot show both price and quantity demanded on the same axis in the same diagram.)

When the amount of the product demanded is small, and prices are therefore high, total outlay increases as price is reduced and quantity demanded rises. Over this range of quantity demanded, from zero to ON in Fig. 1.12, elasticity of demand is greater than one. In Fig. 1.12, this range of quantity demanded is denoted as Zone one. Once quantity demanded reaches ON, demand ceases to be elastic. Numerical elasticity of demand has now fallen to one, and over a range of output it remains at one, namely the range between ON and ON_1. In Fig. 1.12 this is described as Zone two. Total outlay is constant and the total outlay curve is therefore a horizontal straight line.

Finally, price falls to a level where quantity demanded is greater than ON_1. Over this range of output, which is described as Zone three in Fig. 1.12, demand is inelastic. Reductions in price continue to increase the quantity of product demanded beyond ON_1, but not fast enough to prevent total outlay on the product from falling. Over this range of output, total expenditure falls as quantity demanded increases and the total outlay curve therefore slopes downward.

When we gave the formula for point elasticity of demand earlier, we saw that this measure was accurate only if we made our calculation

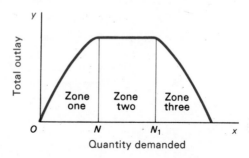

Fig. 1.12

for very small changes in price. We were concerned with elasticity over a small (strictly infinitely small) range of the curve. The formula for measuring point elasticity of demand gave reasonable answers only if the changes in price and quantity were not too large. However, we shall sometimes want to measure elasticity of demand over a substantial range of a demand curve, because a fairly large change in price has occurred. What has just been said about elasticity of demand at various points on a demand curve then becomes important. Provided there is a single numerical elasticity of demand over the whole length of the curve, there is no problem, but this will rarely happen. If we have a demand curve like that in Fig. 1.13, we need a formula which allows us to calculate elasticity of demand over a range of the curve instead of at a point. The point-elasticity formula is likely to give us a wrong answer; obviously, point elasticity of demand will be changing along the range of the curve with which we are concerned.

A second formula for elasticity of demand is therefore used, which allows us to measure what is known as 'arc' elasticity of demand. It measures elasticity of demand over a range, or an arc, of a demand curve, like the range RR_1 in Fig. 1.13.

The second formula is:

$$\text{arc elasticity of demand} = \frac{q_1 - q_0}{p_1 - p_0} \times \frac{p_1 + p_0}{q_1 + q_0}$$

Here, p_0 is the original price, and p_1 the new price. Similarly, q_0 is the quantity demanded at the original price, and q_1 the amount demanded at the new price. This is shown in Fig. 1.13.

We saw earlier that the rule for calculating point elasticity is to take the original price and the original quantity as denominators when calculating the proportional change in price and quantity. With arc elasticity of demand, we take the change in price as a proportion of the average of the original and the new price. The change in quantity is taken as a proportion of the average of the original and new quantities.

The fact that we are taking the average of old and new prices and the average of old and new quantities does not show clearly in the

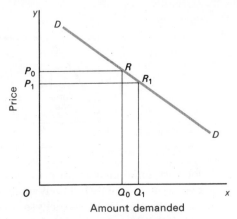

Fig. 1.13

formula. The reason is this. To work out the average of the old and new prices, we should have to divide $p_0 + p_1$ by 2. To get the average quantity demanded, we should have to divide $q_0 + q_1$ by 2. The right-hand side of our formula would then be:

$$\frac{(p_1 + p_0)/2}{(q_1 + q_0)/2}$$

Since both top and bottom of this formula would have to be divided by 2, we can cancel the two's out against each other. We are then left with the expression given earlier, namely, $(p_1 + p_0)/(q_1 + q_0)$.

Numerical measures of elasticity of demand thus enable one to tell whether demand on any demand curve is more or less responsive to price changes than on another curve. It is important to remember, however, that there is no particular economic significance in the fact that elasticity is, say $\frac{1}{2}$ or 2, except that demand is inelastic or elastic respectively, and outlay is thus falling or rising when price falls, as the case may be. Only in three cases is there any important economic significance in the size of elasticity of demand. Elasticity of demand equal to one, with total outlay therefore constant, represents the dividing line between elastic and inelastic demands. Infinitely elastic demand implies a horizontal demand curve for the good in question, with a small fall in price leading to an infinitely large rise in demand. Again, zero elasticity of demand means a vertical demand curve, with exactly the same amount of the good demanded whatever the price.

One further important point to remember is this. As we have seen, only in exceptional circumstances (e.g. where the demand curve is a rectangular hyperbola or a vertical straight line) will a demand curve have a *single elasticity* throughout its length. It will usually have a different elasticity at each point on it. It is therefore usually incorrect to speak of any demand curve as having *an* elasticity. Usually, each has many elasticities. But, at any given point on any demand curve, it will be possible to discover what the numerical elasticity of demand is.

5. Supply

Supply depends on scarcity, just as demand depends on usefulness. Scarcity is a much more difficult concept to discuss than usefulness, because it is more obviously a relative and not an absolute term.. While it is comparatively easy to say whether or not a good is useful, one cannot say whether a good is economically scarce except in relation to the demand for it. Thus while first folios of Shakespeare and genuine Rembrandts are numerically scarce, for their supply is fixed, they may or may not be scarce in the economist's relative sense. If many people want them they will be scarce; if no-one wants them they will be plentiful. Scarcity always means scarce in relation to demand.

Why then is it that economic goods are scarce? Why is there a problem of supply? In the case of those few goods the supply of which is fixed absolutely, the position is clear. What of the enormous number of goods which it is possible to produce? The answer is that all these goods can be produced only with the help of factors of production, e.g. workers, machines, factories, lorries, fields or entrepreneurs, and these factors are themselves limited in amount. The supply of any commodity is limited by the fact that in order to produce it, members from two or more of the four broad groups of factors of production, 'land', 'labour', 'capital' and 'enterprise', must be used. While man's wants are many in number, those which he can satisfy at any given time will be comparatively few, because the supply of productive agents is relatively too small. We shall see later that the process by which equilibrium between demand and supply is brought about determines which of man's wants are satisfied and which are not. For the moment, we may note merely that the supply of factors of production is small compared with the demand for them. There are hundreds of goods with prices, and by definition each one is scarce in relation to the demand for it.

We must now lay down a general rule about the shape of supply curves, like the rule that demand curves normally slope downwards. This general rule is that supply curves slope upwards from left to right. In other words, sellers of a commodity are normally willing to sell more of it if its price is high than if it is low. This is a simple principle, but it needs careful interpretation if its implications are to be correctly understood. Most important, as we shall see, there are major exceptions to this rule.

5.1 Fixed supply Let us first consider the supply of goods whose quantity is fixed and which cannot be increased as a result of economic decisions. The fixed quantity of goods available will be in the possession of certain people. Other people who do not possess any of it at all may want to buy some. We can therefore draw a market demand curve sloping downwards, which shows the readiness of these buyers to take various quantities of the good at various hypothetical prices. This demand curve will be faced in the market by a supply curve for the potential sellers. There is a functional relationship between price and amount supplied of the form $q_s = f(p)$. With fixed supply, the supply curve will normally slope upwards. This is because, if price is high, sellers can acquire a good deal of money, and thus the other goods, in exchange for the good they are giving up. The higher the price of the good in question is, the more worthwhile its sale will seem. The amount supplied will be greater. The situation in the market will thus determine the price. It will do so by the interaction of the downward-sloping demand curve, on the one hand, with the upward-sloping supply curve on the other. Or, as we have seen, one can find what value of q_d and q_s simultaneously satisfies the demand and supply equations.

When one considers the forces determining the shape of the seller's supply curve, however, one finds that, in this particular case, they are of the same kind as those which determine the shape of the buyer's demand curve. Buyers have to decide whether to buy the good in question or to keep their money and use it to buy other goods. In the same way, the sellers have to decide whether to keep the good in question for their own use or whether to exchange it for something else. The willingness or reluctance of sellers to sell is therefore determined by the *sellers' demand for their own good*. Unwillingness to sell something one possesses is determined in much the same way as eagerness to buy something one does not possess, if in each case the motive is to satisfy one's own wants. One can suppose, if one likes, that sellers actually offer their goods for sale in the market, but 'buy them back' at their reserve price. A decision to sell can therefore be expressed, without a change of meaning, as a decision not to demand. It is then possible and legitimate to represent the supply conditions for a good whose amount is fixed, not only by an upward-sloping demand curve but also, alternatively, by a downward-sloping demand curve of sellers for their own good.

In Fig. 1.14 there is a fixed supply, *OX*, of a given commodity. In each diagram the dashed line *XX* shows this fixed supply. The same supply conditions for sellers are represented in Fig. 1.14a by an upward-sloping supply curve *SS*, and in Fig. 1.14b by a downward-sloping demand curve of sellers for their own good, *SOD*. In the case of the supply curve in Fig. 1.14a, market price can be deduced from the intersection of this supply curve with the buyers' demand curve,

Fig. 1.14 <u>a</u>|<u>b</u>
        c|d

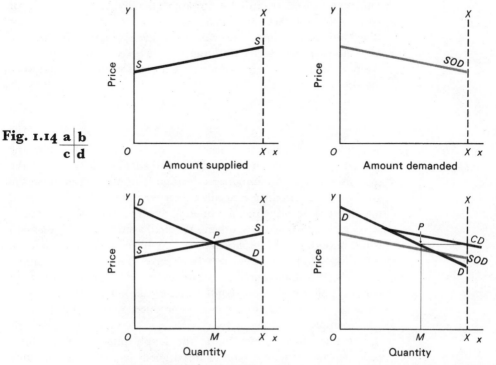

just as in Table 1.1 we deduced the market price from the intersection of the demand and supply schedules. For example, in Fig. 1.14c, the equilibrium price is *MP*, the amount bought by buyers and therefore sold by sellers is *OM*, and the amount not sold by sellers is *MX*. The same result is obtained in Fig. 1.14d where the sellers' demand is added sideways to the buyers' demand. Together they constitute the combined demand curve (the solid black line *CD*) of the market as a whole. This combined demand curve is confronted with the (dashed) vertical supply curve, *XX*, representing the fixed stock of the good available. Price is still *MP* and is determined by the intersection of the combined demand curve *CD* with the curve representing the fixed supply *XX*. The amount bought and sold is still *OM*, and the amount not bought (or bought back by sellers) is still *MX*. When this situation is represented by a vertical supply curve, it can be regarded as the limiting case of inflexible supply. Of course, it 'might happen that sellers had no demand for their own good. In that case, the ordinary sellers' supply curve would take the shape XX and supply would be completely inflexible.

This case of fixed supply has been discussed at length, not only because of its analytical importance as a limiting case, but because of its practical importance. It occurs not only with first editions, etc., but also with the supply of labour. As we shall see later, this can in some contexts be regarded more appropriately as the demand for leisure, since workers are faced with two alternative uses for their (fixed amount of) time. They can either take it as leisure or they can use it to earn income by working. In other words, they can either 'keep' their time for their own use or 'sell' it to someone else and work for him.

5.2 Flexible supply

We now turn to the more usual case of flexible supply. Here the amounts of goods which are produced will alter as price changes. We shall assume that the important decision is whether to produce the good or not to produce it at all. Sellers who have produced a good may be seen, in principle, as choosing whether to consume it themselves rather than sell it to others. We shall assume that this decision is not important. While shoemakers may have demand for shoes, it is not likely to be quantitatively large in relation to the total supply of shoes. We shall therefore ignore sellers' demand for any good where supplies are flexible. For there is here the much more important question of deciding how much to produce, which does not exist where supply is completely fixed.

The main factor determining the supply prices of agricultural products and of many manufactured goods, especially in the long run, is the cost of producing them. To put it simply, if consumers want more of a good to be produced they will have to pay a higher price for it. The reason for this is that to increase the output of a good it is necessary to attract factors of production away from other industries to the production of the good in question. It is likely that these factors will be less efficient, or more expensive, or both. Cost per unit of output therefore often increases as the output of a product rises. This is an over-simplified explanation of the reason why supply curves slope upwards, but we can only give a completely accurate one later. We may provisionally assume for our purpose that a greater amount of any good will be supplied if, but only if, its price is higher.

This implies that sellers' supply curves normally slope upwards from left to right, though they may slope downwards for some manufactured goods, as we shall see. There are thus two limiting cases. At one end of the scale, a vertical straight line represents totally unresponsive, or 'infinitely inelastic', supply. Supply will not increase at all however much price rises. At the other end of the scale, a horizontal straight line represents very responsive, or 'infinitely elastic', supply, such that a small rise in price evokes an indefinitely large increase in the amount supplied. By analogy with elasticity of demand, the first limiting case of totally unresponsive supply can be defined as zero elasticity of supply. The second, representing infinitely responsive supply, can be defined as infinite elasticity of supply.

Along an upward-sloping supply curve, amounts supplied and price both increase together, instead of one increasing while the other diminishes, as with a downward-sloping demand curve. The changes in amount supplied and in price are therefore both in the same direction. Elasticities of supply lying between the two limits mentioned above are both positive and finite. There are no problems over minus signs as there are with elasticity of demand. The general measure of the degree of elasticity of supply is:

Elasticity of supply

$$= \frac{\text{increase in amount supplied}}{\text{amount supplied}} \cdot \frac{\text{increase in price}}{\text{price}}.$$

Thus if the proportionate increase in amount supplied is double the proportionate rise in price, elasticity of supply is 2. The amount supplied changes, proportionately, twice as fast as the price changes. Similarly, if the proportionate change in amount supplied is only half as great as the proportionate change in price, elasticity of supply is $\frac{1}{2}$. On this definition, supply has unitary elasticity if the amount supplied increases in the same proportion as price has changed. Unitary elasticity of supply would be represented graphically by *any* straight line through the origin. Whatever the slope of this straight line through the origin and whatever the scales on the two axes, elasticity of supply will equal one. But it is important to realise that unitary elasticity of supply, unlike unitary elasticity of demand, has no special economic significance.

The distinction between great and small elasticities of supply is important, and we need some measure to show whether one supply curve is more or less elastic than another supply curve over a range, or at a point. But elasticity of supply equal to one, like elasticity of supply of one-half or of two, is only a measure on a scale which divides elasticities greater than zero and less than infinity into arbitrary units. The reason for this asymmetry between supply and demand is that there is no important economic significance, like that of constant outlay, attaching to any particular degree of elasticity of supply, except for elasticities of zero and infinity. It might be concluded that the concept of elasticity of supply is therefore superfluous. However, the idea of responsiveness of supply to changes in price is so important that it is useful to keep elasticity of supply as a technical term with a precise definition.

6.
Equilibrium

Having discussed what factors determine demand and supply, we must now discuss how demand and supply interact in the market to determine the price of a good and the amount of it which is bought and sold. We have seen that demand supply are like two forces pulling in opposite directions. They are balanced, or in equilibrium, at the market price where the amount that is demanded equals the amount supplied. This price is usually called the *equilibrium price,* and the amount demanded and supplied at this price the equilibrium amount. These must be distinguished from other hypothetical prices and amounts, which might satisfy the conditions either of demand or of supply separately, but do not satisfy both simultaneously, and therefore cannot be established in the market. Market equilibrium is shown graphically Fig. 1.16. The demand curve *DD* intersects the supply curve *SS* at the point *R*. In this equilibrium situation, the equilibrium amount of 60 000 bales is exchanged at the equilibrium price of £3·50.

Our main concern in Part 1 will be to explain how the equilibrium prices, first of goods and later of factors of production, are determined. This means that in Part 1 we shall spend our time looking into the factors influencing the shape of the demand and supply curves, for goods and factors, for these curves determine their equilibrium prices.

We shall make one important assumption about equilibrium between demand and supply. We shall assume that the demand and supply curves with which we shall be concerned are such that any disturbance of the original equilibrium situation will set in motion forces which cause a return to that equilibrium. The significance of this assumption can be seen from Fig. 1.15.

In Fig. 1.15 we have a downward-sloping demand curve and an upward-sloping supply curve for a good. The market is in equilibrium when the amount OM of the good is sold at the price of £OP. If the equilibrium is now disturbed and the price rises to £OP_1, the amount of the good supplied, OM_1, will exceed the amount demanded, OM_2. Sellers will be supplying more of the good at the price of £OP_1 than buyers are prepared to buy at that price. They will therefore have to reduce their price. As price falls in this way, the amount demanded will rise and the amount supplied will fall until the two amounts coincide at the equilibrium price of £OP. Similarly, if the price falls to OP_2, the amount demanded, OM_1, will exceed the amount supplied, OM_2, and competition between buyers will force the price up until once again the equilibrium price of £OP is reached. The amount exchanged will once again be OM. When the demand and supply conditions are such that a displacement of the equilibrium situation automatically causes a return to it in this way, the equilibrium is said to be *stable*. Equilibrium will be stable when slightly to the left of the equilibrium position the demand price exceeds the supply price, and slightly to the right of it the supply price exceeds the demand price. Another way of determining whether equilibrium is stable is to discover whether, at a price slightly above the equilibrium level, the amount demanded falls short of the amount supplied. If either of these conditions holds good, any rise in price above the equilibrium level will set in train forces which cause a return to that level, and vice versa.

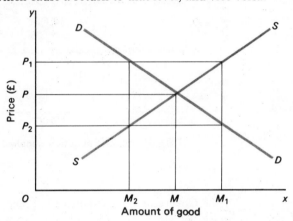

Fig. 1.15

These stability conditions will always be fulfilled if the demand curve slopes downwards and the supply curve slopes upwards. We shall spend a great deal of space in the next few chapters analysing the forces determining the shape of demand and supply curves. This will show why demand curves normally slope downwards, why supply curves normally slope upwards, and why equilibrium is therefore usually stable.

6.1 Flex-price and Fix-price markets

Before doing this, however, it will be a useful exercise to look at the way markets operate where prices are not flexible. Sir John Hicks has described markets where prices are flexible as 'flex-price' markets. Many markets are not like this. They are not flex-price markets but 'fix-price' markets. For example, the Government may intervene in the cotton market, because it is worried by high cotton prices. It could then consider fixing a maximum price for cotton. Let us suppose that the Government sets a price of £2·50 in the market represented in Table 1.1 and Fig. 1.16. Obviously, this will be a situation where there is 'excess demand'. At a price of £2·50, the amount demanded will exceed the amount supplied by M_1M_2. If this were a flex-price market, the excess demand would raise prices. Since the Government has made it a fix-price market, the price cannot now move towards the equilibrium level. Instead, the market is kept in disequilibrium by the Government's decision to fix a maximum price.

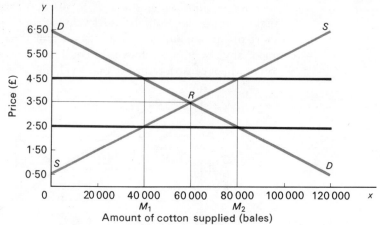

Fig. 1.16

Amount of cotton supplied (bales)

6.2 Maximum prices and shortages

If the Government's fixed price is accepted by all traders, there is no way in which the disequilibrium can be eliminated. Some buyers who would be prepared to take cotton at £2·50 will be unsatisfied. Queues of unsatisfied purchasers may well fill the market and cotton may well be unofficially rationed, as the fairest way of making sure that everybody who is prepared to buy at £2·50 is able to get some. However, we are not here concerned with ethics. The point is simply that a competitive flex-price market has the great economic virtue of ensuring that in the end price will settle at the equilibrium level. Price will settle where all those wishing to buy and all those wishing to sell at that price are able to trade and there will be no queues. The equilibrium price will be that at which the supply and demand curves intersect. This is the only price at which the amount available for sale is exactly equal to the amount buyers wish to buy at that price. Governments may well find it necessary, for social or political reasons, to intervene in markets to fix prices. However, it must be realised that the result is inevitably that there will be disequilibrium.

Indeed, it is likely that the situation will go beyond this. As we have implied already, one of the characteristics of an economic system with flexible prices is that changes in price will tend to eliminate any disequilibrium that develops. If prices are fixed by the Government, disequilibrium cannot be eliminated in that way, unless the Government is disobeyed. This is precisely what is likely to happen. If the Government fixes a price below the equilibrium level, a black-market may well develop where prices are higher than those fixed by the Government. As many governments have discovered in recent years, especially during and immediately after the second world war, only a law-abiding public or an efficient policing system can prevent black-markets from developing where price control leads to an excess demand for a product or range of products.

6.3 Minimum prices and surpluses

So far, we have assumed that the Government imposes a price lower than the equilibrium level. However, especially in markets for primary produce, governments often impose prices above the equilibrium level in order to keep up the incomes of primary producers. Suppose, for example, that the Government decides that the incomes of cotton growers need to be sustained. It may set a price for cotton of £4·50 and make it a 'fix-price' market. Now, there will be an excess supply of cotton at the Government's price. Indeed, Fig. 1.16 shows that the excess supply is M_1M_2. That much more cotton is available at £4·50 than buyers are willing to take. This is the result that will always occur whenever governments think it necessary to impose prices above the equilibrium level. Indeed, they often have to buy up from producers the amount of commodity in excess supply. What the Government will do with the cotton is, of course, another matter. If it feels that the future price of cotton will be higher than £4·50, it may well be able to store it and then use it to meet any excess demand if the equilibrium price rises above £4·50. If the equilibrium price does not rise to £4·50, or to some intervening price at which the Government is prepared to sell the cotton at a loss, difficulties of storing surplus cotton may arise.

6.4 Using algebra

It follows from this discussion that simple demand and supply analyses can deal not only with situations where there is a free market for a commodity. They can also deal with situations where there is Government intervention. Though simple, demand and supply diagrams like this provide powerful tools of analysis.

One can, of course, use algebra instead. Let us see what happens if we again use the demand and supply equations from page namely:

$$q_d = (6·50 - p)\ 20\ 000$$
$$q_s = (p - 0·50)\ 20\ 000$$

If the Government fixes price (p) at £2·50, these become:

$$q_d = (6{\cdot}50 - 2{\cdot}50)\ 20\,000$$
$$= 4 \times 20\,000$$
$$= 80\,000$$
$$\text{and } q_s = (2{\cdot}50 - 0{\cdot}50)\ 20\,000$$
$$= 2 \times 20\,000 = 40\,000$$

As with Fig. 1.16, we have an amount demanded of 80 000 and an amount supplied of 40 000. Excess demand at a price of £2·50 is 40 000. Readers may like to convince themselves that substituting a price of £4·50 into the demand and supply equations gives an excess supply of 40 000 bales of cotton.

Suggested reading

MARSHALL, ALFRED	*Principles of Economics,* 8th ed., London, 1920, especially Book III, chapter 4, and Book V, chapters 1, 2 and 3.
WICKSTEED, P. H.	*The Commonsense of Political Economy,* London, 1933, Volume II, chapter 4.

2

Consumer's demand

1. An elementary theory

We have so far given a simple explanation of the way in which supply and demand between them determine equilibrium prices. We must now discuss in greater detail the forces upon which demand and supply depend. Then, at a later stage, we can study more fully the way in which they interact in the market.

It has already been explained that market demand curves are likely to slope downwards to the right, but we must provide more adequate justification for that statement. Market demand is the aggregate of the demands of individuals, so that to provide such justification we must first of all analyse these individual demands. In this and the following chapter we shall study the demand of an individual consumer for a consumption good and thereby explain the factors on which both individual and market demand curves depend.

In this chapter we give an elementary analysis of consumer demand. We shall assume that:

2. The assumptions

(1) The consumer's wants remain unchanged throughout.
(2) He has a fixed amount of money available.
(3) He is one of many buyers.
(4) He knows the prices of all goods, each of which is homogeneous.
(5) He can, if he wishes, spend his money in very small amounts.
(6) He acts 'rationally'.

3. Choice between alternatives

The first question which we need to answer is, 'How does the consumer decide which of the various available commodities to buy?' To answer this let us assume that the consumer, when he makes his purchases, has the sole aim of obtaining the greatest possible satisfaction from his available money resources. In technical language, we have seen that this means that the consumer obeys the principle of 'economic rationality'. He acts rationally in the sense that he gets the greatest possible satisfaction from his money by deliberately planning his purchases and choosing one good in preference to another. This does not necessarily mean that he is behaving selfishly in any moral sense. He may be buying goods for his family and not for himself. He may be buying shoes for a child or a carpet for the house. But we shall still assume that his decisions about what to buy are taken after deliberate and careful thought.

Basing our argument on these assumptions, we can now discuss the way in which an individual consumer makes his purchases. It will be clear that, since, by definition, all economic goods are scarce, an individual consumer is unable to buy unlimited quantities of any of them. As we know only too well from personal experience, this reduces us in practice to the problem of how to make our money go as far as possible—how to obtain maximum satisfaction from our limited resources. We are compelled to do without this or that good because our incomes are too small to satisfy every desire.

This leads us to an important conclusion. The consumer's basic problem is that he must choose between alternative satisfactions. Since he is not rich enough to be able to buy everything he would like, he can only buy one thing if he forgoes another. The problem of choice between alternatives is the important one. The consumer derives maximum satisfaction from his available money by buying those goods which are most desirable to him. It is clear then that the terms on which these alternative satisfactions are offered are of crucial importance. The questions which consumers ask are: If we buy this, how much must we pay for it? Is it worth it? What alternatives shall we forgo? And what would be their value to us?

In practice, consumers invariably make their choices in the light of existing money prices. A housewife going shopping, who is not certain whether to buy any green peas, will probably allow their price to make up her mind for her. If peas are 25 pence per pound, she will almost certainly refuse to buy any, but at a penny a pound she will take some gladly. Price is the most obvious indicator of the value of the alternative satisfactions which she must forgo if she buys the peas. For the price of peas will determine how many other goods cannot be bought if the peas are bought. And whilst 25p less to spend on, say, groceries may be important, a penny will not.

Yet it is not only the prices of the goods which she is thinking of buying which enter into the housewife's calculations. The price of many other goods which are in the shops will influence her decisions. As Wicksteed says, 'If good sound old potatoes are to be had at a low price the marketer will be less likely to pay a high price for new ones, because there is a good alternative to be had on good terms'.[1] But, although money prices of other goods in the shops are the most obvious indicators of the alternatives sacrificed, other factors may be important too. A decision to buy 1 lb of peas at the high price of 25p may well leave the housewife's purchases of other household goods unaffected, but may deprive her of an afternoon at the cinema, mean one less music lesson for her child, leave the local church with 25p less in the collection plate on Sunday or deprive a charity of a much-needed donation.

The alternative which a consumer finds he must sacrifice may therefore sometimes be the satisfaction of helping a deserving cause. Nor is that all. Instead of deciding to spend 25p on one good instead of on another, the consumer might decide not to spend it but to save it for spending in the future. Or he could, if he wished, simply decide not to earn it at all. To any consumer at any time the range of possible alternatives from which he will be able to choose will be very great indeed. Nevertheless, on our assumption of economic rationality, any satisfaction which is deliberately chosen from this large set of possible alternative satisfactions will clearly be preferred to each and all of the others.

4. Scales of preference

The first step which the consumer takes when deciding which good or goods will give him the greatest possible satisfaction is therefore to rank these goods in order of preference. He must first of all build up '"a scale of preferences" . . . on which all objects of desire or pursuit (positive or negative) find their place, and which registers the terms on which they would be accepted as equivalents or preferred one to the other'.[2] Since people do decide to buy one good rather than another, they must have such scales of preference in their minds. Of course, the fact that people do make choices in a way which suggests that they have scales of preference does not mean that these consumers' preference scales are complete, completely consistent or completely conscious at all times. However, consumers' demand would be much too erratic for us to be able to construct a theory of demand at all unless preference scales were in some degree rational and stable through time, and purchases were made in accordance with them. There is enough stability in consumers' spending patterns in practice to suggest that such a theory is realistic.

One important point must be remembered. While a consumer's purchases at any time are determined by his scale of preferences and his total available money resources, which are fixed in amount, the

[1]P. H. Wicksteed, *Commonsense of Political Economy*, London, 1933, p. 21.
[2]ibid. p. 33.

amount of money which he will spend in the shop or supermarket will not itself be fixed in the same way. It will be closely dependent on whether a number of things are available, for example, houses, flats, holidays, entertainment, education, and on their prices. In the same way, expenditure on these things will depend on prices in the shops. Nor is it only the absolute quantity of money which the consumer spends on any one shopping expedition which is likely to vary according to the details of the situation. It is equally possible for the 'real' value, or 'purchasing power', of the consumer's money resource to change. For example, it may well be that, when the housewife has finished her morning's shopping, prices have turned out to be higher or lower than she expected, and this may either allow her to buy goods she did not expect to be able to afford, or else force her to do without goods she had hoped to buy. Given her scale of preferences, the housewife will arrange her purchases in the light of the realised purchasing power of her resources.

5. Decisions at the margin   In order to keep the exposition as simple as possible, we have so far avoided discussing the actual quantities of any commodity which a consumer will buy. We have seen that a housewife will decide whether to buy any peas or not when she sees their price and the prices of alternatives like cabbage, carrots, or beans. This only shows whether she will buy any peas at all, and not how many pounds. This is the next problem which we must solve.

Let us imagine a housewife with a husband and four children deciding how many pounds of peas to buy for the weekend. We can suppose that her preference might be such that:

if peas cost £0·30 per lb, she would buy   3 lb
,,   £0·20   ,,   ,,   6 lb
,,   £0·10   ,,   ,,   20 lb

If the price of peas is 30 pence a pound, she will feel just willing to take 3 lb as a treat, hoping that there will be enough for Sunday. If the price is 20 pence, however, she will just feel willing to take 6 lb, hoping that there will be more for Sunday and perhaps some left over for another day. If the price falls to 10 pence, she will probably buy some for each day of the week, say 20 lb altogether. The important fact which emerges here is that a single pound of peas *as such* does not occupy a definite position in the consumer's scale of preference.

If peas are being sold at 10p per lb, the housewife is just willing to buy 3 lb, and this clearly means that she regards the first, second and third pounds of peas as occupying a higher position in her scale of preferences than 30 pence. But she regards 30p as being more attractive than the fourth pound of peas. Again, when peas are available for 20p, she prefers the fourth, fifth and sixth pounds of peas to 20p, but thinks that 20p is preferable to the seventh pound of peas. With peas for sale at 10p per lb, her scale of preferences shows that our housewife regards the seventh to the twentieth pounds of peas (inclusive) as worth more than 10p, but regards 10p is worth more than the twenty-first pound of peas.

We may therefore conclude that our housewife thinks that the fourth pound of peas is worth less than 30p but more than 20p; that the seventh pound is worth less than 20p but more than 10p, and so on. But, since we are assuming that the peas are homogeneous, there can be no physical difference between any two individual pounds of peas. This means that the housewife is not deciding whether to buy *a particular* fourth, seventh or twenty-first pound of peas. What she is doing is deciding whether it will pay her to buy 4 pounds of peas in preference to 3, or 7 lb in preference to 6, taking the current price of peas into account.

It is important to remember that throughout the discussion of this section (and indeed this chapter) the purchases of all other goods are assumed unchanged. Although all goods possess the ability to satisfy consumers' wants, we cannot measure their ability to do so except in terms of the price consumers are prepared to pay for them. Even this measure will break down if we consider more than one good. The reason is that, as he extends his purchases over a larger (or smaller) quantity of goods, the consumer finds that the satisfactions given by the expenditure of an extra penny falls (rises). This means that we can use this analysis only to consider the purchase of one good at a time. Money becomes an inefficient measure of the satisfactions given by goods if we look at more than one good which represents a small proportion of consumers' total purchases.

6. The margin defined

This brings us to what is perhaps the most important concept in economic theory—the concept of the margin. We must explain what we mean by the margin before we can fully understand the nature of the decision which we have just seen the housewife making. We may say that the 'part of the thing which he (the consumer) is only just induced to purchase may be called his *marginal purchase* because he is on the margin of doubt whether it is worth his while to incur the outlay required to obtain it'.[1] Similarly, any unit of a commodity which a consumer is momentarily considering whether to buy— whether he in fact buys it or not—may be called a marginal unit. Our housewife reviews each unit of the good in turn, and as she does

[1] Marshall, *Principles of Economics*, (8th Edition), p. 93.

so that unit becomes for a moment the marginal unit. If the housewife buys a unit, it then becomes an 'intra-marginal' purchase. If she refuses any unit, it is clearly worth too little for her to buy it at the current price—it is 'extra-marginal'. The housewife is then in equilibrium, as ours was when she bought 20 lb of peas at 10p per lb. In this equilibrium position, the unit which a consumer is *just* willing to purchase is the marginal purchase.

7. Marginal significance

It is obvious that when we say that the housewife undertakes this review of the value of each unit of the good in succession, we are merely repeating in another way what we have already said about the consumer building up a scale of preferences. But we can now state a more useful conclusion. We may say that when the consumer considers whether any unit of a good is worth buying, he (or she) is working out the *marginal significance* to him of the good he is wondering whether to buy, in terms of the good with which it is to be bought. He is considering what is the value of the marginal unit of the purchased good in terms of the good with which he buys it. Thus, when our housewife was considering whether or not she would buy the sixth pound of peas, that sixth pound had become a marginal pound and the marginal significance of peas in terms of money at that stage was 10p for a pound of peas. For we know that the housewife was just willing to pay 10p for that pound of peas and therefore 10p must just have been the worth of that pound of peas in terms of money.

In this discussion the careful reader will have seen a clue to the solution of our problem: How does the housewife decide how many pounds of peas to buy? We may therefore state the answer briefly here and explain it in detail in the next section. Our housewife is considering whether to buy a particular (marginal) pound of peas. She will do so if the marginal significance to her of peas in terms of money is sufficiently high. It may also be said that, in general, the marginal significance of a good in terms of money will decrease the more of that good one has compared with money and other goods.

8. Consumer's equilibrium

We can now proceed to explain the way in which the decision on how many peas should be bought is taken. It will be recalled that when peas cost 10p per lb, our imaginary housewife took 20 lb. She was willing to give up 10 pence for a twentieth pound of peas, but not for a twenty-first. It is clear, then, that at this point the housewife preferred the satisfaction which 10p could give, through its ability to purchase other goods, to the satisfaction given by a twenty-first pound of peas. This was because the money price of peas insisted on by greengrocers, namely 10p for 1 lb of peas, was too high. It exceeded the marginal significance in terms of money which the housewife herself attached to this twenty-first pound of peas, perhaps 8p for that pound.

Let us look at the problem more closely. In our example, we have assumed that the housewife is just prepared to take the third pound of peas at 30p. This means that the ruling market price (30p for 1 lb of peas) is just equal to the housewife's own marginal significance of peas in terms of money when the marginal pound is the third pound of peas. The housewife is on the margin of doubt whether to buy the third pound at the price of 30p. With price reduced to 10p, the marginal significance in terms of money of the third pound of peas (30 pence) can be presumed to remain the same, since scales of preference are independent of prices. So, since its marginal significance in terms of peas is greater than the current market price of peas, the third pound of peas is now bought without hesitation.

It can also be seen that for the housewife the marginal significance of the sixth pound of peas in terms of money is just equal to its market price when peas are 20p per lb. The housewife is just prepared to take the sixth pound at that price. The marginal significance of peas in terms of money is 20p for the marginal (sixth pound). When the price of peas falls to 10p, the marginal significance of the sixth pound of peas to the housewife, namely 20p, becomes greater than the market price insisted upon by greengrocers. This is now 10p for 1 lb of peas. So she takes the sixth pound at that price.

We see, then, that if the housewife's marginal significance of peas in terms of money is greater for any pound of peas than their market price, she will buy that pound. But if it is less (as for the twenty-first pound of peas when peas cost 10p per lb or more) she will refuse to buy it. Also, if the marginal significance to the housewife of a particular pound of peas is just equal to the market price of peas (as it is with the twentieth pound of peas when their price is 10p) she will just be prepared to take that pound.

9. The rule for consumer equilibrium

We now formulate a vital proposition of consumer demand theory. *A consumer will exchange money for units of any commodity,* A, *up to the point where the last (marginal) unit of* A *which he buys has for him a marginal significance in terms of money just equal to its money price.* This fundamental proposition enables us to explain how a consumer will reach an equilibrium position where he has no desire to buy any more of a good. If he goes on buying a good until its marginal significance in terms of money is equal to its money price, he cannot then make himself better off by buying any more of the good. If he did, he would only become worse off, for he would be obtaining units of the good which, as their marginal significances would show, were lower on his scale of preference than the units of money which he would have to sacrifice in order to obtain them.

For example, our housewife who can buy peas at 10p per lb is in an equilibrium position when she has bought 20 lb of peas at that price. The marginal significance of the twenty-first pound of peas in terms of money is, say, 8p for that pound. That is to say, our housewife regards 8p as being worth only just as much as the twenty-first pound of peas. Yet, in order to obtain that twenty-first pound of peas she would have to pay 10p. She would have to give up 10p, which occupies a higher position in her scale of preferences, to obtain a twenty-first pound of peas which occupies a lower position. She would reduce her total satisfaction if she were to do this. On our assumption that all consumers wish to maximise satisfactions, she will not buy more peas, but will remain in the optimum equilibrium position where she gets twenty pounds of peas at 10p per lb. It is not difficult to see that this analysis will hold for each commodity separately, however many commodities there may be, though the limitations of the human mind make it difficult to apply it to more than two or three goods at once. Only more-advanced mathematical analysis than we are prepared to use in this book would make it possible to apply the analysis to more than two goods simultaneously. Nevertheless, it follows from what has been said that if consumers are to maximise satisfactions they must equate the marginal significance of every good in terms of money with its money price. Goods here include consumer goods, capital goods, services, durable consumer goods from which future satisfactions can be obtained, and leisure (the alternative to working and earning money).

When the consumer has adjusted his (or her) expenditure at all margins in this way, he is in equilibrium, given his wants on the one hand and his income and the set of market prices on the other. So long as the relative importance of his different wants remain unchanged and his income and market price remain constant, he will remain 'at rest' in the same equilibrium position. He has no reason to revise his plans, but will continue to buy the same things in the same quantities, until either his wants, or the opportunities of satisfying them, alter. His wants are adjusted to each other and to his environment.

10. Some limitations of this analysis

The aim in this chapter has been to provide an elementary theory of consumer's demand and the picture given has been one of perfectly rational economic behaviour on the part of the consumer. This picture is unrealistic in three important ways. In the first place, no sensible consumer bothers about making minute adjustments at the margin. Quite naturally, most human beings have not the slightest desire to become calculating machines. Like the law, the normal consumer does not bother about very small things. Even the most careful housewife, with a large family and a very small income, has to draw the line somewhere. Other people will take even less care over the process. The consumer is never completely in equilibrium, even if both his wants and market conditions remain completely stable.

Second, there will usually be frequent small changes in prices (and often in the consumer's income). If he were truly 'rational', the consumer would be continually revising his purchases, making sure that he was using all his money all the time in the best possible way. In practice, there will be many habitual purchases which he will make each week or month and which he will change only if conditions alter markedly. Many purchases are likely to be a matter of habit and to change only at intervals in order to bring the consumer into line with relatively big changes in market conditions.

In the third place, no-one will ever have worked out in detail beforehand how he would reach a new optimum equilibrium position, with given wants, when there had been a large change in his own income or in market conditions. A tramp may dream of becoming a millionaire, but will not have in his mind a detailed scale of preferences between country houses and yachts. The theory of consumer equilibrium is more useful for interpreting adjustments to small, but not minute, changes than for explaining consumers' behaviour in times of violent economic change.

Suggested reading | WICKSTEED, P. H.   *The Commonsense of Political Economy,* London, 1933, Volume I, chapters 1, 2 and 3.

3

Indifference curve analysis

1. Scales of preference

We have so far explained that a consumer makes his purchases in the light of his *scale of preferences*. We must now look at the nature of scales of preference in greater detail, doing this in two stages. In this chapter, we shall use indifference curve analysis. In chapter 4, we shall study revealed preference.

The assumption lying behind indifference curve analysis is that each consumer is able (at least in principle) to set down a scale of preferences and that he can do this quite independently of market prices. We suppose that a consumer can rank combinations, or 'baskets' of the various commodities available to him, in order of importance to him. We also suppose that he does this on the basis of their ability to satisfy his wants and before he knows what their prices are. For example, we may imagine a man going into a green-grocer's shop to buy the week's supplies. It is assumed that this man can, in principle at least, tell us which of the combinations, 'baskets', of fruit or vegetables available to him will give him equal satisfactions, which will give greater satisfactions and which less.

Actually doing this would, of course, be an impossible task. However, the analysis is legitimate provided that it enables us to throw light (as it does) on consumer behaviour. In Chapter 4 we shall provide an analysis which does not require any more of the consumer than that he is able to go out and spend the money he has available.

For the present, let us return to our consumer going into the greengrocer's shop. Before he makes his purchase we ask him to tell us which combinations of the various commodities that are available would give him greater satisfaction than others, which would give him smaller satisfactions, and which equal satisfactions. We suppose that our consumer is able to provide us with a list of the various available combinations of goods, arranged in order of importance. Of course, with his given income, he could not afford to buy all these combinations. When he learned their prices he would rule out some as not worth their cost, but he would be able to say which combinations of the various goods in the greengrocer's shop he would like best, which least, and so on. It would be on the basis of such a list, representing his scale of preferences, that he would ultimately make his purchases. All he has done is to draw up his scale of preferences in a concrete form instead of constructing it mentally, partially and to some extent subconsciously, as he does when he goes shopping.

We now consider what kind of scale of preferences a consumer would be likely to draw up. In order to simplify the problem, let us assume that there are only two goods on sale—grapes and potatoes. This is not very realistic, but it is a useful starting point. If we are concerned with only two goods (grapes and potatoes) we can show the combinations of these goods which give various levels of satisfaction to a consumer in a diagram like Fig. 3.1.

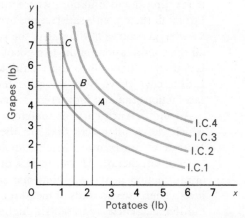

Fig. 3.1

In Fig. 3.1 potatoes are measured along the x-axis, the number of pounds of potatoes increasing from left to right. Similarly, increasing quantities of grapes are measured up the y-axis. The consumer then informs us that if he were at a point A with 4 lb of grapes and $2\frac{1}{4}$ lb of potatoes, he would be just as well satisfied as at point B with 5 lb of grapes and $1\frac{1}{2}$ lb of potatoes, or at point C with 7 lb of grapes and 1 lb of potatoes. These three combinations of grapes and potatoes represent for the consumer the same level of satisfaction—the same position in his scale of preferences.

**2.
Indifference
curves**

Assuming that the consumer is able to give sufficient information, and that the goods are perfectly divisible, it is possible to draw a continuous line through all points representing the same level of satisfactions as at A, B and C. This has been done in Fig. 3.1. The resulting line shows all those combinations of grapes and potatoes which give a particular level of satisfaction to the consumer. We say that the consumer is *indifferent* between all the combinations of grapes and potatoes shown on the line through *A, B* and *C*. This line is therefore known as an *indifference curve*. It shows all those combinations of grapes and potatoes which occupy the same position in the consumer's scale of preferences—which give him the same level of satisfaction. We have labelled it indifference curve number 2 (I.C.2).

We can now draw similar indifference curves showing the particular combinations of grapes and potatoes which represent higher and lower levels of satisfaction than that shown on indifference curve 2. For example, in Fig. 3.1 all points on indifference curves 3 and 4 represent preferred positions to those on indifference curve 2. All combinations of grapes and potatoes shown on indifference curve 3 represent situations where satisfactions are exactly the same. But at all these points satisfactions are greater than at every point on indifference curve 2. Similarly, the consumer is indifferent between all the combinations of the two goods shown on indifference curve 4, but prefers them all to the combinations on indifference curve 3. Indifference curve 1, on the other hand, represents a lower level of satisfactions than on indifference curves 2, 3 or 4.

An indifference curve is therefore like a contour line on a map, which shows all places that are the same height above sea-level. Instead of representing height, an indifference curve represents a level of satisfaction. However, it is quite impossible to *measure* levels of satisfaction in the way that one can measure heights above sea-level. There are no units of measurement. One can say whether one indifference curve represents a higher or lower level of satisfaction than another, but not *by how much* satisfaction is higher or lower. For this reason we give indifference curves numbers to put them in the right order, 1, 2, 3, 4, etc., but do not attempt to label them in terms of units of satisfaction. An indifference map is an *ordinal* system, where levels of satisfaction are ranked, or ordered, but not measured.

3. Our assumptions about indifference curves

We have now described an apparatus which enables us to represent the consumer's scale of preferences by a set of indifference curves or an *indifference map*. While we have drawn such a map in Fig. 3.1, we have not justified our assumptions about the shape of individual indifference curves. We must do this now.

3.1 They slope downwards

We require two assumptions and one definition before we can specify the shape of an indifference curve. The first assumption is that every indifference curve slopes downwards from left to right. This seems eminently reasonable. If indifference curves did not slope downwards, they would either slope upwards or be horizontal. If an indifference curve were horizontal this would imply that the consumer would be equally satisfied with, say, 6 lb of grapes and either 1, 2, 3, 4, 5 or 6 lb of potatoes. This is obviously not likely to be the case. A combination which includes more of one good and no less of another must always be preferred to a combination containing less of the one good and the same amount of the other. Nor is an indifference curve likely to slope upwards to the right, for this would mean that the consumer would regard a combination containing a greater amount of both commodities as giving just the same satisfaction as one containing less of each. This is even less likely to be true. A consumer cannot regard 7 lb of grapes and 3 lb of potatoes as giving the same satisfaction as 6 pounds of grapes and 2 pounds of potatoes. It could only happen if the satisfaction derived from some units of one good were negative, and economics is not concerned with commodities that give negative satisfactions. The very word 'good' implies that satisfactions are derived from goods. The first assumption is realistic. Indifference curves always slope downwards to the right.

3.2 They are concave upwards

Second, it is assumed that all indifference curves are concave upwards, like the curves drawn so far. This is a very important assumption. It can be seen, on reflection, that if one looks at any indifference curve, one can read off from it the marginal significance of one good in terms of the other. For example, suppose that the consumer is on indifference curve 2 in Fig. 3.1, with 4 lb of grapes and $2\frac{1}{4}$ lb of potatoes. The indifference curve shows that he would be equally satisfied if he acquired one more pound of grapes by giving up $\frac{3}{4}$ lb of potatoes. He would then have 5 lb of grapes and $1\frac{1}{2}$ lb of potatoes. The marginal significance of a pound of grapes in terms of potatoes is therefore $\frac{3}{4}$ lb of potatoes when the fifth pound of grapes is the marginal pound. The consumer would just be prepared to give up $\frac{3}{4}$ lb of potatoes for a fifth (marginal) pound of grapes. One can therefore define marginal significance a little more precisely than in the previous chapter. The marginal significance of a purchased good is measured along one indifference curve in terms of the good used to buy it. The marginal significance of the good purchased is the amount of the good with which purchases are made (here potatoes) which a consumer can afford to give up in order to obtain another marginal unit of the purchased good (in this case grapes) if he is to remain on the same indifference curve.

This means that the slope of an indifference curve at any point shows marginal significance at that point. The shape of an indifference curve is important because it is upon this change of slope along the indifference curve that marginal significance at the various points on it depends. The assumption that indifference curves are concave upwards implies something about what change in marginal significance takes place as one moves along an indifference curve. It implies that if he is to increase his stock of one good, Y, by one unit while becoming no better (or worse) off in doing so, the consumer will be able to give up less X in order to obtain that extra unit of Y the more Y he has. For example, on indifference curve 2 in order to obtain a fifth pound of grapes and yet be no better off, the consumer can afford to give up $\frac{3}{4}$ lb of potatoes; to get the sixth pound he can afford to give up only $\frac{1}{3}$ lb of potatoes; for the seventh pound he can afford to give up $\frac{1}{6}$ lb of potatoes, and so on. Thus, as one moves along an indifference curve, the assumption that it is concave upwards, that it gets flatter to the right and steeper to the left, implies that the marginal significance of the one good in terms of the other will always diminish progressively as one acquires more of the former good.

This is clearly a very important assumption and it is necessary to be sure that it is a realistic one. Is decreasing marginal significance as likely to occur as one moves along an indifference curve as this assumption suggests? Clearly marginal significance could not go on *increasing indefinitely*, for one good reason. As we saw in chapter 2, a consumer buys those units of any good for which his marginal significance in terms of money is greater than the price which he has to pay to obtain them. If there were any commodity for which the consumer's marginal significance were increasing indefinitely and he bought any of it all at the current (constant) price, he would find that after he had bought one unit, each succeeding unit would have a progressively higher marginal significance. He would go on buying more and more of the good until he had spent all his money on it. In fact, it is impossible to think of any situation where a consumer does spend all his money on one good in this way. It is therefore reasonable to assume that marginal significance does not go on increasing for ever and that indifference curves are more likely to be concave upwards than concave downwards; for concavity downwards could only occur if marginal significance increased indefinitely.[1]

Marginal significance is therefore unlikely to increase indefinitely. But could there not be limited regions of a consumer's indifference

[1]It must be remembered that even if a consumer did spend all his income on one commodity, this would not necessarily mean that the marginal significance of that commodity was increasing. It might simply mean that the marginal significance of that good, though diminishing, was very high. Even though the consumer bought nothing else, the marginal significance of that good in terms of money would remain higher than that of any other good.

map where marginal significance did increase? It is more difficult to give a definite answer to this. We have seen that the consumer can never be in equilibrium, buying more than one commodity, if marginal significance is always increasing. At points of equilibrium, therefore, marginal significance must be diminishing. But it is quite possible that there may be some parts of the consumer's preference scale where he could never be in equilibrium because marginal significance was increasing. In other words, there might be limited ranges of indifference curves where 'wobbles' or 'bumps of downward concavity' occurred. An instance of this kind of situation is given in Fig. 3.2.

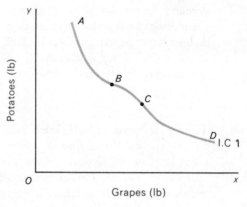

Fig. 3.2

As one moves along the indifference curve from *A* to *B*, the marginal significance of grapes in terms of potatoes declines. The consumer becomes prepared to give up progressively fewer potatoes in order to obtain further grapes. Once *B* is reached, however, a reversal takes place. The consumer suddenly becomes prepared to give up increasing amounts of potatoes to obtain each further pound of grapes. This goes on until point *C* is reached, when conditions again change and the consumer once more becomes willing to give up fewer and fewer pounds of potatoes for each additional pound of grapes. The ranges of the indifference curve between *A* and *B* and between *C* and *D* display normal conditions with diminishing marginal significance of grapes in terms of potatoes. But the range between *B* and *C* is abnormal. The marginal significance of grapes in terms of potatoes increases as the consumer has more grapes.

Our assumption that all indifference curves are convex upwards rules out the possibility that there could be increasing marginal significance, even over small ranges of indifference curves. This does not seem unreasonable. However, we have already seen that a consumer can never be in an equilibrium position, buying some of both goods, at any point on an indifference curve which is concave downwards throughout. Similarly, a consumer will never find it worth remaining on a range of an indifference curve that is concave downwards, however small that range may be. Since the marginal significance of the good he is buying will be increasing, it will pay him to go on buying more and more of it until the indifference curve becomes convex again, when marginal significance will begin to decrease and finally fall below price. One can therefore take consolation from the fact that even if there are isolated segments of indifference curves where marginal significance is increasing these can never be possible positions of equilibrium.

There is more to it even than this. If indifference curves did display 'bumps of concavity' there would be discontinuities in consumers' demand curves, for as we shall see indifference curves lie behind them. One can therefore test the proposition that indifference curves do not have discontinuities. In fact, empirical work suggests that there are few, if any, discontinuities of this kind. Our second assumption is valid. Indifference curves are always concave upwards.

3.3 They do not cross

Thirdly, we need a result which follows from our definition of indifference curves. We define an indifference curve as representing a given level of satisfaction, which is different from that on all other indifference curves. This automatically means that two indifference curves cannot cut each other. In Fig. 3.3, the two indifference curves do cut each other. However, point A is on indifference curve 2, so

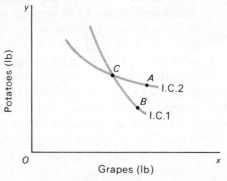

Fig. 3.3

that it represents a higher level of satisfaction for the consumer than does point B, which is on indifference curve 1. Yet point C lies on both curves. This implies that two levels of satisfaction, A and B, which are by definition unequal, have succeeded in becoming equal at point C. This is unacceptable. By definition, indifference curves can never cut each other.

These are the three basic characteristics of indifference curves. All indifference curves in this book will meet the conditions laid down in this section.

4. Consumer's equilibrium

We have now outlined a way in which one can show a consumer's scale of preference for two goods in diagrammatic form. Using this method, we can show how a consumer reaches an equilibrium position. First, we must make one change in our indifference maps. So far, we have assumed that the consumer is considering only two goods—grapes and potatoes. In practice, there are other goods and it will be useful if we can include them in our indifference curve diagrams too. We can do this if we draw indifference maps, not for grapes and potatoes, but for grapes and money, potatoes and money, or indeed any good and money.

Money represents command over all other goods. So, by introducing money into an indifference map we can show the consumer's tastes with respect to, say, potatoes on the one hand and money, representing general purchasing power, on the other. We can do this for money and *any* individual good, and we can do it legitimately, provided we make two assumptions. First, we assume that the prices of all the other goods are given and constant and, second, that the consumer spends all his money on one good or another and does not save any. On these assumptions, we can draw an indifference map where the consumer is represented as choosing between, say, potatoes and all other goods which his money can command.

4.1 Our assumptions

It will be useful to begin by listing all the assumptions we shall make in using indifference curve analysis to show how a consumer decides how much of a particular good to buy—how to reach an equilibrium position. They are:

1. The consumer has an indifference map showing his scale of preferences for combinations of the good in question and of money. This scale of preferences remains unchanged throughout.

2. He has a given amount of money to spend and if he does not spend it on the good we are studying, he will spend all of it on the others.

3. He is one of many buyers and knows the prices of all goods. All prices are assumed to be given and constant, so that money can be treated as command over all goods other than the one the consumer is buying.

4. All goods are homogeneous and divisible.

5. The consumer acts 'rationally' and maximises his satisfactions.

The first step in showing the equilibrium of a consumer diagrammatically is to find a way of depicting on a diagram what his money will buy under the relevant conditions. The consumer's indifference map is shown in Fig. 3.4a. The consumer regards all the combinations of grapes and money on indifference curve 1 in Fig. 3.4a as giving the same satisfactions as each other. Similarly, all the combinations on indifference curve 2 give the same satisfactions, these being greater than on indifference curve 1. Indifference curves 3, 4 and 5 represent progressively higher levels of satisfaction. This indifference map represents the consumer's personal tastes.

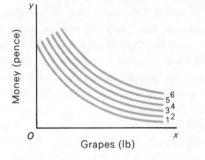
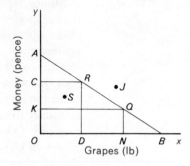

Fig. 3.4 a | b

Figure 3.4b shows the way in which the size of a consumer's income and the price of grapes between them determine his purchases. He has a fixed amount of money, OA pence (shown up the y-axis), which he can spend. The market price of grapes is such that if he spends all his money on grapes he can obtain OB pounds. In other words, the price of a pound of grapes is $\frac{OA}{OB}$p and is shown by the slope of the line AB. The slope of such a line can thus be referred to as its *price slope*.

We are assuming that the consumer spends all his income on one good or another. He must therefore either spend it on grapes or keep it in money to be spent on other goods. This means that, given the price of grapes ($\frac{OA}{OB}$p per pound), the opportunities open to the consumer are shown by the line AB. He could spend all his money on grapes, arriving at point B with OB pounds of grapes. He could keep all his resources in cash, which would leave him with OA pence. Or he could choose any of the various combinations of grapes and money shown on the line AB.

For example, at point R he could buy OD pounds of grapes and keep OCp to spend on other goods. At point Q he could buy ON pounds of grapes and keep OKp to spend on other goods. Assuming that grapes are 'completely divisible', he can acquire any of the combinations of grapes and money shown on the price line *AB*. This line shows the opportunities of acquiring grapes which are open to him with grapes at their current price. It is known as a *price-opportunity line, price line* or *budget line*. The consumer cannot go beyond the price line, say to point *J*, for he is not rich enough. Nor will he remain inside the price line, say at point *S*, for he would not then be spending all his income, and we are assuming that he spends it on one good or another. The price line thus represents the opportunities open to the consumer in the market, given prices and his income. On the other hand, the indifference curves show his tastes quite independently of the prices the consumer has to pay. The price line and the indifference map are completely independent of one another. As we saw in section 1, our customer going into a greengrocer's shop was able to place the goods there on an indifference map before he had any idea what their prices were. The consumer has a scale of preferences which does not depend on prices. Again, in competitive conditions the prices themselves are given and cannot be affected by anything that an individual consumer does. For there are many other buyers, all of insignificant size when compared with the total group of consumers, so that each individual consumer must take the price of every good as given.

4.4 The equilibrium position	The next step is to show how, given his indifference map on the one hand and market conditions on the other, the consumer reaches an equilibrium position. This is done in Fig. 3.5 where we superimpose

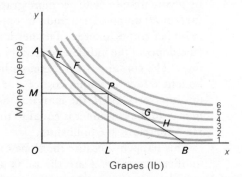

Fig. 3.5

the price line from Fig. 3.4b on the indifference map from Fig. 3.4a. Since we are assuming that the rational consumer always aims at obtaining the greatest possible satisfaction, he will naturally move to the highest possible indifference curve. In doing this he will have to act within the limits imposed by the fact that he has a fixed amount of money OA p, to spend and that the price of grapes is given. In this case the grapes are $\dfrac{OA}{OB}$ p a pound.

The consumer begins at point A in Fig. 3.5[1] with OA p and no grapes. He is on indifference curve 1. He increases his satisfactions by moving to point E, giving up money in exchange for grapes. This increases his satisfactions by putting him on indifference curve 2. If he now comes to point F, exchanging more money for grapes, he again becomes better off, now reaching indifference curve 3. At both E and F the consumer is using all his resources, spending part on grapes and retaining part in the form of money for purchases of other goods. But at F he is better off than at E. He can again increase his satisfactions by moving to P on indifference curve 4. At both F and P he will still be allocating all his money, but at P he will have more grapes relatively to money and will have increased his satisfactions. Having reached P, however, the consumer cannot increase his satisfaction further by substituting more grapes for money. If he did buy more grapes, he would merely find himself back on indifference curve 3 at point G, on indifference curve 2 at point H, and so on. He is not rich enough to be able to reach a position on his scale of preferences higher than indifference curve 4 with grapes at their current price. Hence, at point P on indifference curve 4 the consumer is in an optimum, equilibrium position, where he is maximising his satisfactions.

At any point on the price line above P (e.g. at E or F) the marginal significance of grapes in terms of money to the consumer is greater than the money price of grapes—the indifference curves are steeper than the price line. The consumer therefore increases his satisfactions by giving up money to get more grapes. On the other hand, below P (at G or H) the consumer finds the opposite. The marginal significance to him of grapes in terms of money is now less than the price of grapes (the slopes of the indifference curves are flatter than that of the price line). The consumer will therefore buy no more grapes once he has bought OL lb at a total cost of AM p. This leaves him with OM p for other uses. At P, the marginal significance of grapes in terms of money to the consumer is equal to the price of grapes in the market. He is therefore in equilibrium.

This happens because the slope of the price line and the slope of indifference curve 4 are the same at point P. But this position of equilibrium can now be seen visually from the diagram. The consumer will be in equilibrium where his price line (like AB) is tangent to an indifference curve. For any consumer to be in equilibrium, his price line must be tangential to an indifference curve. At any such

[1]It may prevent confusion if we assure readers that if the straight line AB in Fig. 3.5 appears to be a curve, this is an optical illusion.

point of tangency, the price line and the indifference curve will have the same slope and the marginal significance of the good in terms of money (shown on the indifference curve) will equal its price (shown on the price line). The consumer will retain the combination of the two 'goods' appropriate to this point on his indifference map.

If we consider two consumer goods instead of one consumer good and money, we have to assume that the consumer is paid an income in one of the goods and that their prices in terms of each other are constant. Such a case is shown in Fig. 3.6. Here, units of good X are measured on the x-axis and units of good Y on the y-axis.

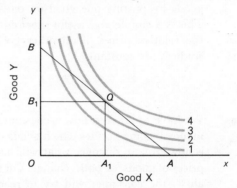

Fig. 3.6

We still assume that the consumer's income, whether paid in X or Y, is fixed, so that he is now able to buy OA of X if he buys nothing but X, or OB of Y if he buys nothing but Y. The price line AB shows all the possible combinations of X and Y which the consumer can afford to buy with his available resources. The steeper the slope of AB, the higher is the price of X in terms of Y, that is, the higher is the relative price of X. If we wish, we can write: $\dfrac{\text{Price of } X}{\text{Price of } Y} = \dfrac{OB}{OA}$. The slope of AB represents the ratio of the money prices of X and Y. In Fig. 3.6, the highest indifference curve which the consumer can reach with his available resources is indifference curve 3. He will be in equilibrium at point Q on this curve, where he buys OA_1 of X and OB_1 of Y. At point Q, the ratio of the prices of X and Y, (namely, $\dfrac{OB}{OA}$), is equal to the consumer's marginal significance of X in terms of Y.

4.5 Consumer's equilibrium with more than two goods

Indifference curve analysis can be extended to cover many kinds of economic problem, and the goods in question can be consumption goods, capital goods, work, leisure or money. In this way, the consumer's indifference maps between all possible commodities can be studied. It follows from our analysis that for him to be in equilibrium with respect to all goods the marginal significance of each good in terms of money must equal its money price. However, diagrammatic representations of consumer equilibrium cannot deal adequately with more than three goods. Each good needs one dimension, so that two goods need two dimensions, three goods need three dimensions, and so on. On the (two-dimensional) page of a book, three dimensions can be shown only by drawing a diagram in perspective. With more than three goods, recourse has to be made to algebra. We shall concentrate our attention on situations where there are only two goods. However, it is always possible to deal by implication with many goods by putting one good on one axis and money on the other. This is a simple and useful short cut. It is legitimate provided that the relative prices of all other goods, apart from the one being studied, are constant.

5. The effects of a price change

We have so far seen how a consumer with given wants and a fixed money income decides which goods to buy and in what amounts. It is now time to discover what will happen if his money income, the prices of goods, or both, change. On the basic assumption of 'rationality', the consumer will try to reach a new equilibrium position where he is once again maximising satisfactions. How will he do this? We shall answer this question by considering the various ways in which the situation facing the consumer can alter. There are three main ways in which the conditions underlying the equilibrium shown on an indifference curve diagram can change.

First, there is the possibility that the consumer may become better or worse off because his income changes but prices remain constant. The consumer's satisfactions will be either increased or decreased according to whether he has a larger or smaller income to spend. The result of this type of change is described as an *income effect*.

Second, it is possible that prices may change, but that the consumer's money income changes at the same time in such a way that he is neither better nor worse off as a result. He will, however, find it worth his while to buy more of those goods whose relative price has fallen. He will substitute the relatively cheaper goods for the relatively dearer ones. The result of this type of change is thus known as a *substitution effect*.

The third possibility is that the price of one good may fall or rise, with money income constant, so that the consumer becomes either better or worse off. In this situation the consumer will not only have to rearrange his purchase as under the substitution effect. His real income, his income in terms of goods bought, will change too. There will now be an income effect as well as a substitution effect. This will make the consumer better or worse off, as the case may be. The result of this kind of change is described as a *price effect*. It is the combination of an income effect and a substitution effect.

We can summarise this in Table 3.1.

Table 3.1

Type of effect	Money income	Price	Real income
Income effect	Changes	Constant	Changes
Substitution effect	Changes	Changes	Constant
Price effect	Constant	Changes	Changes

In this and the next two sections we must discuss these three effects.

5.1 The income effect

First, let us consider the income effect. The effect of a change in the consumer's income can easily be shown on an indifference curve diagram. It will, however, be convenient to carry out this analysis in terms of two goods rather than in terms of one good and money. Let us assume that a consumer has an increased money income to spend, but that the prices of both the goods shown on the indifference map remain constant. The effect of a change of this kind can be seen in Fig. 3.7.

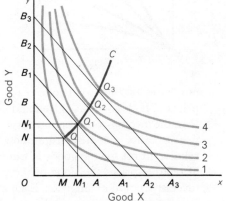

Fig. 3.7

Let us assume that the consumer considered in Fig. 3.7 starts with an income of OA in terms of X (OB in terms of Y). He will be in equilibrium at point Q on indifference curve 1. In this position he will have OM of X and ON of Y. If his income now rises to OA_1 in terms of X, or OB_1 in terms of Y, the consumer will move from the old equilibrium position to a new one at Q_1. He will now be better off, being on indifference curve 2, and will have OM_1 of X and ON_1 of Y. In other words, if we assume that the consumer is paid in X, he will exchange X for Y at the rate of exchange shown by the slope of the price line until he has acquired ON_1 of Y by giving up M_1A_1 of X. He will retain OM_1 of X. As a result of the rise in his income, the consumer has increased his purchases of both X and Y and is at a preferred position on his indifference map. If the consumer's income now rises to OA_2 in terms of X and then to OA_3 in terms of X, he will move to equilibrium positions at Q_2 and Q_3 respectively.

5.2 The income-consumption curve

It is clear that there will be an indefinitely large number of possible equilibrium positions such as Q, Q_1, Q_2, Q_3, one for each possible level of income. The line Q-Q_3 shows all the possible positions of equilibrium over the range of income between OA in terms of X and OA_3 in terms of X, at the given prices of X and Y. Of course, the line can be extended back from Q to O. Any line like O-Q-Q_3-C drawn through the equilibrium points for all the possible levels of income is known as an *income-consumption curve*. It shows how the consumer's

Fig. 3.8 a | b

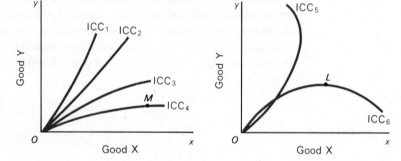

purchases of the two goods react to changing income when the prices of both goods are given and constant. If prices were different, then the income-consumption curve (ICC) would be different. There is a separate income-consumption curve for each different set of relative prices for the goods in question. For with each different set of relative prices the slope of the price line will differ. So will the successive points of tangency. Each income-consumption curve traces out the income effect as the consumer's income changes, with a constant relative price for the two goods.

It would clearly be helpful if we could say what was the most likely shape of an income-consumption curve. With most indifference maps it will be found that all income-consumption curves on them always slope upwards to the right, as happens with three of the low income-consumption curves shown in Fig. 3.8a. This means that a rise in a consumer's income makes him buy more of each of the two (or more) goods he is consuming. Income-consumption curves are usually of the general shape taken by ICC_1, ICC_2, and ICC_3. At the extreme, the consumer may hold his purchases of one good constant over a range of incomes, with the income-consumption curve vertical or horizontal. In Fig. 3.8a, income-consumption curve ICC_4, is horizontal beyond M with the consumer buying a constant amount of good Y as he becomes richer.

It is just possible that, over some ranges, an income-consumption curve might slope upwards to the left, as with the ICC_5, or downwards to the right, as with ICC_6 (in Fig. 3.8b). In these cases, the income-consumption curve shows that, after a point, even though he is becoming richer, the consumer consumes less of one of the goods. This can happen only if one of the goods is consumed in large amounts when the consumer is poor and is replaced wholly or partially by goods of higher quality when he becomes richer. Such a good is known in economic jargon as an 'inferior good'. For example, in Fig. 3.8b, if the income-consumption curve is ICC_5, X is an inferior good; if it is ICC_6, Y is an inferior good. If the income-consumption curve slopes upwards to the right in the normal way, we can say that the income effect is *positive* for both goods. If the income-consumption curve slopes backwards or downwards, we can say that the income effect for one good is *negative*, after a certain point has been reached. In the case of good Y in Fig. 3.8b the income effect is negative beyond point L on ICC_6.

5.3 The substitution effect

A substitution effect occurs, it will be remembered, when the relative prices of goods change but the consumer's money income is altered in such a way that he is neither better nor worse off than he was before. His real income is exactly the same. However, he has to rearrange his purchases in accordance with the new relative prices.

A substitution effect is shown in Fig. 3.9. Perhaps it can best be understood if we use a hypothetical illustration. In the initial situation shown in Fig. 3.9 the consumer is in equilibrium at point Q on indifference curve 2. He is paid in good X and uses it to buy ON of Y. He keeps OM of good X. Let us assume that in this situation a subsidy is being paid on good Y. The price of Y to the consumer is thus kept artificially below its economic level. We now assume that the Government removes the subsidy, so that the relative price of Y rises. Instead of the price of Y in terms of X being $\dfrac{OA}{OB}$, it is now $\dfrac{OA_1}{OB_1}$. Let us further assume that, in order to compensate the consumer for the rise in the price of Y, the Government increases the consumer's income in terms of X. By some fiscal measure, the Government arranges that the consumer's income in terms of X is increased to the extent needed to allow him to be just as well off as he was before—to remain on the same indifference curve. The price of Y has risen, but the consumer's income in terms of X has risen also from OA to OA_1. This rise in income is just sufficient to compensate the consumer for the rise in the price of Y. It is therefore known as a *compensating variation* in the consumer's income. In this case, the compensating

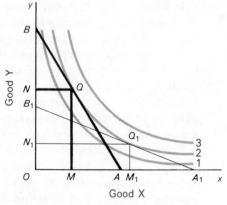

Fig. 3.9

variation in income in terms of X is AA_1. The compensating variation is just large enough to cancel out the change in the consumer's circumstances caused by the rise in the relative price of Y. He remains at exactly the same position in his scale of preferences (on the same indifference curve), because the rise in the price of Y has been compensated for.

As a result of these changes, we have a *substitution effect*. The relative prices of X and Y have changed, while the compensating variation in income has ensured that the consumer is neither better nor worse off than he was before. Although the consumer remains on the same indifference curve, he is on it at a different position. Instead of being at point Q, he is now at point Q_1. This move along the indifference curve from Q to Q_1 represents a substitution effect. The consumer, though neither better or worse off, substitutes X which is now relatively cheaper for Y which is now relatively dearer. A substitution effect can therefore always be represented as a movement along an indifference curve Any change which would have taken place in a consumer's real income because relative prices have changed, is 'compensated' for—just cancelled out—by a change in his money income.

5.4 The price effect

The most interesting consequence of a change in the situation confronting a consumer is known as a *price effect*. Here the relative prices of the goods in question change but there is no compensating variation in income. The consumer's real income therefore either rises or falls. His money income gives him greater or smaller satisfaction than it did before, because prices have altered. A price effect is shown in Fig. 3.10.

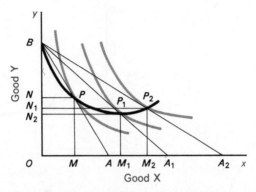

Fig. 3.10

The original equilibrium position in Fig. 3.10 is at P, where the consumer has OM of X and ON of Y. In this original situation, the price of X is such that the consumer could buy OA of X if he spent the whole of his income on it. Let us now assume that the consumer's money income remains constant, but that the price of X falls, so that the same money income will buy OA_1 of X instead of OA. Since the price of Y is constant, the consumer's income in terms of Y is OB all the time. The new equilibrium position will be at P_1 where the consumer has OM_1 of X and ON_1 of Y. If the price of X falls again, so that the given income will now buy OA_2 of X if the consumer buys only X, the resulting equilibrium position will be at P_2. Each change in the price of X alters the slope of the price line by altering the ratio of the prices of X and Y. The cheaper X becomes compared with Y, the less steep is the slope of the price line and vice versa.

5.5 The price-consumption curve

If we now draw a line connecting all the equilibrium positions— P, P_1, P_2, etc.—we have drawn what is known as a *price-consumption curve (PCC)*. It shows the price effect. It shows the way in which the consumption of X changes when its price changes, but the consumer's income in terms of Y and the price of Y are unaltered.

Given any consumer's indifference map and given the prices of the two goods shown on it, one can always construct the consumer's income-consumption curve and his price-consumption curve, as we have done in Fig. 3.11. Let us assume that in Fig. 3.11 the consumer begins with an income of OA in terms of X. With the given prices, he is able to reach point Q on indifference curve 1. We can now construct an income-consumption curve ICC and a price-consumption curve PCC_1 both starting at point Q and showing the income and price effects respectively. Whoever the consumer happens to be, it will always be found that the price-consumption curve PCC_1 lies between the income-consumption curve and the original indifference

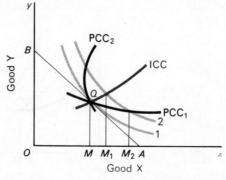

Fig. 3.11

curve, here 1. Similarly, one can draw the price consumption curve PCC_2, showing the effect of a progressive fall in the price of Y, with the price of X, and income in terms of X, constant. One will then find that the curve PCC_2 also lies between the income-consumption curve and the original indifference curve, this time to the left and not to the right of the income-consumption curve. This must happen. It follows directly from the fact that the price-consumption curve represents points of tangency between *progressively flatter* price lines and indifference curves which are all convex to the origin, whilst the income-consumption curve represents points of tangency between the same indifference curves and successive price lines all of which have the *same* slope.

At first sight, the proposition that the price-consumption curve will lie between the income-consumption curve and the indifference curve on which the consumer was originally in equilibrium, looks to be of mere geometrical interest. In fact, it turns out to be of profound economic importance. Let us consider the situation shown in Fig. 3.12. When the price of X falls, the consumer moves from his original

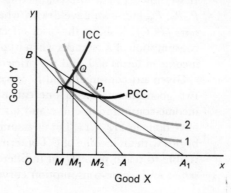

Fig. 3.12

equilibrium at P to a new equilibrium position at P_1. But it is legitimate to look upon this as compounded of a movement from P to Q along the income-consumption curve, and a further movement from Q to P_1 along the indifference curve 2. The movement along the income-consumption curve from P to Q is an income effect, while the movement along the indifference curve 2 from Q to P_1 is a substitution effect.

6. The price effect as the sum of an income and a substitution effect

The effect of a price change is therefore the resultant of the actions of two separate and different forces. The price effect can be looked at in two parts. First there is an *income effect* which causes a movement along an income-consumption curve and which makes the consumer better off. Now that X is cheaper his money goes further—his 'real' income has risen. Second, there is a *substitution effect* which causes a movement along an indifference curve and makes the consumer buy more of the good, X, whose price has fallen. X is now relatively cheaper compared with Y. Since in the initial equilibrium the relative prices of X and Y were equal to their marginal significance in terms of each other, this means that the marginal significance of X in terms of Y is now greater than its price in terms of Y. It therefore pays the consumer to substitute X for Y until once again the marginal significance of X in terms of Y equals the price of X in terms of Y. He does this by moving along the new, higher indifference curve. In Fig. 3.12, this means a move from Q to P_1 because it is X which is relatively cheaper. If Y had become cheaper, the consumer would have moved above Q on indifference curve 2.

It is now standard practice in economics to look upon the price effect as the net result of an income effect and a substitution effect in this way. In Fig. 3.12 the demand for X rises from OM to OM_2 as the consumer moves along the price-consumption curve from P to P_1. But one can legitimately regard MM_1 of this increase in demand as the result of an income effect, and the rest—M_1M_2—as caused by a substitution effect. It is therefore obvious that, as the price of any good, X, falls, the increase in the amount of the good which is demanded depends on the strength and direction of the income effect on the one hand and of the substitution effect on the other. In practice, it will often be found that the amount of a good demanded by an individual consumer increases as its price falls. At the worst, it is likely that the amount demanded of some goods will remain constant while consumption of the remainder rises. This is because the substitution effect and the income effect are normally both positive. They both act to increase the purchases of any good whose price has fallen.

7. 'Inferior' goods

While normally both the income effect and the substitution effect will lead the consumer to buy more of a good whose price has fallen, we must now see what exceptions there can be to this rule. The substitution effect must always be such that the consumer will buy more of a good whose price has fallen. This follows directly from the fact that indifference curves are assumed to be convex to the origin. To remain tangential to the same indifference curve, the price line must move 'round' the indifference curve.

Unfortunately, the income effect is not so reliable. It will not necessarily be positive but *may* work in the opposite direction. Normally, the fact that a consumer's real income has risen will make him buy more of the goods shown in any indifference diagram, including the one which, by its fall in price, has caused the income effect. Where this happens, the income and the substitution effects will both be positive and all is well. The consumer buys more of the good which is cheaper, partly because his 'real' income has risen. He obtains his higher 'real' income by spending more on this good. But he also buys more of a good whose price has fallen because it is now cheaper relative to other goods and he can substitute it for them. For some goods, the income effect can be negative, though the substitution effect can never be. A consumer may actually buy *less* of a good when his real income rises as a result of a fall in the price of that good.

We have already seen that there are some 'inferior' goods of which less and not more is bought when the consumer's income rises. Such goods are consumed mainly when the purchaser is poor, and are entirely or partially replaced by goods of superior quality when he becomes better off. The income effect is therefore negative instead of positive. Margarine is often given as the stock example for the UK. Some consumers apparently replace it by butter when they become richer. There may be other goods of the same kind.

It does not necessarily follow, however, that a fall in the price of an inferior good will lead an individual consumer to buy less of it if its price falls and so raises his real income. Though the income effect is negative, it may well be too weak to outweigh the positive substitution effect so that the consumer's demand curve still slopes downwards to the right in the usual way. This kind of situation is shown in Fig. 3.13. Here, we have a fall in the price of X which causes the consumer to move from an equilibrium point P to a new one at R. He increases his purchases of X from OM to OM_2. But the income effect is negative. Had the consumer merely received an increase in income which took him from P to Q (which would have made him just as well off as at R) he would have reduced his purchases of X from OM to OM_1. It is only because the substitution effect, operating because X has become relatively cheaper, carries the consumer along indifference curve 2 from Q to R that he buys an extra MM_2 of X. Only for that reason is there a net increase in his purchases of X. What happens is that when the price of X falls the negative income effect causes the consumer to buy M_1M less of X. But the positive substitution effect induces him to buy M_1M_2 more of X. The net result, which is a compromise between the income and substitution effects, is that the

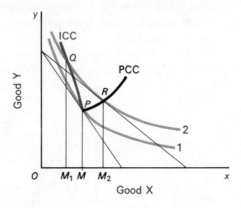

Fig. 3.13

consumer buys more X, but not so much more as he would have bought if the income effect had been either zero or positive.

In practice, though there may be a considerable number of inferior goods, when the price of one of them changes the positive substitution effect usually outweighs the negative income effect. Only where the negative income effect is very strong, which usually happens only when the consumer spends a great deal of his income on the good in question, can the demand for a good *fall* as its price falls.

8. Giffen's paradox

It is, however, possible that there may be a few goods for which the negative income effect is so strong that it can outweigh the positive substitution effect. If this happens, individual consumers will buy less of a good if its price falls and more if it rises. This kind of situation can exist only if the proportion of the consumer's income spent on the good in question is very large. Only then can a fall in the price of a good cause a considerable change in the consumer's real income.

A commodity of this kind, which people demand in smaller quantities when it is cheaper than they do when it is dearer, is clearly an inferior good. But it is a rather special kind of inferior good and is often referred to as a 'Giffen good'. It owes this name to Sir Robert

Giffen,[1] who is said to have claimed during the nineteenth century that a rise in the price of bread often caused such a severe fall in the real incomes of the poorer classes that they were forced to curtail their consumption of meat and other more expensive foods. Bread being still the cheapest food, they consumed more of it, and not less, now that its price was higher. Similarly, if the price of bread fell, people would buy less of it. For their real income would now have risen, and they would curtail their purchases of bread in order to obtain a more varied diet.

The results of a fall in the price of a 'Giffen good' can be seen in Fig. 3.14. When the price of X falls so that the consumer moves from

Fig. 3.14

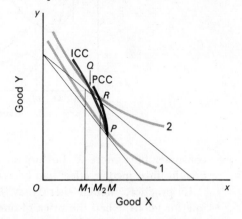

equilibrium at point P to equilibrium at point R, the consumer reduces his purchases of X from OM to OM_2. The reduction in his purchases (by M_2M) is the net result of a negative income effect, which by itself would have caused the consumer to buy M_1M less of X, and a positive substitution effect which, alone, would have caused him to buy M_1M_2 more. The net result is that the consumer buys less X than he did before (OM_2 instead of OM), but not so much less as he would have done had there been no substitution effect. The positive substitution effect would by itself lead to some increase in the quantity of X demanded, but it is swamped by the negative income effect. Less X is demanded now that its price has fallen. Such situations are unusual but it is possible that they occasionally occur.

9. The derivation of market demand curves

The demand curve for a good was defined in Chapter 1 as showing how much of that good would be bought at various prices—assuming

[1]See Alfred Marshall, *Principles of Economics*, (8th Edition), Macmillan; London, 1920; p. 132. See however, Henry Schultz, *Theory and Measurement of Demand;* University of Chicago Press, 1938; pp. 51–2, where the same ideas are attributed to Simon Gray.

all other prices and consumers' incomes to be constant. If one reflects on this, it is clear that an individual's demand curve for a good must be related in some way to his price-consumption curve for the same good. This is so. They both represent the same information except that the demand curve gives it in a more directly useful form. It is not difficult to derive the demand curve of an individual consumer for a good provided only that one knows his indifference map. The way in which this can be done is shown in Fig. 3.15.

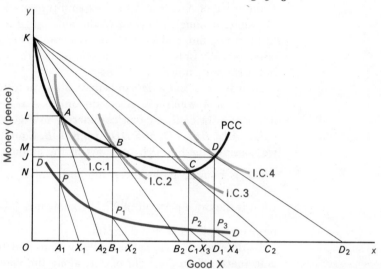

Fig. 3.15

In Fig. 3.15 are shown an individual's price-consumption curve KD together with the relevant parts of his indifference map between money (on the y-axis) and good X (on the x-axis). We now choose at random four points on the price-consumption curve and label them A, B, C and D. At these four positions of equilibrium, the consumer buys OA_1, OB_1, OC_1, and OD_1 units of X respectively. For these quantities he pays prices per unit of $\dfrac{KL}{OA_1}$ p, $\dfrac{KM}{OB_1}$ p, $\dfrac{KN}{OC_1}$ p and $\dfrac{KJ}{OD_1}$ p, the price of X falling progressively as the consumer moves from K to D. In other words, these prices are given by the slopes of KA_2, KB_2, KC_2 and KD_2. Since the consumer has a fixed income of OK p to spend, when he is at A he spends KL p, keeping OL p for other purposes. Similarly at B he spends KM p and keeps OM p, at C he spends KN p and at D KJ p. One can read off all this information from the y-axis. For the consumer's total income is constant at OK p. Since a perpendicular from any point (such as A), to the y-axis tells us how much of his resources the consumer is retaining in money (OL p), we can see at once how much he has spent on X to arrive at A.

A demand curve does not say anything about the size of a consumer's income except that it is constant. Nor does it consider the amount of money left over after the consumer has made his purchases of X. A demand curve tells us only the number of units of X which would be bought at any given price. This can be discovered from the price-consumption curve. The price-consumption curve shows what total expenditure is when any given number of units of X are purchased. We can thus calculate the price of X by dividing total expenditure by the number of units bought. For instance, at K no X is being bought and total expenditure is nil. As one moves from K to B the price of X falls and total expenditure on X increases, as does the amount bought. Beyond C, the amount of X bought continues to increase, but toal outlay now declines. The price-consumption curve is really only a total outlay curve, like that in Fig. 1.5 (p. 21); but it is upside down.

In order to derive a demand curve, all we need to know is the price per unit of X when any given amount of X is demanded. We can find this most easily by first considering in Fig. 3.15, the perpendiculars AA_1, BB_1, CC_1 and DD_1, from A, B, C and D to the x-axis. If we consider the line AA_1, it shows us the amount of X (OA_1 units) which is bought at the given unit price of X, $(\dfrac{KL}{OA_1}=\dfrac{OK}{OA_2}\text{p})$. But what is the price per unit of X? We know it is $\dfrac{KL}{OA_1}=\dfrac{OK}{OA_2}\text{p}$, but it is not easy to plot this on a diagram.

In the present context the easiest way to find the unit price of X is to mark off, to the right of AA_1 along the x-axis, one unit of X; one pound, one can, one bottle as the case may be. Let us assume that in this case one unit of X is represented by the distance A_1X_1. We then draw the line X_1P parallel to KA_2. The slope of KA_2 shows the price of X. Since the slopes of KA_2 and X_1P are the same, they both represent the same unit price of X. And since A_1X_1 represents one unit of X, the distance A_1P represents the price of one unit of X when OA_1 of X is bought. P is therefore a point on the individual's demand curve. It shows how much X he buys when one unit of X costs A_1P p $(=\dfrac{OK}{OA_2}\text{p})$. Similarly, if we mark off one unit of X, B_1X_2, to the right of B_1 and draw X_2P_1 parallel to KB, we can find the unit price of X when OB_1 of X is bought. This price will be B_1P_1 p $(=\dfrac{OK}{OB_2}\text{p})$. Point P_1 is thus another point on the individual's demand curve, showing how much X he will buy when X costs B_1P_1 p per unit. Similarly we can derive the points P_2 and P_3 showing the individual's demand for X when one unit of it costs C_1P_2 p, and D_1P_3 p respectively.

We can then draw a demand curve DD showing the amount of X which the individual consumer will buy at various prices of X. It passes through a series of points like P, P_1, P_2 and P_3 showing price and amount demanded at each price. As we have seen, this demand curve can easily be derived from a consumer's indifference map.

10. The likely shape of a demand curve

10.1 Individual demand curves

In Fig. 3.15 the individual demand curve slopes downwards because, with the indifference map used there, both the income and substitution effects are positive. Individual demand curves will normally be of this general shape. But we have seen that there may be some circumstances in which Giffen's paradox holds good and the demand curve does not slope downwards to the right over the whole of its length. An example of this is shown in Fig. 3.16.

In Fig. 3.16 the demand curve begins by sloping downwards to the right in the normal way. Over this range of prices the income effect is positive. It is likely that *all* demand curves will slope downwards in the normal way to begin with. For total expenditure on the good in question will usually be relatively small at high prices. The income effect (even if negative) cannot therefore be very important. Once price in Fig. 3.16 has fallen to OP, however, the income effect becomes both negative and strong. It outweighs the positive substitution effect, and the demand curve therefore slopes downwards to the left until price has fallen to OP_1. Once this has happened, the demand curve again begins to slope downwards to the right. Prices are so low that total expenditure on the good is very small. The income effect, even if still negative, is again outweighed by the positive substitution effect. This seems to be the most likely shape of the demand curve for a 'Giffen good'. It is most unlikely that any demand curve will slope downwards to the left throughout its whole length. It will only be over those price ranges where a negative income effect is extremely strong that the curve will do this.

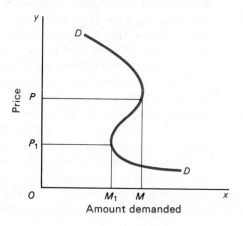

Fig. 3.16

We may sum up this discussion on the shape of the demand curves of individuals by saying that in most cases they will slope downwards to the right in the normal way, because as the price of a good falls the positive substitution effect is reinforced by a positive income effect. Even where the income effect is negative, the demand curve will still slope downwards to the right if the substitution effect is strong enough to outweigh the income effect. Only when the negative income effect is sufficiently strong to offset the substitution effect— a thing which one imagines can only happen over limited ranges of a demand curve—can the curve slope downwards to the left instead of to the right.

10.2 A market demand curve

All that has been said so far relates to the demand curves of individuals. What can we say about market demand curves? Market demand curves are obtained by adding together the demand curves of all the individuals in the market. How this is done is shown in Fig. 3.17.

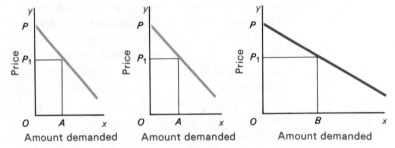

Fig. 3.17 a | b | c

In Fig. 3.17a and 3.17b we have two individual demand curves. These are added together sideways in Fig. 3.17c. Since both the individuals' curves are identical, and both show no demand at all for the good at any price at or above OP, the aggregate curve does the same. At each price below OP the aggregate curve shows the sum of the individual demands at the price in question. For example, at the price OP_1, demand in both Figs. 3.17a and 3.17b is OA. In Fig. 3.17c demand at the price OP_1 is OB, which is twice OA. Because the two individual demand curves are identical, the quantity demanded shown on the market curve at any price equals twice the demand shown on the individual demand curve at that price. It should be noted that *at each price* the elasticity of demand on all three demand curves in Fig. 3.17 is the same.

Any set of individual demand curves for a good—no matter how many individuals there are—can be added together in this way to give a market demand curve for the good. Market demand curves will normally slope downwards to the right, because the individual demand curves will normally slope downwards to the right. Even if the number of buyers in a market does not increase as the price of the good traded falls, the downward slope of the individual demand curves will usually ensure that the market curve (which aggregates them) also slopes downwards to the right. In addition, it is likely that new buyers will enter the market as the price of the good falls. This will be an added reason why the market demand curve should slope downwards to the right.

To sum up: even if an individual's demand curve for a good slopes downwards to the left because of Giffen's paradox, it does not follow that the market demand curve must do the same. One reason is that a good which is sufficiently 'inferior' to some people for their demand curves to slope to the left, may not be inferior to everyone. There may be enough people buying more of the good as its price falls to offset the effects of those who buy less. The market demand curve can still be normal. Again, even if everyone buys less of a good as its price falls over some ranges, they may not all do so over the *same* price ranges. It might well happen, therefore, that a good could be a 'Giffen good' to everyone and yet have a normal market demand curve because only a relatively small number of people regarded it as a 'Giffen good' over the *same* price ranges. Finally, it is likely that even when a good is of the 'Giffen' type, new buyers will enter the market as its price falls. They will either not regard it as a Giffen good at all, or else will not do so over the range of prices obtaining just after they first enter the market.

The conditions which have to be fulfilled for a market demand curve to slope downwards to the left are therefore very stringent. Curves of this type may exist, but they are not likely to be found frequently. Even when all buyers have abnormal demand curves, at any given price, new buyers will usually enter the market as prices fall, and they will presumably have demand curves which slope downwards to the right or they would not be entering the market at all. The assumption that market demand curves slope downwards to the right is the most plausible assumption one can make.

11. Other situations where higher prices may increase demand

There are two other situations where the quantity demanded may sometimes increase when there is an increase in price. The first situation is where a consumer regards the price of a product as an indicator of its quality. If the price of a good rises, and the consumer therefore thinks (rightly or wrongly) that the good has improved in quality, more of it may be bought. There are certainly many examples of this happening. One example was with a scientific instrument. This was selling very unsuccessfully at a moderate price. In the hope of making a reasonable amount of money from his product despite small sales, the producer increased the price of the instrument considerably. The result was a sudden and substantial increase in its sales.

The second situation where an increase in the price of a good may increase the quantity demanded is where expectations come in. If an increase in the price of the good is seen as a reason for expecting a further increase in the future, people may buy more of the good whose price has risen now in the hope of forestalling the price increase.

However, it will be seen that these two examples of situations where an increase in the price of a good may increase the demand for it do not really fit in with the assumptions we have been making in indifference curve analysis. We have assumed that the consumer is able to decide where a good fits into his scale of preferences without needing to know its price. This means that price cannot be treated as an indicator of quality. Second, we have assumed throughout our indifference curve analysis that conditions remain the same. In order that expectations may be brought in, we should have to allow for changing conditions and probably for time as well. The 'Giffen' good is therefore the only example compatible with indifference curve analysis of a commodity for which the demand increases when the price rises. However, our other two examples are important in practice and should not be forgotten.

12. Income-elasticity of demand

We shall find that the understanding of the relationships between income effects, substitution effects and price effects which we have now acquired is very useful in helping us to see more clearly what determines the elasticity of demand for any good. We know that the elasticity of demand for a good depends on the shape of the demand curve for that good. But we have now seen that a demand curve and a price-consumption curve show exactly the same information, though in different ways. Elasticity of demand therefore depends equally on the shape of the price-consumption curve. In its turn, the shape of the price-consumption curve depends on the nature of the income and substitution effects. Thus elasticity of demand depends on two other elasticities. One is the *income-elasticity of demand*. The other is *elasticity of substitution*. Ordinary elasticity of demand, *price-elasticity of demand* as it is often called, is a resultant of income-elasticity of demand and elasticity of substitution, just as the price effect is a resultant of an income effect and a substitution effect. It will be useful now to consider these two factors which determine price-elasticity of demand in some detail.

Income-elasticity of demand shows the way in which a consumer's purchases of any good change as the result of a change in his income. It shows the responsiveness of a consumer's purchases of a particular good to a change in his income. More accurately, we may define the income-elasticity of demand, e_i of any good, X, as

$$e_i = \frac{\text{proportionate change in purchases of good } X}{\text{proportionate change in income}}.$$

It follows that where the income-elasticity of demand for a good is high, a given proportionate increase in a consumer's income of, say, 1 per cent will cause a proportionately much larger increase in the demand for the good of, say, 10 per cent. Here income-elasticity would be $\frac{10}{1} = 10$. Similarly, where a good's income-elasticity is low, a given proportionate increase in income of, say, 1 per cent will cause a much smaller proportionate increase in the demand for the good of, say, $\frac{1}{20}$ per cent. Here income-elasticity will be $\frac{1}{20} / 1 = \frac{1}{20}$. We assume throughout this discussion of income-elasticity of demand that the prices of all goods are given and that it is only the consumer's money income which changes. Now, for all normal goods the income effect will be positive. Income-elasticity of demand will therefore normally be positive too. Changes in a consumer's income and in his expenditure on any single good will usually be in the same direction. All normal income-elasticities therefore have a plus sign in front of them, though their numerical values will vary considerably.

12.1 Some important income-elasticities

With price-elasticity of demand, we saw that elasticity equals one was a very important elasticity because it separated elastic demands from inelastic demands. With income-elasticity of demand, there is no similar dividing line. It is difficult to be certain exactly what are the most important numerical values for income-elasticity of demand. However, the following seem to be interesting ones. First, it is useful to distinguish the situation where income-elasticity of demand is zero. This will occur when a given increase in income fails to lead to any increase at all in the purchases of the good whose income elasticity is being calculated and hence in expenditure on it. On one side of zero income elasticity will be those situations where a rise in income leads to an actual *fall* in the amount purchased—inferior goods. For all such goods income-elasticity of demand, whether large or small, will be negative. On the other side, are all goods with positive income-elasticities. More of such goods are bought as income rises. Whether they are positive or negative, there will be an enormous range of income-elasticities. Each will have a finite, but different, numerical value. Zero income-elasticity is a useful value to select for special comment because it separates positive from negative elasticities.

A second interesting numerical value of income elasticity of demand is where the whole of an increase in the consumer's income is spent on the good in question. In this situation income-elasticity will be equal to $\dfrac{1}{KX}$ where KX is the fraction of the consumer's income spent on any good X. So, if the consumer originally spends $\frac{1}{20}$ of his income on X, and decides to spend the *whole* of an increase in income on X, income elasticity of demand will be $\dfrac{1}{\frac{1}{20}} = 20$. When income elasticity equals $\dfrac{1}{KX}$, then the whole of any increase in the consumer's income is spent on increasing his purchase of good X. This also seems a useful case to bear in mind. If *more* than the whole of any increase in income is spent on any good X, of course, income-elasticity of demand will exceed $\dfrac{1}{KX}$ and vice versa. It will be obvious that while income-elasticity of demand will be greater than $\dfrac{1}{KX}$ in this case, the actual value of income elasticity of demand will differ from situation to situation.

The third, and perhaps the most interesting value of income-elasticity of demand, is where it equals one. This means that the *proportion* of the consumer's income spent on the good in question is exactly the same both before and after the rise in income. If the income-elasticity of demand for any good is greater than one, this means that an increasing *proportion* of the consumer's income is spent on the good as he becomes richer. Similarly, if a consumer's income-elasticity of demand for a good is less than one, the proportion of his income spent on that good falls as his income rises. Unitary income-elasticity thus seems to represent a significant dividing line. It is of some significance if the proportion of a consumer's income spent on any good changes if he becomes richer. It seems reasonable to think that a good with an income-elasticity greater than one, on which a consumer therefore spends a greater proportion of his income as he becomes richer, is in some sense a luxury. A good with an income-elasticity of less than one, on which the proportion of income spent falls as he becomes richer, is in some sense a necessity. One cannot, of course, give a precise definition of necessities or luxuries in terms of income-elasticities of demand, but the notion that goods with income-elasticities greater and less than one are in a general sense luxuries and necessities respectively seems a useful one.

13. Elasticity of substitution

Elasticity of substitution, like the substitution effect upon which it depends, can be measured at any point on any indifference curve. It measures the extent to which it is possible for one good to be substituted for another if the consumer is to remain on that given indifference curve. The numerical elasticity of substitution (e_s) between any two goods, X and Y, can be measured anywhere on a single indifference curve. Its value is given by the following formula:[1]

$$e_s = \frac{\text{relative increase in the ratio between the two goods possessed } X/Y}{\text{relative decrease in marginal significance of } X \text{ in terms of } Y}.$$

13.1 Two limiting cases of elasticity of substitution

Two limiting cases are worth considering. First there is the situation where elasticity of substitution is infinite. This occurs where the indifference curve in question is a straight line and means that the two goods are perfect substitutes; they are identical. As he moves along an indifference curve, the proportionate change in the ratio between the consumer's holdings of X and Y is infinitely large compared with the relative change in the marginal significance of X in terms of Y. For the latter change is zero. The marginal significance of X in terms of Y does not change at all. This means that the indifference curve is a straight line. It is most unlikely that in practice one will ever find a straight-line indifference curve; if goods are perfect substitutes, economically they are the same good. Nevertheless, some goods are likely to possess high elasticities of substitution with other goods and so to have indifference curves with respect to them which are nearly straight lines. If two goods were close substitutes, as, for example, are railway or air travel and travel by long-distance motor coach, then the elasticity of substitution between them is likely to be high. An indifference curve for two goods with very high elasticities of substitution is shown in Fig. 3.18a.

The second limiting case is where elasticity of substitution is zero. In such a situation the two goods cannot be substituted for each other. They must be used in a fixed proportion or not at all. This again is an unlikely case in practice, but there will be some pairs of commodities which are very bad substitutes and have to be used in practically the same proportions. For example, the elasticity of substitution between shirts and trousers may not be very high. One may not want to have more or less than two or three shirts to each pair of trousers. If this proportion holds good for one's current stock

[1]Algebraically $e_s = -\dfrac{d\left(\frac{x}{y}\right)}{\frac{x}{y}} \div \dfrac{\left(\frac{dy}{dx}\right)}{\frac{dy}{dx}}$. It will be noted that elasticity of substitution should strictly have a minus sign, but for simplicity we have ignored this in the text.

and one has, say, twelve shirts and four pairs of trousers, one will not be willing to give up shirts in exchange for trousers (or trousers for shirts) for very long along the same indifference curve. Giving up shirts for trousers (or vice versa) cannot avoid making one better or

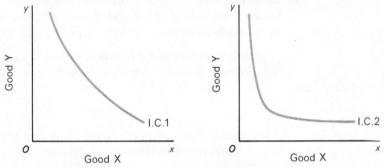

Fig. 3.18 a | b

worse off—putting one on a different indifference curve. If one is to remain on the same indifference curve, one must be offered a large number of pairs of trousers to induce one to part with another shirt, or vice versa. Indifference curves between shirts and trousers will then take the shape shown in Fig. 3.18b. The numerical elasticity of substitution is there very low.

14. Price-elasticity of demand linked to income-elasticity and elasticity of substitution

Price-elasticity of demand—the elasticity of demand normally used in economic theory—depends ultimately both on elasticity of substitution and on income elasticity of demand. It is therefore possible to show the relationship between the three elasticities in a mathematical formula. The relationship between the three elasticities can be given for a single consumer faced with two goods, X and Y, in a single equation.

Where, for good X,

e_p = price-elasticity of demand,
e_i = income-elasticity of demand,
e_s = elasticity of substitution
and KX = the proportion of the consumer's income spent on good X,
then $e_p = KX \times e_i + (1 - KX)e_s$.

This equation holds good in all situations. When one knows any two of the elasticities, one can always calculate the third.

What the first part of the equation means is that the increase in the amount of any good demanded in response to a fall in its price depends first on the income effect. This in turn depends, on the one hand, on the proportion of one's income spent on the good because this determines how much of one's income, previously spent on X, is available for new spending now that X is cheaper. The greater the proportion of one's income spent on the good X whose price has fallen, the greater is the amount of income set free by its fall in price. This is available for new purchases (both of good X and of other goods). Given income-elasticity of demand, the greater the percentage of income spent on good X, the greater is the consequent increase in purchases of X when its price falls. The proportionate increase in purchases of a good due to the income effect depends, secondly, on the size of income-elasticity of demand. This determines what part of income (KX) set free by the fall in price will be spent on the good whose price has fallen and what part will be left over to be spent on other goods. The expression $KX \times e_i$ thus shows the income effect's influence on price-elasticity of demand.

The second part of the formula shows that to the proportionate change in the purchases of X resulting from a change in the consumer's real income must be added the change due to the fact that X is now cheaper relatively to Y. The size of this second element depends first on the extent to which X can be substituted for Y now that it is relatively cheaper—on the elasticity of substitution. Second, it depends on the amount of Y one has been buying and can substitute X for—on the amount of the other good Y, which was being bought before X became cheaper. For, given elasticity of substitution, only to the extent that one was previously buying Y (for which X can now be substituted) will a fall in the price of X result in a switch from the purchase of Y to the purchase of X. If one was *not* buying Y before, one cannot substitute X for it. The expression $(1 - KX)$ in the formula therefore shows the proportion of one's income *not* being spent on X—the proportion of income within which substitution of X for Y is possible.

Perhaps two numerical illustrations will make the meaning of the formula for price-elasticity of demand clearer. First, let us assume that the income-elasticity of demand for any good, X, is 2, that the elasticity of substitution between X and any (or all) other good(s) Y equals 3, and that the consumer in question is spending __ of his income on X. The formula $e_p = KX \times e_i + (1 - KX)e_s$ then becomes $e_p = \frac{1}{10} \times 2 + \frac{9}{10} \times 3 = \frac{2}{10} + \frac{27}{10} = 2\frac{9}{10}$. Price-elasticity of demand for good X is therefore 2·9.

Alternatively, suppose that the income and substitution elasticities for good X are both equal to one, and that one quarter of the consumer's income is being spent on good X. The formula $e_p = KXe_i + (1 - KX)e_s$ then becomes $e_p = \frac{1}{4} \times 1 + \frac{3}{4} \times 1 = 1$. Price-elasticity of demand for X equals one. When both income and substitution elasticity are equal to one, price-elasticity *must* always be equal to one too. That this is so should be intuitively obvious. For, $KX + (1 -$

KX) always equals one, so that $1 \times KX$ plus $1 (1 - KX)$ also equals 1.

Price-elasticity of demand depends both on income-elasticity and on elasticity of substitution, and the formula given above puts the relationship explicitly.

15. What determines the size of price-elasticity

The concepts of elasticity of demand and elasticity of substitution throw light on our previous attempts to discover what determines whether the elasticity of demand for a good is high or low. We saw earlier that the demand for a necessity like salt is very inelastic. We can now say that this is partly because the proportion of income spent on salt is very small. The income effect of a fall in the price of salt will be small partly because the income-elasticity of demand for salt is likely to be small too, but mainly because the proportion of income spent on salt is so minute. In addition, the demand for salt is inelastic, because there are no goods to substitute for salt, and the elasticity of substitution between salt and other goods is therefore small. The demand for goods like colour television sets or motor cars will be much more elastic because such goods, being expensive, will take a larger proportion of income than salt does. The income effect can therefore be great. In addition, the elasticity of substitution between television sets and other forms of entertainment and between motor cars and other forms of transport will be high.

Suggested reading

HICKS, J. R.   *Value and Capital*, O.U.P. (1946). Chap. i and ii.

HICKS, J. R.   'A Reconsideration of the Theory of Value', *Economica*, 1934 (new Series, No. 1), pp. 52–69.

4

Revealed preference

1. Increasing the relevance of demand theory

In Chapter 3 we justified the downward slope of demand curves by an analysis which assumed that it was reasonable to suppose that individual consumers could specify complete and consistent sets of indifference curves. We further supposed that their purchases were made in accordance with these. Many people naturally find this an unreasonable procedure. They do not believe that consumers actually *do* make their purchases by constructing indifference maps and by attempting to reach optimal positions on them.

It seems more reasonable to suppose that, whether or not consumers' scales of preference are complete or completely consistent, it would be better to observe what consumers do when they make their purchases, rather than suggest the unlikely idea that they operate with complete scales of preference set out in the form of indifference curves. Most economists, nowadays, prefer to analyse situations where hypotheses that they make are either tested or, at least, testable. They do this, not least, because of the influence of the philosophical ideas of logical positivism. Like logical positivists, they are concerned only with testable hypotheses.

2. Revealed preference theory

In practice, we do not at this stage need to go even as far as that. As we shall see, we can proceed a very long way provided only that we are prepared to carry out our analysis in terms of an *ideal* consumer whose purchasing behaviour is completely consistent. On this basis, there is little difficulty in providing a justification for the downward-slope of demand curves even though the individual consumer cannot describe his scales of preference by drawing indifference maps. Since this kind of analysis asks the consumer to reveal the nature of his preferences by showing which goods he prefers in any set of circumstances, it is known as *revealed preference* theory.

The fact that one does not need to assume that consumers can define or describe their indifference maps is clearly one advantage of revealed preference analysis. It has also been strongly argued, especially by Sir John Hicks, that one major advantage of revealed preference theory is that it is explicitly designed to allow econometricians to make use of it. Given the growing influence of econometrics, referred to in the Preface, this is an important reason for studying revealed preference theory here.

3. Our assumptions

Before we proceed to consider the effects of a change in the price of a good on the demand for it, using revealed preference theory, we must first make our assumptions explicit and introduce some concepts. For we are still concerned with economic theory, though we want our theory to be one which econometricians, in particular, can test.

Our assumption is again that we are concerned with a consumer who has a given income to spend and is faced with various alternative combinations of goods which he could afford to buy. We assume that he will choose that combination of goods which he ranks highest, the one which he prefers. So, in one set of market conditions he will make one choice; in other situations, he will make different choices. Provided that the consumer maximises his satisfactions we can still, and in this Chapter we shall, suppose that these choices will always be consistent with each other. In other words, we suppose that we are dealing with an ideal consumer. The choices of actual consumers need not be so consistent, but if we observed an actual consumer making different choices, this would at least allow us to describe how an actual consumer differed from the ideal one.

4. Strong and weak ordering

Revealed preference theory also allows us to make explicit a number of distinctions which are derived from the logical theory of ordering. The first distinction is between strong ordering and weak ordering.

(a) Strong ordering

If a set of items is strongly ordered, then each has its own place in that order, which is not shared with any other item. Thus, all the letters in the alphabet are strongly ordered, as are all positive whole numbers.

(b) Weak ordering

Weak ordering, on the other hand, accepts the possibility that it may not be possible to rank some items in a list ahead of or behind each other. A good example of weak ordering, quoted by Sir John Hicks, would be members of the British Parliament. Parliaments of Great Britain are strongly ordered; each is separate, beginning with one election and ending with the next. However, if one arranged all members of Parliament according to the date of their first election, a number of them would always have been elected for the first time at a particular election. Members of Parliament (MPs) are therefore weakly ordered. Some of them are in a cluster, with the same date of first election, though of course some MPs, or groups of them, will be strongly ordered. Some individual MPs will be strongly ordered, because no one else was elected for the first time at the same General Election or at a particular by-election.

5. Strong v weak ordering and demand theory

In Chapter 3 we were concerned with weak ordering. All the combinations of goods represented on a given indifference curve were weakly ordered. One could not arrange the combinations of goods on a single indifference curve in order of preference, since all were equally preferred. The indifference curves themselves were strongly ordered; each was clearly ranked above or below others, and none coincided.

It will be clear from its name that revealed preference theory can most easily deal with situations where the consumer is choosing between strongly-ordered combinations of goods. However, it is not necessary to assume that the consumer can order all the conceivable combinations of commodities with which he might be faced—as indifference curve analysis is usually seen as doing. We simply need to assume that consumers can order (and choose between) those alternative combinations which they actually have to consider in making purchases; or alternatively, that the consumer can rank those alternatives with which we confront him in an experiment that we set up for him.

It is true, of course, that a theory of consumer demand based entirely on strong ordering would be unsatisfactory. Actual consumers must surely be confronted at times by equally-desirable alternatives between which they are forced to choose. Unlike the celebrated ass, associated with the philosopher Buridan, human beings do not hesitate between two combinations of goods, giving equal satisfactions, for so long that they actually starve. They do choose, though choice in these circumstances is perhaps best seen as determined by chance rather than decision. As Sir John Hicks notes, 'chance, in this sense, is not a thing which ought to be excluded'.[1] Economists therefore need theories which do not exclude indifference;

[1] *A Revision of Demand Theory*, Oxford, 1956, p. 21.

which allow for weak ordering. Indifference curve analysis is one example. More advanced analyses, drawing on statistical decision theory, are others. In this chapter we shall begin by confining our attention to consumers choosing between strongly-ordered alternative sets of commodities.

6. Two-term consistency

The final elements in our theory are the notions of two-term consistency and transitivity. Two-term consistency ensures that any two elements in a ranking are consistently placed relatively to each other. If A is above B, then B cannot also be above A. It should be immediately apparent that two-term consistency is a necessary condition for consistent consumer choice.

7. Transitivity

It is not a sufficient condition. Consistent ordering also requires transitivity. For example, suppose that a consumer prefers a combination of various amounts of various goods (combination A) to another combination, B, while he also prefers the B-combination to a third combination (C). The consumer's preferences will be transitive if this means that he also prefers combination A to combination C. The consumer must not, if there is to be consistency in his choices, also prefer C to A. Transitivity ensures that such 'circular' relationships are ruled out.

8. Consumer equilibrium and revealed preference

Having made these distinctions we can now proceed to explain revealed preference theory. As with indifference curve analysis there is no reason, in principle, why we should not extend our discussion to cover as many goods as we wish. As it will be convenient to begin with two-dimensional diagrams, we shall first consider two goods only. As in Chapter 3 we shall look at good X and money. However, since we shall continue to assume the prices of all goods except X to be constant, we can treat money as representing *all* other goods except X.

8.1 The price effect

We can then construct Fig. 4.1. Here, good X is shown on the x-axis and money, representing all other goods, on the y-axis. Initially, the consumer's income is OM. He can therefore afford to choose any of the combinations of X and money shown along the line MX. In fact, he chooses point A, buying OX_1 of X and keeping OM_1 in money. This amount OM_1 is available for spending on other goods. Point A is thus 'revealed' as preferred to all other points on or within the triangle OMX. However, if the 'ideal' consumer seeks to maximise

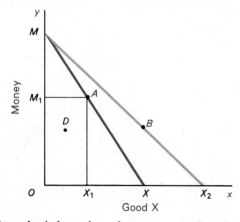

Fig. 4.1

his satisfactions, he is bound to choose some point along MX. If he does not, he is deliberately taking less of at least one good than he might. Provided we continue to assume that each unit of each good gives positive satisfactions (which we have implicitly assumed throughout Chapters 2 and 3) the consumer will not do this. If he chose a point like D, he could always increase his satisfactions by moving out towards the price line MX. Nevertheless, we cannot say where along MX point A will be. That will depend on the consumer's tastes. The more highly he prizes X relatively to all the other goods, the nearer to X will A be. The more X will the consumer purchase.

Let us now suppose that the price of X falls, so that the given income of OM would allow the consumer to buy OX_2 of X if he spent his whole income on it. Let us further suppose that the consumer now moves to point B. Once again, point B could lie anywhere in or on the triangle OMX_2. If the consumer is 'rational', it will lie on MX_2, for the reasons given in the last paragraph. As in Chapter 3, we have a move from A to B which is the result of a price effect; the price of X has fallen, and the consumer has bought more X. The demand curve for X slopes downwards. If revealed preference theory is to be as useful to us as indifference curve analysis is, it must be able to explain why this is likely to happen. Why is it that demand curves are likely to slope downwards? With indifference curves, we showed this by identifying an income effect and a substitution effect which between them made up the price effect. We showed in Chapter 3 that the substitution effect will always be positive, and that only in those rare situations where the income effect was both negative and strong could the demand curve slope upwards.

This distinction between the income effect and the substitution effect was the most fundamental one that we could make. Let us repeat the analysis using revealed preference rather than indifference curves. Consider Fig. 4.2. The consumer begins at A as in Fig. 4.1 and moves

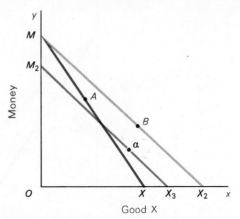

Fig. 4.2

to B as the result of a fall in the price of X. His income remains constant at OM. What indifference curve analysis did was to identify an intermediate position which (following Sir John Hicks in *A Revision of Demand Theory*) we shall call a. What we require of a in indifference curve analysis is that it shall divide the price effect into an income effect and a substitution effect. That is to say, the move from A to a must be a pure substitution effect. The price of X has fallen by the full amount that was required to move the consumer from A to B. At the same time, however, the consumer's income has been reduced by just the amount required to leave him neither better nor worse off than he was at A. He is now on M_2X_3, but since the price of X has changed, M_2X_3 must be parallel to MX_2. We have already defined this reduction in income (in this case of MM_2) as a compensating variation in income. It is a variation in income just big enough exactly to cancel out (to compensate for) the increase in real income caused by the fall in the price of X, and the consequent move of the consumer from A to B. Indifference curve analysis allows us easily to identify the position of a because we can easily find the point where M_2X_3 is tangential to the same indifference curve which was tangential to MX at A.

Revealed preference analysis cannot do this. So long as we are unable to say that all points from which the consumer might choose in Fig. 4.2 are strongly ordered, it is possible that A and a—and indeed other points—may be ones between which the consumer is indifferent. However, we cannot observe indifference, only choice. We know that initially (in what we may describe as the A-situation) the consumer chose to be at A. We also know that, with the lowered price of X but the same money income, the consumer chose to be at B. But revealed preference theory cannot allow us to say more. While it can accept the existence of indifference, provided there is 'weak ordering', it cannot *demonstrate* indifference. We cannot *observe* the consumer 'being indifferent' between A and a. Consequently, a is never observed.

*8.3 The cost-
difference method*

Revealed preference theory therefore must divide up the price effect in a different way. It is a less fundamental division than the one found in indifference curve analysis because it does not allow us to separate out a pure income effect and a pure substitution effect. However, it is an important division for two reasons. First, it provides us with the justification we need for the belief that demand curves usually slope downwards. Second, it is based on a purely mathematical calculation which is one that we can make even though we have no information whatever about the nature of the consumer's indifference map. It is the analytical device we need if we are to base a theory of consumer demand on the observation of consumer purchases and not on a knowledge of his indifference map.

What we do is to make use of what Sir John Hicks has christened the cost-difference variation in income. So far, we have used only the compensating variation in income, which just cancelled out (compensated) the increase in real income which the consumer received because the price of X had fallen. Of course, we could use it in the opposite direction to mean an increase in income which just cancelled out the effect of a *rise* in the price of X.

Let us now see what the cost-difference variation in income is, using Fig. 4.3. Once again, the consumer begins at A. A is revealed to be preferred to all the other points on or in the triangle OXM. Once

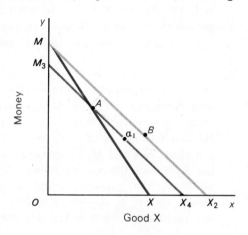

Fig. 4.3

again, the price of X is reduced by enough to increase the amount of X which could be bought, if the whole of income was spent on X, from OX to OX_2. This time, however, we establish our intermediate position by using the cost-difference method. What we do is to introduce a further price line, M_3X_4. This is parallel to MX_2, so that it reflects the B-prices. However, the consumer's income has been reduced by MM_3, so that M_3X_4 passes through A. Because it passes through A, the cost-difference line M_3X_4 just allows the consumer to continue to buy the A-combination of goods, if he wishes. This means that on M_3X_4 the advantage given to the consumer by the lower cost of X is just cancelled out. That explains why this is known as the cost-difference method. The reduction in cost of the A-combination (OX_1 and OM_1) with the B-prices replacing the A-prices, is M_3M. This 'cost-difference' is just cancelled out by the cost-difference variation in income. It also explains why this is such a simple method to use.

Geometrically, all we need to do is to draw a new price line, through the original equilibrium point, A, but with the slope representing the new price of X. This automatically gives us the cost-difference variation in income, by a distance like MM_3 on the vertical axis. Algebraically, what we need to do is also simple. Let us denote the A-prices and quantities by p_0 and q_0 respectively, and the B-prices and quantities by p_1 and q_1 respectively. The A-situation can then be denoted by p_0q_0, where the A-quantities are bought at the A-prices. Similarly, the B-situation can be denoted by p_1q_1, where the B-quantities are bought at the B-prices. If the consumer's income is reduced so that he can, if he wishes, just buy the A-quantities at the B-prices, we can denote this position by: p_1q_0. The cost difference variation in income is then given as:

$$p_1q_1 - p_1q_0$$

It is the difference in cost between the A-quantities and the B-quantities, both at the B-prices. In any empirical work, econometric or not, this calculation can easily be made.

8.4 The components of the price effect

We can now proceed to split the price effect into two parts. With the 'cost-difference' price line M_3X_4 passing through A, the consumer cannot now reach B, even though he is able to buy at the B-prices. He therefore moves from A, not to B, but to a_1. Because the two price lines MX and M_3X_4 cross at A, a_1 cannot lie to the left of A. In the A-situation the consumer chose A. If a_1 now lay to the left of A, on M_3X_4, the consumer would be acting inconsistently. He has already shown, by choosing A with the A-prices, that he prefers A to any position on the line MA. He must, *a fortiori*, prefer A to any point on M_3A. (Now that his income has been reduced by the cost-difference, the triangle AMM_3 is no longer a possible equilibrium area for him. He is not rich enough to move into any part of that triangle.) His preferred position, a_1, could, however, coincide with A. If it did, we could immediately say that there was no substitution effect. The whole of the move from A to B would be an income effect. There could be no income effect in the transition from A to a_1, because both are at the same point. Both represent the same combination of goods: both represent the same real income. There is no income effect *and* no substitution effect if A and a_1 coincide.

What is more likely is that a_1 will lie to the right of A, as in Fig. 4.3. Unfortunately, we cannot now say anything about the respective sizes of the substitution and income effects. If a_1 lies to the right of A, it will lie beyond the original price line MX. Consequently, the consumer must be better off than at A. Given the chance to move to a preferred position beyond MX, he has done so. At a_1, the consumer is consequently better off than at A. A move from A to a_1 represents a combination of a substitution effect *and* an income effect. There has been a positive substitution effect; if the substitution effect were zero, the consumer would have stayed at A. There has been an income effect because the consumer prefers a_1 to A; he is better off at a_1. But we cannot say *how much* of the move from A to a_1 represents a substitution effect and *how much* an income effect. What we *do* know is that the whole of the move from a_1 to B represents an income effect. Since a_1 lies on the price line M_3X_4, the move to the B-prices has already taken place. So, the move from a_1 to B occurs wholly because of an income effect. The cost-difference reduction in income is reinstated, and the consumer moves from a_1 to B. However, the move from a_1 to B does not represent the *whole* of the income effect, *except* in the unusual case where a_1 and A coincide. We have already seen that part of the move from A to a_1 is the result of an income effect; but we do not know how much of it is.

This is why the cost-difference method provides a less-fundamental division of the price effect into an income effect and a substitution effect than the compensating-variation method. Using indifference curves, we can identify the compensating variation in income and so divide the price effect into a pure income effect and a pure substitution effect. With the cost-difference method, the move from A to a_1 will contain the whole of whatever substitution effect there is but, unless A and a_1 coincide, it will also contain part of the income effect. Only if A and a_1 coincide can we be sure how big the substitution effect is: then, of course, it will be zero. If A and a_1 do not coincide, we cannot be sure how much of the move from A to a_1 is the result of an income effect. However, there must be *some* income effect, or a_1 would not be preferred to A.

8.5 The slope of the demand curve

Although the revealed preference theory does not allow us to make the fundamental distinction between the pure income effect and the pure substitution effect, which we can make with indifference curves, it does allow us to show that demand curves will usually slope downwards. For it is immediately obvious that, as we showed in Chapter 3 using indifference curves, the substitution effect can never work to reduce the consumer's purchases of a commodity whose price has fallen.

Figure 4.3 makes it clear why this is impossible. It could only happen if, having chosen A in the A-situation, when all the points along the line MA were open to him, the consumer now decided to choose a point between M_3 and A. Provided the consumer's choice is consistent, the substitution effect can never be negative. At worst, A and a_1 might coincide; a_1 can never lie at the left of A.

As in Chapter 3 we therefore find that the substitution effect will never be the cause of an upward-sloping demand curve. However, again as in Chapter 3, we find that the income effect is not so reliable. If it is positive, it will simply reinforce the substitution effect. Whether or not a_1 lies to the right of A, B will be to the right of A, with more X consumed at the lower (B) price.

The income effect, however, may be negative. If it is, then the consequences spelled out in the previous chapter again follow. If the positive substitution effect is big, and the negative income effect weak, the demand curve will still slope downwards. Only if the negative income effect is big enough to outweigh whatever substitution there is will the demand curve slope upwards. We can again conclude that this is only likely to happen where the negative income effect is rather strong. This in turn is most likely to happen where the proportion of a consumer's income spent on the good in question is very large—as with a Giffen good.

9. The fundamental proposition about demand

We have therefore reached exactly the same conclusions as in Chapter 3, but we have done so in a rather simpler way. It is true that we have been able to say less about the nature of scales of preference than in Chapter 3, but we were there pretending to knowledge of the consumer's tastes which we do not actually have. We have now shown that the fundamental proposition in the theory of consumer demand—the proposition that demand curves are downward sloping—can be obtained quite simply from an analysis of the way a 'rational' consumer would behave. We have shown that the demand curve will usually slope downwards, without any necessity to observe the spending pattern of any actual consumer. It is true that we could not say *how big* the income and substitution effect would be for any consumer or any group of consumers. That would require actual observation. But we have done what we set out to do; we have shown why demand curves usually slope downwards.

It is true that an actual consumer may not behave as consistently as our ideal consumer. There is, however, good reason to suppose that our generalisations hold. Econometric studies suggest that our conclusions are realistic. Consumers *do* seem to behave in this kind of way. If actual consumers behaved very differently from our ideal consumers, there would be more inconsistency than has been observed in consumers' purchasing decisions. More than this, it seems better to begin with a theory of demand which assumes rational behaviour and to allow exceptions to, or qualifications to this, rather than to suggest that consumer demand is inconsistent and unpredictable.

10. Consumer equilibrium with many goods

We must now extend our analysis explicitly to deal with more than two goods. Because we have assumed the prices of all goods except X constant, we have implicitly been treating all goods except X as a composite commodity. We have already written p_0 for the A-prices (the original prices) and q_0 for the A-quantities (the original quantities). We shall continue to do this. Now, p_0 will represent the original prices of all the goods—p_x, p_y, p_z, etc. Similarly, q_0 will represent the quantities of the goods purchased at these prices, namely, q_x, q_y, q_z, etc. For any purchased combination q_0 of commodities to be shown as preferred to another combination q_1, we simply need $p_0 \times q_1$ to be less than $p_0 \times q_0$: $p_0 \times q_1 < p_0 \times q_0$. The total expenditure, $p_0 \times q_1$, required to buy the combination q_1 at the A-prices, is less than the amount actually spent on the q_0 combination. By definition, this was $p_0 \times q_0$. That was what was actually spent and we are assuming total income to have been spent. So, the B-quantities could have been bought in the A-situation; in fact, the A-quantities were chosen. q_0 is a preferred position to q_1.

Similarly, if q_1 is preferred to q_0, we shall have $p_1 \times q_0$ less than $p_1 \times q_1$. The consumer *could* afford to have bought the A-quantities at the B-prices, but chose not to do so. With strong ordering, the only situation in which the consumer could be indifferent between q_0 and q_1 would be when they were identical. Here, $p_0 \times q_1 = p_0 \times q_0$ and $p_1 \times q_0 = p_1 \times q_1$. With weak ordering, however, the two equalities could hold even though the A-combination of quantities was not identical to B-combination: even though q_0 is not identical with q_1. As along a (weakly ordered) indifference curve, two different combinations of goods give the same satisfactions to the consumer. We shall find it more fruitful to work in terms of indifference positions rather than preferred positions from now on, even though this makes what we have to say less easily testable.

What can we say? First, we can be certain that the *total* substitution effect of any price change will tend to be positive. In aggregate, the amounts of the various commodities consumed after a set of price changes has taken place will tend to increase. (By tend to increase we mean that it will rise, or remain constant.) For our purposes, we need only to allow the price of one good to fall. What we *do* need is to identify the other goods individually rather than treating them as a composite commodity labelled M, which is what we have done so far. We need to be able to identify competitive and complementary relationships between the goods other than X, and we cannot do this unless we abandon our composite commodity. We can only define such relationships unambiguously if we eliminate price effects. This is why we must consider indifferent positions rather than preferred positions. To simplify the analysis, we shall consider the relationships between three goods: X, Y, Z where there are no income effects.

<table>
<tr><td>

11.
Competitive goods

</td><td>

Let us assume that the price of X falls, but at the same time there is a reduction in the consumer's income by a compensating variation. We can still say that the quantity demanded will tend to rise. The consumer cannot buy *less* of X now that it is cheaper for there is only a substitution effect. Although we have separated out the individual goods making up the composite good, we have not altered the basic relationship between X and the other goods. We have kept all their prices constant just as we did in section   and we therefore get the same result. The amount of X bought will 'tend to increase' if its price falls.

</td></tr>
</table>

What we *can* now see, however, is the effect on the quantities purchased of the other goods—here Y and Z. Now that the price of X has fallen, the substitution effect will cause the consumer to increase the amount of X which he buys. It will do this even though he is no better off because there has been a compensating reduction in his income. He must therefore buy a reduced amount of at least one of the other two goods. Normally, the consumer will buy less of both Y and Z. He will substitute X for both Y and Z. If this happens, then we can say that *Y is competitive with X against Z, and Z is competitive with X against Y.*

One possibility, therefore, is that if the price of X falls, and the consumer's income is reduced so that his satisfactions do not increase when he moves to a new equilibrium position where he has more X, then any other good of which less is bought is *competitive* with X. Alternatively, the good in question can be described as a *substitute* for X. We can define competitive goods precisely only by doing so in a situation where we have eliminated income effects by making a compensating variation in income. What happens if one takes income effects into account? It is then no longer necessary for a consumer's purchases of Y to fall when X becomes cheaper, even if X and Y are competitive goods. If the reduction in the price of X causes a large income effect, this may increase the demand for Y (or Z), since the consumer's real income will now be much greater. Similarly, if the income-elasticity of demand for Y (or Z), is high, more Y (or Z) may be demanded when X becomes cheaper, even though X and Y (or Z) are competitive. Had there been no income effect, less Y would have been bought. But the 'positive' income effect works in the direction of increasing the consumer's purchases of Y now that his real income has risen. If the income effect is strong enough, it may swamp the substitution effect, which by itself would have worked to reduce purchases of Y now that X is cheaper.

In most cases this will not happen. Either the income effects will be very small or they will be outweighed by the substitution effect. There will be a reduction in the purchases of goods Y and Z whose prices have *not* fallen. Thus, a reduction in the price of, say, tea will reduce the amount of coffee bought and vice versa. It will be realised, of course, that if income effects are *negative* they will merely *increase* the size of the reduction in purchases of the competitive good whose price has not fallen, over and above that caused by the substitution effect.

12. Complementary goods

(a) True complimentarity

Let us now consider what happens where, in the case of three goods X, Y and Z, the amount of X bought by a consumer increases, and the amount of Y he buys also increases. Consider a situation where the consumer is in an equilibrium position, buying some X, some Y and some Z. The price of X now falls, the prices of Y and Z remain constant, but there is a compensating variation in the consumer's income. He will therefore be no better off in the new equilibrium position but will buy more X, less Z and more Y. Here, instead of substituting X for both Y and Z as in our earlier examples, the consumer actually increases his purchases of Y, while reducing his purchases of Z more substantially than before. We may now say that Y *is complementary with X against* Z. Similarly, if in the same circumstances an increase in the amount of X held lead to a substantial reduction in the amount of Y, but was accompanied by an increase in the amount of Z, we could say that Z *was complementary with X against Y*. It is, of course, impossible for *both Y and Z* to be complementary with X. Whenever there is any number of goods (n) at least one of those goods must be competitive with that in which we are interested. It could conceivably happen, that all of the remaining $n-2$ goods were complementary with it, but this is unlikely. It will, of course, be quite possible for $n-1$ of any collection of goods to be competitive with the remaining good.

There are certainly situations where the demand for Y increases in response to a fall in the price of X, where there are *no* income effects. It increases because the consumer uses Y in conjunction with X. He has more X and thus wants more Y to go with it. X and Y supplement or *complement* each other in use. Goods like bacon and eggs; tea and sugar; pipes and tobacco, are examples of complementary goods. If bacon becomes cheaper, and this causes the consumer to buy more bacon, he may well buy more eggs to go with it, even though his real income is no greater than before, because the price of at least one other good has been increased. If this happens, bacon and eggs will be complementary so far as the consumer in question is concerned.

This definition of complementarity, like our definition of competitiveness, ignores income effects. Fortunately, provided income effects are positive they cannot disturb these conclusions. If X and Y are complementary and the price of X falls, more Y is *bound* to be bought, though some of the increased purchases will be the result of the positive income effect. The consumer buys more Y partly because his real income has risen, but partly because Y is complementary with X. Unless the income effect is negative, the consumer will never buy *less* of a good when the price of its complement falls.

It will be useful to sum up this discussion of complementarity. Let us assume that income effects are positive and are *not* eliminated. Then, if the price of X falls and more of it is bought while the amount of Y purchased falls, X and Y must be competitive goods. Had there been no income effect, an even greater reduction in purchases of Y would have occurred. If the price of X falls and purchases of Y *rise,* however, we cannot be so certain whether X and Y are competitive or complementary. It is possible that the goods are competitive but that the positive income effect resulting from the fall in the price of X is strong enough to lead to an increase in the purchases of Y; not the fall which would have occurred without income effects.

(b) Joint demand

It is equally possible that X and Y are complementary, with the income effect working in the same direction as the substitution effect. Where the amount of good Y demanded increases where more X is bought, one can, as a first approximation, say that X and Y are goods in *joint demand*. One has to go on to eliminate the income effect before one can say whether X and Y are competitive or complementary. It follows that, so long as income effects are positive, all complementary goods will be in joint demand. But not all goods in joint demand will be complementary. Some may be competitive goods for which the positive income effect is strong. The essential preliminary to discovering whether goods are competitive or complementary is therefore to eliminate the income effect.

13. Cross-elasticity of demand

It is useful to apply the idea of elasticity of demand to situations where two goods are related in the ways we have been considering, and where a change in the price of one good causes changes in the demand for another. We can do this by discovering whether and to what extent a proportionate change in the price of one good causes a proportionate change in purchases of another good. This gives us a measure of the cross-elasticity of demand between the goods. Where there are two goods, X and Y, the cross-elasticity of demand is obtained by considering the change in purchases of Y resulting from a given change in the price of X—the price of Y being held constant. That is to say:

Cross-elasticity of demand

$$=\frac{\text{proportionate change in purchases of } Y}{\text{proportionate change in price of } X}$$

It will usually be found that any two goods, X and Y, chosen at random, are sufficiently competitive for the (positive) income effect to be outweighed by the substitution effect. A rise in the price of X (or Y) will therefore cause an increase in the purchases of Y (or X); similarly, a fall in the price of X (or Y) will cause a decline in the purchases of Y (or X). In the 'normal' case, then, the changes in the price of X and in the quantity of Y that are purchased will be in the same direction. The numerical measure of cross-elasticity will be positive. Alternatively, if the goods are in joint demand, a fall in the price of X will cause a rise in the amount of Y purchased and vice versa. The numerical cross-elasticity of demand between jointly demanded goods will thus be negative.

Whether cross-elasticities are negative or positive, the limiting cases will be where cross-elasticity is infinite and where it is zero. Where two goods are competitive and cross-elasticity is (plus) infinity, a small fall in the price of X will cause an infinitely large reduction in the amount of Y which is bought. If goods are in joint demand and cross-elasticity is (minus) infinity, a small fall in the price of X will cause an infinitely large increase in purchases of Y. Neither of these limiting elasticities is likely to be observed in empirical studies. Cross-elasticities of varying finite magnitude (positive and negative) will be found. The dividing line between these positive and negative elasticities will occur where cross-elasticity is zero so that a small fall (or rise) in the price of X has no effect whatever on the purchases of Y.

Suggested reading

HICKS, SIR JOHN   *A Revision of Demand Theory*, Oxford, Clarendon Press, 1956, especially chapters 1 and 7.

5

Equilibrium of the firm

1. Profit maximisation

Our analysis has so far shown how the demand curve for an individual, or for a market, can be derived from the relevant scales of preference. We can now discuss the way in which the supply curve for a commodity is built up. We can then, at a later stage, discuss the interaction of demand and supply in more detail. In order to construct a supply curve we shall first study the equilibrium of the individual production unit—the firm—just as when we were constructing a demand curve we first studied the equilibrium of the individual consumption unit—the consumer. We shall find that the concepts which we have to use are rather more complicated than they were for the analysis of consumer equilibrium. We must therefore spend much of the present chapter explaining the meaning and uses of the analytical tools we shall need.

1.1 The assumptions

At the outset we must recall the assumption of 'rationality', as explained in the Introduction. Unless otherwise stated, we shall be concerned with the 'one-man' firm. We shall assume that the owner of the individual firm, the entrepreneur as he is often called by economists, behaves rationally, in just the same way as we assumed that the individual consumer did. For the firm, 'rationality' does not imply maximising satisfaction as it did in demand theory. 'Rationality' now implies that the firm aims at earning the greatest possible money profits. No economist believes that all business men do always maximise profits. Nor does he necessarily believe that they should do so.

What the economist does believe is that the assumption that entrepreneurs maximise profit is the most appropriate one to make in economic theory. What economists want economic theory to do is to enable them to predict how firms and industries will respond to such changes as changes in costs, in demand, in taxation, etc. The assumption that the firm will always maximise profits allows the economist to see the effect of any such change by assuming that both before and after it occurs firms maximise profit. It gives him determinate solutions.

What is more, it is in most cases the best assumption. Where competition is keen, profit maximisation is undoubtedly the most satisfactory assumption. Unless a firm in a very competitive situation maximises profit, there is a danger that it will go bankrupt. The choice is to 'maximise or go bust'. It is true that in less-competitive conditions (what we shall define later as monopoly or oligopoly) there is more choice. Even here, however, the assumption that the firm will try to maximise profit is the most useful initial assumption, which can be relaxed later if desired.

The assumption of 'rationality' is a common factor in the analysis of consumer equilibrium and the equilibrium of the firm. However, there is one important difference. The satisfaction which the consumer attempts to maximise cannot be measured, for there are no units of measurement. The profits of the entrepreneur can be measured in money. It is money profits which the entrepreneur is assumed to maximise.

A corollary of the assumption of rationality is that whatever output the firm produces it always does so as cheaply as possible, given existing technical production methods. We assume that the firm always keeps money costs of production as low as it can. This is another essential part of the theory of the firm. It would be impossible to point to an equilibrium position for the firm if one could not say whether costs had been kept to a minimum or not. One would never know in such conditions what any given output would cost to produce.

We shall also assume for the sake of simplicity that each firm produces only one product. Our results can be applied to multi-product firms, but the analysis then becomes rather complicated and in this book we want to keep it simple. We shall assume, too, that unless an explicit statement is made to the contrary, the price of each factor of production is given and constant. In technical language, we shall assume that all units of each factor of production are equally efficient and that all are in 'infinitely elastic supply' at their current price. Each entrepreneur can hire as many units of any factor as he wishes at that price. This assumption rules out the possibility that higher wages can be paid for overtime work, that lower prices can be given for bulk purchases of raw materials or that differences in cost may arise because some units of a factor of production are more or less efficient than others.

Having made these assumptions, we can deduce the equilibrium position of any firm from two sets of data. First, we need to know how much revenue the firm earns from selling various amounts of its product. Second, we need to know how much it costs to produce these same volumes of output. This information can be given in various ways, but we begin with Fig. 5.1. We draw a firm's total cost curve (*TC*) showing the total costs of producing various outputs, and its total revenue curve (*TR*) showing the total receipts earned from selling these same outputs. This is done in Fig. 5.1. The shapes

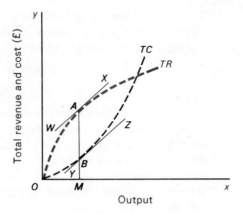

Fig. 5.1

of the curves in Fig. 5.1 are of no special significance, and the conclusion is not affected by this. We shall discuss the likely shapes of such curves later. As Fig. 5.1 implies, it is implicitly assumed in most discussions of the firm in economic theory that stocks of raw materials, components, finished goods, etc. never change. Sales and output are therefore always equal. This assumption is not essential and can be relaxed.

A firm's profits may be defined as the difference between its total revenue and its total costs. It is clear, therefore, that in Fig. 5.1 the largest profits which the firm could make will be earned when the (vertical) distance between the total cost and total revenue curves is as great as possible. This will always be at the output where the slopes of the two curves are the same, that is to say where the tangents *YZ* and *WX* to the cost and revenue curves respectively are parallel. Readers with a knowledge of differential calculus will see that all we have done is to use Fig. 5.1 as a diagrammatic way of maximising the difference between the total revenue and total cost functions. This could be done equally well using calculus.

1.3 Profit maximisation with calculus

The total revenue function shows total revenue as a function of sales, which we are assuming to be always equal to output. Total revenue at any output is equal to price per unit multiplied by quantity sold. If we denote price by p and output by x, we have the total revenue function:

$$px = f(x) \ldots (1)$$

Similarly, if we denote total cost by C, we have the total cost function:

$$C = F(x) \ldots (2)$$

To maximise the difference between the two functions we have to discover that value of x where the derivatives of the two functions are equal. In other words, when:

$$\frac{d(px)}{dx} = \frac{dC}{dx}$$

If we took the particular functions from Fig. 5.1, we should find that this happened where x was equal to OM. Of course, the derivative of the total revenue function can be represented by the tangent WX to the total revenue curve in Fig. 5.1. Similarly, the derivative of the total cost function is given by the tangent YZ to the total cost curve. Where these slopes are equal, as they are in Fig. 5.1 with profits of AB, then profits are maximised. In the diagram, we have equated the slopes of the two tangents; in the calculus, we have equated the two derivatives. Figure 5.1 simply shows that profits are maximised where the derivatives of the total cost and total revenue functions are equal.

What we shall do in this chapter is to elaborate graphically the basic point that profit will be maximised where the derivatives of the total cost and total revenue functions are equal. However, this is useful even for readers with a good knowledge of calculus. The wider implications of the notion of profit maximisation and of the possible shapes of total revenue and total cost curves can be brought out more fully in this way.

1.4 Marginal revenue and marginal cost

While it is perfectly reasonable to use total cost and total revenue curves to show at what output profits are maximised, it is a very cumbersome way of doing so. First, the maximum vertical distance between the total revenue and total cost curve is not always easy to see at a glance. Second, it is impossible to discover price per unit easily—only total revenue (e.g. £AM when output is OM). Total revenue must be divided by output (in this case OM units) in order to discover price per unit.

It is therefore the practice to draw diagrams which provide more information at a glance. They do not show total revenue or total cost at all, but use average and marginal revenue curves, and average and marginal cost curves. The same kind of equilibrium position as that which was shown in Fig. 5.1 can be found by discovering the level of output at which marginal revenue equals marginal cost. For marginal revenue is simply the derivative of total revenue function and marginal cost is simply the derivative of the total cost function. We are applying the general rule for discovering the difference between two functions. A firm will be in equilibrium when marginal revenue equals marginal cost, earning maximum profits. It will be maximising the difference between the total cost and total revenue functions. The 'rational' entrepreneur will therefore fix his output so as to equate marginal revenue with marginal cost.

We must now proceed to explain, in detail, what marginal revenue curves and marginal cost curves are, and what shapes they are likely to take. These are concepts which require some elaboration.

2. Marginal revenue

2.1 Marginal revenue defined

Marginal revenue, at any level of a firm's output, is the revenue which it would earn if it sold another (marginal) unit of its product. Algebraically, it is the addition to total revenue earned if the firm sells n units of product instead of $n-1$, where n is any number.[1] Since marginal revenue can mean the revenue which is earned by selling *any* (marginal) unit of output, we need to draw a marginal revenue curve showing the (marginal) revenue earned by each individual unit of output which the firm produces. In order to construct the marginal revenue curve of a firm, it is desirable to start from the total revenue curve of its product, like *TR* in Fig. 5.1. This total revenue curve shows the total amount of money earned by the firm when output (sales) is at various levels. It is therefore the same thing, from the firm's point of view, as the curve showing consumers' total expenditure on the product of the firm. From this total revenue curve we can derive the firm's average revenue curve. Average revenue, or price per unit of output, is

$$\frac{\text{Total revenue}}{\text{Output}}$$

at each level of output. Average revenue at any output can therefore be discovered from the total revenue curve. The average revenue

---

[1]Alternatively, one could denote it as the addition to total revenue earned by selling $n+1$ units instead of n. Strictly, of course, if one were to reproduce exactly what differential calculus does, one would want to know the *rate of change* of total revenue at a particular level of sales.

E

curve shows what the price of the firm's product is at each level of output. Marginal revenue at the same outputs can also be derived from the total revenue curve. For example, if the total revenue curve shows that two units of output can be sold for the aggregate amount of 95p and one can be sold for 50p, the sale of the second (marginal) unit earns an extra 45p of revenue for the firm. Marginal revenue is 45p at this level of output. A marginal revenue curve can be drawn showing the addition to total revenue earned by selling one extra (marginal) unit of output, if output is at the various levels for which total revenue is known.

2.2 Marginal, average and total revenue related

Let us consider the relationship between marginal, average and total revenue at each level of output more fully, using schedules instead of curves. Let us assume that the situation in an imaginary firm is that shown in Table 5.1. This shows total, average and marginal revenue in pence at all levels of output (sales) from 1 to 10.

Table 5.1
Total, average and marginal revenue schedule

Output	Total revenue (pence)	Average revenue (total revenue ÷ output) (pence)	Marginal revenue (addition to total revenue) (pence)
1	50	50	50
2	95	47½	45
3	135	45	40
4	170	42½	35
5	200	40	30
6	225	37½	25
7	245	35	20
8	260	32½	15
9	270	30	10
10	275	27½	5

Exactly the same information is given by the total revenue (TR), average revenue (AR) and marginal revenue (MR) curves in Fig. 5.2, the curves having been plotted from the figures in Table 5.1. It is not difficult to derive average and marginal revenue curves geometrically from the corresponding total revenue curves. As we have already seen, the slope of a line from the origin to any point on a total revenue (or expenditure) curve shows price per unit, or average revenue, for the output in question.

For example, in Fig. 5.2 the slope of the line OA (i.e. $\dfrac{BA}{OB}$) shows the price of the good in question when output is OB (5) units. Alternatively, one can discover average revenue by marking off one unit along the x-axis to the left of B, shown in this case by the length

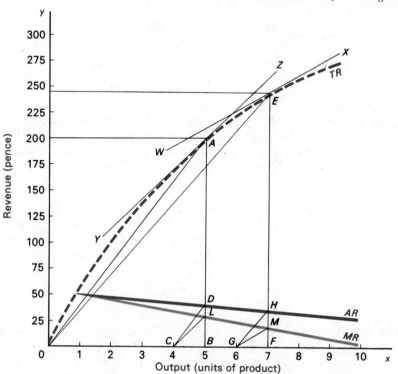

Fig. 5.2

CB. If one then draws CD parallel to OA, one finds price per unit. Since the slope of OA shows price per unit, so does the slope of CD. And since CB represents one unit, BD p (40p) represents the price of one unit, just as BA p represents the 'price' of OB units. D is therefor a point on the firm's average revenue curve, showing price per unit when output is OB. One can derive all the other points on the average revenue curve (AR) in a similar way. For example, when output is OF (7 units) and GF represents one unit of the good in question, average revenue is FHp (35p); OE is parallel to GH.

Similarly, as we have seen, marginal revenue at any output is shown by the slope of a tangent to the point on the total revenue curve appropriate to that output. For example, in Fig. 5.2, YZ is the tangent to the total revenue curve at A, so that its slope represents the rate at which total revenue is changing at the output OB. It shows the net addition to revenue generated by the last unit sold; it shows marginal revenue. So, if we draw CL parallel to YZ, we show how much revenue was added by increasing sales by the unit *CB*. In this instance, marginal revenue is *BL*p (30p). Similarly, if *WX* is tangential to the total revenue curve at *E*, its slope represents marginal revenue when output is *OF*. Here, *GM* is parallel to *WX* and marginal revenue is *FM*p (20p). We can construct the marginal revenue curve for any firm by drawing all the tangents to its total revenue curve, and finding their slope.

2.3 Some useful geometrical relationships

In most of the following analysis we shall be concerned only with average and marginal revenue curves, so that we can ignore total revenue curves. It can be shown that there are geometrical relationships between any average revenue curve and the corresponding marginal revenue curve. The main ones are as follows. So long as

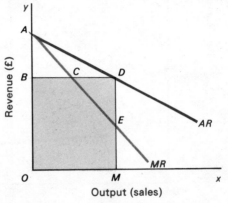

Fig. 5.3

the average revenue curve is falling, marginal revenue must be less than average revenue. The marginal revenue curve itself may be rising, falling or horizontal according to circumstances, but normally it will fall too. The simplest relationship occurs where the average and marginal curves are both straight lines. Where this happens, the marginal revenue curve will cut any line perpendicular to the *y*-axis half-way to the average revenue curve. This is shown in Fig. 5.3, where *BC* equals *CD*.[1] It is perhaps helpful to note at this point that in Fig. 5.3 one can show total revenue in two ways. One can multiply price per unit by number of units sold in a rectangle like *OBDM*, or one can sum marginal revenue over a range of output, in an area like *OAEM*.

In a similar way, where the average revenue curve is *concave upwards*, as in Fig. 5.4a, the marginal revenue curve cuts any perpendicular less than half-way from the *y*-axis to the average revenue

[1]Readers who want a geometrical proof of this can consult, for example, Joan Robinson, *Economics of Imperfect Competition*, Chapter 2.

curve. Where the average revenue curve is *concave downwards,* the marginal revenue curve cuts any perpendicular more than half-way from the *y*-axis to the average revenue curve. For instance, in both Fig. 5.4a and 5.4b, *B* is mid-way between the vertical axis and the average revenue curve.

We have now discussed the relationships between the average and marginal revenue curves along a perpendicular to the *y*-axis, and these relationships are helpful in much economic analysis. From an

Fig. 5.4 a | b

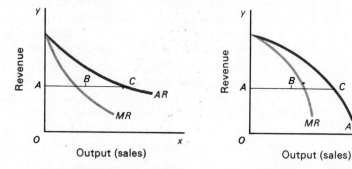

economic point of view, however, it is more useful to analyse the relationships between average and marginal revenue on any perpendicular to the *x*-axis. In other words, it is useful to consider the relationship between marginal and average revenue at *any level of output/sales.* This can be done in terms of elasticity of demand.

First, however, we must clear up a rather important matter of terminology. It will be apparent that the average revenue curve of a firm is really the same thing as the demand curve of consumers for the firm's product. There is therefore a temptation to call the firm's average revenue curve its 'demand curve'. For it shows how much of the firm's product will be demanded at various prices. This is misleading. A consumer's demand curve shows the demand of the consumer for a commodity. It is only reasonable to expect that the firm's demand curve would also show the demand of the firm for something or other. In fact, we shall discover later that the firm does have a demand curve—for factors of production. It therefore avoids confusion if we write of the firm's *average revenue curve* and not of its 'demand curve'. Some economists use the alternative term *sales curve.* We shall reserve the term 'firm's demand curve' for use in the more specialised sense of a demand curve for factors of production later in the book.

*2.4 Average
revenue,
marginal
revenue and
elasticity of
demand*

In order to discuss the relationships between average and marginal revenue and the elasticity of demand on the firm's average revenue curve, we need to extend our definition of elasticity of demand. For the sake of simplicity, we have so far assumed that all demand curves are straight lines. We have just seen that the average revenue curve of the firm is the same thing, looked at from another point of view, as the demand curve by consumers for the firm's product. Consequently, the measure of elasticity of demand which we have already given is perfectly applicable to finding the elasticity of demand on a firm's average revenue curve. However, it is unlikely that all average revenue curves (or for that matter demand curves) will be straight lines. We therefore need to be able to measure elasticity of demand if the average revenue curve really is a curve.

This can be done quite simply. In Fig. 5.5, for example, one can measure elasticity of demand on the average revenue curve AR at the point R, by drawing the tangent tT to the curve at R. Numerical point-elasticity of demand is then given by dividing the length of the portion of the tangent above R (Rt) into the portion below R (RT).

That is to say, elasticity of demand at point $R = \dfrac{RT}{Rt}$.[1] This can be proved from Fig. 5.6 where, for simplicity's sake, we once again draw a straight-line demand curve.

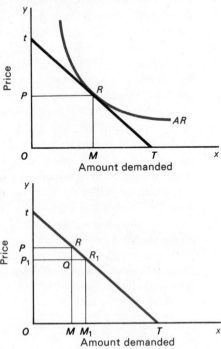

Fig. 5.5

Fig. 5.6

[1] See Marshall, *Principles of Economics*, pp. 102–3.

We know that provided RR_1 is very small (as is the case here) we can define elasticity of demand as:

$$\frac{\text{change in amount demanded}}{\text{original amount demanded}} \cdot \frac{\text{change in price}}{\text{original price}}$$

Thus elasticity $= \dfrac{MM_1}{OM} \div \dfrac{PP_1}{OP}$, or alternatively

$$= \frac{QR_1}{OM} \div \frac{QR}{RM} = \frac{QR_1}{OM} \times \frac{RM}{QR} = \frac{QR_1}{QR} \times \frac{RM}{OM}.$$

But since the triangles RQR_1 and RMT are similar, we can write $\dfrac{QR_1}{QR}$ as $\dfrac{TM}{RM}$. The equation $\dfrac{QR_1}{QR} \times \dfrac{RM}{OM}$ thus becomes $\dfrac{TM}{RM} \times \dfrac{RM}{OM}$. Cancelling out, we get elasticity $= \dfrac{TM}{OM}$. But, since triangles MTR and PRt are similar, $\dfrac{TM}{OM} = \dfrac{RT}{Rt}$. Point elasticity of demand on a demand curve can thus always be found by drawing any tangent tT to the curve at any point R and calculating $\dfrac{RT}{Rt}$. With this measure of point elasticity of demand we can study the relationships between average and marginal revenue curves at any output.

Let us consider the situation shown in Fig. 5.7. We know that

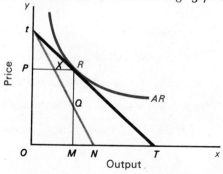

Fig. 5·7

elasticity of demand at point R on the average revenue curve in Fig. $5\cdot7 = \dfrac{RT}{Rt}$. Now the triangles PtR and MRT have equal angles. Therefore $\dfrac{RT}{Rt}$ can be written alternatively as $\dfrac{RM}{tP}$. We now draw a line from t which bisects PR at X and then passes through Q. This (straight) line will in fact be 'marginal' to the tangent tT because it cuts the perpendicular PR, from P to the tangent, at its mid-point, X.

Thus, in the triangles PtX and XRQ,

$$PX = RX,$$
$$\angle PXt = \angle RXQ \text{ (vertically opposite)}$$
and $$\angle tPX = \angle XRQ \text{ (right angles)}.$$

Therefore, triangles PtX and XRQ are equal in all respects, and tP equals RQ. So, instead of writing elasticity at R as $\dfrac{TR}{tR}=\dfrac{RM}{tP}$, we may write it as $\dfrac{RM}{RQ}=\dfrac{RM}{RM-QM}$. At the output OM, $RM=$ average revenue, and $QM=$ marginal revenue. We can thus write elasticity as $\dfrac{\text{average revenue}}{\text{average revenue}-\text{marginal revenue}}$.

Symbolically where, at any output:

$A=$ average revenue,

$M=$ marginal revenue,

and $e=$ point elasticity on the average revenue curve,

$e=\dfrac{A}{A-M}$. It follows from this that $eA-eM=A$;

$\therefore -eM=A-eA$,

$\therefore M=\dfrac{eA-A}{e}=A\dfrac{e-\mathrm{I}}{e}$.

Similarly, since $eA-eM=A$, it follows that $eA-A=eM$;

$\therefore A(e-\mathrm{I})=eM$,

$\therefore A=\dfrac{Me}{e-\mathrm{I}}$,

$\therefore A=M\dfrac{e}{e-\mathrm{I}}$.

The general rule is this: At any output average revenue$=$marginal revenue$\times\dfrac{e}{e-\mathrm{I}}$; and marginal revenue$=$average revenue$\times\dfrac{e-\mathrm{I}}{e}$; where $e=$point elasticity of demand on the average revenue curve.

If the elasticity of a firm's average revenue curve at a given output

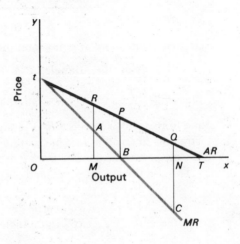

Fig. 5.8

is equal to one, marginal revenue equals average revenue $\times \dfrac{1-1}{1} =$ average revenue $\times\, 0 = 0$. Therefore where the elasticity of demand on the average revenue curve equals 1, marginal revenue equals 0. This can also be seen from Fig. 5.8.

In Fig. 5.8 elasticity on the average revenue curve is equal to one at point P, where output is OB. For $PT = Pt$ and therefore $\dfrac{PT}{Pt} = 1$. At this output marginal revenue is zero. Similarly, when elasticity of demand equals 2 (at point R in Fig. 5.8), where $RT = 2Rt$:

$$M = A\frac{2-1}{2} = \tfrac{1}{2}A.$$

In other words, $AM = \tfrac{1}{2}RM$. Marginal revenue equals half average revenue. Marginal revenue is *always* positive at any output where the elasticity of the average revenue curve is greater than one. This happens in Fig. 5.8 over the range of the average curve between t and P. Similarly, over the range between P and T where elasticity is less than one, marginal revenue is *always* negative. This can be seen from our formula by taking an elasticity less than one, say $\tfrac{1}{4}$—at point Q. Here $QT = \tfrac{1}{4}Qt$ and

$$M = A \times \frac{\tfrac{1}{4}-1}{\tfrac{1}{4}} = A \times \frac{-\tfrac{3}{4}}{\tfrac{1}{4}} = -3A.$$

Marginal revenue is negative and is three times average revenue. In Fig. 5.8, $CN = 3QN$. We therefore know that marginal revenue is always positive where the average revenue curve is elastic and always negative where it is inelastic. It follows that where elasticity of demand equals one marginal revenue is zero. With the aid of these formulae, it is possible to discover marginal revenue *at any output* from average revenue at the same output, provided one knows point elasticity of demand on the average revenue curve.

Table 5.2
Total, average and marginal cost schedules

Output	Total cost (£)	Average cost (£)	Marginal cost (£)
1	1·50	1·50	1·50
2	2·00	1·00	0·50
3	2·25	0·75	0·25
4	2·40	0·60	0·15
5	2·50	0·50	0·10
6	3·60	0·60	1·10
7	5·25	0·75	1·65
8	8·00	1·00	2·75
9	13·50	1·50	5·50
10	22·50	2·25	9·00

3. Marginal cost

3.1 Marginal cost defined

Marginal cost is the cost of increasing the output of the firm's product by a marginal unit. It is the parallel on the supply side to marginal revenue on the demand side. We can therefore derive average and marginal cost curves from a total cost curve of the type shown in Fig. 5.1. Let us first of all construct a table showing total, average and marginal cost in a hypothetical firm at various outputs.

There are one or two points about these figures which should be noted. First, average cost at any output $=\dfrac{\text{Total cost}}{\text{Output}}$. Second, marginal cost is the total cost of n units of output minus the total cost of $n-1$ units.[1] Third, both average cost and marginal cost fall as output rises from 1 to 5 units. They both rise for outputs above 6 units. One can plot the values shown in Table 5.2 on curves in just the same way as one can plot total, average and marginal revenue. We shall not do this here, but the same principles hold with cost as with revenue. We may note that if one starts from any total cost curve, average cost, at any output shown on that curve, is given by the slope of a straight line from the origin through the point in question. Similarly, marginal cost is given by the slope of a tangent to the point on the total cost curve representing a given output.

3.2 Marginal and average cost related

Since marginal cost and average cost are concepts similar to average and marginal revenue, the relationships we set out in the previous section for marginal revenue and average revenue hold equally for marginal and average cost. However, since the average revenue curve for a firm represents the demand function for its product, it follows that average revenue curves (like demand curves) will not normally slope upwards at any point. Average cost curves on the other hand can, and often do, both rise and fall. We have seen that this would happen with curves based on the data in Table 5.2. We shall have to discuss the likely shapes of cost curves in detail soon. For the moment, we shall assume (as in Table 5.2) that average and marginal cost curves are U-shaped like the curves shown in Fig. 5.9 and consider the relationship between such curves.

It will be seen from Fig. 5.9 that so long as the average cost curve (AC) is falling, marginal cost (MC) is less than average cost. Similarly, if average cost is rising, marginal cost is greater than average cost. But one cannot deduce anything about the *direction* in which marginal cost is moving from the *direction* in which average cost is changing. If average cost is falling, marginal cost may be either rising or falling. If average cost is rising, marginal cost may be falling or rising. But if

[1] Or the total cost of $n+1$ units minus the total cost of n.

average cost is constant, marginal cost must be constant. However, this relationship is not reversible. If marginal cost is constant, while average cost *may* be equal to marginal cost, it may also be falling (or rising) towards marginal cost.

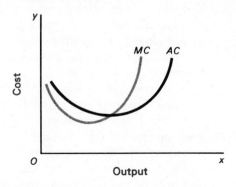

Fig. 5.9

The relationship between marginal and average cost is therefore sometimes found difficult to understand. It may be more easily understood if explained in terms of cricket batting averages. Let us assume that a cricketer's batting average is 60. If in his next innings he scores less than 60, say 52, his average will fall because his marginal score is less than his average score. But this latest marginal score may well be higher than his previous marginal score. He might, for example, have scored 10 in his previous innings, so that his marginal score has risen considerably, by 42 runs. However, so long as his marginal score, whether rising or falling, is less than his average score, that average score must fall. On the other hand, if the average curve is horizontal, the corresponding marginal curve will be identical with it. This can also be illustrated by batting averages. If the batsman's average is 60 as before, but he now plays an innings in which he scores just 60 then his average and marginal scores will be equal. His average score will neither rise nor fall.

Some people find it easiest to remember this relationship between average and marginal values with the aid of Fig. 5.10. Here, where

Fig. 5.10

marginal value is above (greater than) average value, average value rises. It is as though marginal value were pulling average value up towards itself. Similarly, where marginal value is below average value, average value falls, as though marginal value were pulling average value downwards. When marginal value is equal to average value, average value remains constant, as though marginal value were pulling average value along horizontally. The arrows show the direction of these 'pulls'. However, we must stress again that one can make no generalisations of this kind about whether marginal cost will be rising or falling when average cost is rising or falling. The relationships between marginal and average values are 'one-way' relationships. The relationship is between the *magnitude* of the marginal value and the *direction of movement* of the average value. Consequently, if marginal cost is constant, we cannot be sure whether average cost will be equal to it. We cannot relate the *direction of movement* of average cost to the *direction of movement* of marginal cost.

Finally, it is important to remember that when we draw average cost curves which are U-shaped, the corresponding marginal curve will always cut the average curve at its lowest point. This was shown in Fig. 5.9. As we have seen, when average cost is falling, marginal cost will be below average cost. Similarly, when average cost is rising, marginal cost will be greater than average cost. So, at the moment when average cost stops falling but has not yet begun to rise, the marginal cost curve will pass through the average cost curve in order to be above it when average cost does start to rise. On the other hand if, as in Fig. 5.11, the average curve (*A*) were shaped like an inverted U, the corresponding marginal curve (*M*) would always cut the average curve at its highest point.

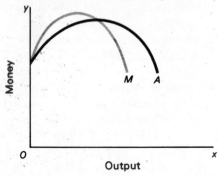

Fig. 5.11

**4.
Equilibrium
of the firm**

On our assumption of 'rationality', a firm will be in equilibrium when it is earning maximum money profits and we know that this will happen where marginal revenue is equal to marginal cost.

In the firm shown in Fig. 5.12, marginal revenue equals marginal cost when the output *OM* is sold. Here, the price which the firm can charge for *OM* is shown on its average revenue curve. It is *MR*, which is the same as *QP*. The amount of profit will be shown by the area of the rectangle *PRLP₁*. This is the largest rectangle which it is possible to draw between the average revenue curve, the average cost curve and the *y*-axis. We may also show profit in Fig. 5.12 by the shaded area *WXD* which lies between the marginal revenue curve, the marginal cost curve, and the *y*-axis. This is because any vertical line between the marginal cost and revenue curves represents the addition to profit resulting from the production and sale of that

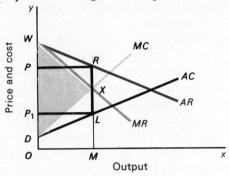

Fig. 5.12

marginal unit of output. Area *WXD* sums these receipts for all units of output between zero and *OM*. Profit at any level of output can therefore be shown in three ways:

Profit = total revenue — total cost (as shown by the line *AB* in Fig. 5.1);

Or,

Average revenue × output — average cost × output (as shown by rectangle $PRLP_1$ in Fig. 5.12);

Or,

$\sum$[1] marginal revenues — $\sum$ marginal costs (as shown by the shaded area *WXD* in Fig. 5.12).

In each case, profit is maximised at the output where marginal cost equals marginal revenue.

The attraction of using marginal cost and marginal revenue curves to show the profit-maximising level of output is that if one is using diagrams rather than calculus this obviates the need for discovering where the largest profit-maximising rectangle can be drawn. In Fig. 5.1, we discovered the profit-maximising output by finding the output where the tangents to the total cost and revenue curves were parallel. As we have seen, these tangents show marginal revenue and marginal cost, which are equal when the tangents are parallel. Figure 5.1 merely provided a rather cumbersome diagrammatic method of doing what we have now done in Fig. 5.12.

[1] The Greek capital 'sigma', meaning 'the sum of'.

Any reader who is still uncertain why profits will be maximised when marginal revenue equals marginal cost may find the following explanations helpful. If, in the circumstances shown in Fig. 5.12, output were increased beyond OM, marginal cost would exceed marginal revenue. Each additional unit of output sold beyond OM could only add an amount of money to the firm's revenue that was smaller than the cost of producing and selling it. An increase in output would therefore reduce profit. Similarly, if output were reduced below OM, marginal revenue would be greater than marginal cost. Units of output which could have added more to the firm's revenue than to its costs, would not have been produced. Profits would be smaller than they could have been. Profits are at a maximum only when marginal revenue equals marginal cost. In Fig. 5.12 profits are maximised when output OM is sold at price OP.

We have now succeeded, by assuming that entrepreneurs always fix output so as to maximise money profits, in giving a determinate solution to a major problem of the individual entrepreneur. He has to answer the question: 'How much of my product shall I produce and what price shall I charge for it?'

It is perfectly reasonable at this stage to ask 'Do business men really equate marginal cost and marginal revenue?' The answer is that only an extremely small proportion of businesses try to do so explicitly, but that the proportion is slowly increasing in the United Kingdom. Many entrepreneurs still fix their price and/or output by working in terms either of total cost and total revenue or, more usually, of average cost and average revenue. For example, they may try to find that output at which the excess of total revenue over total cost is at a maximum. However, provided we decide that it is reasonable to assume that business men seek maximum profits—provided we agree to stand by the assumption of 'rationality'—it makes no difference at all to the actual output produced whether profits are calculated on the basis of total, average or marginal costs and revenues.[1]

5. The firm's average revenue curve

It will be obvious from the analysis of the previous section that if we are to produce a realistic theory of the individual firm we must first discover what shape its cost and revenue curves are likely to take in the real world. In the next two sections, we shall do this.

---

[1]Readers who are interested in the relationship between economic theory and business practice may wish to read a paper by Aubrey Silberston, 'Price Behaviour of Firms', which includes a lengthy bibliography. This paper is to be found in the *Economic Journal*, 1970, p.511.

First, what will be the shape of the individual firm's average revenue curve? The shape of the average revenue curve of the individual firm will depend on conditions in the market in which the firm sells its product. Broadly speaking, the keener the competition of its rivals and the greater the number of fairly close substitutes for its product, the more elastic will a firm's average revenue curve be. As usual, it is possible to be precise about limiting cases. One limiting case will occur where there are large numbers of competitors producing identical products, so that the demand for the product of each individual firm is infinitely elastic and its average revenue curve is a horizontal straight line. The firm can sell as much of its product as it wishes at the ruling market price. If it tried to raise its price, then, owing to the ease with which the same product could be bought from competitors, it would lose all its customers. If the firm were to lower its price, it would be swamped by orders from customers wishing to take advantage of its price reduction. The demand—and the elasticity of demand—for its product would be infinite.

This situation is illustrated in Fig. 5.13. Figure 5.13a shows the demand curves of all consumers for a particular product made by an industry with a large number of firms selling a homogeneous product. The demand curve is originally the dark-brown line *DD*, so

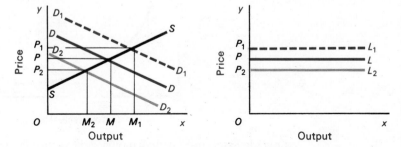

Fig. 5.13 a | b

that the equilibrium price is *OP* and the equilibrium amount *OM* is exchanged at this price. Because there is pure competition, the equilibrium price holds throughout the market and all the firms making the product have to accept it. However, while the individual firm has to accept the price *OP*, it can sell as much as it wants at that price. Average revenue is constant at the price *OP*. So, *PL* (in Fig. 5.13b) represents the average revenue curve of an individual firm. Because average revenue is constant, marginal revenue will also be constant and will be equal to average revenue. The dark-brown line *PL* therefore represents both the average and the marginal revenue curves of the firm.

If the demand for the industry's product increases to D_1D_1 and market price rises to P_1, the average revenue curve of each individual firm rises to P_1L_1. If demand decreases to D_2D_2, and price falls to P_2, the average revenue curve of the individual firm falls to P_2L_2. It should be realised that while the vertical scales of both Fig. 5.13a and 5.13b are the same, the horizontal scale is many times greater in Fig. 5.13b than in Fig. 5.13a. The output of the industry will be many times greater than that of the firm. Each individual firm will produce such a small part of the total output (OM) of the industry that it is unable to influence the price (OP) of the industry's product by its own actions. It must therefore take the price as given. No amount that it could possibly put on the market would alter the price significantly. This situation represents the limiting case of 'pure' competition.

5.3 The average revenue curve in monopoly

The other limiting case is where competition, far from being keen, is absent; where there is monopoly. It might be thought that where a single entrepreneur is the only supplier of a particular product, the demand curve for his product will be a vertical straight line, so that

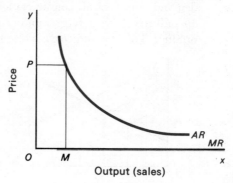

Fig. 5.14

he could extort just as much money as he wished for any given amount of product. This is not realistic. However necessary the product of any firm may be, and however few the competitive substitutes, there must always be some limit to a producer's power to raise his prices. Consumers have only limited incomes, and even if a single producer were able to force each consumer to pay as much as he could, the monopolist could never do more than take the whole of their incomes whatever his output.

The limiting case of 'pure' monopoly, as we may call it, would therefore occur when a producer was so powerful that he was always able to take the whole of *all* consumers' incomes whatever the level of his output. This would happen when, as in Fig. 5.14, the average revenue curve for the monopolist's firm had unitary elasticity and was at such a level that all consumers spent all their incomes on the firm's product, whatever its price. Since the elasticity of the firm's average revenue curve would be equal to one, total outlay on the firm's product would be the same at every price. The pure monopolist could take all consumers' incomes all the time.

It will be seen that even the 'pure' monopolist could not control both the price of his product and the amount which would be demanded. He could fix *either* price *or* output. If he fixed price, say at OP, then the amount which would be demanded (OM) would be decided for him by what consumers would take at that price. If he fixed his output, then price would be decided in a similar way by what his customers would pay when output was at the given level. Even a 'pure' monopolist could never fix both price and output at the same time. Within these limits, however, the 'pure' monopolist's power would be complete. It should be noted that since the total revenue of a 'pure' monopolist would be constant at all levels of output, his marginal revenue would always be zero. The marginal revenue curve coincides with the x-axis. In Fig. 5.14, we show this for the 'pure' monopolist for whose firm we have drawn the average revenue curve.

5.4 Imperfect competition

Pure monopoly has never existed and presumably never will. Pure competition does exist, especially in some world markets for food-stuffs and raw materials where there is no government intervention. But these two types of situation are important rather as limiting cases than as practical possibilities. The great majority of actual firms will be found to be producing in the region of *imperfect* (a better word than 'impure') *competition* lying between these two limits. We shall discuss imperfect competition at great length later. For the moment, we may say the smaller the number of producers making any product, and the smaller the range of close substitutes for that product, the less elastic will be the average revenue curve of any firm producing that product.

In the real world, the average revenue curves of individual firms are likely to range all the way from those depicting almost pure competition, which are almost horizontal, to those denoting very imperfect competition, which are very steep. The actual shape of the firm's average revenue curve will depend on the presence or absence of competing substitutes for the product of the firm in question. Alternatively, we may say the less elastic the average revenue curve of a firm is, the more 'imperfect' is competition in the market to which it sells; the more elastic the demand curve, the more competitive the market is.

5.5 The average revenue curve and time

We have now given a general classification of average revenue curves which will provide a useful basis for our later analysis, but we have so far steadfastly ignored one very important factor—time. The implication throughout our analysis has been that we were studying the firm's average revenue curve in a period of time during which conditions did not alter. What difference will it make if we remove this assumption and allow for the passage of time? So far as average revenue curves are concerned, it is difficult to make satisfactory generalisations. We shall therefore assume for the moment that, if they change at all, demand curves change suddenly and substantially, and then remain constant for a further long period of time. This will enable us to concentrate our attention on changes in *cost* over time, in response to large and sudden changes in demand. As we shall see later, this is a much more interesting and important problem.

6. The firm's short-run average cost curve

The firm's average cost curve is rather more complicated to discuss than is its average revenue curve. There are two reasons for this complexity. First, one cannot now avoid discussing explicitly the problems which arise from the passage of time. This means that we must first discuss short-run cost curves and then long-run cost curves. Second, it is possible for an average cost curve to slope both upwards and downwards, whereas we are assuming that the average revenue curve slopes downward to the right. Indeed, we already know that many cost curves—and *all* short-run cost curves—will be U-shaped. We must now show why this is.

We begin with short-run cost curves. The short run will be more carefully defined later. For the moment, we shall take it to mean a period of time within which the firm can increase its output only by hiring more labour and buying more raw materials. We shall assume that the capital equipment of the firm cannot be altered or added to within this short period of time.

7. A simple analysis

We must now explain why cost curves, or more accurately short-run average cost curves, are likely to be U-shaped. It is possible to discuss this problem either at a simple level or at a more advanced one. It will probably be useful to give both explanations in turn. The more simple explanation requires us to divide the costs of the firm into two broad categories; when added together, these make up total costs. First, every firm has what are known as *fixed* costs. That is to say, it has costs which are independent of output; costs which must be incurred whether output is large or small. 'Fixed' costs cannot be avoided if the firm is to remain in business at all, and include such payments as rent, rates, insurance, depreciation charges (for example, obsolescence) that are independent of the firm's output and depend only on the passage of time. These costs all *have* to be met even if only a very small output is produced. In the short period, the total amount of these fixed costs will not increase or decrease when the volume of the firm's output rises or falls. In terms of our definition of the short period, fixed costs are the costs of all those factors of production whose amount cannot be altered quickly.

By definition, the total fixed costs of the firm cannot fluctuate in the short run, except within very narrow margins, whatever the level of output. This is important. We are interested in the behaviour of average cost, which means dividing total cost by output. The first step is to calculate fixed cost per unit of output, or average fixed costs. To do this, we divide total fixed cost by output. If the fixed costs of the firm are shared equally between the various units of output, each unit will bear a greater amount of fixed cost when output is small than when it is larger. For instance, in the firm shown in Fig. 5.15, total fixed cost is £60 000 whatever the level of output. The curve showing fixed cost per unit of output (average fixed cost) at the various levels of output is the curve AFC. When output is 1 000 units, average fixed costs are £60·00 per unit. When it is 2 000 units, they fall to £30·00 and so on. Average fixed costs fall continuously as output rises. The average fixed cost curve is a rectangular hyperbola, because one is dividing the constant total amount of fixed cost by different levels of output.

This is the main reason why a firm's average cost curve falls when output rises from low levels to higher levels. We must now explain why it rises at a high level of output. To do this, we must consider the costs of the firm which are not fixed. They are variable costs, and include the costs of all those facts of production whose amount can be altered in the short run. Such costs include, for example, payments for wages, raw materials, fuel, power, transport and the like. The total variable costs of a firm therefore vary with output in the short run. Now, if total variable cost always changed in proportion with a change in output, average variable cost (*i.e.* total variable cost ÷ output) would always remain constant. This is not likely to happen. There is a good deal of evidence to suggest that as output rises from zero to the normal capacity level, average variable cost will not change very greatly. Since we are assuming that all factors of production are available at constant and known prices, we are postulating that there is no change in factor prices as output changes. It is likely that the variable factors will produce more efficiently near a firm's capacity output than they do at very low levels of output, but that there will be no great variation in variable cost per unit over this range of output.

Once normal capacity output is being produced, any further increase in output is likely to increase average variable cost quite sharply. Greater output can be obtained but only at much greater cost. Increased output can come only from the use of more of those factors of production whose amount can be altered in the short run.

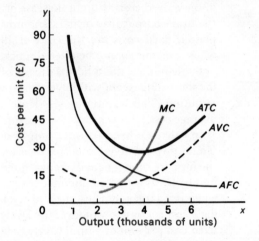

Fig. 5.15

The fact that more and more of the variable factor, say labour, has to be used will lead to overcrowding and to problems of organisation. The fact that existing fixed factors have to be used more intensively means that machines will break down more frequently. Even though we are assuming that overtime rates are not paid when more is done, it is likely that costs will rise. The average variable cost curve will thus take a shape like that of the curve *AVC* in Fig. 5.15. If the curves *AFC* and *AVC* in Fig. 5.15 are now added together, we obtain an average total cost[1] curve *ATC*, or, as it is more usually called, an average cost curve.[2]

It is clear, then, why average cost curves are likely to be U-shaped. At very low levels of output the spreading of fixed costs over more and more units as output rises means that average costs fall quite sharply when production increases; while average variable costs may not fall much, they will certainly not rise. At high levels of output, average variable costs are likely to rise quite quickly because of pressure on the firm's capacity. The continuous fall in average fixed costs will be too small to offset it. The greater the relative size of fixed

---

[1]Average total cost sounds rather like a contradiction in terms, but is probably the best description.

[2]It should be noted that the marginal cost curve in Fig. 5.15 is marginal to both the average variable and the average total cost curves. It therefore cuts both these curves at their minimum points. Since fixed costs are fixed, there is no change in total fixed cost if output alters. If it is reasonable to talk of marginal cost in this context at all, one may say that marginal fixed cost is zero at all levels of output where fixed costs are at a given level.

costs in the firm's total costs, and the more speedy the rise of variable costs once normal output has been passed, the more pronounced the U-shape of the firm's short-run average cost curve will be.

8. A detailed analysis

This simple explanation of the reasons why short-run average cost curves are U-shaped tells much of the story. But it *is* only a simple explanation, and we must now provide a more detailed one. In order to do this, we need to discuss what Marshall called the 'internal economies' of the firm. They are those economies in production—those reductions in production costs—which can be created within the firm itself when its output increases. It seems certain that in all firms average cost will fall to some extent as output rises over low ranges of output. We can discuss the reasons for the internal economies so obtained under three heads.

8.1 Technical economies

(a) The division of labour

In the short-run, with given capital equipment, technical economies can be obtained. First, labour costs per unit of output fall as output rises because of the division of labour. Since the earliest days of economics, great stress has been laid on the principle of the 'division of labour'. Adam Smith, in *The Wealth of Nations*, published in 1776, explained[1] that, if each worker concentrated on a small operation in the manufacture of an article, instead of performing every operation in its construction, production would be greatly increased and greater efficiency obtained. He attributed these results to three facts.

'First, to the increase of dexterity in every particular workman; secondly, to the saving of the time which is commonly lost in passing from one species of work to another; and lastly, to the invention of a great many machines which facilitate labour, and enable one man to do the work of many.[2]

In the short-run, we can only admit the first two of these reasons. The invention of new machinery is a long-run activity. However, even in the short-run the benefits from the division of labour are important.

It was one of Adam Smith's most important contentions that the economies to be reaped from this division of labour were 'limited by the extent of the market'.

[1] *The Wealth of Nations*, chapters ii and iii.
[2] *ibid*, chapter i.

'When the market is very small, no person can have any encouragement to dedicate himself entirely to one employment, for want of the power to exchange all that surplus part of the produce of his own labour, which is over and above his own consumption, for such parts of the produce of other men's labour as he has occasion for.'[1]

This is clearly important for the individual firm. It is possible for a firm to derive economies by dividing up the manufacture of a product into a large number of relatively small operations; but the extent to which such division of labour will be worth undertaking will depend on the scale of output. If only a small total quantity of a product is sold, it will not be worth giving each man one very small job on which to concentrate entirely. If this happened, the man would not be working at all for much of his time.

We have here, in the advantages of the division of labour, one of the reasons why average cost curves will fall over low ranges of output. As output increases, even in the short run with given plant, division of labour, and the greater efficiency it brings with it, will reduce unit costs.

(b) Economies in plant and machinery

Internal economies of a similar kind can be found in the technical sphere. A large electro-plating plant, for example, costs a great deal to keep in operation, and the cost per unit of output plated will clearly be smaller when output is greater. Again, in modern industry, large machines cost a great deal to 'tool up'. Given the complexity of much modern plant and machinery, there are likely to be technical economies in the short run if it is more fully used.

8.2 Marketing economies

Similar internal economies are yielded in marketing. Within fairly broad limits, the total costs of marketing do not alter in the short run. We are assuming in this Chapter that the firm makes only one product, but only for the sake of simplicity. Clearly, if more than one product is made, and especially if the products are closely related, it is not ten times as hard to sell ten different products as to sell one. Even if there is only one product, marketing costs will not vary in proportion to sales. There will be a substantial fixed element in marketing costs, so that economies of scale are realised as sales increase.

8.3 Managerial economies

In just the same way, the cost per unit of management will almost certainly fall as output increases. A good manager can organise a

[1]*ibid.* chapter iii.

large output just as efficiently as a small one and is likely to do so for the same salary. This will be true even though, if the scale of production rises, it may pay to take on a first-rate manager who is worth his higher salary if profits are greater and the job of management more complicated.

For the reasons set out in this section and sections 8.1 and 8.2 above, we can expect average costs to fall as output rises. A little reflection will show that there is not much difference between the reasons for which average costs fall and the reasons for which average fixed costs fall, in response to an increased output. Average fixed costs fall because they are spread over larger volumes of output— because the fixed charges (mainly for buildings and machinery) are being spread more economically. Economies of scale mean much the same thing. Management costs per unit of output fall because they can be spread over more units of output. Advertising costs do not rise in proportion to a rise in output, and so on.

9. Indivisibilities

All this boils down to the fact that most factors of production can be most efficiently employed at the outputs they were designed for and work less efficiently at smaller outputs because they cannot be divided into smaller units. They are *indivisible*. A manager cannot be chopped in half and asked to produce half the current output. Plant cannot be used less fully without being used less economically. It also is indivisible. The reason for internal economies can therefore usually be found in what economic jargon describes as 'indivisible factors of production' or, more shortly, but in a monstrosity of English, 'indivisibilities'. A possible exception occurs in the case of the division of labour. While it is true that the division of labour means that labour efficiency increases as output rises, it is not reasonable to suggest that labour is 'indivisible'.

10. Optimum output

The conclusion from this discussion is that, initially, the firm's short-run average cost curve will fall as output rises. Better use will be made of indivisible factors of production and other economies may be obtained. However, there will be a limit to the possible fall in average costs. In the short run, rising output will sooner or later mean that all the factors used by the firm are being employed as efficiently as possible, so that average cost is at a minimum. This will happen at the output where the factors of production the firm is employing are in the 'right' or 'optimum' proportions. The ratio between the quantities of factors being used is such that short-run average costs are minimised. This output is known as the optimum output. The firm will be producing the optimum output when its average cost is at a minimum.

Once the optimum output is exceeded, average cost will rise. This will now be mainly because indivisible factors are being used to produce too much output. They are again being used in less than optimal proportions with the variable factors. Just as average cost fell when progressively better use was being made of the indivisible factors, so average cost rises when they are being worked too hard. For example, as output exceeds the optimum, management problems will increase and managerial efficiency will decline. The entrepreneur will be unable to manage the firm as efficiently as he could when output was lower. Similarly, there will be too many workers per machine for really efficient production. All this leads to the conclusion that there are good reasons for supposing that the firm's short-run average cost curve will be U-shaped.

11. The law of variable proportions

This is one aspect of a fundamental principle of economics known as the *law of variable proportions*. We shall have to discuss this 'law' more fully in Chapter 10, but a little must be said about it now. Economists have always based their analyses on a belief that the production of a given factory or farm cannot be increased much beyond the optimal level without average cost rising, at least in the short run. This idea, which early economists described as the 'law of diminishing returns', was made the basis of their economic theory. We still retain this 'law' or 'statement of tendency' as an essential element in modern economic theory. Its importance will become clearer as we proceed. For the moment, we see that it enables us to generalise about the shape of short-run cost curves.

The law of diminishing returns, or the law of variable proportions as it is usually now called, can therefore be described in this way. It shows what happens if successive units of a 'variable' factor (one whose amount can vary) are added to a given quantity of a 'fixed' factor (one whose amount cannot be altered). The addition of more and more units of the 'variable' factor will in the end lead to a decline in the additional output resulting from the addition of an extra unit of the variable factor. This 'law' is propounded only on the assumption that the state of technology is given and that no new production methods are introduced during any period in which the 'law' applies. The 'law' is usually 'proved' by empirical evidence. Because the world's food supply cannot be grown on a small field by adding an infinite number of farm workers, the law is held to be realistic. We have ourselves given similar justification for our belief in it.

11.1 The law of variable proportions and the short-run cost curve

The way in which this 'law' helps to explain the shape of the short-run average cost curve should be obvious. In the short-run, one very important factor of production—capital—is fixed in amount for the individual firm. So is management, in the sense of the entrepreneur or the team of managers which runs the firm. So, combining different amounts of variable factor with the fixed factors of capital and management means that, beyond a certain point, returns fall off as output increases—costs rise. Both capital and management are asked to produce too much output for efficient production.

The assumption underlying this statement should be borne in mind. First, we are assuming no changes in factor prices as output increases. Nor are any overtime payments being made. Second, the law of variable proportions does not imply that some units of a factor of production are more efficient than others. We are deliberately assuming that all units of a factor are equally efficient. This may not be true, but it is a convenient simplifying assumption and our aim is to show that the 'law' of variable proportions holds even if it *is* true. It follows that if a firm employs 51 workers where it previously employed 50, each of the 51 produces as much as each other one. Nevertheless, output is smaller than it was when only 50 men were employed. Because the plant is of fixed size each worker will have less elbow-room as the total number of workers increases. The productivity of each, though the same as that of everyone else, falls. Since we are assuming that wages are constant, it follows that average variable costs must rise as total output increases, since output per head is falling. Economists therefore maintain that once a certain level of total output has been reached, average variable cost rises because productivity falls while wages remain constant.

It must be stressed that one can only say that this will happen *after a certain stage*. While only a small number of men is being employed there is the likelihood that productivity per man will rise as output increases. For example, if our hypothetical firm were employing only 20 men, progressively greater specialisation—greater division of labour—might be feasible as employment rose—say to 40 men. Output per man might be higher when 40 men were employed than when 20 were working. Average variable costs would fall if employment rose from twenty to 40 men. All that the 'law' of diminishing returns says is that, given technological conditions, there will be *a point beyond which* the addition of more variable factor(s) to a fixed factor will bring falling returns per unit of variable factor employed. With constant factor prices, this will cause average variable costs to rise. So, while at lower levels of output and employment in the firm it is possible for productivity to increase as more of a variable factor is added to a fixed factor, in the end the return per unit of variable factor must diminish.

12. The short-run marginal cost curve

We have now seen why economists assume that short-run average cost curves are U-shaped. We shall be able to give a more complete explanation of the underlying physical production conditions at a later stage. For our present purposes, this analysis will suffice. It seems desirable to add explicitly at this point that once one knows what shape the average cost curve of the firm is it is always quite easy to draw the corresponding marginal cost curve. The relevant relationships were discussed above in section 3.2.

The conclusion of this section is therefore that short-run average cost curves are U-shaped.

13. Long-run average cost curves

With long-run average cost curves, generalisation is less easy. With unchanging technology, there are good reasons for thinking that long-run average cost curves will also be U-shaped. However, it does not follow that the U-shape is as smooth or regular as in the curves in Fig. 5.17. The curve might be a wavy one. It is more likely that both short- and long-run curves will have a relatively large flat region in the centre, as the long-run curve does in Fig. 5.16. Unfortunately, empirical evidence collected by economists does not show

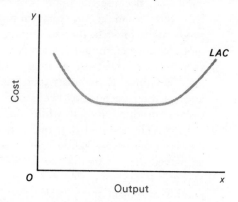

Fig. 5.16

any U-shape in long-run cost curves. The problem is that the empirical evidence is about a world where technology *does* change, while the theory is about one where it does not. We shall begin by outlining the theoretical reasons for supposing that long-run average cost curves will be U-shaped as short-run ones are, but that the sides of the U will be flatter. The U-shape of the cost curve will be less pronounced the longer the period to which that curve relates.

13.1 A simple analysis

This question, like that of the shape of short-run curves, can be dealt with either simply or in a more complicated way. The simple reason for believing that long-run average cost curves will be U-shaped is again in terms of fixed and variable costs. On reflection, it will be clear that as one considers longer and longer periods of time, fewer costs are fixed and more are variable. Over a long period of time there are very few costs which are just as great if output is small as they are if it is large. For, in economics, we define the long period as that during which the size and organisation of the firm can be altered to meet changed conditions.

Over a long period, unwanted buildings can be sold or let to sub-tenants, rent, rates and insurance can all be varied according to changing conditions. Administrative and marketing staffs can be decreased or increased in order to deal efficiently with smaller or larger outputs and sales. As a result, total fixed cost can vary considerably over long periods, whereas in the short run its amount is fixed. In other words, the longer the period under consideration, the fewer costs are 'fixed' and the more become 'variable'. In the long run, the firm is able to adapt the 'scale' of its operations to produce any required output in the most efficient possible way. In the short run, a reduction in output will raise average costs because fixed costs will represent a larger amount per unit of output. In the long run, fixed costs can be reduced somewhat if output continues at a low level. Average fixed costs will therefore be lower, at any given level of activity, in the long than in the short run.

In the short run also, average variable costs are likely to rise sharply once output exceeds the maximum level of output at which the firm was planned to operate. In the long run, the size of the firm can be increased to deal with increased output more adequately. Overcrowding can be dealt with; management can cope with the other problems of high output; and so on. Variable costs are likely to rise less sharply in the long run than in the short run. Thus far, there is no disagreement with the applied economists. Empirical evidence agrees with economic theory. The disagreement is over whether there is any necessity for variable costs, and therefore total costs, to rise *at all* as output *exceeds* the optimal level in the long run.

13.2 A detailed analysis

Before considering this issue, let us spend a little time looking at the more-detailed argument for supposing that long-run average cost curves will be U-shaped. In the long run, the indivisible factors of production can be used more economically, because in the long run they are often to some extent, at least, divisible. In the short run, the shape of the firm's average cost curve depends on the operation of the law of variable proportions, with capital and management fixed (indivisible) factors. In the long run, the cost curve of the firm depends on what are known as *returns to scale*. In the long run, the amount of any fixed factor used by the firm can be altered. Management can be reorganised to run a firm of a different size. Capital can be used differently, and so on. Fixed factors are no longer indivisible.

When *all* factors of production can be used in different proportions in this way, the scale of operations of the firm can be altered. We are now dealing with 'returns to scale' and not with returns to a variable factor. Each time the scale of operation changes we must draw a new short-run cost curve for the firm. For example, in Fig. 5.17, let us

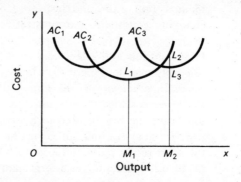

Fig. 5.17

assume that the firm has the short-run cost curve AC_2. The optimum output will then be OM_1. In the short run, an increase in output to, say, OM_2 is perfectly possible, but only by accepting an increase in average cost to M_2L_2. In the short run, the 'scale' of operations is fixed. In the long run, however, a new plant can be built. Let us assume that the firm now has the short-run cost curve AC_3. This means that by increasing the scale of its operations the firm can produce the output OM_2 more cheaply, at a cost of M_2L_3 instead of one of M_2L_2.

The individual short-run average cost curves thus retain their U-shape. At any given scale of operations the firm will encounter regions of rising and falling costs. However, in the long run the firm can produce on a completely different cost curve to the left or right of the original one. For each different scale at which the firm can operate there will, of course, be an output where average cost is at a minimum (*i.e.* a lowest point on the relevant short-run average cost curve). At this output the firm will still be described as producing the optimal output, given its scale of operations. Output will be 'optimal' in the sense that average cost is at a minimum.

In the long run, therefore, the firm will be able to adjust its scale of operations so that it is producing any given output at lowest cost. For instance, in Fig. 5.18, if the firm in question wishes to produce output OM_1, it will find it best to produce at that scale which has the average cost curve SAC_1. If it wishes to produce OM_2 it will be best to produce on the curve SAC_2 and if it wants to produce OM_3 it will produce on SAC_3. In each case, it will be producing the output concerned at the lowest possible cost. It is important to remember, however, that only in the long run can the scale of operations be increased or diminished. In the short run, the scale of operations will be fixed. The firm will be of the short-run size represented by one of

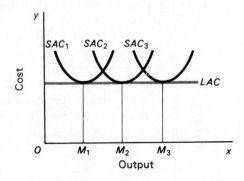

Fig. 5.18

the curves SAC_1, SAC_2 or SAC_3. Consequently, if output moves below or above the optimum level, average costs will inevitably rise as the firm moves along whichever is the relevant short-run curve.

It is therefore possible to draw a long-run average cost curve showing what the cost of producing each output would be when the scale of operations had been completely adjusted to producing any given output as cheaply as possible.

13.3 The divisibility of factors of production

How much can be said about the shape of a long-run average cost curve? We continue to assume that factor prices are constant so that no change in costs can be the result of changes in factor prices, but we can make various assumptions about the divisibility of factors. The simplest case is to assume that all factors are infinitely divisible and that there are no production economies to be obtained, for example, from the division of labour. This means that in the long run the amounts of all factors can be adjusted so that the long-run proportions between them are the same at all levels of output. Production can then take place at the lowest point on the relevant short-run average cost curve; that lowest point is also on the long-run average cost curve. The result is shown in Fig. 5.18. The long-run average cost curve of the firm, LAC, is a horizontal straight line. Returns to scale are constant, even though returns *at a given scale* are variable.

This is not a very reasonable assumption. It is unlikely that all factors are infinitely divisible, even in the long run. Even if they are, there will almost certainly be some economies to be obtained from the division of labour, etc., as output is raised.

It is far more likely that some factors of production will be indivisible. Economists have argued that management in particular is likely to be incompletely divisible. The management of a firm is unlikely to be able to produce twice a given output as efficiently as it produces a given output, however long management is given to get used to having to do so. The total size of the management team can be increased or reduced, but almost certainly not in proportion to output. Of course, if one really is dealing with a firm with a one-man entrepreneur, he will be completely indivisible. It is therefore reasonable to think that firms will still produce more cheaply at some scales of output than at others, even in the long run, if only because beyond a certain point management is difficult. Even in the long run, management is 'indivisible'. Certain combinations of factors will thus produce at lower unit costs in the long run than others. Factor

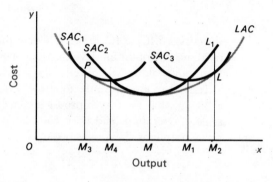

Fig. 5.19

proportions cannot be held at the levels associated with the lowest level of cost possible with any given scale of plant, as in Fig. 5.18.

This means that the short-run average cost curves of the firm will have different minimum points. So, in Fig. 5.19, the plant with the short-run average cost curve SAC_2 has a lower minimum point than the plants with the curves SAC_1 and SAC_3. Its optimum output is produced at lower cost. The long-run average cost curve which is a tangent to all the short-run curves will be the curve LAC. It will be U-shaped itself, but the U will be flatter than on the short-run cost curves—the U-shape will be less pronounced. Such a curve is known as an 'envelope' since it envelops all the short-run curves. In a sense the term 'envelope' is misleading. An envelope is physically distinct from the letter which it contains. But every point on the 'envelope' long-run cost curve is also a point on one of the short-run cost curves which it 'envelops'.

14. Long- and short-run average cost curves related

The relationship between the short-run average cost curves and the long-run average cost curve, when these are of the type shown in Fig. 5.19, needs further explanation. It is clear that, for any given output, average cost cannot be higher in the long run than in the short run. This is because any adjustment which will reduce costs, and which it is possible to make in the short run, must also be possible in the long run. On the other hand, it is not always possible in the short run to produce a given output in the cheapest possible way. If output changes, it is impossible to change the amounts of all factors used in the short run. However, if they can ever be altered, they *can* be altered in the long run. The long-run average cost curve can never cut a short-run average cost curve but it will be tangential to each short-run curve at some point.

It is likely that the long-run average cost curve will lie below any *one* short-run cost curve for most levels of output. But, for any given output, the long-run average cost curve must be tangential to a point on *one* short-run cost curve. It is tangential to the short-run cost curve for that size of plant which produces this output most cheaply. Let us illustrate this. Suppose that the firm shown in Fig. 5.19 has been producing for a long time at the output OM. Given the curves in Fig. 5.19, this output can be produced more cheaply than any other output on the long-run average cost curve. It can also be produced more cheaply than any other output on the curve SAC_2. The firm has adapted its scale to that implied by the curve SAC_2 in order to produce OM at the lowest possible cost.

Suppose that the firm now wants to produce OM_2 units of output. In the short run, it has to expand output along the curve SAC_2 and average cost for the output OM_2 will be $£M_2L_1$. In the long run, however, it can produce this output for $£M_2L$. It does so by adjusting the scale of its plant so as to produce the output OM_2 as efficiently as possible. This happens if it builds a plant of that size which has the cost curve SAC_3 and produces the output OM_2 with it. The short-run curve SAC_2 now ceases to be relevant. If the firm wishes to change output again, in the short-run, it can only do so along the curve SAC_3. At any one time, a firm can only produce along a single short-run cost curve because its plant is of fixed size. In the long run, it can choose the scale of plant which allows it to produce that output at the lowest cost. It will be producing at a particular point on a particular short-run average cost curve, but this point will be on the long-run cost curve as well.

Two further points are of interest. First, it should be borne in mind that, with one exception, the long-run average cost curve is not tangent to any short-run average cost curve at the short-run curve's minimum point. The exception is where a short-run curve is tangential to the long-run curve at the latter's lower point. In

Fig. 5.19, this happens at the output OM when the short-run curve SAC_2 is tangential to the lowest point of the long-run curve. Careful examination of 5.19 shows that for all outputs smaller than OM the lowest long-period costs occur on a falling portion of a short-term average cost curve. For example, the output OM_3 is produced most cheaply in the long run by producing at point P on the short-run

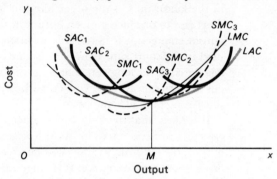

Fig. 5.20

curve SAC_1. But this output is smaller than the optimal output for a plant of this size, which has the curve SAC_1. Its optimal output is OM_4. In the long run, any output less than OM is produced most cheaply by building a plant with a given optimum output and using it to produce at *less* than this optimum output. Similarly, any output *greater* than OM can be produced more cheaply by working a given plant beyond its optimum (short-run) capacity, than it can by building a larger plant and using it to produce its optimum output.

15. Long- and short-run marginal cost curves related

Second if, as in Fig. 5.20, we draw all the short-run marginal-cost curves corresponding to the short-run average cost curves, and if we draw the long-run marginal cost curve appropriate to the long-run average cost curve, we can generalise about the relationships between the various marginal curves. In particular, each short-run marginal curve (SMC) cuts the corresponding short-run average curve at the latter's lowest point. Similarly, the long-run marginal cost curve (LMC) cuts the long-run average cost curve at its lowest point. It is clear from Fig. 5.20 that the long-run marginal cost curve is flatter than any of the short-run marginal cost curves. This is what one would expect because the U-shape of the long-run average cost curve is less pronounced than that of the short-run average cost curves. Thus, if one starts from the long-run optimum output OM, and output increases, marginal costs rise more sharply in the short run than in the long run. Similarly, if output falls from OM, marginal costs fall more substantially (for small changes in output) in the short run than in the long run.

One less-usual type of cost curve is shown in Fig. 5.21. Here, the capital equipment is capable of alteration only discontinuously. The original scale of output gives us the short-run average cost curve SAC_1. The next possible scale gives the curve SAC_2, because capital

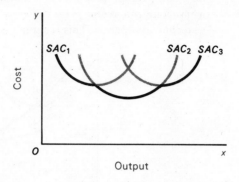

Fig. 5.21

has to be increased greatly. We could assume, for example, that this is a railway, which is working so near to capacity that to carry one extra train would require laying a completely new track. There is no possible short-run curve between SAC_1 and SAC_2. Similarly, there is no possible curve between SAC_2 and SAC_3. The long-run curve therefore takes the shape shown by the thick black line in Fig. 5.21.

16. L-shaped average cost curves

All this assumes that long-run cost curves are U-shaped. As has been explained, empirical investigations do not bear this out. It seems likely that almost all long-run average cost curves are L-shaped, like the one in Fig. 5.22. Here, we have the rather rapid downward slope

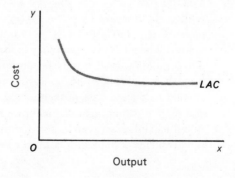

Fig. 5.22

in the early part of the curve, which the analysis earlier in this chapter leads us to expect. However, the curve remains flat, or may slope gently downwards, at its right-hand end.

F

One reason why empirical studies do not bear out the U-shaped curves of economic theory may be that the theory assumes that there is no technological progress, while in practice there is. The existence of technological progress might explain why one would find L-shaped long-run average cost curves in empirical studies, even in a world where long-run average cost curves would be U-shaped if there were *no* technical progress. This is explained in Fig. 5.23.

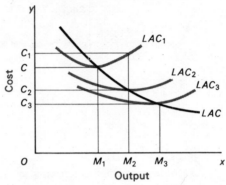

Fig. 5.23

Figure 5.23 shows that initially the firm is producing an output of OM_1 on LAC_1 at a cost of OC per unit. If there is a rise in demand, it may be possible to increase output to OM_2, at a cost of OC_1 per unit. However, if technological progress is occuring, it may be possible to produce an output of OM_2 with a newer plant that has the long-run average cost curve LAC_2. Here, average cost for an output of OM_2 is only OC_2. Similarly, if the firm later decides to increase output to OM_3, technical knowledge may have advanced in such a way that it can do so at an average cost of OC_3, on the curve LAC_3.

Studies carried out by economists at points of time when output was OM_1, OM_2, and OM_3 would therefore suggest that the long-run average cost curve was like the black curve LAC in Fig. 5.23. In reality, the relevant long-run average cost curves would be the grey ones—LAC_1, LAC_2 and LAC_3—one for each different state of technology. The fact that technology changes does not in itself contradict our contention that, if only because it is harder to manage a larger firm than a smaller one, long-run average cost curves will be U-shaped in a *given* state of technology. What the empirical evidence *does* suggest is that technological progress may often be rapid enough to reduce unit costs even in a situation where, with given technology, the problems of managing a bigger firm would increase unit costs.

16.2 'Learning'

However, there may be more to it than this. Economists now emphasise another reason why long-run average cost curves may slope downwards. This is 'learning'. There is a good deal of evidence to show that the cost of a product depends not only on how much of it is produced in each period of time, as in our examples. It also depends on the *aggregate* amount of product produced since the firm first began to make it. This appears clearly in the case of complex products like aircraft. One can draw a 'learning curve' relating cost per aircraft built to the *aggregate* number of aircraft produced to date. The reason is that those making any product 'learn' to produce it more efficiently as the aggregate number of units they have made in total increases. This is not only a matter of learning how to carry out the physical operations performed on a product more effectively. There is improved organisation of the plant or workshop as well. Even with a given technology, a firm can 'learn' to produce at a lower unit cost the longer the period of time that has elapsed since a previous observation and the greater the aggregate amount of that product that has consequently been made. It may be, therefore, that technological change is not the only reason why long-run average cost curves are L-shaped rather than U-shaped.

For our purposes, the reasons why cost curves may be L-shaped do not matter. Nor, indeed, is it very important whether or not they *are* L-shaped. We shall find that if we allow for the possibility that long-run average cost curves can take either shape, this is important for the theory of the firm only when we are dealing with markets where there is pure (or perfect) competition. For the present, we shall take the view that while the short-run average cost curve *must* be U-shaped, the long-run average cost curve can be either U-shaped or L-shaped.

We have now discussed the characteristics of the curves which we shall use in our analysis of the firm. These curves constitute our weapons of analysis. We must now use them to attack our problems.

Suggested reading

MARSHALL, ALFRED	*Principles of Economics*, 8th edn., London, 1920, Book IV, chapters 8, 9, 11, 12 and 13; Book V, chapter 4.
ROBINSON, JOAN	*Economics of Imperfect Competition*, London, 1933, chapters i and ii.
SILBERSTON, AUBREY	'Price Behaviour of Firms', *Economic Journal*, 1970, p. 511.
TURVEY, RALPH	'Marginal Cost', *Economic Journal*, 1969, p. 282.

6

Competitive industry

1. Definition of pure and perfect competition

In Chapter 5 we discussed the meaning and characteristics of the cost and revenue curves which we shall use in discussing the conditions under which the firm or the industry will be in equilibrium. We can now use these curves to see how the firm reaches equilibrium in various conditions. In this analysis, which will be carried out in Chapters 6 to 9, we shall assume unless otherwise stated that there is perfect competition between consumers. What we are looking at is differences in the kind of competition between firms.

We begin with a situation where there is keen competition between large numbers of firms in an industry. This will enable us to see what conditions in a competitive industry are like. It will also bring to light in a very simple context most of the important features of the equilibrium of the firm. For, however competitive or monopolistic the conditions facing the firm are, the main features of the equilibrium of the firm remain essentially the same.

We must first define competitive conditions more carefully than we have done so far. We wrote in Chapter 5 of pure competition where demand curve for the product of the individual firm was infinitely elastic. The firm could sell all it wished at the existing market price, but was unable to alter that price by its own actions. It was too small relatively to the total industry. We saw that in such conditions the average revenue curve of the firm would be a horizontal straight line. Three conditions have to be met if there is to be pure competition between suppliers in any industry. These are as follows.

1.1 The requirements for perfect competition

First, there must be a large number of firms in the industry. This is essential. Only when there are many firms in an industry can each be certain that any action on its own part will have no noticeable effects on the price and output of the whole industry. If there are many firms in an industry, any one can increase or decrease its own

(a) Large numbers

output quite substantially without the slightest fear that there will be a significant change in the price of the product of the industry as a result. The individual firm must take the price of the product as given. It is a 'price taker'.

(b) Homogeneous products

Second, each firm in a purely competitive industry must be making a product which is accepted by customers as identical, or *homogeneous*, with those made by all the other producers in the industry. This ensures that no firm can raise its price above the general level. If it did so, consumers would buy the same good from other producers at a lower price. Best-grade cotton is best-grade cotton whoever grows it. One does not find individual cotton producers advertising their product as better than that of other growers when both are of the same quality. When the goods are homogeneous, uniform price must rule throughout the market.

It is very important to realise that it is the consumer who decides whether or not two products are homogeneous. It is only if buyers agree that all producers are making exactly the same good that their prices must be the same. Wherever buyers find real or imagined differences between two products, their prices can differ, however alike the two articles really are. For example, if a customer wrongly believes that the local supermarket sells goods which are inferior to those supplied by 'Quality Provisions', he may pay the latter 40p for a product which he could have got from the supermarket for 15p, even though the goods are physically identical. Again, Mr Smith may prefer to buy his food from Mr Jones, because they both belong to the same club or go to the same church, even though Mr Jones charges higher prices for the same products than Mr Williams farther down the street. If buyers behave in this way, competition cannot be pure, for the products are not homogeneous in the eyes of the consumers. It is the total conditions surrounding the sale of the product which we must consider. It is important to remember that these conditions in which the product is sold will influence customers as well as the physical constitution of the product. A customer will be prepared to pay more for the identical product sold in more luxurious surroundings or by pleasanter sales staff.

Assumptions *(a)* and *(b)* between them ensure that every firm's average revenue curve is horizontal and at the same level. The fact that there are many producers prevents the individual firm from exerting any influence on price. It has to act as a price taker. The fact that products are homogeneous means that buyers do not regard one producer's product as 'better' than another's. This means that all firms have to 'take' the same price.

It is probably worth emphasising again that we are assuming, and shall continue to assume until further notice, that there is always pure competition *between buyers*. We are taking it for granted that the total numbers of buyers is very large, so that each takes only a small proportion of the total sales of any good. No one buyer is able to alter the price of a good by his own actions. *Buyers* must take prices as given, even where a monopolistic seller can alter prices to suit himself. They cannot bargain with suppliers; they are 'price takers' too. The fact that in this chapter we are assuming perfect competition *both* between buyers *and* between sellers is important and should be borne in mind.

(c) Free entry

The third condition which must be fulfilled if there is to be pure competition in an industry is that anyone who wishes to enter that industry must be allowed to do so. Apart from the obvious restrictions on entry, which we shall discuss below, this means that if the amount of capital required to enter an industry is very great we cannot regard this as an industry where there is free entry.

Even in the more obvious cases, it is difficult to be quite sure what is not a restriction on entry into an industry. For example, in the road passenger transport industry it is desirable that every vehicle should measure up to certain standards of safety. A refusal to allow unsafe vehicles into the industry cannot be regarded as a restriction on entry. It must rather be accepted as essential for the safety of passengers, transport workers and other road users.

Nevertheless, while some difficult cases will arise, it will usually be possible to decide fairly quickly whether or not there is a restriction on entry into an industry. For example, a monopolistic association, which refuses to allow anyone of whom it does not approve to enter an industry is clearly restricting entry. If the association is able to enforce its decisions, this will mean that the number of firms in the industry can be kept at the existing level, or even reduced if some firms leave it. Prices can be maintained at a higher level than would occur with free entry. Our third prerequisite for pure competition thus ensures that the number of firms in a competitive industry can always remain large because newcomers are always allowed to enter if they think it profitable to do so.

These three conditions, large numbers of firms, homogeneous products and free entry, between them ensure that there is pure competition in an industry. This competition is completely free from any monopolistic elements. The three conditions ensure that the average revenue curve of each of the individual firms in the competitive industry is the same horizontal straight line.

2. Pure versus perfect competition

Economists often distinguish pure competition, as we have just defined it, from *perfect competition*. For there to be perfect competition it is necessary to make some additional assumptions. In particular, it is necessary to assume that there is perfect knowledge on the part of all buyers and sellers about the conditions in the market. In addition, it is usual to assume complete mobility of factors of production between industries. It is also convenient, when using perfect competition, to make the assumption that all producers work sufficiently close to each other for there to be no transport costs. Strictly speaking, two identical goods are not homogeneous in an economic sense if they are not in the same place. For example, I may have the choice between buying identical coal from Smith in my village or Brown in the next village. But if the transport charge is £4, Smith may charge me more because he knows it would cost me £4 to obtain the same coal from the next village.

We shall assume that differences caused by transport costs do not exist. Otherwise, prices for identically the same good would differ. These additional assumptions are not essential if we merely want to show what conditions must be fulfilled if monopoly among sellers is to be absent. But they make it easier to build up a hypothetical model of a competitive industry. We shall therefore discuss what happens in an industry where there is 'perfect' rather than 'pure' competition. This is our next task.

3. Normal profit

Two conditions must be fulfilled if there is to be equilibrium in a perfectly-competitive industry. First, each individual firm must be in equilibrium. This will happen when every firm in the industry is earning maximum profit, equating marginal revenue with marginal cost. Second, the industry as a whole must be in equilibrium. This will occur when there is no tendency for firms either to enter or leave the industry. A little reflection will show that this requires that all the entrepreneurs in the industry must earn enough money to induce them to stay there, and that no entrepreneur outside the industry thinks that, by entering it, he could earn enough money to make the move worthwhile.

In what circumstances will this happen? In technical economic language, we describe the situation by saying that every entrepreneur in the industry is at least earning 'normal' profits. 'Normal profits' for any entrepreneur in an industry are therefore those profits which are just sufficient to induce him to stay in the industry. It follows that if an industry is in equilibrium, with no movement in or out, no-one outside the industry sees the possibility of being able to earn 'normal' profits, if he were to enter the industry.

3.1 Our initial assumptions

We shall need to make considerable use of the idea of 'normal' profits. Unfortunately, we shall find that the notion is a tricky one. We therefore proceed by stages, making simplified assumptions to begin with, which we can remove later. In this Chapter, we shall make two assumptions. First, we shall assume that all entrepreneurs in the industry we are studying would prove to be of identical efficiency if they left it and went to another industry, whatever that industry was. On this assumption, normal profits would be identical for every entrepreneur in the industry we are studying. Second, we shall also assume that the entrepreneurs are not necessarily of equal efficiency *within* the industry and that some can therefore earn more money than others. Some may earn 'supernormal' profits. Third, we shall assume that there are no complications because some firms have recently entered the industry and are earning small profits because they have not yet built up to full efficiency; or that other firms have passed their peak and are also earning low profits.

Our assumptions imply that there is a general rate of 'normal' profits for the whole industry—that all entrepreneurs' earnings must fall to exactly the same level before they will leave the industry—but that within the industry some entrepreneurs earn more than others. These two assumptions are not entirely consistent, but they will enable us to simplify the analysis in this chapter.

3.2 Profits and the size of the industry

It follows from the foregoing analysis that if, for any reason, the profits of all entrepreneurs in any industry rise above 'normal' (if they are 'supernormal'), there will be a tendency for the number of firms in that industry to increase. For we may assume that entrepreneurs outside the industry will expect to be able to earn at least 'normal' profits if they enter. On the other hand, if profits for everyone fall below 'normal' (if they are 'subnormal'), there will be a fall in the number of firms in the industry. Some firms will be forced out by bankruptcy and their entrepreneurs will go in search of 'normal' profits elsewhere. We can therefore assume that the industry as a whole and all the individual firms in it will be in equilibrium—in 'full equilibrium' as it is often called—when all firms are maximising profits and when there is no tendency for firms to enter or leave the industry. In such conditions all the firms in the industry must be earning at least normal profits. If profits were greater than normal, new firms would enter. If they were less, some existing firms would leave.

3.3 The average cost curve redefined

The fact that we have introduced normal profits into our analysis means that we must make a slight alteration in the content of our average cost curve. If the firm is to remain in the industry, its decision to do so will not depend on whether it is covering average total cost as we have hitherto defined it. The decision will depend on whether the firm is also earning at least normal profit. In order to be able to decide easily whether or not a firm will be willing to stay in the industry in the long run at the current level of earnings, it will therefore be useful to include 'normal' profits in the average cost curve. In future, the average cost curves which we shall draw will include 'normal' profits. This should be remembered, to avoid the need to point it out specifically on every occasion that an average cost curve is drawn.

The introduction of normal profits gives an additional reason for us to expect average cost curves to slope downwards over low ranges of output. We shall assume that each entrepreneur must earn normal profit if he is to stay in the industry in the long run. It is usual to assume that this sum of money, representing normal profits, is independent of output. We shall assume that each entrepreneur wants the same fixed amount of normal profits, whatever output he is to produce. It follows that, as output rises, normal profit per unit of output falls. For the fixed sum of money representing normal profits is spread over a progressively larger number of units of output as production rises. Here is our additional reason for expecting average cost curves to fall over low ranges of output.

In Fig. 6.1 we have drawn an average cost curve excluding normal profits (AC) and another including them $(AC+NP)$. It will be seen that as output rises, the vertical distance between the two curves steadily diminishes. Normal profit per unit of output declines progressively. For example, when output is OX, normal profit per unit of output is BC; when output is OY it is FG. However, the areas of any rectangles, like $ABCD$ and $EFGH$, showing total normal profit will be equal.

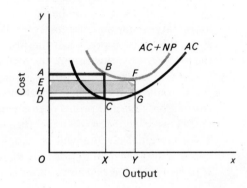

Fig. 6.1

**4.
Equilibrium
of the firm
and normal
profit**

If average cost includes normal profits in this way, the firm will obviously be earning normal profits whenever its cost (including. normal profits) is equal to price. Now we have seen in Chapter 5 that it is reasonable to assume that all average cost curves are roughly U-shaped. We also know that in perfect competition each firm's average revenue curve is a horizontal straight line. So, in perfect competition, the only situation in which the firm can be in equilibrium *and* earning normal profits is when the average cost curve is tangential to the average revenue curve. Only then can average cost equal price. Only then can the firm cover all its costs and just earn normal profits. This is shown in Fig. 6.2.

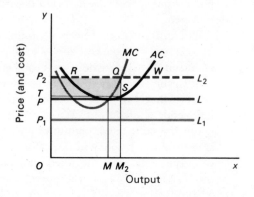

Fig. 6.2

In Fig. 6.2, it is clear that the firm cannot be *both* in equilibrium *and* earning normal profits for any position of the average revenue curve below *PL*. For example, with the average revenue curve P_1L_1 the firm must earn less than normal profits whatever its output. At no output is average cost (including normal profits) equal to price. On the other hand, if the average revenue curve is above *PL*, as with P_2L_2, it is possible for average cost to equal price (in this case at *R* and *W*). But at neither *R* nor *W* would the firm be in equilibrium. At both *R* and *W* profit will be zero, because average revenue equals average cost. The firm will be in equilibrium only when it is equating marginal revenue and marginal cost. With the average revenue curve P_2L_2, this will happen when the firm produces OM_2 and sells it at the price OP_2. At this output, the firm will be in equilibrium but will be earning 'supernormal' profits, equal to the area P_2QST.

The only position where the firm can be in equilibrium while earning only normal profits occurs where it is producing the output *OM*. This will happen when the price of the industry's product is *OP*. Then marginal revenue will be equal to marginal cost but average cost will also be equal to price (average revenue). Since competition is perfect, average revenue will, of course, equal marginal revenue.

A perfectly-competitive firm, which is in full equilibrium, is earning not only maximum profits (equating marginal revenue with marginal costs) but normal profits (equating average cost (including normal profit) with price). This must occur when the average cost curve is tangential to the average revenue curve.

5. Equilibrium in the short run

We have already defined this as a period of time which is long enough to allow the variable factors of production to be used in different amounts so that maximum profits are earned; but during which the fixed factors cannot be altered.

5.1 Our assumptions about costs

We have already implied that it is important, in analysing short-run equilibrium conditions in any industry, to be quite explicit about our assumptions. We have already made clear our assumptions about normal profit. We must now be equally explicit about cost conditions. If costs differ between firms, the equilibrium position of the industry will not be the same as with identical cost curves. We shall therefore consider the short-run equilibrium of the firm and of the industry in three different situations.

(a) All factors homogeneous

First, we shall assume that all factors of production, including entrepreneurs, are homogeneous. This means that, assuming that perfect competition in the market for factors guarantees identical factor prices for all producers buying the same factors, all firms will have identical cost curves. Since all units of all factors, including entrepreneurs, are identical, each entrepreneur will be able to combine the same factors in the same way. And since we are assuming that every firm produces each output at the minimum possible cost, we may conclude that all firms will have identical cost curves when all factors are homogeneous.

(b) All factors except entrepreneurs homogeneous

Second, we shall see what difference it makes if we assume that all factors of production except entrepreneurs are homogeneous, but that entrepreneurship is heterogeneous. This means that costs will differ between firms because some entrepreneurs are more efficient than others, and so can use exactly the same factors to produce a given output more cheaply.

(c) All factors heterogeneous

Third, we shall see what happens when all factors are assumed to be heterogeneous. In this situation, cost differences between firms will be even greater, because all factors are of differing efficiency, and not only entrepreneurs. Let us now consider the short-run equilibrium of the industry under these three conditions.

5.2 All factors homogeneous

(a) The nature of equilibrium

Figure 6.3 shows the short-run position in a firm using homogeneous factors in a situation where there is perfect competition in the factor market and where the prices of all factors are given (and constant). Each firm in the industry has two cost curves shown in Fig. 6.3, because we assume that each produces every output at the lowest possible cost.

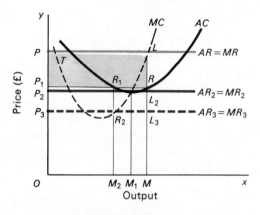

Fig. 6.3

Let us assume, to begin, that the price of the product is £OP. All firms have to 'take' this price of £OP as given. They will therefore set their output so as to maximise profit. The horizontal straight line PL is therefore the average revenue curve of each firm. Since competition is perfect, it is also a marginal revenue curve.

All firms have identical costs, so that each will maximise profits if it produces the output OM and sells it at the perfectly competitive price of £OP. Since average cost is only £MR at the output OM, and price is £OP, each firm earns 'supernormal' profits of an amount shown by the grey area $PLRP_1$. All firms in the industry are in equilibrium, since they are earning maximum profits. The industry is not in equilibrium, because all firms have identical cost curves. They will all be producing the same output and earning the same 'supernormal' profits—£$PLRP_1$. In the short-run the situation will persist, since no firm can create new fixed equipment and no new firms can enter the industry in the short run. In the long run, however, new firms will enter the industry. Having identical costs to those of existing firms, they will compete away the supernormal profits. In the short run, however, the number of firms in the industry is too small for there to be 'full equilibrium'; all earn supernormal profits.

In all the firms in the industry marginal revenue and marginal cost are equal at L. It is by reference to this point that the profit-maximising output will be determined. Marginal revenue and marginal cost will also be equal at point T. Why is it that the firms are not in equilibrium at this level? This becomes clear on examination of Fig. 6.3. At T, marginal cost has only just become equal to marginal revenue and has previously been greater. If output were fixed at this point, the firms would be earning *minimum*, not maximum, profits. The reason for this can be seen if we recall that marginal cost and marginal revenue are the diagrammatic equivalents of the derivatives of the revenue and cost functions. If we do this, we realise that we may have either a maximum or a minimum where the two derivatives are equal. We have to explore the situation more fully, using second derivatives, to know which is which. We may therefore state the conditions necessary for the equilibrium of the firm, whether in perfect or imperfect competition, more explicitly. The marginal cost curve must cut the marginal revenue curve *from below* at the point of equilibrium. A firm can never be earning maximum profits unless this happens.

If price were £OP_2 instead of £OP, all the firms would be in equilibrium when producing the output OM_1. They would just be covering their costs and earning normal profits. This condition can be seen visually from the fact that the average cost curve is tangential to the average revenue curve at the output OM_1. The situation thus represents full equilibrium in the industry, even in the short run. The number of firms is just large enough to ensure that none earns supernormal profits.

On the other hand, if price happened to be OP_3, the firms in the industry would be in equilibrium producing the output OM_2. All would be losing money, losses being equal to $P_1R_1R_2P_3$. The 'maximum profit' each firm could earn would be a loss of £$P_1R_1R_2P_3$. This is the smallest loss each firm could make if it remained in business. It follows that while these firms are in short-run equilibrium, they cannot be in long-run equilibrium. In the long run, firms will leave the industry until those remaining there just earn normal profits.

(b) When to produce at a loss

The obvious question to ask therefore is: 'Does it pay a firm which is losing money to stay in the industry?' The answer is that all depends on the length of time which is being considered. In the long run, if the efficiency of the firm does not improve, it will leave the industry altogether. It will go bankrupt.

In the short run, the firm *may* be able to stay in business. For, given our definition of the short period, the firm cannot, with such a period, alter its fixed capital. This fact will influence the entrepreneur's actions. The fixed costs of the firm *must* be met in the short run, even if the firm closes down altogether (unless it declares itself bankrupt). It will therefore pay the entrepreneur to remain in production if by doing so he earns anything which helps him to cover his 'fixed costs'. He will be reducing his loss, which would be equal to fixed costs if he closed down. This can be seen from Fig. 6.4, which shows two (identical)

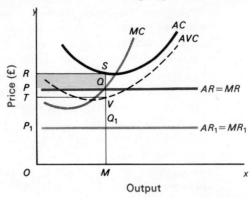

Fig. 6.4

cost curves of all firms in our industry. The firms will remain in business so long as they can cover their variable costs. Since variable costs can be avoided, even in the short run, the firms need not employ any variable factors at all if they do not wish to do so. It will therefore pay the entrepreneurs to take on variable factors only if, after paying for them, they still have something left over to help to meet their fixed costs. However, this will be no more than making the best of a bad job in the short run. It will not provide a long-run solution to their troubles, which can come only from a reduction in costs or a rise in price.

Looking at the short-run problem in greater detail, we can see that, for each firm portrayed, the 'loss minimising' output is OM. For price is $£OP$ per unit of output. Price (average revenue) therefore exceeds average variable cost MV (as shown on the average variable cost curve AVC) by QV. This amount (the difference between price per unit and variable cost per unit) is known as 'unit contribution'. It is the 'contribution to fixed costs', and in more favourable circumstances profit, per unit of output. The fact that (at QV) unit contribution is positive means that it will be worthwhile for the firm to continue running in the short run. Some fixed costs can be covered after variable costs have been met. In such a situation, $£PQVT$ is described as 'total contribution'; it is the total amount by which the firm reduces its loss by staying open. The firm is losing $£RSQP$, which is less than it would have lost if had it closed down altogether, but been forced to go on meeting fixed costs. It would then have lost an amount equal to its total fixed costs; $£RSVT$. Instead, it loses $£RSVT$ minus the total contribution of $£PQVT$.

If short-run price were only OP_1, losses would still be met at every output. For example, if output were OM, average cost would be $£OR$ ($=MS$) and losses per unit $£RP_1$. In this case, average cost cannot be covered. At no output is there any unit contribution. Far from helping to meet fixed costs, the fact that the firm remains in production actually makes things worse. For example, at the output OM the firm is losing more than its total fixed costs—which in this case are $£RSVT$. It loses $£P_1Q_1VT$ more than if it closed down altogether. It will therefore pay the firm to stop producing anything, even in the short run, though it may pay to reopen later.

(c) Some conclusions

What can we conclude from this analysis? We can see that, in the short run, it is possible for the firm to bring itself into a position of equilibrium where it is producing that output which minimises losses, even though in some cases this may mean that production has to stop altogether. One is entitled to assume that it will not be difficult for the firm to reach such an equilibrium even in a short period of time.

It is much less likely that the industry will be able to bring itself into 'full' equilibrium in the short run. 'Full' equilibrium can occur only when all firms are earning normal profits. Only by accident— only if there happens to be just the right number of firms—will the whole industry be in equilibrium in the short run. It is much more probable that there will have to be a long-run adjustment, with a net increase or decrease in the number of firms in the industry, before 'full' equilibrium can be brought about. Since all factors of production are homogeneous, the situation will be the same in every firm in the industry, but it should not be forgotten that the analysis applies only to an industry where a large number of firms is producing a homogeneous product. It must also be remembered that we are assuming that normal profit is the same in all firms.

5.3 Entrepreneurs heterogeneous, other factors homogeneous

While keeping these basic assumptions, we can now move on to consider a situation where entrepreneurs are not all identical in efficiency. Costs can then differ between firms, even though all factor prices are the same to all firms and all factors except entrepreneurs are homogeneous. More efficient entrepreneurs will be able to produce more efficiently than less efficient ones, and their firms' costs will therefore be lower. Even though all firms make the same product, sell it at the same price and seek maximum profits, firms with different costs will maximise profit at different outputs. Maximum profits will, of course, differ too. The kind of situation which is likely to exist in the short run is shown in Fig. 6.5.

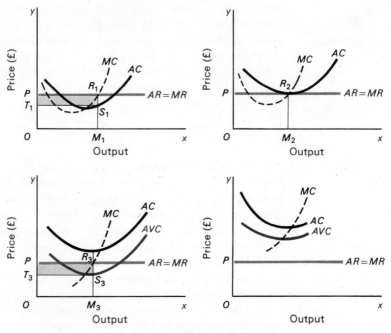

Fig. 6.5 a | b
c | d

Firm A has the most efficient entrepreneur of the four firms shown, and is in short-run equilibrium when producing the output OM_1 and earning supernormal profits of $PR_1S_1T_1$, shown by the grey area in Fig. 6.5a. Firm B, with a somewhat less efficient entrepreneur, produces an equilibrium output of OM_2 and earns only normal profits. Firm C has a still less efficient entrepreneur and loses money. However, since Firm C is covering its variable costs, it pays it to go on producing the output OM_3 in the short run, for losses are thereby minimised. Finally, Firm D has the least efficient entrepreneur of the four firms. Even in the short run, it cannot cover its variable costs at any output. It minimises losses by closing down, even in the short run.

This diagram shows in miniature, and with the simplifying assumptions we are making, the situation in a perfectly-competitive industry when entrepreneurs differ in ability. In the short run, some of the entrepreneurs will be making large losses. In each case, the firm will be in equilibrium earning maximum profits by equating marginal revenue and cost. But the industry as a whole is unlikely to be in 'full' equilibrium in the short run. Profit will either be high enough to attract new entrants, or low enough to drive some firms out.

5.4 All factors heterogeneous

Where all factors of production are heterogeneous, the differences in costs between firms are likely to be even bigger than where entrepreneurs only were of differing efficiency. The same kind of situation as shown in Fig. 6.5 will occur, but the differences between the costs of the various firms are likely to be greater. Those firms which can obtain labour that is more efficient relatively to its wage will have a cost advantage. The more efficient are the factors a firm is using, the greater will its profits be compared with those earned by other firms. The general conclusion, then, still holds. Each individual firm will be able to reach an equilibrium, profit-maximising position in the short run, even though it may (in a very depressed market) have to close down entirely. There is no reason why the industry as a whole should be in full equilibrium in the short run. As we have seen, most firms will usually be earning either supernormal or subnormal profits in the short run. Only in the long run is equilibrium in the industry as a whole likely to come about—by an increase or a decrease in the number of firms in the industry.

6. Long-run equilibrium of the firm and industry

What, then, is likely to happen in a perfectly competitive industry in the long run? We continue to assume that there is perfect competition, that there are no restrictions on entry into the industry and that all factors of production are perfectly mobile. We also assume that there is no difference in normal profit because of the length of time that firms have been in the industry. In the long run, firms will enter or leave the industry until no firm outside the industry thinks it could earn normal profits if it were to enter the industry, and no firm in the industry thinks it could do better by leaving.

6.1 All factors of production homogeneous

Where all factors of production are homogeneous and each factor has a given and uniform price, it is not difficult to see when the industry will be in 'full' equilibrium in the long run. This will happen when each firm has adjusted its output so as to equate marginal revenue with marginal cost. In the long run, each firm will also be in the position shown in Fig. 6.6a, where average cost, average revenue, marginal cost and marginal revenue are all equal to each other and to price. This is the 'full equilibrium' position. Since all firms have identical cost curves and since there is free entry and perfect mobility of factors, entrepreneurs will enter or leave the industry until all firms in it are earning normal profits. Because costs are identical, if any one firm is earning normal profits all firms will be. In perfect competition, with all factors homogeneous, and with our assumptions

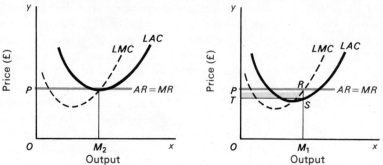

Fig. 6.6 a | b

each firm, and the industry as a whole, will be in full equilibrium where marginal revenue=marginal cost=average cost=average revenue (price).

It is interesting to note that in this full equilibrium each firm will be producing the 'optimum' output where average cost is at a minimum. This is advantageous to consumers since the product in question is being produced in the cheapest possible way without any firm making a loss. But *all* firms can be producing the optimum output only if all have the same minimum point to their cost curves, and this is unlikely to happen in practice since all factors are unlikely to be homogeneous. So we must now turn to the second situation, where all factors are not homogeneous.

6.2
Entrepreneurs
heterogeneous, all
other factors
homogeneous

As we have seen, where entrepreneurs are heterogeneous, some firms will be able to produce every output at a lower cost than other firms. This means that even in the long run it is very likely that some firms will be able to earn 'supernormal' profits. Let us consider the two firms shown in a long-run equilibrium position, in Figs. 6.6a and 6.6b.

Firm B has a more efficient entrepreneur, and therefore lower costs, than Firm A. Let us assume that in the long run Firm A is just efficient enough to remain in this position. It stays in the industry and earns normal profits. We can describe it as a 'marginal' firm. It is 'on the margin of profitability' because any fall in price would, in the long run, send it out of the industry. Since Firm B has a more efficient entrepreneur, it is able to earn supernormal profits amounting to £$PRST$, even in the long run. It can be described as an 'intra-marginal' firm. The only way in which Firm B's profits could be reduced to the 'normal' level in the long run would be if there were an influx of very efficient producers, able to compete more effectively with Firm B than firms like A. This is a possibility, but it not a necessity. It would, of course, drive Firm B out of the industry in the long run. Our conclusion is that even in the long run some firms will be able to earn supernormal profits if they have more efficient entrepreneurs than others.

6.3 All factors heterogeneous

The same result will occur where all factors are heterogeneous. The firms with the most efficient factors will be able to earn supernormal profits even when 'marginal' firms are just earning normal profits. In Chapter 7, we shall complicate the analysis by allowing for the length of time that firms have been in the industry, but this analysis of perfect competition has given us the groundwork we shall need.

7. External economies and diseconomies

We now move on to construct the short- and long-run supply curves of a perfectly-competitive industry. The complications we shall introduce later do not affect this part of our analysis. First, however, we must discuss external economies and diseconomies of production. In the previous Chapter, we discussed the economies of production obtained by altering factor proportions or by altering the internal organisation of the firm as output changes. These are known as *internal economies and diseconomies*. They are the economies and diseconomies which enable the firm to produce more or less efficiently at some outputs than at others, but which result from its internal situation. We must now discuss *external economies and diseconomies*. These are those economies and diseconomies in production which depend on increases in the output of the whole industry and not on increases in the output of the individual firm.

(a) External economies

External economies occur where an increase in the size of an industry leads to lower costs for each individual firm in the industry. For example, in coal mining, the fact that in pumping water from its own workings a mine also pumps water from the workings of other mines, means that the more pits there are in the area, the cheaper it is to keep each pit dry. Another important external economy is to be found where the efficient development of an industry depends greatly on the interchange of technical information between firms. In such a case it is obvious that the larger the industry is, the easier and more worthwhile it will be to set up large-scale information services to publish trade newspapers, magazines, and so on.

(b) External diseconomies

On the other hand, it is quite possible for the growth in the size of an industry to lead to external diseconomies to rises in unit costs. For example, it may well happen that as an industry expands it needs more workers skilled in a particular kind of work. In such conditions, if workers are not all equally efficient, it will be necessary to attract less-efficient ones away from other industries. Even if money wages remain constant, wage costs will rise as less and less efficient labour is taken on. It is more likely that, in order to attract labour away from other industries, wages will also have to be raised for the particular type of labour needed. This will be a diseconomy of increased production which is external to the individual firm—the increased size of the industry as a whole raises costs in the individual firms.

External economies and diseconomies need to be brought into our analysis because we are about to consider the nature of the supply curve of the perfectly-competitive industry. The shape of that supply curve will depend, in part at least, on whether external economies or diseconomies arise as the industry increases or decreases the scale of its operations.

8. The supply curve of the perfectly competitive industry

Our main aim in this chapter and the preceding one has been to bring us to a position where we can build up a supply curve for a perfectly competitive industry. This is an essential step before we return to a discussion of the relationships between demand and supply, outlined in Chapter 1. The shape of a competitive supply curve will not, however, always be the same. It will depend on the production conditions underlying it. We shall therefore consider what the shape of the supply curve will be under different assumptions about these underlying conditions. The simplest assumption we can make is that all factors of production are homogeneous and are in perfect elastic supply to the industry. We shall continue to assume throughout that there is perfect competition in the factor market so that the prices of all units of each factor are the same.

We shall study the supply curve of the industry in three different situations. First, we shall see what it will be like in the short run when not only is the number of firms given, but the scale of the individual firm is given. Second, we shall consider a situation where the firm is able to alter the scale of its operations, but where, for the moment, we shall assume that the number of firms remains constant. Third, we shall consider a long-run situation where we shall assume both that the number of firms and the scale of operations in the individual firm are able to change.

8.1 Firms of constant scale

First, we consider an initial situation where both the industry and the firm are in full equilibrium, with each firm producing at the minimum points of both its short- and long-run cost curves. This situation can be seen in Fig. 6.7.

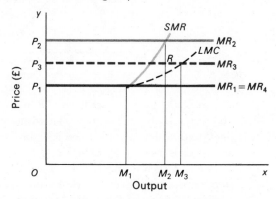

Fig. 6.7

All firms in the industry have identical cost curves because factors are homogeneous. Each firm will therefore originally be in long-run equilibrium, where it is producing an output of OM_1 and selling it at a price of $£OP_1$. Marginal revenue, shown by the curve P_1–MR_1, is equal to both short- and long-run marginal cost for all firms in the industry. All these firms are earning normal profits. Since competition is perfect, marginal revenue will also equal average revenue (price).

In order to discover what the shape of the industry's supply curve is, let us assume that the price of the product rises to OP_2 so that the marginal revenue curve rises to P_2–MR_2. In the short run it is obvious that, in perfect competition, the supply curve of the individual firm is its short-run marginal cost curve (SMC). The only way in which any firm can produce more in the short run is by expanding output along its short-run marginal cost curve. If price rises, as in Fig. 6.7, to OP_2, marginal revenue will equal marginal cost at the output OM_2. Since all firms are identical (our present assumption), the total increase in the output of the industry as price rises to OP_2 will be M_1M_2, multiplied by the number of firms in the industry. To put it another way, the supply curve of the industry will be a lateral summation of the supply curves (short-run marginal cost curves) of the individual firms.

In Fig. 6.8 it has been assumed that the industry consists of 100 identical firms with the cost curves shown in Fig. 6.7. The short-run supply curve of the industry is the black line *SS*. It shows that when price rises from OP_1 to OP_2 because the demand curve shifts from

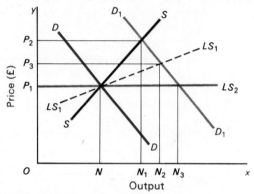

Fig. 6.8

DD to D_1D_1, output rises from ON to ON_1. It rises by NN_1. This is 100 times M_1M_2 in Fig. 6.7. (The distance M_1M_2 in Fig. 6.7 is not one-hundredth of the distance NN_1 in Fig. 6.8, because the scale on the *x*-axis is much greater in Fig. 6.7 than in Fig. 6.8.)

The short-run supply curve of the competitive industry will always slope upwards, since the short-run marginal cost curves of the individual firms which underly it will always slope upwards. The steepness of the industry's short-run supply curve will depend on the slope of the cost curves of the individual firms. Where the cost structures of all the individual firms in the industry are identical, the elasticity of the industry's supply curve will be equal to the elasticity of each separate firm's marginal cost curve. The only general rule one can lay down is that the industry's short-run supply curve must slope upwards to the right, since the firm's short-run marginal cost curve must also slope upwards to the right.

8.2 Firms with changing scale

We now consider the shape of the industry's long-run supply curve, assuming first of all that the number of firms remains constant. With the given number of firms, the long-run equilibrium situation in Fig. 6.7 will be where output is OM_3 and price OP_3. The long-run marginal cost curve of the individual firm (*LMC* in Fig. 6.7) will be less steep than the short-run one, so that output will be able to expand more in the long run than in the short run (by M_1M_3 instead of M_1M_2). Because output is able to expand further, price falls—to

OP_3. The long-period supply curve of the industry (with the number of firms fixed) will be the curve LS_1 in Fig. 6.8. The increase in the output of the industry is now NN_2 compared with the original output of ON. NN_2 is 100 times M_1M_3 in Fig. 6.7. This particular type of long-run supply curve also slopes upwards to the right—though less steeply than the short-run supply curve. It slopes upwards because the long-run marginal cost curves of the individual firms, on which it depends, also slope upwards. It may be noted that in this new long-run situation, with price at OP_3, all the firms in the industry will be earning abnormal profits, as shown in Fig. 6.7. This can happen, even in the long run, because the number of firms in the industry is assumed to be constant.

8.3 Changing number of firms

(a) All factors homogeneous

Finally, we consider the more usual long-run situation where not only can the *size* of all firms in the industry alter, but the *number* of firms is also assumed to change. We assume that there is free entry into the industry, and that new firms continue to enter it until no abnormal profits are being earned. In the short run in Fig. 6.7, a firm in this condition will produce the output OM_2 at the price OP_2. In the long run, the individual firm, shown in Fig. 6.7, will be in exactly the same position as in the original equilibrium. Output will be OM_1 and price OP_1. Marginal revenue will be shown by the curve P_1–MR_4 which is identical with the curve P_1–MR_1. New firms will have entered the industry and all abnormal profits will have been competed away. The output of each firm is once again OM_1 but, because there are now more firms, the output of the industry has increased. This can be seen from Fig. 6.8. The long-run supply curve, where the number of firms can alter, is the curve P_1–LS_2. It will be seen that, in equilibrium, the output of the industry is now ON_3. This long-run supply curve is horizontal because new firms have entered the industry—firms which are identical with those already there—and marginal cost in each firm has returned to the original level. Provided that all factors are homogeneous, the long-run supply curve of the industry (with free entry) will be a horizontal straight line and supply price will be the same at every output. This is the simplest possible kind of long-run supply curve with free entry. It represents a first approximation to reality.

(b) Heterogeneous factors

In practice, it is unlikely that all factors will be homogeneous. It is much more likely that entrepreneurs, at least, will be heterogeneous. If factors other than entrepreneurs are heterogeneous, we can look upon this as an external diseconomy of the industry. All firms will have to hire some less-efficient factors if the size of the industry increases, so that the increased size of the industry will raise the costs of all firms. Even if all units of all factors continue to earn the same money reward, the less efficient factors will produce a smaller output than the more efficient ones. The cost of output will therefore rise. If entrepreneurs alone are heterogeneous there will be no effect on the costs of firms already in the industry if expansion brings in new entrepreneurs. It will be the new firms only which have higher costs. This situation is therefore not the same as where heterogeneity of other factors causes external diseconomies. Let us now consider what will be the shape of the supply curve of the industry where entrepreneurs are heterogeneous, but all other factors are homogeneous.

So far as the short-run supply curve is concerned, the fact that entrepreneurs are heterogeneous will make little difference. The short-run supply curve will still represent a lateral summation of the short-run marginal cost curves of the individual firms. Of course, these marginal cost curves will now be different for each firm, so that the process of summing them will be more complicated than where factors are homogeneous. Since the number of firms is fixed in the short run, and since the short-run marginal cost curve of the firm always rises fairly steeply, the short-run supply curve of the industry will always rise too. Whether or not factors of production are homogeneous, the short-run supply curve is bound to slope upwards to the right. However, with heterogeneous factors it will slope upwards rather more steeply.

In the long run the number of firms will be able to increase, assuming that there is free entry. However, the new firms which enter the industry in the long run will be run by less-efficient entrepreneurs. Their costs will therefore be higher at each level of output than those of existing firms. For long-run equilibrium to occur, the price of the industry's product must have risen above its initial level (OP_1 in Fig. 6.8). Only in that way can less-efficient firms be attracted into the industry and maintained there. The rise in price needed to produce a given increase in output will be smaller than in the short run. This is partly because in the long run each firm will be able to produce a bigger output more efficiently than in the short run. However, it is partly because, in the long run, as the number of firms increases existing individual firms will find that they have to reduce their output. This will lower their marginal cost. The supply curve of the industry, with heterogeneous entrepreneurs and all other factors homogeneous, will therefore slope upwards; with all factors homogeneous it will be horizontal. However, it is likely to slope upwards rather less steeply in the long run than it does in the short run.

(c) External economies and diseconomies

Finally, we must consider what will be the shape of the industry's supply curve where there are external economies and diseconomies. Here, we shall confine our attention to the long-run supply curve. External economies and diseconomies can be important only in the long run; only in the long run can the size of the industry alter without any consequential repercussions on costs of production.

We have seen that if all factors of production are homogeneous and in perfectly elastic supply, the long-run supply curve of the industry will be horizontal. In such conditions, if there are external economies, the long-run supply curve will slope downwards. Alternatively, if there are external diseconomies, the supply curve will slope upwards. We have also seen that where entrepreneurship is not homogeneous in a perfectly competitive industry, but all other factors are homogeneous, the long-run supply curve will slope upwards. In this case, the presence of external diseconomies will accentuate the upward slope of the supply curve. However, external economies will offset the upward slope of the supply curve to some extent. If they are strong enough, they may even reverse it. The long-run supply curve could slope upwards or downwards, or indeed be horizontal, depending on how strong the external economies are.

8.4 A summing up

Let us now sum up. In the short run the supply curve of the perfectly-competitive industry will always slope upwards to the right. In the long run, assuming that there is free entry, it is likely to slope upwards unless all factors are homogeneous. However, it may be horizontal or slope downwards if sufficiently great external economies are obtained as the industry expands.

9. Elasticity of supply again

We have now seen how a supply curve is built up. Our next main task is to analyse the relationship between demand curves and supply curves. A major result of this will be to allow us to study with greater precision the differences between short- and long-run supply curves. First, however, we must say something about elasticity of supply, where supply curves are real curves and not straight lines as we assumed in our discussion of elasticity of supply in Chapter 1.

We saw there that any supply curve which is a straight line passing through the origin, whatever its slope, will possess unitary elasticity of supply. We may now add that any straight-line supply curve which cuts the (vertical) y-axis (or whose projection cuts the y-axis) will have an elasticity greater than one. Any straight-line supply curve which cuts the x-axis (or whose projection cuts the x-axis) will have an elasticity which is less than one. Consequently, the supply curve *SR* in Fig. 6.9a has an elasticity greater than one. The curve S_1R_1 in Fig. 6.9b has an elasticity less than one.

It is simple enough to find the elasticity of supply curves which are true curves. If one draws a tangent to any point on such a curve, the position at which the tangent cuts an axis will indicate whether

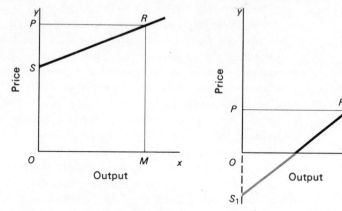

Fig. 6.9 a b

elasticity at the point of tangency is greater or less than or equal to one. If the tangent to a supply curve cuts the *y*-axis, the supply curve has an elasticity greater than one at the point to which the tangent is drawn. If the tangent cuts the *x*-axis, the supply curve has an elasticity of less than one at the relevant point. If the tangent passes through the origin, point elasticity is equal to one where the tangent touches the supply curve. This provides a simple rule for discovering whether elasticity of supply is greater than, less than, or equal to one. The precise numerical elasticity can, of course, be calculated in the usual way from the formula for elasticity of supply.[1]

10. Linear algebra and economics

Throughout the analysis of Chapter 6 we have assumed that the average cost curve of the individual firm is U-shaped. We have also seen that the equilibrium position of the firm can be defined, using differential calculus, as where marginal revenue equals marginal cost. Indeed, because in perfect competition marginal revenue also equals price, profit maximisation takes place where:

$$P = \frac{dC}{dx}$$

Here, P=price, C=total cost, and x=output. One can use differential calculus to state this equilibrium condition because both the

[1]See p. 59.

cost and revenue functions of the firm are assumed to be smooth, continuous curves, with no 'gaps' or 'corners'. If one did have discontinuous functions, differential calculus could not deal with a situation where equilibrium occurred at a discontinuity or 'corner'. However, there is one particular type of situation where there are discontinuities in cost functions but mathematical analysis can still be used.

10.1
Equilibrium
with linear cost
and revenue
functions

A typical example of such a situation is where cost conditions in the firm are as shown in Fig. 6.10. It is assumed here that, in the short

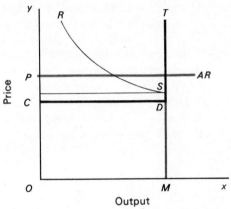

Fig. 6.10

run, marginal cost is constant at OC per unit, until output reaches OM. However, it is not possible to increase output in the short run beyond OM because of some absolute constraint. For example, the product may be made by a machine which can produce a maximum output of OM in a given period of time, but no more. The marginal cost curve is therefore linear up to OM, but there is a 'corner' in the short run at OM. No increase in output can be achieved, however much is spent on trying to do so, so that the curve CDT becomes vertical at D.

For reasons we have explained in Chapter 5, the average fixed cost curve in Fig. 6.10 will be a rectangular hyperbola; it takes the shape RST in Fig. 6.10. In perfect competition, with the price of OP, the profit-maximising output is therefore OM. Indeed, at any price above OC, the profit-maximising output is still OM. With a price of less than OC, the (loss-minimising) output will be zero. Total loss will then be equal to total fixed cost.

It will be clear that if this were all there were to it, this kind of analysis would add nothing significant to what has been said in this Chapter. While the short-run output of the firm would be either a substantial output (like OM) or zero, the supply curve of the industry would be much the same as the one described earlier in this Chapter. Firms would not adjust output minutely, at the margin, when price altered, as we have so far assumed. They would either produce no output at all or they would increase output to a level like OM. However, if each firm's marginal cost for producing up to an output like OM was different, the supply curve would still slope upwards. As price rose, more firms would come into production.

This is a special case of the analysis discussed in this chapter. It is an important special case because it is very useful in programming the short-run output of firms in a number of industries, for example, in oil refining or in engineering batch production, where capacity is limited, but plant or machinery has alternative uses. In this kind of situation, the firm does not make just one product as in Fig. 6.10. However, provided that the price of each product is given to the firm (provided that there is perfect competition or something approximating to it) the cost and revenue situation in the firm can be described by a set of curves, or functions, like those in Fig. 6.10.

If the constraint on the firm was simply that total output was limited because each product required exactly the same amount of the same raw material per unit of output, and if the total supply of raw material was fixed, the firm would operate as follows. First, it

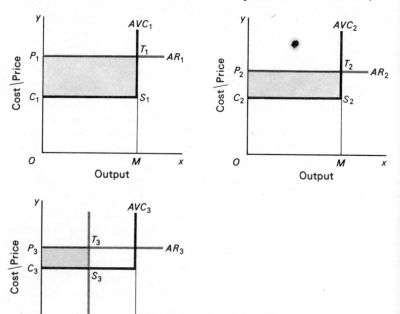

Fig. 6.11 a | b
c |

would produce the maximum possible amount of that product with the highest contribution per unit. It would then move on to produce the maximum possible amount of that product with the second-highest contribution per unit; and so on.

For example, in Fig. 6.11 let us suppose that the firm has enough capacity to produce the amount OM of each of three products: A, B and C. Despite the fact that each unit of each product uses the same amount of raw material and labour, each product provides a different marginal contribution. Let us suppose that there is enough raw material to make an output of only $2\frac{1}{2}$ times output OM. The firm will begin by making the amount OM of product A, whose unit contribution margin is C_1P_1. This is the biggest unit contribution available. The firm then goes on to produce the amount OM of product B, whose unit contribution is C_2P_2. Finally, the firm makes ON of C, where ON is equal to $\frac{1}{2}OM$. This product has the third-biggest unit contribution. The firm has to leave NM of product C unproduced because, although it has enough plant, it does not have enough raw material to make OM. The firm is maximising profit by earning a total contribution of $P_1T_1S_1C_1 + P_2T_2S_2C_2 + P_3T_3S_3C_3$. Since fixed costs are fixed for *each* product, profits are maximised (or losses are minimised) if total contribution is maximised, *whatever* the level of fixed costs. In the short run, the firm can do no better than maximise total contribution.

10.2 Linear programming

This discussion is over-simplified; in practice the situation will be more complex. First, it is likely that plant and machinery will have alternative uses. Machines may be available for producing more than one product. Indeed, it is likely that one will often be concerned with a large plant, able to produce varying proportions of a number of products from the same raw material. This will happen, for example, with an oil refinery. Second, we have assumed so far that 'contribution' per unit of whatever product is being produced by the firm is the important element. This may well not be the case. It will often pay the firm to produce the largest possible amount of a product with a smallish contribution per unit of output because there is a large contribution per unit of the 'bottleneck' factor. For example, suppose that product X has a contribution margin of £10 per unit, but product Y has one of only £5. However, one unit of labour can make three units of Y in one hour but only one of X. If labour (or indeed plant) is scarce, it will therefore pay the firm to make sure first of all that it is producing the maximum possible amount of Y, given the constraint operating on the production of Y. This is because contribution per man is £15 per hour from producing Y, as against £10 for product

X. This is true despite the fact that the contribution from each unit of product X is greater than that from each unit of product Y.

The calculations required in practice are often extremely complicated. They would certainly be complex, if one were concerned, for example, with plant or machinery able to produce a number of different products, each with a different unit contribution margin and each using a different amount of labour, machinery, components, etc. Similarly, the problem will be complex if a firm has to transport large amounts of raw material or product from various sources to various destinations. Nevertheless, if the cost functions are linear (or nearly enough linear for a linear approximation to be reasonably accurate) and if competition is perfect or nearly so, such a problem can be solved by what is known as *linear programming*. Over the last 40 years, a whole new area of linear algebra has been opened up and has made possible the solution of problems of this kind. While mathematically complex, what linear programming does is to proceed, in the way described above, to maximise total contribution or to minimise total cost.

10.3 Linear economics

While all this is important, we are interested here in something else. Linear programming is a practical management technique, not a part of economic theory and this book is concerned with economic theory.[1] This is not to say that linear analysis has no relevance to economic theory. The new mathematical analysis which linear programming and associated developments have brought into being has provided economic theory with new ways of analysing problems —both old and new. If it seemed sensible to do so, one could restate much of this chapter in terms of linear mathematics. One can also explain the operation of a whole economy in terms of input-output analysis, where one has linear relationships between inputs of factors of production and outputs of finished products. Similarly, one can explain new topics, like parts of the Theory of Growth (with which we shall be concerned in Part 3) in terms of linear algebra. While we shall not go into more detail about linear programming in this book, this short description will give an indication of its relevance to economic theory.

However, it is important to realise why we have included this short description of linear algebra at the end of a chapter on perfect competition. In these new developments in mathematics and economics, we are concerned with *linear* algebra. We are maximising, say,

[1] Readers wishing to go further into the applications of linear analysis in business, especially linear programming, may wish to consult D. C. Hague, *Managerial Economics*, Longman, 1969, especially chapters 8, 9 and 10 and chapter 13, section 2.

contribution; or minimising, say, costs in a situation where there is a linear relationship between variables. This means that, on the revenue side, linear analysis can deal only with situations where the firm is selling in perfect competition. Only here, is the total revenue of the function of the firm linear. Linear analysis can be used only to study problems on the revenue side of the firm if it is producing in situations where competition is not perfect, or approximately so, or where, for some other reason, the revenue function is linear.

Suggested reading

MARSHALL, ALFRED	*Principles of Economics*, 8th edn., London, 1920, Book IV, chapters 9 and 13; Book V *passim*.
ROBINSON, JOAN	*Economics of Imperfect Competition*, London, 1933, chapters vi and vii.
CHAMBERLIN, E. H.	*The Theory of Monopolistic Competition*, 5th edn., Cambridge, Mass., 1946, chapter i.
LEONTIEF, W.	*Input-Output Economics*, Oxford, 1966, pp. 13–29. Reprinted in H. Townsend, (Ed.), *Price Theory*, Penguin Modern Economics Readings, Harmondsworth, Middlesex, 1971, chapter 16.

7

Competitive equilibrium

1.
Equilibrium and change

We have seen how the shapes of the demand and supply curves for a product made by a perfectly competitive industry are determined. We must now use these curves to see how equilibrium between demand and supply is brought about. We touched on this problem at the end of Chapter 1 and showed how, with given demand and supply curves, the equilibrium price of a good would be that at which these curves intersected. The amount demanded at this price would equal the amount supplied, and the market would be in equilibrium.

Equilibrium in the market is therefore a state which depends on and satisfies the existing conditions of demand and supply at any given moment of time. In addition, market equilibrium implies a situation of rest, or absence of change, over a period of time. In this sense, the market is said to remain in a state of equilibrium only so long as demand and supply conditions are unchanged. If either demand conditions, or supply conditions, or both of them, alter, the market passes from the existing equilibrium to a new one.

For example, in Fig. 7.1 the demand curve shifts upwards and to the right from DD to D_1D_1, while supply conditions remain exactly the same. For simplicity, we assume that the new demand curve is parallel to the old one. The new equilibrium price is higher and the

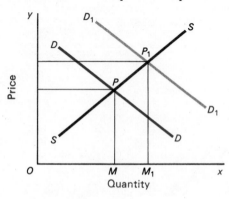

Fig. 7.1

new equilibrium amount demanded and supplied is larger than the old. This shows itself in the fact that P_1 is above and to the right of P. This change can be called, for short, a rise in demand price or an increase of demand. Consumers are willing to buy any amount of the good at a higher price than before. Similarly, at any price they are willing to buy more than in the original equilibrium situation. The effect of an increase in demand is to raise price and to increase sales.

In Fig. 7.2 it is the supply curve which shifts to the right and downwards from SS to S_1S_1, while demand conditions remain unaltered.

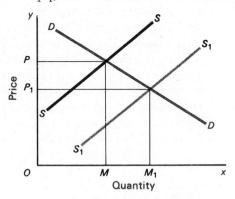

Fig. 7.2

Figure 7.2 shows an 'increase in supply' or a 'fall in supply price'. At each price, sellers will supply a larger amount than before. The result is that sales increase from OM to OM_1 and price falls from OP to OP_1.

However, it is not necessarily true that a given change in demand or supply conditions always causes the same change in price or amount demanded. With a given increase of demand, price rises more and sales increase less the steeper is the supply curve. For example, in Fig. 7.3 the supply curve S_1S_1 is steeper than the curve S_2S_2; P_1 is above and to the left of P_2. This shows that if a given increase in demand takes place, price will rise more and sales will increase less

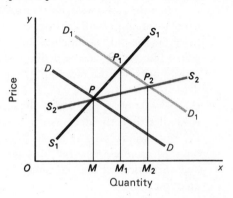

Fig. 7.3

with the supply curve $S_1 S_1$ than with the curve $S_2 S_2$. Since the slopes of both supply curves relate to the same units on the x-axis and y-axis, the steeper curve is less elastic, at each price, than the flatter curve. With inelastic supply, a given increase in demand raises price more than with elastic supply. Similarly, with a given increase of supply, price will fall more with an inelastic demand curve than with an elastic one.

If both demand and supply increase, sales are bound to increase. But price may or may not rise. It will rise if the amount which would now be demanded at the old price exceeds the amount which would now be supplied at that price. But it will fall if the amount which would now be supplied at the old price exceeds the amount which would now be demanded at that price. If the amount demanded at the old price still equals the amount supplied, price will not change. The first case may be called a smaller increase of supply than of demand. The second case represents a greater increase of supply than of demand. The third represents an equal increase of demand and supply. The first two cases are illustrated in Fig. 7.4, where price rises from OP to OP_1 when demand increases more than supply (Fig. 7.4a), but falls from OP to OP_2 when supply increases more than

Fig. 7.4

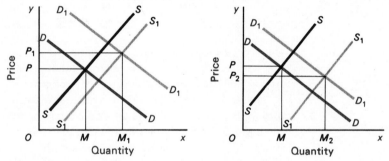

demand (Fig. 7.4b). The amount of the good exchanged rises from OM to OM_1 in the first case and from OM to OM_2 in the second.

In just the same way, an increase of demand with a simultaneous decrease of supply will raise price and increase sales if the new demand price for the old equilibrium amount is higher than its new supply price. Similarly, sales will diminish and price will rise if the new supply price for the old equilibrium amount is higher than its new demand price. In the first case, the increase of demand is greater than the decrease of supply, and in the second case the increase in demand is smaller than the decrease of supply. Both cases are illustrated in Fig. 7.5, where sales increase from OM to OM_1 in Fig. 7.5a, but diminish from OM to OM_1 in Fig. 7.5b. In Figs. 7.5a and 7.5b OM and OP represent the old, and OM_1 and OP_1 the new, prices and amounts.

It is the function of the market to bring about equilibrium at every moment of time between the demand and supply conditions existing at that moment. Since one or other of these forces is continually changing, at any rate in respect of some goods, one or more market prices will be changing at every moment. These price changes may be due to changes in consumers' tastes or incomes on the demand

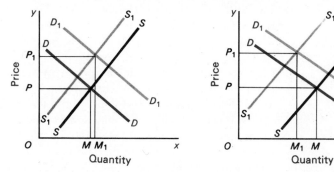

Fig. 7.5 a | b

side, or to changes in technical knowledge and its application, or in the relative scarcity of factors of production on the supply side. All such changes can be represented in the way we have just shown, by shifts of the demand and the supply curves respectively. Such changes may take the form of gradual increases of demand or supply, or gradual reductions of them, rather than large once-for-all changes. If so, they will be accompanied by correspondingly gradual changes in price. Again, they may take the form of alternating increases and reductions of demand or supply. In this last case, market prices will fluctuate through time. Price changes of these types can be adequately explained by the analysis we have discussed in this section.

2. A more dynamic view of the industry

The aim in the remainder of this Chapter is to outline Alfred Marshall's theory of the determination of price and output in a competitive industry. Marshall would clearly have been unsatisfied with the analysis of Chapter 6, because he would have felt it too static. We explained in Chapter 6 that the industry would be in equilibrium if all firms in it were earning normal profit, but we did not allow for firms entering or leaving the industry. Marshall wanted to provide a theory where this could happen, even if the output of the whole industry were constant. In one way, this is easy enough. All that is required is for the output of the firms leaving the industry to be exactly replaced at every point of time by new entrants. However, the necessary analysis is rather more complicated.

What Marshall did was to assume that the profitability of the firm was a function of the length of time it had been in the industry. He argued that firms which entered the industry would take time to build up to full efficiency. Only after a time, would they become profitable. Then, after a period of satisfactory profitability, they would decline again, with falling efficiency and profitability. The implication of this is that each firm, like its own entrepreneur, is mortal. This is an idea that could more easily be accepted in the 1870s and 1880s, when Marshall worked it out, at a time before the full development of the joint-stock company which, as Marshall put it, 'often stagnates but seldom dies'. However, it did imply that in a small, one-man business the development of the firm would sooner or later be halted by a decline in the energy and ability of its owner, and his growing dislike of active work. It also implied that his children would not have the ability and interest required to run the business successfully for more than a short time. It implied, in a term that economists now use but Marshall did not, that there was a 'life cycle' for the individual firm that did not last so very long.

There are reasons for doubting whether this is the whole story, but some of the objections which one could make to the theory are not relevant here. First, one reason why Marshall thought that the firm would take time to reach a peak of efficiency and profitability was that he thought that its marketing activities would be difficult to develop. This cannot be important in perfect competition, because all firms' products are identical, though it does emphasise that when Marshall wrote in his *Principles of Economics* of 'large and open' markets he clearly did not mean perfect competition. There is what we shall later define as monopolistic competition—even oligopoly—in Marshall's competitive industries. In so far as the difficulty of developing marketing efficiency was important in causing the life cycle of the firm, it is not relevant to our analysis of perfect competition. We have to rely on the organisational and managerial problems of achieving and sustaining 'internal economies'. On the other hand, this means that if a firm *did* succeed in becoming very large and maintained its size over a very long period, there would no longer be perfect competition. Firms operating in imperfect competition will be looked at in later chapters. Nevertheless, it will be a useful, and not unrealistic, exercise to look at the way in which a perfectly-competitive industry made up of small firms, each subject to a 'life cycle', will adapt to once-for-all changes in demand conditions.

3. More about normal profit

To do this, we have to extend the concept of normal profit. So far, we have assumed that a spectrum of profitability exists in the industry because of inherent differences in the efficiency of entrepreneurs.

3.1 Profit and the firm

What Marshall did was to suggest that because of the life cycle the profitability of the individual firm would change over time in something like the way shown in Fig. 7.6. Here, profit (both positive and negative) is measured on the y-axis and time along the x-axis. The light brown curve shows an initial period of unprofitability, while the firm obtains the benefit of internal economies. Since all firms in a

Fig. 7.6

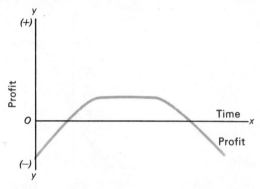

perfectly-competitive industry sell the identical product at the identical price, low profitability must be a result of low efficiency. This initial period passes and the firm enters a long period of acceptable profitability, before the increasing age and disinterest of the entrepreneur leads to a final decline in profitability, and the firm leaves the industry.

Of course, as in our model in Chapter 6, some firms do better than this. Their unprofitable periods may be shorter and their profitability during the profitable periods higher. Other firms may never become adequately profitable at all, but go out of the industry quickly without establishing themselves. However, while we have here the same diversity of efficiency as in Chapter 6, there is not now a completely static position. Even where the size of the output of the industry is constant, so that the situation is stationary in that sense, there is change as well. Some firms are going out of the industry; some firms are entering it. In this way, Marshall not only introduced a measure of change into static economics. He also introduced growth and decline—two of the biological concepts which he found it attractive to introduce into economics.

3.2 Profit and the industry

In this stationary situation, where demand and supply conditions are assumed to be constant, so that price and output in the industry are unchanging, we should find a frequency distribution of profitability among firms. For example, we might find one like the hypothetical profit distribution in Fig. 7.7. Here, we have numbers of firms measured up the *y*-axis and levels of profitability (both positive and negative) along the *x*-axis. The vertical axis denotes zero profit. To the left of it, any firms are making losses; to the right of it, they are earning increasing amounts of profit as one moves to the right. The dark brown curve shows the number of firms earning each rate of profit or loss. In this stationary situation, some firms are losing

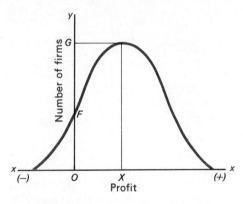

Fig. 7.7

money, some are making a lot of money and larger numbers are earning modest amounts. It is important to note the difference between this diagram and Fig. 7.6. There, we were looking at the profit pattern over time for one firm. The light-brown curve in Fig. 7.6 showed profit at each date during the life of the firm. By contrast, Fig. 7.7 shows the profit position of every firm in the industry, but it shows it at a *single* point of time. At the time when the observation is made, profitability varies considerably from firm to firm. Profit, measured along the *x*-axis, is negative in a number of firms. These are firms that have either not yet established themselves or are on the way out of the industry. Profit is zero, where the *y*-axis cuts the *x*-axis, in *OF* firms. The largest number of firms earning any particular level of profit is *OG;* these *OG* firms are earning a profit of *OX*. They are firms which are well established. Some of them will go on to earn higher profits moving to the right of *X;* others will be in decline, after earning higher profit. Some firms will never earn more than *OX;* some will never earn as much as that.

By this device, Marshall allowed for change as well as stability in static equilibrium. For what we said needs qualification in one way. It is true that the dark-brown curve in Fig. 7.7 represents the situation at a moment of time. Yet if the industry is in stationary equilibrium the curve will continue to represent the profit situation in the industry so long as the equilibrium does not change. Each individual firm may be earning a different amount of profit when the next observation is made. However, the *numbers* of firms earning *each* amount of profit will be the same.

It must be made clear at once that while Figs. 7.6 and 7.7 show what it was that Marshall was saying, he did *not* draw diagrams like this himself. They are our diagrams.

3.3 Normal profit redefined

We shall go on later to see what happens where the frequency distribution of profitability within an industry does alter. What we must do at once is to see how what we have said in this section affects the notion of normal profit. We shall continue to assume, as we did in Chapter 6, that any entrepreneur in this industry would be equally efficient if he left it and went to another. What we do now is to add the assumption that normal profit differs according to the length of time the firm has been in the industry. If the firm has been in the industry for only a short time, its profit will be negative or zero. Moreover, entrepreneurs will not expect more than this. They will realise that it will take time to establish themselves. Similarly, if the firm is in the industry for any considerable time, it will expect to earn, in Fig. 7.7, OX or more. It will be noted that if we draw an average revenue and average cost curve for all firms in an industry in stationary equilibrium, we shall have a diagram like Fig. 7.8. Firms

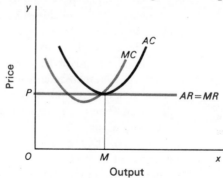

Fig. 7.8

will be earning the profits shown in Fig. 7.7, but since they only *expect* these profits, the existing profits are normal profits for all firms. If we therefore adapt the cost curve, as we did in Chapter 6, to allow for normal profits, all firms will be in an equilibrium position like that in Fig. 7.8. In other words, an industry in stationary equilibrium is one where normal profit is earned by *all* firms. There is therefore no tendency for any firms to enter or leave the industry.

4. Time and supply conditions

With this preparation, we can go on to consider the effects of changes in demand and supply conditions in more detail. There is one kind of change which is important enough to need special study. We have already seen that the reactions of supply to a once-for-all change in demand will be different the longer the period of time which one takes into consideration. For example, if demand suddenly increases, price is likely to rise sharply in the short run because firms will be expanding output along fairly steep short-run marginal cost curves. In the long run, however, firms will be reorganised to produce the new, high output more efficiently. They will now be able to produce along rather flatter long-run marginal cost curves. In addition, there will have been a net increase in the size of the industry, with more new firms entering than existing ones leaving. The initial change in equilibrium price is caused by a change in conditions of demand; the way price then changes over time depends on the response of supply conditions to the new demand situation. The size of such reactions in amount supplied will differ according to the length of time being considered.

Economists find it important to be able to discuss the way in which supply responds to a once-for-all change in demand conditions. The reason can be found in the nature of technical production conditions. It will always take time to make those adjustments in the size and organisation of a firm which are necessary if it is to work as efficiently as possible at a new scale of activity. Once demand has increased (or decreased), a series of adjustments will be put in motion in every firm in the industry. These will bear fruit one after the other as time passes. However, alternations in the amount supplied can be made only after a period of time has elapsed; technical considerations prohibit instantaneous adjustment. Yet there is nothing on the demand side to correspond to this slow process of adjustment on the supply side. There is no reason why demand conditions should not change or, if they do, why they should change differently in the short run and in the long run. Instantaneous changes in demand conditions are perfectly possible. Changes in consumers' tastes are not dependent on technology in the way that supply conditions are. Admittedly, consumers' tastes do change gradually as time goes on. But this will be a change of data, not a change induced by changed supply conditions. There is no reason why the long-run demand curve should differ from the short-run demand curve, however odd the behaviour of supply has been.

This asymmetry between demand and supply explains the apparent preoccupation of economists with adjustments of supply over time to once-and-for-all changes in demand and not vice versa. It does not mean that demand or supply is more important as a factor determining price; both are equally important. What it does mean is that demand and supply do not respond either equally, or equally quickly, to changed conditions. We must expect that more changes will occur the longer is the period during which demand and supply are coming into equilibrium. However, there is a limit to the amount of detail that we can usefully introduce into the analysis. We do not want to consider the various possibilities of adaptation to changes in demand conditions during many successive, very short, periods of time. This would introduce intolerable and unnecessary complexity into the analysis.

To avoid this problem, it is usual to follow the method devised by Marshall. He showed that the most important problems raised by the introduction of time into the analysis of price determination could be dealt with by considering the way in which, and the extent to which, equilibrium between demand and supply was brought about in three periods of time: the market period, the short period, and the long period. The properties of these three types of time period can be summarised as follows.

5. Marshall's time periods

5.1 The market period

Marshall conceived of the market period as being only a single day, or a very few days. The essential element is that it is so short that supplies of the commodity in question are limited to existing stocks, or, at most, to supplies which are 'in sight'. On the basis of this 'market' supply and of the existing 'market' demand for the commodity, a temporary equilibrium will be brought about between demand and supply. With perfect competition between buyers and between sellers, it will be brought about by the establishment of an equilibrium price. This 'market' equilibrium price will only exist temporarily and it is unlikely that it will be the same as the price in preceding or succeeding 'market periods'.

5.2 The short period

Marshall defined the short period as a period which was long enough for supplies of a commodity to be altered by increases or decreases in current output, but not long enough for the fixed equipment producing this output to be adapted in order to produce larger or smaller outputs. In the terminology of the theory of the firm, we may say that output can be altered in the short period only by producing at a different point on a given short-run marginal cost curve. The size and technology of the individual plant has to be taken as unalterable. No change in the scale of operations is possible; nor can new firms enter the industry in the short-run. Equilibrium brought about in this short period represents a 'short period equilibrium'. Supply is able to adapt itself, at any rate partially, to a change in demand. It is therefore possible for a *short-period equilibrium price* to be established. Variations or oscillations in market price caused by factors that are peculiar to each separate market period will still occur, but these will tend to range round a fairly well-defined short-run equilibrium price.

5.3 The long period

In the long period, as defined by Marshall, there is time for firms' fixed equipment to be altered so that output is capable of adapting itself more fully to changes in demand conditions than it was in the short period. There is time to build new machines and factories, and old ones can be closed down or allowed to fall to pieces. A 'long-period equilibrium' between demand and supply will be brought about. In this equilibrium position, supply will be able to adapt itself fully to a change in demand. Market equilibrium price and output will now oscillate round, and vary from, a fairly clearly-defined long-period equilibrium of price and output.

For the sake of completeness, it may be added that Marshall also talked of a secular[1] or very long period. The secular period would see all the changes which occur in the ordinary long period take place. In addition, all the underlying economic factors, such as the size of population, supplies of raw materials, or general conditions of capital supply would have time to alter. These are the issues we shall study in Part 3, in the theory of growth, though using quite different analytical methods from Marshall.

6. 'Normal' price

We must now introduce the concept of 'normal' price. Marshall defines 'normal action' as that which one expects to be taken by a person or group of persons under given conditions.[2] Similarly, 'normal results' are defined as those results which may reasonably be expected as the outcome of a given situation. 'Normal prices' are therefore those prices which may reasonably be expected in given conditions of demand and supply. Time is very important here. A different price will be 'normal' in the long period from the one that is 'normal' in the short period. In our discussion of equilibrium prices in short and long periods we shall really be concerned with short- and long-period 'normal' prices—those prices which one may reasonably expect to occur in the short and long run respectively, given demand and supply conditions.

An important reason for dealing with time using Marshall's methods is that it is thereby possible to throw light on disputes which have raged in the past between economists on whether demand

[1]Derived from Latin *saecula* and meaning age-long.
[2]A. Marshall, *Principles of Economics*, London, 1920, p. 34.

or supply is more important in determining price. Marshall likened this dispute to an argument about whether the upper or lower blade of a pair of scissors actually cuts a piece of paper.[1] He said that if the upper blade is held still and the lower blade moved, it is reasonable, provided one does not wish to be completely accurate, to say that the lower blade does the cutting. Alternatively, if the lower blade is fixed and the upper moved, it is reasonable, provided again that one makes no claim to scientific accuracy, to say that the upper blade is cutting the paper. Similarly, in certain circumstances, it is possible to say, with some justification, that either demand or supply determines price.

For example, a primitive fish market may have a given stock of fish on hand. If there is a danger that it will go bad if kept for more than a few days, the stock must obviously be disposed of quickly. It is then reasonable to say that price is governed by demand. Since supply is fixed, one can say that demand determines price. But while one may use this simplified argument for the sake of brevity, one cannot claim strict scientific accuracy. At the other extreme, in the long run when supply and demand changes have worked themselves out fully, the 'normal' long-period price will be the long-run money cost of production (including normal profits). The long-period 'normal price' around which day-to-day oscillations in price will occur can be roughly described as determined by supply—by costs of production. Again this is not strictly accurate, but it is near the truth.

The only really accurate answer to the question whether it is supply or demand which determines price is that it is both. At times it will seem that one is more important than the other, for one will be active and the other passive. For example, if demand remains constant but supply conditions vary, it is demand which is passive and supply active. But neither is more or less important than the other in determining price.

Of course, in practice, a long-period normal price will never be arrived at. There will always be a change in some of the conditions underlying the long-period equilibrium before it has time to be established. The long run—like tomorrow—never comes.

We may now discuss the way in which prices are determined in these various time periods. We shall employ the usual method of economic theory, proceeding step by step. We shall concentrate our attention on those things which seem most important at each stage of this analysis, by assuming that all other things are equal. As Marshall put it, 'He (the economist) segregates those disturbing causes, whose wanderings happen to be inconvenient, for the time in a pound called *ceteris paribus*'.[2] It should always be remembered

[1] *Op. cit.* p. 348.
[2] *Op cit.* p. 366.

that while this procedure makes it possible to construct a simple theory, it will not be a fully accurate one. The more simple a theory is, the less accurate it will inevitably be. As Marshall said, 'A man is likely to be a better economist if he trusts to his common sense and practical instincts, than if he professes to study the theory of value and is resolved to find it easy.'[1]

7. Market equilibrium

In order to show the value of Marshall's analysis, which uses time periods, in price theory, we shall study the way in which the supply of a commodity adapts itself over time to a once-and-for-all change in the demand for it.

Let us imagine a fish market with a given supply of fish. We assume that the fish cannot be kept overnight and that the whole supply must therefore be sold that day, since none can be kept back. Competition between buyers and sellers will mean that an equilibrium price is established where the amount demanded is equal to the amount supplied. This position is shown in Fig. 7.9 where the supply curve is the vertical straight line MS. This implies that sellers are

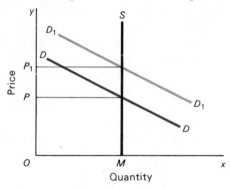

Fig. 7.9

prepared to sell the whole supply of fish, OM, whatever its price. In other words, sellers have no demand for their own fish. This is the assumption which we are making throughout Part 1, and it seems a fairly reasonable one. If the sellers did demand their own fish, the supply curve would slope upwards to the right in the normal way.

In this market, with demand conditions shown by the curve DD, the equilibrium price of OP will be reached, and the whole supply of fish will be disposed of at that price. There is no reason at all to expect this to equal long-run equilibrium price. For example, let us suppose that there were a sudden and permanent rise in the demand for fish to D_1D_1, perhaps because of the sudden onset of a serious

[1] *Op. cit.* p. 368.

cattle disease. The price of fish would rise to OP_1. There would be no increase in the supply of fish, since the only available supplies are already in existence and they cannot be increased until a day or two has elapsed. The whole supply of fish would still be sold, but the price would rise. Owing to the fact that supply is fixed, demand exerts its full influence on the price of fish, which rises considerably.

8. Short-period equilibrium

In the short period, the supply would begin to react to the sharp increase in the demand for fish, which we are assuming to be permanent. In this short-period analysis we shall ignore factors like changes in the weather which would cause daily fluctuations in the number of fish caught and therefore affect market prices from day to day. The influence of the weather can be seen only in periods which are too short to affect our analysis at this stage. Similarly, we shall ignore changes which can only occur over very long periods of time, since these are too long to affect short-run price. We shall, for instance, assume that there is too little time for low wages in the fishing industry to persuade sailors to become bank clerks or farmers instead. Such influences on the supply of sailors are relevant to our analysis only if it relates to long periods of time. We therefore abstract from these problems by 'impounding them' for the moment in *ceteris paribus*.

The problem which has to be faced in the short run is: 'How can we attract sailors into the fishing industry during the period before more of them have been trained? How can we renovate more boats, or otherwise put more into service?' The answer will usually be: 'By offering wages to sailors which are high enough to attract them quickly from jobs on passenger and cargo ships and by ensuring that the owners of old, not very efficient ships can now earn enough to make it worth putting them into service.' By definition, no new firms can enter the fishing industry in the short run; but those already in it can use their existing equipment more intensively.

The price which will solve this short-run problem is the 'short-period normal price' of fish. It is that price for fish which rapidly ensures that all readily-available sailors and ships go out fishing and are enabled to earn the minimum amount of money they are prepared to accept for an average day's work. The market price will still oscillate round this 'normal' price, but the normal price itself will rise sufficiently to ensure that the additional factors of production which have been persuaded to work in the fishing industry find it worth continuing to fish. This short-run 'normal' price must inevitably be higher than the original market price. Sailors can be attracted away from other ships only by higher wages; old, unused boats can be enticed back to sea only by higher returns.

In Fig. 7.10 the curve *MSC*—the market supply curve—shows that in the new demand conditions (given by the light-brown demand curve D_1D_1) the market price rises from *OP* to OP_1 when demand changes. The dashed short-period supply curve *SPS* shows

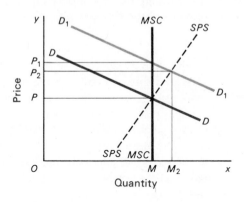

Fig. 7.10

that, in the short period, the increased resources available allow supply to adapt itself in some degree to the changed demand conditions. The short-run normal price will be OP_2. It is higher than the original market price *OP*, but not so high as the second market price of OP_1 after the once-for-all increase in the demand for fish. The supply of fish has also increased slightly from *OM* to OM_2. More fish is sold and price is not quite so high as in the market period.

9. Long-period equilibrium

In the long period, supply conditions can adapt fully to meet the new demand conditions. The problems and changes which have to be considered in the long period are rather different from those which arise in the short period. For example fishermen would have to be attracted from other jobs, and new firms set up. There is no *a priori* reason why the new fishermen entering the industry should be noticeably more or less competent than the original ones. However, it could well be that the entrepreneurs running the new fishing firms proved to be less efficient than those already in the industry. Again, new boats, nets and other equipment would have to be produced, and this might well affect the industry producing them. For example, the increased demand for fishing equipment may lead to a fall in the price of fish if it also allows the industry making it to expand and so to reap external economies of production. It is therefore not easy to decide what effect these factors will have on the shape of the long-period supply curve of the fishing industry, and we must look at the position again later.

The immediate question is what mechanism brings new firms into
an industry where there has been a sudden, large increase in the
demand for its product. To see what happens, we consider Fig. 7.11,
where we have reproduced the dark-brown curve from Fig. 7.7. It

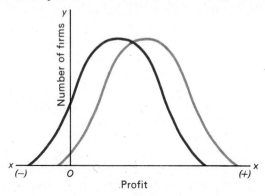

Fig. 7.11

will be recalled that this showed the profits being earned by each of
the firms in a perfectly-competitive industry, at a time when that
industry was in stationary equilibrium. Suppose that this is the
fishing industry which now experiences the sudden long-run increase
in demand. Price immediately rises and settles in the short run at a
higher level than in the original (stationary) equilibrium. In Fig.
7.10, OP_2 is bigger than OP. The short-run profits of all firms therefore rise above their initial level.

Let us suppose that this is shown by the light-brown curve in
Fig. 7.11. Here, all firms make higher profits. Indeed, most firms
previously making a loss now make a profit. The result is that instead
of making just normal profits as in Fig. 7.8, all firms in the industry
would now make supernormal profits—in the sense of making more
money than would be required just to keep them in the industry.
Firms which would have left the industry remain; firms which would
have taken time to become established are established more quickly
and easily. But this is not the end of the story. In the short run, firms
already *in* the industry earn supernormal profit because of the shift in
demand towards their product. In the long run, the number of firms
in the industry will increase. More entrants than usual will be
attracted to the industry. They will come because they see that this
is an industry where supernormal profits are being earned, and will
attempt to earn such profits themselves. Those who enter therefore
do not now merely replace the firms that leave. There is a net
increase in the number of firms in the industry.

The industry is shown to be an attractive one because all firms in
it are earning more than normal profit. The frequency distribution
of profits in Fig. 7.11 is no longer that associated with an industry in

stationary equilibrium. It is now that associated with an industry which is about to expand. This is shown by the fact that the frequency distribution of profits is now well to the right of the original one.

It is this increase in profitability in the short run which attracts new firms to the industry and ensures that in the long run profits fall back to the normal level. When all firms have settled down, the frequency distribution of profits will be similar to the dark-brown curves in Figs. 7.7 and 7.11—the ones associated with stationary equilibrium. It will not be identical, partly because the number of firms in the industry will be larger when long-run equilibrium is reached at a higher output and partly because the efficiency of the new entrepreneurs may be different from that of the older ones. But though normal profit for the new entrepreneurs will be less than for the existing ones if their efficiency is lower, when the industry has settled down to long-run equilibrium all firms will again be earning normal profits given their age and efficiency.

The whole industry will be bigger. More firms in the industry will be producing a bigger total output. However, the industry will again be in stationary equilibrium with new entrants just making up for the loss of output from those firms leaving the industry. Output is bigger, but it has settled down, at the new, bigger level, to stationary equilibrium.

9.2 The shape of long-period supply curves

The question to ask is then what will be the shape of the long-period supply curve associated with this new equilibrium. One possibility is shown in Fig. 7.12. In Fig. 7.12, the long-period supply curve for

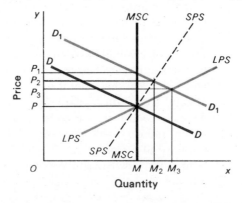

Fig. 7.12

fish (*LPS*) slopes upwards to the right, though less steeply than does the short-period curve shown in Figs. 7.10 and 7.12. The long-period normal price is then OP_3. This is lower than the short-period 'normal' price of OP_2, but higher than the original market price of OP. In the long run, it is possible to obtain fish more cheaply and in larger quantities than in the short run, but only at a rather higher price than in the original situation. This implies that entrepreneurs and/or some other factors of production are less efficient. In the long run, supply is able to adapt itself as fully as possible to the changed conditions of demand. The extent to which the long-run price will differ from the original price will depend on the ease with which extra fish can be caught in the long run. Market prices will still fluctuate, but they do so in the long run round the long-period 'normal' price.

Ignoring the fluctuations here, and concentrating on 'normal' price, it is possible that the long-run supply curve may be horizontal —if the fishing industry is a constant cost industry—or even falling— if there are external economies as the industry expands in the long run. These cases are shown in Fig. 7.13.

Fig. 7.13 a | b

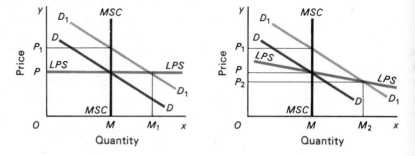

In Fig. 7.13a and 7.13b the original market price is OP. It rises initially to OP_1 when the change in demand takes place. The market supply is OM. In the long run, price falls again to OP, since the industry has a horizontal long-run supply curve (LPS) and the amount OM_1 is now sold. With constant long-run costs, the long-run normal price is therefore the same as the original price. In Fig. 7.13b the long-run normal price is OP_2, and is lower than the original price because of external economies. The amount sold is OM_2.

9.3 Long-period 'normal' prices

It follows, therefore, that the long-run normal price can be higher, lower or the same as the original market price, depending on supply conditions in the industry in question. It depends on whether or not there are internal and external economies or diseconomies of scale and how big they are. The short-period normal price, however, will invariably be higher than the long-period normal price. It is inconceivable that if there is a change in the firm's organisation which will increase its efficiency in the short run, it will be possible to make it in the short period but not in the long run.

It is important to note that 'normal' prices are not the same thing as 'average' prices, unless prices are constant. Normal price is the one toward which one can expect actual prices to tend; average price is the arithmetic average of actual prices. The latter will not only be influenced by fortuitous fluctuations; it will also be affected by the trend towards the 'normal' price.

**10.
Comparative
statistics**

Using time periods, we have now been able to show, in an elementary way, how prices vary over time. We have been able to drop the assumption, made throughout most of the previous chapters, that demand and supply conditions are given, and to assume that both can, and will, change. In technical economic language, we have proceeded from static analysis, where demand and supply conditions were given, to an analysis using *comparative statics*. In comparative statics, there is a once-for-all change in (usually) demand conditions and supply (or demand) is allowed to adjust to that change.

The construction of a truly dynamic theory of economics, where more continuous changes in demand and supply conditions, like those which occur in the real world, are analysed, is the ultimate goal of most theories of economics. We shall move towards such a theory in Part 3. However, so far as the determination of price and output is concerned, simple comparative-static analysis like that outlined in this chapter, using the more-manageable device of Marshall's three different time periods is as powerful an analytical method as we need.

**Suggested
reading**

MARSHALL, ALFRED	*Principles of Economics*, 8th edn., London, 1920, Book V, chapters 5–13.
FRISCH, RAGNAR	'Alfred Marshall's Theory of Value', *Quarterly Journal of Economics*, November 1950, p. 495. Reprinted in Penguin Modern Economics Readings; *Price Theory* edited by Harry Townsend, Penguin, Harmondsworth, Middlesex, 1971, p. 59.
HICKS, SIR JOHN	*Capital and Growth*, O.U.P., 1956, chapters 5 and 7.

8

Monopoly

1. The assumptions

Having seen how price and output are determined in a perfectly competitive industry, we must now see how they are arrived at when competition is not perfect. As we saw in Chapter 5, the two limiting types of market situation are those of pure competition and pure monopoly. The former is not likely to be found very often in practice and the latter never. In the real world, it is the region of 'imperfect' competition lying between these limits which is most important. We turn now to a study of the way in which price and output are determined in conditions of imperfect competition. In making this transition, we shall find it useful to keep some of the assumptions we have made so far, but to drop others. We must therefore make it clear which of the assumptions will be kept in this discussion of imperfect competition.

1.1 About the consumer

We shall continue to assume that there is perfect competition *between buyers*. We shall assume that there are so many consumers buying each product that no one consumer is able to have any influence on the price of that product by his own actions. So far as the individual consumer is concerned, the prices of all goods must still be taken as given. We shall continue to assume that each consumer is 'rational' and seeks to maximise his satisfactions. We shall assume that he bases his purchases on a scale of preferences so that if one had enough data one could construct demand curves showing how much of each commodity he would buy at various prices. These individual demand curves could then be added together to give a market demand curve. It follows that the demand curve for the product of any individual *industry* means exactly the same thing under imperfect competition as it does under perfect competition.

1.2 About the firm

(a) Profit maximisation

We now turn to the individual firm. We shall continue to assume that the sole aim of the entrepreneur is to earn maximum profits. In other words, we keep the fundamental assumption of 'economic rationality'. When we draw diagrams showing the equilibrium position of the firm, such an equilibrium will always require marginal revenue to equal marginal cost, whether competition is perfect or imperfect.

(b) The average revenue curve

There is, however, one important difference between the equilibrium position of the individual firm in perfect competition and that in imperfect competition. When competition is imperfect, there are no longer sufficient firms in the industry to ensure that a change in the output of any one of them has only a negligible effect on the output of the industry as a whole. Thus, while the nature of the demand curve for the product of the industry as a whole is not affected if competition becomes imperfect, it will be found that the average revenue curve of the individual firm does take a different shape. In imperfect competition, we can no longer assume that the average revenue curve of the firm is a horizontal straight line. In conditions of pure competition, where each individual firm has to take the price of the industry's product as given, the firm's average revenue curve must be a horizontal straight line. In imperfect competition this is no longer the case.

When there is imperfect competition, the average revenue curve of the individual firm slopes downwards throughout its length. This has an important corollary. In perfect competition, since the firm's average revenue curve is a horizontal straight line, marginal revenue and average revenue are always equal. In imperfect competition, average revenue is falling at all levels of output. Therefore marginal revenue falls as well, but even more swiftly. In geometrical terms, the marginal revenue curve always lies below the average revenue curve and slopes downwards more steeply. It will also be remembered that when, in perfect competition, the industry as a whole is in 'full' equilibrium, not only does marginal cost equal marginal revenue. These are themselves both equal to average revenue and to average cost. In imperfect competition this is not the case. In equilibrium, marginal revenue still equals marginal cost, but since marginal revenue is less than average revenue, marginal cost is also less than average revenue—than price.

1.3 Differences between perfect and imperfect competition

These are the main differences between the assumptions made in analysing perfect and imperfect competition. They are not very great differences. Unfortunately, there is no single representative case of imperfect competition as there is of perfect competition. The fundamental distinguishing characteristic of imperfect competition is that the average revenue curve of the firm slopes downwards throughout its length. But the average revenue curves of different firms will slope downwards at different rates. We do not have a single case of imperfect competition to compare with the single case of perfect competition. We can find some instances of firms in imperfect competition where the average revenue curve slopes downwards only very gently and where competition is almost perfect. There are other cases where the slope of the average revenue curve is very steep and competition is extremely imperfect. There is not one, single case of imperfect competition, but a whole range or series of cases representing progressively more and more imperfect competition.

Since the general term, imperfect competition, covers all situations where there is neither 'pure' competition nor 'pure' monopoly, it is usual to distinguish several separate types of competition within the broad concept of imperfect competition. We shall discuss each of these narrower types of imperfect competition in turn.

We begin with a type of market form which has always attracted the attention of economists—that of *monopoly*. Strictly interpreted, a 'monopolist' is the sole producer of his product. In monopoly, the distinction between the firm and industry, so important in perfect competition, goes. The monopolist's firm is not only a firm, it is also an industry. It is the only firm producing the product in question. The firm, that is to say, takes on the characteristics of the industry and has an average revenue curve which slopes downwards just as the demand curve for the product of an industry slopes downwards.

2. Pure monopoly

As we shall see, while in monopoly each firm is the only producer of a given good, this good still has to compete indirectly with all other goods. For each of these is competing for the same consumers' incomes. In this sense, there will usually be *some* competition between all goods, even though it will often be so small that it can be ignored. Before embarking on the analysis of monopoly, it will be useful to look first at the limiting case of pure or perfect monopoly, where competition even in this limited form is completely absent. We have already given a definition of 'pure' monopoly, and have shown that it would occur when the average revenue curve of the firm was a rectangular hyperbola with an elasticity of demand equal to one, and when the monopolist took the whole of the community's income all the time.[1] It is important to remember that unlike perfect competition, which is a reasonable approximation to reality in certain industries, pure monopoly is merely a theoretical limiting case.

[1]See pp. 105–6.

No-one is a complete monopolist, because in the end all producers must be competing for the limited incomes of consumers. Ultimately, all goods compete with each other, however distantly or indirectly. This means that the only way to be a perfect monopolist would be to produce *all* goods. It is therefore useful to distinguish 'monopoly' where the producer faces competition but not very close competition, and 'pure monopoly' where there is no competition at all. A real-world monopolist is an imperfect competitor rather than the sole, absolute seller of all commodities.

Our explanation of the way in which a 'pure' monopolist would fix his output and price need not detain us long; the answer is very simple. Since a 'pure' monopolist earns a fixed and constant amount of money (the whole of all consumers' incomes) whatever price he charges, his profits will be at a maximum when his total costs are as low as possible. This will happen when he is producing a very small output (presumably only one unit) and selling it for an extremely high price. It could never pay a pure monopolist to produce more than a very small output so long as his costs were positive.

One merely has to state the kind of price-output policy a pure monopolist would follow to see how unrealistic the idea of pure monopoly is. No one producer in any country is in such a powerful position that he can sell a minute amount of his product for a fantastically high price, taking the whole of consumers' incomes in the process. Pure monopoly is merely a theoretical limit. For a more realistic analysis, we turn to a producer who is called a 'monopolist' in the real world. We consider the producer who controls the whole supply of a *single* commodity which has no close substitutes. The question of how such a monopolist will fix his price and output is much more important.

3. Monopoly equilibrium

If we define a monopolist as the sole producer of a product which has no closely-competing substitutes, it is possible to generalise about his price-output policy and to compare the equilibrium of the firm under monopoly with its equilibrium under perfect competition. It is important to remember at the outset that monopoly is an extreme form of imperfect competition. It follows that the average revenue curve of the firm will slope downwards throughout its length.

One can at once say two things. First, no monopolist will ever fix the output of his product at any level where the elasticity of his average revenue curve is less than one. If he were to do so, it would always be possible for him to increase his total receipts by restricting his output. We have seen that when elasticity of demand on any average revenue curve is less than one, the monopolist's total receipts will always fall if his sales increase—marginal revenue will always be negative. It follows that total revenue will rise if his sales are decreased. Conversely, provided that a monopolist's marginal costs are not negative (which is most unlikely), he will always be able to earn larger profits by reducing his output whenever he is producing an output at which the elasticity of demand for his product is less than one.

The reason is simple. Since marginal costs are invariably positive, a reduction in output will reduce total costs. At the same time, since elasticity of demand is less than one, a reduction in output will also raise total revenue. Profits must therefore rise as output is reduced. So long as a monopolist has positive marginal costs, the usual situation, it will never pay him to produce an output where the elasticity of demand for his product is less than one.

If the elasticity of a monopolist's average revenue curve were equal to one over a small range of outputs, he would be completely indifferent which of those outputs he produced *only* if marginal cost were zero. Since marginal cost will normally be positive, it will pay the monopolist to reduce his output until the elasticity of demand for his product becomes greater than one. Over the range where elasticity of demand is one, any reduction in output will reduce total costs. Since elasticity is equal to one, it will leave total revenue at exactly the same level as before. We are assuming here that, as with all normal average revenue curves, a range where elasticity is equal to one will have elasticity greater than one at all points to the left of it.

To sum up, a monopolist's equilibrium position will always be where the elasticity of demand for his product is greater than one. Only where elasticity of demand is less than one, will a monopolist with positive marginal costs he able to find an output where, if he decreases production, revenue falls by more than cost. If elasticity were equal to one or greater than one, the reduction in output would always raise profit.

3.1 Monopoly equilibrium in diagrams

Figure 8.1 shows an extreme situation where a monopolist has no costs of production. He may possess a mineral spring. This is a time-honoured example in economics of production without costs. The equilibrium position will be where the monopolist produces the output OM and sells it at OP pence per unit. This will maximise his receipts. Since he has no costs, it will also maximise his profits. At point R, the average revenue curve will have an elasticity equal to one and the monopolist's total receipts will be at a maximum. Marginal revenue will be zero, as it always is when elasticity of demand equals one. It will equal marginal cost.

Figure 8.2 shows the more usual situation where the monopolist has positive marginal costs. We have assumed that these costs are constant at OC, but only to simplify the analysis. Here, the monopolist is not interested in any part of his average revenue curve beyond

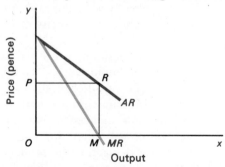

Fig. 8.1

point R, because beyond R elasticity of demand is less than one. Between R and R_1 the curve has an elasticity equal to one. Since his marginal costs are positive, it will pay the monopolist to reduce output at least as far as R_1. If the producer's average revenue curve had an elasticity of demand equal to one at all points to the left of R, it would pay him to reduce his output until he was selling as little as possible (presumably one unit) for an extremely high price. This would not, of course, mean that the producer was a 'pure' monopolist. As we have seen, such a producer must not only have an average revenue

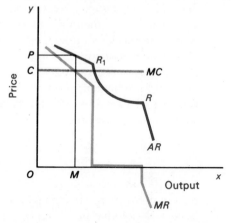

Fig. 8.2

curve of unit elasticity; he must also take all consumers' incomes all the time.

In practice, it is likely that every monopolist will have a range of his average revenue curve (in Fig. 8.2 to the left of R_1) where elasticity of demand for his product is greater than one. A monopolist like the one in Fig. 8.2 will therefore produce where output is OM, marginal revenue equals marginal cost and the elasticity of the average revenue curve at this output is greater than one. Since demand curves with unit elasticity throughout are unlikely to occur, the real world monopolist (unless he has zero marginal costs) will normally produce where elasticity of demand is greater than one.

4. Monopoly and perfect competition compared

The scope and nature of the range of individual situations covered by the general term, monopoly, means that it is not possible to find a single, typical case of monopoly or to generalise about monopoly so as to be able to compare it simply with perfect competition. Nevertheless, we can point to some differences between monopoly and perfect competition. The first common feature is that in both equilibrium occurs at the output where marginal revenue equals marginal cost. However, even here, there are differences between the two types of competition.

4.1 The marginal cost curve at the equilibrium output

In particular, where there is perfect competition, the marginal cost curve must always be rising at or near the output where the firm is in equilibrium. This follows from the fact that there are many firms in a perfectly competitive industry so that the average revenue curve and the marginal revenue curve of the firm are both horizontal and are, indeed, identical. As was shown earlier,[1] the perfectly-competitive firm is in equilibrium only where the marginal cost curve cuts the marginal revenue curve from below. If the marginal cost curve cuts the marginal revenue curve from above, profits are at a minimum, not at a maximum. Since the marginal revenue curve is horizontal in perfect competition, this means that if the marginal cost curve is to cut it from below, then marginal cost must be rising at and near the equilibrium output. Falling cost curves are incompatible with equilibrium under perfect competition.

As we have seen, Marshall tried to find reasons for supposing that the firm's cost curve in perfect competition would not continue to slope downwards as the firm's expansion continued over a period of time. For if the firm's marginal cost curve did fall continuously over a very large range of output, it could never cut a horizontal average revenue curve from below. There could never be equilibrium. With its continually falling cost curve, the firm would expand until it became so large that its average and marginal revenue curves ultimately began to fall too. The firm would have become so large that competition had become imperfect and would increasingly affect the price of its product if it made further increases in its output.

[1] See p. 173.

Consequently, its marginal revenue curve would slope downwards and would ultimately slope steeply enough to cut the downward-sloping marginal cost curve. In the end, an equilibrium position would be reached because competition ceased to be perfect. Perfect competition is incompatible with a continuously downward-sloping marginal cost curve.

This is the first difference between perfect and imperfect competition. While in perfect competition the marginal cost curve of the firm must be rising at or near the equilibrium output, in imperfect competition this need not be so. A monopolistic firm can be in equilibrium with rising, falling or constant marginal costs. The only conditions which must be satisfied if there is to be equilibrium are that marginal revenue shall equal marginal cost, and that the marginal cost curve shall cut the marginal revenue curve *from below*.

5. Monopoly equilibrium in more detail

Let us analyse monopoly equilibrium in more detail.

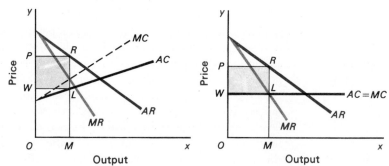

Figs. 8.3 | 8.4

5.1 Rising marginal costs

In Fig. 8.3, marginal cost is rising. This ensures that there is equilibrium in monopoly, as it does in perfect competition. The equilibrium output in Fig. 8.3 is OM and the monopoly price is OP. The 'super-normal' or 'monopoly' profits being earned are shown by the grey rectangle $PRLW$.

5.2 Constant marginal costs

In Fig. 8.4, marginal costs are constant and are equal to average costs. This condition is incompatible with equilibrium under perfect competition. If a firm could afford to produce at all under these circumstances, there would be no limit to its size in perfect competition. The monopolist in Fig. 8.4 *is* in equilibrium. Equilibrium output is OM, monopoly price is OP and monopoly profits are shown by the area $PRLW$.

5.3 Falling
marginal costs

Monopoly equilibrium is also possible with falling marginal costs, as in Fig. 8.5. Again, monopoly output is *OM*, monopoly price *OP* and monopoly profits *PRLW*. The marginal cost curve must cut the marginal revenue curve from below (or from the left), but so long as it does so there can be equilibrium. If marginal costs are falling more rapidly than marginal revenue, with the marginal cost curve cutting the marginal revenue curve from above, equilibrium is clearly impossible even in monopoly. In practice, if this happened the growing size of the firm relatively to its market would mean that ultimately the marginal revenue curve fell more rapidly than the marginal cost curve. The only situation incompatible with monopoly equilibrium is thus where marginal costs are falling more swiftly than marginal revenue. This cannot happen except over short periods of time; before long, the firm begins to dominate its market so strongly that marginal revenue falls faster than marginal cost.

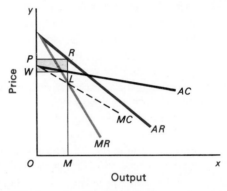

Fig. 8.5

5.4 A summing
up

To sum up, equilibrium for the firm under perfect competition can occur only when the marginal cost curve of the firm is rising at and near the equilibrium output. Equilibrium under monopoly can occur whether marginal costs are rising, falling or constant. The only situation in which monopoly equilibrium is impossible is when the firm's falling marginal cost curve is steeper than its marginal revenue curve.

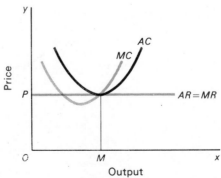

Fig. 8.6

The second major difference between equilibrium under perfect competition and under monopoly lies in the size of profits. We have seen that in perfect competition the entrepreneur will, in the long run, be unable to earn supernormal profits.

In Fig. 8.6 the perfectly competitive firm is in long-run equilibrium, earning only normal profits. Supernormal profits can be earned in the short run, but in the long run they will be competed away by new entrants into the industry. Thus the long-run conditions of equilibrium for the firm in perfect competition can be summarised as follows:

Total cost=Total revenue.
Average cost=Average revenue.
Marginal cost=Marginal revenue.

In addition, these last four items will be equal to each other and to price. In the short run, if demand for the industry's product increases, price rises and supernormal profits are earned. In the long run, these supernormal profits disappear, and only normal profits are earned.

In monopoly it is quite possible for the firm to earn supernormal profits in the long run. The firms shown in Figs. 8.3, 8.4 and 8.5 were in short-run equilibrium and were earning supernormal profits. But it is not necessary to assume that such profits will be competed away even in the long run. Free entry may not be possible in monopoly situations for institutional or technical reasons, and if free entry is absent then the monopolist may be able to protect himself against competition for a very long time. Of course, if there is freedom of entry and competitive firms begin to produce close substitutes for the monopolist's good, the firm ceases to be a monopolist. The second difference between competition and monopoly is therefore that monopoly profits can be maintained even in the long run. This does not mean, however, that a firm cannot, even under monopoly, be earning only normal profits.

In Fig. 8.7 we have the interesting case of a firm producing with a

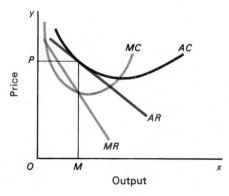

Fig. 8.7

downward-sloping average revenue curve denoting imperfect competition, but earning only normal profits—for its average cost curve is tangent to its average revenue curve. It will be noted, however, that such a firm must be producing at less than optimum size. In other words, it will not be producing at minimum average cost. A downward-sloping average revenue curve can never be tangent to a U-shaped average cost curve at or beyond its lowest point. The second difference between competition and monopoly is that in the long run a competitor can never earn abnormal profits whilst a monopolist can do and usually does.

6. Degrees of monopoly

We have seen that in monopoly the firm's average revenue curve will always slope downwards. This means that its marginal revenue curve will always lie below its average revenue curve. Since the firm is in equilibrium where marginal revenue equals marginal cost, it follows that in equilibrium marginal cost is less than average revenue; marginal cost is less than price. The size of this difference between marginal cost and price is sometimes used to measure the extent of the firm's monopoly power. In perfect competition, when a firm is in long-run equilibrium, marginal cost equals price. When a firm is in a strong monopolistic position, marginal cost is considerably less than price. Economists therefore refer to the difference between marginal cost and price as measuring the *degree of monopoly*. The larger the difference between marginal cost and price, the greater is the firm's monopoly power.

This gap between marginal cost and price will depend ultimately on the elasticity of demand for the firm's product—on the elasticity of its average revenue curve. This follows from the equations which we gave on page 136 to show the relationship between marginal and average revenue. The lower the numerical elasticity of demand, the farther does marginal revenue at any output lie below average revenue—the farther, when the firm is in an equilibrium position, does marginal cost fall short of price. Differing elasticities of demand, shown by varying differences between price and marginal cost, are useful measures of the degree of monopoly. The lower is elasticity of demand, the greater is the 'degree of monopoly'.

A second indication of the strength of a monopoly is the size of the supernormal profits the firm is able to earn. In perfect competition firms will be unable for long to earn more than normal profits, because, if they do, competitors will enter the industry. With monopoly, new entrants will not normally compete monopoly profits away in this manner. But there will usually be some level of profits at which new firms will find it worth taking the risk of trying to break the monopoly. The stronger the monopolist's position, the greater the profits he will be able to earn without attracting rivals. The size of monopoly profits is thus another (perhaps more reliable) measure of the monopoly power possessed by any firm.

7. Monopoly in practice

We have seen that, for monopoly to exist, the only condition required is that within whatever is the relevant market area there shall be no close substitutes for the products of the firm in question. For example, the monopolist may own the whole stock of some mineral which is not found elsewhere in the world. Or is may perform a distinctive service which no one else within easy (and cheap) travelling distance can perform. It may, for example, be an exclusive furnisher or decorator.

7.1 Who are the monopolists?

It follows that many firms which are described as monopolists in discussion in the press, radio or television are not monopolists in the economist's sense of the word at all. A large chemical firm may well be a monopolist in the production of a few particular drugs or chemicals, but probably only a few. Many of its products will be competing, often indeed quite fiercely, with similar products made by other large firms. Indeed, the best example of a monopoly, defined as an economist defines it, may be a small business supplying a service to a limited area. One example will be a restaurant which supplies food and drink at the top of a high mountain. If the only competitors are at the foot of the mountain, the restaurant will be able to take advantage of its isolated position by charging high prices. So will the caterer at a football, cricket or baseball match. Unless spectators leave the ground, they have to choose either to pay whatever price the caterer asks for food or drink or go without. There is no competition within the ground. In both these cases, the caterer is likely to decide to charge higher prices than other food suppliers nearby, who face more competition from other restaurants, shops or supermarkets. Such a firm is a monopolist within a limited area, and perhaps for a limited period of time, in the sense in which the term is used by an economist.

This is not to say that no large firms are monopolists in the economist's sense. In the United Kingdom, for example, British Oxygen supplied virtually the whole of the market for oxygen for a long period. Other firms have had monopolies of particular, often patented, products for differing periods. For most products, however, there is some competition from similar if not identical products made by other firms. Competition is clearly not pure where there is monopoly in the economist's sense, but limited competition often does exist. Indeed, in the strict sense, there will always be *some* competition for the monopolist, since all products compete, if only indirectly, for consumers' limited incomes. The point that is being made is that, in the real world, it is often the small monopoly which is likely to be the most effective.

7.2 Potential competition

It is also important to point out that an important factor influencing the monopolist's price-output policy will be his fear of *potential* competition. The highly profitable monopoly, by making other firm's feel that this is a chance for them to make large profits also, will represent a strong force attracting new firms to any field. No monopolist will dare to ignore the possibility that if he makes very large profits, by equating marginal revenue with marginal cost, this will merely make it more certain than ever that he will attract the competition of rivals. Obviously, the likelihood that competition will be attracted in this way will depend on the source of the monopoly. Where technical factors are the foundation of monopoly, in the sense that the smallest technically-possible production unit can easily supply the whole market, a 'natural' monopoly of this kind will be hard to break. However, the most widespread basis of monopoly to-day is institutional factors, like patents and trade marks. With these, one can never be sure how safe one's monopoly is. Patents, for example, do not last for all that long, and may not represent a complete protection even while they do. Certainly, for a monopolist to rely on institutional support to protect his profits is to invite competitors to find loopholes in his legal protection, or to find ways of producing close substitutes for his product without breaking the law. The best and most profitable course for any monopolist may be to preserve that monopoly by being content with reasonable prices and moderate returns over a long period of time. Trying to earn as much as possible in a short period may simply lead to a price fall brought about because the high returns attract new entrants into the monopolist's market. *Potential* competition is the most important constraint on the monopolist.

The safest conclusion about monopoly may well be that there is no simple explanation of monopoly policies. One cannot expect precise and clear-cut answers in a situation where, because of the lack of competition, the individual producer has considerable freedom of action and could, if he wished, follow any one of a variety of different policies.

8. Discrimi-nating monopoly

'Discriminating monopoly' or 'price discrimination' occurs when a monopolist charges different prices for different units of a commodity, even though these units are identical in their physical characteristics. The extent to which such discrimination can occur will obviously depend on the circumstances. In a very favourable situation, it is just conceivable that the price charged could be different for every individual unit of a homogeneous commodity. Such a situation is described as 'perfectly discriminating monopoly'. It is much more likely that one will find that different *individual consumers* are charged different prices for their purchases. It would be most unusual to find a single consumer being offered a number of units of an identical good each at different prices. Discrimination between buyers is more usual than is discrimination between units of a homogeneous good. However, it will be more usual still for a different price to be charged to different groups of consumers' Each member of such a group will be offered goods at exactly the same price as each other.

It should be clear at once that discrimination between customers is incompatible with perfect competition. If there are many sellers of a homogeneous good, it is a quite simple matter for a consumer who feels that he is being overcharged by one supplier to go to another. It would be impossible in perfect competition for one seller to charge 10p for an article and the others 5p. Any customer who was asked for 10p could easily go to other sellers to get the good for 5p. Price discrimination can only occur where there is imperfect competition; but the relationship is not reversible. Price discrimination does not always occur when there is imperfect competition.

Of course, a number of imperfectly-competing sellers may carry out a jointly-agreed policy of price discrimination. If they do, this will lead to the same results as discriminating monopoly. In this analysis of discriminating monopoly, we shall assume that it is a single monopolist in whose policy we are interested. Our results hold good without significant qualification if discrimination occurs through collective agreement between firms in other types of imperfect competition. We shall assume throughout this analysis that the monopolist always maximises his profits.

We must first decide in what conditions price discrimination is possible at all. We have seen that it is impossible under perfect competition. It may also be impossible even under monopoly. The fundamental condition which must be fulfilled if discrimination is to take place is that there can be no possibility of resale from one consumer to another. If the same product is supplied to Brown at 14p and to Smith at 5p, and if Brown and Smith can exchange goods freely, discrimination will break down. Smith will buy the product for both of them. If price discrimination is to succeed, communication between buyers in different sectors of the monopolist's market must be impossible, or at any rate extremely difficult. In technical language, there must be little or no 'seepage' between the discriminating monopolist's different markets.

9. Conditions for price discrimination

It follows that if price discrimination is to succeed there must always be some reason why consumers in different parts of the monopolist's market cannot communicate. This limits the possibilities for price discrimination fairly narrowly. There are three main situations where price discrimination between consumers can occur, even though there is no fundamental difference between the goods offered to these consumers. These are as follows:

9.1
Discrimination owing to consumers' peculiarities

Discrimination of this type can occur for three main reasons:

1. It can happen where consumer A is unaware that consumer B gets the same goods more cheaply. To put this more generally, discrimination can happen when consumers in one part of the market do not know that prices are lower in another.

2. It can exist where the consumer has an irrational feeling that though he is paying a higher price he is paying it for a better good. For instance, it is probably irrational to think that one gets a better view of a film from the front row of the 100p seats than from the back row of the 50p seats, if these are two consecutive rows.

3. Discrimination can occur if price differences are so small that the consumer does not think it worth paying attention to them.

9.2
Discrimination based on the nature of the good

This type of discrimination occurs particularly when the good in question is a direct service. While it is possible for butter to be resold by a customer who is charged a lower price to one who pays a higher price, it is impossible to do this with haircuts or manicures. The resale of direct services is impossible. Of course, what may appear to be homogeneous goods are often not really homogeneous. For example, it is clearly not realistic to think that a film is just as enjoyable when seen from the front row of a cinema as it would be from farther back. The service provided to the consumer is not the same; it is not homogeneous.

It may be noticed in passing that in the past an important example of this type of discrimination in the UK was of the doctor who charged a poor man £1 for removing his tonsils, while he charged a rich man £100. The establishment of the National Health Service has largely robbed us in Britain of this practical illustration, though it may still hold for private patients in Britain and for other patients in other countries. In any case, it may be that doctors are not quite as anxious to maximise profits as are business men.

9.3
Discrimination
because of
distances and
frontier barriers

Discrimination often occurs where consumers are separated by distance or where the fact that a national frontier separates two markets means that tariffs can be levied at that frontier. In such cases, prices can diverge. A good may be sold in one town for 10p and in another for 20p. So long as the cost of transport is at least 10p per unit, resale will not be profitable. Again, where a monopolist serves two different markets, say, a home market with a tariff and a world market without a tariff, he can take advantage of the tariff barrier to raise his price in the protected market. Similarly, tariffs on imports into a country would allow a monopolist producing in that country to keep up the price in his home market. Clearly, none of this results from the nature of the goods sold but is a result of artificial or geographical barriers between one of the monopolist's markets and another.

It should be noted that all these forms of price discrimination depend ultimately on the monopolist's power to ensure that no-one else sells his products to his customer at a lower price. His ability to discriminate will depend on his ability to retain his customers, even if rivals enter his market, because enough customers prefer to patronise his firm. In many cases, however, discrimination will be possible only because *all* producers discriminate in the same way. In the case of doctors, for example, the practice of charging high fees to rich people depends ultimately on enough members of the profession accepting this as a convention. In other cases, there may be legal sanction for price discrimination—as with the sale of electricity at different prices for different purposes. In this case, the customer will be liable to penalties if he tries to save money by taking electricity at one price for one purpose and using it for another.

10. The analysis of price discrimination

We have now seen the conditions in which price discrimination is possible. When will it be profitable? This question can be answered by applying the ordinary theory of the firm to a case where there are two (or more) markets instead of one. This complicates the analysis but does not affect its fundamentals. We can still base our theorising on the assumption that the monopolist seeks maximum profits and therefore fixes his output so as to equate marginal revenue with marginal cost. Now, however, the firm has two separate markets, so that marginal revenue and marginal cost must be looked at simultaneously in both of them. We shall assume that there are large numbers of buyers in each market so that there is perfect competition between buyers within each of them. We shall also assume that buyers in the one market are unable to trade profitably by selling the commodity to buyers in the other.

On the sellers' side, we assume initially that the monopolist is a monopolist in both markets. This means that his average revenue curve will slope downwards in each market. We also assume that price discrimination is physically *possible*. It will be *profitable* only if elasticity of demand in the one market is different from elasticity of demand in the other. In general, it will pay a monopolist to discriminate between two markets only if elasticity of demand is different in each market, though there may be exceptions even to this rule. Let us examine the two possible cases.

10.1 Elasticity of demand the same in each market

Let us assume that elasticity of demand in each market is the same at each price as elasticity of demand in the other. This means that the average revenue curves in the two markets both slope downwards, each changing its elasticity at the same rate. The fact that the two markets are unable to communicate with each other then does not matter. Demand in each is of the same quality and price discrimination will not pay. The monopolist will treat the two markets as one. He will add together horizontally the two average revenue curves and the two marginal revenue curves and his profit-maximising price will be where marginal cost equals marginal revenue. He will then sell all output at this price.

10.2 Elasticity of demand different in each market

If the elasticities of demand in the two markets at all the relevant prices are different, the monopolist may be able to profit from price discrimination. Provided he wants to earn maximum profits he normally will discriminate. It is possible, of course, that the monopolist may be legally forbidden to pursue a policy of price discrimination. If this is so, he would generally charge the monopoly price which would maximise profits. He would equate marginal cost with marginal revenue for the two markets added together.

We shall assume here, however, that discrimination is not prevented by law. The question which the monopolist now asks is: 'Is elasticity of demand the same in both markets at the single monopoly price?' If elasticity *is* the same in each market at that price, the monopolist will not discriminate, even though the elasticities may be different at *all other* prices. For if elasticity at the single monopoly price is the same in each market, marginal revenue will also be the same. This follows from the formula Marginal Revenue=Average Revenue $\times \frac{e-1}{e}$, where e is point elasticity of demand. If average revenue (single monopoly price) is the same in each market and elasticity of demand is also the same, then it follows immediately from the formula that marginal revenue in each market will be the same. This means that if a marginal quantity of output is transferred from one market to the other, there will be no gain in total revenue. What is gained in the one market will be lost in the other; there is no motive for discrimination here.

Let us now assume that at the single monopoly price the elasticity of demand is different in each market. Even now, discrimination may not pay, as can be seen from Fig. 8.8. In Fig. 8.8a for Market 1 marginal cost equals marginal revenue at the output of OM_1, and the monopolist will maximise profit if he charges the price OP and sells the quantity OM_1. However, in Market 2 in Fig. 8.8b there is *no* output at which marginal revenue equals marginal cost. The only price at which *any* quantity of the good can be sold is less than marginal cost. It will therefore pay the monopolist to sell only in Market 1,

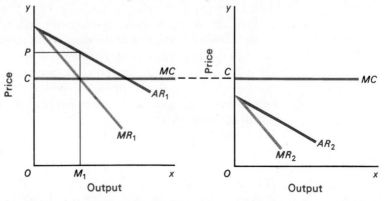

Fig. 8.8 a | b

where he will sell the quantity OM_1 at the price OP. This will maximise his profits.

However, if at all prices, including the single monopoly price, elasticity of demand is different and it is profitable to sell in both markets, price discrimination will pay. If the elasticity of demand is lower in one market (Market A) the price there will be raised even above the single monopoly price for the two markets together. Since demand in Market A is relatively inelastic, it is relatively insensitive to price changes and a rise in price will not cause much fall in demand. Similarly, if elasticity of demand is greater in the other market (Market B) demand will there be more responsive to price reductions. It will therefore pay to lower the price of the good in Market B below the single monopoly price. For, since elasticity of demand is lower in Market A, an increase in price and a decrease in sales will decrease revenue only a little. In Market B, elasticity of demand is higher and a reduction in price will add more to revenue than it does to cost. It will pay the monopolist who is charging the single monopoly price to transfer goods from Market A with the inelastic demand to Market B with the elastic demand. The loss of revenue from reducing sales by one (marginal) unit in Market A, which has inelastic demand will be smaller than the gain in revenue from expanding sales by one (marginal) unit in the Market B, which has elastic demand. Prices will consequently rise in Market A while they fall in Market B. This follows from the formula cited above. When average revenue is given, marginal revenue will be greater the greater is elasticity of demand. So where average revenue (single monopoly price) is exactly the same in each market, marginal revenue will be greater where elasticity is greater (Market B) and vice versa. How long will it be worth while continuing this process of transferring units of the good from the market with the low elasticity of demand to the one with the high elasticity? Let us analyse this problem in two stages.

(a) Output already produced

Let us first assume that the monopolist has a given output already produced and merely wants to distribute it in the most profitable way between the two markets. Let us consider a situation where the elasticities of demand in the two markets are different and where marginal revenues in the two markets are therefore different also, but where the monopolist begins by distributing his output between the two markets in such a way that the single monopoly price obtains in each. In order to maximise profit, the monopolist will restrict his sales in the market with the less elastic demand (Market A), and expand it in the market with the more elastic demand (Market B). He will do this because he is adding more to his revenue in Market B than he is taking away from his revenue in Market A. Since to begin with price (single monopoly price) is the same in each market, so marginal revenue is greater in Market B than in Market A. This follows from the formula given above.

The discriminating monopolist will therefore move up the marginal revenue curve in Market A (by restricting sales and raising price) and down the marginal revenue curve in Market B (by expanding sales and lowering price) until the marginal revenues in each market are equal. Once marginal revenue in the two markets is equal, he will stop switching sales from one market to the other. He will gain nothing in switching a marginal unit of output and will actually lose if he continues the process because marginal revenue in the market with low elasticity of demand will eventually become less than marginal revenue in the other.

It should be noted that in this equilbrium position price will be different in the two markets. Elasticity of demand will differ also. It follows from our formula that if marginal revenue in each market is to be the same but price is to be different, elasticity of demand will also differ. Price will be higher in the market with the less-elastic demand and vice versa. We therefore see that if the output to be distributed between his two markets is fixed in amount, it will be most profitable for a discriminating monopolist to divide it between the markets in such a way that the two (or more) marginal revenues are equal when the whole output is just being disposed of in one market or the other(s). Only when the marginal revenues in two markets are equal will it become unprofitable to shift output from one market to the other. It will be realised that since the output is supposed to have been produced already, cost is irrelevant. All cost is 'sunk' cost. What is relevant is opportunity cost—the sacrifice of profit if output is sold at a lower price in one market than could have been obtained in the other. For example, if price is 10p in one market and 6p in the other the opportunity cost of selling a unit at 6p is the 10p which could have been earned in the other market.

(b) Variable output

Let us now assume that total output is not already available and fixed in this way but has not yet been produced. Once again, marginal revenues in the two markets must be equal if profits are to be maximised. But it is essential now not only that marginal revenue should be the same in each market, but that this marginal revenue should also be equal to the marginal cost of producing the whole output. This is the condition of equilibrium in discriminating monopoly. The position may be shown in a rather complicated diagram, Fig. 8.9.

Figure 8.9 refers to a producer selling in two different markets. For simplicity, we assume that he is a monopolist only in one market and that the other is perfectly competitive. In Market H, the home market, the producer is a monopolist and the elasticity of demand for his product is not very great. His light-brown average revenue curve AR_H slopes downwards. So does the dashed marginal revenue curve MR_H. In the world market, W, there is perfect competition, and elasticity of demand for the product is infinite. The dark-brown average revenue curve AR_W is a horizontal straight line and coincides with the marginal revenue curve for the world market MR_W.

In Fig. 8.9, the marginal cost curve for the monopolist is the dashed curve MC. In order to discover how much output it is worth producing altogether, the monopolist must find where this marginal cost curve intersects the combined marginal revenue curve $ARTD$. Once the

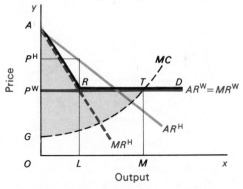

Fig. 8.9

size of total output has been determined, the shares to go to each market can be decided by allocating the output in such a way that marginal revenues are equal in each market. In Fig. 8.9 the combined marginal revenue curve $ARTD$ is a composite curve. On this curve, marginal revenue in the world market is added sideways to marginal revenue at home. The intersection of the monopolist's marginal cost curve with the combined marginal revenue curve (at T) gives a total output of OM as that which maximises profits.

This output OM must now be shared between the two markets. It is clear from Fig. 8.9 that the only way in which the marginal revenues in each market can be equal to each other and to marginal cost (MT) is for OL to be sold in the home market at a price of OP_H and a marginal revenue of RL. This leaves LM to be sold in the world market at a price of OP_W and with a marginal revenue (MT) equal to OP_W. MT is also the same as RL. Price is thus higher (OP_H) in the monopolistic home market than in the competitive world market (OP_W). The monopolist's total profits are represented by the grey area $ARTG$. These profits are at a maximum and are contributed to by both markets.

When both markets are monopolistic, it is still possible to show what the monopolist's price and output will be in Fig. 8.10. Figures 8.10a and 8.10b show the average and marginal revenue curves of this firm for two separate markets (Markets 1 and 2). These markets have different elasticities of demand at each price. In Fig. 8.10c the profit maximising output is shown to be determined by the inter-section of the dashed black marginal cost curve for the monopolist's whole output (MC), with the dashed brown curve showing the combined revenue earned from the two markets (CMR). The curve CMR is obtained by adding the curves MR_1 and MR_2 together sideways. In this equilibrium situation, output is OM and marginal revenue is $OL = MR$. This output of OM has to be distributed between the two markets in such a way that marginal revenue in each is OL. This means that OM_1 must be sold in Market 1. With sales at that

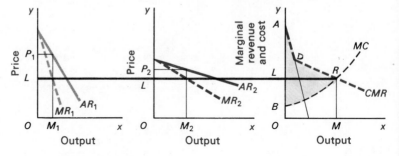

Fig. 8.10 a b c

level, marginal revenue in Market 1 is OL. Price is OP_1. Similarly, OM_2 must be sold in Market 2, at a price of OP_2. Marginal revenue here is OL. The monopolist's profit is shown by the grey area $ADRB$ in Fig. 8.10c and is at a maximum. This same solution in terms of marginal and average revenues and costs could, of course, be shown by combining Figs. 8.10a, 8.10b and 8.10c in a single diagram, but it would be somewhat complicated.

We have seen that if a discriminating monopolist is to be in equilibrium, three conditions have to be fulfilled. First, it must be profitable for him to sell output in more than one market. Second, marginal revenue in both (or all) markets must be the same. Third, these marginal revenues must also equal the marginal cost of producing the monopolist's aggregate output. We have looked at these three conditions separately but it is important to remember that they have to hold simultaneously. In other words, $MR_1 = MR_2 = MC$ is nothing more than an application, for situations where price discrimination is worthwhile, of the general principle. It applies the rule that: 'in equilibrium marginal revenue equals marginal cost' to the special case where discrimination between different parts of the market is possible.

Suggested reading

ROBINSON, E. A. G.   *Monopoly*, London, 1948, *passim*.

ROBINSON, JOAN   *Economics of Imperfect Competition*, London, 1933, especially chapters iii, iv, v, xv and xvi.

9

Monopolistic competition

**1.
Monopolistic
competition**

In our analysis of imperfect competition, we have so far concerned ourselves with the problems of firms run by individual monopolists, producing products which do not compete closely with any other goods. We have seen that in such firms the extent of monopoly power will be indicated by the shape of the average revenue curve. However, we have assumed that the position and shape of the monopolist's average revenue curve is given. We have not needed to say anything more about the way in which it will be determined, apart from emphasising that it depends ultimately on the nature of consumers' tastes and on the number and significance of rival goods competing indirectly for consumers' incomes. There is no direct competition for a monopolist.

In the real world, imperfect competition does not usually mean that there is only one producer with no closely related goods competing with his own, as we imply when we talk of a monopolist. The great majority of imperfectly-competitive firms sell goods which are very similar to those made by their rivals. It follows that these firms are always very interested in the way in which the actions of their rivals affect their own profits. This kind of situation is dealt with in economic theory by the analysis of what is called *monopolistic competition*. One is concerned with *large-group equilibrium* where there is keen, though not perfect, competition between many firms making similar products.

The concept of monopolistic competition was introduced into economic analysis by Professor E. H. Chamberlin.[1] In monopolistic competition, it is reasonable to suppose that the shape of the firm's average revenue curve will be determined not only by the tastes of

[1]Professor E. H. Chamberlin in *The Theory of Monopolistic Competition* uses this term in the sense in which we have used 'imperfect competition' in this book. (*op. cit.* p. 9, footnote.) It has, however, become the convention to use the words *monopolistic competition* to mean a large group of firms making similar products. Since this is the main type of market situation which Professor Chamberlin analyses this seems a justifiable procedure, although he does have a good deal to say as well about competition between small numbers of firms.

consumers, but also by the pricing, output and product decisions of rival producers. The problems of monopolistic competition are therefore more complicated than those of perfect competition. In perfect competition there is only one, homogeneous commodity. In monopolistic competition there is differentiation of products.

1.1 Product differentiation

Product differentiation is an important concept in modern economic theory and we must explain it. Where products are differentiated, they are not homogeneous, as in perfect competition; neither are they remote substitutes, as in monopoly. The emphasis is on the word 'differentiated'. The products of a monopolistically-competitive group of firms are not so different that consumers regard them as quite separate products. Neither are they so similar that customers can remain indifferent about which particular firm's product they buy. Differences are big enough to make consumers prefer the product of one manufacturer in the group to those of another, but they are small enough to allow the consumers to regard the total group of competing products as quite separate from all other products of all other firms or groups of firms.

A good example is breakfast cereals. In the 1960s, one US cereal producer advertised his cereal as: 'Just a little bit better than any other cereal happens to be'. This is an excellent example of product differentiation through advertising. The product is clearly identified as a breakfast cereal but it is identified as one which is just sufficiently better than its competitors to be the one to buy. While advertising of this kind is designed to make sure that each breakfast cereal is 'differentiated' from the others, the whole group of breakfast cereals is deliberately distinguished from other foods. Otherwise, the advertising of the monopolistically-competitive group would actually be creating competition for itself. Advertising represents each product as being different enough from the others in the group to be the one to buy; but similar enough to be a member of the 'breakfast-cereal group', not another group.

In the UK, good examples of monopolistic competition are perhaps some parts of the textile, clothing, food, electronics, and engineering industries, which make consumer goods. With intermediate and capital goods, product differentiation will not be so common and will usually depend on the physical characteristics of the various products. With consumer goods, 'branding', selling in attractive packets and wrappers and the use of trademarks and tradenames are the most usual methods by which products are differentiated. This can be done even if physically they are identical, or almost so. With detergents, for example, during the 1950s and 1960s in the UK there were attempts to design packets which were the same size as those of their rivals, but which looked bigger. In addition, firms will make small improvements in or additions to the physical characteristics of the product to persuade consumers that it is rather superior to other, similar products.

To analyse monopolistic competition, we must discuss the market situation where an imperfectly-competitive producer meets keen competition from a large number of close rivals, even though none of them produces products which are identical with his own. 'Product differentiation' is a key element in the competitive situation. The analysis of monopoly given so far does not apply to this kind of situation. The average revenue curve of a firm in monopolistic competition must be considerably influenced by the price, output and product policies of rival firms.

1.2
Assumptions
about costs

Apart from this, the cost curve poses a problem too. In monopoly, we could assume that the firm's cost curve was given, since we were studying only one firm. In monopolistic competition, since many rival firms are producing rather similar products, they will all be using rather similar factors of production. The firms' cost curves must be somewhat related to each other. For example, an increased demand for factors of production because the number of firms in the monopolistic group increases, may well raise the prices of these factors to other firms in the group. The idea of independent cost curves, even if it seems acceptable under monopoly, can never be completely satisfactory in monopolistic competition. In order to simplify the analysis, we shall assume in this book that all firms in the same 'group' of monopolistically-competitive firms have identical cost curves and that these curves remain at exactly the same level whatever the number of firms in the group. In other words, we assume that all factors of production are homogeneous and in perfect elastic supply to the monopolistic group. We also assume that no external economies or diseconomies of production occur as the number of firms in the group increases. Professor Chamberlin initially makes this same assumption[1]; an 'heroic' assumption as he calls it, though he later relaxes it.

2. Where the idea of monopoly is realistic

Before we begin our analysis of monopolistic competition, it will be helpful if we try to discover the conditions in which the notion of the 'classical' monopolist, as outlined in the previous chapter, is realistic. The fundamental feature of monopolistic competition is

[1] E. H. Chamberlin, *Theory of Monopolistic Competition*, Cambridge, Mass., p. 85.

that a large number of 'differentiated' goods compete quite keenly with each other, and this seems to suggest that the idea of a single monopolist is untypical. However, there must be some situations where the idea of 'classical' monopoly is useful. Let us see what these are.

The idea of monopoly as we discussed in Chapter 8 is quite appropriate where there are several firms (let us call them A, B and C) whose products are not at all closely related—whose products are only very bad substitutes for each other. In such a situation there is no close competition between the producers. It is therefore perfectly legitimate to regard the average revenue curve of each firm as independent and given. Each of these average revenue curves will be downward-sloping. Its shape will depend on the tastes of consumers and on the reaction of *all* other producers in the economy, whatever their products, when the monopolist changes its price. It is the reactions of *all* other producers *taken together* which guides the action of the simple monopolist.

It is obvious that, in this particular case, where there are no close substitutes for the monopolist's product, he will need only to consider the large range of very distant competitors, including other monopolists. So far as A is concerned, the other monopolists, B and C, are no more serious rivals than other, even perfectly competitive, producers. Since his competitors are so distant and so many in number, it is both impossible and unnecessary for the monopolist to isolate the influence of any one of them and treat it separately. He can regard the shape of his average revenue curve as entirely determined by consumer demand and will not find it worthwhile to probe into the way in which the actions of other firms determine its position and shape.

2.1 Monopoly profit

What happens, then, if a monopolist in such a situation makes monopoly profits? Since all other goods are only very distant competitors of his own, it is not very likely that large earnings on the part of any one monopolist will cause his rivals to change their policies. There is very little reason to suppose that they will alter their own prices, outputs or products merely because he happens to be earning high profits. By definition, they do not produce the same product, nor even close substitutes. The monopolist's profits are therefore safe. He can justifiably look upon his average revenue curve as unaffected by the actions of his rivals. He has no reason to think that they will compete away his monopoly profits, *provided* there is no possibility of breaking his monopoly. This is why monopolists do worry about the *potential competition* of possible new entrants, as we saw in Chapter 8.

3. The monopolistically-competitive 'group'

In a case like this, the idea of a single monopolist is realistic. It is *not* realistic when the firm faces a large number of rivals, each producing a very close substitute for his own product. It is then impossible to analyse the situation realistically if one looks at individual producers in isolation. As in perfect competition, one is forced to concern oneself not only with the firm but also with the industry. The problems of the group of closely-competitive rivals—the monopolistic 'group', as we shall call it—must now be faced. This is much more relevant in practice than the idea of an independent monopolist. In the real world, one does often find situations where there is competition between a number of producers, each making something a little different from each of the others. Where there is a range of competing (differentiated) substitutes of this kind, elasticity of demand for each individual product will be much greater than in 'classical' monopoly, where competition is with more remote rivals. The actions of competitors will have significant effects on one's own firm and the analysis needed will be different.

4. Group equilibrium

4.1 Relations within and between groups

We begin our discussion of monopolistic competition by considering the nature of competition in the monopolistic 'group' or 'industry'. When one has imperfect competition between a group of producers all making similar products, it turns out that the limits of the industry are not so easy to define as they were under perfect competition. There is some degree of competition *between* monopolistic groups of firms. Since the characteristic feature of monopolistic competition is product differentiation, the simplicity of perfect competition disappears. There is no longer a clear dividing line between an industry making homogeneous products and the rest of the economy. In monopolistic competition, there are bound to be many cases where firms could be legitimately classified as belonging to two or more industries.

The assumption used in Professor Chamberlin's theory of the monopolistically-competitive group is that one can nevertheless discover situations where a number of firms are making very similar products, all competing with each other. Beyond this group of firms there is a large 'gap' in the chain of substitutes, so that one can reasonably regard the closely-competitive producers as forming an 'industry' or 'group' of monopolistic competitors. For example, let us assume that each clothing and each textile firm produces only one product (which is of course untrue). It is then reasonable to regard the products of the various clothing firms as competing very closely with each other, but it would not be sensible to think that there was equally close competition between clothing firms and, say, firms making furnishing fabrics or man-made-fibre used as tyre-cord for automobile tyres. While furnishing fabric and clothing are very similar technically, they are not regarded by consumers as closely competitive goods. So far as consumers are concerned, competition between clothing, on the one hand, and the products of the textile 'groups', furnishing fabric, carpets, etc., on the other, is not much greater than competition between clothing and cinemas, automobiles, houses and so on.

Each firm in the monopolistic 'group' making up the 'clothing industry' has a downward-sloping average revenue curve. This is first because clothes will not be identical, as they would be if there were perfect competition. Second, it is because there will presumably not be quite as many firms in the 'industry' as there would be if competition were perfect. The shape of each firm's average revenue curve will now be determined not only by the competition of distant rivals in other 'industries', about whose actions the individual firm need not worry. It will also be determined by the actions of the very close rivals within the same monopolistic 'group', whose actions will need to be carefully watched.

In monopolistic competition, the firm earning monopoly profits has to be very alert if it is to safeguard them. If one firm is making large monopolistic profits by producing a popular new product, there will clearly be a temptation for other firms in the same group to manufacture products which are similar to the products of the successful firm, but not so similar that they cannot be 'differentiated' in sales campaigns. The more directly other firms can compete with the firm making large profits, the more money they will be able to earn for themselves. Since all firms in the group are making similar products, they will all be in a position, should they wish to do so, to compete away part of the profits of the innovator by making their products more similar to his.

It is therefore reasonable to assume that all products made by a group of monopolistic competitors can, if necessary, be made more like each other, even though they will not be made identical. One can also assume that any very profitable product made by one member of the group will soon be made by many others, though with slight variations in design. If the products of the group are, say, motor cars and one firm starts to make a fortune by introducing a new kind of engine, other firms will follow. This means that in monopolistic competition large profits earned by individual firms will be competed away in the long run. Since the products made by firms in the group cannot be identical, it is unlikely that abnormal profits will be eliminated completely. The fact that these products are very similar, in conjunction with our 'heroic' assumption of identical cost curves, means that high profits earned by one firm are bound to be eaten into. If *all* existing firms are making large profits, then, unless the industry is protected by restrictions on entry, new firms will be able to enter the group and compete away these profits by producing yet more rather similar products.

The conclusion to be drawn from this analysis is thus that, in the short run, when there is monopolistic competition in an industry but the number of firms is fixed, they can all earn abnormal profits or losses. In the long run, however, the position will be similar to the long-run position in a perfectly-competitive industry. Large profits will be competed away. The result will be that in monopolistic competition the long-run equilibrium position will be one where the profits of the firms in the industry represent a 'normal' frequency distribution of profits. Or, perhaps, the general level of profits will be slightly 'above-normal' because there is some successful innovation. Different firms will earn different profits, these being larger the more profitable the firm's own product currently is.

*4.2 The
equilibrium
situation*

The process by which the short- and long-run equilibrium position is reached by a firm in monopolistic competition is shown in Fig. 9.1. We assume that the average and marginal cost curves for its own

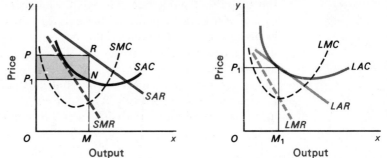

Fig. 9.1 a | b

particular product (*SAC* and *SMC*) remain the same in both the short and long run. So do those of all other firms. In the short run (Fig. 9.1a), the firm finds that marginal revenue equals marginal cost at the output OM and is able to earn abnormal profits of $PRNP_1$. The firm is in short-run equilibrium. It is able to make abnormal profits because not enough closely-competitive substitutes are being sold by other firms to compete these profits away.

In the long run (Fig. 9.1b), at that level of output where marginal cost equals marginal revenue (OM_1), the average revenue curve has become tangential to the average cost curve and the firm is now earning only 'normal' profits. Competitors (both old and new) are producing similar products, and the firm's abnormal short-run profits have been competed away. This situation is similar to that of long-run equilibrium in perfect competition. The main difference is that whereas in perfect competition the average revenue curve of the firm is a horizontal straight line, in monopolistic competition it slopes downwards. It follows that, so long as its average cost curve is U-shaped, the long-run equilibrium of a firm producing in monopolistic competition must occur at a smaller output than in perfect competition.

It is impossible for a downward-sloping average revenue curve to be tangential to a given U-shaped average cost curve except to the left of the position where a horizontal average revenue curve would be tangential to it. This means that, in long-run equilibrium in monopolistic competition, output must always be smaller than at the 'optimum' perfectly competitive output. However, one has to be careful in drawing any conclusion about the efficiency of the firm from this. For example, consumer satisfactions derived from being able to buy 'differentiated' rather than homogeneous products have to be considered.

It is clearly desirable that we should separate those features of Fig. 9.1 which are of purely geometrical significance from those which are economically important. First, it should be noted that the only reason why the average revenue curve is a straight line is that this simplifies the diagram. The equilibrium conditions would hold equally if it were a true curve. Second, it is important to note that, again for the sake of simplicity, the long-run average curve has been drawn parallel to the short-run one. This again will not necessarily happen in practice.

It is arguable that the average revenue curve of a firm producing in monopolistic competition will be more elastic in the long run than in the short run, as in Fig. 9.2. The firm shown in Figs. 9.2a and 9.2b

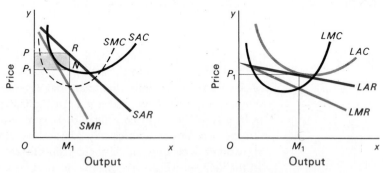

Fig. 9.2 a | b

has a short-run average revenue curve (SAR) which is rather less elastic than its long-run average revenue curve (LAR). The case for thinking that the long-run average revenue curve in a monopolistically-competitive firm will be more elastic than the short run one is that, as we have seen, the products made by a monopolistic group or industry will tend to become more similar as time goes on. Everyone will be looking for what is currently the most profitable type of article, and all will be trying to make it. Similarly, if new producers enter the industry, this is likely to mean that instead of, say, a hundred similar types of clothing being produced, there will now be, say, one hundred and fifty. Each of the garments is likely to be more similar to each of the others than it was previously. The more closely-competitive substitutes there are in the 'group', the more elastic the demand for the product of any one firm in the group will be.

It can therefore be seen that since monopolistic competition implies considerable competition between many firms producing slightly different goods, it is really more like perfect competition than monopoly. For practical purposes this is important. To use perfect competition, in economic theory, as anything more than an artificial case is unrealistic, since it is unreasonable to think that many firms in a real-world industry make homogeneous products, or that abnormal profits are completely eliminated. Since there is undoubtedly a certain degree of imperfection of competition through-out all industry, monopolistic competition may well often be found in practice. So long as there are no institutional or technical restrictions on entry into an industry, and so long as most of the firms in it produce goods similar to those of the firms already there, every producer must always be prepared to meet the competition of similar products made by rivals. There will then be monopolistic competition. Where it occurs one can assume that abnormal profits will usually be competed away fairly quickly, perhaps to be recreated by innovation in products or processes.

5. Advertising

As we have seen, the characteristic feature of monopolistic competition is that products are differentiated. Everyone tries to make a product which is just a little different from everyone else's in his own 'group'. This inevitably means that producers do their best to ensure that their own products are different (and if possible superior) in some way or other from those of their rivals. This is how abnormal profits are competed away. In some cases, it may be possible to alter the physical nature of the product. Whether or not this can be done, it is usually worth trying to persuade customers that one's own product is different from the others—even though it may be physically identical. We must therefore discuss the problems that arise when *selling costs* are incurred. They may take the form of advertising expenditure, or of other types of sales promotion, like undertaking door-to-door selling, or sending out sales leaflets or tokens offering '5p off', and so on. We shall concentrate here on advertising. In monopolistic competition, this is often undertaken with consumer goods to persuade customers that one product is preferable to another. It is undoubtedly true that the producers of many goods, toothpaste or cigarettes for example, spend a good deal of time and energy trying to convince consumers that their own brand is better than the others.

We have already implied that a producer who is working in conditions of monopolistic competition has to make two important decisions. First, he has to decide how much of his product to produce and at what price to sell it. This is a decision common to all producers, whatever sort of market they are producing in. Second, he has to decide whether to produce one good with one set of physical characteristics or another with a slightly different set. For example, a man-made fibre producer might have to decide whether to make his brand of yarn dull or shiny. This sort of decision is important only in monopolistic competition (and oligopoly to which we turn later). In perfect competition, all the products of the industry are identical. In monopoly, there are no closely-competing products at all. The design of the monopolist's good is not so crucial, and advertising will be needed more to remind consumers that the product exists than to call attention to its competitive features. Only in monopolistic competition will changes in design and in advertising be a major competitive factor.

If the product is an intermediate good or capital good sold to other firms, changes in design are likely to be more important than changes in advertising. With consumer goods, the producer in monopolistic competition too will have to decide whether or not to spend money on changing his product. He will also have to decide what to spend on advertising to persuade people to buy his products rather than others. How much money will he decide to spend? This problem is unimportant for the producer in perfect competition or for the monopolist. Since there are no close substitutes for his product, the monopolist need not worry very much whether he can convince people that his good is different from other goods. Everyone knows that it is. He may or may not decide to advertise, but he will not be 'differentiating' his product when he does.

On the other hand, advertisement of this kind is quite incompatible with perfect competition. Since in perfect competition all producers are making identical goods it is not usual to try to persuade consumers that one firm's product is different from another's. If this were done and consumers *did* become convinced that, say, Williams's wheat was better than Jones's, even though they were homogeneous, that would immediately destroy perfect competition. Of course, there can be advertising of a kind in perfect competition. There can be advertising undertaken by all producers together—by the whole industry—to persuade consumers to take that industry's product instead of those of other industries. There is what we may call 'promotional' advertising. The exhortation to 'eat more fruit' or 'drink more milk' and the advice that 'there is *no* substitute for wool' are examples. But 'competitive' advertising *within* an industry is incompatible with perfect competition in that industry.

5.1 Promotional and competitive advertising

It is now time to discuss the costs of advertising, or *selling costs* as economists usually call them, in a monopolistically-competitive group. There are two kinds of advertisement. First, there is what we may again describe, now in monopolistic competition, as *promotional* advertising. For example, in the UK there has been advertising by the whole hat-making industry, intended to increase sales of hats in general, not those of any one particular producer. Promotional advertising of this kind may include the provision of a certain amount of information, intended only to tell consumers about the general class of products being promoted. What is more typical of monopolistic competition is the type of advertisement which does not primarily give information about a class of product, but tries to persuade the consumer to change his attitude to the good in question. This is *competitive* advertising. We all know what toothpaste is and what it does, but the various producers try to persuade us that their own brand is better than the rest. 'Competitive' advertising is often successful. It follows that if a producer can persuade people to buy his product, say, by producing appealing T.V. commercials, our assumption that the demand curve is an objective fact given by consumers' tastes on the one hand and by the number and activity of rivals on the other, is no longer realistic. Where successful advertisement is undertaken, this demand curve is replaced by one which can be altered or shifted by the producer's own efforts—if he is prepared to spend money and effort on advertising.

5.2 Promotional advertising

We now discuss these two types of advertising in rather greater detail. Promotional advertising, insofar as it merely gives information, is not incompatible with the analysis we have used so far. We have assumed that there is perfect competition between buyers. This means that we have assumed that all buyers are in possession of all relevant information about all the products which are available. This may well be the case in the capital-good markets and in markets for other intermediate or finished products where the consumers are businessmen with expert knowledge. It is less likely to be the case where an ordinary consumer is buying the finished product. Here, there is great scope for informative promotional advertising telling the consumer what the product is, what it does and how it does it. This type of advertising is clearly desirable since it makes possible a more rational choice between goods, of the kind we have continually assumed that consumers do make. It also helps to increase the sales of all firms in the 'group', because it makes consumers more aware of the potentialities of the product made by the 'group'. Even where promotional advertising does attempt to 'sell' the product, it does not attempt to increase the sales of one brand of that product relatively to those of another.

5.3 Competitive advertising

Much advertising is not of this kind but of the second kind. It is not promotional advertising but 'competitive' advertising. The aim is to persuade consumers that X's product is better than all others in the 'group'. Our analysis is not concerned with value judgments and it does not concern us whether these advertisements are strictly truthful or not. The important thing from our point of view is the effect of advertising, and we can realistically say that the fundamental aim of all 'competitive' advertising is to attract the consumer's attention and to imprint the name of a particular product on his mind; the aim is to persuade the consumer to put his hand in his pocket and buy the product in question. Advertising of this kind can help to increase the sales of all firms in the 'group' if it brings the product of the whole 'group' to the notice of consumers. In this sense, even persuasive advertising can also be promotional. But the main aim is to increase the sales of one firm at the expense of others, and not to increase the sales of the 'group' as a whole.

6. The analysis of selling costs

It follows that the aim of 'competitive' advertisement is to induce consumers to buy more of a particular firm's product. The producer who is deciding whether to advertise is making a decision of fundamentally the same kind as when he decides what price to charge for his product or how large an output to produce. It is not very important to him whether his firm increases its profits by changing the price and output of its products; by altering their physical constitution; by spending money on advertising; or by other forms of sales promotion.[1] These are all examples of maximisation decisions.

[1] We shall not show in detail how a firm will adapt the nature of its product—'differentiate' its product—in order to maximise profits. For a fuller analysis of this problem, the reader should consult Chamberlin, *op. cit.*, pp. 94–7.

We continue to concentrate on advertising decisions. In this case, a two-dimensional diagram is rather clumsy, but it does show the fundamental features of the problem from the point of view of the individual firm. In Fig. 9.3 sales of a given good, which we call good X, are measured along the horizontal x-axis and its price up the vertical y-axis. We shall assume that the nature of good X is unchanged throughout the analysis. In practice, as we have seen, the main reason why advertising is undertaken is that it does change the nature of the good, so far as the consumer is concerned. This assumption is therefore not entirely realistic. However, provided that the physical make-up of the good is given and that its production cost curve is therefore unchanged by the alteration in its physical make-up, the problem is not very important, though it is desirable to bear in mind what is being done.

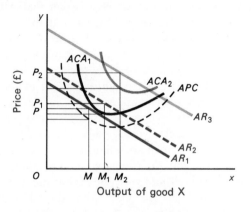

Fig. 9.3

In Fig. 9.3 the original situation is one where the firm is in equilibrium. The average revenue curve for the firm's product is the brown curve AR_1. This is the basic average revenue curve before any advertisement is undertaken. Similarly, the dashed black curve APC is the basic cost curve. It represents only average *production* costs, and is the curve which we are assuming to be identical for all firms in the 'group'. It includes no advertising costs. We assume throughout this analysis of selling costs that the firm's objective is to earn maximum profits. The initial equilibrium position in Fig. 9.3 is therefore where output is OM and price is £OP. In this position, maximum profits are being earned.

If advertisement is now undertaken a new equilibrium position will be reached. Let us assume that £1 000 is spent on advertising. The cost of advertising per unit of output will depend on the size of that output. Advertising cost per unit of output would be £1 000 with an output of one unit, but would fall to £1 at an output of 1 000 units. This means that the black average cost curve which includes the £1 000 spent on advertising (ACA_1) gradually moves closer to the average production cost curve (APC) as output increases.

However, the effect of spending the £1 000 on advertising is to increase demand. At every price, a larger quantity of the advertised product can be sold than before. The new (dashed) average revenue curve AR_2 is therefore to the right of the original one. The equilibrium position of the firm will now be where output is OM_1, price is £OP_1 and profits are again maximised. In the firm depicted in Fig. 9.3, this new equilibrium position will be where output is greater and price higher than in the original equilibrium. However, this need not happen. If the average production cost curve is downward-sloping, price may not rise and could even fall. The important question is not what happens to price or output but whether profits are larger in the new equilibrium than they were in the original one. This will depend on whether total revenue minus total production cost is increased by more than £1 000 when the selling costs of £1 000 are incurred. If more than £1 000 is added the advertising has proved worth while. If it is not, the move was unwise.

If profits have risen because of advertising, this means that further advertising expenditure might increase them still more. The firm may then consider spending £2 000 on advertisements instead of £1 000. The same analysis can be repeated. Will the second £1 000 spent on advertising lead to a further increase in profit? If the answer is yes, then spending the second £1 000 is worthwhile. Indeed, it will pay the firm to go on increasing selling costs in this way so long as each increment of advertising expenditure adds more to revenue than to costs. Only when the additional revenue generated (net of production costs) equals the extra (marginal) amount spent in order to generate that net revenue, will profit be at the highest possible level. This would happen in Fig. 9.3 with selling costs of £5 000. The cost curve would then be the grey curve ACA_2, and the (light-brown) average revenue curve AR_3. Output would be OM_2 and price OP_2. Beyond this, it would be found that profits began to decline in response to any further expansion of advertising outlay. An extra pound added to selling costs would not yield an equal increase in revenue net of production costs. There is, therefore, for each firm producing in 'monopolistic competition', a whole set of average revenue curves and average cost curves, each pair of curves corresponding to a different level of selling costs. The producer's problem is to decide which pair of curves represents the position where money profits are maximised, and which is the point on this pair of curves where output should be fixed.

It will be useful to consider more carefully the way in which, and the extent to which, the firm's average revenue curve is likely to be affected by advertising expenditure. It can be seen that, in drawing

Fig. 9.3, we have made two assumptions. First, we have assumed that demand increases when advertising expenditure is increased. This is a reasonable assumption but it is not inevitably true. A bad poster or television commercial might alienate customers. However, we shall assume that advertising will never reduce demand. The question is, by how much will demand increase? A small increase may not be worth the cost incurred in obtaining it; it is by no means axiomatic that increased selling costs are always worthwhile.

The second assumption which we have made is more dubious. While we have assumed that the average revenue curves are straight lines only for the sake of simplicity, we have also assumed that the new average revenue curve is parallel to the old. This is also an assumption made on grounds of convenience, but its implications need to be considered. It implies that elasticity of demand is lower at each price on the new curve than on the old one. This seems reasonable, though the difference may be bigger than in Fig. 9.3. If a producer's advertisements succeed in their intention they will inevitably make people look upon his product as rather more different from other products than they originally did. The most reasonable result to expect from this will be for the elasticity of demand for his product to fall. Consumers will now regard his product as being more desirable, even if its price is rather higher than the prices of close substitutes, for they have been persuaded that his product is rather different from the others. They now believe that these other goods are not nearly such good substitutes for it as they had hitherto supposed. It is therefore highly probable that the elasticity of demand for the advertised product will decline. The extent to which it will decline is, of course, uncertain. In any case the producer is likely to be less interested in his ability to reduce the elasticity of demand for his product than in his ability to raise its sales. Increases in sales caused by shifts of the whole demand curve are more likely to cause significant increases in profits. Changes in elasticity of demand are likely to be of only secondary importance.

The effects of advertising on prices and output are equally uncertain. It is possible that, by beginning an advertising campaign, the producer may be able to increase the sales of his product and yet not lower its elasticity of demand. This will mean that if he now lowers the price of his product he can increase output considerably, so long as his cost curve does not slope upwards too steeply. On the other hand if, as seems more likely, elasticity of demand falls sharply as the result of advertising, it may pay the producer to raise his price a good deal and be content with a relatively small increase in sales. The most probable result for a profit-maximising firm will be that the elasticity of demand will fall somewhat at each price, that the volume of demand will increase at each price and that price and output will both increase to some extent as a result of the advertising campaign.

We have so far assumed that advertising takes place in an industry already producing under conditions of monopolistic competition. It must be remembered, however, that monopolistic competition with product differentiation may well be the result and not the cause of advertising. There are endless possibilities, but two limiting cases are apparent. On the one hand, if there is a monopoly, this means that there are no firms producing closely competitive substitutes. In such circumstances, if the monopolist feels that he is not earning enough profit, the only way for him to increase his sales is to persuade consumers that his product is a good substitute for some distant rival's products. In other words, the monopolist will try to increase both the volume of demand and the elasticity of demand for his products at any price. At the same time, of course, he will break down his monopoly. On the other hand, if there is perfect competition in an industry so that all firms' products are homogeneous, an individual producer may try to persuade consumers that his product is *not* identical with those of other firms. Here the aim is to lower the elasticity of demand for the product in question. Between these limits there are endless possible situations and one cannot *a priori* say anything very useful about them.

One final point is interesting. In practice, advertising of the kind envisaged in this second limiting case may have been rather widespread during the last seventy years. Producers in perfectly competitive industries may, in the early part of the twentieth century, have become dissatisfied with their opportunities for earning increased profits. In perfect competition, increased profits can result only from an increase in the demand for the output of the whole perfectly-competitive industry. An entrepreneur producing in perfect competition may well find it very attractive to increase his profits by persuading consumers that his particular product has some special characteristic which distinguishes it from the general product sold by his industry. A case in point seems to be tea. During this century, tea, which had hitherto been regarded as a number of homogeneous products, has been packed in various different packets. The intention has been to persuade consumers that, since the packets are different, so is the tea. There is reason to think that other previously homogeneous products have been differentiated in the same way. Flour seems to be a further example. If it is true that this kind of change has taken place, then it is reasonable to conclude that in practice the aim of much advertising since 1900 has been to reduce the elasticity of demand for the product (from infinity to a finite level), as well as to shift the firm's average revenue curve bodily to the right.

7. Oligopoly   We have been concerned in this chapter and in the previous one with a discussion of the different types of imperfect competition which are likely to occur. Such a discussion is often referred to as study of 'market forms'. The final type of market form—the final species of imperfect competition—is known as *oligopoly*. This piece of economic jargon is derived, by analogy, from the more respectable term, monopoly. A monarchy has a single ruler; an oligarchy has a small group of rulers. A monopolist is therefore a single seller, while oligopoly occurs where there are only a few sellers. It differs both from monopoly, where there is one seller, and from perfect and monopolistic competition, where there are many. We are now introducing the notion of a small group of producers, in distinction to the large group which we studied in the three previous sections.

7.1 Duopoly   The simplest case of oligopoly occurs when there are only two sellers and is known as *duopoly*. Duopoly analysis raises all the fundamental problems of oligopoly. These are basically different from the problems of monopoly, perfect competition and monopolistic competition. The analysis of duopoly, moreover, provides a simplified model for an explicit statement of the problems of oligopoly. Our conclusions from the study of duopoly can be extended to cover situations where there are three, four, five or more sellers. We shall assume to begin with that the products made by the various oligopolists are identical. Where products are homogeneous in this way, one can speak of *oligopoly without product differentiation*. At a later stage, the analysis will be extended to study oligopoly situations where the products of the firms concerned are not identical but are differentiated; where they are close, but not perfect, substitutes for each other.

It will be readily appreciated that oligopoly with product differentiation is in reality only a rather special case of monopolistic competition. The important difference is that, since the number of producers is smaller, the actions of rival firms need more careful and individual attention. One firm in the large group of producers in monopolistic competition can legitimately look at its many rivals within the group *en masse*. Since the numbers of competitors in oligopoly is small, the reactions of individual producers are both more easily discernable and more important than in monopolistic competition.

8. Oligopoly without product differentiation   As explained, we shall approach the analysis of oligopoly without product differentiation through an analysis of duopoly without product differentiation. The first important feature of duopoly is that the individual producer has to consider very carefully what the indirect effects of a decision to change his price or output will be. Since in duopoly without product differentiation there are only two producers of identical goods, any price or output change by the first producer is bound to affect the second very significantly. The latter's reactions will in turn change the position of the first, and so on. The individual producer therefore has to acknowledge that he will change the whole situation in which he is producing, in this indirect way, if he changes his own price.

*(a) How
duopoly differs
from monopoly*

Such a chain of reactions does not occur either with monopoly or with perfect competition. The monopolist can fix his price and output so as to maximise his profits and is able to ignore the effect on his rivals as he does so. These rivals are producing only extremely distant substitutes for the monopolist's own good. So, while a monopolist's price change might conceivably affect his rivals' sales and profits to a very small extent, they are most unlikely to alter their prices in retaliation. Any consequential effects on the demand for the monopolist's product, resulting from his rivals' reactions to his initial move, will be so small that he can ignore them entirely. Similarly, in perfect competition, the producer is a price taker, who simply adjusts his output to fit in with a given market price which he can do nothing himself to alter. This is because the basic assumption of perfect competition is that the number of firms in the industry is very large. Any change in the output of a single producer will have a negligible effect on the profits and prices of other producers. The consequence is that both in monopoly and perfect competition it is possible to regard the individual producer's revenue and cost curves as given and unaffected by his own actions. The profit-maximising output of the individual producer can be read-off from these curves without difficulty.

In duopoly without product differentiation the position is quite different. It would be extremely dangerous to assume that, with identical products and with only two producers (let us call them A and B), A can ignore the policy of B. It would also be dangerous to assume that A could ignore the indirect effect on his own price and profits of changes made by B in response to his own (A's) decisions. A must always have at least one eye on B. The position may well be likened to that in a game of cards. It is impossible to say beforehand what is the best way of playing any given hand, since one does not know in advance which cards the other players hold. The best way of playing the hand will not depend entirely on how likely it is that particular cards will be played. It will also depend on how anxious and able one is to keep one's opponents guessing about which cards one has and which one does not have.

It will be clear from this analogy that there is no simple solution to the question: How will a duopolist, where products are identical, fix his output and price? The answer will depend on which assumptions are made about how the two producers act. There is no single, determinate solution as in monopoly, perfect competition or monopolistic competition. There is a whole series of possible solutions, each depending on different assumptions. In particular, the solution will depend on whether A thinks that he can persuade B to make a foolish response to any change which he (A) makes. The key to any solution of the problem of duopoly lies in the kind of assumptions which A makes about B's reactions to a change in his (A's) price and output, and vice versa. It is not surprising, therefore, that economists have produced several different explanations of what happens in duopoly, each based on different hypotheses about what A might expect B to do. There is no need, here, to give a list of these different solutions.[1] The more useful procedure will be to find which are the most realistic ones.

(b) Our assumptions

The search for plausible assumptions about duopoly without product differentiation is not easy. A simplified model is so simple that it is difficult to illustrate from practical experience. However, it is possible to make some reasonable assumptions. We shall assume first that the two producers are of equal intelligence. We shall also assume that the costs of each firm are the same, or at any rate not very different. Of course, the simplest assumption of all is to assume that each producer has no costs at all. This was done in the original analysis by Cournot,[2] of duopoly in the ownership of mineral springs, but it is not very realistic. However, it is quite sensible to think that the only two producers of an identical good will have similar costs.

It is more difficult to make assumptions about demand conditions in oligopoly. In duopoly without product differentiation (as in other types of oligopoly) there is no objective average revenue curve for the individual producer. Both firms are producing identical goods. The result is that if we assume (as we must) that consumers are indifferent about which producer they patronise when prices are the same for each firm's good, we cannot say how many consumers will buy from A except on some assumption about what B's price is. We cannot draw a demand curve for A's product, unless we know what price B will charge when A's price is at each possible level.

[1] Readers who are interested in the solutions to this duopoly problem will find a survey of them in E. H. Chamberlin, *Theory of Monopolistic Competition,* chapter iii, and in William Fellner, *Competition among the Few,* chapter ii.
[2] *Recherches sur les principes mathématiques de la théorie des richesses,* chapter vii.

What we *can* say is that if consumers really are indifferent whether they buy from A or B at a given price, we may reasonably assume that, when both firms charge the same price, half the consumers will buy from A and half from B. It will be a matter of pure accident which *individual* consumers go to A or to B. However, if the products are homogeneous and prices are different, we must assume that the firm with the lower price will attract *all* the custom.

(c) The equilibrium price

On these assumptions, where will the price actually settle? Since consumers are indifferent between the two producers' products, each must in the long run charge the same price. If this were not so, the producer charging the higher price would be unable to sell anything at all. Nevertheless, it is difficult to say what this single price will be. A cannot be assumed to begin by charging the same price as B, since B will also be attempting to charge the same price as A, and he will not know what A's price is until after A has set it. Once both prices are set, and if they are set at different levels, then whichever duopolist has set the higher price will reduce it to equal the lower. But will the other firm then cut its price further? Will there then be a price war? What are we to assume about the 'equilibrium' price which two duopolists will finally charge, perhaps as a result of bitter experience in a price-war, perhaps by independent decisions or perhaps by actual (or tacit) discussion and agreement?

The simplest solution will satisfy the duopolist and the economic theorist, but not any anti-monopoly legislation there may be. This is that the single monopoly price will be charged by both firms, either as a result of consultation or of independent decision, perhaps following some (jointly-agreed) experiment.

(d) Maximising joint profits

Both parties will be wise if they set the price which would be charged if a single monopolist were producing both their outputs. For that price will give maximum joint profits, shared equally. It would not be in the joint interests of the duopolists to charge any other price. For the monopolist is assumed to fix his price at that level which will maximise his profits. The joint profits of the duopolists will therefore also be maximised at this level. We are assuming, of course, that the total costs of the monopolist would be the same as the total costs of the two duopolists when producing the monopolist's profit-maximising output, which need not be the case. The fact remains that the best that the duopolists (jointly) can do is either to make a monopoly agreement, or else to behave independently just as they would if there were one. Of course, if duopolistic price-cutting begins, as is quite possible, profits will be lower than they would be in monopoly.

Assuming that their costs are the same, the duopolists will together earn smaller profits than the monopolists would, if they raised their price above the monopoly level. Nor would it pay them to charge less. At any price less than the monopoly one, their combined profits must be below the maximum, monopoly level. They will be foolish to take less since, with identical products and cost, they will share the total profit equally. Why share less than the maximum? If there is an actual or tacit agreement between the duopolists, it is unlikely that they will pursue a policy of price reduction, for then they will merely lose money.

This is one answer to the question 'What happens where there is duopoly without product differentiation?' If each producer wants to make as much money as possible, and if the market is shared equally between them at any price, they will fix the same price as would have been fixed by a single monopolist. This gives us a determinate solution showing an optimum equilibrium position. Of course, what happens in this situation depends on our assumption that the cost curves of the two producers are identical, and that the monopolist's total cost at the equilibrium output is equal to the combined costs of the duopolists. However, so long as the duopolists' costs are identical, the best solution is to produce the output that maximises joint profit, even if their costs are higher than the monopolist's.

(e) Price cutting

We must now consider what will happen if one duopolist tries to earn more than the other by raising or lowering his price. If both duopolists are intelligent they will not try to do this, since they will see that they are both bound to lose. They will merely take equal shares in a smaller pool of profits. It is possible, however, that both duopolists *are* unintelligent. If so, each will attempt to gain at the expense of the other in this way, at least until bitter experience teaches him to stop. If A cuts his price, B, having lost all his customers, may respond by cutting his own price by more than A. A will reply with a further price cut and so on, each duopolist cutting prices in an attempt to regain the market.

If, on the other hand, the duopolists were of unequal intelligence, A, the less intelligent, might make a series of price cuts to each of which B would be forced to reply. Being more intelligent, B would realise that the best thing to do would be to make an identical cut, hoping that A would then realise that a further cut would not pay. In any case, whether both duopolists were determined to cut each other's throats (or only one of them!) the effect would be to reduce profits below the maximum. It is difficult to say where equilibrium would be reached. All one can say is that, if both are to stay in business, the price cannot for long fall below the point at which both duopolists are earning only normal profits. In the long run, they would not both want to remain in the industry if price fell below this level. The least satisfactory of the possible equilibrium positions for two duopolists is thus where each is earning only normal profits. Anything worse can only be a short-run solution.

This normal-profit equilibrium is one where the follies of the duopolists have artificially created a position similar to that of a firm which is in equilibrium in perfect competition. It is not an optimal equilibrium position, but it is nevertheless a possible one. The difference between this situation and that of equilibrium in perfect competition is as follows. In perfect competition, inexorable market forces bring about a long-run equilibrium situation where only normal profits are being earned. In duopoly such a situation has been artificially created because there has been a price-war between the duopolists. However, it is not *necessary* that there should be price war.

Once again, our result depends upon the assumption of identical costs in the two firms. If costs are different for the two duopolists, the firm with lower costs may be able to undercut the other and, by forcing it to earn less than normal profits, drive it out of existence in the long run. Then duopoly would become monopoly. Alternatively, even if costs are the same, but one firm is very big or has considerable financial resources, it may be able to force the other out of business and take over its market share by cutting prices below the normal-profit level for a sufficiently long period.

(f) Conclusions

To sum up: the best course for the duopolists will be to charge the monopoly price, to earn the maximum profit and to share it equally. This does not necessarily imply any formal agreement between the two firms. There may well be such an agreement (if the law does not forbid it), but the same result could come about if each producer independently worked out the best possible solution, assumed that his competitor had done the same, and charged the monopoly price. It is possible, however, that, in the long run, the duopoly price may settle at any level between the monopoly price and the perfectly competitive price according to how far any price cutting goes. In the short run, the duopoly price may even fall below the competitive price with both firms failing to earn even normal profits if they indulge in competitive price cutting.

8.2 Oligopoly with homogeneous products

The solution to the problem of what happens in oligopoly without product differentiation, where three, four, etc., producers make identical goods, is at least as uncertain. With three producers, the monopoly solution is rather less probable. Agreement between three producers will usually be harder to obtain than with only two, and it is rather less likely that all three will decide independently to charge the monopoly price. With four producers the same arguments hold; the likelihood that they will fix the monopoly price is a little less.

As the numbers of firms increase they must sooner or later become sufficiently numerous for something approaching perfect competition to occur, unless one of the firms is run by a very strong personality able to form a single large firm from a number of them. The situation will then revert to one of oligopoly, perhaps with price-leadership from the large firm holding prices above the perfect-competition level. The price which will be fixed in oligopoly without product differentiation is thus indeterminate. It is likely to be lower the larger the number of producers so that, in the end, there will be enough firms for a perfectly-competitive equilibrium to be reached.

9. Oligopoly with product differen- tiation

Where there is oligopoly *with* product differentiation in any market not only is the number of firms small; their products are also differentiated. The main generalisation which can be made about this situation is that, in general, monopoly agreements are less likely to be reached than in oligopoly without price differentiation. Since the products of the various firms are not identical, a monopoly arrangement will probably be harder to arrive at. Now that products are differentiated, each firm will have its own clientele and it will be harder for any firm to know the position and shape of its own and the others' average revenue curves. Once again, of course, this discussion assumes no anti-monopoly legislation preventing collusion.

9.1 Duopoly with differentiated products

Let us consider the simplest case first. What happens in duopoly with product differentiation? It will still always pay the two producers to refrain from undercutting each other's price's in such a way as to cause a price-war. However, it is no longer so certain that a change in price on the part of one producer will provoke an immediate retaliatory change by the other. We have seen that in oligopoly *without* product differentiation the fact that products are identical means that if one producer raises his price he loses *all* his customers. He will therefore never do this. On the other hand, if a producer lowers his price his rival will immediately lose all *his* custom and will make a price cut in retaliation.

In oligopoly *with* product differentiation, the fact that products are somewhat different means that it is possible for one producer to raise or lower his price without needing to fear either the loss of all his customers, on the one hand, or an immediate response by his rival, on the other. The latter may keep some of *his* customers, even if he now has the higher price.

9.2 Oligopoly with differentiated products

(a) The kinked average revenue curve

Fig. 9.4

In analysing oligopoly *with* product differentiation, economists therefore often use an average revenue curve, like that in Fig. 9.4. This is known as a *kinked average revenue curve.* In a sense, there is no revenue

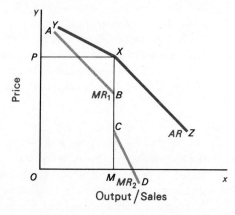

function for an oligopolist at all. The amount he sells depends on the prices charged by other producers, and unless these can be specified in advance he cannot know what demand for his product will be. As time goes on, it seems likely that more and more mathematics will be used in analysing the decision problems of the oligopolist. However, the 'kinked' demand curve does provide a simple way of conceiving an average revenue curve for an oligopolist which helps us to understand oligopoly pricing problems.

Figure 9.4 assumes that there is a small group of firms, each producing a similar product. We assume that the price charged for every firm's version of this product has settled down at OP. At this price, our particular firm sells OM of its own product; other firms may sell more or less than OM, depending on the relative popularity of their particular products and the extent to which they are being advertised and promoted.

The brown average revenue curve (YXZ) of our firm has a kink at point X. The reason is this. We assume that if our firm raises its price none of its competitors follow, because they feel that a higher price would give too low a level of sales. Since the firms are producing very similar products, a small increase in the price of our firm's product will therefore lead to a very large fall in its sales; demand is very elastic if one firm alone increases its price. However, if our firm cuts its price, the assumption is changed. We now assume that all the rivals will cut their prices to exactly the same extent. They will feel that while it may be unprofitable to cut prices, the danger that they will lose market share if they do not do so is too great for them to be able to allow our firm's price cuts to go unmatched. The result is that beyond X the kinked average revenue curve slopes downwards very steeply. Since all firms are assumed to be charging the same price, any one of them gains extra business only to the extent that the sales of the whole oligopoly group can be expanded through price cutting at the expense of the rest of the goods and services in the economy. In some trades, such an oligopoly group might be able to expand its sales a good deal as price was cut. Over the last 30 years, for example, sales of new products like television sets have risen rapidly as their prices have fallen. However, unless the product is a new one where the market is currently very small, it is more reasonable to assume that the lower portion of the kinked average revenue curve will be rather steep.

We must say a word now about the shape of the light-brown marginal revenue curve which is associated with this kinked average revenue curve. This also is shown in Fig. 9.4. Again, it is a composite curve. The upper, left-hand part (AB) which slopes downwards fairly gently is the section of the marginal revenue curve associated with the shallow curve YX in Fig. 9.4. The second, right-hand part (CD) is the section of the curve which is marginal to the steep curve XZ in Fig. 9.4. The left-hand part of the marginal revenue curve in Fig. 9.4 ends, at B and the right-hand part begins, at C, both immediately below the kink. There is a 'gap' or 'hole' (BC) in the marginal revenue curve. A little reflection will show why this is. The curves which are marginal to the sections YX and XZ of the kinked average revenue curve have very different slopes and positions. At the level of the output where there is the kink, the firm switches suddenly from the curve which is marginal to the gently sloping line YX to the one which is marginal to the much steeper line XZ. Hence the 'gap'.

(b) Depressed markets

In fact, this kinked average revenue curve is likely to be found mainly where trade is relatively depressed. It is when business is bad that a group of oligopolists will be reluctant to follow a price increase by one of their members. They will feel that by raising his price he is likely to lose market share, and profit as well, so that they will be well advised to maintain their prices. It is in these circumstances, too, that they will feel compelled to follow a price cut by one member of the group. They will then feel that unless they follow the price cut they themselves will lose market share, and that in the long run at least they will lose profit as well.

(c) Boom conditions

We may use the same kind of curve to analyse what happens in boom conditions. The relevant 'kinked' average revenue curve (*ABC*) is the one shown in Fig. 9.5. Here we make the opposite assumption

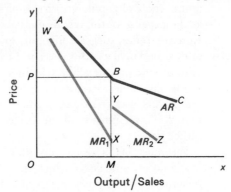

Fig. 9.5

from that made in Fig. 9.4. We assume that if one oligopolistic firm raises its price the others will follow; if it lowers its price they will not. Since trade is good, they will feel no need to expand sales by cutting price, but will be prepared to take higher profits by collectively raising prices; unless, of course, profits are already maximised.

Once again, the average revenue curve is a composite one, as indeed is the marginal revenue curve. This time, the left-hand part of the average revenue curve (*AB*) is steep while the right-hand part (*BC*) is flatter. The marginal revenue curve is again composed of the relevant parts (*WX*) and (*YZ*) of the marginal revenue curves that are marginal to the two sections of the average revenue curve. Once again, the marginal revenue curve has a 'gap' (*XY*) in it, again immediately below the kink. But, in Fig. 9.5, the right-hand part of the marginal revenue curve begins at *Y*, which is higher than *X*, where the left-hand part ended.

(d) Equilibrium in a depressed market

With these kinked curves, we can now go on to analyse oligopoly. In Fig. 9.6, price has settled down at *OP* and the firm is currently selling the amount *OM*. Should it alter its price? As we have seen, this kind of average revenue curve implies that there is a rather depressed market. If the firm cuts its price, its rivals will follow; if it raises its price, they will not. The marginal revenue curve is the light-brown line, with a gap between point B and point C, vertically below point X. If the grey marginal cost curve (MC) is then as shown, there will be no reason to alter price. The marginal cost curve passes

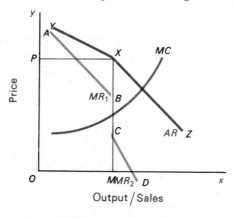

Fig. 9.6

through the 'gap' in the marginal revenue curve. Only if marginal cost rises far enough for the marginal cost curve to pass through the marginal revenue curve above B, will there be a case for raising price. Therefore, if the general level of costs in the industry is rising, as so often happens in an inflationary world, in the end it will pay the oligopolist to raise his price. Indeed, when he does this it may well be that contrary to what the diagram suggests, the other oligopolists will match the price increase. The 'kinked' average revenue curve will then move upwards bodily to a new position, with the kink opposite the new, common price. At this new price level, there will again be no incentive for the individual oligopolist to alter his own price. If he makes any price cut, his rivals will follow it; if he increases his price, they will refuse to follow. There is again a 'kink' in the oligopolist's average revenue curve, but this is now opposite the *new* common price. Vertically below the kink, there will still be a 'gap' in the marginal revenue curve.

Alternatively, if in Fig. 9.6 the marginal cost curve *falls* far enough to cut the marginal revenue curve below C, it may pay the firm to cut its price. Even after the competitors have matched the price cut, costs may have fallen far enough to leave substantial profits. The danger is that rivals may react to the oligopolist's price cut by cutting their own prices even further. The best way to insure against this, is clearly for each firm to keep its own costs as low, or lower, than those in any other firm. This is one reason why 'technological competition' is likely to be very keen in oligopoly. Firms will strive to see that by using new production methods and introducing new products their costs are low, their productivity high and their products attractive by comparison with those made by other firms. If a price war does then break out, the firm that has concentrated on using technology to improve its position will be strong enough to come out well.

(e) Equilibrium in a buoyant market

The same kind of analysis can deal with the situation where the oligopoly average revenue curve is like that in Fig. 9.7. Here, the kink is in the opposite direction. We have seen that this implies that

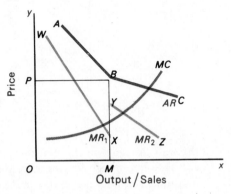

Fig. 9.7

there are very buoyant conditions in the market. If our firm raises its price, its rivals will follow; if it cuts price, they will not bother to change their own prices since business is already good. Yet, the tendency may again be for price to be stable, though this is less certain now. Our firm may not want to be accused of earning 'excessive' profits either by its customers or by the Government. Nevertheless, if costs rise for *all* firms the tendency to pass these increased costs on to customers will be greater than in the situation shown in Fig. 9.6. The restraining factors will be a reluctance to charge 'high prices' to consumers and the fact that the Government may well be trying to keep prices down by persuasion or exhortation. If the firm's costs fall, consumers may be given the benefit of cost reductions, especially if the situation for our firm really is that implied by the right-hand part of the average revenue curve. This suggests that rivals will not match any price cut. It is obviously a good time for a firm with a cost advantage to risk making a price cut, especially if it has spare capacity during a period when demand is strong.

However, it is clear that we have to be more cautious in generalising about oligopoly pricing when the market is buoyant, than we did for a depression. Purely economic considerations make price changes much more attractive than when trade is depressed, or relatively depressed. Figure 9.7 makes it clear why this is. While the grey marginal cost curve (MC) does pass through the 'gap' in the marginal revenue curve, the marginal cost curve cuts both parts of the marginal revenue curve. Profits are therefore increased whether prices are raised or lowered. The situation looks very unstable, and in purely economic terms it will pay the firm in Fig. 9.7 to join its competitors, increasing price far enough above OP to equate marginal revenue and cost at the lower output. It may be even more profitable to 'go it alone', cutting price to equate marginal revenue and cost at the higher output. (Since the marginal cost curve cuts two quite different marginal revenue curves, one cannot say in advance, for any particular instance, whether profit will be maximised at the lower or the higher output where marginal cost equals marginal revenue.)

(f) Equilibrium   To summarise, the purely economic analysis of oligopoly suggests that, except in very buoyant market conditions, prices will be stable.

(g) Conclusions   We may therefore conclude that if prices in oligopoly are currently satisfactory, then, unless there is a major change in costs, no price change will be made. If each producer continues to earn adequate profits, he may argue that to lower his price would be to start a price-war and to bring ruin. On the other hand, unless business is very buoyant, he may well feel that if he were to raise his price he would also lose. He is not sure how closely competitive with his own the rival products are, but will fear that they are as competitive as the kinked average revenue curve for depressed conditions suggests. He is therefore not very keen to experiment with changes in price and output, in order to discover what the optimum price is. This type of experimentation may be suitable for a monopolist, who need not fear the reactions of his rivals. For the oligopolist, it may mean a catastrophic fall in sales if he raises his price and alienates consumers; or a serious price-war if he lowers price very far and provokes his rivals.

The analysis has important implications. It suggests that oligopolists producing differentiated goods may be content, unless trade is very buoyant, to leave price and output exactly as they are for the sake of a quiet life—provided profits are reasonable. They may do this even if, because of the way the market has developed, different firms have come to be selling at different prices.

This type of situation is not likely to occur in oligopoly without product differentiation since the individual producer must always immediately follow any price cut by his rivals. Otherwise he would lose *all* custom. In oligopoly with product differentiation, the idea that oligopolists want above all to avoid trouble seems an attractive one, though we shall see that economists disagree over what actually happens. The kinked demand curve certainly suggests that while occasional price wars may occur, prices will soon return to the old levels once everyone sees that they are merely cutting each other's throats.

This notion is interesting because it throws doubt on our basic assumption of profit maximisation. It could be that this picture of oligopoly with product differentiation gives a realistic picture of what happens in reality. Perhaps producers prefer a quiet life to the hazards of always seeking maximum profits in conditions where the results of any price change are uncertain. The real world entrepreneur, especially if he is an oligopolist, may be more anxious to avoid the perils of price wars than to earn maximum profits.

(h) A 'quiet life' In this book, we have largely ignored political and social influences on pricing. If there is more stability in reality than this analysis of oligopoly implies, it will be because governments or consumers put pressure on manufacturers to keep prices (and profits) down or because they prefer a 'quiet life'.

(i) Are prices 'sticky'? Certainly, unless demand is high, economic analysis implies that prices will be 'sticky' in oligopoly. Unless there are considerable changes in cost conditions, there will be no incentive for the oligopolist to alter his price. There has been a good deal of argument between economists over whether or not this is a realistic explanation of what happens. Some empirical work, particularly that by Professor Stigler of Chicago University, suggests that prices are much less 'sticky' than this implies. However, in this book we are dealing very much with a world where purely economic motives are followed. Professor Stigler's analysis is concerned with the real world where political influences come in too.

9.3 Conclusions What conclusions can we reach? In duopoly *with* product differentiation, consumers are likely to be attached more firmly to one product *(a) Duopoly* than another. The assumption that the two producers will share the *with product* market equally, which we could make for duopoly without product *differentiation* differentiation, no longer holds. We have seen, too, that the monopoly solution is less probable, too, because we are now dealing with two different products. However, there may be less danger of a price war in depressed conditions, since neither producer needs to respond quite so readily to a price cut by the other as where there was no product differentiation.

(b) Oligopoly with product differentiation

If there are three, four or five producers of differentiated goods, the kinked oligopoly demand curve remains a useful analytical tool. The monopoly solution becomes progressively less probable. The difficulties of forming a monopoly organisation, already considerable where there are more than two firms, is complicated by the fact that no two of them produce exactly the same product. As was noted earlier, each firm will have its own clientele and its own goodwill. On the other hand, there may be cut-throat competition, with a final solution analogous to that of monopolistic competition.

(c) Differences from oligopoly without product differentiation

For example, Fig. 9.8a shows the equilibrium of a single firm earning normal profits in conditions of oligopoly *without* product differentiation. A price-war has forced price down to *OP*. At this price the firm can sell an output of *OM* and earn normal profits. Its average cost

Fig. 9.8

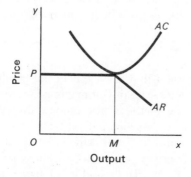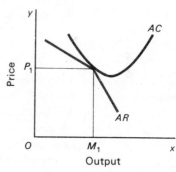

curve just touches the kink in its average revenue curve. Because the products are identical, the left-hand section of the average revenue curve is horizontal. If it were to raise its price the firm would lose all its customers, assuming that its rivals did nothing. If it were to lower its price it would go out of business in the long run.

Figure 9.8b shows the position of a similar firm but this time one producing in conditions of oligopoly *with* product differentiation. The equilibrium after a price war is again where the kink in the average revenue curve touches the average cost curve. The firm is earning only normal profits, but is producing less than the optimum output. The price war has eliminated abnormal profits but the final equilibrium is not like that associated with perfect competition. This is not surprising. Conditions are similar to those under monopolistic competition. The average revenue curve is not horizontal at any point. In fact, since products are differentiated, firms with 'better' products can still earn small supernormal profits in the short run at least, even in this situation.

The few producers in oligopoly with product differentiation, though they could have agreed to band together to protect each other's profits, may deliberately decide to compete the general level of prices down, while each may hope that product differentiation will enable him to earn more than the others. Profits will then be smaller than they would have been with a monopoly agreement— unless one or more firms retire, or are forced to retire, from the competitive struggle, when prices may be raised again. It is only too obvious that the best interests of all the oligopolists lie in making an agreement to ensure that there is no price war. As we have seen, however, the problems which would arise in doing this are often great, especially where monopoly agreements are frowned on by the law. In addition, now that products are not identical each producer has an interest in keeping his own particular customers; he may find that a price other than the monopoly price enables him to do this. It is therefore likely that the final price will lie between the monopoly price and the cut-throat competition price. The actual price will depend on the conditions prevailing, and will differ from case to case.

10. A military analogy

Despite our conclusion that in oligopoly the equilibrium situation may well be one where firms do not maximise profits, we have nevertheless followed the methods of economic theory in reaching it. However, it could be that oligopoly will turn out in the end to be best treated by a quite different kind of analysis. This may be a mathematical one, perhaps 'game theory'. One interesting suggestion has been made by K. W. Rothschild in the paper quoted at the end of this chapter. He there suggests that one interesting aspect of oligopoly is the ease with which we use military terminology when discussing it. We talk of price wars, sales campaigns, marketing strategies, industrial espionage, etc. It may be that an analogy could help business men to analyse their problems. If he were writing now, Dr Rothschild would no doubt be equally impressed by the way in which military strength has developed since he wrote in 1947. The distinction is now made between 'nuclear' and 'conventional' weapons. So far, the countries with nuclear weapons have mercifully been reluctant to use them. The nuclear bomb is not used, partly because the other side can scarcely fail to notice that it has been. A President of the United States could not overlook the fact that Washington had been wiped out. The challenge would be both too obvious and too serious. Perhaps there is a commercial parallel. Maybe one reason why prices do not change often in oligopoly (why prices are sticky) is that competitors cannot overlook the fact that price has been cut. The newspapers will have told everyone that it has been. Once again, the challenge is both direct and serious. A price war (the oligopolist's counterpart of a nuclear war) may well break out. So, because of the seriousness of using price changes they may, like hydrogen bombs, be used only in extreme situations, if at all. Perhaps this is why some oligopoly prices remain unchanged for long periods.

Maybe we can carry our analogy further. Because nuclear weapons are so powerful, they are rarely used. However, this makes it more, not less, likely that smaller-scale military activity and, even more, espionage may take place. The same may be true in business. Perhaps firms which are reluctant to alter prices spend a great deal of money on market research, advertising, cut-price offers and other forms of sales promotion. The fact that a price war is unlikely makes it more, not less, important continually to probe the rival's position, to erode his market and (through market research) to be well informed about his market share and his general competitive position. There is nothing very precise in these ideas, but perhaps they give new insights into the nature and problems of oligopoly. Perhaps, also, they show that economists can find analogies like this military one useful in studying business problems.

11. A classification of market forms

The characteristics of the various market situations which we have discussed in the last few chapters are summarised in the Table 9.1.

Although Table 9.1 should be self-explanatory, perhaps a few comments on it will be helpful. First, it is important to note that apart from perfect competition all other types of market situation can be grouped under the general heading of imperfect competition. Monopolistic competition is then the 'least imperfect' or 'most nearly perfect' type of competition. Monopoly is the 'most imperfect' type of market situation. Second, we have ignored 'pure' monopoly in this classification since it is only a theoretical limiting case. Third, it will be noted that the situation where a single firm produces differentiated products does not seem to have any meaning at all—especially since we are assuming that each firm produces only one product.

Table 9.1
A classification of market situations

Number of firms	Type of market situation	
	Homogeneous products	*Differentiated products*
Many firms	Perfect competition	Monopolistic competition
Few firms	Oligopoly without product differentiation	Oligopoly with product differentiation
One firm	Monopoly	

Finally, it is worth noting that one can distinguish between these various types of market situation by considering cross-elasticities of demand. In perfect competition the cross-elasticity of demand for the product of a single firm with respect to a change in the price of the rest of the industry will be infinite. That is to say, the proportionate fall in the demand for the product of a single firm will be infinitely large compared with any given proportionate fall in the price of the product of the whole industry. Similarly, in monopolistic competition the cross-elasticity of demand for the product of a single firm with respect to a change in the price of the other products made in the monopolistic 'group' will be very high. The cross-elasticity of demand for the product of a monopolist with respect to a fall in the price of other products in the economy will be very low. A given proportionate change in the prices of other goods will cause only an extremely small proportionate change—if indeed it causes any change at all—in the demand for the product of a monopolist.

12. 'Full cost' and a fixprice market

During most of this analysis of the equilibrium of the firm, we have assumed that firms maximise profits by equating marginal cost with marginal revenue. However, we saw in the discussion of oligopoly with product differentiation that there was some indeterminacy in pricing. While our analysis implied that once prices had settled at any level they would tend to stay there, we found it harder to explain how prices reached that particular level in the first place. The oligopolistic group clearly had some discretion in determining what price should be.

12.1 Full-cost pricing

Partly as a result of empirical studies of oligopoly pricing, some economists have suggested that, instead of equating marginal cost with marginal revenue, many firms engage in what economists call 'full-cost' pricing. They suggest that having worked out what average total cost would be if the level of output expected for the next period of time were actually achieved, firms add to this a 'satisfactory' profit margin. This is known as 'full-cost' pricing. The price is equal to 'full' cost, including an acceptable profit.

If full-cost pricing exists, it does not necessarily mean that firms behave very differently from the way economic theory suggests. Even if there is a widely-held convention, in any industry charging 'full cost' prices, about what a 'satisfactory' profit margin would be, this may well have been arrived at through an understanding, built up over time, of the sort of profit margins that competitive conditions in that industry usually allow. The 'conventional' profit margin may simply enable firms to charge roughly the level of price which competitive conditions would themselves have brought about in the kind of market the industry is operating in. Working out price by applying a 'full-cost' formula may simply be an easy way of achieving roughly the result the firm would have achieved had it equated marginal cost with marginal revenue. If so, this is understandable. Firms find it difficult to work out marginal cost in practice, and marginal revenue is even more elusive.

It may be that 'full-cost' pricing was widespread in the 1950s and early 1960s, but is now less generally used. More and more firms, certainly in the UK, are moving towards pricing based on average variable cost and on the 'contribution' over and above average variable cost that each product makes towards the firm's fixed costs at various levels of price. It may be no accident that 'full cost' pricing was most in evidence in the writings of economists during the long period after World War II when there was full employment in most countries. With full employment and moderate inflation, there was relatively little pressure on firms to maximise profits. Perhaps it is increased competition, as well as a growing understanding of the principles of variable-cost pricing, that has led in recent years to an increased willingness to base prices on marginal cost, in the way that economic theory suggests.

12.2 Equilibrium in a fixprice market

Nevertheless, perhaps firms do have more discretion in pricing than our analysis has suggested, especially in oligopolistic conditions. We therefore conclude this chapter by looking at what might happen if a number of firms were producing similar products under oligopoly or monopolistic competition, and were also using full-cost pricing. In these circumstances, we have a Fixprice market rather than the Flexprice market studied in Chapter 1. Firms can set their own prices; they do not have to 'take' them. We can therefore look at the same time, in a more general way than we have so far done, at a Fixprice market.

The problem in a Fixprice market is that any outside observer finds it very difficult to predict what the short-run level of prices will be, even if he knows as much about supply and demand schedules as we assumed we did in Chapters 1 and 7. In the medium to long run, prices will have to cover costs; even in the short run, most prices will cover costs. But these requirements can be met with price at a number of different levels and some levels of price will be much more profitable than others. The fact that some prices are not very profitable, makes the firm less willing to charge them; it does not make it impossible for the firm to charge them. It is true that there will be a tendency for high profits in any industry to be reduced. If profits are high, firms already in the industry will increase their outputs; the number of firms in the industry will rise because new firms will enter in greater numbers relatively to the numbers of firms moving out.

We described this kind of process in Chapter 7. In practice, it will be a slow and complex one. While there will be a continual tendency for high profits in the industry to be competed away, it will take a long time to happen. Despite what we have said in this book so far, in practice the level of profits across the economy is unlikely to become uniform in each industry. This is true, even after one has allowed for differing degrees of risk in different industries; and we shall see in Chapter 15 that higher risk usually goes with higher profit.

Nor can we suppose that, even in full-cost industries, prices will never change. They will change, but they will do so infrequently. They will change more frequently in some industries than in others. They will certainly not, as in a competitive Flexprice market, change whenever there is a small shift in the balance between demand and supply. This raises the important question: What does happen if supply and demand are out of balance in a full-cost Fixprice market?

(a) Excess demand

Let us suppose that a number of firms are producing similar products. Let us further suppose that the general level of price for these products is below that at which the quantity of output supplied by this industry, and the quantity of output demanded by consumers, would be equal. The 'full-cost' price is below the equilibrium level; more output is demanded by customers than is supplied by the industry. There is excess demand. If, as is likely with a manufactured product, stocks of that product are available, they can be used to meet the excess demand. Prices do not have to change, because stocks can change. In this situation, they may be reduced. However, if stocks are too small to meet the excess demand, as they will be if the excess demand is both large and persistent, there will be a much greater likelihood of prices being increased, rather than the whole burden being put on the running-down of stocks. There have certainly been occasions in recent years when prices were held stable by firms and industries for considerable periods, even though excess demand had developed in their markets. This was true, for example, in the UK with motor cars in the immediate post-war period and with man-made fibres in the early 1950s. Prices will be held below the equilibrium level if producers think that the increase in demand is temporary; if there is new production capacity which will become available in the fairly near future; or if imports can be safely increased to meet the excess demand.

However, the firms supplying the market (and those attracted by the level of prices in it) will not be satisfied with this situation. We have seen in Chapter 7 that in the long run there are many industries where unit costs will be roughly the same, even if there is a substantial rise in long-run output. The long-run cost curve is horizontal, or nearly so. This means that where there is excess demand, and where this is expected to persist, the industry will be able to meet the whole of this high, future demand, at much the same level of costs and prices as at present. The result is that the group of producers in the industry will plan to meet the whole of the long-run demand which they expect will materialise if the current price is still charged in the future. Any increase in price is likely to be a rather short-term expedient, holding the position until new capacity can be installed. Such a short-run increase in price will be carefully considered. Price will be increased if this will reduce short-run, but not long-run, demand. Price will almost certainly not be increased if the result of a price increase would be to divert a good deal of demand permanently to products made by other industries or to imported goods.

(b) Excess supply

A similar situation will occur in a full-cost Fixprice market if demand falls off, so that there is *excess supply* at the ruling price. The price is now above the equilibrium level, but may again not be allowed to fall in order to bring supply and demand back into equilibrium, as it would in a Flexprice market. In one sense, the situation is easier with excess supply than it is with excess demand. When demand is greater than supply, stocks can be drawn on to keep the quantity supplied equal to the quantity demanded only so long as there are stocks. Once they are exhausted, then either price must be raised or shortages will develop. With excess supply, stocks can, in principle, always be increased to keep the excess supply off the market. However, the difference is one of degree only. Stocks are expensive to finance and to store. There is also the danger, in a market where there is technical change, that products put into stock will be out of date before demand revives. Stocks can take the strain of excess supply only for a time. Once they have reached what is regarded as the highest tolerable level, there will be pressure on the industry either to reduce prices in order to create more demand, or to reduce output.

What actually happens will vary from industry to industry. If the fall in demand is expected to be temporary, output is more likely to be cut than price. Only where demand has fallen permanently, or for a substantial period, is price likely to be reduced as each producer tries to keep his share of the smaller market. Indeed, prices may be cut below the firm's 'full' costs of production—there may be 'weak selling'. It is unlikely that prices will be cut below out-of-pocket costs, because this would mean that the firm would be better off if it closed down altogether. In the end, the number of firms in the industry will be reduced if there is a permanent fall in demand. In terms of the analysis in Chapter 7, the level of profits in the industry will be below normal, and there will be a net reduction in the number of firms in it. On our assumption of perfect competition, of course, this process could take place painlessly. In the real world, the obstacles to easy contraction in most industries are great. The fact is that neither men nor equipment can move easily from one line of activity to another. A woollen mill cannot move into the electronics industry; a shipyard cannot become an airline. In practice, therefore, when an industry declines there is often no obvious alternative to continuing to produce at very low prices, running the industry's equipment until it wears out. In practice, the time taken for a declining industry to decline may be very long—a matter of decades. This is why governments find it difficult to deal with the problems of declining industries. There are strong pressures on governments to keep men at work in such industries by subsidisation. Deciding exactly when and how to stop supporting a declining industry is an agonising problem for all governments.

In this final section, we have linked the analysis rather more closely to the real world than we have been doing elsewhere in this book. It has seemed useful to give readers an understanding of the way in which economic analysis can deal with situations where firms are not maximising profits. Nevertheless, as we have explained on several occasions, we believe that in many industries, for much of the time, an analysis assuming that firms equate marginal cost and marginal revenue will not be far from the truth.

Suggested reading

CHAMBERLIN, E. H.	*Theory of Monopolistic Competition,* Cambridge, Mass., 1946, especially chapters 4–7.
FELLNER, WILLIAM	*Competition among the Few,* New York, 1949, especially chapters 1 and 4–7.
TRIFFIN, ROBERT	*Monopolistic Competition and General Equilibrium Theory,* Cambridge, Mass., 1940, *passim.*
ROTHSCHILD, K. W.	'Price Theory and Oligopoly', *Economic Journal,* September 1947, p. 299.
HICKS, SIR JOHN	*Capital and Growth,* Oxford, 1965, chapters 5 and 7.
TOWNSEND, HARRY	*Price Theory,* Penguin Modern Economics Readings, Middlesex, 1971, chapters 11, 12 and 13.

10

Laws of returns

1. The theory of factor prices

We have now reached an important stage in our analysis. We have concluded our study of the way the prices of goods are determined in conditions of both perfect and imperfect competition. We now come to another broad field of economic theory, to how the prices of factors of production are determined.

In the past, ideas about the determination of factor prices were often referred to as the *Theory of Distribution*. Nineteenth-century economists were extremely interested in the problem of how much of the receipts of industry and agriculture went to each factor of production. For political and social reasons they felt it important to know how the relative incomes of the various social groups were determined. For a time, in pure economic analysis at least, the centre of interest shifted, partly because economic theory became rather more 'pure', not least under the influence of logical positivism. Economic theory became more concerned with what determined the prices of factors of production than with what determined their respective shares of the national income, especially if this implied judgements on whether they were the 'right' shares. Applied economists remain interested in both questions, but in Chapters 11–15 we shall put more emphasis on a study of the way in which the prices of factors of production are determined, than on their respective shares in the national income.

Our analysis of the pricing of factors of production will exactly parallel our analysis of the pricing of commodities and services. For, although on social and political grounds one may feel some qualms about saying so, each broad group of factors of production—land, labour, capital and entrepreneurship—has its 'price' in the form of rent, wages, interest and profits respectively.

This chapter is in a sense a digression from the main line of argument. We are entirely concerned with physical production conditions. But this discussion will enable us to look both backwards and forwards. Physical production conditions underlie the firm's cost curves—already considered in Chapter 5. They also underly the returns to factors of production—the subject of the next few chapters.

2. Equal product curves

We shall find that the easiest way to discuss the laws of returns is to use an analysis similar to the one used in Chapter 3. In Fig. 10.1 we we assume that two factors of production, X and Y, are being used to produce a given product. Amounts of factor X are measured along the x-axis and amounts of factor Y along the y-axis. Physical production conditions are such that if OL units of factor Y and OM units of

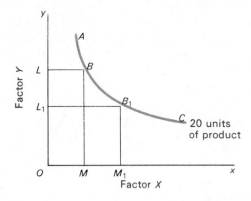

Fig. 10.1

factor X are being used, 20 units of the product are produced. Again, if OL_1 units of factor Y and OM_1 units of factor X are being used, 20 units of product are produced. Similarly, the co-ordinates of any other point on the curve AC apart from B and B_1 show the other quantities of the two factors X and Y needed to produce 20 units of product. The curve AC, that is to say, shows all those combinations of the two factors which, with given technology, will produce 20 units of output. As in Chapter 5, we assume throughout this analysis that physical production conditions are unchanged, and that the factors of production used are being combined as efficiently as possible in these given production conditions. The curve AC thus shows the set of the smallest combinations of the two factors needed, in the existing state of technology, to produce a given output. Curves like AC have been variously described as equal product curves, iso-product curves and isoquants. We shall call them equal product curves.

2.1 Equal product curves defined

The equal product curve AC in Fig. 10.1 is similar to an indifference curve. It shows all those combinations of factors which yield a given quantity of product, just as an indifference curve shows all those combinations of goods which provide a given level of satisfaction. However, there are important differences between equal product curves and indifference curves, which we must note. First, and most obvious, there is the fact that, unlike indifference curves, one can easily label equal product curves; one does it in amounts of product.

While there is no way of measuring consumer satisfactions in physical units, one can measure the number of units of a homogeneous good produced without difficulty. This is extremely helpful. Similarly, if one draws 'higher' and 'lower' equal product curves, as in Fig. 10.2 — if we draw equal product 'maps' — it is easy to say by how much production is greater or less on one equal product curve than on another.

For example, the second equal product curve in Fig. 10.2 shows that output is 40 units—20 units greater than on the first equal product curve. The third equal product curve represents an output

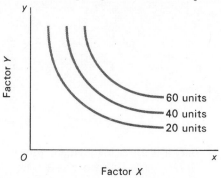

Fig. 10.2

20 units greater than on the second—60 units instead of 40—and so on. So, equal product maps not only enable us to measure physical quantities of output. We can also compare the size of physical output at various points on equal product maps, in a way one could not with satisfactions on indifference maps. We can label equal product curves in units of product and do not have to content ourselves with the non-commital numbers 1, 2, 3, 4, etc., as with indifference maps.

2.2 Equal product curves slope downwards

We must now consider the probable shape of equal product curves, just as in Chapter 3 we considered the probable shape of indifference curves. They will be of the same general shape and for the same kinds of reason. First, equal product curves will slope downwards to the right. This must be the case so long as additional units of any factor of production do not produce *negative* amounts of product. Now this is not an impossibility. One can imagine situations where, with two factors, say land and labour, so many men might be employed that they would all get in each other's way. The result of adding more men would be actually to reduce total output. An increase in the other factor of production, land, would be needed to prevent this.

However, while this might happen, it would never pay an entrepreneur to produce in such a situation. What an upward-sloping equal product curve shows is that a given product can be produced with less of *both* the factors of production. Since factors of production have positive prices, it could also be produced at lower cost. No entrepreneur who is maximising profits would use any combination of factors shown on an upward-sloping portion of an equal product curve. So, while it is quite possible that, over certain ranges, equal product curves will slope upwards, no point on such a range could ever represent an equilibrium position. We can therefore ignore this possibility. Similarly, a horizontal range of an equal product curve, though it could exist, could never represent a possible position of equilibrium. The same output could be obtained with less expense by reducing the amount of one of the factors. A profit-maximising firm will reduce employment of one factor whenever it reaches a downward-sloping portion of an equal product curve. We can therefore assume that, over those ranges in which we shall be interested, equal product curves slope downwards to the right.

2.3 Are equal product curves convex or concave downwards?

Second, we shall assume that equal product curves are convex downwards. This is important, but it is not immediately apparent why equal product curves should be like this. We are clearly implying something about the marginal significance of one factor in terms of another. Let us be quite clear, first, what marginal significance means in this context. In terms of ordinary indifference curves, the marginal significance of one good in terms of the other means the amount of the one good which a consumer can give up in exchange for more of the other, and yet remain on the same indifference curve. With equal product curves the marginal significance of one factor, X, in terms of another factor, Y, is the amount of the factor Y which it is possible to give up in exchange for one more unit of factor X without altering the amount of product made—while remaining on the same equal product curve.

For example, let us imagine a situation where one unit of factor X and ten units of factor Y are being used to produce twenty units of product. What is the marginal significance of factor X in terms of factor Y? If the product is to be kept constant while one unit of factor X is added to the factor combination already being used a certain quantity of factor Y must be dispensed with. Otherwise the total product would increase. It might, for example, be necessary to dispense with two units of factor Y, now that an additional unit of factor X had been taken on, if the amount of product were to be kept constant. In this situation, the marginal significance of X in terms of Y is $X = 2Y$. So, we can calculate the marginal significance of one factor in terms of the other at any point on an equal product curve.

This marginal significance will always depend on the slope of the equal product curve. It follows that the way in which the slope of an equal product curve changes, as one moves along it, will determine the way in which the marginal significance of one factor in terms of the other alters.

What does the assumption that equal product curves are convex downwards imply about the marginal significance of one factor in terms of the other? It implies that the marginal significance of one factor in terms of the other will always diminish along any equal product curve. On any equal product curve, the more of factor X is being used, the less of factor Y it will be possible to give up at the expense of a further unit of X, if product is to be kept constant. Similarly, of course, the more units of Y are being used, the less X it will be possible to give up in exchange for yet one more unit of Y. This assumption that equal product curves are convex downwards, and that the marginal significance of one factor in terms of the other therefore always diminishes along an equal product curve, is important. But is diminishing marginal significance of one factor in terms of the other likely to occur as a general rule? Our fundamental assumption about production conditions is that it is.

This assumption that equal product curves are convex downwards —that marginal significance always diminishes—can be justified in exactly the same way as can the convexity of indifference curves —so long as competition between buyers of factors is perfect. When we discussed consumer's equilibrium in terms of indifference curves we assumed that the prices of all goods were given, so that all price lines were straight lines. Whatever the volume of purchases made by a single consumer, it was assumed to leave the relative prices of the goods he bought unaltered. By making this assumption, we were able to show that convexity downwards of indifference curves was an essential condition for equilibrium of the consumer and to report that observation of consumers' buying patterns fitted in with it.

As we shall see in a moment, the 'perfectly competitive' buyer of factors of production makes his purchases in accordance with an equal product map, just as a consumer does with an indifference map. He is in equilibrium where his (straight line) price line is tangential to a convex-downwards equal product curve. In this way, he just reaches the highest possible equal product curve. But this means that, at the point of equilibrium, the relative prices of factors of production equal the marginal significance of one factor in terms of the other. In consequence, the purchaser buys each factor until its marginal significance in terms of money is just equal to its money price. If, however, the marginal significance of a factor *increased* as one hired more of it, as it would on a concave equal product curve, and it was worth buying any of the factor at all, it would be worth spending the whole of one's outlay on it. For each succeeding unit of the factor would have a progressively higher marginal significance and would be correspondingly more worth hiring—given the relative factor prices shown on the (straight) price line. Equal product curves that were concave downwards would make it worth hiring only one of the factors. In practice, one does not find large numbers of men, large areas of land or even large capital-intensive factories producing output entirely on their own and without any co-operating factors at all. It is therefore reasonable to assume that equal product curves are concave upwards so long as competition between buyers of factors is perfect.

This does not, of course, rule out the possibility of 'bumps' or 'wobbles' on an equal product curve. On the other hand, as with indifference curves, a producer would never be in equilibrium on such a range of an equal product curve. Only where marginal significance is diminishing can he be in equilibrium. Since economists are not interested in situations where equilibrium is impossible, we have good reason to ignore such unusual portions of equal product curves. The fundamental assumption of diminishing marginal significance along an equal product curve is therefore reasonable in conditions of perfect competition between buyers of factors.

It is, however, possible that competition between the buyers of factors may not be perfect. Indeed, this is more likely to happen with buyers of factors of production than with buyers of consumption goods. It is reasonable when dealing with consumers to assume that there are large numbers of them—that competition between them is perfect. But there may well be only a few firms, or even only one firm, buying factors. If there is only one purchaser of certain factors of production, their prices will almost certainly be influenced by his own purchases of them. So, a price line need not be a straight line, but may be concave downwards. The more of one factor of production the firm buys compared with the other, the higher will the former factor's relative price be and vice versa. It follows that such a producer could be in equilibrium, with the price line tangential to an equal product curve that was concave downwards, provided that the concavity of the price line was greater than that of the equal product curve. The concave-downwards price line would show that relative prices were varying and not constant. While equal product curves that are concave downwards cannot represent equilibrium positions in perfect competition, they can do so in imperfect competition. We shall assume here, however, that though a single monopolistic firm buying two factors might be in an equilibrium position on an equal product curve that was concave downwards, all equal product curves are actually concave upwards. This is our second assumption about equal product curves. But it is an *assumption* and it cannot be justified on *a priori* grounds.

Finally, there is a definition. Equal product curves, like indifference curves, can never cut each other. If they did, there would be a logical contradiction.

3. Returns to scale

Before going on to use equal product curves to discover how returns to factors of production will change as the amounts of factors used are altered in certain ways, there is a point which needs discussion. The equal product maps we have used so far, and shall use in this section and in section 10.4, show two factors. This is not altogether realistic. The idea that labour and capital can produce a product with no-one to supervise them is unreasonable. It is therefore important to be able to use an analysis where there are three or four factors of production, with the entrepreneurs one of them. The others could then be labour, land or capital, as one wished. While we shall confine our attention here to two factors only, the analysis can be extended easily to situations with more than two.

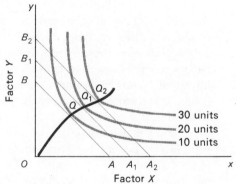

Fig. 10.3

We are interested in the laws of returns and shall look at the problem in two stages. In this section, we shall consider returns to two factors of production where both can vary—returns with two variable factors. In section 10.4, we shall consider returns to two factors where one can vary and the other is in fixed amount. We are then considering returns to one variable factor, as we did in the 'law of variable proportions'.[1] We shall assume throughout that competition between buyers of factors is perfect—that all *price lines* are straight lines.

Let us discover how a firm will change its output in the long run in response to a change in the demand for its product, assuming that it can alter the amounts of both factors. To do this we must introduce the prices of the factors in question into the analysis, for the amounts of factors hired by the firm, in a given situation, will depend on the relative prices of these factors as well as on the technical conditions

[1]See p. 152.

shown in Fig. 10.3, and that in the existing situation the price of factor X divided by the price of factor Y is equal to $\dfrac{OB}{OA} = \dfrac{OB_1}{OA_1} = \dfrac{OB_2}{OA_2}$.

3.1 Scale lines

We shall continue to assume that the firm wishes to produce each output as cheaply as possible.

If this is so, and if the firm wishes to produce 20 units of product, it will be in equilibrium at point Q_1 on the equal product curve representing 20 units of output. Here, the price line A_1B_1 is tangential to the equal product curve. Only at point Q_1 will the firm be producing the 20 units of output as cheaply as possible. To reach any point other than Q_1 on the equal product curve representing 20 units of output, the firm will have to spend more than OA_1 in terms of X, or OB_1 in terms of Y, for appropriate combinations of factors. Similarly, if the firm wishes to produce 30 units of the product, it will be in equilibrium only at point Q_2. OA_2 in terms of X, or OB_2 in terms of Y, represents the lowest cost at which 30 units of output can be produced. It will be noted that at all points such as Q, Q_1 and Q_2 the marginal significance of X in terms of Y is equal to the relative money prices of factors X and Y. This is shown by the fact that each equal product curve is tangential to the relevant price line. Such equilibrium positions are therefore analogous to those shown in consumers' indifference maps.

Given the relative price of factors X and Y, a firm which is able to vary the amounts of both these factors by small amounts always fixes its scale of output as its scale of operation increases at some point along a line like O–Q–Q_1–Q_2 in Fig. 10.3. This line is known as a *scale line*. It is analogous to the income-consumption curve in Chapter 3. It shows the way in which the entrepreneur adjusts the scale of his operation with given relative factor prices. It shows the cheapest way of producing each output in these circumstances. Where both factors are variable, as they may well be in the long run, the firm will always produce at some point on such a scale line. The shape of the scale line will depend both on the relative prices of the factors concerned and on the shape of the equal product curves. The point on the scale line at which a firm will be in equilibrium will depend on the output it wishes to produce. This in turn will depend on the level of output which conditions in the product market make it profitable to produce.

However, one can be certain that where both factors are variable the profit-maximising entrepreneur will be producing somewhere on a scale line like the one shown in Fig. 10.3. A scale line therefore shows the way in which factor combinations alter, where both factors can be varied in response to changes in the output which the firm is producing, but where the relative prices of the factors are given. It must be remembered, of course, that on every equal product map there will be a different scale line for *every* different relative price of the factors.

From such an equal product map we can find two things. First, having obtained the scale line corresponding to any particular ratio of the prices of the factors, we can tell whether *returns to scale* (returns along the scale line) will increase, diminish or remain constant as output varies. Second, we can tell whether the proportion between the amounts of the two factors of production used will remain the same or will vary as one moves along any one scale line. These two problems should not be confused, for they are in essence quite separate.

3.2
Homogeneous
production
functions

Let us consider the way in which these two influences affect the nature of scale lines by studying first a very simple equal product map. Let us assume that if we start from any given combination of two factors of production and increase the amount of each factor in a given proportion, this increases the amount of product in that same proportion. For example, if we treble the amount of each factor, we treble the product. Such a production function, that is, the function which relates the amount of output to the amounts of the factors needed to produce that output, is homogeneous of the first degree.

We can write *any* production function in the general form $P = f(X, Y)$, where P is the amount of product and X and Y are the amounts of factors of production used. The general form of a production function of the first degree would then be $P = t^k f(X, Y)$ where k is a constant and t any positive real number. A specific example of a production function which is homogeneous of the first degree would be: $P \sqrt{AB}$. The production function giving the relationship between factors used and product produced in the conditions shown in Fig. 10.4 will also be homogeneous of first degree. As can be seen by inspecting the diagram, if the factors X and Y are both increased in any proportion, the product increases in that same proportion.

The equal product map for a homogeneous production function of the first degree will *always* be one where *all* scale lines are straight lines through the origin and where returns to scale along every scale line on the equal product map are constant. The constancy of returns to scale is displayed by the fact that the distance between successive equal product curves along any one scale line such as $OABCD$ or $OA_2B_2C_2D_2$ is always the same. So, in Fig. 10.4, $OA = AB = BC = CD$;

$$OA_1 = A_1B_1 = B_1C_1 = C_1D_1; \quad \text{and} \quad OA_2 = A_2B_2 = B_2C_2 = C_2D_2, \quad \text{etc.}$$

Alternatively one could say that, with given relative factor prices and therefore with a constant slope of the price line, *returns to outlay* are constant. If factor prices are constant and one doubles the amount

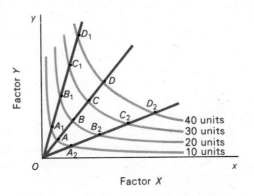

Fig. 10.4

of each factor, one also doubles outlay on the two factors together. With this particular type of equal product map, one can use the terms returns to scale and returns to outlay interchangeably. As we shall see later, with other kinds of equal product map it is more meaningful to speak of returns to outlay rather than returns to scale.

3.3 Constant factor proportions and returns to scale

A homogeneous production function of the first degree is a useful one to study first because it is simple, but it does imply that, with constant relative factor prices, the proportion between the two factors is always the same whatever output is being produced. It is difficult to say how frequently this will actually happen in practice. Returns to scale will clearly not always be constant. Even if there are constant returns to outlay (or scale) along a scale line, the proportions between the factors of production need not be constant. It would be perfectly possible for a scale line to curve in one direction or another, even though there were constant returns to outlay along any individual scale line.

It is when the scale lines cease to be straight lines (when the proportions between factors vary as output changes) that it immediately becomes necessary to talk of returns to *outlay* instead of returns to *scale*. For, when this happens, it is impossible to speak unambiguously of doubling the scale of operations along that scale line, in the usual sense of doubling the amount of each factor. To increase the amounts of both the factors in the same proportion would now mean moving to a different scale line. The only unambiguous comparison is now a comparison of *changes in outlay on factors* with the *changes in output* to which they give rise. For example, if outlay on the factors is doubled and the product doubles also, one can say that returns to outlay are constant.

Now it is quite possible that, although returns to outlay are constant along any scale line, the proportion between the amounts of factor used along that same scale line will alter. Constant returns to outlay and constant proportions between the two factors are not the same thing. Nor is there any good reason why constant proportions between factors at all levels of output should often be found in practice. In this chapter, it will be convenient to assume that the proportion between any two factors remains the same whatever the scale of output is. This will keep the argument simple. It will also enable us to use the terms returns to scale and returns to outlay interchangeably. But it must be borne in mind that this is only a convenient simplification. One will not always find constant proportions between factors even with constant returns to scale; nor do returns to scale and returns to outlay always mean the same thing.

One can easily think of instances where the proportions between factors will vary as the scale of activity changes. For example, the output of a single-storey factory could be doubled by adding a second storey. This would change the proportion between land and capital. Constant proportions between factors will not necessarily occur, though we shall assume here that they do.

3.4 Increasing and decreasing returns to scale

Having made this assumption, we can now return to the question whether returns to outlay are likely to be constant in practice. It does not seem very sensible to assume that this will always happen, as we have assumed, even when there are only two factors of production. It seems more reasonable to think that a change in the scale of operations will often mean that there are increasing or decreasing returns to outlay. Over relatively low levels of output it is likely that increasing returns to outlay will occur, because as output rises there are economies of scale to be reaped. It is likely, for example, that where one of the factors is labour, the division of labour will increase output as the number of men employed rises. There are likely to be increasing returns to outlay in some parts of an equal product map, whether or not the scale lines are straight lines. There will be diminishing returns to outlay over other ranges of output. The characteristics of an equal product map where this happens are shown in Fig. 10.5.

Here, we have drawn the scale line as a straight line purely to simplify the construction of the diagram. Up to the point R on the scale line, returns to outlay increase as output rises. Beyond R, returns decrease as outlay continues to increase. It *does* seem to be justifiable to assume that returns to outlay will vary as output alters. We saw in Chapter 5 that increasing returns are likely to occur as output rises from low levels to moderate ones. To that extent, Fig. 10.5 seems to be correct. What is less certain is what happens to returns to scale as output continues to increase. It may well be that Fig. 10.5 is not

Fig. 10.5

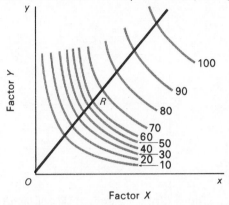

realistic because it shows diminishing returns to scale rather than constant ones. The discovery of L-shaped long-run cost curves in empirical studies suggests that, at high outputs, returns to scale in the long run may be constant.

We have noted that there are similarities between scale lines on equal product maps and income-consumption curves on indifference maps. They both represent points of tangency between successive price lines of constant slope and successive equal product curves and indifference curves respectively.

4. Returns to a variable factor

So far, we have seen how factor proportions and returns to outlay may behave as output changes, with two variable factors. This kind of analysis is of limited use in economics. In practice, at least one factor of production is usually fixed in amount. In the discussion of U-shaped cost curves in Chapter 5, for example, what we spoke of as 'returns to scale' were, strictly speaking, returns to a number of variable factors. For we assumed that, even in the long run, entrepreneurship is a fixed factor of production. True 'returns to scale', in the sense of returns where *all* factors vary, will be found very rarely in the real world. It is more realistic to study the case of only one variable factor in order to discover what can be said about the way physical returns to that factor will alter. So long as one factor at least is fixed and at least one is variable, the results can be easily extended to situations where there are more than two factors.

4.1 Marginal physical productivity

Let us assume that a firm uses a fixed amount of factor Y in conjunction with varying amounts of another factor, X. In Fig. 10.6a, OM of the fixed factor Y is used in conjunction with varying amounts of factor X. The way in which returns to factor X change as the amounts of factor X vary can be discovered by studying what happens along the horizontal line MM in Fig. 10.6a. At each point on this

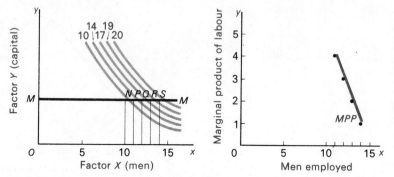

Fig. 10.6 a | b

line, a fixed amount (OM) of factor Y is being used in conjunction with a different amount of the variable factor, X. We can represent the physical returns to the variable factor in several ways. Just as we can represent costs and revenues by total, average and marginal cost curves, we can also portray the physical productivity of a variable factor of production by drawing total, average or marginal physical productivity curves. We now go on to consider the shapes of physical productivity curves—especially marginal physical productivity curves.

A marginal physical productivity curve shows how the marginal physical productivity of a variable factor alters, as the amount of it which is used in conjunction with a fixed factor changes. This marginal productivity curve will form the basis of our analysis of the pricing of factors of production.

We can discover the marginal physical productivity of any variable factor from an equal product map in the way shown in Fig. 10.6a. In Fig. 10.6a, there is a fixed amount (OM) of factor Y, say capital. This is used in conjunction with varying amounts of factor X, say labour. As employment increases from 10 men to 11, total production rises from 10 units to 14. The marginal physical productivity of labour is therefore four units of output. This is shown by the fact that the horizontal line MM intersects the equal product curve representing 14 units of output at point P, representing 11 men, on the x-axis. Total output rises from 14 units to 17 units as one moves from P to Q. The thirteenth man adds two units (from Q to R), the fourteenth adds one unit (from R to S), and so on.

We now construct Fig. 10.6b to show the marginal physical

productivity of factor X (labour) on a curve. This marginal physical productivity curve, which is coloured dark brown in Fig. 10.6b, shows how total physical productivity increases as extra individual men are added to the number already employed. In this particular instance, the marginal physical productivity curve of labour (MPP) slopes downwards. As we shall see later, the marginal physical productivity of any variable factor is assumed usually to diminish (at least in the end) as more variable factor is added to the fixed factor (or factors). It is also possible to draw an average physical productivity curve (derived from the equal product map by dividing total output at each level of employment by numbers of men employed). This bears the usual average-marginal relationship to the marginal physical productivity curve and can indeed be derived from the marginal curve instead. The total physical productivity curve could also easily be derived either from the equal product map or from the average and marginal physical productivity curves.

4.2 Diminishing marginal physical productivity and the law of diminishing returns

The assumption that the marginal physical productivity of a variable factor used in conjunction with one or several fixed factors will diminish is important. Such an idea has always had a place in economics. In the past, it has usually been known as the 'law of dminishing returns', or, more recently, the 'law of variable proportions'. One can state the 'law of diminishing returns' thus:

> 'An increase in the amount of a variable factor added to a fixed factor causes, in the end, a less than proportionate increase in the amount of product, given technical conditions.'[1]

The 'law of diminishing returns' is not couched directly in terms of diminishing marginal productivity, though it comes to the same thing. Nor must diminishing marginal productivity be confused with diminishing returns to scale where both (all) factors alter. We are here concerned with returns to a single variable factor used in conjunction with a fixed factor. However, diminishing marginal productivity is probably not as ubiquitous as some earlier economists seem to have thought. There may well be ranges of marginal physical productivity curves where marginal physical productivity is increasing and not diminishing. Instead of falling throughout, as in Fig. 10.6, the marginal physical productivity curve may rise for a short time before it ultimately falls. Diminishing marginal physical productivity does not always occur. Some modern economists therefore speak of *eventually* diminishing marginal productivity. This is the general condition. While it is conceivable that before diminishing marginal physical productivity may rise, in the end it will fall.

[1] Cf. Alfred Marshall, *Principles of Economics*, p. 150.

In order to see more fully under what conditions marginal physical productivity will diminish and in what conditions it will increase, let us first consider a situation where the production function is homogeneous of the first degree. Here, there will *always* be diminishing marginal physical productivity along any horizontal or vertical line like *MM* in Fig. 10.6a. That is to say, whenever there are varying proportions between factors, with one fixed and the other variable, marginal physical productivity will always diminish. This must be the case, but perhaps it will be useful to prove why. It will help us to do this if we first derive the marginal physical productivity of a variable factor from an equal product map rather differently from the way we did it in Fig. 10.6.

4.3 When marginal physical productivity always diminishes

In Fig. 10.6, equal increments of a variable factor were added to a given amount of a fixed factor. We defined the resulting increments of product as the marginal physical productivity of the variable factor. In Fig. 10.7, with a homogeneous production function of the first degree, we instead consider several equal increases in production along any horizontal, such as *MM*. We then discover how many

Fig. 10.7

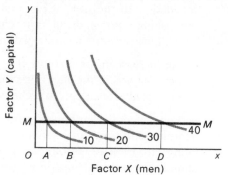

men are needed to bring about these equal increments of output. If this is done, we can see that to increase output from 10 to 20 units along *MM* in Fig. 10.7 requires the addition of *AB* men to the fixed amount of capital *OM* and to the *OA* men who are already employed. To increase production from 20 to 30 units needs a further *BC* men, and so on. The number of extra units of the variable factor (labour) needed to raise output by the same absolute amount, here 10 units, therefore increases as we move along the horizontal *MM* from left to right. In other words, the marginal physical productivity of labour diminishes.

What we want to show is that with a homogeneous production function of the first degree, the distance between two successive equal

product curves along a horizontal such as *MM* (like *BC*), is always
greater than a similar distance immediately to the left of it, in this
case *AB*. In other words, as more of a variable factor is added to a
fixed factor, the marginal physical productivity of the variable factor
falls progressively with this type of equal product map. We can prove
this from Fig. 10.8.

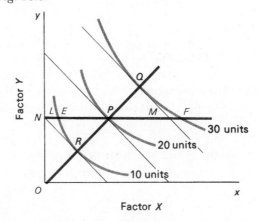

Fig. 10.8

In Fig. 10.8, there are three equal product curves, showing 10,
20 and 30 units of output respectively. Along the *x*-axis are measured
differing amounts of the variable factor *X*, applied to a fixed amount
(*ON*) of factor *Y* shown on the *y*-axis. A scale line showing constant
returns to outlay passes from the origin through point *P*. Tangents
have been drawn to the equal product curves at the points *R*, *P* and
Q, where the equal product curves and the scale line intersect. Since
these tangents must touch the equal product curves where the scale
lines cut them, they must be parallel to each other; all equal product
curves have the same slope on the same scale line.

We wish to prove that the intercept *PF*, between the equal product
curves representing 20 and 30 units of output, is greater than the
intercept *EP* between those representing 10 and 20 units. Since the
production function is homogeneous of the first degree, *RP*=*PQ*.
As we saw earlier, with this type of production function, returns to
scale are always constant. Because *RP*=*PQ* and because the tangents
are parallel to each other, the intercepts *LP* and *PM* on the horizontal
line *NF* are also equal. Now *LP* is obviously greater than *EP*, because
the equal product curve representing ten units of output is concave
upwards, while the tangent to it is a straight line. *EP* is consequently
smaller than *PM*, because *PM*=*LP*. Similarly, *PF* is greater than
PM and is therefore also greater than *EP*. This proof holds with any
equal product map for a homogeneous production function of the
first degree. On any such equal product map the marginal physical
productivity of a variable factor always falls as more of it is added to

a fixed factor. So, if production functions were always homogeneous of the first degree and if returns to scale (and outlay) were always constant, marginal physical productivity would always fall. Since returns to outlay are not always constant, marginal physical productivity of the variable factor may rise over some ranges of output.

4.4 When marginal physical productivity may increase

Figure 10.9a shows an equal product map where the horizontal line MM shows the returns to differing amounts of a variable factor X, used in conjunction with OM of a fixed factor Y. Figure 10.9b shows the marginal productivity curve of the variable factor X. In Fig. 10.9a, returns to outlay rise to begin with as one moves up the scale line OP; once outlay exceeds 19 units, returns to outlay fall. It can be seen from Fig. 10.9b that the marginal physical productivity of the (variable) factor first rises and then falls. If fewer than 13 men are employed, the marginal physical productivity of labour is rising.

Fig. 10.9 a
⎯
     b

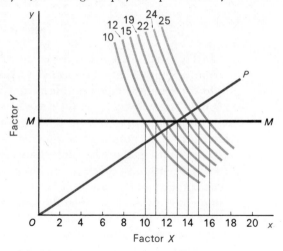

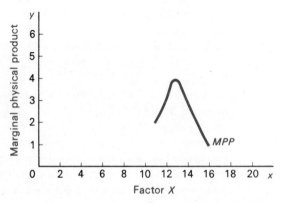

For example, the eleventh man adds two units of output to the firm's total product, which rises from 10 units to 12; the twelfth adds three; and the thirteenth adds four (output rises from 15 to 19 units). Once 14 men are employed, the marginal physical productivity of labour begins to fall. The employment of this fourteenth man adds only three units of output (which rises from 19 to 22), that of a fifteenth only two (22 to 24), and that of a sixteenth only one.

It will probably be valuable if we can show in a more general way under what circumstances returns to a variable factor (marginal productivity) can increase as more of that factor is employed in conjunction with a fixed factor. This has been done in Fig. 10.10.

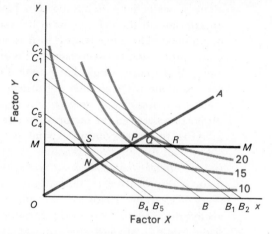

Fig. 10.10

Here, there are three equal product curves representing 10, 15 and 20 units of output respectively and all scale lines (like OA) are straight lines through the origin. It is along such scale lines that the firm will expand output (given the relative prices of factors) so long as both factors can be freely varied in amount as output is increased. Returns to outlay (scale) are clearly increasing along the one scale line shown (OA). Since NP is greater than PQ, a smaller increase in outlay on factors is required to raise output from 15 to 20 units than from 10 units to 15. Similarly, marginal productivity is increasing along MM (SP is greater than PR).

Let us assume that initially the firm is producing fifteen units of output at point P. With given factor prices, if the firm now wishes to produce twenty units of output, and both factors can be freely varied, it will proceed to produce at point Q on the scale line OA. This will require an outlay of OB_1 in terms of factor X (or OC_1 in terms of factor Y). If factor Y is fixed in amount at OM and factor X only can be varied, the only way to produce 20 units of output is to do so at point R. This would require a greater additional expenditure (BB_2 in terms of X or CC_2 in terms of Y) than would be necessary to produce at Q (BB_1 in terms of X, or CC_1 in terms of Y). Since returns are increasing strongly along the scale line, the additional outlay needed to raise output along the scale line from 15 to 20 units (BB_1) is smaller than the outlay needed to raise output from 10 units to 15 (B_4B). Similarly, to increase output from 10 to 15 units along MM (from S to P) requires an additional outlay of B_5B, while to raise it from 15 to 20 units (from P to R) costs only an additional BB_2. In other words, returns to outlay do not increase so rapidly along MM as along OA. The excess of B_4B over BB_1 is greater than the excess of B_5B over BB_2. Even so, returns to outlay do still increase along MM.

To put the point more generally, since the move from P to Q is along a scale line, the proportion between the factors which is appropriate to the existing ratio between the factor prices can be maintained. The move from P to R is one which disturbs this 'optimum' proportion between factors. Production increases less rapidly along MM than it would have done if output could have been increased along the scale line OA instead. However, since returns to scale are *increasing very strongly*, this departure from the 'optimum' proportion between the factors does not cause an actual decrease in marginal product as output expand along MM.

One can sum up thus. *Whenever all the scale lines on an equal product map are straight lines through the origin,* the following conditions will hold. If returns to scale (outlay) are *constant*, the marginal productivity of a variable factor used in conjunction with a fixed factor will always diminish as more of the variable factor is used. If returns to scale (outlay) are *decreasing*, marginal productivity will likewise always diminish; when returns to scale (outlay) are *increasing*, marginal productivity will still diminish *unless the returns to scale are increasing sufficiently strongly* to prevent this.

Even if the scale lines are not all straight lines through the origin, the above rules will always hold (though now for returns to *outlay*) provided that all scale lines slope upwards to the right. If scale lines take any other shape (*e.g.* are horizontal, or slope downwards to the right), there will be exceptions to the above rules. It is impossible to say intuitively whether such exceptions will be numerous, but one must allow for the possibility that they will occur.

5. Eventually diminishing returns

It follows from this discussion that the 'law of diminishing returns' does not hold with all types of production function. In some situations, marginal productivity may rise before it ultimately falls. However, there is no *a priori* reason for believing that marginal productivity will not ultimately fall. The 'law of eventually diminishing marginal productivity' seems to be valid. While one cannot be certain that marginal productivity will be diminishing over all ranges of output, there is no reason to doubt that in the end the addition of more and more units of a variable factor to a fixed factor will cause marginal productivity to decrease. The field will ultimately be overcrowded with farm labourers; the factory will be filled with workers, and so on. What is quite possible is that this may happen at an output *larger* than that at which the firm has already reached equilibrium, so that empirical investigations would not show diminishing marginal productivity.

However, the law of diminishing returns comes to the same thing as the law of variable proportions. In the short run, the firm's marginal cost curve is bound to rise in the end. Ultimately, marginal physical productivity will fall as the firm expands output along a given short-run marginal cost or marginal productivity curve. All the empirical evidence supports this view. There is as much certainty over the fact that in the short run marginal cost ultimately rises and marginal physical productivity ultimately falls as there is doubt over what happens in the long run.

While the argument of section 10.5 was throughout in terms of only two factors, we have already explained that the results can be extended to cover situations were there are more than two without difficulty.

Suggested reading

CARLSON, SUNE	*The Theory of Production*, London, 1939. (For readers with a good knowledge of calculus.)
LERNER, A. P.	*The Economics of Control*, New York, 1946, chapters 12 and 13.

11

Marginal productivity

Armed with the findings of Chapter 10, we may now return to the main trend of our argument and analyse the way in which factor prices are determined. We shall discover that the key to the pricing of factors of production lies in marginal productivity. The rewards of a factor of production depend in the end on what it produces. Before turning to the detailed analysis it will be useful to explain its basic principles.

We simplified our study of the pricing of goods by assuming that prices of all factors needed to make them were constant and given. In analysing the determination of factor prices, we must allow explicitly for the fact that the price of a factor of production is determined not only by conditions in the market for it, but also by conditions in the market where the product made by the factor is sold. We shall also show what happens if there are differing degrees of imperfection of competition in both factor and product markets.

It is clear that it would be possible to undertake a lengthy and intricate analysis of factor prices by assuming many different combinations of conditions in the markets for factors on the one hand, and for the products they make on the other. In order to simplify the analysis, we shall confine our attention to situations where there is either perfect competition or monopoly in one or both markets. The curious reader will no doubt be able to extend the analysis for himself to cover cases of oligopoly and monopolistic competition.

2. Monopsony

One final point is important. We have seen that monopoly in the market for a product means that the monopolist is the only seller of a particular article. He does not need to worry about the reactions of rivals to changes in his price-output policy because they produce only very remote substitutes for his own product. We must now envisage the possibility that in the market for a factor of production, where the buyers are firms, there may be one firm which is large enough to have a unique position on the buying side. To describe such a situation, Professor Joan Robinson coined the word *monopsony*,[1] which is now generally used. A monopsonist is the only firm on the buyers' side of a market just as a monopolist is the only firm on the sellers' side. A monopsonistic firm is the only firm demanding a particular factor of production.

In this chapter we shall find in every case we discuss that the answer to the question: 'What determines the prices of factors of production?' can be framed in terms of marginal productivity. The essence of our theory is that the price of any factor of production depends on its marginal productivity. What precisely we mean by marginal productivity—a concept already met with in the previous chapter—is the next topic we must discuss.

3. Marginal productivity

It seems best to divide this explanation of the meaning of marginal productivity into two parts.

3.1 Productivity

First, let us discover why we are interested in productivity at all. The answer is that the productivity of factors of production is important because they are not hired or bought because they are *directly* useful in the way that consumption goods are. They are useful only indirectly. They can produce goods which do satisfy wants directly. This is why the demand for factors of production depends on what they can produce—on their productivity.

For example let us consider labour, because it was largely in connection with wage theory that the idea of productivity as the fundamental determinant of factor prices was originally worked out. The economist finds the basis of his analysis of wages in labour productivity. He assumes that if the wage paid to one man is greater than that paid to another, then the first man produces more. This does not, of course, provide a complete solution to the way in which wages are fixed. The theory which we shall outline is more complicated than this, but productivity does provide a convenient starting-point for a theory of factor prices.

One important point must always be borne in mind. So far as economic theory is concerned, it is assumed that the relation between productivity and wages is a one-way relation. That is to say, it is assumed that wages depend on productivity, but that productivity does not depend on wages. Yet the relationship is by no means so simple as this in practice. It is perfectly reasonable to look upon low

[1] *The Economics of Imperfect Competition*, p. 215.

wages in poor countries as the cause as well as the effect of low productivity. Malnutrition among workers is often one cause of low output. Nevertheless, it would be difficult to devise a theory of factor prices if *wages* depended on productivity but *productivity* also depended on wages. Our theory will therefore hold that wages are determined by productivity and not vice versa.

3.2 Productivity and the margin

We have now seen why productivity is important in determining factor prices. What we must now see is why it is *marginal* productivity matters. Why not average productivity? Why not productivity per man or per machine? The answer to this is the same as to the question: 'Why do we study marginal revenue and marginal cost in the theory of the firm?' Just as an entrepreneur maximises profits when he equates marginal revenue and marginal cost, he also maximises profits if he equates the marginal productivity of each factor with its marginal cost. We are back to the fundamental rule for maximising the difference between two functions in differential calculus. One equates the derivatives of the two functions.

4. A model of factor pricing

Let us now build up an analytical scheme, based on marginal productivity, with which we can outline the theory of factor prices. We must first make clear several assumptions, some of which we shall relax later.

4.1 Our assumptions

First, we assume that there is perfect competition in the market for a factor of production, say, labour. There are large numbers of buyers and sellers of labour, none of whom is important in relation to the total of buyers and sellers. Second, we assume, for the present, that there is perfect competition in the market for the product which the labour is making. Third, we assume that the labour is homogeneous in the sense that all workers are equally efficient. This is not an entirely reasonable assumption, but it will simplify our analysis greatly. Fourth, we shall assume that the number of hours which will be worked each week by any one man is given and that problems of overtime can be ignored. This will enable us to measure amounts of labour in terms of numbers of men, each working a fixed number of hours per week. In this way we can ensure that additional labour comes onto the market only in the form of more men and not in the form of longer hours worked by each man. We have a measure of homogeneous labour which enables us to measure amounts of the factor in the same way as we measured output in terms of units of a homogeneous product in value theory. Finally, we shall for the present concern ourselves only with explaining what determines the price of a *single variable factor* which is applied to a given amount of one or more fixed factors. This must be borne in mind so as we are making this restrictive assumption.

4.2 Labour productivity in the firm

On the basis of these assumptions let us begin by considering the marginal physical productivity of labour for a single firm. This can be derived from the firm's equal product map, as we saw in the previous chapter. Let us assume that we are concerned with a farm which produces potatoes and that as the number of men employed increases from one to ten, the weekly product of the farm changes as follows:

Table 11.1

Schedules of total and marginal physical productivity

Men employed	Total product (kg of potatoes)	Marginal physical product (kg of potatoes)
1	6	6
2	13	7
3	25	12
4	45	20
5	70	25
6	100	30
7	127	27
8	152	25
9	170	18
10	180	10

The important feature of these schedules is that the marginal physical product of labour—the increase in the total product of the firm as additional men are taken on—rises when these additional men are taken on, until there are six men. Once more than six men are employed, the marginal physical productivity of labour begins to decline. This is the same situation as that discussed in our analysis of the 'law' of variable proportions in the previous chapter. As increasing amounts of the variable factor (labour) are applied to a combination of fixed amounts of other factors, the marginal product of labour increases up to a point (here where six men are employed) and then declines. Empirical evidence suggests that this is correct;

it is the counterpart of the U-shaped short-run marginal cost curve. We shall assume that all marginal physical productivity curves are of this shape.

If more men are employed after the point of maximum marginal physical productivity has been reached, the marginal physical productivity of labour begins to decrease. This is simply another instance of the 'eventually diminishing returns' discussed in Chapter 10. After a certain stage has been reached, it must become unprofitable to go on applying more and more men to a given amount of, say, land and entrepreneurship, though when that stage will be reached we cannot say. One important point must be remembered. The seventh man is assumed to be just as efficient as the sixth, even though marginal physical productivity begins to fall when he is taken on. Seven equally efficient men produce just as much as each other, but each produces a little less than each of six equally efficient men had been able to produce. This is a result of physical production conditions and has nothing to do with inefficiency on the part of any of the workers. Perhaps each of seven men has less 'elbow-room' than each of six men and marginal productivity falls off because of this.

We begin from this hypothetical schedule of the marginal physical productivity of labour, showing how the marginal physical productivity of labour changes in response to changes in the number of men employed. It would be quite simple to go on to turn this schedule into a diagram of the kind we drew in Chapter 10. However, for our purposes we do not need a diagram showing the marginal productivity of a factor in terms of physical units—in this case kilogrammes of potatoes. We are not interested in marginal physical productivity so much as in the money which a firm earns from the sale of its physical output. The entrepreneur does not normally pay his worker in potatoes but in cash. What interests the entrepreneur most is how much he can add to the *revenue* of his firm when he progressively increases the size of his labour force. He has to compare two things. The first is what the employment of each additional (marginal) unit of each factor (in this case labour) adds to the revenue of the firm; the second is what it costs him when he hires an additional unit of the factor.

We shall therefore find it more useful to draw what is called a *marginal revenue productivity curve*. This shows the addition to the total revenue of the firm caused when successive marginal units of labour are added to the fixed amounts of the other factors which it employs. Such a curve can easily be constructed from a marginal physical productivity schedule like that in Table 11.1, if one knows the price of the firm's product. Let us assume that potatoes are 50p per kg. Since we are assuming that competition between sellers in the potato market is perfect, we can take this price of 50p as given and unalterable whatever the output of the firm we are studying is. Thus marginal revenue product, in perfect competition, is simply marginal physical product multiplied by price. The marginal revenue productivity schedule of the firm in question is therefore as follows:

Table 11.2
*A marginal
revenue
productivity
schedule*

Number of men	*Marginal physical productivity (kg of potatoes)*	*Marginal revenue productivity (physical productivity × price (£0·50 per kg))*
1	6	3·00
2	7	3·50
3	12	6·00
4	20	10·00
5	25	12·50
6	30	15·00
7	27	13·50
8	25	12·50
9	18	9·00
10	10	5·00

This marginal revenue productivity schedule can be shown, alternatively, on a diagram like Fig. 11.1. Here, the marginal revenue productivity curve (*MRP*) shows the addition to total revenue when successive extra marginal units of labour are employed by the firm in question. Numbers of men are measured along the *x*-axis and marginal revenue product (in pounds) up the *y*-axis. Marginal revenue productivity curves like the one in Fig. 11.1 will form the basis of our analysis of factor prices. One can, of course, draw an average revenue productivity curve bearing the usual average-marginal relationship to the marginal revenue productivity curve. The curve (*ARP*) in Fig. 11.1 does this. Such a curve shows, for any level of employment measured on the *x*-axis, the average amount of

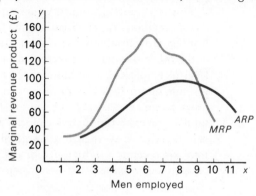

Fig. 11.1

revenue earned for the firm by each man. That is to say, the average revenue productivity of labour at any level of employment is total revenue divided by the number of men employed. Since the marginal revenue productivity curve is shaped like an inverted U, it cuts the average revenue productivity curve at its highest point.[1]

One important problem has so far been ignored. We have already seen that a factor of production can produce output only when used in conjunction with other factors. The output of a firm is not the consequence of using a *single* variable factor in isolation. It is produced by that factor only when it is combined with other factors. The average revenue productivity curve we have drawn in Fig. 11.1 shows total amount of revenue divided by the number of men. It does not take account of the fact that some of the revenue earned by the firm is due to the productivity of the other factors—land, capital or enterprise—used in conjunction with labour. We therefore need to distinguish between the *gross* and the *net* product of a factor. The average *gross* revenue productivity of the factor labour is the total revenue of the firm at any level of employment divided by the number of men employed. The average *net* revenue productivity of, say, labour is the *total net revenue* attributable to labour divided by the number of men employed. We therefore need to ensure that the revenue productivity curves we draw show only the productivity of the factor whose price we are interested in. If we are concrned with labour we need to draw curves showing the *net*, and not the *gross*, revenue product of labour.

There are two possible ways of discovering the *net* productivity of a factor. It would be perfectly legitimate, in an elementary analysis like this, to assume that only negligible amounts of the co-operating factors were being used. If this were the case, their contribution to the gross revenue of the firm would be so small that it could be ignored. One could justifiably regard labour as the only factor producing revenue. Gross and net revenue productivity would amount to the same things.

This is an unrealistic procedure and there is a rather more satisfactory method. We can discover the net productivity of, say, labour from its gross productivity, if we assume that the aggregate rewards of the other co-operating factors are independently known. At each level of employment of labour we can deduct from the total *gross* revenue of a firm a sum of money equal to the aggregate of all the other factors except the one we are considering. This gives us the total *net* revenue productivity of the factor under consideration. We can then derive average and marginal *net* revenue productivity from total *net* revenue productivity in the usual way. This reduction of gross to net revenue is not easy when the amounts of more than one

[1]See p. 140

factor can vary, as they may do. We shall postpone these difficulties until Chapter 16. With a single variable factor, the task of translating gross into net revenue productivity is fairly simple.

We shall therefore assume for the present that the amount of capital and entrepreneurship used by each firm is fixed. If we know the 'prices' of capital and entrepreneurship, we can assume that a fixed amount of money represents the 'normal' profit of entrepreneurship plus the 'price' of the given amount of capital. If we deduct this from the total *gross* revenue of the firm at each level of output, we can discover total *net* revenue at these levels of output. It is then not difficult to derive the average gross and average net revenue productivity curves. We simply divide total gross and total net revenue at each level of employment by the number of men employed.

In Fig. 11.2, the curves *AGRP* and *ANRP* respectively represent the gross and net average revenue productivity curves of labour (the single variable factor). Since the factors other than labour are fixed in amount, any rectangles in Fig. 11.2 like *KLMN* and *PQRS* have

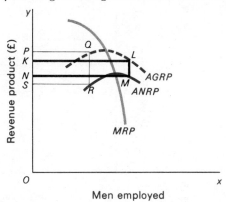

Fig. 11.2

the same area. The same fixed sum of money representing the combined, constant costs of capital and entrepreneurship together is associated with a progressively larger volume of labour as output rises. We have not shown marginal *net* and *gross* revenue productivity separately in Fig. 11.2 because with only one variable factor there is no difficulty in calculating marginal revenue productivity. When only one factor is variable, marginal revenue productivity is the same whether one is considering net or gross revenue productivity.

Until further notice, we shall refer to marginal revenue productivity curves and not to marginal *net* revenue productivity curves since the two are identical when one is studying a single variable factor. Since the amounts of the other factors are the same whatever the level of output, it is only by changing the amount of the *variable* factor that the revenue of the firm can be altered. This is essentially the same problem as with the marginal costs of the firm. In the short run, the costs of entrepreneurship and capital are fixed; they do not enter into the firm's marginal cost curve. We can therefore analyse the pricing of a single variable factor with the productivity curves shown in Fig. 11.2. Labour is the only variable factor, and we do not need to complicate our analysis further until Chapter 16, when we have to allow for more than one factor being used in varying amounts.

We have spent a great deal of time explaining the meaning of marginal and average revenue productivity curves because they represent the chief weapons of analysis which we shall use in our discussion of the pricing of factors of production. In fact, the marginal revenue productivity curve of a factor of production to the firm is really *the firm's demand curve for that factor of production*. In this analysis we shall consider the marginal revenue productivity curve of labour because labour seems to be the factor which is most likely to be variable. What we have to say applies, in principle, to any other variable factors of production as well. The marginal revenue productivity of labour to the firm is the firm's demand curve for labour. It is

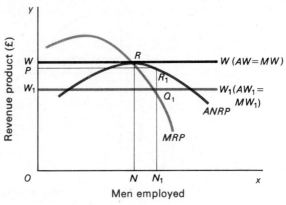

Fig. 11.3

often said that the demand for labour is a *derived demand* because labour is hired only for what it will produce. So in Fig. 11.3 the marginal revenue productivity curve (*MRP*) shows the 'derived' demand curve for labour of a hypothetical firm. It is a demand 'derived' from the demand for the product labour is helping to make.

Since we are at present assuming perfect competition between the firms demanding labour, the supply side of the entrepreneur's problem is simple. The supply conditions confronting each firm are represented by the horizontal straight line WW. This shows the supply curve of labour to the individual firm. Since there is perfect competition in the labour market, the firm can hire just as much labour as it wishes at the ruling wage of £OW per man. Just as a perfectly competitive firm can take the price at which it can sell its product as given, so it can take the wage per man as given too. The firm's demand for labour is so small compared with the total demand for labour that any change in the individual firm's demand, even a proportionally large one, does not affect the price of labour. This is a perfectly legitimate assumption since we are concerned only with the problems of a single competitive firm.

In these circumstances the firm can regard the curve WW as representing both the average and the marginal wage (AW and MW). The average amount of money paid to such a worker is £OW. Similarly, the addition of every marginal unit of labour increases the wage bill by £OW too.

The firm will be in equilibrium—profits will be maximised—*when the marginal revenue productivity of the factor (in this case £NR) is equal to the marginal cost of the factor—the marginal wage (in this case OW).* In Fig. 11.3 this happens when ON men are employed. If fewer men were employed the firm could add more to its receipts than to its costs by increasing the employment it offered. For the marginal revenue productivity of labour would then exceed its marginal cost. Similarly, if more than ON men were employed, the marginal cost of labour—the marginal wage—would exceed its marginal revenue productivity. The firm would be paying more to its marginal employees than their employment was adding to its revenue. The firm is in equilibrium, in Fig. 11.3, when ON men are employed. At that level of employment profits are at a maximum. It should be noted that, with perfect competition between buyers of labour, equilibrium is possible only if the marginal revenue productivity curve of labour is falling at and near the equilibrium position. This explains why economists have been so anxious to show that marginal physical productivity must eventually diminish. Otherwise equilibrium would be impossible. Of course, if there is imperfect competition in the labour market, equilibrium could occur without there being diminishing marginal productivity of labour, because the supply curve of labour would slope upwards.

In perfect competition, since we shall continue to assume 'rationality' on the part of the entrepreneur, a firm will be in equilibrium when the marginal revenue productivity of any factor to the firm equals its marginal cost. Profits will then be maximised. With perfect competition between firms buying in the factor market, this means that in 'full' equilibrium the average cost of the factor will also equal its marginal revenue productivity. The condition for full equilibrium of the *firm* when there is perfect competition in the labour market is thus:

Marginal revenue productivity of labour
=Marginal wage=Average wage

It will be seen in Fig. 11.3 that, with wages at £OW, the average net revenue productivity of labour is also equal to the wage. This implies that the *industry* is also in full equilibrium, with entrepreneurs earning only normal profits.

The position is analogous to that shown in diagrams which represent the equilibrium of the firm in terms of costs and earnings. In a perfectly-competitive industry where entrepreneurs are homogeneous, every firm's average revenue productivity curve will, in 'full' equilibrium, be tangential to the 'wage-line', as in Fig. 11.3. In the short run, the 'wage-line' might be below or, of course, above WW, in which case greater or less than normal profits respectively would be earned. In the long run, firms would then enter or leave the industry until normal profits only were being earned.

For example, if the wage-line is below WW, as at W_1W_1, employment will be ON_1 and abnormal profits of $W_1Q_1R_1P$ will be earned. The firm is in equilibrium but the industry is not. In the long run, firms will enter the industry until only normal profits are being earned. The entry of new entrepreneurs into the industry will lower the price of its product and this will lower the marginal and average net revenue productivity curves. Similarly, an increase in the demand for labour by the expanding industry may raise wages and/or reduce labour productivity. The average revenue productivity curve will then fall and the 'wage-line' rise until they are tangential to each other. In the same way, if firms in the industry are earning less than normal profits, entrepreneurs will leave the industry until equilibrium is reached.

It should be apparent on reflection that Fig. 11.3 is closely related to the sort of diagrams we used in analysing the equilibrium of the firm in terms of price and output in Chapters 5 and 6. It will therefore be useful to study the similarities and differences between these two kinds of diagram.

In Fig. 11.4a we reproduce the essential parts of Fig. 11.3. In Fig. 11.4c we have shown the cost and revenue curves of the same firm. To simplify the analysis, we assume that instead of paying a fixed amount of money for entrepreneurship and capital the firm pays nothing. This makes the interpretation of the diagrams simpler, but makes no difference in principle. The productivity and cost curves thus represent labour productivity and cost only. Fig. 11.4b shows the production conditions for the good in question and provides a link between Figs. 11.4a and 11.4c. The total product curve TPC shows how the total output of the good made by the firm changes as employment is increased.[1]

In Figs. 11.4a and 11.4c it is assumed that the firm is in equilibrium, maximising profits, and also that the industry is in equilibrium with each individual firm earning normal profits. The two diagrams show

[1]It will be noted that the scale on the y-axis in Fig. 11.4b is larger than on the x-axis in Fig. 11.4c.

us that the firm is in equilibrium when OM units of output are produced and ON men are employed. Figure 11.4b shows that production conditions are such that when ON men are employed a total output of OM units of output will be produced. What the entrepreneur is doing in Fig. 11.4c is to find how many units of output he must produce in order to maximise profits by looking at

Fig. 11.4

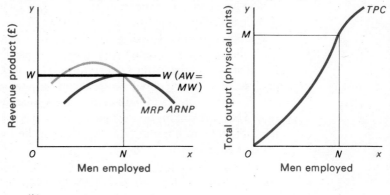

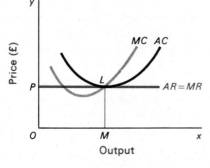

his cost and revenue curves. The size of the labour force needed to produce this output is shown by Fig. 11.4b. In Fig. 11.4a the entrepreneur is deciding how many men to employ in order to maximise his profits. He does this by taking the number of units of output produced by various labour forces, as given to him in Fig. 11.4b. The two diagrams 11.4a and 11.4c thus represent the same equilibrium position for the firm in different ways. Since each diagram shows different variables on the two axes, there is no direct or obvious link between them. Figure 11.4a shows the revenue productivity and the wage per man. Figure 11.4c shows labour cost (there being no other costs) and revenue per unit of output. It is impossible to translate one diagram directly into the other. The diagrams represent the same equilibrium position, but in different ways.

To sum up, an entrepreneur will take on more units of any variable factor of production until its marginal revenue productivity is just equal to its marginal cost. If the factor is labour he will employ more men until the marginal worker adds to the firm's revenue just as much as he adds to its wage bill. The firm is in equilibrium in its purchases of labour when the marginal wage equals the marginal revenue productivity of labour. In perfect competition, with full equilibrium, this also means that the wage equals the average (net) revenue productivity of labour.

The first step in our theory of the pricing of factors of production, then, has been to show that a firm will act in a determinate way to maximise its profits. It will go on hiring more factors of production until the marginal revenue productivity of each factor equals the marginal cost of that same factor. But this has been a very simplified analysis. We have ignored the problem of how to price more than one factor at a time and have assumed that there is perfect competition. These are assumptions which we must keep for the moment, but it is now time to find out what happens in the industry as a whole rather than the firm.

We have so far taken wages as given, and have shown that the volume of employment offered by the firm depends on the marginal revenue productivity of labour. We now want to find how the wage of labour itself is determined. We can do this only by looking at all entrepreneurs on the one hand and all workers on the other. It is impossible for the level of wages to be affected by the action of a single entrepreneur when there is perfect competition. We are therefore justified in assuming the level of wages to be constant when we are dealing with the single firm. But wages can be taken as given only by the individual firm. For the industry as a whole, they are not necessarily so given. We must therefore find how they are determined.

5. Wages and marginal revenue productivity

The individual firm's demand for labour at any wage depends on the marginal revenue productivity of labour. As one would expect, in the whole industry wages also depend in part on the marginal revenue productivity of labour. (We shall continue to assume that there is perfect competition in both factor markets and product markets.) As with all prices, the price of labour depends on supply and demand. We have seen that the problem of the individual entrepreneur in the product market is to equate supply, in the form of marginal cost, with demand, in the form of marginal revenue. In the factor market, the individual entrepreneur has to balance supply in the form of the marginal cost of the factor against the demand for it in the form of its marginal revenue productivity.

When we turn from the individual entrepreneur to the whole industry the price of a factor to the industry, like the price of the product of the industry, also depends on demand and supply. We now have supply in the form of labour available at various wage rates whilst demand depends on the marginal revenue productivity of that labour—this time to the whole industry. Since it is the price of labour which is now being determined, we have to discover the shape of the demand and supply curves for labour. As usual, it is reasonable to think that the demand curve for labour will slope downwards and that the supply curve will slope upwards. We could, of course, consider all conceivable shapes of demand and supply curves for labour, but that would not be very useful. We are mainly interested in the way in which wages are influenced by marginal productivity—in the way in which the demand for labour influences wages. It will therefore pay us to ignore complicated conditions of labour supply for the moment. We shall assume that the total supply of labour is fixed whatever the wage offered; that the elasticity of supply of labour is zero.

This will not always be the case. Indeed, it will not be the normal case, but it will allow us to simplify the analysis. Let us consider what this assumption means. First, it means that there is a fixed number of men who will work for the industry quite irrespective of the wage offered. Second, it means that the labour is 'specific' to the industry. The men can work in the industry only and cannot do the jobs required in another industry, even if wages there are higher. There is, in other words, no mobility of labour *into or out* of the industry we are considering. Third, the vertical supply curve of labour implies that all workers are prepared to do a full week's work whatever the level of wages. We shall ignore for the moment the possibility that some workers (coal-miners are supposed to be the chief offenders) will work for five days a week if paid £10 a day, but if they are given £20 a day will work for three days and spend two days in bed or at the races. We shall also continue to assume that there is no overtime working. While these assumptions mean that our analysis is simple, a simple analysis does at least have the virtue of showing just how the various influences work.

We start then in Fig. 11.5 with a vertical supply curve for labour

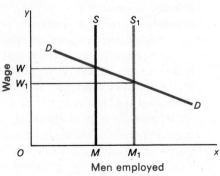

Fig. 11.5

(*MS*) showing that there is a fixed number of men (let us call this *OM*) willing to work whatever the wage. We must now discover what will be the shape of the demand curve for this labour. To do this let us consider two cases; first, where the demand curve is downward-sloping; second, where it is horizontal.

First, let us try to discover when the demand curve for labour will slope downwards. Let us consider the situation shown in Fig. 11.6.

Fig. 11.6

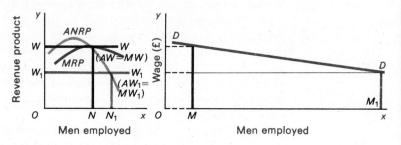

Men employed   Men employed

In Fig. 11.6a we show the demand curve of a firm for labour. This demand curve, the marginal revenue productivity curve of labour for the firm (*MRP*) has the usual humped shape. The average (net) productivity curve of labour (*ANRP*) is also shown. Current wages are assumed to be at the level denoted by the line *WW*. The firm is therefore in 'full' equilibrium, earning only normal profits and employing *ON* men. If we now assume that wages fall to W_1W_1, the demand for labour increases from *ON* to ON_1.

Let us now assume that the industry is composed of ten identical firms. If this is the case, then, for a given fall in wages, the demand of the industry for labour will increase by ten times the amount (NN_1) by which it increases in the individual firm. This is shown in Fig. 11.6b. The fall in wages raises the amount of labour demanded from *OM* to OM_1. It can be seen that the demand curve for labour of the whole industry here slopes downwards. The elasticity of demand for labour in response to the given fall in its price will be the same both for the firm and the industry in this particular case. (Elasticity of demand is concerned with proportional, not absolute, increases in demand as a result of changes in price.)

In adding the marginal revenue productivity curves of the individual firms together sideways, as we have done in Fig. 11.6b to obtain the demand curve for labour, we have assumed that the price of the industry's product is given whatever the output. For the individual firm, shown in Fig. 11.6a, this assumption that the demand for its product is infinitely elastic is reasonable. For the industry, it is not reasonable. The demand curve for the product of the industry is almost certain to slope downwards. What we have done in Fig. 11.6b is to depict the marginal *revenue* productivity of the factor (labour) to the industry at each level of output as equal to marginal *physical* productivity of the factor multiplied by price of product. The correct definition would be marginal physical productivity per unit of factor × *marginal revenue to the industry*. The demand curve for the industry, and therefore the marginal revenue curve for its product, *must* slope downwards. Nevertheless, this simplifying assumption that price, and therefore marginal revenue, is constant for the industry whatever the level of output, will ease our task now. We shall abandon it later.

Let us assume that when the *firm* in Fig. 11.6a was in the original position with a wage of WW, it was in full equilibrium. We know that the *industry* was also in full equilibrium because we are assuming that all firms are homogeneous. If we also know the supply curve for labour, we can tell what the wage would actually have been. For our assumption, made above, that wages fell from OW to OW_1 was made simply to show the shape of the demand curve for labour. Having discovered the shape of that demand curve, we must now use it in conjunction with the supply curve of labour to discover what the wage will actually be. This can be seen from Fig. 11.5, where DD is the demand curve for labour, MS is the supply curve, and OW is the wage at which supply and demand are in equilibrium.

Let us now assume that while the demand for labour remains the same the supply is increased. Let us imagine that to begin with we are considering a colony with a fixed labour supply of only OM men willing to work in the industry with which we are concerned. Now let us assume that an immigrant ship brings MM_1 new workers who are willing to work under exactly the same conditions as the existing workers. The supply curve shifts from MS to M_1S_1 but remains a vertical straight line. Elasticity of supply of labour is still zero. The result of this change, seen in Fig. 11.5, is to lower wages from OW to OW_1. Wages fall because the supply of labour has risen, but demand conditions have not changed. Wages are still equal to the marginal revenue productivity of labour, but that marginal revenue productivity itself has fallen now that more men are employed. The implication of this is, of course, that the number of firms in the industry remains constant. This further implies that entrepreneurship is assumed to be a fixed factor of production for the whole industry, while labour is assumed to be variable in amount.

Diminishing marginal revenue productivity in an industry thus does not result from the fact, taken in isolation, that the supply of labour has increased. It follows from the fact that we have assumed labour and entrepreneurship to be used in varying proportions. Diminishing returns are a corollary of the fact that the number of entrepreneurs did not increase as the supply of labour rose. This is an important fact to remember. It is important, not least because traditional economic theory often based itself on this assumption and derived generalisations about wages from it.

Two clear conclusions may be drawn. First, if it is hoped to maintain wages at the existing level, the immigrant ship should be sunk. Or, to put it another way, if parents want their children to follow them in the same industry, the way to keep up wages of future generations in that industry is to restrict the size of families. Second, if future entrepreneurs are the sons of the present entrepreneurs, workers should encourage entrepreneurs to have large families. The more entrepreneurs there are, the higher the level of wages. If the supply curve of labour is given, the more entrepreneurs there are, the farther to the right will the demand curve of the industry for labour lie and the higher will wages be.

If one thinks carefully about this second case, it is clear that if the supply of entrepreneurs is infinitely elastic at the current rate of profits in the long run, the long-run demand curve for labour will be a horizontal straight line. Indeed, this is the horizontal demand curve for labour which we set out to discover. In the first case, that of the downward-sloping demand curve for labour, we were implicitly assuming that entrepreneurs could earn abnormal profits when wages fell because the number of firms in the industry was limited. Now, we are assuming that (in the long run) there is an infinitely elastic supply of homogeneous entrepreneurs, all of whom are equally efficient. In this case there will be no (long-run) abnormal profits and the long-run demand for labour will be infinitely elastic. In the long run, the number of firms will expand and the demand for labour will increase whenever there is a tendency for wages to fall and so far abnormal profits to be earned.

One may therefore sum up as follows. The demand curve for labour will always slope downwards if the number of firms (and thus of entrepreneurs) in the industry is fixed, as it must be in the short run. But even if the number of firms in the industry is not fixed, as will normally happen in the long run, the demand curve for labour can only be horizontal if entrepreneurship *of the same quality* is in infinitely elastic supply to the industry at the existing level of normal profits. If entrepreneurs are heterogeneous, those outside the industry being less efficient than those within it, the demand curve for labour must slope downwards. Wages have to fall in order that less efficient entrepreneurs can enter the industry and earn normal profits in it. Only if 'homogeneous' entrepreneurs are available in sufficient numbers at the existing rate of normal profits can the demand curve for labour be horizontal. We are, of course, assuming throughout that labour is homogeneous.

This situation where the demand curve for labour is a horizontal straight line is, however, even less probable than it appears at first sight. It can only exist at all on our assumption that the price of the product made by the competitive industry is constant, however large or small the industry's output is. But it is unreasonable to think that, even though the industry expands, the price of its product can remain the same. The only hope of maintaining wages if the supply of labour increases is therefore that when the immigrant ships bring new workers they will also bring a shipload of consumers. That is to say, there must be an increase in the demand for the product of the industry in which we are interested, from those working in other industries. We are making the usual assumption of partial equilibrium analysis that the demand for labour in a single industry is independent of the supply. This means that workers do not buy the production of their own industry. So, if the supply of labour to an industry increases, then unless consumers as a whole increase their demand for its product the price of the product must fall and the money wages of workers in the industry will drop. Wages will be constant only in terms of product made and to measure any worker's wage in terms of the product he makes is not very helpful. He will be unlikely to buy substantial quantities of the product; if indeed he buys any at all.

It is clear that a horizontal demand curve for labour is a most unlikely occurrence. We shall therefore assume that the demand curve for labour (and indeed for any other factor) slopes downwards both for the firm and for the industry. This demand curve will, of course, show the elasticity of demand for labour, which can be measured in the normal way. Broadly speaking, the more rapidly the marginal physical productivity of labour falls as employment increases, and the more rapidly the price of the product made by labour falls as its output rises, the less elastic the demand for labour will be. The opposite will, of course, also be true.

We have now seen that the wage of labour in a perfectly competitive industry depends on demand and supply. Demand conditions are represented by the marginal revenue productivity curve of labour to the industry. Supply conditions are represented by a curve showing, for each level of wages, what the volume of labour offered will be. Wages are determined by the intersection of these two curves.

6. Monopsony   We must now go on to see what will happen when competition between the firms buying labour is not perfect. To some extent our analysis will be simpler in this situation. We shall no longer need to study first the individual firm, to see how much labour it will employ at a given wage, and then the industry, to see what that wage will be. In monopsony, demand by the monopsonist is the only demand for the factor of production. The monopsonist's demand for, say, labour will determine wages in conjunction with the supply conditions for that labour. We have already discovered that where there is perfect competition both in the factor market and in the product market, the price of any factor of production is equal both to its marginal revenue product and to the price at which its marginal physical product is sold. It is determined by demand and supply conditions. Let us now see what forces determine factor prices for a firm which is a monopolist in the product market.

For the firm that is a 'monopolist-monopsonist' the demand for labour will still depend on the marginal revenue productivity curve of labour. But the marginal revenue product of any unit of labour cannot be so easily calculated when there is monopoly as it could be when there was perfect competition in the product market. With perfect competition, marginal revenue product equals marginal physical product multiplied by the (constant) price of the product. Suppose that the employment of an additional unit of labour adds ten wheelbarrows to the output of a firm, and that the price of a wheelbarrow is £10 whether the individual firm produces 10 or 1 000 wheelbarrows. It is clear that the marginal revenue product of labour is then £100. The sale of the ten wheelbarrows has added £100 to the earnings of the firm. With monopoly, the price of the product is not constant but varies with output. A further complication is therefore introduced.

A marginal worker may still produce ten wheelbarrows. The marginal physical productivity of labour may therefore still be 10 units of output. But the price of wheelbarrows will now fall as output rises. The ten additional wheelbarrows produced by employing a marginal worker who raises a firm's output from, say, 100 to 110 may be sold for £10 each. The value of the marginal physical product is still £100, but the price of wheelbarrows may be lower now that output is 110 and not 100. For example, it may be that when 100 wheelbarrows were being sold, the price of each was £10·50. Now that output is 110, suppose that the price of each falls from £10·50 to £10. When this marginal worker is taken on, the firm earns £50 less on the existing output, *i.e.* £0·50 less on each of 100 wheelbarrows. The employment of the marginal unit of labour has therefore added only £50 (net) to the firm's revenue. Ten more wheelbarrows have been sold for a total amount of £100, but £50 less has been earned on the other 100 wheelbarrows. They were previously sold for £1 050 but are now sold for only £1 000. The marginal revenue product of labour is thus £50, while the value of the marginal physical product of labour, *i.e.* the price at which the marginal physical product is sold, is £100.

In monopoly, therefore, the marginal revenue product of a factor at any level of employment is not marginal physical product × price of product; it is marginal physical product × marginal revenue from selling that physical product. It is still the net addition to the revenue of the firm resulting from the employment of a marginal unit of the factor, but we now have to allow for the fall in the price of the firm's product. This results from the fact that the monopolist's average revenue curve is downward-sloping and not horizontal as the perfect competitor's average revenue curve is.

The result of this is to make the marginal revenue productivity curve of a factor to a monopolist slope downwards more rapidly than it would do if he were producing in perfect competition. Figure 11.7b

Fig. 11.7

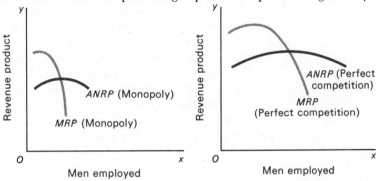

shows the demand curve (marginal revenue productivity curve) for labour of a firm producing in conditions of perfect competition. Figure 11.7a shows the demand curve of a firm with an identical marginal physical productivity curve but which is a monopolist and not a firm producing in perfect competition. The difference between the shapes of the two curves results entirely from the fact that the first firm has a horizontal average revenue curve for its product whereas the second has a downward-sloping one.

The supply curve of labour to the firm is also different for our 'monopolist-monopsonist' from what it would be for the perfect competitor. Where the firm is buying in conditions of perfect competition in the labour market, the supply curve can be shown as a horizontal straight line. Where a firm is a monopsonist, it is the only buyer of labour and it influences the price of labour by altering its own purchases—by changing the level of employment. Wages rise and fall as the firm hires more or less men, whereas in perfect competition they remain constant however many men it employs. This raises a further problem. When there was perfect competition in the labour market it was possible for the firm to ignore differences between average factor cost—the price paid to each unit of factor—and marginal factor cost—the addition to the total cost of the factor when a further unit was engaged. These were all the same thing. Now there is a difference between marginal and average factor cost.

Where a firm is a monopsonist it can lower the average cost of labour —average wage—by reducing its demand for labour. Average wage (total wage bill divided by number of workers employed) is not equal to marginal wage. This is the addition to the wage bill when another worker is employed. If employment rises under monopsony, the addition to the wage bill—marginal wage—will be greater than the average wage. The reason is the same as the reason why marginal cost rises faster than average cost when average cost is increasing with output increases.

Let us consider an example. Suppose that a firm hires ten men at £30 per week and therefore has a weekly wage bill of £300. If the firm now takes on another man, the fact that it is a monopsonist may mean that it has to raise the average wage to £32. If so, the total wage bill of the firm will rise to £352. There will be the £32 paid to the man who has now been taken into employment. There will also be a further £20 going to the ten existing employees now that wage per man has risen by £2.

The supply conditions facing a monopolist in the labour market are shown in Fig. 11.8. The position is analogous with that for any

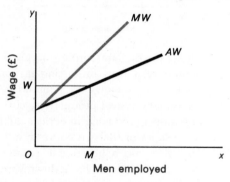

Fig. 11.8

rising cost curve. The average wage curve shows the amount of money paid to each worker when various numbers of workers are employed. For example, when OM men are employed, they have to be paid £OW each. As our example has shown, the marginal wage curve *does not show the wage paid to a marginal worker; all workers receive the same wage*. It shows the *addition to the total wage bill of the firm* when an additional unit of labour is taken on. Where there is monopsony, an extra worker can be engaged only if a higher wage is paid to *all* other workers in the firm. The wage paid to each marginal unit of labour (and of course to each other worker) will be less than the addition to the total wage bill when he is employed. Since the average wage curve rises as employment goes up, the marginal wage curve will be above the average curve.

What, then, is the connection between the two sets of curves shown in Figs. 11.7 and 11.8? If they are drawn together as in Fig. 11.9 we can find the equilibrium of the firm in question. We assume that the firm will still wish to maximise profits. The monopsonist will therefore increase employment until the amount added to revenue (marginal revenue product) when a marginal unit of labour is taken on is equal to the total addition to the wage bill (marginal

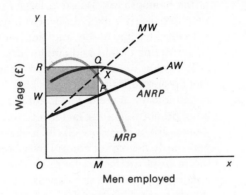

Fig. 11.9

Men employed

wage). The marginal wage allows for the rise in the wages of *existing* workers when the extra man is taken on.

This equality of marginal revenue product and marginal wage will occur at point X in Fig. 11.9 when OM men are employed at the wage £OW. Abnormal profits earned by the firm will be £$WPQR$, normal profits having already been deducted from total revenue, in order to derive the average net revenue product from the average gross revenue product. What, then, is the difference between this situation and equilibrium under perfect competition? The marginal revenue product of labour must still equal the marginal cost of labour (marginal wage). But there are two important differences. A change in the output of the product will lower its price because of monopoly in the product market. An increase in the number of workers employed in making the product will therefore lower its price. This makes it impossible to go on expanding employment as long as might have happened without monopoly—the marginal revenue product curve of labour is steeper. Second, the marginal wage curve slopes upwards instead of remaining horizontal as in perfect competition.

There are other differences too. Let us sum these up. If there is perfect competition in the factor market then, first, the marginal revenue product of labour equals the marginal wage; but that marginal revenue product also equals the average wage. Second, not only does the marginal wage equal the marginal revenue product of labour, it also equals the price at which the marginal *physical* product of labour can be sold.

If there is monopoly in the factor market then, first, the average wage is less than the marginal wage. Second, the marginal revenue product of labour is less than the price at which the marginal physical product of that labour can be sold.

The causes of this are to be found in the downward-sloping average revenue curve of the monopolist and the rising average wage curve of the monopsonist. Where a large firm is both a monopolist and a monopsonist, it is likely to benefit in two ways. It can raise the price of its product, and at the same time lower the wage paid to its workers, by restricting output and employment.

It is only reasonable to think that a monopolist will also be a monopsonist. If a producer is making a large proportion of the product of an industry, it seems fair to think that he will also be employing a large proportion of the factors of production used by the industry. A monopolist is therefore likely to have a similar kind (though not necessarily degree) of control over both the price of his product and the price of the factors he uses. This may well enable him to earn abnormal profits at the expense of consumers and workers alike, though we shall see that if labour is unionised this may keep wages up.

It is this feature of the monopolist's position which has led economists and others to talk of 'monopolistic exploitation'. Unfortunately the idea of exploitation implies some kind of moral judgment. It is an emotive phrase and it is far from easy to make moral judgments, especially in a book where there has not been the space required to lay a foundation for making such judgments. We therefore make no moral judgments whatever about the role of a monopolist.

We have described the equilibrium of the 'monopolist-monopsonist' in terms of marginal and average revenue curves and marginal and average wage curves. Perhaps this does not show the position quite clearly enough. It may therefore be useful to show the same equilibrium position in terms of revenue and cost curves. We shall therefore approach the problem in two ways, with two different types of diagram. In Fig. 11.10 the position of the firm is set out in terms of the usual concepts of money receipts and money costs for

Fig. 11.10

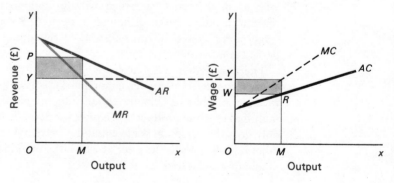

various outputs, assuming for the sake of simplicity that the only costs are labour costs.

Figure 11.10a needs no explanation. It shows the average and marginal revenue curves of a monopolistic firm. It shows what average and marginal revenue are when output is at various levels. Figure 11.10b shows average and marginal costs. Since wages are the only cost, it also shows average and marginal wage, but it shows them per unit of output and not per unit of labour as is more usual. In other words, it shows marginal and average (wage) cost per unit of output. At output OM, wage cost per unit of output is MR. Wage cost per unit of output is a concept that is used less frequently than is wage per man, but it is exactly the same (when labour is the only cost) as average cost.

The dotted line joining the two diagrams shows the output at which marginal revenue per unit of output equals marginal wage cost per unit of output. The firm therefore produces OM units of output, selling tham at £OP each. Its wage bill is OW per unit of output. It earns abnormal profits of $(£PY+£WY) \times OM$. Since the firm is a monopolist, these profits may well not be competed away, but go on being earned so long as the monopoly is maintained.

An alternative way of showing the same equilibrium position for the firm is given in Fig. 11.11. In Fig. 11.11b average and marginal

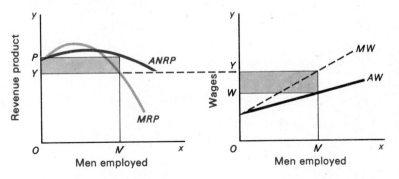

Fig. 11.11

wage per man are shown. Figure 11.11a shows average and marginal revenue, not per unit of product but per man. It uses the same concepts as we have used throughout this analysis of the theory of factor pricing—marginal and average revenue productivity curves.

Here again, the dotted line connecting the two diagrams shows the equilibrium position of the firm. From it we can deduce how many men will be employed in the equilibrium position. ON men will be employed at a wage per man of £OW. Average revenue per man is £OP and profits are £$(PY+WY) \times ON$. The equilibrium of the firm can therefore be shown both in terms of revenues and costs of products and in terms of revenues, productivities, and costs of factors. Figure

11.10 shows an example of the former type of equilibrium and Fig. 11.11 shows the latter.

We have now provided, in outline, a theory which can be generalised to show how the rewards of all factors of production are determined. Yet, although this theory can be applied equally to all the broad groups of factors—land, labour, capital and enterprise—there are distinctive features of each factor which make it important to apply the general analysis outlined above to each group of factors in turn. This we now do.

Suggested reading

ROBINSON, JOAN   *Economics of Imperfect Competition,* London, 1933, especially chapters 17, 18, 21 and 22.

12

Wages

1. Labour as a factor of production

Although our analysis of the pricing of factors of production has so far been carried out very largely in terms of the wages of labour, the theory we have outlined applies equally to *all* factors of production. However, each factor does have its own peculiarities and problems. In this chapter, we shall explicitly apply the conclusions of the theory of factor pricing to labour, explaining at the same time what are the main differences between labour and other factors of production. We can then see how far the theory of the pricing of factors of production needs modifying if it is to take account of these differences.

In Chapter 11 we gave general rules by which to explain the pricing of all factors of production. We saw that an entrepreneur will continue to purchase more of any factor until its marginal revenue productivity is equal to its marginal cost—the addition which its purchase makes to the costs of the firm. With perfect competition in both the factor market and the product market, this means that for the firm the price of the factor is equal to the value (price) of its marginal physical product. For the whole industry, the price of any factor is determined by the marginal productivity curve of that factor on the one hand, and by its supply curve on the other. With monopoly in the product market, the value of the marginal product of a factor is greater than its marginal revenue productivity. Similarly, with monopsony in the factor market, the marginal cost of the factor exceeds its average cost—its price. This means that if there is monopoly and monopsony at the same time, employment in the firm is still set at the level where marginal revenue product equals marginal cost. However, in the equilibrium position, both of these are less than the price of the marginal product and greater than the price of the factor.

This formal statement applies equally to any and all factors of production. It is our task now to apply it specifically to labour. Are there any differences between labour and other factors? If so, can we make valid generalisations about them?

The characteristic of labour which distinguishes it from other factors of production is a sociological one. It has been the tradition in economics to divide the factors of production into four broad groups. One discusses the wages of labour, the rent of land, interest on capital and the profits of enterprise (or entrepreneurship). Some economists have suggested that there is no difference economically between the return to labour and the return to the other factors of production. It is said that since returns to all factors of production depend on the marginal productivity of the factor and its supply conditions, there is no difference in principle between them. Indeed, one economist has gone so far as to claim that the classification, land, labour and capital, is no more useful than would be the classification animal, vegetable and mineral.

In this chapter, we shall argue that a number of problems arise when one studies the wages of labour which do not arise with other factors of production. It does seem justifiable to distinguish labour from the other factors. Of course, there are bound to be some difficulties in being quite certain whether a specific unit of production factor is labour or not. For example, does labour mean only manual labour? Or does it include clerical, 'white-collar' workers? How should managers be classified? We should apparently have to include a £20 000 a year manager in labour; yet Mrs Jones earning £1 500 a year from a snack bar or shop would be a capitalist, or entrepreneur.

We shall select a typical case in order to avoid these border-line problems of definition. We shall consider the problems of those whose sole income is obtained from the work of their hands or brains, and who spend their lifetime working for an entrepreneur or, more generally, as subordinates to senior, or even middle-management, in a large firm. They are people who may well not be very interested in their work as such, but who carry on fairly cheerfully with rather dull jobs under fairly detailed supervision.

It seems reasonable to think that this type of factor of production differs from other factors in three main ways. First, this kind of labour will usually be found combining together in trade unions to urge wage and salary claims on entrepreneurs. Second, such people, are, within limits, free to choose whether they will work on a particular day or not, though they will usually have less freedom of choice in deciding how *long* they will work on a given day. Third, they can decide whether or not to perpetuate themselves by having children. All these choices are out of the question for land or capital. Machines and fields, being inanimate, cannot combine together. They cannot refuse to work because they are too tired or too bored; nor can they choose whether to replace themselves or to increase their numbers. Labour can and does. The main task of this chapter will be to discuss the consequences which result from the ability of labour to influence the conditions of its own employment in these ways.

However, before looking at these issues let us consider some of the more general issues of wages and salaries using the kind of analysis set out in Chapters 1 and 7. Let us use this analysis to explain differences in wages between industries and occupations. We have seen that the usefulness of labour to employers depends partly on its physical productivity—on the amount of physical product produced —and partly on the price at which this physical output can be sold. The first factor is probably more important in explaining differences in wages between occupations, the second in explaining differences between industries. However, in both cases, the nature of the supply conditions of labour will represent an additional and important factor.

Let us first consider the differences in the wages paid in different occupations. To take an obvious example: Why are the wages of skilled workers higher than those of labourers? Much of the explanation lies in differences in productivity; the skilled worker is more 'productive'. This does not necessarily mean that he produces more physical units of output. Indeed, with the division of labour an essential feature of all industrial activity today, few people produce the whole of any product themselves. What we mean is that skilled workers will usually be more 'productive' in the sense that their contribution to industrial activity is a more essential one. However, merely to say this gives away the fact that it is almost impossible to separate the superior productivity of skilled workers from their supply conditions. At most times, skilled labour will be scarcer, and therefore more expensive, than unskilled labour. Not everyone is willing or able to spend the necessary time and money required to acquire skills which are useful to industry. Yet anyone can take on an unskilled job. To a large extent, the greater productivity of the skilled worker is simply a different way of expressing his scarcity. If there were more skilled men and women in industry, their individual contributions would be less 'essential'. However, whatever the reason, the productivity of skilled workers is higher than that of unskilled workers. It is this difference which explains their higher wages.

Having explained why, in *general*, skilled workers will earn more than unskilled ones, there appears to be one important reason why some *types* of skilled worker earn unusually high incomes. This may be the result of unusually high productivity. In many cases it seems to be the result of deliberate restrictions on entry into a particular occupation. Especially where there is a strong trade union, workers in a particular trade may restrict the number of entrants to it. This is often said to have happened in the British printing trade. The result is obvious. Given any individual industry's demand for a labour of a particular kind, the smaller the number of men of that type who are available, the higher will be the wage that they will earn.

Differences in wages between *industries* may also result from differences in productivity and skill. In the medical profession, where skill is great and expensive to acquire, salaries will be higher than, say, in refuse collection where no special skill is needed. However, the most interesting examples of difference in wages between industries seemed to be the result of differences in the prosperity, and therefore the price level, in particular industries. Our analysis has already shown that the marginal revenue productivity of labour depends not only on the amount of physical output but also on the price at which this output can be sold. So, for example, in the second half of the nineteenth century British agriculture was declining while manufacturing industry was growing. Abstracting entirely from differences in the physical productivity of labour one found that wages were low in agriculture where prices were low, but higher in manufacturing where prices were higher. Again, of course, labour supply enters into the analysis. Even if there is little difference between the skills required in the declining and the expanding industries, which may not always be the case, workers may find it difficult to leave the areas where industry is declining and move to areas where it is expanding. If the declining industry also requires particular skills—if labour is *specific* to it—the problem is even more acute. So, for example, people who have been trained to work in the cotton industry will find it hard to move to jobs, say, in engineering factories, even if these are nearby. Low wages in cotton will fail to reduce the supply of 'specific' labour in the cotton areas very substantially. Wages may well fall to extremely low levels, unless government action is taken. Similarly, a scarcity of a 'specific' labour in an expanding industry means that wages there will be even higher than the prosperity of the industry itself—working through a high marginal revenue productivity of labour—would have guaranteed.

2. Collective bargaining

2.1 *The assumptions*

We now move on to look at the results of the fact that workers are able to combine in trade unions to press wage claims. Let us assume that the workers in a particular industry, who have not previously been unionised, decide to set up a trade union. There has previously been perfect competition between workers in the industry. The trade union is now formed and goes to the employers. They agree that every man whom they employ will, in future, be paid £35 a week, neither less nor more. Let us also assume that the agreement is put into force completely, and that once it is in operation the trade union indulges in no strikes, and the employers in no lockouts. Work goes on as usual. What will be the result?

We shall confine our attention to situations where a trade union presses for a higher wage but does not make any stipulations about the numbers of workers to be employed. In fact, of course, being a monopolist, a trade union will have to take account of the fact that a rise in the price of labour will probably alter the amount demanded. In practice, the main concern of trade unions is with the level of wages, if only because it is almost impossible to control levels of employment. We assume here that when a wage-bargain is made, all members of the union are prepared to offer their services at the agreed wage. The supply curve of labour is therefore a horizontal straight line at this wage.

Clearly, the conditions of demand and supply for labour are altered. Instead of perfect competition between sellers in the labour market, there is monopoly. If the marginal revenue productivity curve for labour slopes downwards, there is a distinct possibility that fewer workers will now be employed. For the supply curve of labour will become horizontal instead of being vertical or upward-sloping, and we are assuming that the equilibrium wage will rise too. Workers are unlikely to combine in trade unions except with the aim of raising wages.

However, the problem is complex. The results of collective bargaining will differ according to circumstances in the markets for the factor and the product. There are four main combinations of circumstances, assuming as we shall do throughout that there is perfect competition between *buyers* in the product market. Now that there is collective bargaining, we are also assuming that there is monopoly instead of perfect competition between *sellers* in the labour market. The four possible situations are these: *(a)* Perfect competition between sellers in the product market and between buyers in the labour market. *(b)* Perfect competition between sellers in the product market, but a monopsonist buying in the labour market. *(c)* A monopolist seller in the product market but perfect competition between buyers in the labour market. *(d)* A monopolist selling in the product market and a monopsonist buying in the labour market. We shall consider the results of the advent of a trade union in each of these four cases.

(a) Perfect competition in both markets

Where there is perfect competition in both the factor and product markets, then, for the individual firm, the wage will be equal to the value of the marginal physical product of labour, both before and after collective bargaining is introduced. The result of the introduction of collective bargaining will depend on whether the new wage is the same, higher than or lower than the existing wage. If wages are merely frozen where they were, there will be no effect at all. The new agreement will merely underwrite the existing situation.

Nevertheless, it is possible that even if wages were unaltered the

L

introduction of collective bargaining would have some effect. If collective bargaining were instituted in an industry with a large number of small firms, it is possible that the perfection of competition between them has not been complete. Hard-hearted business men in some small firms may have been holding down the wages of their unorganised workers below the general level. In this case, the new wage obtained from collective bargaining would improve the position of such underpaid workers by ensuring that they earned the negotiated wage. This sort of problem is really one of imperfection of competition, but it may exist in conditions of apparent perfection. The effect of collective bargaining will be to eliminate such accidental imperfections.

What happens when as we are assuming, and as will normally happen, collective bargaining is introduced and does more than merely underwrite the existing situation but leads to an actual rise in wages? If all firms in the industry are homogeneous, the amount of labour used by each firm will be reduced by the same amount. The wage paid to each worker in each firm will still be the same as that paid to each other worker, but it will be higher than it was. Since the marginal revenue productivity of labour in each firm decreases as employment increases, the amount of employment in each firm must be reduced as wages rise, if firms are to maximise profits. In the industry as a whole, less employment will be offered at the new, higher wage than at the old one. We are, of course, assuming that everything else, except wages and employment in the industry we are studying, remains the same.

How much less employment will be offered now that wages have risen will depend on the speed with which the marginal revenue productivity of labour rises as employment falls. The steeper the marginal revenue productivity curve of labour (the lower the elasticity of demand for labour) the smaller will be the fall in employment as wages rise. This can be seen from Fig. 12.1.

Figures 12.1a and 12.1b show two different hypothetical firms, A and B. Firm A has a steep marginal revenue productivity curve of

Fig. 12.1 a | b

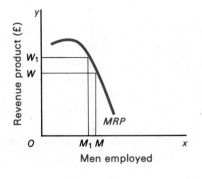

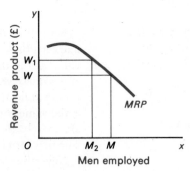

labour, and Firm B a flat one. In Firm A, a rise in wages from OW to OW_1 decreases employment by the small amount M_1M. In Firm B, the same rise in wages reduces employment by the much larger amount M_2M. If all firms in an industry are homogeneous and all have marginal revenue product curves like those in Fig. 12.1a, a given increase in wages will lower employment by less than if all curves are like those in Fig. 12.1b. So long as other things remain equal, the effect of an increase in wages resulting from collective bargaining, with perfect competition in both markets, will be a certain amount of unemployment. It is therefore possible that the action of philanthropists who raise wages will cause unemployment.

If all firms in the industry are homogeneous and start from a position of long-run equilibrium, the short-run effect will be to reduce profits below normal. Firms can only off-set this fall in profit to a small extent, by reducing employment along their marginal revenue productivity curves. In the long run, however, because profits have fallen below normal, there will be a net reduction in the number of firms in the industry as a result of the rising wages. If there really is complete homogeneity among these firms, it will be sheer accident which determines which firms leave the industry. If the firms in the industry are not homogeneous, the solution is easier. The least profitable will leave. In either case, the reduction of the advent of collective bargaining must be some unemployment.

We must now consider what will happen in the market for the product. Since employment has fallen now that wages have risen, the supply of the product at each price will be reduced, the equilibrium price will rise slightly, and a smaller amount of the product will be sold. The fact that the price of the product has risen will, of course, cause the marginal revenue product curve of labour to move to the right, reducing the fall in profit to some extent. Employment need not fall as far as it would have done if the price of the product had been constant; but the rise in price cannot increase marginal revenue productivity sufficiently to prevent some fall in employment.

The conclusion one has to draw where collective bargaining is introduced into an industry with perfect competition in both the product market and the factor market is therefore that wages will be raised, but that this will not be an unmixed blessing. On our assumptions a certain amount of unemployment is inevitable. This has been the traditional case of economists against collective bargaining. It is important to remember, however, that this case *does* depend on the assumption that there is perfect competition in both markets, and also on the fact that we are concerned only with a partial-equilibrium analysis, with everything outside this particular industry remaining exactly the same. We shall see in Part Two that the problems of a *general* wage reduction cannot be completely discussed except through a general equilibrium analysis.

(b) Perfect competition in the product market, monopsony in the factor market

Where there is perfect competition in the product market and monopsony in the factor market, the situation will be as in Fig. 12.2. Figure 12.2 shows a firm which is the only purchaser of a particular type of labour, but which sells in a perfectly-competitive market.[1] Since the firm is a monopsonist in the labour market, the average wage curve is not horizontal. The average and marginal wage curves (AW and

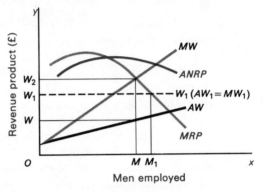

Fig. 12.2

MW) both slope upwards. The monopsonist will maximise profits when he hires OM men at the wage of £OW. If there is now a collective agreement fixing wages at £OW_1, the average wage curve will cease to slope upwards but will be horizontal as shown, say, by the dashed black line W_1W_1 in Fig. 12.2. This is because the entrepreneur will have to pay the given wage of £OW_1 however few or many men he employs. Marginal and average wage will now be equal, as under perfect competition, because of the collective agreement. The wage *has* to be £OW_1, however few or many men are employed.

What happens when this collective agreement is introduced? Earnings per man rise from £OW to £OW_1, but the volume of employment rises from OM to OM_1. There is an increase and not a decrease in employment now that wages are higher. The reason is that the new marginal wage curve (MW_1), representing the addition to the wage bill caused by employing one more worker at each level of employment, is the horizontal line W_1W_1. It is identical with the average wage curve (AW_1). Thus, at the old level of employment, the marginal wage is now less than the marginal revenue product of

[1] It is improbable, though not impossible, that a firm could be the only buyer of labour of a particular kind and yet sell in a competitive market. Its competitors might use a different production process.

labour. If the entrepreneur wishes to maximise profits he must increase employment to OM_1. Marginal revenue product will then equal wage. Employment has risen because collective bargaining has reduced the marginal wage at the old level of employment. Only if the wage fixed by collective agreement were greater than OW_2 would employment fall. For only if this were to happen would the new marginal wage exceed the marginal revenue product of labour at the old level of employment (OM). It is quite possible that where there is monopsony in the factor market and perfect competition in the product market, a rise in wages, resulting from the advent of collective bargaining, will cause a rise in employment.

(c) Monopoly in the product market and perfect competition in the factor market

The results of an increase in wages caused by collective bargaining will be similar, in this case, to the results where there is perfect competition in both markets. Employment will fall, since the marginal revenue curve of labour will be downward-sloping; the marginal (and average) wage curve will be horizontal, both before and after wages are increased. The size of the fall in employment will depend on the amount of the increase in average (and marginal) wages; on the slope of the marginal revenue productivity curve of labour; and on the elasticity of demand for labour.

(d) Monopoly in the product market and monopsony in the factor market

The effect on employment of a rise in wages in these conditions can be deduced from the conclusions of the three previous sub-sections. If the new marginal wage (which is now the same as the average wage) is less than the old marginal wage at the original level of employment, then employment must increase. Only if the new marginal wage is greater than the old marginal wage at the original level of employment will employment fall off. It is thus possible that *both* wages *and* employment will increase when a collective agreement comes into force.

3. The supply curve of labour: (1) The short run

The second special feature of labour as a factor of production which we must now consider is the fact that workers can decide whether or not they will work on a particular day or on particular terms. In order to carry out this part of our analysis we shall assume that workers can decide how many hours they will work each day. We shall assume that the contract they make with employers is to work for Xp per hour, but that they are free to choose for themselves how many hours they will work. This is not entirely realistic. In reality, the number of hours worked will be fixed by negotiations between groups of workers or their trade unions and individual employers or employers' associations. We also abstract from the problems raised because, in practice, overtime can be worked and higher payments are received if it is. The simplifications are drastic, but they do not detract from the validity and importance of the general principle which we shall enunciate. They apply, with little change, to a situation where the worker can decide now many days to work each week, but the hours worked on each day in the week when he does work are fixed.

Our analysis of the supply of labour to an industry as a whole has been based almost wholly on the assumption that the supply curve of labour will be a vertical straight line. It is unlikely that the supply curve will really be like this. At first sight, it seems more probable that the supply curve of labour will vary in response to wages, sloping upwards to the right. This certainly seems a plausible assumption. People often appear to work longer hours if they are paid more for *each hour* that they work. However, while it seems likely that the supply curve of labour will rise, it will not always slope upwards towards the right. Over some ranges it may slope upwards and backwards; it may rise to the left. If wages rise, workers may sometimes work fewer hours. Such a phenomenon may, of course, happen with entrepreneurs too. They may decide to spend more time at home or playing golf when profits rise. However, this phenomenon is most likely to be important with labour.

If a backward-sloping supply curve of labour is a widespread phenomenon, it is essential to understand why and how it can occur. We shall now analyse this type of behaviour, working in terms of the supply curve of labour for an individual worker.

We must consider the worker's demand for income in exchange for effort. As his wages rise, his income in terms of money will rise also. Since he will be better off, he will normally spend more money on goods of various kinds. It does not follow, however, that he will work a larger number of hours each day now that his income is greater. The worker's standard of living will also depend on the amount of leisure he is able to enjoy; leisure is just as much a good to be 'consumed' as are clothes, television sets and cigars. Our worker will want time to amuse, enjoy or educate himself in his own way. When wages rise he may therefore take the opportunity to decide that he will take more time off—that he will spend longer not working.

The worker's ability to make decisions of this kind makes it important to consider the relationship between the demand for leisure and the demand for the more usual kinds of consumer goods. It is quite likely that, now that his standard of living is higher, he will want both more leisure *and* more ordinary consumer goods. Leisure is needed in order that many consumption goods can be enjoyed at all. Consider the case of visits to the theatre. Higher wages or salaries make it possible to raise ones standard of living by visiting the theatre more often. But this can be done only if one has enough time during the evening to go to see the play. Again, a Bach concerto cannot really be appreciated if it has to be heard in the factory or office as background music. Most of the good things of life must be enjoyed at leisure if they are to be enjoyed at all.

We can analyse this kind of behaviour, where an individual worker works fewer hours as wages rise, diagrammatically, in the Fig. 12.3.

In Fig. 12.3a we show the worker's total supply curve of labour (effort) in exchange for income. As his weekly income rises from zero to £24, the number of hours he works each day rise too, reaching a maximum where weekly earnings are £24 and 10 hours a day are worked. Once weekly wages exceed £24, however, the number of hours worked begins to decline. The black curve *SL* in Fig. 12.3a shows how the worker's supply of labour varies as his income changes. In Fig. 12.3b the same information is shown, but the axes are reversed. The curve (now coloured dark brown and called *DI*) which in Fig. 12.3a showed the supply of labour (effort) in exchange for income, now shows the total demand for income in exchange for effort (labour). It will be seen that the demand for income, measured in terms of effort offered in exchange, rises steadily for every increase in income until 10 hours a day are being worked, and then declines. For example, when the weekly income demanded rises from £28 to £32, the number of hours of work offered each day falls from 9 to 8 hours.

In Fig. 12.3c the way in which a curve giving the same information as that in Fig. 12.3b is derived is shown. This curve shows the demand for income in terms of leisure. As in Fig. 12.3b, income is measured along the *x*-axis. Instead of measuring daily hours of work up the *y*-axis, daily hours of leisure are shown. Since there are only 24 hours in a day (shown here as *OK*), the number of hours worked can be measured *down* the *y*-axis from *K*. For example, if *OM* (14) hours per day are taken in leisure, *KM* (10) hours must be worked. This diagram also shows the worker's indifference curve system between income and leisure. By drawing a series of straight lines radiating from the point *K* on the *y*-axis, which shows the total number of hours available each day, one can show all the possible 'price ratios' between income and leisure.

The points of tangency between these various price lines and successive indifference curves show the equilibrium position of the worker with respect to income and leisure at the various 'price ratios'.

If all such points are joined by a price-consumption curve, one can see the worker's equilibrium position at all possible levels of income. When the price line is very steep—when it coincides with the y-axis—income is so expensive in terms of effort, leisure is relatively so 'cheap',

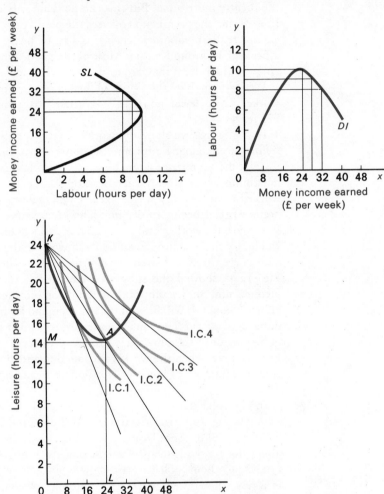

Fig. 12.3 a | b
c

that no work is done and the whole day is taken in leisure. As the price line becomes progressively less steep, income becomes less expensive in terms of effort (leisure becomes 'dearer') and more and more hours are worked. Finally, with the price line KA, the relative 'prices' of income and leisure are such that OM (14) hours are taken as leisure; KM (10) are worked and £OL (£24) is earned. Any further increase in wages (i.e. any further reduction in the price of income in terms of effort) reduces the number of hours worked. If this price-consumption curve is turned upside down so that K coincides with the origin, the total demand curve shown in Fig. 12.3b is obtained, with work measured upwards on the y-axis instead of downwards as in Fig. 12.3c. It should be remembered that all that this analysis means is that, while the elasticity of demand for income in terms of effort is normally greater than one, it may sometimes be less than one. In our example, the elasticity of demand for income becomes less than one once 10 hours a day are being worked. The total demand curve for income in terms of work offered therefore slopes upwards once income reaches £24.

It is likely, then, that a wage rise will at times reduce the number of hours worked by labour. This is a point which must never be overlooked. It is not a theoretical curiosity, like 'Giffen's Paradox', but a hard fact of real-world behaviour. Nevertheless, it does not follow that this peculiarity in the behaviour of labour is necessarily unfortunate. There are two important qualifications which should be borne in mind.

First, an increase in income may well raise the efficiency of the worker. If he has previously been badly fed, he may now be able to afford a proper diet. This will probably increase his productivity per hour. Such an effect is certainly likely in underdeveloped countries where standards of living are very low. The possibility that this may be the case has long been recognised by economists, who speak of the 'economy of high wages'. Second, a reduction in the number of hours worked by an individual may increase his productivity. It has often been found that a reduction in weekly hours worked actually increases total weekly output; hourly output rises more than in proportion to the fall in the number of hours worked. Consequently, a reduction in hours may raise output as well as enabling workers to enjoy the fruits of their work at leisure.

What general conclusion can be drawn from this analysis for the whole economy? It is that, in the short run, while the total number of workers is fixed, the supply curve of labour showing hours of work offered at various wages will usually slope upwards to the right. However, over some ranges it may slope upwards to the left.

4. The supply curve of labour: (2) The long run

In the long run, the number of workers in the economy can alter, so that the shape of the supply curve of labour can alter by net additions to, or reductions in, the population. It is not certain what shape this supply curve will take. Economists in the early nineteenth century believed that the supply curve of labour to the economy was horizontal because they thought that every increase in wages would, over the longer period, call forth a sufficient increase in population to return wages to the original level. This original level was conceived as the minimum amount needed to maintain their existence—the subsistence level of wages. It was thought that there was an 'iron law' which ensured that, in the long run, wages always equalled the cost of subsistence; that the long-run supply curve of labour was horizontal at this level, because any rise in wages would evoke a proportionate increase in the size of the population.

This is not the accepted view now. It is agreed that a rise in wages will not always induce a correspondingly large long-run increase in population. In developed countries, at least, people are willing to allow their standard of living to rise and do not always increase their families in such a way as to cancel out the effect of any rise in wages on their standard of living. In many poorer countries, especially in Asia and Latin America, this still seems to happen. All that one can say is that in developed countries the supply of labour to the whole economy will not be infinitely elastic to changes in wages and salaries in the long run, though one cannot be sure exactly how responsive it will be. Its response will depend on too many psychological, moral and social factors to permit satisfactory generalisations. In general, it seems that the richer a community is the less correlation there will be between wages and the size of the population.

Perhaps the relationship differs between countries. Some communities may be more willing to take out part of a potential increase in the standards of living by increasing the size of the population, than others are. Indeed, the same community may respond differently to an increase in the standard of living at different periods of time. It seems to be impossible nowadays, to point to any clear, universal relationship which links the size of the population to the level of wages and salaries.

What is more, with public opinion in many countries becoming worried about the 'population explosion', the relationship may well alter during the 1970s and 1980s.

Suggested reading

MARSHALL, ALFRED	*Principles of Economics*, 8th edn., London, 1920, Book VI, chapters 3, 4 and 5.
ROBINSON, JOAN	*Economics of Imperfect Competition* London, 1933, chapter 26.
ROBBINS, LIONEL	'On the Elasticity of Demand for Income in Terms of Effort', *Economica*, 1930, p. 123.

13

Rent

We now move on, in our discussion of the factors of production and
their prices, to consider the rent of land. In colloquial English, the
word 'rent' can refer to any periodic payment made regularly for the
hire of a good. Examples are the rentals paid for the hire of automobiles or television sets and the rents paid for houses, flats, shops
and the like, where these are not bought outright. In economic
theory, on the other hand, rent means something different. The term
is applied only to payments made for factors of production which are
in imperfectly elastic supply—with land as the main example.

The type of payment ordinarily known as rent may, of course,
include a payment for the hire of land. The total rent of a house, for
instance, will usually include a sum large enough to cover the annual
value of the land on which the house stands, but it is a payment for
other things as well. The landlord has invested his money in the
materials of which the house is built and he expects a return on that
investment. The 'economic' rent we shall discuss in this chapter takes
account only of payments for the use of land. It excludes any return
on a landlord's capital investment in buildings. We shall therefore
ignore the problems of returns on investments for the moment. We
shall consider them in detail in the next chapter.

The kind of model which will enable us to see most clearly what
'economic' rent is and why it is paid is one where a tenant farmer
rents his farm from a landowner. This is still an important institutional
arrangement in most countries. It is also the standard case which
was discussed for over a century by economists in developing the
theory of rent. Of course, relations between landlord and tenant
differ from country to country. What we are interested in is any
payment to the landlord as owner of the land.

This is 'economic' rent. It is sometimes described as a 'surplus'
because it does not result from any effort or activity on the part of the
landowner. This idea that rent is a reward for the mere ownership of
a factor of production and not a payment for effort expended is both
well-established and important in economic theory. Adam Smith

commented that 'the landlords like all other men love to reap where they never sowed'.[1] Perhaps the metaphor is a little misleading, since reaping is by no means an effortless operation. Apart from this, the statement does not explain why rent exists. How is it that landlords are able to reap where they have not sown when other members of the community cannot? Most of us would be only too happy to earn our incomes as easily as this implies.

One of the earliest explanations of the nature of rent, and one which is still regarded as coming very near to the truth, was provided by David Ricardo in the early years of the nineteenth century. It is not surprising that rent should have been regarded as important in Britain in the early 1800s. The scarcity of food, resulting partly from the Napoleonic wars and partly from the pressure of increased population, had raised food prices considerably. Rents had risen sharply and it was widely felt that landlords were profiting from the misfortunes of the rest of society.

It has therefore been suggested that Ricardo developed his theory of rent as an attack on the landed aristocracy as distinct from the tenant farmers. It is sometimes said that Ricardo was a member of the new bourgeoisie and, as such, antagonistic to the aristocracy. There may be some justification for this idea, but it should not be given too much stress. Ricardo was bourgeois by upbringing and inheritance, but he is one of the few economists who has made a great deal of money. Going on to the Stock Exchange he made a fortune in a very few years and, retiring very young, bought an estate in Gloucestershire, becoming a landlord himself—as well as a Member of Parliament. It is therefore dangerous to represent Ricardo as being an unrelenting opponent of landowners.

2. Ricardo and rent

It will be useful to take these Ricardian ideas as our starting-point in this discussion of rent. What was the essence of Ricardian theory? Where were Ricardo's ideas right and where were they wrong? Ricardo's two main contentions were these. First, rent is a return for the use of the 'original and indestructible powers of the soil'.[2] Second, high rents are not a sign of the bounty of nature. On the contrary, they are an indication of the niggardliness of nature.

It will be easiest to take the second point first. This part of Ricardo's doctrine was probably intended largely as an attack on a group of French economists known as the 'physiocrats'[3] who laid great stress

---

[1]Adam Smith, *The Wealth of Nations*, chapter 6.
[2]David Ricardo, *Principles of Political Economy* (edited by Piero Sraffa), p. 67.
[3]For a study of their doctrines see *A History of Economic Doctrines*, Gide and Rist, chapter 1.

on the bounty of nature as the reason for the rent of land. In modern terms, Ricardo was arguing that while land is clearly useful, it is also scarce. While the productivity of nature may be a sign of its usefulness and of the bounty of nature, the fact that the total supply of land is more or less fixed is a sign of nature's niggardliness. As we have seen, Ricardo lived at a time when high rents were causing great anxiety. He saw only too clearly that these high rents were caused by the scarcity of agricultural land and its produce and not their abundance. It is scarcity and high prices which cause high rents, not plenty.

What, then, can we say about Ricardo's first point? The assertion that rent is a payment for the 'original and indestructible powers of the soil' is more difficult to judge. Admittedly, the fact that to economists rent is payment for the use of natural resources and not of consumption goods makes it easier to use such terms. A major difficulty is how one can decide which of the powers of the land are 'original' and which are not. By the term 'original powers' Ricardo probably meant that it is both desirable and possible to distinguish, for example, between payment for land with drainage facilities supplied by the landlord and payment for land with natural drainage only. The former is really a return on the landlord's capital investment; only the latter is rent. For example, the landscape of most countries has been changed enormously by man since prehistoric times. The present landscape is certainly not attributable to the original powers of the soil and to nothing else. What land is today depends not only on what nature has given but also on the actions of successive generations of farmers, manufacturers and civil servants. The concept of the 'original' powers of the land is, to say the least, nebulous.

Can it then be said that the powers of the soil are 'indestructible'? In these days, when atomic energy has been discovered, it is dangerous to assert that anything is indestructible. But even on a more ordinary plane it is unreasonable to claim that the fertility of the land is unalterable. Changes in climate, farming methods or the introduction of irrigation can turn good arable land into dust-bowls or deserts into farmland. It is not reasonable to regard the powers of the land as indestructible.

3. Rent and elasticity of supply

It is therefore now agreed by economists that rent is a payment not for the original and indestructible powers of the soil but rather one which results from the fact that land is one factor of production which is in almost completely inelastic supply in response to changes in its price. More land cannot be produced to meet a greater demand for it. Such expedients as reclamation from the sea are quantitatively unimportant, except perhaps for a country like the Netherlands. What Ricardo was really searching for was an explanation of the fact that, when the demand for land increased, the supply was incapable of changing in response to that increased demand. The idea that there are 'original and indestructible powers' of the land implies inelasticity of supply with respect to changes in price. It is therefore much more satisfactory to explain the rent of land in modern terms. The rent of land is a payment to a factor of production with an extremely low elasticity of supply. For, while the Ricardian idea of rent as a result of the original indestructible powers of the soil implies very inelastic supply, very inelastic supply does not necessarily imply original and indestructible powers in the soil. This is all to the good.

4. A model with pure scarcity rent

In order to explain the theory of rent more fully, we shall find it useful to construct a simplified model which will not, in its early stages at least, be a Ricardian model.

4.1 Our assumptions

Let us assume that there is an island of finite size and that this island is made up of homogeneous land. This means, first, that every acre is equal in fertility to every other acre and, second, that no acre is in a superior situation to any other acre or more suited to growing any particular crop. We imply, for example, that there is no inherent difference between the situation of one acre of the island and that of another, as there clearly is between a site, say, in the middle of London and one in a remote rural area of Great Britain. These assumptions are not realistic, but they are useful at this early stage in our discussion. They enable us to rule out the possibility that some parts of the island are better situated than others for serving particular markets. We shall also assume that all the land on this imaginary island is agricultural land and is able to grow only one product. We shall call the product wheat, again for the sake of simplicity. We assume that none of the island will be of any use for country parks, children's playgrounds or airports, and that none of it can produce carrots and potatoes as well as wheat.

So far as ownership of the land is concerned, we assume that it is divided between a large number of landowners. We rule out the possibility of a monopoly in the ownership of land, which has some-times led to confusion in theories of rent. We can assume, for example, that each acre of the island is owned by a different person. Let us assume that the ancestors of the present landowners came to the island centuries ago. They were then granted pieces of land which have remained in the hands of the same families ever since, though none of the descendents actually live on the island. This enables us to postulate that no landowner ever wants to farm the land himself or to buy or sell parts of the island. Finally, we assume that the island is uninhabited.

4.2 When scarcity rent is zero

Let us now imagine that a farmer arrives and wants to farm on the island. It would be easiest to suppose that he merely needed two factors of production—himself and some land—in order to commence production. It is rather more realistic to think that he will bring a plough. Let us therefore assume that every farmer has one tractor and plough which can only be used by him. We then have a 'fixed production coefficient' between farmers and ploughs.

Finally, we must introduce demand into our model. Let us assume that there is a perfectly competitive world market for wheat and that our hypothetical island is small compared with the world market. Then, even if the whole island is cultivated, we can assume that any change in the island's output of wheat does not change the world price. This is a realistic assumption. Any group of farmers on a small island would have to take the world price as being given, and quite unaffected by their own actions.

When the farmer arrives he will be unlikely to want to farm the whole island—we assume that it is too large. Nor, since there is perfect competition between the landlords, will he need to pay rent. If any one landlord tries to charge him rent, the farmer simply moves along to another piece of land. Perfect competition between landlords ensures that the price of land is zero. Since no rent need be paid, a profit-maximising farmer will go on extending his farm until the last acre he takes into his farm produces no addition to his revenue.

4.3 The extensive margin

In other words, he will employ more and more land until its marginal product is zero (and equal to rent). He will then be maximising profits. It is often said that when the farmer is cultivating just that area of land where the last acre he takes into cultivation produces exactly what it costs to hire, the *extensive margin of cultivation* has been reached.

The situation can be seen from Figs. 13.1a and 13.1b. Figure 13.1a shows the demand and supply curves for land on the whole island. The demand curve *DD* is given by the (falling) marginal revenue productivity curve of land to the one farmer who is farming on the island. For simplicity we have drawn this curve as a straight line. The supply curve of land, *SM*, is a vertical straight line showing that there is only a fixed amount of land, *OM* acres, available—the whole island. In this initial situation, Fig. 13.1a shows that there is no positive price for land at which the demand for land equals its supply.

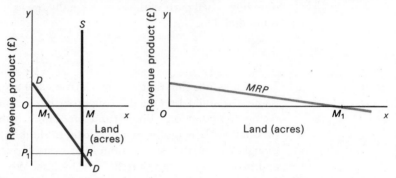

Fig. 13.1 a | b

If all the island were to be cultivated, the landowners would have to pay the single farmer £OP_1 (=£MR) per acre to cover his losses from farming the whole island—which is too big for him to farm profitably. Since no landlord is likely to pay anyone for farming his land, the one farmer uses OM_1 acres of land and pays no rent.

4.4 Marginal productivity and rent

Figure 13.1b shows the equilibrium position for this single farmer. Since he has no rent to pay, he hires more and more land until the marginal acre brings him no additional revenue. He equates the marginal revenue product of land with its marginal cost. In Fig. 13.1b this happens when the farmer uses OM_1 acres but pays no rent for them. He then stops increasing the size of his farm. It will be seen that when there is only one farmer the marginal revenue productivity curve of land to the farmer is the same thing as the demand curve for land. The two curves look different in Fig. 13.1a and 13.1b only because the scale along the *x*-axis in Fig. 13.1b is ten times larger than in Fig. 13.1a. This is because the individual farm is only one-tenth the size of the whole island.

4.5 When scarcity rent is positive

Let us now assume that the success of this pioneer farmer attracts new entrants to the island's farming industry. We shall further assume, for simplicity, that all the farmers are equally efficient. So long as there are not enough farmers to make it worth while farming the whole island, no rent will be paid. This is because we are still assuming that there is perfect competition between landowners.

However, even when all the land (*OM* acres) is taken there may still be farmers who want to farm land on the island and who are willing to pay a rent for it. Rent will then be charged. All the farmers will have to pay rent—and all will pay the same rent—because all the land is homogeneous, all farmers equally efficient and there is perfect competition between landowners. The increase in the number of farmers demanding land will reduce the amount of land used by each individual farmer. Each will still use only those acres of land which yield a marginal revenue product at least as great as their rent. But there are now more farmers and rent is therefore paid. It is obvious that, given the marginal revenue productivity of land, an individual farmer will now find that if he is to maximise profits he can afford to farm only a smaller amount of land than when the price of land was zero. The increase in the number of equally-efficient farmers thus reduces the amount of land used by each. For each farmer the revenue product of his marginal acre of land will be the same; for each it will be equal to the rent of an acre of land. All farmers, being equally efficient, will have exactly the same acreage of land.

The situation when the whole island is being farmed is shown in Figs. 13.2a and 13.2b. These are similar to Figs. 13.1a and 13.1b. In

Fig. 13.2 a | b

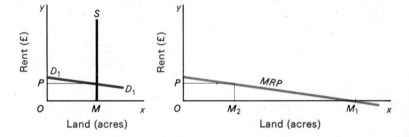

Fig. 13.2a, the curve *SM* still shows the same fixed supply of land, *OM* acres, as in Fig. 13.1a. D_1D_1 is still the demand curve for land for the island's whole farming industry, but there are now a number of producers and not simply the individual farmer shown in Fig. 13.1a. D_1D_1 is obtained by adding the marginal revenue productivity curves of all the farmers together sideways. This demand curve slopes downwards because we assume that the number of farmers on the island is still relatively small. We are continuing to assume a given and constant world price for wheat. The whole island (*OM* acres) is now used and a rent of £*OP* per acre is paid. In Fig. 13.2b we see the position of the individual farmer, as in Fig. 13.1b. The marginal revenue productivity curve of land to each farmer is the same as it was to the single farmer in Fig. 13.1b, because all farmers are assumed to be equally efficient and the world price of wheat

unchanged. Rent per acre has risen from zero to £OP and each individual farmer now finds it profitable to farm only OM_2 acres instead of the OM_1 farmed by the original farmer. The 'extensive margin' of cultivation has retreated for the individual farmer.

We may now sum up this part of the discussion. If he wants to maximise profit, every farmer will farm land up to the point where the revenue product of the marginal acre he farms is equal to the cost of a marginal acre. In perfect competition, this 'marginal cost of land' will also equal the rent of an acre.

5. The intensive margin

We have so far studied the problem of rent mainly from the point of view of an individual farmer deciding how many acres to farm. We can also consider it from the point of view of the farmer wondering how many hours to work or, to put it in the terms we are using, how many 'doses' of labour and capital to apply to the land. Each 'dose' may be, say, one hour's work by the farmer with his plough.

5.1 'Doses' of labour

This is not so simple as it sounds. What we are interested in is the marginal productivity of additional 'doses' of labour and capital applied to land. However, we have seen that, strictly speaking, the amount of land used by an individual farmer will change every time rent changes. This means that, strictly, we should reconstruct the marginal productivity curve for 'doses' of labour and capital applied

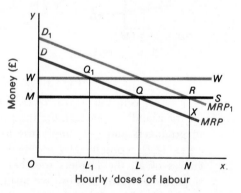

Fig. 13.3

to land each time rent changes. For the 'doses' would then be applied to a different amount of land. This would be inconvenient. The simplest case to consider is therefore where the amount of land used is fixed in amount. This will show the main principles involved, but will avoid the difficulties encountered when the amount of land farmed by each farmer changes. We shall also, for the sake of simplicity, talk only of 'doses' of labour—though in fact each unit of labour will use a fixed amount of capital.

In Fig. 13.3 the marginal revenue productivity curve of 'doses' of labour applied by a single farmer to a given area of land is originally the curve MRP. The farmer is then in equilibrium when he applies OL hourly 'doses' of his own labour to the fixed amount of land. The supply curve of labour (MS) shows the amount of money per hour (measured up the y-axis) which the farmer must be paid if he is to be induced to work for any given (marginal) hour (measured along the x-axis). It represents his supply curve of labour in terms of (hourly) income. For simplicity, it is assumed that the farmer asks a constant return of $£OM$ per dose of labour (and capital), however many or few hours' 'doses' he supplies.

5.2 The marginal 'dose'

The farmer therefore applies his labour to the farm until the 'marginal dose', in this case the OLth, brings no greater reward than he asks. Because his supply curve is horizontal he receives the same reward for *each* 'dose'. A more intensive effort on his part, say, working for ON hours, would bring a smaller return than he requires, namely, $£NX$ for the ONth hour instead of $£OM$ ($=£NR$). So he does not work so hard as that. The marginal (OLth) dose yields just as much as the farmer requires from it. On all the 'intra-marginal' doses, however, the return yielded is greater than the farmer asks. It is from these 'intra-marginal' doses that rent is paid. The 'doses' yield more to the farmer than the $OMQL$ he asks, and competition for land between farmers ensures that this 'surplus' goes to the landlord. In Fig. 13.3, the triangle MQD represents the rent paid. The 'marginal dose' of labour makes no contribution to this rent. It is only just worth applying.

5.3 The intensive margin defined

If the farmer now becomes less inclined to work, the supply curve of his labour may rise to WW. He still works up to the point where the marginal revenue product of his labour is equal to the reward he demands for applying that marginal 'dose' of labour. But since the reward that he asks for is now greater than it was, he supplies only OL_1 'doses' instead of OL, getting Q_1L_1 for each—total earnings of OWQ_1L_1. When this marginal dose of labour (the OL_1th) has been applied it is said that the *intensive margin of cultivation* has been reached. Rent is now WQ_1D. It will be seen from Fig. 13.3 that the 'intensive margin' is reached sooner when the 'marginal cost' of the farmer's labour rises: that is, when the supply price of a marginal 'dose' of labour and capital is higher. It follows that if the labour used is not the farmer's own but it is hired by him, a rise in wages will cause a fixed amount of land to be worked less intensively. Fewer men—fewer 'doses' of labour—will be used on it.

We now return to the farmer's original supply curve of 'doses' of labour (MS). If the marginal revenue productivity curve of labour now rises to MRP_1 (whether because the farmer becomes more efficient or because the price of wheat rises), it will pay the farmer to apply ON 'doses' of labour and capital to his land instead of the original OL. He still gets a marginal return per unit of QL, but his total income is now $OMRN$; rent is MRD_1. The intensive margin is thus extended when the marginal revenue productivity of labour increases, unless the terms on which labour is supplied alters. A farmer will always push the 'intensive margin of cultivation' to the point where the marginal 'dose' of labour and capital brings a return just equal to the payment demanded by it—to the point where the marginal revenue productivity of labour equals the marginal cost of labour.

6. The extensive and intensive margins

We have now seen that farmers must adjust their operations in two ways if they are to earn maximum profits. First, at each level of rent they must cultivate an area of land of such a size that the *extensive margin* is just reached. Second, with a given supply curve for doses of their own or other peoples' labour and capital, they must apply so many doses that the *intensive margin* is just reached. It must be remembered, of course, that adjustments at both these margins will take place simultaneously to meet changed conditions. We have considered the adjustments separately only to simplify the exposition.

7. Some conclusions about scarcity rent

The main conclusions we have reached are these. First, since in our model land has zero elasticity of supply, no change in rent can bring more land into cultivation. Second, on our assumption that all land is homogeneous and that there is perfect competition both between landlords and between tenants, all farmers will pay the same rent. The size of this rent will be determined by the demand for land and the supply of land. It follows that a rise in rents will occur in three main situations or any combination of them:

(*a*) if the number of farms increases but the price of the product and the physical productivity of each farm remains constant;

(*b*) if the price of the product rises but the number of farms and the marginal physical productivity of land remain constant;

(c) if the marginal physical productivity of land rises but the price of the product and the number of farms remain constant.

Rent in the situation so far studied is pure scarcity rent, resulting from the scarcity of homogeneous land. The characteristic feature of pure scarcity rent is this. While a rise in the prices of other factors of production will often cause an increase in their supply, at any rate in the long run, a rise in rent cannot increase the supply of land. Higher earnings for land can therefore persist even in the long run; with other factors, their supply will usually increase to meet an increased demand. It is the fixity of supply which distinguishes the scarcity rent of homogeneous land from the prices of other factors of production. Scarcity rent results from the fact that, both in our model and in the real world, land is in inflexible supply.

8. A model with differential rents

We have shown how scarcity rent can be analysed in a model where land is both homogeneous and scarce. This is not a very realistic model. Land is rarely homogeneous over large areas. We shall therefore drop the assumption that it is.

8.1 Our assumptions

We continue to simplify the analysis by discussing our hypothetical island, but assume that a new area is uncovered by the sea. There is then no problem of how to treat the cost of reclamation. It is reasonable to assume that the new land is less fertile than the rest of the island, since until recently it has been covered by the sea. There will therefore be land of two qualities. We have already assumed that the whole of the original island is being cultivated and that, since all the land is homogeneous, each acre pays the same rent.

8.2 How differential rents are set

If more new farmers now arrive on the enlarged island, they will obviously consider using the less-fertile land. Since the new land is less productive, the farmers cannot afford to pay the same rents as for the better land. If the same rent were charged for both types of land, it would clearly be sensible for the new farmers to use the better land, bidding up its price. Assuming perfect competition between both landlords and farmers, rent on the less-fertile land must be appropriately lower than on the better land. For we are still assuming all farmers equally efficient, and therefore want equal (normal) profits.

For example, if the rent of the better land is £20 per acre, while the fertility of the inferior land is such that the farmers' earnings are £12 less per acre than on the better land, the rent of the inferior land must be £8 per acre. If rent on the inferior land were less than £8, it would pay farmers to farm it instead of the better land. Competition between farmers wishing to farm on the cheaper land would then raise its price. If rent on the inferior land were more than £8 per acre in rent, it would pay farmers to farm the better land instead. Only at £8 per acre will there be no flow of farmers to or from the inferior land. Competition between farmers establishes an appropriate difference between the rents of the two types of land. It follows that if there are *more* than two grades of land, each will earn its own different rent.

This situation represents the one in which Ricardo was interested. We now have a rather more complicated model than where all land is equally fertile and all rent is pure scarcity rent; but it is more realistic. It can allow for differing fertilities between different pieces of land. This type of situation is said to cause *differential rents*. Rent is different on each grade of land. The grade of land which is only just worth cultivating is said to be *on the extensive margin of cultivation* for the island's farming industry. If the area under cultivation increases, for any reason, far enough to use all land of a given grade, rents on all grades of land will rise proportionately and the extensive margin will be pushed onto an inferior grade of land.

8.3 'No rent' land

However, rent is *not* due to the existence of land of differing fertility. We have shown that rent is caused by the fact that land is scarce. It can be paid even when land is homogeneous. Nevertheless, *differences* between the fertilities of different types of land will cause *differences* in their rent. Rent will be lower on less-fertile land and higher on more-fertile land. At the same time, the most infertile land will pay no rent at all if all land is not of the same quality and not all of this most-infertile land is farmed. Ricardo considered this kind of situation and showed that where land is on or beyond the 'extensive margin of cultivation' for the whole farming industry, it will pay no rent. It will be 'no rent' land.

8.4 Differential rent in reality

The idea that different areas of land are of differing fertility is quite realistic. A typical case can be considered if we assume that there is a fertile valley containing several farms and that, on either side of the valley, there are less-fertile hillsides with less and less productive farms as one moves up them. Let us continue to assume that only wheat is grown. If the price of wheat rises, progressively less-fertile land farther and farther up the hills will be cultivated. The extensive margin of cultivation will move up the hillsides. 'Marginal land,' as farmers have come to call it following economic terminology, will be brought under cultivation. Rents will rise everywhere. However, the effect of the increased prices—and hence the increased rents—will be felt on both the extensive and the intensive margins of the wheat-farming industry. More land will be used—the extensive margin will spread. Land will also be used more intensively now that wheat is more expensive—the intensive margin will alter too.

It is very important to remember that, whenever circumstances change, every farmer has to adapt his activities at both the extensive and the intensive margins so as to bring himself back into equilibrium. If agricultural product prices rise, he will want *both* to farm more land *and* to farm all his land more intensively. The result of these changes is to ensure that he continues to earn normal profit. Because individual farmers always behave in this way, it follows that the farming industry as a whole will constantly maintain equilibrium at both its extensive and intensive margins.

We have shown how some land can earn no rent. As the extensive margin of cultivation advances, there will always be some land 'on the margin of cultivation'; so infertile that it pays no rent. It will only be worth cultivating if it can be farmed free of charge. If rent had to be paid for it, the farmer would find it more profitable to work on the better land instead. Although there would be a rent to pay on this better land, it would be sufficiently fertile to allow the farmer to pay the rent and still earn larger profits than on the inferior land.

9. Why rent exists

We have seen throughout our analysis of rent that there are three main circumstances which can lead to a rise in rents. These are: (*a*) an increase in the number of farmers; (*b*) an increase in the productivity of each farmer not outweighed by a fall in the price of the product; and (*c*) a rise in the price of the product which the farmers are growing.

Each of these will be caused either by an increase in demand or, in the case where rising productivity does not lead to an offsetting fall in prices, *either* to a rise in demand *or* to a demand which allows an increase in rents, despite the fact that the increasing output of the product being cultivated tends to lower its price. In our model, if the price of an agricultural product rises, it rises equally for all farmers, however much or little they produce. For we are assuming that competition is perfect. Unless productivity rises, the higher agricultural prices are the less fertile is the 'marginal' land which it is just possible to cultivate and still earn normal profits. Consequently, the higher agricultural prices are, the higher are rents on the better grades of land. It is usually rises in the prices of agricultural products, and consequently rises in the marginal productivity of land, which cause changes in rent. Since land is in fixed supply, such changes in the prices of the products of land cause increases in rent. High prices are the cause of high rents—not vice versa.

10. Rent and taxation

It will always be possible experimentally to show whether the earnings of a given piece of land is rent by taxing those earnings. Since the supply of land is completely inelastic, no rise or fall in the receipts of landlords can affect the supply of land. Landlords cannot produce more land however high rents are. If a tax were imposed on land, this would in itself have no affect on rents. So long as there was perfect competition between landlords, they would always find it worth leaving their land under cultivation, paying the tax and keeping what was left, however little that might be. The land exists whatever the landlords do and they will feel that it is sensible to take what rents they can—even if these are taxed. There will be no reduction in the supply of land. There is, however, little likelihood that the supply of *other* factors of production would remain unaltered in this way if their earnings were to be taxed. Land *is* different in this respect.

11. Some conclusions

This analysis of rent has been very abstract but it has enabled us to distinguish two different types of rent.

11.1 Scarcity rent

First, we have seen that rent can be earned where all land is homogeneous—provided that it is also scarce. If there is perfect competition between landlords, homogeneous land like that on our hypothetical island is in *perfectly elastic* supply until all of it is used. Until it is all used, no rent can be charged. Once all the land is used, however, land is in *perfectly inelastic* supply to changes in the demand for it and scarcity rent begins to be paid. This accrues equally to each and every acre of land. The rent is a pure scarcity rent and no differential elements exist at all. It will be remembered, of course, that we are assuming that our land can only grow wheat. In technical language, it is 'completely specific' to wheat-growing. We shall see soon what difference this simplifying assumption makes.

11.2 Differential rent

Second, when there is a supply of land large enough for some of it to pay no rent at all, there is no scarcity rent as such. But this land may not be homogeneous. If one part is more fertile than the rest, differential rent can be earned by the better land. Obviously, land of differential fertility might or might not be specific to wheat-growing, though for the moment it will be easier to assume that it is. What *is* clear is that land cannot be in completely elastic supply if it is not all of the same quality. Some acres are only imperfect substitutes for others. More-productive acres will therefore earn more rent than inferior acres, because of the differences in fertility between them. Land is in *imperfect elastic* supply to changes in its price and in such circumstances it is always possible for rent to be earned. As Marshall has said, 'in a sense all rents are scarcity rents, and all rents are differential rents'.[1] Differential rents arise only because land of each particular quality is scarce. Nevertheless the distinction between differential rent and scarcity rent is worth making.

12. Rent and situation

Another qualification is also needed to the theory of rent outlined above. We have relaxed our initial assumptions a little, but only to allow for the fact that land is heterogeneous. We must now make a similar change in our assumptions to allow for the fact that not all land is in the same place. Some areas of land are therefore less accessible than others and differential rents can occur because of differences in situation.

To some extent differences in the situation of land come to the same thing as differences in its fertility. Land may be described as bad for wheat-growing either because it is situated in the Sahara Desert or because it is half-way between Algiers and Lagos. Both come to the same thing in the end, but the first explanation is in terms of soil fertility and the second in terms of situation. However, even where land is homogeneous in its inherent fertility, there may be differences in rent because of differences in situation. As we have seen, the rent of land is determined in the last resort by what consumers will pay for the product of the land. Receipts from a particular crop will therefore depend in part on how much it costs to transport it to market. The result of transport charges is that land near a market can pay a higher rent than land farther away. Those farming

[1] *Principles of Economics*, p. 422.

the more-accessible land have to pay less to send their produce to market, and competition between farmers will ensure that rent on this land is higher than on less-accessible land.

The same type of situation can arise with perishable foods. It may be more profitable to grow vegetables, milk and fruit for a town market near that particular town than to grow them many miles away. A smaller amount of the goods will go bad in transit. However, with cheaper air-freight rates and better refrigeration, this is now less true. For example, vegetables can be profitably transported from California and sold in England. In competitive conditions, then, two market gardens of equal fertility and run with equal efficiency will pay different rents if one is much nearer to the London market than the other, only to the extent that there are differences in transport costs, including the cost of physical deterioration of the product transported.

It is therefore necessary to allow for differences in situation in constructing a satisfactory theory of rent. Differential rents are likely to exist because of differences in situation as much as because of differences in the innate fertility of the land.

Since we have drawn our illustrations of the importance of the situation as a cause of differences in rents from agriculture, it is important to emphasise that rents in industry will differ in the same way. A factory near a large market will pay a higher rent for the land it occupies than an identical factory far away. Similarly, there are big differences in rent between shops in the centre of London and shops in rural areas of England. Rents are higher where trade is more easily attracted. The advantages of a site in a good shopping or trading centre have to be paid for in the form of high rents.

13. Transfer earnings

One final and fundamental qualification remains to be made to our theory of rent. It should be obvious to the reader that by confining our attention to the payment made for land which is completely 'specific' to growing one crop we have been able to avoid a very important problem. We have been able to treat the whole of rent earned by land as a payment for a 'free gift of nature'. Being a 'gift of nature' land is not reproducible: no payment of rent is necessary in order to keep land in existence. There is therefore no problem, as there would be if some of the earnings of land were devoted to keeping it alive. If that happened, only some of the earnings of land would be a rent due to its scarcity; the remainder would be a 'wage' to keep it alive. An analogous problem does arise if we look at the rent of land from the point of view of a particular 'industry'. This is the problem we have avoided by assuming so far that land can do nothing but produce wheat.

Since all land was assumed to be valueless for any other use, we could assume that there was no need for wheat farmers to make any payments to keep land in the 'wheat industry'. It would remain in existence whether paid for or not and its earnings could therefore be described as rent. This is not realistic. Most land can produce more than one crop. To keep it in any one crop-growing 'industry' it must be paid enough to prevent it from leaving that particular 'industry'. For example, let us assume that a marginal acre of wheat land would remain profitably in the wheat-farming industry so long as rent was £6 an acre or less. However, it could profitably turn to the production of turnips if only rent were to fall to £4 an acre. In this situation, the wheat farmer must pay at least £4 an acre in rent to the landlord or the latter will hand over the land to the turnip industry.

13.1 Transfer earnings defined

This £4 per acre is known as the land's *transfer earnings*. Unless each acre earns at least £4 in the wheat industry it will transfer to the next most lucrative occupation, in this case in the turnip industry. We may therefore define the rent from the point of view of any one industry more accurately than we have done so far. It is *any payment to a factor of production in excess of its transfer earnings*. In our example, from the point of view of the wheat industry paying £6 an acre for land, the 'true' rent is £2. The remaining £4 are transfer earnings. If there is now a change in the supply or demand conditions for turnips, the most profitable alternative crop, it might become possible for turnip growers to pay £10 an acre for land. With unchanged supply and demand conditions for wheat, wheat-farmers can still only offer £6. Land will therefore move into the turnip industry. From the point of view of the turnip industry, the transfer earnings of any acre of land will now be the £6 required to prevent it from returning to the wheat industry. Its rent will be £4—the difference between its transfer earnings of £6 and the £10 it actually earns.

The same factors explain why, for example, rents of the available land are too high in urban areas to allow profitable farming. Unless farmers are willing to pay the same rents as are factories, offices and shops, land will 'transfer' to these activities. Such rents are too high in large towns to allow farmers to produce there profitably when they have to sell in competition with farmers from rural areas where there is little or no competition from other activities.

13.2 Transfer earnings and the industry

The concept of transfer earnings leads to interesting conclusions. Only land which is in *perfectly inelastic* supply to the economy as a whole will earn nothing but rent from the point of view of that economy. Yet this same land can be in *perfectly elastic* supply from the point of view of a particular industry and so be earning no rent at all so far as that industry is concerned. To illustrate this let us revert to our original imaginary island of homogeneous land. Let us imagine that it is all used to grow wheat and that the rent per acre is £6. If a small group of farmers now decides to grow, say, turnips, this group will be able to obtain as much land as it wants for slightly more than £6 an acre, so long as it does not want to use the whole island. From the point of view of the 'turnip industry' the whole payment of a little over £6 will be needed to entice the land away from wheat-growing. It will all be transfer earnings and the land will earn no rent so far as the 'turnip industry' is concerned.

Now, as we have seen, land can earn more than its transfer earnings. Any such excess over transfer earnings is rent from the point of view of the industry using the land.

It must be remembered that this analysis of transfer earnings has been undertaken only from the point of view of a single industry. The individual industry *does* have to pay money to keep land from transferring to the next most profitable use. For the economy as a whole, however, land has no alternative use at all. The transfer earnings of land from the point of view of the economy as a whole will be zero. All the earnings of land will be rent.

13.3 Transfer earnings and the individual producer

The same kind of problem can be studied from the point of view of the individual farmer. To him land has a cost in just the same way as any other factor does. Unless he pays whatever rent per acre is established by competition between landlords and between farmers, the land will go to someone else. *For the individual farmer the whole rent will be a cost—the cost of preventing the land from transferring to someone else.* This concept of transfer earnings helps to bring the simple Ricardian theory—where transfer earnings are zero because it is the whole economy which is being studied—into closer relation with reality.

14. Rent of ability

We have now seen that land earns rent because it is a factor of production which is in inelastic supply to changes in its price. Of course, there are other factors of production which cannot be reproduced at will—or at all—and which are therefore also in imperfectly elastic supply so far as changes in their prices are concerned. All such factors can earn rent. Rent can therefore be defined, more accurately than we have done so far, as the difference between the reward of *any* factor of production which is in imperfectly elastic supply with respect to changes in its price and its transfer earnings. Natural ability, which cannot be reproduced even if earnings rise, is frequently found in some units of the factor of production labour. A genius possesses scarce and non-reproducible ability. While this ability is not 'indestructible' (though it may be original), it is undoubtedly born and not made. The supply of genius over periods of time may well be variable, but it certainly does not vary in response to changes in its price. Human ability just happens.

Natural ability of this kind cannot be produced by even the best education. From this point of view of the whole economy it is therefore in completely inelastic supply to price changes. This ability may be either general or specific. If the skill is completely specific to one occupation, the person concerned will earn a very large income in that occupation. For example, consider a brilliant violinist. Suppose that his talent is natural and he is able to earn £200 a week by his playing but nothing at all by doing anything else. The money he earns then represents a true economic rent. It is a payment for a completely 'specific' ability.

However, it is much more likely that the violinist's talent will not be specific in this way, but that he will be able to earn a smaller income in another occupation. As a soloist he earns £200 a week. If he had to choose some other job he could, say, earn £40 a week by playing in a group. So long as he is paid at least £40 a week he will remain a soloist. Since we are assuming that he is 'rational', he will turn to playing in a group if he is offered less than £40. This principle can be tested if we apply the acid test of a tax. If a special tax of £160 a week is levied on concert soloists, our violinist will continue to play his Bach and Brahms. Only if the tax on solo violinists exceeds £160 will he (being 'rational') join an (untaxed) group. The £160—the difference between his total earnings and his transfer earnings—is the violinist's economic rent from the point of view of the 'solo violin industry'. It represents his *rent of ability*.

15. Quasi-rent

We have so far assumed that a factor of production that is in inelastic supply in the short run is also in inelastic supply in the long run. However, there are some factors of production whose supply is elastic in the long run but inelastic in the short run. In Marshall's words, these will be 'machines and other appliances made by man'.[1] They are not in fixed supply like land, so that the earnings from their use cannot be called rent in the economic sense. Nevertheless, in the

[1] *Principles of Economics*, p. 74.

short run their supply cannot be increased or decreased, since they are relatively durable in use and take time to make. The reward from them is therefore not quickly adjusted to changes in market conditions. It is not a rate of interest on free or floating capital, but is rather some kind of rent. Marshall attached great importance to the analysis of these earnings from machines, and coined a special term from them, namely, 'quasi-rents.' Marshall never defined quasi-rent explicitly and formally. The term has been used both by him and by other writers in a variety of related, but not identical senses. In Marshall, the most important example appears to be typified by the following 'model'.

15.1 Our model   An entrepreneur hires a machine, on an annual contract, and pays a given weekly sum for its use. This payment is a fixed and not a variable cost for the entrepreneur. However, by using the machine in conjunction with one or more variable factors, the entrepreneur

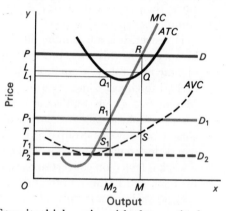

Fig. 13.4

earns a profit from it which varies with changes in demand conditions and in other cost conditions—for example, wage rates. If the entrepreneur has only one fixed factor (the machine) and one variable factor (labour), his total receipts from sales of the product minus his total wage bill is a quasi-rent earned by the machine. Now this quasi-rent may be less than, equal to, or greater than the weekly rental of the machine. In Fig. 13.4 the firm initially faces the average revenue (demand) curve PD. Total weekly wages are $OMST$; weekly rental of the machine is $LQST$; quasi-rent is $PRST$. In this case the entrepreneur is doing well. He is earning abnormally high profits or 'abnormally high quasi-rent' in the short run. He can pay the rental of the machine and have something left over. It is only in the long run that the numbers of machines in existence can be increased, and such abnormally high quasi-rent competed away. If the demand curve fell, in the shorter period, from PD to P_1D_1, the machine would still be earning a positive quasi-rent of $P_1R_1S_1T_1$, but this would be smaller than the weekly rental of $L_1Q_1S_1T_1$ ($=LQST$). The quasi-rent would now be 'abnormally low'; it would not be enough to pay the rental. In the long run, the number of machines in existence would fall so that quasi-rent returned to the 'normal' level. It should be noted that if demand fell still further, quasi-rent might become zero; this would happen with the demand curve P_2D_2. With a demand curve below P_2D_2, it would pay the firm to close down altogether, in the short run at least, rather than produce in a situation where total receipts were less than the total wage bill (total variable cost) for all positive outputs. We have already seen that in such circumstances a firm will minimise its loss by closing down temporarily. It may be noted that, on this assumption, quasi-rent can never be negative.

15.2 Quasi-rent defined

Let us attempt a formal definition of quasi-rent. The quasi-rent of a machine is its total short-period receipts less the total costs of hiring the variable factors used in association with it to produce output, and of keeping the machine in running order in the short run. In long-run equilibrium, quasi-rent will become equal to the (constant) normal earnings of the machine. Quasi-rent, in other words, will be at its 'normal' long-run level, where it is just equal to the cost of keeping the machine in continued existence; just equal to the rental in our model. In these circumstances an entrepreneur would be just willing to replace the machine by an identical one, when it wore out.

It follows that while, in the short run, any receipts of a machine in excess of the prime costs of running it can be regarded as akin to rent, over the longer period such earnings are quite essential to the continued operation of the machine. In the long run, any quasi-rent 'is expected to, and generally does, yield a normal rate of interest . . . on the free capital, represented by a sum of money that was invested in producing it'.[1] As Marshall says, 'it is . . . just as essential in the long run that the price obtained should cover general or supplementary costs as that it should cover prime costs. An industry will be driven out of existence in the long run as certainly by failing to earn even a moderate interest on the capital invested in steam-engines, as by failing to replace the price of the coal or the raw material used up from day to day.'[2] Consequently one may say that 'the confident expectation of coming quasi-rents is a necessary condition for the

[1] Marshall, *op. cit.*, p. 424 (footnote).
[2] *ibid.*, p. 420.

investment of capital in machinery and for the incurring of supplementary costs generally.'[1]

**16. Rent and
quasi-rent
compared**

The principles lying behind rent and quasi-rent are well illustrated
by what is known as Marshall's 'parable' of the meteor stones.[2] We
shall use Marshall's analysis as the basis for our own.

16.1 Rent

Let us assume in the first instance[3] that a single shower of homogeneous meteoric stones falls in a particular area. All the stones fall
within a very small radius and they are all immediately found. It is
then discovered that since the stones are harder and more durable
than diamonds they are very valuable in industrial uses. The owners
of the stones are therefore able to charge a 'scarcity rent' for them.
They own a 'free gift of nature' in perfectly inelastic supply to changes
in its price.

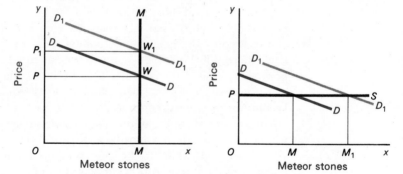

Fig. 13.5 a | b

This hypothetical situation is depicted in Fig. 13.5a. The fixed
(long- and short-run) supply of stones, *OM*, is demanded by entrepreneurs who are willing to pay for varying amounts of them the
amounts of money shown on the demand curve *DD*. This is the
marginal (net) revenue productivity curve of stones to the entrepreneur. It slopes downwards for the usual reasons. The price of each
stone, in perfect competition, is therefore *OP* and all the stones are
used. The owners earn an amount of rent *OMWP*. If the demand for
these stones now increases, perhaps because of an increase in the
price of industrial output, the demand curve may rise to D_1D_1. The
price of a stone would then increase to OP_1 in both the short and the

[1] *ibid.,* p. 424 (footnote).
[2] *ibid.,* pp. 415–21.
[3] cf. Marshall, *op. cit.,* p. 415.

long run and an additional amount of rent PWW_1P_1 would be earned. Since the supply of stones is completely fixed there can be no change in the supply curve MM. All the earnings of the stones are rent—both in the short and the long run. This limiting case is therefore analogous to the case of scarcity rent with homogeneous land. Since we assume that the stones are homogeneous it is a 'pure scarcity rent'. Each stone earns rent and each earns the same rent.

16.2 No rent

At the other end of the scale is the case[1] where the meteor stones fall in such a way that they are available in unlimited quantities, provided that the buyer pays the cost of finding them. If we assume that the stones are all equally easy to find, the production cost of stones will be constant and their supply curve PS will be horizontal, as in Fig. 13.5b. In the original demand conditions in Fig. 13.5b, shown by the demand curve DD, the price of stones is OP and the amount of stones OM is demanded. Suppose that the demand curve rises D_1D_1. Since the supply of stones is perfectly elastic, even in the short run, supply adjusts itself completely to the changed demand conditions and the quantity of stones OM_1 is supplied. The price of stones remains at OP. As already explained, this price is just high enough to pay for their production, so that the owners of the stones earn no rent as a result of the increased demand. This is the other limiting case. Because supply is perfectly elastic, rent is entirely absent, both in the short and the long run.

16.3 Quasi-rent

Let us now consider an intermediate case where supply takes some time to react to a changed demand and where quasi-rent is therefore earned in the short run. In Fig. 13.6, the original situation is one where a quantity of OM stones is available at a price of OP, but where no more stones at all are available whatever price is offered in the shorter period.

In the long run, however, further stones can be provided at the same cost as the original ones. The short-period supply curve PWR therefore rises vertically, as soon as more than OM stones are demanded. Short-run supply is infinitely inelastic. If the demand curve DD now rises to D_1D_1, the price of stones will rise to OP_1 but whatever happens to their price only OM stones are available in the short period. Assuming that there are no short-run costs of maintaining the stones in working order, all the short-run earnings of the stones (OMW_1P_1) represent quasi-rent. There are no variable costs.

[1] cf. Marshall, *op. cit.*, p. 418.

This quasi-rent is earned only because the homogeneous stones are in imperfectly elastic supply in the short run. Over the longer period, the supply curve PWL is horizontal and the price of stones falls to OP again. OM_1 stones are now supplied, and no rent at all is earned in excess of costs of production. The short-period return is therefore a 'quasi-rent'. Only in long-run equilibrium can it be regarded as part

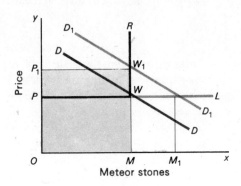

Fig. 13.6

of costs of production. Quasi-rent will be earned whenever any factor of production is in fixed short-run supply and earns something more than its prime costs. In Fig. 13.6 these are zero. Of course, if prime costs are positive, quasi-rent will be correspondingly less than OMW_1P_1.

16.4 Summing up

These hypothetical illustrations, using Marshall's example of meteor stones, emphasise that a situation where factors of production earn 'pure' rent is only a limiting case. The other limiting case is the situation where no rent at all is earned because factors are in perfectly elastic short-run supply. Between these limits, there are various different situations where, because factors are in imperfectly elastic supply in the short run, they earn quasi-rent in excess of prime costs. In the long run, prices will fall again. But they may not fall to the original level if the supply curve for them slopes upwards—if the factors of production are being produced under conditions of increasing costs. In this case, differential rents will be earned. Those factors which were produced most cheaply will earn a surplus payment over and above their cost—even over the longer period. Those factors whose production is only just worth while (in the long run) will be 'marginal stones' and will earn no rent.

17. Quasi-rents and human ability

Two further points about quasi-rents are important. First, quasi-rent can be earned by humen beings just as easily as by inanimate capital goods. Possessors of ability which is in imperfectly elastic supply in the short run will earn quasi-rent. This quasi-rent will be of two kinds. First, there will be scarcity rent, where all units of the human factor are homogeneous. Let us assume, for example, that a new method of teaching entrepreneurs is discovered by one business school which is able to prevent any other business school from finding out what the method is. The graduates of the innovating business school will be able to go into business and, having been taught with the new methods, will make large profits. We shall assume, to begin with, that all these new entrepreneurs are equally able so that the new 'factor of production' is homogeneous. All graduates of the innovating business school will then earn exactly the same amount of money; this will be a larger amount than can be earned by business men taught elsewhere. In the short run, these extremely large earnings will persist because there will be very few of these 'super-entrepreneurs'. They all earn a quasi-rent. In the long run, however, the innovating business school is unlikely to be able to maintain its monopoly of the new teaching methods. Its secrets will leak out and other business schools will make use of them. Quite apart from this, the business school will itself be turning out increasing numbers of 'new' business men and they will ultimately cease to be in limited supply. The quasi-rents will then disappear.

17.1 Quasi-rent and transfer earnings

The second important point is that transfer earnings enter the picture with quasi-rent just as they do with rent. Maintenance costs arise too. From the point of view of the economy as a whole, rent is *any* earning over and above what is required to keep a factor of production in existence. It is true that capital goods, like land, remain in existence in the short run whether paid for or not. But they will deteriorate if left unused, even in the shorter period, and it may well be worth spending just enough money on them to keep them in good running order. Some short-run earnings of machines will represent maintenance costs and not quasi-rents, from the point of view both of an individual industry and of the economy. Similarly, human beings must be paid something if they are to be kept alive. Even from the point of view of the whole economy, labour has 'transfer earnings'. It must be paid something or it will 'transfer' to the next world.

From the point of view of an individual industry, of course, all factors of production, including labour, will have their transfer earnings and these must be carefully separated from quasi-rents. For example, let us suppose that the new method of business training which we discussed above is more suited to the automobile industry than to others. A man trained in the new way might earn £30 000 a year making cars, while he might be able to earn £20 000 a year in several other industries. In this case, his transfer earnings from the point of view of the motor industry will be the £20 000 needed to keep him in the motor industry. His quasi-rent will be £10 000.

18. Are land and rent peculiarly related?

We have now seen that the theory of rent can be generalised so that it will apply to all types of factors of production. However, it is usually assumed that rent is in some way peculiarly connected with land. Is this true? The usual justification is that land is the only 'original' factor of production. This is not the case. As we have seen, outstanding human ability is also 'original' in the sense that more cannot be created if its 'price' rises. Again, it is reasonable to think that the connection between wages and the birth-rate is now less close than many people, especially during the nineteenth century, imagined. It is difficult to maintain that land is the only factor of production which is a 'free gift' of nature and which cannot be 'produced' in larger quantities if its price changes. Nevertheless, it is likely that land is the only factor whose total supply is *completely* inelastic in response to *everything*, including its own price. There does seem to be some justification for regarding the rent of land as rather different from the rents of other factors—in describing the rent of land, as Marshall did, as 'the leading species of a large genus'.[1]

Suggested reading

RICARDO, DAVID *Principles of Political Economy* (edited by Piero Sraffa), Cambridge, 1951, chapter 2.

MARSHALL, ALFRED *Principles of Economics*, 8th edn., London, 1920, Book V, chapters 9, 10 and 11; Book VI, chapters 9 and 10.

ROBINSON, JOAN *Economics of Imperfect Competition*, London, 1933, chapter 8.

[1] *Op. cit.*, p. 421.

14

Interest

1. Capital

In our study of the pricing of the factors of production, we have so far discussed the wages of labour and the rent of land. This chapter deals with interest on capital. It is important at the outset that we should be quite clear what is meant by capital. The fundamental distinguishing features of capital are that it is made by man and that its amount depends mainly on economic decisions. Land is a gift of nature and 'test-tube babies' remain part of science fiction. Again, while people can decide that they will have more or fewer children, there is no clear link between economic conditions and the size of the population.

The term capital is used to describe all those instruments of production which are deliberately made by man to carry on production in the future. Examples of capital assets are machines, factories, aircraft, lorries, trains and so on. Capital is unique among the factors of production in that man exercises complete control over its creation.

In the past, economists have argued at considerable length about whether such things as houses are capital goods or not. It will be seen from the previous paragraph that we have excluded them from our definition of capital. It seems better, at present, to treat them as durable consumer goods. For, while capital goods and durable consumer goods have many characteristics in common, they serve rather different purposes. In this chapter, we shall confine our attention to those capital goods which are built, bought or sold as direct factors of production—in order to produce consumer goods or further capital goods.

We shall discover that the problems of capital and interest are rather more difficult to solve than those of other parts of the theory of factor pricing. This is partly because a deliberate decision has to be taken to make each capital asset. It is partly because capital goods often have long lives, so that the timing of expenditure on them and receipts from them have to be carefully predicted in deciding to create them. This complicates the analysis. In the case of land and labour, such deliberate decisions on the part of their owners are usually not possible.

The early economists, Adam Smith and David Ricardo, could offer no real solution to the problem of how the return on capital was determined, and the first broad outline of the modern theory of capital was given by Nassau Senior some twenty years after Ricardo had made his own contribution.

The essence of the theory put forward by Senior was that interest—the price of capital—depended on the forces of demand and supply. In Senior's view, the supply of capital goods depended on the willingness of consumers to abstain from consumption in order that resources might be freed to produce capital goods. The demand for capital, Senior thought, depended on its productivity. As in the case of other factors of production, it was the output of the consumer goods which entrepreneurs expected capital goods to produce that determined the demand for them.

Senior's theory of capital was not accepted by everyone. In particular, Karl Marx objected to the idea that the rich underwent anything meriting the title of abstinence. The notion that the capitalist practised virtuous thrift or suffered from the rigours of deprivation struck Marx as ridiculous. It was largely to avoid such criticisms that Marshall[1] substituted the colourless term 'waiting' for the more doubtful 'abstinence'. This term 'waiting' has the added advantage of reminding us that the passage of time is crucial where capital is concerned. It reminds us that production with capital means using lengthy processes. The investor will 'wait' for the machine to produce its return only if the machine gives a bigger reward than he would obtain if he made the consumer goods directly. Spending time making machinery which can ultimately be used to make consumer goods, instead of producing the consumer goods directly, is rather like choosing to have a birthday present next year instead of this year. The choice of a present next year will be worthwhile only if one gets a better present than one would have had this year. For it is a fundamental feature of human nature to prefer the satisfactions obtained from consuming a good or service now rather than waiting a year to do so. A birthday present this year is normally regarded as worth more than a promise of exactly the same present next year.

The essence of the services rendered by machines, then, is that they represent productive and efficient processes. The return on most machines *is* positive. However, they also represent 'roundabout' processes. We shall have a good deal to say in the next few pages about roundabout processes. What we may note at once is that the time-lag between the moment when work is started on building a new machine or factory and the moment when it is actually in operation is often

[1]See his *Principles of Economics*, p. 233.

considerable. At the extreme, a steel works or power station will take years to build. In other words, production is carried on in a 'round-about' way, with energy and time expended on making an asset (or assets) which will produce the final consumer goods, instead of being expended directly on producing the consumer goods themselves. It is the roundaboutness of production using capital which causes most of the difficulties met with in constructing a simple capital theory.

In this book so far we have largely succeeded in evading the problem of time. Production and consumption has been studied on a short-term basis. We have, of course, made use of the distinction between long and short time-periods—a distinction concerning the response of supply over time to a change in demand conditions which takes place at a particular moment of time. Now, with capital goods, we meet a whole class of factors of production which is intimately and peculiarly connected with time. This is the second characteristic, in addition to the fact that capital is man-made, which we can identify as distinguishing capital from other factors of production. It also accounts for the difficulty of capital theory.

Because capital theory is not easy, it is hard to construct an analysis which is useful but also simple. Economists have expended a great deal of energy on constructing precise models which have turned out to be very complicated.[1] Even so, the results have not been altogether happy. We shall therefore content ourselves with the construction of simple, not very rigorous, models.

2. Robinson Crusoe investment

The simplest model one can imagine is of a man shipwrecked on a desert island. We shall assume that the island is completely un-inhabited and that it grows no food. The only possible food is fish, which can be caught from the sea or from rivers. We shall also assume that the castaway has been unable to salvage any capital equipment (fishing rods, lines or nets) from the wreck. If he wants to live he must catch fish, but unless he makes himself a net he will have to catch the fish by hand. We therefore have only one consumption good—fish. Robinson Crusoe has to decide how to catch enough fish to remain alive. At first, he will doubtless catch fish by hand until it strikes him that it ought to be possible to make some sort of net from twigs and creepers. What will it cost him to make the net—his primitive capital asset? Assuming that it takes Crusoe a day to produce the net, the cost will be an opportunity cost. It will be the number of fish which he has to forego because, on that one day, he has no time to go fishing. It will be an opportunity cost, because he

[1] Readers who are anxious to see one such model for themselves should consult F. A. Hayek, *Pure Theory of Capital*.

will have to sacrifice the opportunity of spending a day catching fish in order to make the net.

The decision which Crusoe has to make is therefore whether the opportunity cost of the net—one day without fish—is worth paying. This will depend on the returns which Crusoe expects to obtain from the net if he makes it. If he is able to catch five fish a day by hand and still expects to catch only five when the net is made, it will clearly not be worth making. Crusoe will sacrifice five fish today and he will not make up any of this deficiency in the future. However, if there are prospects of catching more fish each day once the net is made its construction may be worthwhile. Crusoe will have to decide whether to make the net on the basis of what economists call his 'rate of time preference'. This shows how highly he rates the desirability of having fish today rather than tomorrow—how strongly he prefers present to future satisfactions. If Crusoe's rate of time preference is such that he regards five fish today and five fish each day in the future as worth more than no fish today but ten fish every day in the future, then he will still not make the net. However, the choice may not be between five fish every day, on the one hand, and no fish today but ten fish every day after (including) tomorrow. Crusoe may be able to have either five fish every day or no fish today and twenty fish every day after (including) tomorrow. Then, he might well decide to go hungry for one day and make the net. Whatever his decision, he reaches it by comparing the returns from investment in the capital good with its cost—the day without food. Since the undesirability of a day without food can be taken as given, the more productive the net is expected to be the more likely it is to be made.

However, the productivity of the net will depend not only on how many fish can be caught with it each day, but also on the number of days for which it can be used. So far, we have implied that it will last for ever. Let us consider two possible situations in which the net may not be worth making. First, if the castaway is certain that he will be rescued within a week he may feel that even the extra eighty-five fish which the 'twenty-fish' net would catch during those seven days will not repay him for a day's hunger. On the other hand, if he expects to be stranded for a year, the extra fish he will catch will run into thousands, and will make a day's hunger seem a trivial price to pay. A second possibility (indeed probability) is that the net will not last for very long. Suppose that Crusoe thinks that the net will fall to pieces after a week. He will again feel less inclined to make it (to catch eighty-five extra fish) than if he thinks that it will last for a year.

This raises an important point in capital theory. It is what the investor *expects* to happen, rather than what will happen, which matters. The fact that the net would last for much more than a week is irrelevant if Crusoe is convinced that it will not. What the investor making the net has to compare are not two figures for fish caught, one for today and the other for tomorrow. He has to compare two supplies of fish, of different sizes, that stretch into the future, probably over different periods of time. It is between these that he must choose.

Perhaps the most important point to note about Crusoe's (and any other) investment decision is this. The cost of a capital good is likely to be easily discovered, since it is in the present. The returns expected from it—its *prospective yield*—are inevitably a matter for conjecture rather than accurate estimate. This is because the prospective yield of any asset depends on *expectations* of what the future holds in store. A Crusoe making a net, or a business man buying a machine, will both have to base their actions on their own estimates of the future earning powers of these capital assets. Both may prove to be wrong. Crusoe may expect to catch twenty fish a day but may actually only catch ten. A firm may build a new steel works expecting to earn a fortune, but be sent bankrupt by the development of competitive products like plastic or aluminium, whose growth it had not been able to predict. Investment in capital assets depends very largely on businessmen's expectations of the future. If these are wrong, a capital asset may be incapable of fulfilling the hopes of those who acquired it. This close connection between investment and expectations must never be overlooked.

Finally, even on his island, Crusoe would be able to choose between nets with different productivity. Assuming that both lasted for the same length of time, he might be able to make a rather useless one in a day but a very productive one in a week. Which would be better? Again, he would have to balance the opportunity cost of going hungry for longer against the expected, *incremental* returns from the better net. How many *more* fish would the better net catch? On our assumption of 'rationality', he would choose that net which promised to give the greatest satisfactions compared with its cost.

This is an extremely simple model of a Robinson Crusoe economy, but it is none the less useful. The problems which Crusoe faces are essentially the same as those faced by a modern economy. In both cases demand and supply have to be taken into account.

Let us therefore sum up what we have learned so far about the Crusoe economy under the heads of demand and supply. The conditions of supply of capital assets depend on their cost. In the Crusoe economy, this is measured in terms of the number of fish he sacrifices to make the net and his rate of time preference between fish today and fish tomorrow. On the demand side, we first have to establish that the capital asset is more productive than the unaided man. It is reasonable to think that a net would be more productive than Crusoe fishing with his hands, but it does not necessarily follow that a larger, more-complicated net will be correspondingly more productive. It may be too elaborate to work at all. The main element determining 'demand' for the net will therefore be its expected productivity, which will have to be balanced against its cost. As we have seen, human beings normally prefer a thing today rather than the same thing tomorrow or next year; the individual's rate of time preference is normally in favour of the present. For this reason, a capital asset must promise a return over and above its cost if it is to be considered worth making. The investor must be offered a positive reward for his 'waiting' in order to be persuaded to postpone his consumption. It is this positive reward which economists call 'interest'. Unless interest is expected from it, neither a Crusoe nor a businessman will acquire a capital asset.

Perhaps the nature of interest in a 'Crusoe Economy' can be seen more clearly from a more-rigorous, hypothetical model. Let us assume that Crusoe knows that he will be shipwrecked only for six days, during which time he can catch thirty fish by using his hands only. He can, however, choose to spend one day making a net and five days using it to catch fish. If the net is to be made, it must catch at least thirty fish, or Crusoe will be worse off. In order to make the net, Crusoe will have to go without food for one day, and since we may reasonably assume that he prefers present to future satisfactions, will need to be offered more than thirty fish to make the postponement of satisfactions worthwhile. If he catches thirty-three fish with the net, the interest on it will be three fish. If these fish are just sufficient to induce Crusoe to make the net, we can say that his rate of time preference is such that one day's hunger must be repaid by three extra fish—representing interest—within the following five days. Crusoe calculates whether the net is worth making by comparing the interest he expects to earn from it with his rate of time preference. If the two are equal, the net is just worth making.

Alternatively, we may say that Crusoe 'discounts' the future receipts from the net. Since the fish which Crusoe will catch with the net can be caught only in the future, he will prize them less highly than the fish he could have caught at present. He will therefore have to decide how many fish caught with the net (after a day's lapse) equal the thirty fish he can catch by hand, some of which can be caught today. Suppose Crusoe decides that thirty-three fish caught with the net, over five days, are worth just as much as the thirty present fish, spread over a week, in the way we have predicted. What we are saying is that anyone can compare the future yield of an asset with the cost of that asset, either by discovering what 'interest' it will yield or, alternatively, by deciding how heavily its returns— being future returns—must be 'discounted' if it is to be just worth its cost, or its opportunity cost. He can calculate a lump sum value for these future returns (a present value) which can then be compared with the (present) cost of the asset. One of the main issues in capital theory is therefore how to capitalise the returns from an asset so that this capitalised 'present value' can be compared with its cost, which is itself a given capital sum in the present.

3. Socialised investment

We have now seen how the process of creating capital assets will be carried on in a one-man economy. This is the simplest possible case to study. It has the virtue of showing very clearly that a decision to invest means that there must also be a decision to refrain from consumption. The necessity for such a choice between consumption and investment is made perfectly clear because the consumer and the investor are the same person. Perhaps the greatest difficulty in analysing investment in a real-world economy is that the people who refrain from consumption, at any given moment, and the people who invest at that moment are rarely the same. This causes complications. While it is clear that (in a closed economy) the whole economy *has* to refrain from present consumption if capital goods are to be created, it is very hard to see just how and where the necessary 'waiting' is being generated. Because one individual who is investing may not be 'waiting' at all, it is easy to reach the false conclusion that *no one* needs to 'wait'. Yet the fact is that if new capital assets are to be created the economy as a whole must postpone enough consumption to free the resources needed to construct them. It is therefore important to stress the direct connection between a rise in investment, on the one hand, and the consequent fall in consumption, on the other.

Fortunately, there is one kind of economy where the connection between investment and consumption can be seen very easily. This is the 'socialist' economy. By a socialist economy we mean an economy, like that of the USSR, where all economic activities are controlled by the State. In such a society, the State is the only body able to decide to increase investment in capital assets. Because it is the only decision taker, the State is well aware that to increase investment it has to reduce the consumption of at least some members of the community.

A socialist country may well be aiming to industrialise itself rapidly. The alternative courses between which its government has to choose are then clear. On the one hand, it can use the existing capital equipment to produce as many consumer goods as possible in the short run. On the other hand, it can use the greatest possible proportion of the existing resources to produce more and better investment goods, reducing the proportion which is currently producing consumer goods in order to release productive resources to produce capital goods.

If the socialist country chooses the second course, this means that the flow of consumer goods is reduced below the level which it could have reached in the short run. Only thus can the stock of capital goods be increased. There is a deliberate act of self-denial and abstinence in the present so that the future standard of living may be raised. The cost of investment in the socialist economy is thus a reduced standard of living in the present, just as on the desert island it is a day without food. In neither case is it possible *both* to make a large increase in one's stock of capital assets *and* to increase one's standard of living at the same moment. One has to 'wait'.

The rulers of a collective economy often disapprove of the idea that there is such a thing as interest on ideological grounds. Nevertheless, they have to base their choice between current and future satisfactions on a magnitude which is actually interest, whatever they may like to call it. The planners have to decide how great a surplus of revenue (or benefit) over its cost any act of investment will yield, if they are to decide whether it is worth the sacrifice it entails. This surplus over cost is interest. It shows how great the net rise in the standard of living at a later date is expected to be if the investment is undertaken. More accurately, one may say that socialist planners have to 'discount' the future yields of assets and compare these 'discounted values' with their present costs. The choice between present and future satisfactions has to be made in every collective economy. In the case of those where the original standard of living is low, it is a painful choice.

4. Marginal productivity and investment

We have now reached a position where we can discuss capital and interest in a modern market economy in an elementary way. At a later stage, in Chapter 21, we shall see that if we consider all forms of investment in a modern economy—in housing, public transport, schools, hospitals, etc., as well as in private industry—the determinants of investment are very complex. In this section, we concentrate our attention on investment decisions in private manufacturing industry, where it is not unreasonable to assume that the main objective is profit. This will pave the way for the more general analysis of Chapter 21.

What we need to know is how the return from a capital asset should be calculated, and how it can be compared with the cost of the asset. We shall find in Chapter 21 that in a market economy a major analytical and practical difficulty is that decisions to invest and decisions to refrain from consumption are not made by the same people. In both the Crusoe economy and the planned economy a decision to invest means a simultaneous decision to refrain from consumption: both decisions are made by the same person or body of persons. In a market economy, decisions to invest and decisions to refrain from consumption are not necessarily made by the same person. Some firms may be investing their own retained profits, 'waiting' for a return on them. But others may be borrowing money from investors (who then must 'wait') in order to acquire capital assets.

This important difference between the one-man and the market economy will make for some difficulties in Part Two. For the moment, we can avoid these pitfalls by making two assumptions. Throughout the rest of this chapter we shall assume, first, that all money which is saved at a given rate of interest is immediately used to buy capital assets. This rules out the possibility that people may save their money and put it aside (that is, hoard it) in the form of cash. Second, we shall assume, as we are entitled to do in particular equilibrium analysis, that the demand for capital assets is entirely unconnected with the supply of savings with which they have to be purchased. We shall assume, for instance, that if savings increase and people spend less money on consumer goods, this does not cause any falling off in the demand for capital goods. Since capital goods are bought in order to produce consumer goods, this is not a very realistic assumption, but we shall find it useful as a first approximation. In particular equilibrium analysis like this, any other assumption would be difficult to handle. With these two simplyfying assumptions, we may now consider investment in a market economy.

We have already seen that in the short run there can, by definition, be no change in the volume of capital goods in an economy. Because of this, in the short run the earnings of machines are quasi-rents, and we have already discussed them. Only in the long run, when investment *can* be undertaken, is a change in the stock of capital goods possible. To study these long-run problems we must again look at supply and demand. Capital assets are both scarce and useful; that is why they earn a return.

5. Interest: demand factors

Let us first consider demand. Why are capital assets demanded? Capital assets are demanded only when they can be profitably used to produce consumer goods. They have a revenue product like all other factors. For any given type of capital asset—say a machine tool—it will thus be possible to draw a marginal revenue productivity curve. It will be possible for an entrepreneur to calculate how much he expects the employment of an additional machine tool to add to the total revenue of his firm at each level of employment.

The marginal revenue productivity of capital is not a simple concept. In particular, the problem of time enters at two stages. First, capital goods, as we have seen, are not used up when they are hired, in the way that consumer goods are used up over a working life measured in years. If a firm is to borrow money in order to buy a machine, it must feel certain that it can repay the money with interest over a period of time. The businessman has to consider the productivity of the machine, not now, but in the future. What matters is the productivity of the machine over time—its expected future productivity or 'prospective yield'. Second, the machine itself takes time to build. It is some time before anything at all is produced. Money has first to be spent on building the machine, installing it and running it in, before it is ready for full-scale production. Investors must be paid interest on this money.

5.1 Models of investment

(a) Our first model

The easiest way in which to study the act of investment will be to construct a series of models, beginning with a very simple one and introducing successive complications. In our first model, let us assume that a businessman is considering whether to buy a machine. This machine costs £1 000. It has a working life of one year, all of which is spent in producing a single product which is completed on the last day of that year. The entrepreneur thinks that when all other factors used with the machine have been rewarded, the *net* product of the machine will be worth £1 060. Having produced this product worth £1 060, at the end of the year the machine immediately drops to pieces. The entrepreneur therefore finds that the machine has a product of £1 060, to be compared with its cost of £1 000.

Now we shall have to wait until later to see what determines the rate of interest in the economy as a whole, but it is clear that any individual entrepreneur has to take that rate of interest as given. If there is perfect competition in the capital market, every entrepreneur has to pay exactly the same interest rate in order to borrow money. Let us assume that everyone has to pay interest at 6 per cent to borrow money for a year. In order to pay for the machine, the entrepreneur will need to borrow £1 000 for a year. At the end of the year, he has to find £1 000 to repay the loan. The machine has now ceased to exist and must have repaid its cost, as well as £60 interest, if it is to be worth buying. Since we have assumed that the machine is expected to produce just £1 060, the entrepreneur will find it just worth his while to buy it. It will be a 'marginal' machine. If the machine is expected to produce more than £1 060, he will buy it cheerfully; if less, he will decide not to buy it. An entrepreneur will therefore buy a machine only if he expects it to earn at least enough to repay the money borrowed to buy it, as well as the interest on this loan. The revenue product of a machine must at least equal its cost, plus interest at the market rate, if the machine is to be bought.

We may say, alternatively, that the entrepreneur is discounting the future yield of the machine. If the machine costs £1 000, and over its one-year life earns interest at 6 per cent (£60 on £1 000) we can say that the machine's future return of £1 060 can be discounted at 6 per cent. The discounted value of its future earnings (£1 000) will then be just equal to its cost. If one discounts £1 060, earned exactly one year hence, at 6 per cent one obtains a present value of £1 000. The entrepreneur will be prepared to buy the machine only if the expected value of its earnings, when discounted, is at least equal to its cost. In our hypothetical model, the entrepreneur will just be prepared to do so if the 'market' rate of discount is 6 per cent. Then, the present value (£1 000) of the machine's future net earnings of £1 060 will be just equal to the cost of the machine.

(b) Our second model

In our second model, let us assume that a farmer is buying a sheep which will live for ten years. It is expected to produce wool worth £6 at the end of each year for ten years and, at the end of the tenth year, £100 worth of meat. The sheep costs £100. Now, if the market rate of interest is 6 per cent per annum, the sheep will be able, each year, to cover the interest charge of £6 on the loan required to buy it. It will also be able to pay off the whole loan (by the sale of £100 worth of meat) at the end of the tenth year. The 'asset' will earn interest of £6 each year on the investment of £100. Alternatively, if one discounts the future earnings of the sheep at 6 per cent, they will have a present value of £100. If he is rational, the farmer will buy the sheep if the market rate of interest (or discount) is 6 per cent or less. This second model is useful, because it avoids the problems of compound rates of interest and discount, but it assumes that the annual returns from the asset are constant from year to year. This is most unlikely to happen in practice except, say, where land or buildings have been rented out at a constant annual rent.

(c) Our third model

The third model we shall consider is where an entrepreneur is deciding whether or not to buy a machine costing £1 000, which will last for ten years. We assume that this machine produces nothing until the end of the tenth year, when it produces a product worth £1 078. The machine then falls to pieces. The entrepreneur who is wondering whether it will pay him to install the machine will have to borrow money to do so. Having borrowed it, he will have to pay interest on it. If he borrows the capital at a compound interest of 6 per cent per annum, the total amount owing at the end of ten years, including the £1 000 loan, will be £1 078. So long as the rate of interest is less than 6 per cent, the entrepreneur will find the machine worth buying. For the total amount owing at the end of the year will then be less than the £1 078 which the machine yields. Similarly, if the rate of interest is more than 6 per cent, it will not be worth buying the machine. Alternatively, one can say that the machine will certainly not be bought so long as its future earnings have to be discounted at more than 6 per cent per annum. If the rate of discount is 6 per cent, the present value (£1 000) of the machine's yield (£1 078) is just equal to its price of £1 000. In this model we have been able to allow explicitly for the existence of compound rates of interest, but have simplified the problem by assuming that no repayments of capital are made for ten years.

(d) A digression on how to 'discount'

In our final model we shall try to be more realistic. However, in order to do this we must first spend some time learning the principles of discounting. So far in this chapter we have talked in a rough and ready way about the need to 'discount' the future earnings of any asset. We must now be more precise about what discounting is and how it is carried out. Readers will find that this section provides a useful technical skill as well as being essential to an understanding of the remainder of Chapter 14.

All of us are familiar with the principles of interest. We know that if we lend someone £100 and ask him to pay £108 in *exactly* one year's time, we are earning interest of exactly 8 per cent on our loan. We add the £8 interest to the principal of the loan in order to work out what we must receive after exactly a year. We are much less used to working with rates of discount. However, once we have learnt to do so, the calculations turn out to be very easy.

The reason why rates of discount will be useful to us is that both in this chapter and in Chapter 21 we shall be looking at investment decisions. All investment means is deciding whether it is profitable to spend money on a capital asset in the present in the hope of receiving a series of returns in the future—a future *cash flow*, or a *prospective yield*. Since the asset has to be paid for in the present, the decision is made as simple as possible if the expected future cash flow —the prospective yield—can be reduced to a sum of money in the present. This is exactly what discounting allows us to do. We *discount* the expected future cash flow from the asset in order to obtain its *present value*. This present value we compare with the cost—the 'supply price'—of the asset.

The first step in calculating the present value of the expected future earnings from any asset is to write down what one expects to earn in each year of the asset's life. Suppose that a firm is deciding whether to spend £1 000 on a new machine, which will last for four years. Having sold the products made by the machine, the firm expects to earn the gross amounts shown in column 2 of Table 14.1.

Table 14.1

Year	Gross cash flow (£)	Cost of cooperating factors (£)	Net cash flow (£)
1	3 500	3 200	300
2	4 000	3 300	700
3	4 000	3 400	600
4	4 000	3 500	500
5	3 000	3 500	−500

We simplify the analysis by assuming that the machine can begin to produce immediately. If not, and it is more than a year before the machine has to be paid for, then the investment in the machine would also have to be discounted. Column 2 does assume that there will be some difficulty in getting the machine into full production during its first year. It produces only £3 500 worth of product in that year. After the first year, the machine runs to capacity and produces £4 000 (gross) in Years 2, 3 and 4. Finally, in its last year, Year 5, there are some breakdowns and the machine produces only £3 000 worth of product. This pattern of working up to peak efficiency, and then experiencing a decline at sometime towards the end of its life, seems to be typical of most plant and machinery.

These figures do not represent the earnings of the machine alone. They include the sums earned by the labour working with the machine, the cost of maintaining it and the cost of raw materials and the components it uses. These costs of the cooperating factors are shown in column 3 of Table 14.1. In order to calculate the returns to the machine alone, we therefore deduct the amounts in column 3 from those in column 2. This gives us the net cash flow in column 4.

For the next stage in the analysis we turn to a *discount table*. On the top of this discount table we have various possible rates of interest. Down the side, we have the number of years which will elapse before a sum of £1 is received. The discount factors in Table 14.2 show the value, in present money, of £1 received at that time. Thus, £1 received one year ahead when the rate of interest is 8 per cent is worth £0·926. The remainder of the £1 is interest of £0·074; this is 8 per cent on £0·926 over one year. The remainder of the table works

Table 14.2

Discount table (present value of £1 received as a single payment in the future)

No. of years before receipt	Discount rate 1%	2%	4%	6%	8%	10%	12%	14%	15%	16%	18%	20%	22%	24%	25%	26%	28%	30%	35%	40%	45%	50%
1	0·990	0·980	0·962	0·943	0·926	0·909	0·893	0·877	0·870	0·862	0·847	0·833	0·820	0·806	0·800	0·794	0·781	0·769	0·741	0·714	0·690	0·667
2	0·980	0·961	0·925	0·890	0·857	0·826	0·797	0·769	0·756	0·743	0·718	0·694	0·672	0·650	0·640	0·630	0·610	0·592	0·549	0·510	0·476	0·444
3	0·971	0·942	0·889	0·840	0·794	0·751	0·712	0·675	0·658	0·641	0·609	0·579	0·551	0·524	0·512	0·500	0·477	0·455	0·406	0·364	0·328	0·296
4	0·961	0·924	0·855	0·792	0·735	0·683	0·636	0·592	0·572	0·552	0·516	0·482	0·451	0·423	0·410	0·397	0·373	0·350	0·301	0·260	0·226	0·198
5	0·951	0·906	0·822	0·747	0·681	0·621	0·567	0·519	0·497	0·476	0·437	0·402	0·370	0·341	0·328	0·315	0·291	0·269	0·223	0·186	0·156	0·132
6	0·942	0·888	0·790	0·705	0·630	0·564	0·507	0·456	0·432	0·410	0·370	0·335	0·303	0·275	0·262	0·250	0·227	0·207	0·165	0·133	0·108	0·088
7	0·933	0·871	0·760	0·665	0·583	0·513	0·452	0·400	0·376	0·354	0·314	0·279	0·249	0·222	0·210	0·198	0·178	0·159	0·122	0·095	0·074	0·059
8	0·923	0·853	0·731	0·627	0·540	0·467	0·404	0·351	0·327	0·305	0·266	0·233	0·204	0·179	0·168	0·157	0·139	0·123	0·091	0·068	0·051	0·039
9	0·914	0·837	0·703	0·592	0·500	0·424	0·361	0·308	0·284	0·263	0·225	0·194	0·167	0·144	0·134	0·125	0·108	0·094	0·067	0·048	0·035	0·026
10	0·905	0·820	0·676	0·558	0·463	0·386	0·322	0·270	0·247	0·227	0·191	0·162	0·137	0·116	0·107	0·099	0·085	0·073	0·050	0·035	0·024	0·017
11	0·896	0·804	0·650	0·527	0·429	0·350	0·287	0·237	0·215	0·195	0·162	0·135	0·112	0·094	0·086	0·079	0·066	0·056	0·037	0·025	0·017	0·012
12	0·887	0·788	0·625	0·497	0·397	0·319	0·257	0·208	0·187	0·168	0·137	0·112	0·092	0·076	0·069	0·062	0·052	0·043	0·027	0·018	0·012	0·008
13	0·879	0·773	0·601	0·469	0·368	0·290	0·229	0·182	0·163	0·145	0·116	0·093	0·075	0·061	0·055	0·050	0·040	0·033	0·020	0·013	0·008	0·005
14	0·870	0·758	0·577	0·442	0·340	0·263	0·205	0·160	0·141	0·125	0·099	0·078	0·062	0·049	0·044	0·039	0·032	0·025	0·015	0·009	0·006	0·003
15	0·861	0·743	0·555	0·417	0·315	0·239	0·183	0·140	0·123	0·108	0·084	0·065	0·051	0·040	0·035	0·031	0·025	0·020	0·011	0·006	0·004	0·002
16	0·853	0·728	0·534	0·394	0·292	0·218	0·163	0·123	0·107	0·093	0·071	0·054	0·042	0·032	0·028	0·025	0·019	0·015	0·008	0·005	0·003	0·002
17	0·844	0·714	0·513	0·371	0·270	0·198	0·146	0·108	0·093	0·080	0·060	0·045	0·034	0·026	0·023	0·020	0·015	0·012	0·006	0·003	0·002	0·001
18	0·836	0·700	0·494	0·350	0·250	0·180	0·130	0·095	0·081	0·069	0·051	0·038	0·028	0·021	0·018	0·016	0·012	0·009	0·005	0·002	0·001	0·001
19	0·828	0·686	0·475	0·331	0·232	0·164	0·116	0·083	0·070	0·060	0·043	0·031	0·023	0·017	0·014	0·012	0·009	0·007	0·003	0·002	0·001	
20	0·820	0·673	0·456	0·312	0·215	0·149	0·104	0·073	0·061	0·051	0·037	0·026	0·019	0·014	0·012	0·010	0·007	0·005	0·002	0·001	0·001	
21	0·811	0·660	0·439	0·294	0·199	0·135	0·093	0·064	0·053	0·044	0·031	0·022	0·015	0·011	0·009	0·008	0·006	0·004	0·002	0·001		
22	0·803	0·647	0·422	0·278	0·184	0·123	0·083	0·056	0·046	0·038	0·026	0·018	0·013	0·009	0·007	0·006	0·004	0·003	0·001	0·001		
23	0·795	0·634	0·406	0·262	0·170	0·112	0·074	0·049	0·040	0·033	0·022	0·015	0·010	0·007	0·006	0·005	0·003	0·002	0·001			
24	0·788	0·622	0·390	0·247	0·158	0·102	0·066	0·043	0·035	0·028	0·019	0·013	0·008	0·006	0·005	0·004	0·003	0·002	0·001			
25	0·780	0·610	0·375	0·233	0·146	0·092	0·059	0·038	0·030	0·024	0·016	0·010	0·007	0·005	0·004	0·003	0·002	0·001	0·001			
26	0·772	0·598	0·361	0·220	0·135	0·084	0·053	0·033	0·026	0·021	0·014	0·009	0·006	0·004	0·003	0·002	0·002	0·001				
27	0·764	0·586	0·347	0·207	0·125	0·076	0·047	0·029	0·023	0·018	0·011	0·007	0·005	0·003	0·002	0·002	0·001	0·001				
28	0·757	0·574	0·333	0·196	0·116	0·069	0·042	0·026	0·020	0·016	0·010	0·006	0·004	0·002	0·002	0·002	0·001	0·001				
29	0·749	0·563	0·321	0·185	0·107	0·063	0·037	0·022	0·017	0·014	0·008	0·005	0·003	0·002	0·002	0·001	0·001	0·001				
30	0·742	0·552	0·308	0·174	0·099	0·057	0·033	0·020	0·015	0·012	0·007	0·004	0·003	0·002	0·001	0·001						
40	0·672	0·453	0·208	0·097	0·046	0·022	0·011	0·005	0·004	0·003	0·001	0·001										
50	0·608	0·372	0·141	0·054	0·021	0·009	0·003	0·001	0·001	0·001												

in the same way. Thus, with an interest rate of 12 per cent, £1 received exactly two years hence is worth £0·797 now; the remaining £0·203 is *compound* interest at 12 per cent on £0·797 over two years.

Three points should be remembered about a discount table like Table 4.2. First, if the sum received lies more than one year in the future, the interest element is *compound* interest on the *present value* of £1 received at that point in the future. Second, Table 14.2 gives the discount factors only to three places of decimals. For our purposes, and indeed for most investment decisions in business, this is enough. However, tables going to more decimal places are available if required. Third, all the figures in Table 14.2 assume that the amount of £1 is received *exactly* the given number of years ahead.

Table 14.3

Year	Net cash flow (£)	Discount factors (12%)	Discounted net cash flow (£)
1	300	0·893	267·7
2	700	0·797	557·9
3	600	0·712	427·2
4	500	0·636	318·0
5	−500	0·567	−283·5

Present value of cash flow (column 4) £1 287·5.
Net present value of project: £1 287·5—£1 000 (cost of machine)= £287·5.

With these figures, we can go on to calculate the present value of any sum which is to be received in any given number of years time. The time is shown in the first column of Table 14.2, while the appropriate interest (discount) rate is shown on the top. So, £1 received ten years hence with an interest rate of 14 per cent is worth £0·270 now; £2 500 (at the same rate) received ten years hence is worth £675 now.

We now return to the figures in the final column of Table 14.1, which are reproduced in second column of Table 14.3. It will be recalled that these figures show the *expected* earnings of the asset whose purchase is being considered. What we now want to do is to find the present value of these expected earnings. Let us suppose that the firm has to pay 12 per cent to borrow money to invest. We therefore multiply each amount in the second column of Table 14.3 by the discount factor for the number of years ahead that it will be received, assuming a 12 per cent interest rate. The discount factors are written down in column 3 of Table 14.3, having been taken from

Table 14.2. The results of multiplying the figures in column 2 by the discount factors in column 3 are then given in column 4 of Table 14.3. For example, the net cash flow in Year 1 is expected to be £300. This is expected to be received after exactly one year. The discount factor for one year hence, with an interest rate of 12 per cent, is 0·893. The *discounted net cash flow* for Year 1 is therefore £267·9. In Table 14.3 we discount the net cash flows for each individual year to obtain a discounted net cash flow over the whole life of the asset. The net present value of this cash flow is the (algebraic) total of the individual figures: £1 287·5. The present value of the prospective yield of the asset (to be compared with its supply price) is £1 287·5.

The most usual way of finding whether the purchase of the asset will be profitable is to deduct the cost (supply price) of the asset (here £1 000) from the present value of the prospective yield (here £1 287·5). This gives us the *net present value* of the project. In this case, the net present value is: £1 287·5—£1 000=£287·5.

Alternatively, one can calculate what is expected to be the percentage rate of return on the asset if it is purchased. For example, suppose we use the procedure outlined above and discover that the net cash flow from an asset has a present value of £1 000, when the discount rate is 14 per cent. Suppose, also, that the cost of the asset is £1 000. The net present value of investing in the asset is then £0 (£1 000—£1 000). This allows us to say that the rate of return, known as the *internal rate of return,* on the asset is exactly 14 per cent. Discounting the cash flow at 14 per cent gives a present value just equal to the cost of the asset. The rate of return on the asset is therefore just equal to 14 per cent. It is, however, important to remember that this calculation implies that the firm will replace the asset, at the same price as it cost, at the end of its life. In this example, at the end of the life of the asset, the firm will have earned enough *both* to buy a further asset worth £1 000 *and* to give a return of just 14 per cent on the funds tied up in the asset at any point during its life.

This is important. The return on the asset will *not* be 14 per cent on £1 000, compounded annually. It will be a return of 14 per cent *on that part of the initial investment of £1 000 which has not been 'released' through the earnings of the asset.* For example, in Year 1, the net cash flow might be £100. With a 14 per cent interest (discount) rate this £100 has a present value of £87·7. The discounting procedure assumes that £12·3 of this £100 is interest; it also assumes that it is interest on the £87·7 represented by the present value of £1. Similarly, if the net cash flow in Year 2 were £500, it would have a present value of £384·5. The discounted cash flow (D.C.F.) calculation assumes that £115·5 out of the £500 is interest (compounded over two years) on the £384·5. Since the D.C.F. calculation works in this way, one will find that over the life of an asset, interest at the internal rate of return will have been earned on those funds *not shown by the D.C.F. process* to have been 'released' from the investment project. That is to say, where in Year 1, the net cash flow is £100, £12·3 is treated (with a 14 per cent interest rate) as the interest element in this £100; and the remaining £87·7 as being released from the project at the end of the first year.[1]

(e) Our fourth model

With this elementary understanding of discounting we can return to our main argument in this study of interest. Let us assume that an entrepreneur is considering installing a machine which will have a life of five years. It costs £1 000 and the rate of interest at which the entrepreneur can borrow is 8 per cent. We assume that in the first year the machine takes time to build up to its full efficiency and has net earnings of only £86·3. In the next four years, the machine earns £300 per annum. The net cash flow is therefore that shown in column 2 of Table 14.4.

Table 14.4

Year	Net cash flow (£)	Discount factors (8%)	Discounted net cash flow (£)
1	86·3	0·926	79·9
2	300	0·857	257·1
3	300	0·794	238·2
4	300	0·735	220·5
5	300	0·681	204·3

Present value of cash flow (column 4) £1 000.
Net present value of project: £1 000—£1 000 (cost of machine)=£0.

Making the calculations we have now learned to make, we see that the discounted net cash flow has a present value of £1 000. This is exactly equal to the cost of the machine, so that the net present value of the project is zero. It follows that if the rate of interest is more than 8 per cent the entrepreneur will lose on the investment. If he predicts the earnings of the machine accurately, he will not buy it. On the other hand, if he predicts the earnings accurately and the rate of interest is less than 8 per cent, he can buy the machine. Finally, if the rate of interest is 8 per cent, the future earnings of the machine, when discounted, will just equal its cost and the firm will be on the margin of doubt whether to buy it or not.

[1] For a detailed explanation of this point see D. C. Hague, *Managerial Economics*, London and Harlow, 1969, Section 6.4.

(f) A summary

We can sum up this discussion as follows. An entrepreneur wishing to buy a particular asset will have to consider: first, the prospective yield of the asset, calculated by adding together all the earnings from it over its whole working life; second, the cost of the asset; and third, the rate of interest (discount). The entrepreneur can compare the internal rate of return represented by the prospective yield of the asset (*net* of the cost of cooperating factors) with the interest which he will have to pay on the money borrowed to buy the machine. Alternatively, he can compare the cost of the asset at the present time with the present value of its prospective yield. In either case, he will reach the same decision about whether to buy the machine or not. If the internal rate of return on the asset exceeds the interest which he will have to pay in order to borrow the money; or if the present value of the prospective yield exceeds the cost of the asset, it will be bought. On the other hand, if the interest payable on the loan required to buy the machine is greater than the internal rate of return on it, or if the cost of the asset is greater than the present value of its prospective yield, the asset will not be bought.

5.2 The demand for capital goods

Since for any single kind of asset an entrepreneur can calculate the prospective returns which any given unit of it is expected to produce, the yields from owning various amounts of an asset of a given type, either to the entrepreneur or the industry, can be similarly calculated. Let us, for example, consider the prospective yields of differing amounts of a particular kind of asset to a given entrepreneur. We assume that we can draw a marginal productivity curve for the asset we are considering, showing how much will be added to the receipts of the firm when, with any given stock of the asset, another unit is added. However, it should be clear that this is the marginal revenue productivity obtained from employing another marginal asset of this kind, with a given initial stock of assets.

The marginal revenue productivity of an asset can be shown in two ways. It can be looked at *either* in terms of the internal rate of return on the asset *or* in terms of the present value of its prospective yield. The first will mean that we work in lump sums in the present; the second will mean that we work in rates of return. Before going on to look at the demand for capital goods in both these ways, there are two important points which need to be borne in mind when one speaks of the prospective yield of an asset.

First, while this prospective yield is determined by the returns to the asset over a period of time, the returns *per unit of time* will not necessarily be equal. Indeed, in a dynamic world, this is most unlikely to be the case. Second, it must always be remembered that prospective yields are *anticipated* yields, not realised yields. Businessmen can make wrong guesses about such yields; if they do, capital assets will not yield what was expected of them.

Since assets do not always have the same length of life, the returns expected at the end of the life of a long-lived asset have to be more heavily discounted than those earned sooner. If two machines are both expected to yield the same total amount of money during their lives, but one earns this money more slowly, it will be less profitable. Larger interest payments will be needed to acquire the second machine because the money borrowed to pay for it will be needed for a longer period of time. One way of calculating and comparing the productivities of different kinds of assets, with different lengths of life, is to compare not their marginal productivities (prospective yields) but their *discounted* marginal productivities (*discounted* prospective yields). What we do is to work with the current rate of interest (discount). One brings the yields of assets of different kinds, with different prospective yields and different lengths of life, to a comparable basis by discounting them. As will be realised from what we have done so far, this process gives us, for each unit of each asset, a capital sum representing the present value of its prospective yield. The marginal revenue productivity curve—the demand curve for capital assets—will then show the *discounted* marginal productivities of the assets. It will show the present value of the additional receipts which an entrepreneur expects to earn in the future if he employs another unit of any given asset, these receipts being discounted at the current rate of discount.

(a) Present value

The curve of discounted marginal revenue productivity for an asset will show the entrepreneur's demand function for the asset. It will show the discounted present value of the returns an entrepreneur expects to receive from employing successive additional units of a particular kind of asset. This demand curve will slope downwards from left to right in the normal way, as is shown in Fig. 14.1. This diagram shows that the more machines of a given kind an entrepreneur has, the less money he will expect to earn by hiring one more machine of the same kind. Thus, for example, if the entrepreneur has already acquired OM_1 machines, then machine OM_1 will be offering him a prospective yield with a present value of £OA. Similarly, if he were to acquire OM_2 machines, then machine OM_2 would be offering him a prospective yield with a present value of £OB.

We now need to look at supply conditions. The supply curve for the same kind of asset will be given by its price. For each asset, this curve will be a horizontal straight line to the individual entrepreneur, assuming that competition in the market for each asset is perfect. In Fig. 14.1, the entrepreneur can buy as many machines as he wishes provided he pays £OC for each of them. The supply curve for this particular kind of machine is represented by the horizontal black line CC. A profit-maximising entrepreneur will obviously increase his purchases of the asset until the last one he buys has a discounted

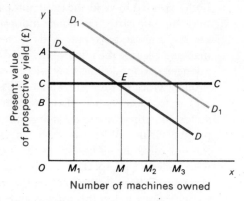

Fig. 14.1

marginal productivity just equal to its cost. In Fig. 14.1 this happens when the entrepreneur buys OM machines. The OMth machine costs £OC. At the same time, it has a prospective yield whose present value, at the current interest rate, is £EM (=£OC). When the rate of interest is at the current level, the entrepreneur will buy OM machines, each costing £OC.

We can go farther than this. If we take the price of the machine as given, it follows that a fall in the rate of interest (discount) makes the entrepreneur willing to buy more of this particular kind of asset. Indeed, we can extend the argument to all assets. With a lower rate of interest, the cost of borrowing money to buy any assets falls and the returns expected from it therefore have to be discounted less heavily. Entrepreneurs find that units of the asset which they did not think it worthwhile buying at higher rates of interest can now be bought. Their discounted prospective yields exceed their supply price, because these yields do not have to be discounted so heavily. In other words, the demand curve for capital assets of each kind shifts bodily to the right. For example, if the rate of interest were to fall in Fig. 14.1, the demand curve for assets might move from DD to the light-brown curve D_1D_1. Given their cost (£OC), the entrepreneur will buy more assets (here OM_3) at the lower rate of interest.

(b) Internal rate of return

As we have explained, we can put all this another way. We can express the demand for capital goods by showing how many units of each will be bought (given their price) at varying rates of interest. What we do is to show the internal rate of return, on a marginal asset with a given capital cost, when different amounts of that asset are owned by the entrepreneur. Anticipating the terminology of Chapter 21, we may call the demand curve for capital assets shown in Fig. 14.2 a *marginal efficiency curve* (*MEC*) for capital assets of this particular

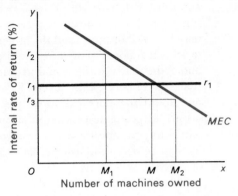

Fig. 14.2

kind. We again see that this demand curve slopes downwards. If the firm is considering buying the OM_1th asset, the internal rate of return on it will be Or_2 per cent. On the other hand, if the firm is considering buying the OM_2nd asset, the internal rate of return on that will be lower, at Or_3 per cent. The position shown in Fig. 14.2 is such that, if the rate of interest is Or_1, the entrepreneur will buy OM machines.

This analysis can be extended. It holds for individual firms, for individual industries and for the community as a whole. The lower the rate of interest, the more capital goods will be demanded. We can construct a downward-sloping demand curve for both capital goods and for loanable funds—for money to be used to buy capital assets. Both will slope downwards from left to right. The latter curve will show that the more loanable funds are demanded—by all entrepreneurs in the country taken together—the lower the rate of interest is. Since more assets are demanded as the rate of interest falls, more money is required to purchase them. The curve shows us the demand for 'money capital' at various rates of interest.

6. Interest: supply factors

We must now see what will determine the supply conditions for money capital. How will the amount of money which people will lend out to businessmen wanting to build machines and factories vary as the rate of interest changes? It will be remembered that we are assuming that all money which is saved is lent to entrepreneurs to enable them to build capital assets. But if people are to be persuaded to save money and to lend it to entrepreneurs, they must be offered interest. We have already seen that if anyone is to be persuaded to save and to put his money into capital assets, he will ask for some future return over and above the initial loan, because he is being asked to abstain from present consumption. But if a man has £100 and is asked to part with it for a year, he is not only foregoing consumption. He is also running the risk of losing his money. The risk may be small or large, and the larger it is the less anxious he will be to lend his money. For if he could put his money in a stocking or under the mattress, he would at least be sure that it would be safe (barring robbery). If he invests it, he cannot be so certain. Interest on capital therefore has to be paid, partly in order to persuade people to postpone consumption and invest in capital assets, but partly to persuade them not to *hoard* their savings. Savings do not have to be risked in business; they can be hoarded to avoid any risk of capital loss.

The supply curve of loanable funds to all industry will therefore slope upwards to the right. On the one hand, the more money capital people lend out, the more consumption they have to postpone; the greater will be the reward (per cent) they will ask to make such a postponement worthwhile. In other words, as more money is borrowed it has to come from people whose 'rate of time preference' is progressively more strongly weighted in favour of present satisfactions. On the other hand, as more money is borrowed it will have to be borrowed from people who are progressively more worried about the risks being run. More money can be borrowed if, but only if, a higher return is offered. Thus if more money is to be lent out, rates of interest normally have to rise to induce 'marginal lenders' to forego present satisfactions and allow their resources to be tied up in machines and factories instead of being kept in the form of more 'liquid' capital assets.

7. Interest: supply and demand

The actual level of the rate of interest will therefore be determined by the intersection of a downward-sloping demand curve for loanable funds (to be used to buy capital goods) and an upward-sloping supply curve for such funds.

Suggested reading

FISHER, IRVING   *The Theory of Interest*, New York, 1930, especially chapters i–ix.

15

Profits

In this chapter, we shall discuss the profits of the entrepreneur—
the profits of enterprise. We shall then have completed our study of
the pricing of factors of production. The word entrepreneur is not a
pleasant one, but, compared with the alternatives 'undertaker' and
'enterpriser', it seems the most desirable. The word and the idea
behind it are both hangovers from an earlier stage in the development
of the economy theory.

The entrepreneur was assumed in earlier economic theory to be
the owner of a one-man business. He was also regarded, as we have
regarded him so far, as a human calculating machine. Of course,
many modern firms are not one-man businesses. Indeed, although
there are still many one-man businesses in all economies, the one-
man business accounts for a progressively smaller proportion of total
national output as the economy becomes richer. A few large firms
produce a large proportion of total output. Later in this chapter we
must deal with the problem this poses for the concept of the entrepreneur. For the present, we continue to assume that he is the one
person in the firm who hires factors of production and that his
decisions are always based on an attempt to maximise profits. It is
clear, therefore, that the entrepreneur is a special type of factor of
production. He is the only factor of production whose role it is to
combine and organise other factors of production. Nevertheless, the
entrepreneur is a human being and not a true calculating machine.
No calculating machine would be described as *attempting* to maximise
profits. It *would* maximise them. There are two reasons why this may
happen. First, the entrepreneur may not wish to maximise profits.
Second, even if he does want to maximise profits, he will rarely have
sufficient information to know what he would have to do in order
to maximise them.

One fundamental difference distinguishes the entrepreneur from
other factors of production. While land, labour and capital are all,
at least in principle, hireable, enterprise is not. For this reason the
entrepreneur is not on all fours with other factors of production. We

shall not place great stress on this feature of entrepreneurship, particularly since the one-man firm is of declining significance, but it is quite important and should be borne in mind.

2. Profit and uncertainty

We have written so far as though the entrepreneur bases his actions on objective and completely certain figures of cost and revenue. The data on which the real-world entrepreneur has to make his decisions are not objective. He has to decide, in advance, what revenues and costs will be. His ideas about them are therefore subjective estimates embodying his own guesses and hunches. Like all guesses, they may well turn out to be wrong. The best that the entrepreneur can do is to equate his estimate of marginal cost with his estimate of marginal revenue. He can never be certain in advance what either marginal cost or marginal revenue will be.

This realisation of the true nature of the data on which entrepreneurs' decisions are based brings us explicitly face to face with a new element in economic theory. We must study expectations under uncertainty, in this case the expectations of the entrepreneur. Despite our attempts so far to avoid the problem of uncertainty we have not altogether succeeded. In our discussion of interest we found it necessary to acknowledge that businessmen's estimates of the prospective yields of the capital assets they are wondering whether to buy or construct are uncertain. In this discussion of the earnings of the entrepreneur, we shall be forced to devote a major proportion of the analysis to studying the way in which uncertainty about revenues and costs influence businessmen in deciding the levels of their prices, outputs and marketing activities.

It is important to realise that uncertainty enters economics immediately one allows for the fact that conditions can change. So long as one is concerned with a static or changeless world, uncertainty can be ignored. When, as in capital theory, the future enters in to it, change has to be allowed for and uncertainty automatically appears. With profit, uncertainty is the essence of the problem. The entrepreneur can never be certain what he will earn from producing goods until *after* he has decided to produce them. He is never certain whether he will make a profit or suffer a loss.

3. Risk and uncertainty

Once he looks upon the entrepreneur as more than a mere calculating machine, the economist can argue that the entrepreneur does fulfil a useful social function in the productive process—that he *is* productive. The entrepreneur can be considered as possessing a marginal revenue productivity in just the same way as any other factor of production. What, then, is the function of the entrepreneur in the economic system? Why is he productive? An answer to this important question has been given by Professor F. H. Knight.[1] We shall base the following analysis of profits on his explanation.

Some idea of the difficulty in finding an answer to this question, 'Why do entrepreneurs earn profits?' can be seen from the fact that the economists of the nineteenth century failed to answer it. The main reason for their failure to provide a satisfactory theory of profit seems to have been that they did not distinguish profits from interest. Because the typical entrepreneur of the nineteenth century was also the owner of the capital of his firm, economists confused the returns which he received *qua* entrepreneur with the returns he earned *qua* capitalist. They did not realise that the receipt of interest as a reward for investing his capital and the receipt of profit as a reward for taking the risks of business are not the same thing.

The modern theory of profit regards the entrepreneur's contribution to the process of production as that of bearing *non-insurable risks and uncertainties*. The distinction between insurable and non-insurable risks is an important one. Every entrepreneur faces many risks besides the most important risk—that he may lose money as a result of misjudging market conditions. There is always the risk that fire, theft, death and the like may cause business losses. But these latter risks can be insured against. Indeed, the modern economy provides a whole industry to deal with insurance against risks of this kind. The businessman need not worry about what will happen to his dependants if he dies, for he can insure his life. Nor need he lose sleep over the danger of losing plant or stock through fire. Fire also can be insured against.

The entrepreneur has to meet only those risks which *cannot* be insured against. We must therefore discover what kind of risks these are and why they cannot be insured against. We must discover what is the difference between insurable and non-insurable risks. The answer is that the difference lies in the fact that the probability that some events will occur can be predicted statistically, while the probability that others will occur cannot. For example, statisticians are able to calculate the probability of fires occurring quite accurately. An insurance company knows that, say, 1 per cent of factories in the country will have a fire each year. It is impossible to say which particular factory will catch fire; but it is possible to predict with considerable accuracy what percentage of factories in general are likely to suffer from fire in any one year. It is therefore possible for businessmen to insure against this type of risk. The insurance company knows how high a premium it must charge in order to be able to meet

[1] F. H. Knight, *Risk, Uncertainty and Profit*, especially chapters v–xi.

fire insurance claims. The businessman knows what the premium is and what the risk of fire is. Since no-one deliberately wants to take risks which can be avoided, the entrepreneur is only too pleased to pay the premium and avoid the risk. The reason why this can be done, as has been stated, is that an accurate quantitative estimate of the danger of fire can be made. The fire insurance premium is a cost of production just as much as payments for labour or raw materials are.

We must now move away from these definite and calculable risks to risks which are vague and more uncertain. What are these risks, taken by entrepreneurs, which are unpredictable and which no insurance company will dare to insure against? The kinds of decision made by entrepreneurs are decisions about, for example, whether it will pay to introduce a new product or build a new plant. The entrepreneur has to guess what his cost conditions will be, which is usually quite simple. He also has to guess what demand conditions will be, and this is often extremely difficult. He may earn a profit or he may make a loss. But no-one can say which with any real degree of certainty. Nor can anyone say with certainty how large the profit or loss will be.

It is no accident that it is impossible for entrepreneurs to insure against commercial losses. It is possible for an insurance company to estimate accurately that, say, 1 per cent of all firms will have a fire each year. It is quite impossible to say whether no firms at all, 5 per cent, or 25 per cent of firms in an industry will lose money that year or how much will be lost. It is possible that all will make profits or even that all will suffer losses. No statistician can work out the numerical probability that a given group of firms will make profits or losses in any year. It is therefore impossible for any organisation to insure firms against loss. It would not know what premium to charge and in a slump might well go bankrupt.

We can now explain why entrepreneurs earn profits. It is because they have to trust their own judgment about the likelihood of success or failure if they expand or contract their output, raise or lower their prices, introduce new products and so on. If a businessman refuses to insure against fire but relies on his ability to design efficient fire-fighting devices, he is fulfilling the function of a true entrepreneur. Since fire insurance is not expensive, there is no need for him to do this; so he will normally not do so. The real function of the entrepreneur is to take those risks where the unknowns to be dealt with are more intangible than the danger of fire. The sort of question which the entrepreneur has to answer is: 'Will consumers buy my new refrigerator?' or 'Will my new advertising campaign prove profitable?' The responsibility for making this kind of decision cannot be shifted. It is because this kind of decision is typical of entrepreneurial decisions in general that being an entrepreneur is much more risky than being a wage earner or capitalist.

We have now succeeded in isolating a specific function which may be attributed to the entrepreneur. He has to take the risks of making product, pricing and production decisions. Having drawn this sharp distinction between the function of the entrepreneur and the functions of the other factors of production, we must now consider the similarities between the entrepreneur and the other factors of production. There is no such thing as a disembodied entrepreneur. Entrepreneurs usually own some other factors of production. Let us take the case of the owner of a small shop. He is clearly an entrepreneur, for he decides what to sell and at what prices. He may also own some, at least, of the capital of the shop, if only the stock, and is likely to serve in it too. He owns labour as well. Such an entrepreneur is therefore the supplier of capital and labour as well as enterprise. His reward is made up of wages and interest as well as profits. Again, in theory at any rate, it is possible for an entrepreneur to be his own labour force and yet to own none of the capital of his business. It is quite conceivable that he might borrow the whole of his firm's capital at a fixed rate of interest. On the other hand, an entrepreneur might own part of the capital of the business, or even all of it, and yet not provide any labour. He would take decisions about the firm, but hire a manager to run it. It is not always easy to sort out the rewards of labour and capital from the rewards of enterprise.

Nevertheless, the problem is not insoluble. It is always possible to make some estimate of the share of the various factors of production which the entrepreneur owns in his earnings. So far as his capital is concerned it is not difficult to decide what the return on it would have been if it had been invested elsewhere. The market price for loans— the interest rate—shows the general level of returns on investments. So if an entrepreneur, who also owns the capital of his firm but provides no labour for it, discovers that his earnings exceed the current rate of interest on his capital, one may assume that he is earning profits for his enterprise in addition to interest on his capital. It is a sign that he is performing a useful function for the business in addition to providing capital. Taking business as a whole, most firms do earn 'profit' in this strict sense of the word. Most businessmen who put capital into their firms do get returns in excess of the market rate of interest. In the short run, of course, there will be a rent element in entrepreneurial earnings. Profits may be abnormally high or low. In the long run, provided there is a fair degree of competition, any excess of the earnings of entrepreneurs over the rate of interest represents the reward of enterprise. We see, therefore, that while the rewards of the businessman *qua* capitalist are not always immediately distinguishable from his rewards *qua* entrepreneur, this certainly does not mean that the distinction between the two rewards is not valid.

The same sort of procedure of separating true profits from the other earnings of entrepreneurs can be used where the entrepreneur provides labour to the firm. Where a shopkeeper serves behind the counter as well as making entrepreneurial decisions it is not likely that he will pay himself two separate amounts of money, one for his labour and the other for his entrepreneurial skill. Yet his earnings will be made up of two amounts. In the long run, there will be a sum of money, about as large as he could have got elsewhere as a general manager in a shop, representing the wage for his labour.Otherwise, if he is rational, he will *become* a general manager for someone else. Also there will be a further sum earned by his entrepreneurial skill.

The most realistic model to use therefore seems to be one where the entrepreneur invests some capital in his business and also provides his own labour. However, there usually is difficulty in deciding on the border-line between enterprise and labour. It is not easy to separate the functions of the entrepreneur from those of the manager, who is really only a special type of labour. The duty of a manager is to coordinate hired factors as effectively as possible and most business-men do this. It is not the true function of the entrepreneur. The true entrepreneur, the output and price fixer, is the man who risks losses and earns profits. It is not necessary for him to coordinate and manage factors of production at all. He can easily hire a manager to do that and pay him a wage for doing so.

The idea that the entrepreneur is essentially a coordinator is sometimes put forward by economists, but coordination is not an *essential* part of the entrepreneurs duty. He can choose whether or not to act as a manager coordinating factors of production; he cannot ever escape the danger of loss if he makes wrong product, pricing or output decisions. This type of confusion is best avoided by being quite clear what one means by coordination. If coordination is stretched to include decisions about the best scale of activity, the best mix of products and the best price to charge, it is being widened to include the true entrepreneurial function. This is why economists sometimes speak of the entrepreneur as a coordinator.

In practice, of course, the distinction between the entrepreneurial and the coordinating function is very difficult to make. The typical entrepreneur does not sit on the Costa Brava while the dividends roll in. Such persons cannot justly be described as entrepreneurs at all— though they may occasionally reap the reward of other people's entrepreneurial decisions. Most entrepreneurs find it possible to make entrepreneurial (product, pricing or output) decisions only if they are inside their businesses for much of the time. If this is the case, they are likely to make large and small *managerial* decisions as well—as a matter of course. Some time spent as a coordinator is just as necessary for most real-world entrepreneurs as is the ownership of some or all of the capital of the firm. It is for this reason that the earnings of entrepreneurs will usually include what are often described as 'the wages of management'. These are payments earned for performing the tasks of general management and organisation. The entrepreneur is not a disembodied spirit.

4. Ownership and control

The objection will probably be made that this analysis of the entrepreneur is unrealistic in these days. There is much justification for such an objection. In the modern economy, with the growing scale of industry, its own creation, the limited liability company, has replaced the one-man entrepreneur of the nineteenth century. The twentieth-century joint-stock company functions through the shareholders' meeting, the board of directors and the managing director or chief executive. Who performs the function of the entrepreneur in this type of organisation? The shareholders are the people who actually make profits or losses when entrepreneurial decisions turn out to be right or wrong, but the shareholders do not make the decisions themselves. The most that the shareholders can do is usually to start a row afterwards if losses have been made. Even so, it would usually be necessary for the shareholders to be 'quasi-entrepreneurs' themselves if they were fully to understand and appraise the decisions which had been made. Rows of this kind occur less often than one might expect: they rarely achieve much, simply because shareholders lack information and expertise.

It is also difficult to decide how far the board of directors really is responsible for making entrepreneurial decisions. The board will often give final approval to price changes, but will usually do so on the basis of proposals from senior management. It would be very difficult for many boards of directors to act as more than 'rubber stamps' for decisions already taken by senior executives. While in theory the board of directors has sole power to make entrepreneurial decisions, it will often be greatly influenced by others lower in the firm in deciding what decisions to make. The real decisions on products, prices, output and so on in most modern firms are made by the managing director and his senior colleagues. Such men may or may not own shares in the firm. Even if they do, it is likely that only a small part of their income will be derived from their shareholdings. Most of their income will come from a fixed salary. This means that the man who really makes entrepreneurial decisions in the modern business rarely receives a payment which is large when he guesses rightly and small when he guesses wrongly. Of course, it often happens that a manager who has made several wrong decisions is sacked or

N

demoted and thereby suffers a reduction in income, while a man who has made several right decisions is given an increase in salary. But there is no automatic connection between the correctness of the manager's decisions and his income. The 'managerial revolution' predicted by James Burnham seems to be upon us.

Though many 'small men' remain in business, the largest and most important firms today are not run by *an* entrepreneur. It is therefore difficult to decide whether the entrepreneurial function in these firms is fulfilled by the managers, who make (or at the least suggest) entrepreneurial decisions, or by the shareholders, who lose money if these are unwise decisions. Modern industry cannot point easily and unequivocally to *the* entrepreneur. How, then, can there be an entrepreneurial function?

What one can say is that the analysis of the entrepreneurial function is internally consistent. Its only real fault is that it is about a hundred years out of date so far as large businesses are concerned. It is the development of joint-stock companies which has altered the picture. However, this criticism can be overdone. Although the one-man entrepreneur is less important now, decisions do have to be taken even in large businesses. Entrepreneurial decisions have to be made and profits and losses are earned. The role and the rewards of the entrepreneur are there, though they will be difficult to pinpoint and the rewards may not necessarily go to those who take the decisions. The theory outlined in this chapter still explains why it is that profits exist. If there were no risks in running a business, the rewards to enterprise would be lower than they are.

5. Marginal productivity and profits

Our theory of the pricing of factors of production is based on the argument that each factor earns a reward that depends on its marginal revenue productivity—that the demand curve for any factor is the same thing as its marginal revenue productivity curve. This holds equally true for enterprise. The number of 'entrepreneurs' in an industry will depend on how much they can earn there—on their revenue productivity. What, then, will the marginal revenue productivity curve of entrepreneurship look like? This question can best be studied by continuing to use the simplifying concept of the entrepreneur and by studying the marginal revenue productivity of entrepreneurs in a particular industry. This is important. With land, labour and capital it is possible to calculate the marginal revenue productivity of each of these factors to an individual firm. With entrepreneurship this is not possible. One cannot, where a single firm is concerned, compare the revenue product of half an entrepreneur with that of a whole one or the revenue product of three entrepreneurs with that of four or five. Nor can one measure the contribution of the entrepreneur to a firm by the length of time he takes to make his decisions or to measure it in any other physical units. There are no rules for measuring entrepreneurial activity. It is therefore unrealistic to try to estimate the marginal revenue productivity of entrepreneurship for a single firm.

While it is useless to try to calculate the marginal revenue productivity of entrepreneurship for a single firm, it can be done, in principle, for the industry. In an industry, the numbers of entrepreneurs can be assumed to alter and the results of such alterations can be studied. Let us assume that in the industry with which we are concerned all entrepreneurs are homogeneous. This means that we can measure enterpreneurship in homogeneous physical units along the x-axis, as is done in Fig. 15.1.

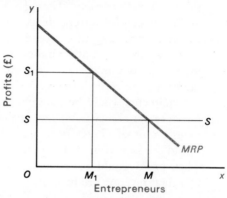

Fig. 15.1

In Fig. 15.1, the marginal revenue productivity curve of entrepreneurship to a particular industry is shown by the curve *MRP*, which is drawn for convenience as a straight line. It is reasonable to think that such a marginal revenue productivity curve will fall throughout its length. The more entrepreneurs there are in an industry the smaller will be the profits each is likely to be able to make. The marginal revenue productivity of entrepreneurship, like that of all other factors, is lower the more entrepreneurs there are. The supply curve of entrepreneurship is shown by the curve *SS*. Since we are assuming that all entrepreneurs are equally efficient, all must earn the same amount of profit (in this case £*OS*) if they are to remain in the industry. This profit of £*OS* represents their transfer earnings. All the entrepreneurs, being identical, can earn £*OS* in another industry and all will leave this particular industry and go to the other one unless they can earn £*OS* in the long run. The supply curve of entrepreneurship is a horizontal straight line.

It can be seen from Fig. 15.1 that equilibrium will occur where there are *OM* entrepreneurs in the industry, so that each is earning just his transfer earnings of £OS; so that each is earning normal profits. This will be the long-run equilibrium position in perfect competition. In the long run, entrepreneurs (and firms) will enter or leave the industry until all are earning normal profits. In the short run, however, the industry might contain only OM_1 entrepreneurs so that each would be earning £OS_1. Each would be earning abnormal profits of £SS_1. Such abnormal profits would be competed away, in perfect competition, in the long run. If there were imperfect competition in the industry, however, entrepreneurs could still earn abnormal long-run profits. Because there would not be completely free entry to the industry, newcomers would be unable to compete all existing profits away.

It is, of course, possible for entrepreneurs to earn rent of ability in addition to profit. A Henry Ford would earn much more than a third-rate entrepreneur. There are two ways of analysing the rent of ability earned by entrepreneurs. First, one could assume, as we did in Chapter 6, that all entrepreneurs are equally efficient from the point of view of all other industries except the one in which one is interested, but that their abilities differ so far as this particular industry is concerned. In such a situation, the transfer earnings of all entrepreneurs would be the same. Since some entrepreneurs would have greater ability (which was specific to this industry), they would earn a rent of ability over and above their transfer earnings. It would be the marginal entrepreneurs alone who would earn no rent. Their profit would just be equal to their transfer earnings and their marginal revenue productivity.

Second, one could assume that entrepreneurs were of unequal ability, both in the particular industry one was studying and in all other industries. This is a more realistic assumption. The simplest way of putting the position would then be to assume that the entrepreneurs who were most successful in one industry were equally successful in all others; that those who were least successful in a given industry would be equally unsuccessful in all others, and so on. In other words, we can assume that entrepreneurial skill is never completely specific but always completely general. Entrepreneurial rent is now unlikely to exist, so far as the individual industry is concerned. For, although some entrepreneurs earn more than others in any given industry, they could do the same in other industries too. For the industry, differences in entrepreneurs' earnings then represent differences in transfer earnings, not differences in rents of ability. The entrepreneurs who earn most money in any industry also have the highest transfer earnings and vice versa.

This assumption that entrepreneurs have general rather than specific ability seems the most sensible one to make. Entrepreneurs who are most successful in one industry would probably be equally successful in others too, so that those who have the highest earnings in one industry also have the highest elsewhere. They may be among the first to leave a declining industry rather than the last. Entrepreneurial skill is not likely to be 'specific' to an industry, because running one firm is very much like running another. Only the technology differs.

One final point is noteworthy. We have seen that profits are earned as a reward for taking risks, so that where there are no risks there can be no long-run profits, provided that competition is perfect. It follows that in an economy where nothing changes there can be no profits. There is no uncertainty about the future, so that there are no risks and no profits. If there were changes, but all of them were foreseen correctly by omniscient entrepreneurs, there could again be no long-run profits. Every entrepreneur would be able to adapt completely to the foreseen changes and none would earn long-run profits. Thus, in a static or omniscient society no entrepreneur would earn long-run profits, as distinct from wages of management or interest on capital, so long as there was perfect competition. In the long run, the marginal revenue product of entrepreneurship would be zero.

This is an interesting idea because it suggests that in a static world long-run profits could exist only because imperfect competition prevented abnormal profits being competed away. In other words, there could only be 'monopoly profits'. 'Pure profits'—the reward for risk-taking—would not occur. In such a world, it might appear that profits were being earned by some entrepreneurs who managed their own firms. These would turn out, on examination, to be 'wages of management'. Similarly, entrepreneurs might earn interest on money invested in their firms and any such rewards should not be confused with 'pure' profits. So long as such confusion is avoided, long-run profits will be found to be earned only because we live in a dynamic, changing world. With our lack of knowledge, uncertainty about the future must always be present. Those who risk their capital in business activities in such a world will therefore earn profit.

Suggested reading

KNIGHT, F. H.   *Risk, Uncertainty and Profit,* London, 1933, chapters v–xi.

16

Interrelations between factors and markets

1. Relations between marginal productivities

We have now completed our analysis of the demand for a single variable factor of production, and have studied the individual peculiarities of each of the four broad groups of factors. We must now study the interrelations between two or more variable factors. In this chapter, we look at two approaches to the problem of how the prices of factors of production and of products are interrelated. The first approach concentrates on factors of production. It shows how marginal productivity can be calculated where there are two or more variable factors, and what the relationship between the marginal products of factors is.

1.1 The assumptions

In the first part of the chapter, we shall assume that it is possible to vary the amounts of all factors freely. Thus when the amount of one factor is altered the amounts of the other factors can be altered less than in proportion or not at all. We have already noted[1] that there may be fixed production coefficients between factors of production, so that the factors in question have always to be used in a given proportion, if they are to be used at all. This is the same kind of situation as where the elasticity of substitution between consumer goods is zero. However, if factors do have to be used in fixed proportions, there is no way of discovering what the marginal product of either factor is. Without a fixed amount of the one factor the other is of no use at all. We therefore assume now that all factors can be used in varying proportions. This condition is necessary if the marginal productivity of a factor is to be measurable. In this situation, the marginal product of any factor can be defined as the addition to the total product when a small additional amount of that factor is used, *the amounts of all other factors remaining constant*. We shall therefore assume throughout the first part of this chapter that each and every factor can be varied separately and that its marginal productivity

[1]See p. 313.

can be thereby discovered. We shall also assume, throughout the whole chapter, that there is perfect competition.

To study marginal productivity in this kind of situation we shall consider an entrepreneur using two hired factors. One can deal with all the important problems which arise when there are several factors of production so long as there are at least three of them: an entrepreneur and two hired factors, which we shall call A and B. We are not looking at the whole economy, but can generalise the discussion to the whole economy if required. If the entrepreneur's firm is to be in equilibrium maximising profits, he must be equating the marginal revenue product of each factor with its marginal cost, in the way shown in Chapters 11 to 15. On our assumption that factors can be used in varying proportions the firm can then always vary freely the amount of each factor which it uses. It follows that when the firm is in equilibrium the ratio between the marginal physical productivities of the various factors will be equal to the ratio between their prices. Since with perfect competition the price of the firm's product is given, it follows that if the ratio between the marginal physical products of any number of factors is not equal to the ratio between their prices, the firm can always increase its profits by expanding or contracting its use of one or more factors until the two sets of ratios are equal. Since there is perfect competition, the marginal revenue product of each factor will be equal to the value (or price) of its marginal product. We can express the marginal product of a factor either as the addition to the revenue product resulting from the employment of one more unit of factor, or as the addition to the physical output of the firm (resulting from the employment of the same additional unit of factor) multiplied by the price of the product.

2. When the sum of the marginal products equals the combined marginal product

On the basis of these assumptions we can proceed to analyse the relationship between the productivities of two hired factors, A and B. First, we can say that the marginal product resulting from a unit increase in the amount of factor A (with factor B held constant) plus the marginal product resulting from a unit increase of factor B (with factor A held constant) is approximately equal to the addition to the product resulting when both factors are simultaneously increased by these same amounts. We shall call the addition to the product when both factors are increased simultaneously in this way the *combined marginal product*. More shortly, the sum of the marginal products of the hired factors equals their combined marginal product.

This proposition holds strictly only where the changes in the amounts of the factors are very small. Then, neither the proportions between the factors, nor the scale of the firm's operations is significantly changed *either* when the amounts of the factors are altered separately *or* when they are changed simultaneously.

If the changes in the amounts of factors are very large, to change the amount of factor A, with factor B held constant, will mean that the proportion of factor A to factor B increases greatly. An analogous result would occur for a change in B. The upshot will be that if an entrepreneur increases the employment of factor A by, say, 25 per cent (with factor B held constant), he may find that this raises total output by 200 units. If he then alters the amount of factor B by 25 per cent (with factor A held constant at the original level), he may find that this also yields an increase in total output of 200 units. But if he increases the amounts of both factors simultaneously by 25 per cent, total product may rise by more or less than 400 units.

Let us look at this in more detail. We first consider a situation where the production function is homogeneous of the first degree. This means that along every scale line the proportions between the factors and returns to outlay are constant. Where the proportions between the factors are altered, returns to outlay diminish. There will therefore be a greater increase in output if both factors are increased in the same proportion than if each is changed separately. If both factors are increased in the same proportion, returns to outlay will be constant; if each factor is increased separately, returns will diminish.

A similar relationship will exist where returns to outlay are increasing along each scale line, so long as these scale lines slope upwards to the right. A (large) increase in the amount of factor A alone gives a smaller increase in output than would the same increase in outlay along the scale line. The same is true for B alone. If both factors are increased at the same time in the proportions given by the slope of the scale line, there will be the same proportionate increase in total outlay. There will now be a (large) composite increase in the amounts of both A and B along the scale line. The combined marginal product will exceed the sum of the individual marginal products, since returns to outlay are increasing. With diminishing returns, it is not possible to generalise in this way. However, unless returns to scale are diminishing very rapidly the conclusion will not be reversed.

The first proposition, then, is that the sum of the individual marginal products of any number of variable factors will equal their combined marginal product. This will hold approximately for small changes in the amounts of factors and holds strictly for infinitesimally small changes in their amounts.

3. The 'adding-up problem'

Our second proposition about the relationship between factors of production is this. Assume that returns to scale in any firm are constant, as happens at the minimum point of the firm's cost curve: if each unit of each factor used by the firm is then paid a reward equal to its marginal product, the rewards of all factors when added together will just equal the total product of the firm. In other words, the marginal product of factor A multiplied by the amount of factor A employed, plus the marginal product of factor B, multiplied by the amount of factor B used, equals the total product of the firm. In competitive equilibrium, factors of production *will* be paid a reward equal to their marginal products. They will therefore just exhaust the total product of the firm. The problem of demonstrating that this proposition will hold, and why, has been called the 'adding-up problem'. We must now see how the 'adding-up problem' can be solved.

3.1 The first model

We begin with a firm where returns to scale are constant and there is only one factor of production. The production function can then take the particular form $P = kA$. Product (P) equals a constant (k) times the amount of factor (A) employed; as the amount of factor A is increased, the product always increases in the same proportion. To show that the adding-up problem is solved in this case we need to show that the marginal product of A, multiplied by the amount of A used, is equal to the total product (P). The only unknown is the marginal productivity of factor A. If we use calculus, the marginal productivity of factor A is given by the *differential coefficient, or derivative, of* P *with respect to* A. If we derive the differential coefficient, we can discover whether the product is exhausted when each unit of factor A is paid a reward equal to its productivity.

The rule for obtaining the derivative of a function is to reduce the power of the function by one, and multiply it by the original power. So, kA becomes $1 \times k \times A^0 = 1 \times k \times 1 = k$. It follows that, with the production function $P = kA$, the marginal product of factor A is k. This marginal product will be the same at all levels of output, because the production function is linear. We know that the total product (P) equals kA. Therefore, if each unit of factor A is paid its marginal product (k), the total product (P) is just exhausted.

3.2 The second model

We now consider a second case, where there is still only one hired factor, but its returns to scale vary, when it is combined with an entrepreneur. For simplicity, let us assume that he has no marginal product. The production function can here be written as $P=f(A)$. Total product still depends on the amount of factor A used, but does not now vary in exact proportion with the amount of A. We need to show that the total product will just be exhausted when, in competitive equilibrium, each unit of the factor is paid a reward equal to the marginal product of the factor. Since we are concerned only with the competitive equilibrium position,[1] we know that the average product equals the marginal product. That is to say, $\frac{P}{A}=\frac{dP}{dA}$. If we now multiply both sides of the equation by A, then $P=A\times\frac{dP}{dA}$, which is what we set out to prove. The total product is exhausted when the factor is paid its marginal product, assuming that the firm is in 'full equilibrium'.

3.3 The third model
(a) Partial derivatives

We now turn to the more interesting case where there are two hired factors, so that the production function is $P=f(A, B)$. Here, the amounts of factors A and B can both be varied separately in a large or small degree. We now have to calculate the *partial differential coefficient* or *partial derivative* of P with respect to A or B, according to which factor we are interested in. The partial derivative of P with respect to A is similar to the derivative used in the first and second models, except that we now regard B as held constant while A is varied. The partial derivative of P with respect to A shows the rate of change of P compared with the rate of change of A, when the amount of A is altered but that of B remains unchanged. Since

$$P=f(A, B), \qquad . \qquad . \qquad . \qquad . \qquad (1)$$

it follows that $\qquad P+\delta P=f(A+\delta A, B+\delta B) \qquad . \qquad . \qquad . \qquad (2)$

Subtracting (1) from (2) we have

$$\delta P=f(A+\delta A, B+\delta B)-f(A, B) \qquad . \qquad . \qquad . \qquad (3)$$

By subtracting $f(A, B+\delta B)$ from each term on the righthand side of the equation (so that the total is not affected) we can rewrite the equation as

$$\delta P=[f(A+\delta A, B+\delta B)-f(A, B+\delta B)]+[f(A, B+\delta B)-f(A, B)] \quad (4)$$

In equation (4) the first pair of terms (in the first square bracket) differ only in the amount of the first factor, factor A. This difference is approximately equal to the change in the amount of the factor

[1] As we have seen, at any point except that of competitive equilibrium, returns to scale will not be constant. If each unit of each factor is paid an amount equal to the marginal product of the factor, total payments to factors will *not* equal the total product.

$A(\delta A)$ multiplied by its rate of marginal productivity $\dfrac{\partial P}{\partial A}$.[2] Similarly, the difference between the second pair of terms (in the second square bracket) is approximately equal to the change in the amount of the factor B used (δB), multiplied by its rate of marginal productivity $\dfrac{\partial P}{\partial B}$. We can therefore rewrite equation (4) as

$$\delta P = \delta A \times \frac{\partial P}{\partial A} + \delta B \times \frac{\partial P}{\partial B} \text{ (approximately)}.$$

The reason why this relationship is only approximate springs from two different sources. First, there is the usual fact that $\dfrac{\partial P}{\partial A}$ gives the rate of marginal productivity only for infinitesimal changes in factor A $\left(\text{and similarly with } \dfrac{\partial P}{\partial B} \text{ for factor } B\right)$. However, what we are interested in is small but finite changes in A (and B). Second, as we have seen, the first pair of terms in equation (4) differ only in the amount of factor A, which is being used with a constant amount of factor B. But this amount of B is $B+\delta B$, and not the original amount of B to which the partial differential strictly refers.

(b) The differential

An exact relationship can, however, be obtained by using *the differential*, written as dP, dA or dB according to whether we are considering P, A or B. The differential dA means a finite increment in factor A. The differential dP shows what the finite increment of product (∂P) would have been if, over the whole range of the finite increment of the factor δA, the rate of marginal productivity $\left(\dfrac{\partial P}{\partial A}\right)$ had been the same as at the original employment of factor A. We can thus write a further equation, using the differentials, where $\text{d}P = \text{d}A \times \dfrac{\partial P}{\partial A} + \text{d}B \times \dfrac{\partial P}{\partial B}$. This is known as the equation of the complete, or total, differential. It is simply another way of saying that the relationship $\delta P = \delta A \times \dfrac{\partial P}{\partial A} + \delta B \times \dfrac{\partial P}{\partial B}$ holds approximately, being a better approximation the smaller the finite changes δA and δB.

With the aid of the equation of the complete differential we can solve the adding-up problem for a production function with two independent variables. Let us consider a homogeneous production function of the first degree where, as we know, returns to scale will always be constant and the proportion between the two factors along any scale line will always be the same. If the production function is

$P=f(A, B)$, we can say that, since we are considering a homogeneous function of the first degree, $f(\lambda A, \lambda B)=\lambda f(A, B)$ for any value of λ. That is to say, if we increase the amount of each of the factors A and B in a given proportion, we increase output in the same proportion. Let us now give λ the particular value $\lambda=1+\dfrac{dA}{A}=1+\dfrac{dB}{B}$, so that the amounts of the factors become $A+dA$ and $B+dB$. Then:

$$P+dP=f(\lambda A, \lambda B)=P\left(1+\frac{dA}{A}\right)=P\left(1+\frac{dB}{B}\right) \qquad . \quad (1)$$

Dividing through by P, we get $\dfrac{dP}{P}=\dfrac{dA}{A}=\dfrac{dB}{B}$. Substituting for dA and dB in terms of dP in the equation $dP=dA\times\dfrac{\partial P}{\partial A}+dB\times\dfrac{\partial P}{\partial B}$ (the equation of the total differential), we have:

$$P=A\times\frac{\partial P}{\partial A}+B\times\frac{\partial P}{\partial B}.$$

As we have seen, the fact that we are considering the differential dP and not the actual increment of product δP in the equation (1) means that the proof is not entirely rigorous.[1] For $f(\lambda A, \lambda B)$ refers to the actual output corresponding to $\lambda A, \lambda B$, while dP shows what the output *would be* if $\dfrac{\partial P}{\partial A}$ and $\dfrac{\partial P}{\partial B}$ were the same at the increased employments $A+\delta A$ and $B+\delta B$ as at the original employments A and B. This result, showing that when the production function is homogeneous of the first degree and each factor is paid a reward equal to its marginal product, the whole product is just exhausted, exemplifies what is known as Euler's Theorem on homogeneous functions of whatever degree. This is often quoted as:

$$A\times\frac{\partial P}{\partial A}+B\times\frac{\partial P}{\partial B}=nP.$$

This formula gives the result for a homogeneous function of the nth degree, by which we mean a function such that $f(\lambda A, \lambda B)$ is equal to $\lambda^n f(A, B)$. In our particular case, of course, $n=1$.

(c) Homogeneous production functions

The above proof relates to homogeneous production functions of the first degree in the general form $P=f(A, B)$. It may be useful if we consider a particular function of this form in some detail. Let us consider the function $P=\sqrt{(AB)}$. It is not difficult to show alge-

[1] Students requiring a rigorous proof should consult R. G. D. Allen, *Mathematical Analysis for Economists*, pp. 317–18.

braically that with this function the adding-up problem is solved. Since:

$$P=\sqrt{(AB)},$$

then
$$\frac{\partial P}{\partial A}=\tfrac{1}{2}\sqrt{\left(\frac{B}{A}\right)}[1] \text{ and } \frac{\partial P}{\partial B}=\tfrac{1}{2}\sqrt{\left(\frac{A}{B}\right)},$$

therefore
$$A\times\frac{\partial P}{\partial A}+B\times\frac{\partial P}{\partial B}=\tfrac{1}{2}A\times\sqrt{\left(\frac{B}{A}\right)}+\tfrac{1}{2}B\times\sqrt{\left(\frac{A}{B}\right)}$$

$$=\tfrac{1}{2}\sqrt{(A)}\times\sqrt{(A)}\times\sqrt{\left(\frac{B}{A}\right)}+\tfrac{1}{2}\sqrt{(B)}\times\sqrt{(B)}\times\sqrt{\left(\frac{A}{B}\right)}$$

$$=\tfrac{1}{2}\sqrt{(AB)}+\tfrac{1}{2}\sqrt{(AB)}=\sqrt{(AB)}=P.$$

Therefore, if each factor is paid its marginal product, the total product is just exhausted.

3.4 The fourth model

The proofs so far given for the case of two hired factors relate only to firms with constant costs at all scales of output. Since in perfect competition such firms can never be in equilibrium, it will be useful to give a further solution for the adding-up problem in the more realistic case where a firm using two hired factors is in competitive equilibrium. The general form of the production function for this kind of firm, with decreasing costs to begin with as the scale of operations increases, and increasing costs after the optimum output has been passed, can be written as $P=f(A, B)$. The total cost of production will be Ap_A+Bp_B, where p_A and p_B are the prices of factors A and B respectively. Let us write the average cost per unit at an output of P units as π_P. Then:

$$\pi_P=\frac{1}{P}(Ap_A+Bp_B) \qquad . \qquad . \qquad . \qquad . \quad (2)$$

Since we are considering a competitive equilibrium position, $\pi_P=p_P$ or, in other words, average cost of production=price of product.

In order to obtain the conditions for π_P to be a minimum (as in competitive equilibrium) we must differentiate π_P partially with respect to A, that is holding B constant. The partial differential coefficient of π_P with respect to A is $\dfrac{\partial \pi_P}{\partial A}$, which can be written as

$$\frac{\partial \frac{1}{P}(Ap_A+Bp_B)}{\partial A}.$$ We therefore wish to differentiate the product

---

[1] This is equivalent to differentiating $kx^{\frac{1}{2}}$ where, in our particular case, $k=\sqrt{(B)}$ and $x=A$. With this type of function the differential coefficient can again be obtained by reducing the power by one and multiplying by the original power. Thus the differential coefficient of $kx^{\frac{1}{2}}$ is $\tfrac{1}{2}kx^{-\frac{1}{2}}=\tfrac{1}{2}\dfrac{k}{\sqrt{(x)}}$.

$\frac{I}{P}(Ap_A+Bp_B)$. This we can do by using the well-known rule for differentiating a product. If we consider the product uv, where u and v are both functions of A, then:

$$\frac{\partial(uv)}{\partial A}=u\frac{\partial v}{\partial A}+v\frac{\partial u}{\partial A}.$$

In our particular case $u=\frac{I}{P}$ and $v=Ap_A+Bp_B$, so:

$$\frac{\partial(uv)}{\partial A}=u\frac{\partial v}{\partial A}+v\frac{\partial u}{\partial A}$$

can be written

$$\frac{\partial\pi_P}{\partial A}=\frac{I}{P}\times\frac{\partial(Ap_A+Bp_B)}{\partial A}+(Ap_A+Bp_B)\frac{\partial\frac{I}{P}}{\partial A}.$$

This can be rewritten as:

$$=\frac{I}{P}\frac{\partial(Ap_A+Bp_B)}{\partial A}+(Ap_A+Bp_B)\frac{d\frac{I}{P}}{dP}\times\frac{\partial P}{\partial A},$$

since $\frac{\partial\frac{I}{P}}{\partial A}=\frac{d\frac{I}{P}}{dP}\times\frac{\partial P}{\partial A}$. For $\frac{\partial\frac{I}{P}}{\partial A}$ means the rate of change of $\frac{I}{P}$ compared with the rate of change of A. This can be split up into the rate of change of A. This can be split up into the rate of change of $\frac{I}{P}$ compared with the rate of change of P and the rate of change of P itself compared with the rate of change of A.

Now $\frac{\partial(Ap_A+Bp_B)}{\partial A}$ is equal to p_A, since in the partial differentiation p_A, B and p_B are treated as constant. Also $\frac{d\frac{I}{P}}{dP}=-\frac{I}{P^2}$, by the usual rule for differentiation.[1]

Therefore $\qquad \frac{\partial\pi_P}{\partial A}=\frac{I}{P}p_A-\frac{I}{P^2}\frac{\partial P}{\partial A}(Ap_A+Bp_B)$

$$=\frac{I}{P}p_A-\frac{I}{P^2}\frac{\partial P}{\partial A}(P\pi_P).$$

Therefore $\qquad \frac{\partial\pi_P}{\partial A}=\frac{I}{P}\left(p_A-\frac{\partial P}{\partial A}\pi_P\right).$

For this equation to relate to a competitive equilibrium where π_P (average cost) must be at a minimum, we must have $\frac{\partial\pi_P}{\partial A}=0$, or alternatively $\frac{I}{P}\left(p_A-\frac{\partial P}{\partial A}\pi_P\right)=0$. Now since P (output) must be a

---
[1] See footnote 4, p. 371.

finite quantity, $\frac{1}{P}$ cannot be 0. So, if the whole term is to equal 0,

$\left(p_A - \frac{\partial P}{\partial A} \pi_P \right)$ must equal 0, therefore:

$$P_A = \frac{\partial P}{\partial A} \pi_P = \frac{\partial P}{\partial A} p_P.$$

Similarly, $$p_B = \frac{\partial P}{\partial B} \pi_P.$$

Substituting for p_A and p_B in equation (2), we have:

$$\pi_P = \frac{1}{P} \left(A \frac{\partial P}{\partial A} \pi_P + B \frac{\partial P}{\partial B} \pi_P \right)$$

Multiplying both sides by $\frac{P}{\pi_P}$, we have $P = A \frac{\partial P}{\partial A} + B \frac{\partial P}{\partial B}.$ Q.E.D.

Thus in competitive equilibrium where there are two hired factors the adding-up problem is solved.

4. The demand for factors of production

The remaining problem which we must discuss is the nature of the demand for several variable factors of production. We have seen in the last few chapters that the demand curve for a single hired factor is its marginal revenue productivity curve. But not all factors will have the same shape of marginal productivity curve, so that the size of the increase in the demand for a factor when its price falls (and hence the elasticity of demand for the factor) will vary according to the circumstances. In particular, the demand for any factor will be less elastic the lower the elasticity of demand for the product it makes, and the more quickly the factor's marginal physical productivity falls off when its employment rises and vice versa.

We have also seen that when there are several variable factors of production, the demand for any one of them will still depend on its marginal revenue productivity. We have shown, in our discussion of the 'adding-up problem', how marginal revenue productivity can be measured when there are more than two factors. If we vary slightly the amount of factor A while holding the amount(s) of the other(s) constant, we can calculate the marginal (net) physical (and hence marginal (net) revenue) product of factor A in any given situation. Similarly, with any other factor, if we vary its employment by a small amount, holding the amount of the other factors constant and find the resultant addition to the revenue of the firm, we shall have discovered its marginal (net) revenue productivity. It will always pay an entrepreneur to go on hiring more and more of any factor until its marginal net revenue product equals its marginal cost. Thus, in equilibrium, the marginal net revenue products of all factors will equal their marginal costs.

4.1 Derived demand

Let us now consider what will be the main effect on the demand for any given variable factor when its price changes, assuming for the sake of simplicity that the prices of all other factors remain constant. It is important at the outset to stress again the fact that the demand for every factor of production is a *derived* demand. Factors of production are useful only because they can help to produce consumer goods and the demand for factors is 'derived' from the direct demand for those consumer goods. This is an important difference between the demand for factors of production and the demand for consumer goods. There are, however, some similarities between the two cases. In particular, some factors of production will be competitive and others complementary.

4.2 Factor substitution

Where there are only two factors of production, shown, for example, on an equal product map, these factors must be substitutes for each other in the sense that, if the product is to remain constant, less of one factor must be used when more of the other is employed. In these circumstances, if the price of one factor falls, more of it will be bought. The size of this increase in purchases will depend partly on the scale effect and partly on the extent to which substitution between the factors is possible—just as the extent to which a fall in the price of a consumer good leads to an increased demand for it depends partly on the income effect and partly on the extent to which it can be substituted for the good. If the factors have to be used in a given proportion, elasticity of substitution between the factors will be zero. If the factors are perfect substitutes, elasticity of substitution will be infinite. Between these limits, substitution between factors will be possible in differing degrees.

4.3 Competitiveness and complementarity

Where there are three (or more) factors of production, the relationships between them will be more complex than where there are two. First, some factors will be closely competitive; for example, hand looms and power looms, or paint brushes and paint sprays. A fall in the price of one relationships of each of these pairs of factors will have a considerable effect, both on the demand for the factor itself and on the demand for its substitute.

4.4 Competitive factors

Let us consider the likely effects of such a fall in price, by studying a problem discussed at length by nineteenth-century economists. This is the introduction of power looms in the place of hand looms in an industry making woollen goods. Let us assume that the demand and supply, both for woollen goods and for looms, are originally in equilibrium. The equilibrium is now disturbed. Suppose that the price of power looms has fallen as the result of an improved design. Since power looms are cheaper, the number of hand looms used will fall and more power looms will be used. The extent to which the demand for hand looms falls will depend on the extent to which power looms can be substituted for them. There is one good reason why we should expect such substitution to take place on a large scale. The two kinds of loom were very close substitutes in the conditions that existed in the early nineteenth century.

(a) Scale effects

We can ascribe this result partly to a substitution effect and partly to a scale effect. Since hand looms are now relatively dearer, it would have paid to use fewer hand looms *even if* the output of the industry had remained unaltered; power looms and hand looms are 'competitive' factors of production. They are competitive in the sense that (the level of output remaining constant) if the price of power looms falls, more power looms will be used and fewer hand looms. However, there is more to it than this. If the price of power looms has fallen, it is likely that costs of production in the woollen industry as a whole will have fallen; this will increase the output of woollen goods. More woollen goods will be bought now because they are cheaper. Because of this 'scale effect' more factors of all kinds will be used. It is just possible that more hand looms may be used as a result. While if output had not increased fewer hand looms would have been used, the fact that output has risen *may* mean that more hand looms are used *as well as* more power looms. This would be analogous to the possibility of an increase in the demand for a consumer good when the prices of competitive goods fall—if the income effect is strong enough. However, it seems unlikely that in this particular case any practicable increase in the scale of operations would be sufficiently large to offset the strong substitution effect. In practice, the demand for hand looms will fall now that they are dearer relatively to power looms.

(b) Employment

This is not the whole story. We have so far considered only the relationship between the demand for power looms and that for hand looms. What of the effects on the employment of weavers, assuming they can work either loom? With fewer hand looms being used, it is likely that the demand for weavers will fall off. One weaver per hand loom must be used as a minimum, while with power looms one man can look after several looms. Only if there is a *considerable* increase in the output of woollen goods will the demand for weavers increase. The fact that power looms and hand looms (and hand-loom weavers) are close substitutes means that a fall in the price of power looms reduces the demand for hand looms and for weavers, though how much it reduces it will depend on how far it is possible to substitute power looms for hand looms. Only if the scale effect is extremely strong can it outweigh the substitution effect and raise the employment of weavers. Since fewer men are needed to work each power loom, and since power looms will be at least as productive as hand looms, the number of weavers employed is likely to fall.

Because there are so many influences to be considered, it is wise not to be too dogmatic about the effect of a fall in the price of power looms either on the employment of weavers or on the demand for hand looms. Both are likely to fall. But both could increase if the scale effect were sufficiently strong. An early analysis of this kind of problem can be found in Ricardo's *Principles of Economics,* in the chapter 'On Machinery'.[1]

5. Joint demand for factors of production

Some factors of production are not competitive in the way that hand looms and power looms are. Instead of at least one factor being used in smaller quantities if the price of one other has fallen, more of every factor is used. Such factors are, for example, sugar, flour and butter used together in cake-making; and malt and hops used in brewing beer. Such factors of production are in *joint demand*. We have already used the term to describe related demands for consumer goods, but joint demand was a term originally applied by Marshall to factors of production. He said, 'there is a *joint demand* for the services which any . . . things render in helping to produce a thing which satisfies wants directly and for which there is therefore a direct demand.'[2]

5.1 An example of joint demand

In discussing joint demand Marshall[3] studied the effects of a strike by plasterers on their wages and on the prices of other factors of production, say, carpenters and bricklayers, when all are being used together to build houses.

[1]*Op. cit* (Sraffa edition), chapter 31.
[2]Marshall, *Principles of Economics* (8th edition), p. 381.
[3]*Op. cit.,* pp. 382–7.

(a) The model

Let us use a similar model. Consider the effects of a claim for higher wages by plasterers who are building houses in conjunction with bricklayers and carpenters. We shall assume, as Marshall did, that the demand curve for houses remains unaffected throughout, and that the supply curves for bricklayers and carpenters do not alter. Bricklayers and carpenters continue to offer their labour in the same amounts as before, at the same wage levels.

(b) The effect on wages

If the plasterers' claim for higher wages succeeds, the effects will depend ultimately on how far the price of houses rise, and how far the wages of bricklayers and carpenters fall once the demand for them has declined. The price of houses having risen, and the wages of other factors having (at most) remained constant, house-builders will be able to pay higher wages to plasterers and still earn normal profits.

Marshall listed the following conditions as being conducive to a large increase in the wage offered to a factor of production if the amount supplied is reduced. The first condition is that there should be no competitive substitute for the factor in question available at a similar price. Second, the demand for the product which the factor is making should be very inelastic so that a small reduction in its output causes a large rise in its price. Third, it is necessary that the cost of the factor should represent only a small proportion of the cost of the product. For example, if the wages of plasterers represent only 1 per cent of the cost of houses, an increase of 100 per cent in wages will raise the cost of producing houses by only 1 per cent. Fourth, it is necessary that the supply of other factors should be very inelastic so that a small fall in house-building, and hence in the employment of the other factors causes a large drop in their wages.

Marshall pointed out that if there were good substitutes for plasterers, the rise in their wages might be quite small. The demand for plasterers would be elastic, so that to obtain large wage increases they might have to be prepared to see a large fall in their employment. The analysis thus relates to a situation where all factors are in joint demand, and where a fall in employment of one factor (plasterers) causes a fall in the number of cooperating factors (bricklayers and carpenters) demanded. Similarly, an increase in the number of plasterers hired (if their wages fell) would cause an increase in the demand for bricklayers and carpenters.

5.2 Joint demand and complementarity

Let us consider in greater detail the reasons why factors of production are in joint demand. We saw in Chapter 4 that consumer goods may be jointly demanded either because they are complementary or because, though they are competitive, there is a strong income effect when the price of one good falls. A similar point can be made here. In the example given above it seems likely that plasterers and brick-layers will not be very competitive—they will not be very good substitutes for each other in house-building. The scale effect resulting from a reduction in house-building thus easily overcomes the sub-stitution effect. This will tend, in our example, to work in the direction of increasing the demand for both bricklayers and carpenters now that plasterers are more expensive to hire. The factors are in joint demand because the scale effect is considerable. In addition, they are only moderately, and not *highly*, competitive as, for example, power and hand looms are likely to be.

(a) True
complementarity

It is quite likely, however, that some factors of production will bear a truly complementary relationship to each other. One can discover whether or not factors are complementary if one first eliminates the scale effect (by keeping output constant). For example, continuing to discuss house-building, consider the three factors—bricks, wood and bricklayers. Let us suppose that the price of bricks falls, that the prices of all other factors remain constant and that there is no change in the number of houses produced. It is likely now that less wood, but more bricks and more bricklayers, will be used. Bricks and bricklayers will be complementary factors. Although the number of houses pro-duced remains unaltered, bricks and bricklayers are used in greater amounts and less wood goes into each house. As with consumer goods, it is impossible for *all* the factors making a particular product to be complementary. Given any number (n) of factors, it is impossible for more than ($n-1$) of these to be complementary. One factor, at least, must be competitive with the rest.

It is thus possible to discover whether factors of production are competitive or complementary only by eliminating any scale effect, just as we had to eliminate the income effect when considering complementary relationships between consumer goods.

6. General-
equilibrium
analysis

6.1 Two
traditions

Throughout Part One, we have concentrated on particular-equilib-rium analysis. This is the tradition of Marshall and it has been accepted by most British and American economists. There is, how-ever, another tradition—that of Europe. This finds perhaps its most explicit form in the work of Léon Walras of Lausanne, notably in his *Elements d'Economie politique, pure*.[1] Walras developed a general-

[1]Lausanne, 1874.

equilibrium system, simplifying his analysis by assuming perfect competition in all markets.

6.2 Partial equilibrium

We have constructed the theory of Part One from a study of the behaviour of the basic economic units—the consumer and the firm. We have shown how consumers and firms reach equilibrium in perfect competition, on the assumption that the prices of goods (in the case of consumers) and of factors (in the case of firms) were given. Even when we went beyond this to look at the way the price of an individual product (X) was set in a Flexprice market, we saw that *ceteris paribus* we could regard the price of good X as determined quite independently of all other prices. We assumed that if the price of X fell, this would not lead to a change in the demand for Y. This is how particular-equilibrium analysis works—by assuming all other things equal.

6.3 General equilibrium

It is a big assumption. While particular-equilibrium analysis has allowed economists to develop the strong body of theory outlined in Part One, the assumption that 'all other things are equal' is not strictly correct. For example, while the demand for X depends on the price of X, so does the demand for Y, if only to a small extent. In partial-equilibrium analysis we assume that a change in the price of X has no significant effect on the demand for Y. This may not be true. If X and Y are either strongly complementary or strongly competitive, a fall in the price of X can have a substantial effect on the demand for Y. General-equilibrium analysis attempts to take account of such relationships. It looks at multi-market equilibrium. It considers the way in which the prices of all goods in an economic system are set simultaneously, each in its own Flexprice market.

7. A pure-exchange economy

7.1 The assumptions

Like Walras, we begin with a *pure-exchange* system, ignoring production. Suppose we have an economy where a given quantity of each good has been made available to consumers; each consumer is provided with an initial stock of at least one product. In the language of Chapter 3, we assume that each consumer has an initial income, but in commodities rather than in money. Given these 'incomes' consumers are assumed to be free to buy or sell as much of each commodity as they wish at prices determined in the perfectly-competitive system of Flexprice markets. We can treat all these exchanges as barter transactions because all that matters to us, as we have insisted throughout Part One, is *relative* price. We need only to know the rate at which one good can be exchanged for any other.

7.2 Consumer behaviour

As we saw happening in Chapter 3, each consumer will exchange the goods he has for those he does not possess until he has made the marginal significance of each good in terms of each other good equal to its relative price. It is virtually certain that everyone will do some trading, since it is most unlikely that any consumer's initial stock of goods will represent his optimal stock. He will therefore want to obtain those goods whose marginal significance to him in terms of other goods is in excess of their relative price, and to give up some other goods to obtain them. However, in a general-equilibrium system, the consumer has to do this in a situation where prices are in turn determined by demand and supply for each good from all consumers. They cannot now be taken as given; they will result from the process of exchange in the Flexprice markets.

7.3 Multi-market equilibrium

The whole set of markets, one for each good, will be in equilibrium only when the quantities supplied equal the quantities demanded in each market. This will give the set of equilibrium prices. Mathematically, this means that we have a set of simultaneous equations, one equation for each market. Each equation will state that in a given market, the value of the quantity demanded at the equilibrium price must be equal to the value of the quantity supplied. Let us denote the quantity of X that is demanded by Dx; the quantity of X that is supplied by Sx; the price of X by px. Then, equilibrium in the market for X requires us to have:

$$Dx \times px = Sx \times px$$

(a) Two markets

This must be true simultaneously for all markets. Let us consider a simple example. Let us suppose that an economy contains only two markets, one for good X and one for good Y. Using the notation given above, this means that the economy can be represented by two simultaneous equations:

$$Dx \times px = Sx \times px$$
$$Dy \times py = Sy \times py$$

If this economy is to be in equilibrium, the equations must be satisfied simultaneously. However, since this is a pure-exchange economy, the demand for X is the amount of Y supplied in exchange for it. Similarly, the demand for Y is the amount of X supplied in exchange for Y. This means that the demand for X (which is the supply of Y) is equal to the supply of X (which is the demand for Y). It follows automatically that when the demand for X equals the supply of X, the demand for Y must equal the supply of Y. We can obtain all the information we need to show when there will be equilibrium in the *two* markets from only *one* of the demand and supply equations—either that for X or that for Y. We do not need both.

This condition can be extended. Suppose there are n goods in a 'pure-exchange' system. The equations representing that system are then:

(b) N *markets*

$$D_1 P_1 = S_1 P_1$$
$$D_2 P_2 = S_2 P_2$$
$$\cdots\cdots$$
$$\cdots\cdots$$
$$\cdots\cdots$$
$$\cdots\cdots$$
$$D_n p_n = S_n p_n$$

If we have n commodities, the reasoning in the previous paragraph shows that we can establish the conditions for all markets to be simultaneously in equilibrium by considering only $(n-1)$ of the n equations. As in our above example, if $(n-1)$ of the n markets are in equilibrium, then the remaining market must be in equilibrium as well.

7.4 A system of relative prices

However, there is more to it than this. The system of equations does not tell us anything at all about the *absolute* level of prices, only about *relative* prices. This is not surprising. Since we are concerned with a pure-exchange system, *relative* prices are all that matter. Provided each consumer can be told the rate at which he may exchange, say, commodity X for commodity Y, that is all he needs to know. A money system and money prices would be a convenience, since all prices could then be expressed in terms of the same money, but money does not have to exist in a barter system.

In order to reduce the number of variables from n to $(n-1)$ so that the system is not over-determined, it is usual to divide all n prices by the price of one of the n goods, selected at random. The price of the chosen good (in terms of itself) is obviously one; its own price can therefore be ignored. The remaining $(n-1)$ exchange ratios (prices) can then be derived from the remaining $(n-1)$ equations. In the process of determining the equilibrium exchange ratios in this way, the equilibrium quantities for each market will be determined.

8. A system with production

8.1 The assumptions

In an economy where there is production as well as exchange, we can assume that each consumer has an initial endowment of one or more factors of production, land, labour, etc. A consumer can then be seen as selling the factors he owns in order to obtain commodities. Indeed, if he sells his labour, he will be selling it in order to work to supply commodities and services. He may well not sell the whole of his factor endowments, but keep some for his own use. This is especially likely with labour, where the consumer will keep a part of his endowment to be 'consumed' in the form of leisure. In addition, it is possible for the consumer to sell one factor and buy another. For example, a landowner might rent out land and use the proceeds to hire labour to provide him with personal services.

8.2 Consumer behaviour

As in the previous section, we can now suppose that consumers maximise satisfaction. This will give us the demands of individual consumers for products (and their supplies of factors) as functions of the prices of factors and products. To keep the argument simple, we ignore the fact that entrepreneurs may be buying intermediate (or indeed final) goods to sustain production. Now that each consumer can be assumed to have an initial endowment of factors of production, he will maximise his satisfactions by selling (or keeping for his own use) factors of production which he owns. He uses them to buy consumer goods (including services). Totalling these for the whole community in the way described will not only show the demands for final output; it will also allow one to calculate the incomes received by consumers from the factors they sell. In total, these incomes will equal the values of commodities and factors consumed. It will be seen that this includes the values of those amounts of factors that are consumed directly.

8.3 Behaviour of the firm

The big difference from the situation of pure exchange is that we now have to allow for the conversion of factors into products. The Walrasian model assumes perfect competition in both product and factor markets. It also assumes that each firm converts factors of production into commodities at the lowest possible costs achievable with a given production function. As in the analysis of Chapters 10 and 11, we assume that the firm attempts to maximise profits. With perfect competition in all markets, this means employing each factor up to the point where the value of its marginal physical product is equal to its price.

The result is that the demand for factors by all entrepreneurs taken together is the function of their prices, the prices of products and of the numbers of firms in each industry. Entrepreneurs are assumed *not* to possess any initial endowments of factors, so that their demands for factors *must* be non-negative. As we have seen, firms may buy their own products. This can be allowed for, but we are assuming that there are no intermediate products. If there were, the analysis would obviously have to allow for more of the firms buying their own products, but the principles would not be altered. One can set down a system of equations which gives the demands of entrepreneurs for factors and their supplies of products.

8.4 Multi-market equilibrium

We can then aggregate these demands and supplies of both entrepreneurs and consumers for commodities and factors. We discover the demands for commodities and the supplies of factors from consumers; and the demands for factors and the supplies of products from entrepreneurs. We can again divide the economy into a number of Flexprice markets, one for each commodity and one for each factor. We then obtain a demand and supply equation for each market. If we solve these equations simultaneously, we obtain a set of short-run equilibrium prices at which the demands and supplies for every product and every factor are in short-run equilibrium. However, the individual firms in the system need not be in long-run equilibrium. If this is to happen, profit in each industry must be zero (normal). This will happen only if the number of firms in those industries where profits are not zero (normal) alters. This will be brought about, in the long run, by prices falling in those industries where profits are greater than zero and rising in those industries where they are negative. This will increase the profitability of unprofitable industries and reduce the profitability of industries where profits are above zero.

8.5 Relative prices again

When equilibrium has been reached, we have the same kind of situation as under pure exchange. The prices of the (m) factors of production and the (n) commodities will be set by the demands and supplies for them. Once again, it is relative, not absolute, prices that have to be determined. Again, the $(n+m)$ equations for the $(n+m)$ commodities and factors can be reduced to $(n+m-1)$ equations if one divides through by the price of any randomly-chosen product. All prices are then relative prices, giving exchange ratios in terms of that product.

In this general-equilibrium system, the long-run equilibrium position has four characteristics. First, every consumer is maximising satisfactions. Second, every entrepreneur is maximising profit. Third, this profit is normal in every firm. Fourth, every market is an equilibrium, with the quantity demanded equal to the quantity supplied.

9. The role of money

9.1 The numéraire

In both the preceding sections we have described an economy where there is no money. The price at which each market was in equilibrium was an exchange ratio. The prices of $(n-1)$ out any collection of (n) commodities and/or factors of production were expressed in terms of the nth, which was chosen arbitrarily. The good in terms of which all these exchange ratios are stated is known as the *numéraire*. The numéraire acts as a standard of value. It is the unit in which the prices of all other goods and factors are measured. However, this is only an accounting function. Apart from performing this function it is assumed that the numéraire is used by consumers and entrepreneurs as a factor or commodity in exactly the same way as all other factors and commodities. In particular, it is assumed that the numéraire cannot be stored: it cannot act as a store of value, as money does.

(a) The classical dichotomy

In this sense, an economy with a numéraire does not take on any of the characteristics of a monetary economy. It is impossible for such an economy to suffer from the problems that arise in the real world because people can hold their wealth in the form of money from one period of time to another. Nineteenth-century economists distinguished a 'real' sector of an economy of the kind outlined in section 16.4 and 16.5, where relative prices only were set. In addition, they distinguished a 'monetary' sector of the economy where money prices were determined in the way we shall consider in Chapter 24. We shall postpone a fuller discussion of this dichotomy until then.

9.2 Existence theorems

The only additional point we need to make here is that even if a set of equations representing the kind of multi-market system we have just outlined can be formulated, this does not necessarily mean that it has an equilibrium solution. Even if there is a *mathematical* solution, there may not be an economic one. For example, negative prices are perfectly acceptable mathematically, but not economically. Nor can amounts of commodities consumed or of output produced be negative. Economists have therefore spent a great deal of time formulating *existence theorems* which show that equilibrium solutions exist which meet given constraints. This is not as simple as it sounds, though existence theorems have been provided for a number of different multi-market systems, including linear economic systems like those discussed at the end of Chapter 6.

The complexity of the problem can be seen by the restrictive nature of the assumptions that have to be made. For example, Arrow and Debreu considered a system like the one described in section 16.6.[1] They made the following assumptions. Increasing returns to scale do not exist. At least one primary factor of production is required for the production of each commodity. The consumer has a continuous scale of preferences, and his wants are infinitely great. Indifference surfaces are concave upwards. The restrictiveness of these assumptions shows that there is still a great deal of work to be done before we fully understand the nature of equilibrium in general-equilibrium systems.

Suggested reading

ALLEN, R. G. D.	*Mathematical Analysis for Economists*, London, 1937, chapter 12.
ROBINSON, JOAN	'Euler's Theorem and the Problem of Distribution', *Economic Journal* 1934, p. 398.
MARSHALL, ALFRED	*Principles of Economics*, 8th edn., Macmillan, London, 1920, Book V, chapter 6.
RICARDO, DAVID	*Principles of Economics* (edited by Piero Sraffa), Cambridge University Press, 1951, chapter 31.
CASSEL, GUSTAV	*The Mechanism of Pricing*, reprinted in Penguin Modern Readings, *Price Theory*, Harry Townsend (ed.), Harmondsworth, Middlesex, p. 93.
HICKS, J. R.	*Value and Capital*, Oxford University Press, 1946, chapters 4 and 5.
(For mathematical readers)	
HENDERSON, J. M. and QUANDT, R. E.	*Microeconomic Theory*, McGraw-Hill, 1958, chapter 5.

[1] K. J. Arrow and G. Debreu, 'Existence of an Equilibrium for a Competitive Economy', *Econometrica*, 1954, pp. 265–90.

Part 2

Macro-economic theory

17

General equilibrium and employment

1. Say's Law   Part One was concerned with how the prices of individual goods and factors of production are determined. As we have seen, it is possible to analyse such problems by using 'partial' (or 'particular') equilibrium theory, though we also touched on one kind of general-equilibrium analysis. So far, we have not tried to show how the general level of income and activity in a country will be determined, or whether it will be high or low. We must do this now. It is impossible to provide an adequate explanation of the forces determining the general level of employment in a country on the basis of partial equilibrium analysis. Partial equilibrium analysis can show that unemployment may occur in particular industries; but it is impossible to show whether employment in *all* industries will be high or low, except by using a general-equilibrium analysis, though of a rather different kind from that outlined in Chapter 16. We need to use a *macro-economic* analysis which looks at the whole economy and not parts of it as micro-economic analysis does.

Until the 1920s and 1930s economists usually assumed that general unemployment was impossible. The 'classical economists'[1] tended to ignore the problem of what determines the general level of employment. Nevertheless, on the few occasions when they discussed the possibility of general unemployment, they seem to have taken the optimistic view that general over-production—and hence general unemployment—were impossible. In 1936, however, J. M. (later Lord) Keynes wrote his *General Theory of Employment, Interest and Money*,[2] refuting the 'classical' optimism and showing that, far from being a logical impossibility, general unemployment is logically quite

[1]Keynes argued that '"The Classical Economists" was a name invented by Marx to cover Ricardo and James Mill and their *predecessors,* that is to say for the founders of the theory which culminated in the Ricardian economics. I have become accustomed, perhaps perpetrating a solecism, to include in "the classical school" the *followers* of Ricardo, those that is to say, who adopted and perfected the theory of the Ricardian economies.' These economists include (for example) J. S. Mill, Marshall and Edgeworth. *General Theory of Employment, Interest and Money,* London, 1936, footnote, p. 3.
[2]For brevity, this book is referred to hereafter as *General Theory.*

possible. Economists now see full employment as only a limiting case. Just as perfect competition is a limiting case to differing degrees of monopoly, or imperfect competition, so full employment is merely the limiting case to various possible situations of under-employment equilibrium, each with a different amount of unemployment. In Part Two of this book we shall summarise contemporary macro-economic theory. Before doing so, however, it will be useful to look in greater detail at the kind of conclusion about unemployment which some earlier economists draw from theories of relative prices similar to that outlined in Part One. We can then see what are the short-comings of particular-equilibrium analysis if one attempts to use it to deal with the problems of unemployment.

One of the most important conclusions provided by the 'classical economists' is known as 'Say's Law of Markets'. It was this so-called 'law' which gave a concrete formulation to the idea that general over-production, and hence general unemployment, were impossible. J. B. Say (1767–1832) was a French economist whose *Traité d'Economic Politique* passed through several editions and was the first popular treatise on political economy published in France. In the chapter in his *Traité* on 'Des Debouches', Say gives his reasons for refusing to believe those businessmen and merchants who think that general over-production and unemployment are common occurrences. He rejects this view by arguing that 'supply always creates its own demand', as the currently-accepted version of his 'law' runs. Un-fortunately, it is difficult to find an apt quotation from Say himself, though the phrase 'supply creates its own demand' certainly sums up accurately the drift of his argument in this chapter. The nearest one can come to an explicit statement by Say is that 'it is production which creates markets for goods'.[1] It does not need very free trans-lation to render this as 'it is supply which creates its own demand'. Say is prepared to agree that the supply of the products of particular industries may temporarily outrun the demand for those particular products, if entrepreneurs misjudge demand. However, *general* over-production is impossible, according to Say.

Say's Law was explicitly accepted as the true explanation of the working of the economic system by many English economists during the early part of the nineteenth century. It implicitly underlay most economic writings prior to the 'Keynesian Revolution' of the 1930s. James Mill included a chapter in his *Elements of Political Economy*, showing that 'consumption is coextensive with production', and claimed that 'production is the cause, and the sole cause, of demand. It never furnishes supply without furnishing demand, both at the

---

[1] 'C'est la production qui ouvre des débouchés aux produits.' *Traité d'economic politique* (2nd edition), p. 144.

same time and both to an equal extent'.[1] Mill claimed that 'whatever the amount of the annual produce it can never exceed the amount of the annual demand'.[2] David Ricardo, in a letter to T. R. Malthus,[3] another eminent economist of the early nineteenth century, spoke approvingly of Mill's claim that 'in reference to a nation, supply can never exceed demand'.

Perhaps the most explicit statement of Say's Law given by any English economist appears in John Stuart Mill's *Principles of Political Economy*, published in 1848. J. S. Mill, the son of James Mill, took great pains to refute the idea that the demand for commodities in general might fall short of supply and thus cause over-production and unemployment. He said:

> Is it . . . possible that there should be a deficiency of demand for all commodities, for want of the means of payment? Those who think so cannot have considered what it is which constitutes the means of payment for commodities. It is simply commodities. Each person's means of paying for the productions of other people consists of those which he himself possesses. All sellers are inevitably and *ex vi termini*[4] buyers. Could we suddenly double the productive powers of the country we should double the supply of commodities in every market, but we should by the same stroke double the purchasing power. Every one would bring a double demand as well as supply: everybody would be able to buy twice as much because everybody would have twice as much to offer in exchange . . . It is a sheer absurdity that all things should fall in value and that all producers should, in consequence, be insufficiently remunerated.[5]

It is difficult to find explicit statements of this kind in later writings, but the idea that demand in general might fall short of supply in general and cause general over-production was regarded as heretical. Not, of course, that heresy had been absent even in the earliest days of Say's Law. T. R. Malthus, in particular, had tried to convince Ricardo who, as we have seen, took the same kind of view as Say, that demand might be deficient and cause unemployment, but without success. As Keynes said:

> Malthus, indeed, had vehemently opposed Ricardo's doctrine that it was impossible for effective demand to be deficient; but vainly.

---

[1] *Elements of Political Economy*, 3rd edition, p. 237. The chapter from which this quotation is taken, chapter iv of Section 3, is devoted to a discussion of the impossibility of general over-production, and is worth reading in the original.
[2] *Op. cit.*, p. 233.
[3] Letter of 16 September, 1814.
[4] By the meaning of the word (our footnote).
[5] *Principles of Political Economy*, Book III, Section 2, chapter xiv.

For since Malthus was unable to explain clearly (apart from an appeal to the facts of common observation) how and why effective demand could be deficient or excessive, he failed to furnish an alternative construction; and Ricardo conquered England as completely as the Holy Inquisition conquered Spain. Not only was his theory accepted by the City, by statesmen and by the academic world. But controversy ceased; the other point of view completely disappeared; it ceased to be discussed. The great puzzle of Effective Demand with which Malthus had wrestled vanished from economic literature.[1]

2. Wages and unemployment

2.1 Wage cuts in individual industries

It will be seen from the quotation from J. S. Mill given above that, for economists like him, the demand for good X is exactly the same thing as the supply of other goods Y, Z, etc., in the economy. Similarly, the demand for good Y is the supply of other goods X, Z, etc., in the economy. Therefore the demand for all goods together is identical with the supply of all goods together. General over-production is ruled out by definition. Such economists would admit that it was possible for there to be a temporary excess of the supply of X over the demand for X, or of the supply of Y over the demand for Y. But an excess of the supply of X, Y and Z together over the demand for X, Y and Z together was seen as a contradiction in terms. Even the over-production of any one good alone, say good X, was conceived by 'classical economists' as being possible only because the ruling price of X was too high. It was only at a price above the equilibrium price of X that the supply of X could exceed the demand for X. Once the price of X had fallen relatively to the prices of Y, Z, etc., this excess supply would disappear. The conclusion which one would obviously draw from this kind of analysis was that if the price of a particular commodity were high, compared with other prices, thus causing over-supply, the solution would be to reduce costs in the industry making the product in question. In these circumstances the 'classical economists' would advocate a reduction in the wages of workers in the industry suffering from over-production. This would reduce the cost of the product to an extent depending on the importance of wages in the total costs of the industry. Now since in partial equilibrium analysis one can assume that the individual industry is a relatively small part of the whole economy, one can also assume that the demand curve for the product of a single 'over-producing' industry remains the same after the wages of its workers have been cut. The amount of the product demanded would increase and would catch up with the supply. Over-production would therefore dis-

[1] *General Theory*, p. 32.

appear, provided only that wages (or other costs) were reduced sufficiently.

2.2 General wage cuts	This kind of conclusion is perfectly valid when one is applying partial-equilibrium analysis to the problems of over-production in a particular industry. However, 'classical economists' who used this kind of analysis often extended their conclusions to the economy as a whole. They suggested that *general* unemployment and over-production could be met in the same way by a *general* cut in wages. They did not see that if there is general over-production it may be unreasonable to try to solve the problem by applying partial-equilibrium analysis. The suggestions that wages should be reduced may now be unsound. When there is general unemployment, a general cut in wages in *all* industries *cannot* be assumed to leave demand unaltered, for part of that demand results from spending out of wages. It is thus quite likely that a *general* cut in wages will merely cause a reduction in demand and will not in itself remove unemployment. In fact, things are much more complex than this. This kind of problem can be adequately analysed only by the sort of theory which we shall outline in Part Two. We shall therefore postpone a complete discussion until that theory has been explained. What *is* clear is that partial-equilibrium theory cannot be used to analyse the problem thoroughly. Some kind of general-equilibrium analysis is needed. We cannot go further here.

2.3 Limitations of partial-equilibrium analysis

This criticism of particular-equilibrium theory holds much more widely. General-equilibrium analysis shows that every part of the economy is connected with every other part and that the repercussions of a change in one part of the economy on conditions in another cannot be ignored. It is therefore unreasonable, in general equilibrium theory, to regard the demand for consumption goods and investment goods as independent of each other, as we did in Chapter 14. We assumed that if saving increased, that is if the demand for consumption goods decreased, the demand for capital goods would rise because entrepreneurs had more money to spend on investment goods. In partial-equilibrium analysis this is a valid procedure; in general-equilibrium analysis it is no longer legitimate. One has to look in detail at the links between consumption and investment.

To see why this is, let us assume that money wages throughout an economy are constant. It should be clear that, since all workers must work in either the consumption goods industries or the investment goods industries, the volume of employment in the community depends on money expenditure on consumption plus money expenditure on investment. Only if money is paid to firms in return for consumer and investment goods will labour be demanded. It follows that if consumption expenditure remains constant while investment expenditure increases, employment will rise. More money will be paid to entrepreneurs who are making capital goods and they will hire more labour. Similarly, if investment expenditure is constant but consumption expenditure is increased, employment will again rise. The demands for consumption and investment goods are interdependent. The relation between them is similar to that of complementarity between consumer goods. When consumption expenditure increases, investment expenditure will increase too. Since consumers are buying more consumption goods, entrepreneurs will feel willing to purchase machines and factories to produce consumer goods. Similarly, if investment expenditure rises, consumption expenditure rises too. When there is more investment expenditure, more money is paid to workers in the investment industries, and they spend this money on products made by the consumption goods industries. This complementary relationship between consumption and investment is important in employment theory, but it cannot be analysed except by a general-equilibrium analysis.

2.4 The relationship between consumption and investment

It is important to recognise that this condition of complementary relationship occurs only when there is less than full employment. With unemployment, it is possible for a rise in investment expenditure to pull up consumption expenditure and vice versa. However, once full employment is reached there are no longer resources available to meet increased demand. A rise in consumption will now be competitive with investment. If it occurs, the only way of avoiding inflation, because overall demand is now greater than overall supply, is for investment to be cut. The fact that the economy is asymmetrical in this way is important. With unemployment, consumption and investment are complementary; with full employment, they are competitive.

3. 'The money illusion'

We saw in the previous section that when there is general unemployment, theoretical analysis shows that *general* wage cuts may fail to remove it. However, quite apart from this technical point, there is an important practical objection to cuts in wages in any economy where money is used. For in such an economy, there may well be what is known as a *money illusion*. That is to say, money is often regarded as having a fixed purchasing power in terms of commodities. The term money illusion is due to Professor Irving Fisher, who explained in 1927 that there is a money illusion, 'a failure to perceive that the dollar or any other unit of money expands and shrinks in value.'[1] We simply take it for granted that 'a dollar is a dollar', that 'a franc is a franc', that all money is stable.

3.1 Reactions to falling real wages

It follows from the existence of the money illusion that if general unemployment is caused by wages everywhere being too high, the solution will probably be to cut labour's real wage but not its money wage. As Keynes said, 'whilst workers will usually resist a reduction of money wages, it is not their practice to withdraw their labour whenever there is a rise in the price of wage-goods.'[2] It is obvious, not least from experience in the UK in the early 1970s, that a very sharp rise in the cost of living causes considerable discontent among the labour force and that this can lead to many claims for high wages, and perhaps long strikes.

3.2 Reactions to cuts in money wages

Even so, disturbances caused by the falling purchasing power of money are likely to be less serious than those which would result from an attempt to cut money wages directly, unless the fall in purchasing power is very rapid. An attempt to cut money wages can lead to very serious labour unrest, as it did in the UK in 1926 when cuts were made in coal miners' wages.

One reason for the existence of the 'money illusion' may be that while workers in one industry realise that a rise in prices does reduce their real wages, they also realise that rising prices have an equal impact on workers in other industries. It is possible that, within limits, workers are more concerned with maintaining their position relatively to workers in other industries than with maintaining their absolute real wages.

A further reason why cuts in money wages are resisted so strongly may be this. Labour may feel that a cut in money wages must be resisted by strikes since it is imposed by their own employers. However, they know that a fall in real wages is a result of more general economic forces which may be much more difficult to alter by strike action, though this certainly does not mean that trade unions will be

[1] *The Money Illusion*, p. 4. This book is based on a series of lectures given in the summer of 1927 at the Geneva School of International Studies.
[2] *Op. cit.*, p. 9.

silent or impassive if they feel that changes in government economic policy threaten their interests. All these reasons taken together make it likely that even *if* extra employment could be created only by a reduction in real wages it would be preferable for this reduction to be brought about by a rise in prices rather than by cuts in money wages.

3.3 Money as a store of value

These considerations suggest that the existence of money can be an important factor influencing the level of employment, incomes and prices in an economy. As we explained, the 'money' used in Part One was merely a 'measuring rod', introduced in order to enable us to compare the prices of different goods and factors of production. Money in the real world is a much more active force than the 'standard of value' of Part One. For example, we assumed in Part One that it was impossible for people to save out of their incomes and to hold these savings in the form of money. In practice, people may well save part of their incomes and hold them in the form of money, spending this money neither on consumption goods nor on investment goods. This situation can occur because money performs the function of acting as a means of storing purchasing power in addition to its function of acting as a standard of value, or numéraire. This means that the quotation from J. S. Mill[1] does not fully describe the situation. The money demanded for commodities can increase or decrease, *without* any change in the total money supply, simply if people decide that they will hold more or less of their wealth in the form of money. Money serves more than one purpose, and this is what the quotation from Mill overlooks.

4. Two fundamental issues

The *General Theory* raised the issue of the role of money in two ways. In the most fundamental sense, it raised the question whether an economy with money was different in any essential respect from a barter economy. There was also the more specific question touched on above—whether general unemployment is possible only where money wages are rigid. We shall return to both these questions later. In order to be able to do so, we must first understand what money is. We go on to look in detail at the nature and role of money in Chapter 18.

Suggested reading

KEYNES, J. M.	*General Theory of Employment, Interest and Money,* chapter 2.
FISHER, IRVING	*The Money Illusion,* London, 1928.

[1] *Principles of Political Economy,* p. 355.

18

Money

1. The nature of money

In Chapter 17 we explained that the economy studied in Part One was an economy in which complications caused by the existence of money were absent. We must now bring money explicitly into the analysis since many problems arise only because modern economies are monetary economies. In this chapter we consider the nature and importance of money.

1.1 How money has developed

Throughout the history of the world, communities have found it necessary to begin to use money at an early stage of their development because of the extreme inconvenience of exchange by direct barter. The most troublesome feature of trade carried on by direct barter is that it means that there must always be a coincidence of wants between buyers and sellers. A man wanting to exchange goats for cabbages may spend several weeks before he finds anyone who has cabbages for sale and happens to want goats. This inconvenience can be avoided by the use of money. The seller can sell his goats for money and keep the money until he finds cabbages for sale. From very early times, civilised societies have found that the most satisfactory method of carrying on trade is through the medium of one particular good which then becomes money. All members of the society become prepared to receive payment in the form of this good, which is demanded even though it may not be edible, wearable or capable of being consumed in any other way. Everyone knows that everyone else will accept the 'money good' in payment for all other goods or services. This is what gives the money good its value.

Several questions naturally arise at this stage. First, what exactly decides whether a particular good is money? Second, what are the functions of money? Third, how does money differ from other goods? In answering these questions, we must consider the demand for money and the supply of money. We begin by discussing the nature and uses of money; by discovering what it is and why it is demanded.

Later, we shall consider the supply of money and the factors which influence that supply.

Like all other goods, money is demanded because it is useful. Money and other goods therefore have this one feature in common. But the reasons why money is useful are rather different from those which make other goods useful. We have already seen that these other goods can be divided into two categories. First, there are consumer goods. These are goods which we can eat, wear, burn or otherwise consume. Second, there are capital (or producer) goods which assist in the production of consumer goods. It is because machines and factories are useful indirectly that they are essential for efficient production in modern economies.

1.2 How money differs from consumer goods

How, then, does money compare with ordinary consumer and capital goods? Money is not usually a consumer good. It cannot normally be consumed in any way. It is true that there are exceptions to this, but they occur only in primitive societies or in unusual circumstances. For example, in Germany, in the months just after defeat in 1945, cigarettes took on the function of money. Nevertheless, even in such exceptional situations consumer choice, operating through the price system, ensures that the price of the 'money good' is high enough to enable it both to perform its function as a normal consumer good and to act as money as well.

In Germany in 1945, consumers had to choose between smoking cigarettes or keeping them as 'money'. This choice had to be made in the usual way. The consumer had to ask whether the satisfactions obtained from smoking a cigarette would be greater or less than its value as money, carrying as it did the ability to buy consumer goods other than cigarettes, either now or in the future. However, if cigarettes were the *only* commodity capable of use as money, and if consumers smoked a significant percentage of the 'money stock', there would then be a 'shortage' of money. The value of 'money' in terms of goods would rise. Unlike paper money, cigarettes would not be denominated in money terms. Their value would have to be determined by the interaction of supply and demand. If the rate of smoking relatively to the rate of production of cigarettes led to a reduction in the stock of 'money' over time, the price of 'money' would rise. Each unit of 'money' would buy more other goods and people would increasingly use cigarettes as money, rather than smoking them. Indeed, one can picture the price of cigarettes rising far enough to establish an equilibrium where the 'money stock' was at the required level. In normal circumstances, however, money has its separate and distinct function. It is not an ordinary consumer good. It will be a piece of metal or paper, a mark on a ledger, data in a computer, and so on.

1.3 How money differs from capital goods

Nor is money quite like a capital good. The essential feature of capital goods is that they manufacture products by transforming them physically. Grains of wheat are made into flour, or steel slabs into steel sheet, by physical processes. Money, on the other hand, cannot perform any feat of physical transformation. It performs an essentially different operation from that performed by capital goods.

First, then, modern money differs from both consumer and capital goods. Because of this, some economists have denied that money is useful at all. This view is wrong. Money *is* useful, but its usefulness is of an unusual sort. Once commodity money is abandoned in favour of what we may call *token money*, money becomes *the* exchange good. It is useful only in an economy where exchange takes place. Other goods are useful, at any rate in principle, in a one-man economy where there can be no exchange. A Robinson Crusoe finds food useful for the same reasons as we do. He finds capital goods useful in the same way. But token money is of no use to him at all. Not until Man Friday arrives does money become useful to a Crusoe. Token money is useful in an exchange economy, but only in an exchange economy.

1.4 General acceptability

The *sine qua non* of any kind of money is that it must be *generally acceptable* to every member of the society which uses it. Money is useful to *A* because he knows that he can pay his debts to *B* with it. It is useful to *B* because he can pay wages to *C* with it, and so on. But acceptability of this kind is not a physical attribute possessed by some goods and not by others. This sort of acceptability is essentially a social phenomenon. Goods of all kinds have become money, at various times and places, simply by acquiring this social quality. They then become acceptable to everyone, in payment of debt.

1.5 Social attributes of money

(a) Physical characteristics

It is not necessary to be an anthropologist to see that it is society, and not any of their own physical characteristics, which decides which goods do and which goods do not become money. There is no common physical characteristic between coin, bank notes and bank deposits. Indeed the bank deposit, which is much the most important kind of money in a modern society, has scarcely any physical constitution at all. Bank deposits are simply numbers printed in ledgers or stored in computers. Yet bank money is accepted by everyone in payment of debt. It is for that reason, and for that reason alone, that it is worth keeping stocks of money. The history of money, the study of all the goods which have been money at various times, is fascinating. But ours is a study of economic theory and we must ignore history. All we need for our present purpose is a broad understanding of the nature and importance of the various kinds of money in modern societies.

(b) Bank deposits are the main kind of money

The main type of money in Great Britain at the moment, and indeed in all other developed countries, is not coin or notes, but bank credit —the deposits which people hold with 'commercial' banks.[1] There are large numbers of notes and coins in existence, but there is much more bank credit. Moreover, since the monetary authorities in countries like the UK allow the public to hold cash and bank deposits in whatever proportion the public wishes, the important changes in the amount of money nowadays are changes in the volume of bank deposits. While accepting that many transactions are still carried out with notes and coin, we shall therefore concentrate our attention on bank deposits.

1.6 Some unimportant types of money

(a) Legal tender

Another useful simplification we can make is to rule out one or two complications which are historically and legally important but economically insignificant. First, we shall find it convenient to ignore the concept of legal tender. In England, the only forms of legal tender are Bank of England notes to any amount and coins to restricted amounts. Businesses do sometimes refuse to accept cheques and insist on payment in bank notes and coin instead. Bank deposits are therefore not perfect substitutes for legal tender for all purposes in all countries, but they are almost perfect substitutes.

(b) Fiat money

It must always be remembered, however, that even legal tender may not function as money. Though the State may give its sanction, or 'fiat', to a particular kind of legal tender, this will not function as money unless it is generally accepted. During the German inflation of the early 1920s marks were legal tender, but they were losing value so rapidly that they ceased to be generally acceptable, and therefore ceased to be money. From the point of view of the economist, the notion of legal tender is not very important.

[1] The 'commercial' banks are independent institutions which are quite separate from the 'central' bank—in the UK the Bank of England.

(c) Gold

Second, we shall ignore the precious metals which have for so long played an important part in monetary systems. It seems inevitable that human ideas should lag somewhat behind events. This is especially true of ideas about money. Some people still think of money as in some way 'backed' by gold. This is not now the case in most countries. Of course, it is not very long since even the relatively small change in many economies was in the form of gold coins. Now they scarcely exist. Only in international trade is gold still important, though even here 'man-made gold' in the form of the Special Drawing Rights of the International Monetary Fund is beginning to supplement it. In Part Two, we are concerned with a closed economy and shall ignore gold. It should be remembered, however, that gold is nowadays not often used even as a basis for the credit structure. Yet the fact that gold has ceased to 'back' currency has not weakened confidence in it. The conventional foundation of the credit system has been taken away, but the structure itself remains firm and strong. People have ceased to worry whether notes are backed by gold or not. Money has only to be 'generally acceptable' to be money.

1.7 The basis of 'general acceptability'

This idea that the sole prerequisite of any form of money is that it should be 'generally acceptable' worries some people. They feel that this is far too slender a basis to bear the heavy burden of anything so important as money. The idea that you trust money because I do, and that I trust money because you do, sounds improbable to them. There may be some justification for such scepticism, but there is obviously not much. There are many conventions of this type in our modern society. A university professor, for example, arrives promptly at 10 a.m. each Wednesday to lecture on economics. He does so because he has confidence that his class will come to hear him. Similarly, the class arrives each week because they have confidence in the fact that there will be a lecture. The convention stands because each side has confidence in it. So it is with money. As long as the convention holds and money is generally acceptable to everyone, it retains its usefulness.

2. The functions of money

2.1 A unit of account

Having seen what are the essential characteristics of money, we must now see what functions it performs. There are four functions of money. First, it serves as a unit of account. The individual member of the economy has to have some common denominator with which he can measure the relative values of such different commodities as wheat and wash basins, swimsuits and sardines. This task is performed by money. We have already seen that the main disadvantage of a barter economy is that needs must always coincide. Another is that rates of exchange between commodities cannot easily be worked out. It is extremely difficult to do this, except in terms of some standard measure, for precisely the same reasons that it would be very difficult to compare the heights of Westminster Abbey and St. Paul's Cathedral if there were no unit of linear measurement. One would have to resort to some standard of measurement, such as a length of string or a piece of wood. Since one would have to use a standard each time one measured the length or height of any object, it is only sensible that one particular standard should be accepted as *the* standard. Money is *the* standard for measuring value, just as the yard or metre is *the* standard for measuring length. We have already defined money which is acting as a standard measure of value as a *numéraire*. This is a disembodied money; money with no function other than that of measuring value. It was for this purpose alone that we used money in our analysis in Part One.

2.2 A medium of exchange

On reflection, it will be clear that if a particular commodity is used as a unit of account, it will be convenient for it to serve also as the commodity through which exchange is carried out. This leads us to the second function of money. It acts as a medium of exchange. This is the central function of money and it is in performing this function that the notion of general acceptability is most clearly brought out. A good will not act as a convenient medium of exchange unless it is accepted by everyone. But it is important that just because this is the most obvious function of money it should not be thought of as the only function of money. The other functions are also important.

2.3 A store of value

Third, money functions as a store of value. The good chosen as money is always something which can be kept for long periods without deterioration or wastage. It is a form in which wealth can be kept intact from one year to the next. Money is a bridge from the present to the future. It is therefore essential that the money commodity should always be one which can be easily and safely stored. This explains the popularity of gold in the past; it does not suffer from physical deterioration. It also explains the present popularity of bank deposits, for they are perfectly safe unless the banks' ledgers and/or its computer data are destroyed or stolen—both unlikely contingencies.

2.4 A standard of deferred payments

Fourth, and last, money acts as a standard of deferred payments. Loans are usually made in money rather than in, say, tobacco or chocolates. But since this is the case, it would be a little odd if repayments were made otherwise than in money. It is also always important for debts to be measured in terms of a stable store of value, which money usually is.

2.5 The functions of money in an unstable system

One of the conveniences of using money, then, is that it often represents a stable medium in which debts can be contracted and repaid. The importance of this stability can be seen when one considers the consequences of an inflation which is sufficiently serious to cause a monetary breakdown because money is losing its value very rapidly. The first consequence is invariably that money ceases to fulfil its function as a standard of deferred payments. Instead of being contracted in terms of the currency of the country in question, debts are incurred in terms of the currencies of other countries whose monetary systems are more stable, in terms of precious metals or in terms of commodities. Money ceases to function as a standard of deferred payments even if at the time it fulfils its other functions. Logically, these functions can be separated. If necessary, each can be performed by a different good, but in practice they are connected and in any normal economy all the functions are performed by the same good. In our analysis we shall assume that this is always the case.

In practice, once money has ceased to function as a standard of deferred payments, it also ceases to act as a store of value. If it is not worth agreeing to have one's loans repaid in money because it is losing value too rapidly, it will not be worth storing money. The value of the store will be falling too fast. Money *ceases* to be a bridge between the present and the future and the way to protect the value of one's assets is to store wealth in forms other than money.

Once money ceases to fulfil this third function, its ability to perform the first two functions will be called into question as well. Money may cease to act as a unit of account. When prices become very high, calculating them will be harder. Individuals, and even businesses, will long to return to the simple arithmetic of the days when a loaf of bread cost two francs and not 29 234 768 221. Quite apart from this, when inflation has reached this stage, the sheer labour of recalculating prices daily, or even hourly, will be unbearable.

The last function which money is likely to fail to fulfil is that of acting as a medium of exchange. So long as one can spend one's money fast enough to prevent prices rising too far before one's dealings are complete, money will still be exchanged for goods. But when inflation is really serious—when there is *hyperinflation*—the

position will soon arise where no one wants to keep money at all—
even for a few minutes. Once this happens, a completely new money
will have to be found.

3. The demand for money

The exposition of the four functions of money given above is the
traditional one, and it remains useful. For our purposes in discussing
macro-economic theory, we shall also find it useful to discuss money
in more modern terms. Economists often look at the reasons why
money is demanded—why people want a stock of money to hold.
We are defining the money stock as coin, notes and bank deposits.

Keynes said that the demand for money, or *liquidity preference* as he
called it, depended on three motives. These are: (i) the transactions
motive; (ii) the precautionary motive; and (iii) the speculative
motive. As we shall see later, the emphasis attached to these three
motives by contemporary economists is rather different from Keynes's,
but the three motives remain important concepts, from which more
recent developments in this branch of economic theory stem. In this
chapter, we outline Keynes's ideas.

3.1 The transactions motive

People receive their income weekly, monthly, quarterly or even
yearly. They spend this money at much shorter intervals. Although
some payments—for rent, hire-purchase instalments, gas or electricity—are made weekly, monthly or quarterly, many payments are
made daily—for food, travel or amusement. Because income is
received at discrete intervals but is paid out more continuously,
people need a stock of money all the time, to enable them to carry
out their transactions. The sorts of inconvenience which people
would suffer if they held no money to satisfy the transactions motive
are typified by those of the man who finds himself in a shop with no
money at all. Everyone holds some money, however little, to satisfy
the transactions motive.

The transactions motive can be looked at from the point of two
sets of people: (*a*) consumers and (*b*) businessmen.

(a) The income motive

From the consumer's point of view, the amount of money which he
will hold to satisfy the transactions motive will depend: (i) on the size
of his income, and (ii) on the intervals of time between the receipt of
the various instalments. His demand for money can be said to depend
on the *income motive*. It is easy to show why the amount of money held

will depend on the length of time between the receipts of consecutive instalments of income. Let us consider two men, both earning £30 per week, one being paid weekly and the other every two months. Assuming that they both make expenditures of £30, evenly spread over each week, on average the first man will hold £15. At the beginning of the week he will have £30, and at the end he will have nothing. On average he will have £15. The second man will receive £240 every two months. If he spends £30 each week throughout the two months, he will have an average of £120 in his bank account or in notes. Even if, as is likely, expenditure is not spread evenly over time, the man with the weekly income will still hold less money on average for transactions purposes. The demand for money under the transactions motive by consumers as a whole thus depends, mainly, on the length of the interval of time between successive pay days, averaged over the whole population.

It may not be quite so clear why the amount of money held under the income motive will vary with the *size* of a person's income. Let us assume that there are two men, one earning £120 a month and the other £240, and that each spends one-thirtieth of his income on each day during the month. The man with the larger income will then hold £120 on average, as compared with the other's £60. While it is again unlikely that anyone spends his income evenly through the month, it does seem reasonable to think that a richer man will hold more money to satisfy the income motive than a poorer one. The income motive is likely to mean that there is a greater demand for money, both by individuals and by society as a whole, if income is higher. The relationship may not be a proportional (linear) one; but there will *be* a relationship.

In total, then, a community's demand for money under the income motive will be a function of the size of personal incomes, and of the average time between successive pay days.

(b) The business motive

Businesses will also wish to hold a certain amount of money in their bank accounts. They will need money in the bank to pay for raw materials, components, wages and salaries and to meet the other current expenses incurred by businesses. Money held by firms in this way is said to be required to satisfy the *business motive*. Clearly, the amount of money held under the business motive will be a function of the turnover of the firm. The larger the turnover, the larger will be the amount of money the firm needs if it is to be reasonably certain of covering its current expenses. Keynes thought that the amount of money needed under the business motive would be roughly proportional to the total volume of business transactions carried out.

More recent thinking suggests that the relationship will be more complex, because the firm (and indeed individuals) should be seen as holding an 'inventory' of money like its inventory of raw materials, etc. We shall look again at the nature of this more complex function in Chapter 22, and at its implications for the behaviour of the demand for money.

The average length of time between the receipt by individuals of successive payments of salaries or other forms of income will not change frequently or substantially in any country. It follows that the amount of money held under the transactions motive will mainly depend on: (*a*) the size of personal incomes and (*b*) the turnover of business. As incomes rise, and as businesses increase their turnover, the amount of money demanded under the transactions motive will increase, though the relationship may well be rather complex.

3.2 The precautionary motive

Keynes argued that the amount of money which people held under the precautionary motive would be devoted, broadly speaking, to fulfilling the function of a store of value. It is possible to liken the amount of money held under the *transactions* motive to water in a tank. It is as though water is being fed into the tank through one hose-pipe and being taken out of it through another. The aim of the individual concerned is to see that there is enough water in the tank all the time for something to be able to run out, even when nothing is running in. Carrying on the simile, money held under the precautionary motive is rather like water kept in reserve in a separate tank. Money held under this motive is kept to provide for emergencies. The individual holds a certain amount of money to provide against the danger of unemployment, sickness, accident and other more uncertain perils. The amount of money held in this way will depend on the individual and on the conditions in which he lives. If he is nervous, he will hold much money; if he is sanguine, he will hold little. The amount of money held for this purpose is not likely to represent a constant proportion of a man's income, though in general a rich man is likely to hold more than a poor one. But this is not necessarily so. The amount held will depend on the individual.

Similar considerations may lead businesses to hold money under the precautionary motive. They may want to hold more cash to use if unexpected events occur. Again, it is likely that the amount held under the precautionary motive will be directly related to the firm's attitude to risk. Firms in risky industries may hold more than others. A firm with a reputation for prudence may hold more money relatively to its turnover than another. Similarly, a firm which is prepared to run greater financial risks is likely to hold less.

As with the transactions motive, money held under the precautionary motive will be a function, maybe a complex function, of income.

3.3 The speculative motive

The third motive for holding money is the speculative motive. The notion of the speculative motive for holding money was not an evolution from the traditional functions of money but a new, Keynesian, idea. There has been some reaction against early enthusiasm for it. As we shall see in Chapter 22, the speculative motive plays a less important role in contemporary economic thinking than it did in Keynes's. In particular, Keynes simplified his theory by assuming that there were only two kinds of financial asset that people could hold: money and bonds (fixed-interest securities). Contemporary economists have relaxed this simplifying assumption.

Money held under the speculative motive constitutes a store of value just as money held under the precautionary motive does, but it is a store intended to fulfil a different purpose. The aim of the holder of a precautionary balance is to help himself, or his firm, through times of difficulty and disaster. He is able, perhaps, to avoid selling his car if he falls on hard times.

(a) Bonds

Money held under the speculative motive is quite different. It constitutes a liquid store of value—a readily-realisable asset which the holder intends to use for gambling, to make a speculative gain. The money is held in a bank account to be invested in securities at an opportune moment. As we have observed, Keynes assumed that if people wanted to hold wealth over time, their choice was either to hold cash or to hold a financial security which yielded a fixed annual sum of money and is known as a 'bond'.[1] For simplicity, we shall consider only *undated* bonds, where the interest is received in perpertuity. Good examples of undated bonds are British government securities—4 per cent Consols or $2\frac{1}{2}$ per cent Treasury Stock. The *debentures* of businesses are also bonds, but they are usually 'dated'.

(b) Bond prices and interest rates

Now since the annual yield on bonds is fixed, a change in the rate of interest will alter the price of all bonds. For example, suppose that an undated bond[2] is issued at a time when the rate of interest is

---

[1]Securities which do not yield a fixed and known amount of interest each year are known as 'equities'; they include the ordinary shares of businesses.

[2]This means that whoever issues the bond has an obligation to pay a fixed amount of interest annually to the lender, but that there is no obligation to 'redeem' (repay) the bond on a particular date.

6 per cent. The government (or whoever issues the bond) will offer £6 each year, until redemption, to every purchaser of the security who is prepared to pay the face value (the *nominal value*) of £100. Let us suppose that the rate of interest then falls to 3 per cent. A new purchaser of bonds now has a choice. He can buy a new bond with a nominal value of £100 and receive £3 interest on it each year until redemption. Alternatively, he can buy an existing 6 per cent bond. Since the government is committed to pay £6 interest on each £100 (nominal) of such a bond, the only way in which the return on the two bonds can be equated is for the price of a 6 per cent bond with a face value of £100 to rise to £200. The rate of interest must hold throughout the whole market for any bond with a given life, or 'maturity'. A government can borrow from lenders at any given moment at a single rate of interest only for a security with a given life. If the return on 'second-hand' bonds is different from that on new bonds they will be bought (or sold) until the rates become the same.

Similarly, if the rate of interest rises to 12 per cent, the price of the 6 per cent undated bond must halve. Borrowers will now be able to earn £12 by investing £100 in a new bond. They will not be prepared to buy the old, 6 per cent bond unless its price falls to £50. They will then obtain the same rate of return as from a new, 12 per cent bond.

Two things follow from this. First, changes in the rate of interest inevitably mean changes in bond prices. Second, with undated bonds, changes in the rate of interest will be in inverse proportion to changes in bond prices. If the rate of interest doubles, bond prices will be halved; if the rate of interest is halved, bond prices double. While this is strictly true only if bonds are undated, the general principle is important and this generalisation is good enough for our purposes in this book. Prices of 'dated' bonds will move in the same direction, but to a smaller extent. The 'longer' a bond with a given interest rate is, the greater the change in its price for any change in the rate of interest.

(c) Speculation in bonds

It is therefore possible to make money by buying bonds when they are cheap (when the rate of interest is high) and selling them again when they are dearer (when the rate of interest has fallen). Keynes argued that individuals and firms who believed that the rate of interest was likely to rise in future would hold money under the speculative motive in order to buy bonds with it. When the rate of interest had reached such a high level that they felt it must fall again, they would buy bonds. If the rate of interest then did fall, they would make capital gains because the price of bonds had risen. They speculated in bonds, hoping to gain from predicting accurately what future interest rates would be.

(d) Interest rates and the speculative demand for money

The amount of money held under the speculative motive therefore depends on the rate of interest. If almost everyone expects the rate of interest to fall—if they expect the price of bonds to rise—they will buy bonds, hoping to sell them later when the price is higher. At such times, the amount of money held under the speculative motive will be relatively small. Similarly, if most people expect bond prices to fall—if they expect a rise in the rate of interest—they will hold a good deal of cash under the speculative motive. When the slump in bond prices has run its course, people will switch into bonds again at what they hope is the psychological moment, making speculative gains as bonds become dearer once more. However, if there are differing views on future bond prices, and some people expect them to fall even farther, these people will continue to hold cash. At what other people regard as high rates of interest, they will be holding cash in the hope that interest rates will rise even farther, and bond prices fall even lower, before there is a reversal of the trend. There is unlikely to be unanimity over the future course of bond prices. This will affect the total amount of money held for speculative purposes throughout the economy at any interest rate. It will not affect the general principle: more money will be held at low interest rates than at high ones.

As we shall see later, this 'pure' Keynesian model with only two assets—cash and bonds—will need to be elaborated. We have outlined it because it is important to begin by understanding how the 'pure' Keynesian speculative motive worked.

3.4 The demand for money is a 'stock' concept

These three motives, the transactions, precautionary and speculative motives, between them determine the demand for money. They are important in macro-economic theory because, as we shall discover, changes in the demand for money can cause alterations in interest rates which, in turn, can lead to changes in GNP (gross national product).

There is, however, one important aspect of the demand for money which we must stress. This is the essential difference between the demand for money and the demand for a commodity. When we speak of a consumer *demanding* a good, we envisage him deciding how much he can afford to buy, then giving up money to obtain it.

Drawing a parallel, it might be thought that when we considered the demand for money, we should explain it by analysing the reasons for which people were prepared to give up goods in order to obtain money. There is one sense, of course, in which there is such a demand for money. It is constituted, in a given period of time, by the supply of all the goods offered in exchange for money during that period. But this is much more conveniently described as the *total production of the community*.

The demand for money, in economic analysis, is the demand for the existing stock of money which is available to be held. The demand for money means the demand for money *to hold*. So, when one speaks of an increased demand for money, one means that the community wishes to hold a larger amount of money. We are concerned with a *stock* of money that is held, not with a flow. It is important to remember that the demand for money—or *liquidity preference*—is always a demand for a money stock to hold.

4. The supply of money: another 'stock' concept

The supply of money is defined in a similar manner. In the case of the supply of a commodity, we mean the amount which entrepreneurs sell at current prices in a given time period. This supply is a flow over time because goods are being continually produced. With money it is different. The supply of money, like the demand for money, is a stock. It is the supply of money *to hold*. Unless money is held by someone, it cannot exist. So, the supply of money is the existing stock of money, all of which is held by someone. The supply of money at any moment is the sum of all the money holdings of all the members of the community.

Again, there is one sense in which there is a supply of money which in a given period constitutes a demand for goods. All the money spent in a given period is a kind of demand for all the goods bought. But this is more conveniently regarded as the *total money expenditure of the community*.[1]

We shall therefore use the terms demand and supply of money to denote the demand for and the supply of a stock of money. An increase in the supply of money does not mean the spending of money by those who possess it. This simply alters the *ownership* of the existing supply of money. An increase in the supply of money means an increase in total money stock. We shall find later that, quite apart from the convenience of enabling us to distinguish easily between the 'supply

[1] This is *not* the same as gross national expenditure as defined in chapter 19. It is the total value of transactions carried out in a period, and will therefore include, for example, Stock Exchange transactions which are excluded from gross national expenditure, as well as purchases of raw materials, components, etc. The latter cannot be included in gross national expenditure or there would be double counting.

of money' and 'total money expenditure', this method of denoting demand and supply of money as the demand and supply of money to hold is especially appropriate in the case of money.

4.1 The importance of bank deposits

What, then, constitutes this supply or stock of money? We shall concentrate our attention on bank deposits. Currency and coin are much less important in most countries. In the UK, the number of notes and coins in circulation is now decided automatically, by the demand of the community for them, given the total of coin, notes and bank deposits. The community decides to hold so much of its money in the form of notes, and the central bank issues them. When, as at Christmas, people want more currency to use for Christmas shopping, the required amount is automatically increased. At each moment, the community decides to hold a certain percentage of its total money stock in the form of notes and the rest in the form of bank deposits. The Bank of England issues enough notes to allow this decision to become a reality. From an economic point of view, the distinction between bank notes and bank balances is unimportant.

The supply of money, then, is the total amount of money which is held. Ignoring the number of currency notes and coins in circulation, the supply of money is the supply of balances in the commercial banks. It is therefore time to discuss the nature of bank balances—or bank deposits—and the way in which the total amount of bank deposits is determined.

5. Bank deposits

A bank deposit is a liability to the bank but an asset to the customer. The banker is bound to make the deposit available to his customer in whatever form the latter wishes. The customer, on the other hand, can regard it with satisfaction as good, solid money. A community's supply of bank money is thus the sum total of all the bank deposits of all the members of the community. An increase or decrease in the supply of bank money means a rise or fall in the total volume of bank deposits. To understand the significance of such changes in the supply of money, we must discover how the volume of bank deposits in a country can vary.

5.1 What determines the amount of bank deposits

Bank deposits, as we have seen, are supplied by banks but the latter cannot issue just as many as they wish. The volume of bank deposits is ultimately controlled by the central bank—in the UK the Bank of England. Whether nationalised, like the Bank of England, or not, each central bank has considerable control over the volume of bank deposits in its own country. Our search for the factors determining the volume of bank deposits therefore leads us to study the policy of the central bank. There are three stages in our analysis. First, given the policy of the central bank, why can the commercial banks supply bank deposits at all? Second, to what amount? Third, how can the central bank increase or decrease the volume of bank deposits when it thinks it necessary to increase or decrease the supply of money?

The first question, then is: How do commercial banks create deposits? The answer, in the words of the old banking maxim, is that 'every advance creates a deposit'. Every time a bank lends, or 'advances', money to a client it creates a deposit.

5.2 Advances create deposits

The plain man's idea of the way in which bank deposits are created is probably as follows. Somehow one gets hold of some bank notes, perhaps having been given a student grant or started one's first job. One then goes to a bank and asks to be allowed to open an account. One hands over the notes. A record of the amount of money deposited is written in a ledger or fed into a computer and the account is there. A bank deposit has been created.

This is *not* the way bank deposits are created. Deposits are created by a businessman with little or no spare cash going to a bank, explaining what good prospects he has and asking for a loan of, say, £10000 to enable him to engage in business. Having proved that he is honest and reputable, and perhaps having left collateral security, the businessman is given an advance of £10000. With this he opens or increases his account. This time a deposit really has been 'created'. Bank deposits are not given in *exchange* for currency. They are created because banks allow business men to open accounts, because money is 'advanced'.

A bank deposit is created entirely by the banking system. The borrower deposits the advance in his account and is able to use it to finance his business. By making this advance, the banker has therefore created a corresponding deposit. The two things happen simultaneously. The granting of an advance implies the creation of a deposit and vice versa.

5.3 The limiting factor on credit creation

What is it, then, that puts a limit on the amount of credit which bankers can provide? This is the second problem which we set out to solve. We shall look at the question in two stages. First, we shall look at the way in which this has happened historically. Second, we shall look at recent developments.

It might be thought that the limit on the creation of credit lies in the credit-worthiness of borrowers. This does enter into a bank's decision to lend, but it is not fundamental. On occasion, bankers refuse to make advances even to first-class borrowers. Money is 'tight', it is said. There must be other limits on the ability of bankers to make advances. Historically, the ultimate limiting factor has been a convention of the banking profession which is still a very important, though not usually the only, factor.

(a) The cash ratio

Banks keep a definite ratio between the volume of deposits which they issue and the amount of 'cash' which they possess. This is known as the 'cash/deposit ratio', or 'reserve ratio'. In the UK, it was for many years the convention that banks held £1·00 of 'cash' for every £12·50 of their deposits. Part of this 'cash' was in the form of bank notes and coins in their tills, while the rest took the form of 'bankers' deposits' with the Bank of England. The cash ratio was therefore 1 : 12½. Since the autumn of 1971 banks have been free to set their own cash ratios and these have been reduced below 8 per cent.

Let us look at how a banking system would operate with a 1 : 12½ cash/deposit ratio. We shall discuss the size of the commercial bank's deposits with the central bank in the next section. The essential thing about them is that the commercial banks can look on deposits with the central bank as 'cash', because the central bank will always supply bank notes in exchange for them if asked to do so. So long as the commercial banks abide by the 'cash ratio', the volume of commercial bank deposits in a country must bear a fixed proportion to the amount of 'cash' which the banks hold. Since the proportion of 'cash' which is 'till-money' is likely to remain roughly constant over longish periods of time, it will be on changes in deposits with the central bank that changes in the volume of bank deposits depend.

It follows that so long as the commercial banks strictly maintain the existing 'cash ratio', a rise in the volume of bank deposits can result only from a rise in the amount of 'cash' and vice versa. If we can see how such a change in cash can come about, we shall have moved towards explaining why changes in the supply of money occur—the third stage of our analysis.

(b) The irrelevance of the 'circular flow'

First, however, we must notice how the change does *not* take place. A fall in the 'cash' held by a bank does not usually result from the fact that customers draw out cash from the banks to spend on household and personal expenditure, that firms draw out money to pay wages to labour or that shops draw out till-money. This money is engaged in a circular process. It will soon be spent and will return to the bank, whence it will be withdrawn once more. Only over long periods, or in exceptional circumstances, will the amount of cash used for this purpose change significantly, assuming that the size of total national expenditure remains the same. People will usually draw out and pay in roughly the same amount of cash to their banks week after week and month after month. The 'circular flow' will average out. The fact that money is drawn out of bank accounts provides no explanation of changes in the volume of bank deposits. Advances are created or destroyed because of changes in the amount of 'cash', and the reasons for such changes cannot be found in the actions of customers of the banks. We must turn our attention instead to the deposits which commercial banks hold at the central bank.

6. Open-market operations

Under the traditional system we are discussing, the crucial factor controlling the volume of deposits in the commercial banks was the size of the latters' own deposits with the central bank. These 'bankers' deposits' are included in the 'cash reserve' of the commercial banks. So, if the central bank can alter the amount of bankers' deposits, it can *ipso facto* affect the banks' ability to create deposits. The central bank can indeed do this. It does so through what are known as 'open-market operations'. The central bank goes into the public or 'open' market for either long or short-term government securities, and buys or sells them according to whether the aim is to create or destroy bank deposits.

6.1 Credit creation

The way open-market operations work can be seen most clearly if one considers a simplified system with a central bank and only one commercial bank. If the central bank buys securities worth £1 000, it pays the seller with a draft on itself. This draft is paid into the seller's account with his commercial bank, so that the latter's deposits with the central bank increase by £1 000. On this basis, the commercial bank can create extra deposits worth £1 000 by making loans. This is the essence of open-market operations. By buying securities, the central bank can increase the deposits of the public with the commercial bank; it can increase the money supply.

However, the process of credit creation does not stop there. The existence of the 'cash ratio' means that the commercial bank can create more deposits than the equivalent of the value of open-market purchases of securities. With a 1 : 15 cash/deposit 'reserve' ratio one might suppose that the addition of £1000 to the 'cash' of the commercial bank would enable it to create not £1000 but £15000 of new deposits. This is not so. The effect of open-market operations is certainly greater than if there were only a 1:1 cash ratio, but the extent to which the original open-market purchase will be magnified in its effect on bank deposits will not depend simply on the size of the cash/deposit ratio. We have so far ignored the fact that some 'cash' created by the purchase of securities will get into the hands of the public and will not stay in the tills of the bank. There will be a 'drain of cash into circulation'. Central bank purchases of securities worth £1000 on the open market may ultimately increase the commercial banks' deposits with the central bank by only, say, £250. The remaining £750 will stay in the hands of the public.

(a) The drain of cash

Just how quickly this 'drain of cash' will occur is a matter for debate. Sir Ralph Hawtrey, who stressed the importance of the phenomenon, suggested that it would occur only slowly. In the short run, open-market operations may exert the full effect of a 1:15 cash/deposit ratio on bank deposits while, subsequently, more and more cash may slowly 'drain' into the hands of the public. However, if the bankers realise that the drain of cash will occur sooner or later, they may create no more new bank deposits than they feel they will be able to sustain in the long run. In practice, the drain of cash *does* reduce the credit-creating effects of open-market operations. In Britain, if there were a 15:1 deposit/cash ratio, a given open market by the central bank would probably increase total bank deposits not by fifteen times, but by four or five times the amount of that purchase.

This is how open-market operations work. By buying government securities, the central bank increases the money supply, provided that the commercial banks observe the cash ratio and that not all the extra 'cash' is 'drained' into circulation. Since banks earn interest on all advances they make, it pays them to create extra deposits to the full amount that the drain of cash will allow.

6.2 Credit contraction

If the central bank sells securities, the effect will be of the same kind but in the opposite direction. Assuming that there is still only the one commercial bank, if the central bank sells securities worth £1000, these have to be paid for out of the deposits of the commercial bank. Whoever buys the securities will pay £1000 to the central bank. This will reduce the commercial bank's balance with the central bank by £1000. Since this balance is part of the bank's 'cash' it will have to reduce its deposits to maintain the cash ratio. Allowing for the drain of cash, this time *out* of the hands of the public and *into* the commercial bank, a fall in 'cash' of £1 000 in the UK, would reduce the commercial bank's deposits by about £4 000 at a time when the deposit/cash ratio was 15 : 1. The actual size of the reduction, as with the increase, will depend on the current cash ratio and on the size of the drain of cash.

6.3 More than one commercial bank	We have so far assumed a system with only one commercial bank. However, we have seen that though, in practice, there will be more than one commercial bank, in principle this makes no difference to the argument. The central bank can still alter the aggregate deposits of the commercial banks. The extent of the alteration will depend on the banks' current cash/deposit ratio as well as on the relative amounts of cash and bank deposits which the public wishes to hold. At any given time, open-market operations may have a big effect on the deposits of one commercial bank, because its clients happen to be selling or buying a large proportion of the securities being bought or sold by the central bank. However, the total amount of deposits in all commercial banks, as distinct from those in individual banks, will be unaffected. The central bank can carry out open-market operations just as effectively with ten commercial banks as with one. There is, however, the fact that if the central bank is contracting deposits by selling securities for cash, and if most of this cash consistently comes from one commercial bank, its relative size will be contracting. There is no *a priori* reason why contraction should particularly affect one bank in this way, but the possibility should be mentioned.
6.4 Contraction is often easier than expansion	This leads to a major point. An important element in the discussion has been the fact that if banks are to be trusted by their clients the 'cash ratio' must be carefully observed. In practice, this means that open-market operations can reduce the money supply rather more easily than they can increase it. If the central bank sells securities and so *reduces* 'bankers' deposits' with it, the legal or conventional cash ratio will *force* the commercial banks to reduce their clients' deposits in order to restore the cash ratio. They will not be allowed, or will not dare, to keep too little cash in hand. If the central bank buys securities, the commercial banks can now expand deposits while still maintaining the cash ratio. However, there is no guarantee that the banks' clients will be willing to borrow. As we shall see later, central

banks will normally undertake the purchase of securities only in times of recession, in the hope of stimulating business activity by making more credit available to business. Yet it may not be easy to find enough credit-worthy businesses to borrow these potential deposits. The central bank's control over the money supply is often more effective in a downward than in an upward direction.

7. The theory of money as a theory of choice

7.1 The traditional theory of money

We have now outlined the traditional theory of money, which sees the supply of money as determined by two ratios. One is the cash/deposit ratio between the amount of cash held by the commercial banks and their deposits: this is the reserve ratio. The other is the ratio in which the public wishes to hold bank notes and bank deposits. It is this ratio which determines the proportion of total 'cash' which is available for the commercial banks to use as the basis for credit creation.

Both these ratios reflect choices. The proportion of reserves held in cash rather than in bank deposits is determined by the proportions in which the individuals who make up the community choose to hold them. Similarly, while reserve ratios may or may not be legally required, they will reflect the amount of cash which past experience has shown it is prudent for banks to hold. The amount of cash the commercial banks hold will also depend on how much more cash they feel it is necessary to hold, over and above the legally-required amount or the amount shown to be necessary by past history, in the light of their hopes and fears for the future.

7.2 The modern theory

This means that our study of the money supply leads us again into problems of capital theory. The public's choice between holding assets in the form of cash rather than of bank deposits is clearly of this kind. So is the bank's choice of a reserve ratio. Cash held by a bank against the possibility of withdrawal represents an inventory just as much as does the stock of finished goods which a firm holds against the possibility of future increases in demand. As we shall see later, this means that the theory of the supply of money is developing in the same direction as is the theory of the demand for money.

8. The bank's asset structure

There is more to it than this. Like all businesses, a bank has assets as well as liabilities. Indeed, being a financial business, a bank's balance sheet is an even more important indicator of its activities and problems than is the case with other businesses. So far we have looked mainly at the bank's liabilities—its deposits. (A bank will usually have some capital of its own as well, but we have ignored this element on the liability side of its balance sheet.) However, we have looked only at one of its assets—'cash'.

When we extend our attention to the whole range of assets that banks hold, we find that we are moving once again into capital theory, with the bank concerned ensuring that the proportion of each individual asset to its total assets is what it thinks desirable. Banks can therefore be seen as concerned with building up an optimal portfolio, containing the right proportions of the various assets. Apart from cash, there are three main kinds of asset which banks hold.

8.2 Liquid assets

First, there are short-term government and commercial securities— especially treasury bills and commercial bills. In England, a con- siderable proportion of these are likely to be held at one remove, via loans to the discount houses in London. The banks lend money to the discount houses in short-term loans, and the discount houses use these loans very largely to hold treasury and commercial bills. As for the banks' own holdings of bills, these will normally have less than three months to run, so that while they will usually offer relatively low rates of interest, they will be redeemed without capital loss within a relatively short period of time.

(a) The liquidity ratio

Together with cash, short-term assets (including loans to the discount market) will make up what are often called the bank's liquid assets, or liquidity. For example, in recent years British commercial banks have found it desirable to hold about 30 per cent of their assets in this form. Their *liquidity ratios* have been around 30 per cent.

(b) The British reserve-asset ratio

In September 1971 the Bank of England introduced a new *reserve- asset ratio* to replace the older liquidity ratio. The new arrangement no longer includes cash in the commercial banks' tills as part of the reserve ratio. Nor does it include all of the money lent to discount houses, with which the latter hold bills and other short-term assets. The ratio does now include government bonds with only a year to run. The reserve-asset ratio is therefore not the same as the liquidity ratio but serves much the same purpose. On the new definition, the

banks have to maintain, day by day, a uniform minimum reserve
ratio of $12\frac{1}{2}$ per cent of their eligible liabilities.[1]

8.3 Bonds

The second main group of assets held by banks are long-term, fixed-
interest bonds—often government securities. While these will usually
bring a higher rate of return than short-term securities, they will also
be less liquid—less easily converted into cash without capital loss.
Many of these long-term securities will have several years to run.
For example, British commercial banks hold government bonds,
about half of which have up to five years to run and the remainder
between five and ten years. A bank cannot be certain of being able to
exchange any bonds for cash without capital loss if it needs money.
These bonds are readily saleable in that they can easily be sold on
the Stock Exchange, but may not be 'liquid' in the sense that they
can be sold quickly without any capital loss. If interest rates rise,
waiting until the greater proportion of a bank's bonds can be redeemed without capital loss may take several years. Certainly, if
interest rates have risen, selling bonds bought recently at short notice
on the Stock Exchange will be possible only at a loss.

8.4 Advances

The final kind of commercial bank asset is advances to individuals,
firms and other organisations, private or public. It is likely that the
rate of interest earned on advances will be as high or higher than the
rate of interest on long-term bonds. At the same time, these advances
may be less liquid—less easy to redeem quickly and without capital
loss. To take money away from firms to which it has been lent,
because the bank needs it for other purposes, may be easy; but it may
be difficult. To insist on rapid repayment of a loan may even send
the borrowing firm bankrupt, so that banks are often reluctant to

[1] Eligible liabilities are defined as the sterling deposit liabilities of the banking system
as a whole, excluding deposits having an original maturity of over two years, plus
any sterling resources obtained by switching foreign currencies into sterling. Inter-
bank transactions and sterling certificates of deposit (both held and issued) will be
taken into the calculation of individual banks' liabilities on a net basis, irrespective
of term. Adjustments will be made in respect of transit items.

Eligible reserve assets will comprise balances with the Bank of England (other
than special deposits), British Government and Northern Ireland Government
Treasury bills, company tax reserve certificates, money at call with the London
money market, British Government stocks with one year or less to final maturity,
local authority bills eligible for rediscount at the Bank of England and commercial
bills eligible for rediscount at the Bank of England (up to a maximum of 2 per cent of
eligible liabilities).

ask for their advances back quickly. Whatever the nominal position, many of a bank's advances will be among its least-liquid assets.

8.5 Portfolio choice

In building up its portfolio of assets, then, a bank will be faced with the classic problem of portfolio selection. To earn satisfactory profits for its shareholders the bank will need to see that a significant proportion of its assets are relatively illiquid but profitable ones. To avoid the danger of failing to meet its liabilities through illiquidity, the bank will also have to invest an adequate proportion of its assets in liquid, but relatively unprofitable, securities. Banks are continually concerned with balancing profitability against liquidity. Every bank's shareholders will judge it by its success in doing so. Like so much of economics, the problems of banking reduce in the end to problems of portfolio selection—of choice between different assets.

9. Monetary policy

9.1 Secondary reserve ratios

Of course, bankers have to do all this within the constraints imposed by government policy. Indeed, because of the banks' asset structures, government policy can operate in several ways to affect the money supply. Over the years, the traditional method of open-market operations outlined earlier in the chapter has been increasingly supplemented, or replaced, by other devices. In the UK, for example, the 'primary' reserve ratio between cash and deposits has been supplemented by secondary ones. Thus, for example, during the 1950s and 1960s, British governments imposed a liquidity ratio at varying rates around 30 per cent. While Britain has now replaced the liquidity ratio by the $12\frac{1}{2}$ per cent reserve-asset ratio, the new system works in a similar way. Since the liquidity ratio is a simpler concept, and is more like the secondary reserve ratios used in other countries, we shall discuss the way the liquidity ratio has been used in Britain. The same principles apply to secondary reserve ratios in other countries and, indeed, to the new reserve-asset ratio.

9.2 A rise in the required liquidity ratio

(a) Sales of bonds

Suppose that the banks have previously been required to hold 30 per cent of their assets in liquid form (including cash) and that the government now raises the legally-required liquidity ratio to 32 per cent. This means that the banks have to convert some other assets into liquid assets. They can do this either by selling bonds or by calling in advances. The effects of the change in the liquidity ratio may therefore be of several kinds. If the banks are forced to sell government securities they must either sell them to the central bank or to the non-bank public. If they sell to the central bank, this will usually mean a switch from holding long-term government securities to holding treasury bills. However, if it wishes to reduce the liquidity of the banking system, the central bank will not buy the securities in question. If the banks then try to sell the securities to the non-bank public, the result may be a rise in the rate of interest. Purchasers for these securities may well not be found without there being a fall in the price of government bonds, especially if it is known that monetary policy is becoming more restrictive.

(b) Cuts in advances

If the banks do not wish to sell their securities, or if the price falls so sharply when they try to do so that they cannot sell except at a capital loss and so become 'locked in' to their existing holdings, the banks may see no alternative to reducing advances.

(c) Changes in asset structures

This may, for example, mean that the banks reduce the amount of money that they lend to private industry and take up treasury bills with it instead. If the treasury bills are newly issued, this will mean that money previously lent to private industry has gone to the government; if the treasury bills were previously held by private individuals the latter will now hold bank deposits instead of treasury bills. Changes in the structure of the banks' assets will then not alter the total money supply; but they will alter the type of asset held by various individuals and institutions. This is the way that monetary policy most often works at present. The aim is usually not so much to increase or reduce the money supply as to alter the asset structure of the community.

As we have seen, the change may be that the banks lend more to the government and less to individuals or to business. Or they may hold liquid assets previously held by the non-bank public who now hold bank deposits instead. Consequently, even if changes in the required liquidity ratio of the banks do not alter the money supply, they do affect the quantities of different assets held by different individuals, banks and other organisations. This is likely to affect their spending and therefore the level of the GNP.

For example, suppose that bank deposits previously held by industry now come into the hands of the non-bank public, which previously held treasury bills. The rise in the liquidity ratio may then result in the replacement of 'active' balances used by businesses with holdings of 'idle' cash by the public. Activity will fall. While monetary policy today is aimed more at affecting asset structures in the economy than at changing the volume of bank deposits, the monetary authorities can still affect the level of activity by changes in monetary policy.

9.3 Special deposits

In the UK, a further device is used. While not altering the required liquidity ratio, the government can compel the banks to put a certain proportion of their total liabilities, or of some part of their assets, into 'special deposits' with the Bank of England. While 'special deposits' earn interest comparable to that available on alternative assets like treasury bills, the former do not count as part of the liquidity ratio. By requiring the banks to make special deposits, the British government can ensure that adequate, or even comfortable, liquidity ratios become inadequate. For example, suppose the banks have been required to hold 25 per cent of their assets in a liquid form. The government now requires the banks to deposit 1 per cent of their assets in special deposits. The only way the banks can obtain funds to do this quickly will be by reducing their liquid assets. This means that the liquidity ratio will fall 1 per cent below the required level. The banks will therefore be forced to take the kinds of step we have outlined above to restore the liquidity ratio.

In practice, of course, the effect of changes in the liquidity ratio, or in special deposits, is not so much on the existing level of bank deposits as on the banks' opportunities to increase them. In the UK, the Bank of England will not refuse to allow the banks to run down treasury bills and increase cash. This means that so long as the liquidity (or reserve-asset) ratio is adequate, if the banks wish to increase their deposits they can do so by reducing their holdings of treasury bills and increasing the amount of cash that they possess. Given the cash/deposit ratio, this will enable multiple credit creation to take place. If the government does not want this to happen, an increase in the required liquidity (or reserve-asset) ratio will prevent the banks from expanding deposits. Its effect must therefore be seen as being aimed as much at preventing an increase in bank deposits as at bringing about a reduction.

9.4 The role of the central bank

Obviously, a great deal depends on who buys the assets that the banks have to sell in order to restore their reserve ratios. As we have seen, if banks are forced to sell gilt-edged securities and these are bought by the central bank, then, not only will the banks' liquidity position have improved; they will actually have more cash and will be in a position to increase the volume of bank deposits. To operate an increase in the liquidity ratio in a restrictive way, the central bank must force the banks either to sell their long-term securities to non-bank individuals or institutions, or to reduce the volume of their advances.

9.5 A restrictive effect

Of course, we have so far been discussing various ways in which the government can restrict the money supply, or otherwise work to reduce the level of activity. An increase in the level of activity can be brought about by reversing one or more of these policies. An increase in the money supply can be brought about by open market operations, where the central bank *buys* government securities. The liquidity position of the banks can be eased by a *reduction* in the required liquidity (or reserve-asset) ratio. It can be brought about by *repayment* of special deposits.

9.6 Quantitative credit control

Finally, governments in some countries have imposed detailed requirements on the rate of growth of particular kinds of asset. For example, some governments have announced that in the current year, the total of bank advances to businesses and individuals must not exceed, say, 106 per cent of the level at the end of the previous year. This is a much more precise method of control, and one British banks dislike intensely. However, it is a weapon that governments can use if they wish.

10. A summary

To sum up: the supply of money depends on the ratio of currency to bank deposits that the public wishes to hold; and on the ratio between their balances of cash and their total deposits that banks are legally-required, or find it prudent, to keep. Given these ratios, the banks will try to build optimum portfolios, balancing liquidity against profit-ability for each kind of asset. However, they have to do this within constraints imposed by the government. Among the methods of controlling the money supply that governments can use are: changes in (primary) cash/deposit ratios; changes in (secondary) liquidity or reserve ratios; and quantitative control over the size of particular types of banks' assets.

Between them, these devices ensure that governments can control the supply of money within fairly narrow limits if they are prepared to do so. In this book, we shall therefore assume that the supply of

P

money is determined by the government, working through the banking system.

Suggested reading

SAYERS, R. S.   *Modern Banking,* 5th edn., Oxford, 1960, chapters 1, 2 and 5.

JEVONS, W. S.   *Money and the Mechanism of Exchange,* London, 1875, chapter 3.

ROBERTSON, D. H.   *Money,* London, 1948, chapters 1 and 3.

JOHNSON, H. G.   *Essays in Monetary Economics,* London, 1967, chapter 1. This paper includes a lengthy bibliography which students will find extremely valuable.

19

Employment and income

1. A general theory

Having explained what money is, we can now return to the main theme of Part Two and explain the contemporary theory of macro-economics. What is it that determines the level of income, employment and activity in a *closed* economy, that is, an economy without international trade? Many of these ideas found their first expression in English in the *General Theory of Employment, Interest and Money,* by J. M. (later Lord) Keynes, published in 1936. The *General Theory* was intended to provide a more systematic and realistic explanation of the causes of unemployment than that given by the 'classical' economists, whose main ideas on this subject we outlined in Chapter 17. Keynes maintained that, especially by their acceptance of Say's Law, the 'classical' economists had assumed away the problems of unemployment.

The Keynesian theory was intended to be 'general' in the sense that it would apply equally to economies with less than full employment, in a way that the 'classical' theory did not. It is difficult to be sure whether Keynes' indictment of the 'classical' economists on this score is entirely fair, but they certainly discussed the problems of the general level of economic activity on so few occasions that it appears that they did not think them of particular importance. We shall have more to say later about the differences between contemporary macro-economic theory and 'classical' ideas. First, we must outline contemporary macro-economic theory as it has developed from its Keynesian origins.

2. Aggregate demand and aggregate supply

The essential idea is that, like all other economic problems, the level of activity in an economy is a matter of demand and supply. For any economy, one can construct an aggregate demand curve showing, for each possible level of employment in the economy, what the total demand for the products made by those employed in that economy will be. This curve will show the aggregate sums of money which all firms in the economy, taken together, *really do expect to receive* during the next period of time, if they sell the output produced by each different number of men. It represents expected receipts when different volumes of employment are offered to the labour force.

Similarly, the aggregate supply schedule shows what all firms in any economy *must expect to receive* from the sale of the output produced by those same numbers of men, if it is to be just worth employing them. Unless firms as a whole expect to cover their costs when they employ, say, X men, they will reduce the number of jobs they offer.

What we are saying is that for each possible level of employment there will be both an aggregate demand price and an aggregate supply price. This can be seen from Fig. 19.1. Up the y-axis are shown various

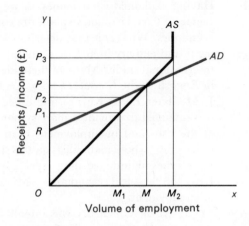

Fig. 19.1

amounts of receipts (income) earned by all firms in the economy taken together from the sale of output. This is, of course, the same thing, looked at from the other side, as the total expenditure by the community on the total output of goods and services. Along the x-axis are measured volumes of employment. The aggregate supply curve (AS) shows, for each possible amount of income received by firms from the sale of output, how many men it would be just worth employing at that level of income.

Let us consider the level of employment OM_1. The relevant point on the black aggregate supply curve shows that in order to find it worth while employing OM_1 men, all firms in the economy together *would have to receive* a total of £OP_1. £OP_1 is the aggregate supply price at the level of employment OM_1. Similarly, aggregate demand is shown by the brown aggregate demand schedule (AD). At the level of employment OM_1, the aggregate demand schedule shows that all firms taken together *really do expect to receive* £OP_2.

2.1 The level of employment

Let us look again at Fig. 19.1. We shall go further into the shape of the aggregate supply and demand curves later. For the present let us assume that, as employment rises from zero to a level where the whole labour force is employed, the total cost of output rises in proportion with employment. Once the whole labour force is employed, no more output is available and no increase in aggregate demand can increase employment further. The elasticity of supply of labour falls to zero once national expenditure (income) is £OP_3. The black, aggregate supply curve becomes vertical. Similarly, we assume that while there would be an aggregate demand of £OR if employment were zero, any rise in employment above zero will be accompanied by a proportionate increase in aggregate demand. The aggregate demand schedule is the straight brown line.

The aggregate supply and demand curves for any community therefore between them determine the volume of employment that all employers in the economy together will offer. Since we are assuming throughout Part Two that there is perfect competition, then, so long as profitable opportunities for providing extra employment exist (and they will exist so long as aggregate demand price exceeds aggregate supply price) competition between employers will force employment up. Thus, in Fig. 19.1, so long as employment is below OM, competition between employers will raise it. For, with employment less than OM, aggregate demand price is always greater than aggregate supply price. It pays to offer more jobs. Similarly, if employment is greater than OM, the aggregate demand curve lies to the right of the aggregate supply curve. All employers together expect to receive less at each level of employment than the minimum amount of money they require to make that amount of employment worth offering; they would lose money if they were to employ more than OM men.

2.2 Equilibrium of the economy

The level of employment in the community is therefore set at the intersection of the aggregate demand curve with the aggregate supply curve. Only if the amount of proceeds which firms *expect to receive* from providing any given number of jobs is just equal to the amount which they *must receive* if the employment of those men is to be worthwhile can the economy as a whole be in equilibrium? In Fig. 19.1, this will happen when employment is OM and total receipts of £OP are expected by employers. This is the only possible equilibrium position with the curves AD and AS in Fig. 19.1. However, while there will normally be only one position of equilibrium in any economy at any moment, this need not be at the full-employment level.

For example, in Fig. 19.2, two different equilibrium situations are shown. There is only one (black) aggregate supply curve (AS), but there are two different aggregate demand curves. With the dark-brown aggregate demand curve AD_1, the economy is in equilibrium with the expected receipts of producers at £OP and employment at OM. Since there are OM_1 men who want work, there is unemploy-

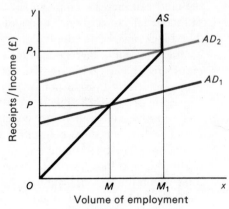

Fig. 19.2

ment of MM_1 men in this equilibrium position. It is perfectly possible for an economy to be in equilibrium and yet have men out of work. In this instance, only if aggregate demand is expected to be £OP_1, will all the available OM_1 men be employed. The light-brown aggregate demand curve AD_2 is one where employers *do* expect to receive just enough money to make it worth their while to give a job to everyone who wants one. OM_1 men are employed and, in the aggregate, firms receive £OP_1.

2.3 Under-employment equilibrium

This shows that nothing makes full employment inevitable. There will be full employment in an economy only if aggregate demand is large enough to make it worthwhile employing everyone who wants a job. The situation where equilibrium is at the full-employment level is an 'optimum' one, but full employment does not always occur by any means. An economy may just as easily be in equilibrium with some (or many) men unemployed.

2.4 Types of unemployment

An important point must be made here. The type of employment we have just described is *involuntary* unemployment. There are other kinds of unemployment too. There is *frictional* unemployment, where men are unemployed because they are changing jobs and are temporarily out of work. There is *structural* unemployment, where employment in one or more declining industries is falling. And there is *voluntary* unemployment, where some people are unwilling to work at all—at least unless wages rise. These three types of unemployment can be adequately dealt with on the basis of ordinary partial-equilibrium theory. Indeed, we discussed structural employment in Chapter 9. What we are concerned with here is the problem of involuntary unemployment—where workers from all (or most) industries in the country would be willing to work for the current wage, or even for less, but simply cannot find jobs. It is this which cannot be explained by partial-equilibrium price theory.

3. Aggregate supply

We have seen that the level of employment depends on the aggregate demand and the aggregate supply schedules. The aggregate supply schedule in turn depends ultimately on physical production conditions. As we saw in Part One, increased output in any industry is usually associated with increased employment. However, that increased output and employment must be paid for. So long as marginal costs are positive, increased output is worth producing only if extra payment is made for it. It follows that if more men are to be employed by any industry, enough extra receipts must be expected by that industry to make it worthwhile taking them on. The aggregate supply curve will therefore slope upwards to the right. More men will be employed if, but only if, employers expect to be paid more money for the larger output produced by these men.

3.1 The shape of the aggregate supply schedule

The aggregate supply schedule will slope upwards to the right. But what shape will it be? This is a difficult question to answer, but we shall ease our problems by making two simplifying assumptions which we shall retain until we reach Chapter 24. First, we shall assume that the money prices of all goods and factors of production are constant. Second, we shall assume that employment and national expenditure (measured at these constant prices) rise and fall in proportion with each other. That is to say, if national expenditure in money terms doubles, we assume that employment also doubles. This will make our task easier, but we must remember that the assumption is not altogether realistic. An extra £1 000 spent on the products of the economy will not always have exactly the same effect on employment. £1 000 spent on a capital-intensive product like steel would create less employment than £1 000 spent on services where little capital is used. Thus, while national expenditure and employment are likely to rise and fall together, there is no reason why they should rise and fall exactly in proportion. In other words, the aggregate supply function which relates the number of men employed to the level of national expenditure is unlikely to be linear. It is only for simplicity that we shall make the assumption that unemployment and expenditure change in exact proportion to each other.

On these assumptions, the aggregate supply schedule will have the shape shown in Fig. 19.2, though its steepness will depend on production conditions in the economy in question.

3.2 When aggregate supply should be ignored

The aggregate supply schedule, then, depends on technical production conditions. It depends on the productivity of the men, machines and raw materials available to the community. Now, while we are considering the static macro-economic problems studied in Part Two, the aggregate supply schedule is not worth studying in detail. The problems with which Part Two is particularly concerned are relatively short-run ones, and technical production conditions are likely to change only over longer periods. Keynes, of course, had another reason for largely ignoring the aggregate supply schedule. He was writing at a time of high unemployment (the early 1930s). He saw no point in discovering how to use resources more effectively (to produce the same output with fewer men) when there were men unemployed already. He largely ignored the problems of aggregate supply because he felt that it was aggregate demand which had received too little attention in the past.

We shall ignore supply conditions too, because we have discussed them fully in Part One. Nevertheless, because we shall ignore aggregate supply this does not mean that it is unimportant. It is only in studying the relatively short-run problems of an economy where there is a good deal of unemployment that one can ignore aggregate supply. There is then no point in supplying goods more efficiently. When there is full employment—and even more when there is inflation—an improvement in productive efficiency is the only hope for raising living standards. We therefore return to aggregate supply when we study inflation in Chapter 24 and in our analysis of economic growth in Part Three.

The aggregate demand schedule is the relationship we shall enphasise in Part Two.

4. Aggregate demand

Economists divide aggregate demand in a modern economy into three main parts. These are private consumption; public expenditure on current account (public consumption); and investment (public and private). We shall look at these in more detail soon. First, it will be useful to see how they link with the other main elements of national income and expenditure. We shall do this by considering a simplified, interlinked set of national income and expenditure accounts for a hypothetical economy, in Year X. This will be a closed economy, where there are no exports or imports. The country's currency happens to be the pound, but its national income figures are not the same as those for the UK, though they do bear some resemblance. Readers will find it useful to compare the figures for national income and expenditure in their own countries with these hypothetical ones.

5. Simplified national income accounts

The starting point of national income accounting is the fact that any 'mixed' economy, with public and private activities, can be divided into the sectors shown in Fig. 19.3. The proportions between the various sectors there are not intended to be realistic; the aim of Fig. 19.3 is only explanatory.

Fig. 19.3

5.1 The personal sector

We look first at the personal sector, made up not only of private individuals but also of private businesses—for example, partnerships, one-man firms and farmers. The income and expenditure of the personal sector is shown in Table 19.1. On the left-hand side, we list the sources of private income. The biggest proportion, as in all economies, is from wages and salaries (£30000m) but there is also a substantial income from rent, dividends and interest (£4000m). Our hypothetical economy is one where substantial social security benefits are paid by the government to those who are retired, ill or unemployed. These represent income for those who receive them, but we shall see that there is a substantial contribution towards these benefits (covering exactly 75 per cent of them) shown on the right-hand side of the account. These contributions come from those who have not yet retired and are neither sick nor out-of-work.

Table 19.1
Personal income and expenditure: Year X

£m			£m
Income		*Expenditure*	
Wages and salaries	30 000	Consumers' expenditure	27 000
Rent, dividends and		Taxes on income	5 000
interest	4 000	Contributions to	
Benefits received from		government benefits	3 000
the government	4 000		
			35 000
		Personal savings	3 000
	£m38 000		£m38 000

(a) Personal expenditure

We now turn to personal expenditure. Most of this is expenditure on consumer goods—food, clothing, accommodation, consumer durables (radio sets, television sets, automobiles, washing machines, etc.), travel, entertainment, holidays etc. There are problems of classification here. While cars bought by the personal sector are shown as consumer goods, cars bought by businesses are classified as part investment. Similarly, while the benefits from living in houses or other accommodation in Year *X* are included in consumers' expenditure, expenditure on houses themselves is classified as 'investment'. These problems of definition are important, but provided that the agreed definition is strictly applied they do not lead to serious problems.

(b) Disposable income

As we can see from Table 19.1, total consumer expenditure in our hypothetical economy in Year *X* was £27 000m, out of total personal incomes of £38 000m. However, this is not the relevant measure of income where consumer expenditure decisions are being made. The relevant measure here is *disposable income*.

Before a consumer is able to spend, he will have had deducted, or will have to deduct for himself, an amount to cover his income tax payments, and his contributions towards government pensions and other benefits. In Table 19.1, £5 000m is paid in income tax; while £3 000m goes in contributions to government benefits. This amount —personal income minus income tax and contributions towards government benefits—is known as *disposable income*. It is from this that consumers decide how much they will spend on consumer goods and how much they will save. They are free to 'dispose' of this income as they will. They cannot choose whether to pay tax; it is compulsory. It is the relationship of consumers' expenditure to disposable income that we shall look at in Chapter 20 when we discuss consumption. Here, disposable income is: £38 000m minus £5 000m (income tax) and £3 000m (contributions towards government benefits). It is £30 000m.

(c) Savings

The only item in Table 19.1 that is likely to cause any difficulty is 'savings'. In macro-economics, the standard definition of savings is that it is income minus consumption expenditure. We shall see later there are some ambiguities in this. For the moment, we can only appeal to the reader to accept this standard definition. Above all, readers should resist the temptation to identify what is done with savings: whether they are put in a bank account or a hire purchase company; invested in government securities; or spent on equities, houses or works of art. We shall see later that it is quite unnecessary to do this. Moreover, trying to do so leads to very great problems. Theoretical analyses which attempt to identify the sources and uses of savings in detail turn out to be extremely complicated. And any national income statistician will vouch for the fact that calculating the precise figures for savings disposed of in particular ways is impossible.

Fortunately, macro-economic theory does all we require of it without any need to identify the sources and uses of savings in detail. We simply define savings as income minus consumption. In the personal sector of our hypothetical economy, savings is therefore defined as the relevant income, here disposable income, which is £30 000m, minus consumers' expenditure of £27 000m. Saving is therefore £3 000m.

5.2 The corporate sector

We turn now to the corporate sector. Figure 19.3 shows that this is divided (though not necessarily equally) into private companies, large and small,[1] and public corporations (nationalised industries or other publicly-owned organisations). It will be noted that Fig. 19.3 shows that the total private sector is made up of the personal sector and the *private* part of the corporate sector. In Table 19.2 we therefore show the corporate income account of our hypothetical economy. This differs from Table 19.1 in that it is an income-appropriation account and not an income and expenditure account.

Table 19.2
Corporate income appropriation account: Year X

£m	Income		Expenditure	£m
Profits of private companies	6 000	Dividends and interest		3 000
		Taxation on profits		1 000
Profits of public corporations	2 000	Undistributed profits (corporate savings)		4 000
	£m8 000			£m8 000

(a) The appropriation of profits

Table 19.2 shows how the profits of corporations are allocated between payments to shareholders, taxation and earnings retained in the business. The reason why it is profits, and not the gross receipts of corporations (on the left-hand side), that interests us is this. It is true that firms spend money on raw materials, components, labour, etc., in making goods that earn gross revenue. It is also true that those who make raw materials, components and indeed the products from which the corporations themselves earn their gross receipts, receive income for doing so. However, we have already taken account of these incomes in constructing the income and expenditure account of the personal sector in Table 19.1. To include them again in corporate income would be to commit the cardinal sin of any national income statistician; we should be double-counting.

The left-hand side of the corporate income account therefore shows the profits of the corporate sector: these are £6 000m for private corporations, £2 000m for public corporations. On the right-hand side, we show how this £8 000m has been allocated. We see that £3 000m is paid out in dividends and interest and £1 000m in profits tax. We are *not* double-counting by including this £3 000m here. The £3 000m is part of the receipts (totalling £4 000m) from rent,

---

[1] British readers should note that what Companies' Act describes as a 'public company' is here being described as a private company, along with all other private companies. The point is that these are private bodies, not government corporations.

dividends and interest, shown in Table 19.1, as part of the income of the personal sector. Nor should it be deduced that total rents in the economy are £1000m. There are two reasons for this. First, rents, dividends and interest are also received by business and government as well as by the personal sector. Second, profits are calculated after any receipts of dividends and interest by companies, including, for example, interest on government debt held by companies. The personal sector will receive less than £3000m in dividends and interest from bonds and debentures. Again, the personal sector will receive interest from the public authorities.

(b) Corporate savings

After making allowances for all receipts from trading, property and other assets, corporate profits are £8000m, of which £4000m is paid out in dividends, interest and tax. Once again, we follow our rule about saving. Here, it is altered slightly to be: savings equals income after tax minus payments of dividents and interest. On our definition, the £4000m representing *retained earnings* are defined as savings.

5.3 The Public Authorities

We now turn to Table 19.3. Here, we again have an income (more accurately revenue) and expenditure statement, this time for the Public Authorities—Central and Local government. As Fig. 19.3 shows, the bulk of the public sector is made up of the Public Authorities—Central and Local government. The total public sector comprises the Public Authorities and Public Corporations.

Table 19.3
Current account of the Public Authorities: Year X

£m			£m
Receipts		*Expenditure*	
Taxes on income and profits	6000	Current expenditure on goods and services	10000
Taxes on expenditure	5000	Transfer payments:	
Taxes on property (rates, etc.)	4000	Subsidies	1000
Contribution to government benefits	3000	Benefits and grants from government	4000
		National debt interest	1000
		Current surplus (government saving)	2000
£m18000		£m18000	

*(a) Current
revenue*

Our hypothetical government obtains its tax revenue from three sources. First, there are income taxes. These are divided into income taxes proper, raising £5 000m from the personal sector, as shown in Table 19.1, and profits taxes, raising £1 000m from the corporate sector, as shown in Table 19.2. This gives total receipts from income taxes of £6 000m. Second, a further £5 000m is received from taxes on expenditure: sales taxes, value-added taxes, etc. Third, there is £4 000m raised from taxes on property. These include rates and other property taxes. There is also what can, in most contexts, be treated as another kind of tax—contributions towards government pensions and other benefits. There is no Public Authority income from property etc. If there were, it would appear on the receipts side. This gives total government revenue of £18 000m.

*(b) Current
expenditure*

More than half of this is spent on the current account by the government in purchasing goods and services. This includes payments for the services of members of the armed forces, doctors (our hypothetical government runs a national health service), teachers, civil servants and so on. It also includes current expenditure on military equipment (which is treated as current rather than capital expenditure), and expenditure on goods for hospitals, schools and offices, like bandages, books and paper. This is the government equivalent of the personal sector's expenditure on consumption: it is government consumption.

*(c) Transfer
payments*

The concept of government consumption should by now be a fairly familiar concept, but the next is not: transfer payments. We must explain what *transfer payments* are. Much of most people's incomes are made up of income from work (e.g. wages) or income from property (e.g. rents or dividends). However, some (or all) of many people's incomes is received in the form of pensions, unemployment benefits and so on. These are not incomes from work or property, but incomes paid to their recipients by society because of past work (pensions) or because of unfortunate circumstances (unemployment benefits). They are 'transfers' from one section of the community to another. They do not create national income, though they do create national expenditure. Indeed, national-debt interest (interest on government bonds, treasury bills, etc.) comes into the same category. It is a 'transfer' from those who do not hold national debt to those who do. Finally, subsidies are also transfers. They are payments from the rest of the community to supplement the incomes of farmers and others who would otherwise be paid less than it is thought desirable for them to earn. For example, farmers may earn less from producing food than is thought necessary, because prices are deliberately kept down by subsidies. In our hypothetical economy, total transfer payments—subsidies, pensions and other benefits and interest on government debt, total £6000m.

(d) Public Authority savings

Once again, we apply our general rule that savings are equal to investment minus current expenditure. This gives us savings of £2000m from the Public-Authority sector. It should be noted that this will not necessarily be equal to the size of the budget surplus announced by the Chancellor of the Exchequer or the Finance Minister. The definition of the budget surplus differs from country to country. Governments and legislatures do not always distinguish, as we are carefully doing, between current and capital expenditure. So, in arriving at a figure for government savings, we are simply applying our general rule: savings equal income minus consumption. Here, we are deducting from total government income (£18000m) an amount of £10000m for government consumption (expenditure on current account) and £6000m for transfer payments (which make particular private individuals' consumption possible).

Table 19.4
The combined capital account: Year X

£m			£m
Receipts		*Expenditure*	
Savings:		Gross fixed capital	
Personal	3000	formation	8000
Corporate	4000	Increase in volume of	
Government	2000	stocks (inventories)	1000
	£m9000		£m9000

5.4 The combined capital account
(a) Fixed investment

Next, we turn to Table 19.4. Up to now, we have been concerned with the incomes of the personal, corporate and government sectors and with their current expenditure. We now look at expenditure on investment. The right-hand side of the table shows the total amount devoted to investment in Year *X*. The first item is £8000m spent on fixed investment. This not only includes investment in plant, machinery and vehicles for the manufacturing (including nationalised) industries, for distribution and services. It also includes large amounts spent on houses, roads, hospitals, schools and other public buildings, as well as amounts spent outside the manufacturing, distributive and service sectors on vehicles, ships and aircraft. We have already explained that we are combining investment in the public and private sectors. In a country like the UK, large amounts of investment are made by the Central government in roads, schools, hospitals and other public buildings. There is also a large amount of investment in housing by Local government. In most countries, a very large amount of investment is required, especially in the early stages of development, on 'infrastructure': roads, railways, houses and other buildings of various kinds. Especially in the early stages of development, there are also large expenditures on investment in fuel and power, whether nationalised or private.

(b) Investment in stocks

The other item on the right-hand side of Table 19.4 is investment in stocks (inventories). All countries have large amounts of money tied up in holding stocks of raw materials, work in progress and finished goods—money tied up in working capital. Without this, no economy could operate. These are the buffers against fluctuations in the economy. If there are sudden increases in demand for some products, or strikes in industries supplying raw materials or components, stocks can be drawn on for a time. Supplies of raw materials and components do not run out immediately. Time is provided during which the economy can take whatever remedial action is necessary. The difficulties that can arise in an industry where only small stocks are held can be seen from the British motor industry. Strikes in one plant very soon lead to men being laid off in other plants depending on it for supplies.

In the UK, total stocks have a value equal to something like half the total national income. However, it is not total stocks that concern us here. What matters is that each year there will be an *addition* to these stocks. This can take place only if goods that might have otherwise been consumed are allowed to go into inventories. An increase in stocks is just as much an example of a country putting aside current output in order to be able to obtain future benefits as is fixed investment in the construction of a factory or a machine. In our hypothetical economy, total stocks have increased by £1 000m in Year X; there is investment in additional stocks of this amount.

(c) Total savings

In total, then, investment on our hypothetical economy is £9 000m. We now turn to the left-hand side of Table 19.4, where we show total savings. It must be obvious that at each stage in the construction of the simplified national income accounts we have been using the word savings to describe claims on resources which have *not* been exercised in the current period. In the personal sector, for example, the fact that total income was £38000m meant that goods and services to that value were available for consumption. The government took part of these through taxation and through contributions to government benefits, but this still left consumers with disposable incomes of £30000m. Consumers could have spent that total amount, since goods to that value have been produced in earning those incomes. What happened was that consumers did not exercise their potential claims in full. Instead, they left unspent £3000m of the money which could have been spent on consumer goods; they saved it. At this stage, therefore, we add together all these amounts of unexercised expenditure (of savings), by the personal sector, by firms and by government. These are the amounts which the various sectors have *not* spent on current expenditure: they show the value of resources left available for investment.

In other words, we have taken another step in what we are saying about savings. We are now saying not only that savings are equal to income minus consumption: we are also saying that savings are equal to investment. Again, things are not quite as simple as they might seem, but at this stage this is all we need to say. Just as any income which is not spent on current account can be defined as having been saved so, on our definition, savings and investment will always be equal.

Table 19.4 shows how many investment goods the economy has created during the year. At the same time it shows the extent to which the different sectors have refrained from exercising their ability to spend their incomes on current consumption, in order to leave resources available for the community to invest. Of course, the decision to refrain from consumption is not really as closely matched with the decision to invest as this implies. We looked at the problems which arise from this in Chapter 14 and shall return to them again in Chapter 20. For the moment, all we need to note is that, in national income accounting, savings and investment are always equal.

5.5 National income and expenditure (a) Gross national product

Finally, we consider Table 19.5. The left-hand side of this table will now be easily followed. What we do is to calculate national income by adding together the incomes of all the individual sectors. Thus, the left-hand side is made up of the following items: the wages and salaries of the personal sector, *as well as* their rents, dividends and interest, and the total profits of the whole corporate sector. We do not include any government income. Whether government income is from taxation or from contributions to government benefits, these are payments out of incomes that have already been included in those of the personal and corporate sectors. The only exception would be if, as some governments do, the government earned an income from its own trading. This would then be income of the government, to be included on the left-hand side of the national income account in just the same way as anyone else's income would be. Since there is no government profit here, we have only the four items on the left-hand side of the national income account, totalling £42 000m. This is *gross national income* or *gross national product*. Since all the incomes of the community are earned from producing the total national product —the total output of goods and services—then, by definition, gross national income must be equal to gross national product.

Table 19.5
National income and expenditure: Year X

£m			£m
Income		*Expenditure*	
Wages and salaries	30 000	Consumers' expenditure	27 000
Rent, dividends and interest	4 000	Government expenditure on current account	10 000
Profits:		Gross fixed capital formation	8 000
Private companies	6 000	Increase in the volume of stocks (inventories)	1 000
Public corporations	2 000		
		Total national expenditure at market prices	46 000
		Less taxes on expenditure	5 000
		Plus subsidies	1 000
Gross national product	£m42 000	Gross national product at factor cost	£m42 000

National income statisticians collect information about the income side of the account from such sources as the tax authorities. They also, partly as a check on the accuracy of these figures, collect information from the expenditure side. This comes from producers and traders about their sales. If all the information is accurate, then the two sides will be equal. However, before this can happen we have to make an adjustment.

*(b) Gross
national
expenditure*

On the right-hand side of Table 19.5, we list the figures for all sectors
of expenditure, obtained by collecting information from firms, shops
and other organisations which sell to the public. (We are assuming
here that the figures are accurate.) What we do is to take the relevant
items from Tables 19.1, 19.3 and 19.4, where information about
expenditure would be collected in this way. We then discover that
total national expenditure is made up of three main elements:
(i) consumers' expenditure; (ii) government consumption (government expenditure on current account); and (iii) investment (private
and public) in fixed capital formation and increasing the volume of
stocks (inventories). The total of these is £46 000m, made up in the
way shown in Table 19.5.

*(c) Market
price and factor
cost*

This £46 000m is known as gross national expenditure at market
prices. It is this item on which we shall concentrate in the rest of
Part Two. Readers will see that the figure of £46 000m for gross
national expenditure at market prices is different from the £42 000m
for gross national income. The difference is that the figure for *gross
national expenditure is at market prices*; the figure for gross national income
is at what is known as *factor cost*. We need to explain the difference.

We can best approach this by two examples. Suppose that a firm
sells a motor car for £1 200 but that £200 of this represents an
expenditure tax levied on motor cars (perhaps a value-added tax).
The market price of the car is £1 200. While this represents what
the purchaser pays, it does not show the value of the factors of production going into making the car. These are worth only £1 000. The
rest of the payment for the car is a payment of tax and does not
represent a payment to the factors of production which made the
car. The *market price* of the car is therefore £1 200; the *factor cost* of
the car is £1 000.

Now this is not to say that the market price actually paid for a
product (like this car), or indeed for total national expenditure on all
products at market prices, is not an important figure. As explained,
we shall use it in the rest of this part of the book. However, for many
purposes, economists find it convenient to know the other amount:
gross national expenditure at factor cost. It follows from what has
been said that we shall have to deduct from the figure for gross
national expenditure at market prices an amount equal to total
expenditure taxes to reduce the figure to gross national expenditure
of factor cost.

However, this is not all. Some goods are subsidised and not taxed.
Suppose that a loaf of bread costs 15p in a shop; its market price is
15p. The cost incurred by producers in making it will be 20p, if there

is a subsidy of 5p being paid to keep down bread prices. Here, we have the opposite case from the automobile. The market price is now less than the factor cost and we need to adjust upwards the figure for gross national expenditure at market prices in the national income accounts.

This explains the last two items on the right-hand side of Table 19.5. We have to adjust the figures for gross national expenditure at market prices. We have to deduct expenditure taxes in order to show the value of the factors of production going into the taxed products. We must add back subsidies for the same reason. This means deducting £5000m for expenditure taxes but adding back £1000m for subsidies (see Table 19.3). We end with the same amount as on the left-hand side: £42000m. We now have *gross national expenditure* (or *gross national product*) at factor cost, but it is now arrived at from the expenditure side.

This analysis makes clear that gross national income, gross national product and gross national expenditure represent the same sum of money. However, the way these are arrived at is different in each case. National income is the total of all personal and other incomes; national product is the value of the total output of goods and services; national expenditure is the total expenditure of the community.

6. How GNP is determined

As has been explained, we shall concentrate here on total expenditure. This gives us the basic macro-economic equation:

$$Y=C+G+I$$

where, Y is gross national income, or GNP; C is total personal consumption; G is total government expenditure on current account; and I is total gross investment, both private and public.

In the remainder of Chapter 19, we shall begin to explore the relationships between these four variables. Later, we shall look at consumption, investment and government expenditure on current account in more detail.

6.1 Consumption
(a) The consumption function

We begin by looking at consumption. In Chapter 20, we shall study the relationship between income and consumption in detail; we shall call this relationship the *consumption function* or, in Keynesian terminology, the *propensity to consume*. For the moment, let us suppose that the consumption function is of the form:

$$C=b+aY$$

This means that consumption is a function of GNP where b is a constant (OE) whatever the level of GNP. As income rises, consumption increases by a constant proportion of income: precisely, by aY. This is shown in Fig. 19.4.

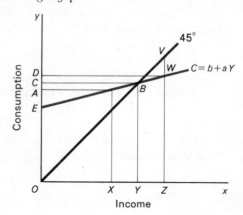

Fig. 19.4

(b) Equilibrium

An important element of the construction of this diagram is the black 45° line. Only when the function representing the variable we are considering (here consumption) cuts the 45° line is the economy in equilibrium at any level of income. The reasons are similar to those we looked at in explaining why aggregate demand equals aggregate supply earlier in this chapter. In Fig. 19.4, if income is greater than OY it will fall to that level. If it is less than OY, it will rise towards it. This is because the consumption function cuts the 45° line at B. Only here will expenditure on consumption (OC) continue to generate a level of income (OY) which will continue to give consumption expenditure of OC. The economy is an equilibrium because $OC = OY$. If GNP is initially bigger than OY, say at OZ, consumption out of this income of OZ will be only OD, given by the point where the brown consumption function cuts the line ZV. Income cannot be sustained at OZ. It will fall to OD. But out of an income of OD, less than OD will be consumed. It will fall again. If there is no expenditure except consumption expenditure (as this diagram implies) GNP will gradually fall to OY ($= OC$).

An expansion process will operate if GNP is less than OY. For example, at an income of OX, consumption will be OA. Income will rise to OA. But consumption will now be above OA. Income will rise again. A process of expansion will raise income until it reaches OY.

(c) A multiplier process

Observant readers will have noticed that OC is bigger than b, which is here equal to OE. With this consumption function, we do not simply have an income of OE. Yet it is only because there is this fixed element (b) in the equation, that OC *is able* to be bigger than OD. Let us look at this more closely, using algebra. We shall start from the basic equation: $Y=C+G+I$. For the moment, we are assuming that there is no government expenditure or investment. Our basic equation reduces itself to:

$$Y=C \quad . \qquad . \qquad . \qquad . \qquad . \quad (1)$$

Now, our consumption function is $b+aY$. We therefore replace C in equation (1) with $b+aY$. This gives us equation (2):

$$Y=b+aY \quad . \qquad . \qquad . \qquad . \quad (2)$$

We can now manipulate equation (2). Moving aY to the left-hand side, we obtain:

$$Y-aY=b$$

therefore

$$Y(1-a)=b$$

therefore

$$Y=\frac{b}{(1-a)}$$

Not only is income greater than b. There is a precise relationship between the level of income and b. Income will be $\frac{1}{(1-a)} \times b$. Moreover, a positive income can exist at all only because there *is* this fixed amount of b to be multiplied. If the consumption function had been $C=aY$, income would have been zero. We can therefore see that a multiplier 'process' is at work, where GNP is greater than the fixed elements like b. The size of this 'multiplier' is equal to $\frac{1}{(1-a)}$.

It is worth noting, at this point, that if income is to be sustained at OZ, in Fig. 19.4, then some other kind of expenditure of an amount WV will have to be made. This is the basic problem Keynes lighted on in the 1930s. The higher income is the bigger will be the gap between income and consumption; the bigger income is the more investment or government expenditure will be needed to sustain it. If there is difficulty in sustaining a high enough level of either or both, then income will fall, and employment with it.

6.2 Government expenditure

Before looking at the multiplier in detail, let us see what happens if there is some government expenditure on current account and some investment, as well as consumption. The simplest way to do this is to add constant amounts of investment and government expenditure to the amount of consumption we had in Fig. 19.4. In Fig. 19.5, we therefore draw the line $Y=C+G$ parallel to $C=b+aY$. We have increased expenditure at all levels of consumption by the constant amount of G. We can see at once that income rises by more than G. It rises from OC $(=OY_0)$ to OD $(=OY_1)$; and CD is bigger than G.

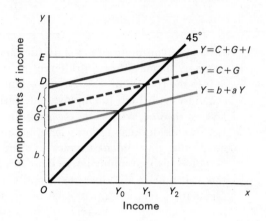

Fig. 19.5

6.3 Investment   Similarly, we now add a constant amount of investment (I) at all levels of expenditure, by drawing the line $Y=C+G+I$ also parallel to $C=b+aY$. We have an equilibrium income of OE $(=OY_2)$. Again, the increase in income (DE) is bigger than the amount of investment (I). Again the multiplier is at work, and again we can see its size by a little algebra.

Now, we really do have the basic equation:

$$Y=C+G+I$$

where $C=b+aY$, and G and I are constants. Again, we can rewrite the equation as:

$$Y=b+aY+G+I. \qquad . \qquad . \qquad . \qquad (3)$$

This equation can now be manipulated to give us:

$$Y-aY=b+G+I$$

therefore $\qquad Y(1-a)=b+G+I$

therefore $\qquad Y=\dfrac{b}{(1-a)}+\dfrac{G}{(1-a)}+\dfrac{I}{(1-a)}$

Again, the multiplier is at work. Again, it multiplies all the fixed elements (here b, G and I) by the same amount $\dfrac{1}{(1-a)}$. Indeed, this is a general principle. In any economy, the level of gross national product will be a multiple of the total of the constant elements in expenditure like b, G and I. The size of the multiplier will depend on the size of a. Economists have often denoted the multiplier $\dfrac{1}{(1-a)}$ by the letter k. Let us now look more closely at what a is and how the multiplier works.

7. The multiplier

Instead of continuing to explain the multiplier in terms of a whole economy, it may throw a different light on this concept if we look at it in the context in which it was originally developed. This was an economy with high unemployment. Instead of looking at the *total* level of income, we look at *changes* in investment, and so in income. Let us consider a situation where, because there is high unemployment, the government decides to spend £1m on building roads. National income immediately increases by £1m, but we have seen this will not be all. Investment and consumption stand in a complementary relationship to each other, so long as there is less than full employment. If there is unemployment and investment rises, consumption will rise with it. It is only when there is full employment that consumption and investment become competitive. An increase in one must then reduce the other.

7.1 The relationship between consumption and investment

Here, because there is unemployment, consumption and investment are complementary. When £1m more is spent on investment, workers in the investment industries spend their extra money on consumer goods. This raises the incomes of the consumption-goods workers, who in turn spend their money on further consumer goods. The initial extra expenditure of £1m results in a rise of several million pounds in the income of the community. This is the multiplier effect. The initial expenditure leads to bigger incomes for, in this case, road builders. This leads in turn to higher incomes for those on whose products road builders spend their extra incomes. GNP rises by more than £1m. Similarly, the total increase in employment resulting from the extra government expenditure will be greater than the number of men working on the original road-building scheme. The precise relationship between such an original increase in income (or employment) and the ultimate, total increase is given by the 'multiplier'. The multiplier is now an accepted part of macroeconomic theory. It was developed in the early 1930s by Mr. R. F. (now Lord) Kahn.[1] The essence of the multiplier is that it compares the relative sizes of an initial increase in investment and the total (direct and indirect) ultimate increase in income.

[1] 'The Relation of Home Investment to Unemployment', *Economic Journal*, June 1931, p. 173.

There are, however, two points which it will be useful to make here. First, we shall calculate the size of the multiplier, assuming that there is a net increase in investment over and above the preceding level. However, we shall assume that there are no further indirect effects on investment, or, alternatively, that any such indirect effects have been counted back into the original increase in investment. We can then confine our attention to the relationship between investment and consumption.

Second, we continue to assume that we are dealing with a 'closed' economy without international trade. If this were an 'open' economy, and if those employed within that economy could spend their money on imports, some of the increased consumption would provide income in other countries, and some of the multiplier effects would be lost. Any expenditure on imports constitutes a 'leakage' which reduces the size of the multiplier. Taxation constitutes a similar 'leakage'. It will, however, be offset to the extent that any extra money raised by taxation leads to an increase in government expenditure. It is not inevitable that there must be detrimental effects on employment.

7.2 The investment and employment multipliers

The effect of an increase in investment, working through the multiplier, is to increase both income and employment. There is both an investment (or income) multiplier showing the effect of an increase in investment on income, and an employment multiplier showing the effect on employment. The latter shows the total (direct and indirect) increase in employment divided by the direct initial increase in employment. Lord Kahn's original multiplier was an 'employment' multiplier and there is no reason why, in practice, the two multipliers should be the same. As we saw in Chapter 19, an increase in income may yield different increases in employment in different parts of the economy or at different times. However, for simplicity, we assume that the effects of any absolute increase in income on employment are always identical whatever the original level of income is. This means that while we concentrate our attention on changes in income, all that we have to say will apply equally to changes in employment.

7.3 The mathematics of the multiplier

We now turn to the mathematics of the multiplier. We have seen that the multiplier equals $\dfrac{1}{(1-a)}$, but what is a? The answer is that a is the *marginal propensity to consume*. Mathematically, if δY represents a small increment in income, and ∂C the resultant increase in income, then $\dfrac{\delta C}{\delta Y}$ is the marginal propensity to consume. It is the proportion of a small increment in income that will be consumed. So if a community's income rises by £1m and it spends £750 000 on consumption, the marginal propensity to consume is $\dfrac{£750\,000}{£1\,000\,000} = \frac{3}{4}$. This is what we have been denoting as a. Since the consumption function we have been using so far is linear, and of the specific form $C = b + aY$, it follows at once that a is the proportion of any extra income that is consumed. If one extra pound is received, the fraction a of that pound will be consumed. a is the marginal propensity to consume.

The multiplier, then, depends on the marginal propensity to consume; it is the reciprocal of one minus the marginal propensity to consume. However, there is an even simpler way of putting this. We have seen already that savings are equal to income minus consumption. It follows that if there is an increment in income δY and a proportion of this (a) is consumed, then the proportion saved is $(1-a)$. This proportion $\dfrac{\delta S}{\delta Y}$ is called the marginal propensity to save. We can see immediately that where k is the multiplier and s is the marginal propensity to *save*, then $k = \dfrac{1}{s}$.[1] With these formulae we can compute the numerical size of the multiplier, once we know the size of the marginal propensity to save or to consume. Suppose that, in a given economy, the marginal propensity to consume is $\frac{4}{5}$ and the marginal propensity to save thus $\frac{1}{5}$. Out of any increment of income of £100 the community will consume £80 and save £20. Now since the multiplier:

$$k = \frac{1}{\text{marginal propensity to save}}$$

and the marginal propensity to save is $\frac{1}{5}$:

$$k = \frac{1}{5},$$

therefore

$$k = 5.$$

This means that, for an investment outlay of, say, £1 000 the resulting total increase in income will be £5 000. A given increase in investment

---

[1] We know already that $Y = C + I$. It follows that $\delta Y = \delta C + \delta I$ (i.e. an increase in income is made up of an increase in consumption plus an increase in investment). Now we know that the multiplier, $k = \dfrac{\delta Y}{\delta I}$, and that the marginal propensity to save (s) $(=1$ minus the marginal propensity to consume) equals $1 - \dfrac{\delta C}{\delta Y}$. But since $\delta C + \delta I = \delta Y$, the marginal propensity to save $(s) = 1 - \dfrac{\delta C}{\delta Y} = \dfrac{I}{Y}$. So $\dfrac{1}{s} = \dfrac{\delta Y}{\delta I}$, which is the definition of the multiplier. Thus $k = \dfrac{1}{s}$, and $s = \dfrac{1}{k}$.

(and in employment) will cause a five-fold increase in total income (and in total employment).

If we want to work directly in terms of the marginal propensity to consume, we know that $k=\dfrac{1}{(1-a)}$. If $a=\frac{1}{3}$, then $k=\dfrac{1}{(1-\frac{1}{3})}=\dfrac{1}{\frac{1}{3}}=3$. We can always calculate k, provided we know either the marginal propensity to consume or the marginal propensity to save.

7.4 *The marginal propensity to consume*

In these calculations, we have ignored one very important point. In order to simplify the arithmetic we have assumed that the marginal propensity to consume remains constant over the relevant range of income. In practice, of course, this need not be the case, though we shall see in Chapter 20 that the assumption that the marginal propensity to consume is constant seems to be a realistic one. The marginal propensity to consume may fall once the initial investment raises income, and may continue to fall as income rises further. This in no way invalidates the result which we have obtained, though it does mean that the calculations involved become more complicated. The multiplier will change with each change in the marginal propensity to consume, as the process works itself out. In practice, one would need a measure of the 'average' marginal propensity to consume over the range of income in question. We shall ignore this here.

7.5 *Some complications*

It is also important to remember that the multiplier relates to a *net* increase investment (or indeed government expenditure). We have not considered what will be the effect of an increase in public and private investment together. We have ignored the possibility that instituting any particular government investment project might lead to a rise or a fall in other investment activity. Total investment (private and public) might rise by more or less than the amount spent on public works. Some economists even argued in the 1930s that it might decline, since the introduction of government-financed investment might discourage private investment. The net effect of any public works scheme therefore depends on whether private investment is discouraged or encouraged by the advent of a public works scheme and, if so, by how much. However, it must be emphasised that even if private investment falls off more than public investment has increased, this has nothing to do with the size of the multiplier itself. It merely means that the thing to be multiplied (the net increase in investment) is negative. In practice, all the evidence suggests that increased public investment, by raising employment, will lead to greater business confidence and hence to greater private investment. But again this has nothing to do with the multiplier. It means that the multiplicand (investment) has grown larger through the repercussions of the increased public investment on private investment.

7.6 Time-lags

The multiplier was an important part of the macro-economic system which Keynes set out in the *General Theory* and has remained an important part of modern macro-economics. However, Keynes ignored time-lags. These will be of two kinds. First, it will obviously take time before the full effects of an increase in, say, investment work through into GNP, by the operation of the multiplier. We shall look at this question again in Chapter 25. Meanwhile, we may note that for many purposes it is sufficient to use comparative statistics. Much economic theory is of this kind. What we do is to compare the stable situation, before the increase in investment took place, with the situation when the full effects of the multiplier process have worked out. This is precisely what we have been doing. When we say that the multiplier$=\dfrac{1}{(1-a)}$, we mean that the effect of an increase in investment on income will be multiplied by $\dfrac{1}{(1-a)}$ when sufficient time has elapsed for the process to work through completely.

Second, and more serious, of course, is the fact that there will not necessarily be a single discrete increase in investment. Before the multiplier has worked itself through, fresh investment projects may well have been undertaken and themselves be causing multiplier effects. The formulae given above show the level of income reached when the whole multiplier process has had time to work itself out. Where there are lags, the final equilibrium position will take longer to reach. The multiplier will still determine the size of the increase in income but the process will be more complicated than it would be if there were no lags.

7.7 Imports

Let us look, briefly, at the effect of imports and taxation on the situation. Let us suppose for the moment, that the economy is open and that out of each extra pound of income not only is the fraction (s) saved. The proportion (m) is also spent on imports: m is the marginal propensity to import. Suppose that $s=\frac{1}{4}$ and $m=\frac{1}{4}$. The marginal propensity to consume (a) is $(1-s)=\frac{3}{4}$. However, the proportion of an extra £1 spent within the country is not $(a=\frac{3}{4})$ but $(a-m)=\frac{1}{2}$.

The multiplier is now smaller than in an open economy. It is:

$$k=\frac{1}{1-(a-m)}.$$

In our example, where $a=\frac{3}{4}$ and $m=\frac{1}{4}$:

$$k=\frac{1}{1-(\frac{3}{4}-\frac{1}{4})}$$

therefore $\qquad k=\frac{1}{\frac{1}{2}}$

therefore $\qquad k=2.$

Instead of being 4 (as it would be in a closed economy) the multiplier is only 2.

7.8 Taxation

Taxation represents a similar leakage. Suppose that we have an economy where the budget is always balanced. So, if government expenditure $=G$, taxation is also G. We can now presume that consumption is out of *disposable* income (i.e. income minus taxation), as we saw in Table 19.1. For simplicity, we assume that the consumption function is $C=aY$. Consumption is now not aY; it is $a(Y-G)$. It is not the fraction a of income (Y) but the fraction a of *disposable* income, which is ($Y-G$). With taxation of G, government expenditure of G, and a balanced budget, income is:

$$\begin{aligned} Y &=a(Y-G)+G\\ Y &=aY-aG+G\\ Y(1-a)&=G-aG\\ Y(1-a)&=G(1-a)\\ Y &=\frac{G(1-a)}{(1-a)} \end{aligned}$$

therefore $\qquad Y \quad =G.$

GNP will equal government expenditure. Similarly, an increase in government expenditure of δG will raise income by δG. There is now a multiplier of 1, not of $\frac{1}{1-a}$.

7.9 The balanced-budget multiplier

A balanced-budget increase in government expenditure *does* have an expansionary effect, but only one equal to G. The reason is that although each extra £1 of government expenditure is matched by an extra £1 of taxation, the fraction a of that extra taxation comes from saving and *not* from consumption. The consumer does not reduce his consumption by G, when government expenditure is introduced, but only by aG. There *is* an expansionary effect which is known as the *balanced-budget multiplier*. On our assumption, the balanced-budget multiplier is always 1. GNP rises by exactly the same amount as government expenditure. Part of the money which would otherwise have been saved is being taken in taxation and spent by the government. This is why, although the budget is balanced, there is an expansionary effect. The lesson, of course, is that where budgetary policy is being discussed, things are not always as simple as they look. In particular, the effect of any increase or reduction in taxation will depend on how far that taxation is paid out of income that would otherwise have been saved.

7.10 The size of the multiplier

In conclusion, it may be worth saying something about the size of the multiplier. Obviously where the marginal propensity to consume is high, the multiplier will be large, and vice versa. If the marginal propensity to consume is $\frac{9}{10}$, the multiplier will be 10. If it is $\frac{1}{10}$, the multiplier will be 1·1. This dependence of the multiplier on the marginal propensity to consume is what one would expect. Where the marginal propensity to consume is low, any increase in wages paid, let us say, to road builders will be mostly saved. There will be little additional employment for those making clothes, electricity, washing machines, etc., as a result of this increase spending by road builders.

One limiting case will occur where the marginal propensity to consume is zero. Here none of the income created by employing more road builders will be spent at all. The total increase in income will be equal to the increase in the income of road builders. The marginal propensity to consume is 0 and $k=1$. The multiplier will therefore usually be greater than 1, because it is unlikely that the marginal propensity to consume will be zero.

The other limiting case is where the marginal propensity to consume is equal to 1. Here, all of any increased incomes earned by road makers employed on public works will be spent. This will add to the incomes of shopkeepers who will in turn spend *all* their increased incomes, and so on. The multiplier will therefore be infinitely large, $k=\infty$. The process will continue for an indefinite length of time if no further change in data takes place. In such circumstances, the government would need to employ only one road builder to raise income indefinitely, causing first full employment and then a limitless spiral of inflation. This case is just as unlikely as the one when $k=1$. It is certain that the real-world multiplier will be greater than one but less than infinity.

7.11 The multiplier in practice

Keynes's view of the size of the multiplier was that 'in actual fact, the marginal propensity to consume seems to lie somewhere between these two extremes' (i.e. 0 and 1), 'though much nearer to unity than to zero; with the result that we have, in a sense, the worst of both worlds, fluctuations in employment being considerable, and at the same time, the increment of investment required to produce full employment being too great to be easily handled'.[1] Recent evidence suggests that, for the UK, the multiplier is around 2. It is as low as this, not least because of progressive taxation. Progressive taxation means that when the multiplier raises income, an increasing proportion of this income is taken in taxation. The higher income is, the smaller the *net* effect of an increase in investment on income, unless the government spends the extra income it raises from taxation. If the government does *not* spend the extra revenue, we do not have the balanced-budget multiplier at work. Indeed, economists talk of progressive taxation as a 'built-in stabiliser'. If income increases, higher marginal rates of taxation tend to keep consumption down; if income falls, lower marginal rates of taxation tend to keep consumption and income up. If the aim is stability, this is attractive. If the aim is to increase gross national product in times of unemployment, some of the attractiveness of progressive taxation disappears. After all, a multiplier as small as 2 will mean that a substantial part of the task of increasing income is likely to fall on increases in investment or government expenditure.

Suggested reading

KEYNES, J. M.   *General Theory*, London, 1936, chapter 3.

BAUMOL, W. J.   'More on the Multiplier Effects of a Balanced
and   Budget', *American Economic Review*, 1955, p. 140.
PESTON, M. H.

[1] *Op. cit.*, p. 118.

20

Consumption

1. The consumption function

We have seen that, leaving aside government expenditure on current account, the GNP is the sum of the amounts spent on private consumption and on investment (private and public). For the moment, we shall ignore investment and concentrate on consumption. Total private consumption expenditure in any country will depend on the consumption decisions of individual members of the community. The sum total of the amounts which separate individuals spend on consumption is the amount spent by the community as a whole. This sounds obvious, but it is important to begin from individual decisions.

We start this chapter by considering the factors which determine the consumption of an individual and proceed to discover what determines the consumption of the whole community. Statistical investigation shows a fairly stable functional dependence of consumption on disposable income for the whole community, just as the amount of a good that is demanded shows a functional dependence on price. There also appears to be a fairly stable relationship for the individual. So where, for an individual consumer, C=consumption and Y=disposable income, the consumption function is: $C=f(Y)$. Here, f shows the functional relationship between disposable income and consumption. As we have seen, Keynes called f the *propensity to consume*, but the term *consumption function* is more often used now. If we can discover the nature of the consumption function for an individual, we shall know how much he will spend on consumption out of any given income.[1]

1.1 The function: $C=aY$

Our task is to discover what generalisations can be made about the consumption function. While the evidence suggests a fairly stable functional relationship between consumption and income both for

---

[1] We have seen that, strictly, we are concerned with *disposable income*. For simplicity, we shall henceforth write income and leave readers to remember that throughout this chapter we are really concerned with disposable income.

the individual and the community, the actual relationship appears to differ according to the length of the period of time studied. We begin by looking at some possible functional relationships between consumption and income, and proceed to explain which of these relationships econometric studies have identified in practice. The simplest possible relationship would be of the form:

$$C = aY \qquad . \qquad . \qquad . \qquad . \qquad . \qquad . \qquad (1)$$

(a) The marginal propensity to consume

Here, C will always represent a constant percentage (a) of income, Y. If a were $\frac{3}{4}$, this consumer would always consume £0·75 out of any extra £1 of income. Every time he received an extra hundred pounds, he would spend seventy-five of it on consumption. This is the marginal propensity to consume, and here it is a constant. It will be a. The marginal propensity to save (s) will be $(1-a)$.

(b) The average propensity to consume

We may sometimes wish to look, instead, at the consumer's *average propensity to consume*. This is the proportion of his *total* income which he consumes at any level of income. If a consumer has an income of £2000 and spends £1500 on consumption, his average propensity to consume is $\frac{3}{4}$. He is spending $\frac{3}{4}$ of his total income on consumption. It follows from what we have said already that the average propensity to save is $\frac{1}{4}$.

We can now say a little more about our simple consumption function. In equation (1) $C = aY$. With this *particular* consumption function the marginal propensity to consume always equals the average propensity to consume. If the consumer always spends the same fraction (a) of any *extra* income on consumption goods, he obviously spends the identical fraction (a) of his *total* income on consumer goods. However, it is important to realise that the marginal propensity to consume equals the average propensity to consume only in simple cases like this where the consumption function is linear and passes through the origin.

(c) A diagram

We show the simple consumption function in equation (1) diagrammatically in Fig. 20.1, where we have income on the x-axis and consumption on the y-axis. The consumption function shown here is $C = aY$, with a equal to $\frac{3}{4}$. It will be seen that we are assuming, as we shall do throughout this chapter, that the consumption function has no 'kinks' in it. It is not merely stable, but smooth as well.

R

All this can be summarised algebraically. Where dY represents a very small increase in income, and dC represents the resultant increase in consumption, dC divided by dY is positive but less than 1. That is:

$$1 > \frac{dC}{dY} > 0.$$

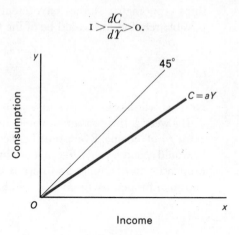

Fig. 20.1

We are here making the one assumption that *must* be correct in the long run, namely, that everyone consumes something, and that no one consumes more than his total income. This may happen for a time, though it is not normal. As Mr. Micawber and others have pointed out, the long-run result is usually disastrous. Our rule seems valid: everyone consumes something and hardly anyone consumes more than he earns for very long.

1.2 The function: $C = b + aY$

A little reflection on these issues will lead one to doubt whether any consumption function *can* be of the form $C = aY$. If income is zero, consumption is zero too, so that the consumer will starve to death. In the long run, at any rate without social security systems or rich benefactors, this is what would have to happen. In the short run, the consumer will do all he can to stay alive; to keep his consumption above zero. He will do this, if necessary, by drawing on his savings or by borrowing. Indeed, in most countries social security benefits paid by the state will ensure that his income does *not* fall to zero.

(a) A diagram

Reflection may well lead to the conclusion that the consumption function ought to be of the form met with in Fig. 19.4:

$$C = b + aY \qquad . \qquad . \qquad . \qquad . \qquad . \qquad (2)$$

In Fig. 20.2, the line BL denotes such a consumption function. If income, measured on the x-axis, falls to zero, consumption does not fall to zero, but to OB. In equation (2), b is represented by the amount OB; aY is represented by the straight brown line BL. Its slope is equal to a in equation (2). Again, a represents the marginal propensity to consume; once more it is constant.

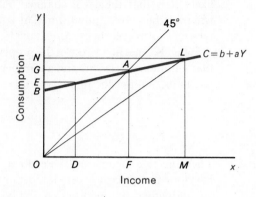

Fig. 20.2

(b) The marginal and average propensities to consume

However, we now have to distinguish between the marginal and average propensities to consume. Since equation (1) for the consumption function was $C=aY$, the average propensity to consume was always equal to the marginal propensity. In equation (2), we have to allow for the constant element b. While the marginal propensity to consume (a) is again constant at all levels of income, the average propensity to consume falls steadily as income rises.

At low levels of income, consumption is greater than income, so that the average propensity to consume is greater than 1. In Fig. 20.2, with an income of OD, consumption is OE. The average propensity to consume (the proportion which total consumption bears to total income) is $\dfrac{OE}{OD}$. This is obviously greater than 1, since OE is longer than OD. As income rises to OF, consumption rises more slowly to OG. OF equals OG, because A lies on the 45° line. At A the average propensity to consume is 1; the whole of income is consumed. Once income exceeds OG, the average propensity to consume falls below 1. It continues to diminish as income rises. For example, when income has risen to OM, the average propensity to consume, represented by the slope of OL, has fallen considerably below 1. This was its size (shown by the slope of OA) when income was OF.

2. Factors underlying the propensity to consume

Our aim in this chapter is to discover a general relationship between income and consumption—the consumption function. It will therefore be helpful if we can rule out any other factors (apart from income itself) which affect the propensity to consume. We can then concentrate our attention on changes in income. We must therefore discover what are the other factors which may affect consumption and how likely it is that they will change. This will enable us to discover whether the consumption function is likely to be the rather stable relationship which the statistical evidence suggests.

When Keynes first wrote of the propensity to consume, he suggested that a number of *objective* and a number of *subjective* factors lay behind it. Let us consider the important ones.

2.1 Objective factors
(a) Prices

The objective factors are these. First, there are prices. We saw in Part One that prices are very important in determining the amount of any individual commodity that will be consumed. If we assume that his income and the characteristics and prices of all other goods are given, a consumer's purchases of any individual good can be assumed to depend solely upon its price. A substantial change in its price will lead to a substantial change in purchases, unless elasticity of demand is low. When we consider all goods together, any individual price is less important. Admittedly, a substantial rise or fall in the general price level cannot be ignored, since it will change real incomes considerably; it will alter the real value of money substantially. But even if there is a quite large change in one individual price, the effect on the general price level will be quite small. At present, we shall assume that all prices are constant. Any proportional change in money income will then be equal to the resulting proportional change in real income. This is important, because the consumption function is ultimately a relationship between *real* income and *real* consumption. Our assumption allows us to look at this relationship without being distracted by differences between changes in real and in money income or consumption. We can add the complications of a changing price level later.

(b) Fiscal policy

A second objective factor is fiscal policy. Changes in fiscal policy, especially in taxation, are likely to be much more important for consumption expenditure than changes in prices. We must allow for fiscal policy later, but we ignore it here.

(c) Depreciation allowances

The third possible change in objective conditions is a change in the amount of their earnings which businessmen set aside to cover depreciation on their factories, machines, vehicles, etc. If these amounts were increased, and were invested, this would raise investment. If they were saved, it would probably reduce the size of some other variables in the economy, perhaps spending out of dividends. However, we can safely assume that the amount of earnings retained in order to cover depreciation will not change very significantly in the short run, except where the price level is changing rapidly. Since we are assuming a constant price level, we can also assume that depreciation allowances are constant.

So far, we have seen that the two objective factors which are most likely to lead to changes in the consumption function are the level of prices and fiscal policy. We have explicitly ruled out the possibility of such changes at this stage.

(d) The rate of interest

The fourth of the objective factors we must consider is the rate of interest. In practice, changes in the rate of interest are unlikely to have a very important effect on the level of consumption. However, we cannot leave the matter there. In the analysis in Chapter 14, we gave an outline of the partial-equilibrium theory of interest. We showed that if consumers were to be persuaded to consume less the rate of interest would have to rise, assuming that the income of the community was constant. Pre-Keynesian economists put some emphasis on their belief that if the rate of interest rose, people would save more and consume less; if it fell, they would consume more and save less. This sounds reasonable enough. How can we now maintain that the direct effect of the rate of interest on consumption is negligible?

So far as the individual consumer is concerned, it certainly does seem to be dangerous to assume that a fall in the rate of interest will increase consumption, and vice versa. This could be the normal response, but it is by no means certain. Suppose, for example, that a man with an income before tax of £4000 p.a. is saving for his old age and invests his savings in gilt-edged government securities. He hopes, at the end of his life, to have £2000 (before tax) coming from his investments. If the rate of interest is 5 per cent, he will know that he must buy £40000 worth of securities. Over his lifetime he will then save £40000, which will give him the necessary retirement income of £2000 a year. If the rate of interest now rises to 10 per cent, what will happen? Our investor can, of course, continue with his plans to save £40000. On this, he will now receive £4000 a year and will enjoy a merry old age. However, if he is quite content with £2000 a year, he need save only £20000 instead of £40000. Similarly, a man wishing to leave a given income from government securities to his children will need to save less if the rate of interest rises. Even if the rate of interest does have a marked effect on the savings of some people, the effect will not always be in the same direction. If the interest rate rises, some people may save more but others will save less. For the community as a whole, there is bound to be a certain amount of cancelling out and there may not be much net effect either way.

We shall therefore assume that people make their decisions about how much to save and how much to spend almost independently of the rate of interest. We shall suppose that the amount of money which people put aside to prepare for whatever the future may hold in store does not depend significantly on the rate of interest. Certainly, rainy days in the metaphorical sense are not closely related to the rate of interest. We shall argue, as Keynes did, that the rate of interest can and should be ignored as a factor directly affecting the propensity to consume.

We have now given the reasons for our provisional assumption that with the exception of changes in money income, no change in *objective* economic conditions will significantly affect the individual's propensity to consume. We have admitted that the propensity to consume may not remain stable over long periods, because external changes may well have some effect on the individual's long-run consumption. Since we are concerned only with outlining a relatively simple theory of employment, and since we are concerned with the short run rather than the long run, we can exclude the possibility that big changes in objective economic conditions will affect the consumption function. ·

2.2 Subjective factors

We must now proceed to consider the possibility that changes in *subjective* factors will affect the consumption function. Fortunately, we can be quite confident that any such changes which do take place will occur only in the long run. Short run changes are likely to be quite unimportant. In considering the subjective factors which affect the propensity to consume, Keynes was much more realistic than earlier economists. The 'classical' economists tended to over-simplify the psychological background to any decision to save. They represented it merely as a choice between present and future consumption. They stressed the virtue of thrift and made all decisions of this kind into choices between 'jam tomorrow and jam today'.

(a) For the
individual

Keynes brought a welcome breath of realism. He regarded decisions to consume or save as far more than choices between the present and the future. He maintained that the individual who decides to save is often motivated by such feelings as price and avarice, caution or greed. He may wish to have enough wealth to be able to hold his head high, to bequeath a fortune to his heirs, to provide a reserve for meeting such unforeseen difficulties as illness or unemployment, or merely to satisfy his miserly instincts. Nor did Keynes think that all these subjective motives were ones which increased savings. Each subjective motive which increased savings had a counterpart which reduced them. He pointed out that the desire for ostentation may lead to high expenditure. An extravagant or a careless man may waste his money. A generous man may give it away. A man who cares little for his heirs may bequeath them nothing.

(b) For the firm

Similar motives will lead businesses to put aside much or little. Firms with careful or cautious managements will put aside more of their funds than other managements do. Firms will set aside funds for emergencies, or to carry out investment and expansion in the future. This will reduce the community's consumption. Some firms, being more cautious or more far-sighted than others, will save more. Others will save less. Some firms may pay the biggest dividends they can. Some will not be interested in expansion and therefore will not put funds aside to finance investment. The strength or weakness of all these motives will affect the propensity of the community to save (and consume).

Fortunately, significant short-run changes in the subjective factors influencing the propensity to consume are unlikely. Keynes said that these subjective consumption habits depend largely on 'those psychological characteristics of human nature and those social practices and institutions which, though not unalterable, are unlikely to undergo a material change over a short period of time except in abnormal or revolutionary circumstances'.[1] We shall therefore assume in what follows that, in the short run at any rate, the propensity to consume will be unaffected by changes in subjective factors.

3. The
Keynesian
consumption
function

We can now go on to study the consumption function, but one point first needs to be emphasised about national income statistics. It is important to realise just how recent a phenomenon they are. In the USA, there were no national income figures at all before 1934, while

[1] *General Theory*, p. 91.

in the UK official national income statistics were published only after 1939. It follows that when Keynes was writing about the propensity to consume in the 1930s, he could not rely on much statistical information in deciding what its character might be.

3.1 Keynes's view

Keynes thought that the propensity to consume was like that shown in Fig. 20.3. He thought that if income rose by a given absolute amount, say £100, consumption would rise by a smaller absolute amount. Mathematically, $1 > \dfrac{dC}{dY} > 0$. Keynes also believed that the

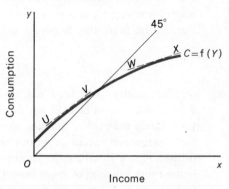

Fig. 20.3

marginal propensity to consume would decline as income increased. This means that, in Fig. 20.3, the 'Keynesian' consumption function is like the brown curve. A tangent closer to the origin, like UV, is steeper than one farther away, like WX. And, at any level of income, a tangent like UV or WX, represents the marginal propensity to consume.

(a) A diminishing marginal propensity to consume

Let us put this in words. While Keynes assumed that no one would consume the whole of any increase in income, he did assume that the richer a person was the less he would consume out of any absolute increase in income. For example, a man with an income of £1 500 might be spending £1 400 on consumer goods. If his income now rose to £1 550, he might consume only, say, £40 of the increase. Out of a further increase of £50 in his income, he might consume only £35, and so on. The assumption of a diminishing marginal propensity to consume was an important part of Keynesian theory. It assumed, among other things, that as income increased a progressively bigger proportion of national income would be saved. In order to maintain full employment, therefore, an increasing proportion of expenditure would have to be devoted to investment. This might well lead to difficulties, if such investment was hard to provide. The difficulties which we saw in Fig. 19.4, with a linear consumption function, would be even bigger. The intention of investment is to produce benefits of one kind or another for the consumer; an economy where increasing investment was accompanied by proportionately smaller increases in consumption, would probably be one where business became progressively less profitable and investment correspondingly more difficult to generate as GNP rose.

Let us look more carefully at the kind of consumption function Keynes was concerned with in Fig. 20.4. As with our linear consump-

Fig. 20.4

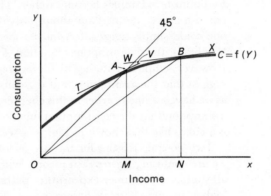

tion function in Fig. 20.2, there is some consumption expenditure even when income is zero. The excess of consumer expenditure over income then declines steadily until, when income is OA, income and consumption are equal. This is shown by the fact that the 45° line passes through A. The average propensity to consume at any point on the consumption function $C=f(Y)$ is shown by the slope of a straight line from the origin to a point like A or B. It will be seen that at higher levels of income the slope of a line like OB is flatter than that of the line accompanying a lower level of income, like OA. The average propensity to consume is lower when income is ON than when it is OM. The marginal propensity to consume is given by the slope of the tangents to the points A and B. As we have seen, it is lower when income is higher. It also follows, and this will be true of any consumption function that is not linear through the origin, that at all levels of income the average propensity to consume is higher than the marginal propensity to consume. This is clear in Fig. 20.3 because, at any point like A or B, the tangent showing the marginal propensity to consume is flatter than the line from the origin (like OA or OB) showing the average propensity to consume. So, for example, the tangent TV at A, is flatter than the line OA. Because of his assumption of a diminishing marginal propensity to consume,

Keynes was bound to assume that this was the case. Finally, like us, Keynes believed that the consumption function was a smooth, continuous function of income.

3.2 Family budget data

Keynes's assumptions were not based on any rigorous theory. They seemed to depend on an intuitive feeling, no doubt influenced by what Keynes knew of studies of family budgets. However, for the individual consumer, or family, they do seem to be supported by empirical studies. The marginal propensity to consume does seem to diminish as families become richer. The doubts are over whether one can aggregate the data about individuals. Keynes assumed that one could simply aggregate what happened to individuals in order to obtain the consumption function for the whole community. However, empirical studies of the aggregate consumption function suggest that the assumption that the consumption function is linear, as we have assumed earlier in this chapter, is more accurate. Keynes's assumption that the consumption function for the whole community is a curve like that shown in Fig. 20.4 seems to be wrong.

Two possible reasons for this are as follows. First, it may be that we are confusing *differences* in income with *changes* in income. Almost all studies of consumer expenditure patterns show that families with higher incomes save a higher proportion of those incomes than families with lower incomes. These studies do not look at the same family at different points of time; they look at different families at the same point of time. They are therefore valid for *differences* between the incomes, and therefore consumption expenditures, of a number of families all observed at the same point of time. What such studies cannot show us, because we cannot trace what happened to *individual* families over time, is what would happen if the income of *every* family were to increase by the same proportion at a given point of time.

(a) Relative versus absolute income

Statistical evidence suggests that, certainly after a longish period of time, the whole cluster of families would save roughly the same *proportion* of income as before. In other words, if the incomes of a whole spectrum of families increased in the same proportion, the savings of the poorer families would rise a little. Their savings would not rise to reach the same proportion of income as had previously been saved by richer families in the spectrum, when they were at those income levels. The average propensity to consume of the whole group of families would not change much.

Perhaps an example will help to show what this means. Let us suppose that there are two families, one with an income of £1 500 and the other with an income of £2 000 per annum. Suppose that the family with the income of £1 500 is saving £100 per annum, while the family with the income of £2 000 is saving £200. Now suppose that the income of the poorer family rises to £2 000. Its savings are unlikely to rise to £200. If the aggregate savings of all families are initially $\frac{1}{10}$ of their aggregate incomes, they are likely to remain at $\frac{1}{10}$ of these aggregate incomes once everyone has adapted to the rise in incomes.

3.3 The demonstration effect

These facts suggest the hypothesis, put forward by Professor Duesenberry, that consumer expenditure depends on *relative* rather than absolute incomes. The reason why the consumption function may be linear rather than curved, as income rises, may be that it is the income of a family *relative to that of other families* which determines how much it saves. Families may base their spending not only on their own tastes but on the tastes, and so the expenditures, of their neighbours. This idea, put forward by Duesenberry soon after World War II, has been christened the 'demonstration effect', or the 'Duesenberry effect'. We might call it the 'keeping up with the Joneses effect'. People want to *appear* to others to be able to spend as much money as the Joneses. The demonstration effect certainly provides a possible explanation of the observation that consumption functions are linear rather than curved.

If it is true, this hypothesis explains why the consumption function is linear for increases in income.

3.4 The ratchet effect

A reason why the consumption function may be linear, and not curved, if income falls has also been provided by Duesenberry. He suggests that when income falls consumers try hard to maintain their consumption expenditure at the highest level previously reached. They may again do this because they do not want their neighbours to see that they can no longer afford that previous level of consumption expenditure. They may do it simply because they have grown accustomed to the previous level of consumption. Whatever the reason, if this is what happens it means that a fall in income leads to a smaller reduction in consumer expenditure than one would expect from family expenditure studies. The reduction in consumer expenditure will also be smaller than one would expect if one had traced the way in which consumption, as a proportion of income, had gone up earlier as income increased. There is what is often called a 'ratchet effect'. The consumption function is not reversible.

Duesenberry therefore suggests reasons why the consumption function for the whole community may be flatter than family budget surveys would suggest. If income increases, savings may not go up very much because of the 'demonstration effect'. It is *relative* rather than absolute incomes which determine the size of consumption expenditure. If income falls, consumption expenditure may not fall much, because of the 'ratchet effect'. People try hard to cling to their previous levels of consumption expenditure, and reduce savings to some extent in order to do so. Although not accepted by all economists, particularly Professor Milton Friedman, Duesenberry's hypothesis does provide a coherent explanation of what econometricians appear to have discovered, namely, that the aggregate consumption function is linear rather than non-linear.

4. The short-run and the long-run consumption function

However, there is another puzzle to be unravelled as a result of econometric studies. Some economists have looked at the behaviour of the consumption function over long periods of time—decades or longer. The most important studies, perhaps, are those of Nobel prize-winner Simon Kuznets, in the USA. His studies suggest that, in the long run, the marginal propensity to consume in the USA is reasonably constant and not far from 1; usually between 0·85 and 0·95. The long-run consumption function appears to be of our simple form:

$$C = aY$$

with a around 0·9.

For shorter periods of time, it seems that our second equation:

$$C = b + aY$$

is the right one, with a substantially less than 1·0. How can we resolve this apparent contradiction? Why does the consumption function appear to be a straight line, but steeper over long periods than over short ones and with a vertical intercept only in the short run?

4.1 Smithies' ideas

One possible answer has been suggested by another American economist, Arthur Smithies. In 1945 he suggested that, as shown in Fig. 20.5, the short-run consumption function may move gradually up the long-run one. While in a short period of time an increase in income would increase savings substantially, say along CF_1; over longer periods the kind of proportion (around 0·9) discovered by Kuznets would apply. The long-run consumption function (LCF)

is the dark-brown straight line in Fig. 20.5. The explanation Smithies suggested was that factors like the movement of the US population from urban to rural areas or the introduction of new products might, over time, lead to changes in consumption patterns.

We may suggest a rather naive, but more general variant on this, which seems to be fairly near the truth. Perhaps it does take time to

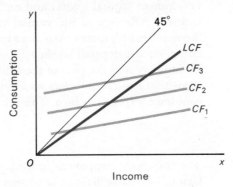

Fig. 20.5

get used to a higher level of income. After a period of two or three years, when consumption has been fairly stable, *either* the fact that consumers become used to higher incomes, *or* that fact plus the fact that new products have been introduced, moves the flatter short-run consumption function up the steeper long-run one, as in Fig. 20.5. After a time, it moves up to CF_2; later, it becomes CF_3. Certainly a study of statistics for the USA suggests that the short-run consumption function shifts upwards fairly sharply, at discontinuous intervals of perhaps three or four years. Something similar may happen in the UK.

However, these are not coherent theories. A number of economists have provided such theories and we must look at some of them.

5. The permanent income hypothesis

First, there is the *permanent income hypothesis* put forward by Milton Friedman.[1] Friedman argues that both income and consumption are better treated as divided into two parts: a permanent and a transitory part.

5.1 Permanent income

There is permanent income, which one expects to go on receiving over time; there is transitory income, which is made up of positive or negative amounts added to (subtracted from) this level. Friedman

[1] Milton Friedman, *A Theory of the Consumption Function*, Princeton, 1957.

argues that the permanent component of income is very much a reflection of the capital value, or wealth of the consumer. In other words, there is here part of the development, which we shall meet again on several occasions, which is increasingly moving economics towards emphasising the importance of capital theory. Here, Friedman argues that the income of the consumer depends on his non-human capital assets; and on his earning-ability, which is of course a reflection of his 'capital value'. The consumer is seen as 'human wealth', rather than as an income earner. The income of the consumer also depends on the type of job he does; on his occupation, his industry and the part of the country where he works. Friedman holds that it is these factors which determine the income which the consumer 'expects' to earn. This is his permanent income.

5.2 Transitory income

The transitory component in income is seen as reflecting 'all other factors' which are likely to be treated by the consumer as representing 'accidental or chance' occurrences. He will see them in this light even though, to an outside observer, they may be the predictable result of, for example, fluctuations in economic activity. Examples of transitory components of income which Friedman gives are: illness or a bad estimate about when to buy or sell some commodity or capital asset. His view is that, over the population, these transitory elements in income tend to cancel out over time.

Perhaps two examples will make it a little clearer what Friedman means. One criticism of the normal measure of income—the amount of money earned in a particular period of time—is that one's income is not always best seen as one's cash receipts in a given period. For example, suppose that we concern ourselves with people who are paid once a week. This would mean that the average consumer in that group would have no income at all on six days a week and a very large income on the seventh. An attempt to devise a consumption function based on this data would reveal the fact that on six days he is spending without receiving; on the seventh day, he is receiving a large amount of income and spending very little of it. In one sense, therefore, Friedman is concerned simply with obtaining a proper definition of income and indeed of consumption.

Another example would be that of an author receiving a royalty from a book. He would face a situation very similar to that of the wage earner, but with a longer time span. If the author receives his royalty annually, and has no other income, then on one day of the year he will have a very large income from the book; on the other 364 days, he will have no income whatsoever. This example can be taken further. Unless the author believes that the book will go on selling roughly the same number of copies from year to year, he may well find it unwise to treat the whole of the royalty from the book as permanent income. If he does, he may be building up his standard of living to a level that he cannot sustain if the income from the book falls after a time, unless he can replace that 'transitory' income by royalties from another book, or some other activity. It may well be, therefore, that the author will treat part of the royalty as a 'transitory' income and use it to buy rather special capital assets—as, for example, a record player or an oil painting would be—rather than using it to increase the level of what Friedman would call his 'permanent' consumption.

Although those transitory elements in income which are specific to particular consumers, like illness, may cancel out, Friedman argues that there are other factors which will not cancel out. Two of his examples of factors that do not cancel out are unusually good or bad weather, or a sudden shift in the demand for a product. A group of farmers in the relevant geographical area, or producing the relevant product, may then find that there is a substantial transitory element in their incomes. If the factors causing it are favourable, it will be positive; if they are unfavourable, it will be negative.

5.3 *Permanent consumption*

This leads us to the notion of permanent consumption. Friedman believes that just as there is a notion of permanent income, so there is a notion of permanent consumption. His definition of permanent and transitory consumption are similar to those for income. Permanent consumption would be that part of consumer expenditure which a study of the data showed to be regarded as permanent by the consumer.

5.4 *Transitory consumption*

Transitory consumption is the remainder of consumption. Friedman argues that some of the factors producing transitory consumption are specific to particular consumers: sickness, a favourable opportunity to purchase, and so on. As with transitory income, he thinks that these elements will tend to cancel out over the community. On the other hand, he thinks that there are other transitory elements in consumption, like those resulting from unusually cold weather or a good harvest, which will not cancel out. A spell of cold weather might have the effect of keeping consumers at home and away from shops so that it reduced consumption; or it might lead them to indulge in once-for-all purchases of warm clothing.

Consumption

*The
influence of
durable
consumer goods*

Friedman's analysis leads one to see that there is a further difficulty in defining consumption, which we have not emphasised until now, but which we shall consider again in Chapter 21. This difficulty stems from the distinction between non-durable and durable consumer goods. Expenditure on the latter is really concerned with purchasing a capital asset. With a non-durable good, one is buying something that the act of consumption itself will destroy. So, buying a cabbage is one thing; buying a washing machine is another. The purchase of the washing machine is best seen as the consumer *investing* in a capital asset. A distinction is therefore necessary. There is 'ordinary' consumer expenditure on goods which are used up quickly in consumption; these are flow items. A 'flow' of them is continually being consumed. On the other hand, there are stock items. These include not only savings held over time in the form of a stock of cash or other financial assets; they also include the accumulation of consumer durables.

*5.6 The
permanent
income
hypothesis*

We shall look in a moment at another theory which takes this distinction into account more explicitly. For the moment, we set out Friedman's permanent income hypothesis. Friedman puts this into three equations. If we denote income by Y, we can denote permanent income as Y_p and transitory income as Y_t. Similarly, if we denote consumption by C, we can denote permanent consumption by C_p and transitory consumption by C_t. Friedman's first two equations are simply definitions. They are:

$$Y = Y_p + Y_t$$

and
$$C = C_p + C_t$$

All these two equation do is to tell us what we know already; that both income and consumption have permanent and transitory elements. The remaining equation sums up the permanent income hypothesis. It is:

$$C_p = k(i, w, u)\, Y_p$$

This equation gives the relationship between permanent income and permanent consumption. It states that the ratio between the two does not depend on the size of permanent income, although it does depend on other variables.

*(a) The rate of
interest*

In particular, Friedman believes that the relationship is affected by the rate of interest (i); the relationship between the consumer's in-

come from his property and that from his own abilities and efforts
(w); and the consumer's preference for immediate consumption as
opposed to additions to his wealth (u). As we have seen, economists do
not now believe that the rate of interest has much effect on consumption. However, Professor Friedman does not agree. It remains for
econometric work to resolve the position. So far as this book is concerned, we shall continue to assume that consumption depends much
more on income than it does on the rate of interest.

(b) Human and non-human wealth

The second element, the relative amounts of income earned from
capital assets and from the consumer's inherent abilities and efforts,
is symbolised by the term w in the equation; this gives the ratio of
non-human wealth to income. As this book proceeds, we are seeing
that this is an element which is going to play a role of growing importance in economic theory. Statistical work suggests that the size of
consumption expenditure does depend on the value of the consumer's
assets. While we shall ignore it in this book, the consumption function
should therefore include a term which allows consumption to depend
on wealth.

(c) An optimal stock of assets

The simplest way of seeing the relationship is perhaps as follows.
Suppose that a consumer has £20000 in various forms of easily-
realisable assets, yielding £1 200 p.a. He is then likely to save a rather
lower proportion of his income than someone who has no assets at
all, but has the same *desire* to hold assets. The second consumer is
likely to save in order to try to accumulate capital assets, while the
first has already accumulated what he wants. This also explains the
importance of the final term (u) in Friedman's equation, which
depends on the desire of the consumer to add to his wealth rather
than to satisfy his wants by immediate consumption.

(d) Income and wealth

Finally, it is worth emphasising that Friedman is essentially concerned with discovering a way of defining income in terms of wealth.
As we have seen, permanent income is to be seen as income earned by
the human and non-human capital of the consumer. In defining
permanent income, one is in effect defining wealth rather than
income. The most important aspect of the permanent income
hypothesis is therefore that it moves economic theory towards
treating both income and consumption as closely linked to the con-

sumer's wealth. It seems safe to predict that economic theory will increasingly concern itself with capital and wealth (human and non-human) rather than purely with income, as time goes on.

6. The life-cycle hypothesis

Another important approach to consumer expenditure is that of Modigliani, Brumberg and Ando.[1] These authors take the view that consumption is most satisfactorily related not to the current income of a consumer but to his income over his whole life. The permanent income hypothesis emphasises the consumer's cash receipts over recent years, because the incomes consumers expect in the future will be significantly determined by what they have earned in the recent past. It also implies that present consumption will depend on expectations of future earnings (and wealth). The Modigliani-Brumberg-Ando model looks at the pattern of income over the consumer's whole life in a much more explicit way.

In his early years, the assumption is that the consumer will be spending money without earning income; he will be kept by his parents or some other relation. He then begins to work and earns income. Although there will be certain stages during middle-life when the consumer is spending a good deal, for example, on his children's education, middle-life is a time when on balance the consumer will be earning more than he spends. His aim will be to accumulate enough assets to allow him to continue at what he sees as a satisfactory standard of living after he stops working, after allowing for state pensions, etc. In the final stage of his life-cycle, after the individual has finished working, he will spend a good deal and earn little or nothing. In other words, over the whole life-cycle, the consumer is trying to organise his uneven flows of cash receipts so that they make possible a much more regular pattern of expenditure. To the extent that he does this consciously, he will be arranging his receipts and expenditures into a pattern which best supports the flow of consumption expenditure he wishes to enjoy.

6.1 No net savings

The simplest model of an economy will then be where the average individual aims to save nothing at all (net) over his lifetime. His savings will be made during those periods when he is earning more money relatively to his desired consumption expenditures, and will

[1]F. Modigliani and R. Brumberg, 'Utility Analysis and the Consumption function: An interpretation of cross-section', pp. 383–436 in K. K. Kurihara (ed.), *Post-Keynesian Economics*, New Brunswick, 1954; and A. Ando and F. Modigliani, 'The "Life-Cycle" hypothesis of saving: aggregate implications and tests', *American Economic Review*, 1963, pp. 55–84.

be intended to support him towards the end of his life. Ideally, this 'average' consumer's last pound would be spent at the moment when he died. What this would mean for a community is not certain. If everyone were able to predict exactly when he and his dependents would die, an economy of people like this would make no net savings at all over a lifetime. Whether the economy as a whole was making savings would then depend on changes in the size and age-structure of the population and on incomes.

6.2 Net savings

However, since death cannot be predicted accurately, it is likely that most people would die holding more non-human wealth than they intended. Some net saving would occur. A less-simple model would be where most people wished to leave money to their heirs. There would then be net savings, whose amount would depend on how much people wanted to leave to their heirs, on the age-structure and growth of population and on income.

6.3 Saving, population growth and rising income

The life-cycle theory leads to some interesting conclusions. For example, it links net saving in any economy closely to the growth rate of the population and to the rate of increase of incomes. Even where each individual plans to use up his total savings by the end of his life, if population is rising so that more and more individuals are doing this, at any moment of time there will be net saving. Moreover, net savings will increase as time passes; more income will be saved in each year than in the previous one. Similarly, if people today have higher incomes than those of their parents, then savings out of those incomes will also be higher. Those who are making today's net savings out of higher incomes will be saving more than their parents are dis-saving, because the parents saved out of lower incomes.

The life-cycle hypothesis sounds plausible. Moreover, statistical tests suggest that it is realistic. However, we must note that it is another move away from the idea of income as represented by receipts of cash towards income as closely related to wealth. It also emphasises the fact that consumers have to choose between accumulating assets or deriving their satisfactions from current consumption.

7. An optimal stock of assets

As we have said, it appears certain that economics will move progressively farther towards a theory of consumption that is essentially a branch of the theory of capital. A life-cycle theory is likely to be developed which not only allows for the fact that consumers build up a capital stock which they hold in cash or invest in various kinds of assets over their lives. It will also allow for the fact that a part (perhaps a major part) of the consumer's capital stock is 'invested' in consumer durables. One example of this kind of theory is a paper by Alan Spiro, who suggests that every consumer aims at a certain total stock of assets that he wants to accumulate, *given* the size of his income. In other words, if a consumer's income is constant, he will want to build up a stock of assets of a particular size which he regards as appropriate to his level of income. Given long enough, he will achieve this. From then on he will consume the whole of his income. If his income were then to fall, the consumer would gradually *reduce* the stock of assets, consuming more than he was earning until again the stock of assets had been reduced to a size which was appropriate to the reduced level of income. Consumers can be seen as adjusting their capital stock to the level which is required if that capital stock is to match current income.

Tests of this kind of model suggest that it describes reality quite accurately. This is why we believe that future developments in the theory of the consumption function are likely to take place along the lines which these two models—the Modigliani-Brumberg-Ando model and the Spiro model—suggest. The theory of the consumption function is in future likely to be firmly linked to capital theory.

8. Government consumption

So far, we have said nothing about government expenditure on current account: what in this context we are calling government consumption. The reasons for this should be clear. The size of government consumption—expenditure on defence, health, education, administration, etc.—depends very much on political attitudes and decisions. The amount spent on defence will depend on the country's role in the world, on the likelihood of attack and on the degree to which the community feels it worth spending money to be able to meet that attack. Similarly, the amounts of money spent in different countries on health, education, and general administration will differ considerably. In the same country, they will differ over time. All we can say is that, somehow, the community as a whole will determine the size of government expenditure on current account which it thinks is acceptable, given current attitudes on the desirability of the public sector rather than individual meeting particular needs. Thus, in a country like the UK there will be a National Health Service; in the USA there will be a changing mixture of public and private provision for health, and so on.

Perhaps one point should be made on this. It is important to remember that if the community decides to set up a National Health

Service spending £1 000m per annum on it, this does not necessarily mean a net addition of that amount to gross national expenditure. If private individuals had previously been spending exactly £1 000m themselves on health, there would be no net change in total national expenditure at all, though its pattern might alter. Exactly the same amount of money would be spent, but by the government and not by individuals. What determines the level of income and activity is the total amount of expenditure on consumption, public or private. The precise division of the economy into public and private sectors is unimportant for income and employment, though it may be important for efficiency and for politics.

9. Savings and investment

9.1 The adjustment process

The careful reader will have noticed that this discussion has avoided any precise definition of the relationship between income, consumption, savings and investment and, more particularly, between savings and investment. In Chapter 19 we saw that, leaving aside government expenditure, gross national product (viewed from the income side) is made up of consumption and savings. We also saw that, from the expenditure side, gross national product is made up of consumption plus investment. Since consumption is included in both concepts, it follows that savings equal investment. At the same time, we implied that things were not quite so straightforward as this makes it seem. We must now go a little further into the question.

The main problem, as anyone who thinks about these issues for very long will discover, is this. We have defined savings and investment as being equal by definition. Yet in many discussions of economic problems or policy one soon finds oneself explaining how two things, which are equal by definition, are brought into equality. How can one say that savings and investment are equal by definition, and yet find it difficult to explain how they become equal?

The first point is that, as our simplified national income accounts have shown, defining income as $C+I$ is different from defining it as $C+S$. As we suggested in Chapter 14, the act of saving is *not* identical with the act of investing, at least in a monetary economy. It is because of this that we have to study the connection between savings and investment with care.

(a) Ex-post magnitudes

For, although saving and investing are not activities that are always performed by the same people, they are nevertheless equal after the event. Economists therefore say that, after any time period is ended, *ex-post*, savings and investment are equal. What we must do is to discover the way in which, despite being carried out by different people, savings and investment are brought into this *ex-post* equality.

The *ex-post* equality between savings and investment derives from that fact that, on the one hand, income received in any year must, by definition, be either spent on consumption or saved. On the other hand, income received in that same year will be derived either from selling consumption goods or from selling investment goods. Savings must equal investment.

9.2 Savings—
the passive
element

Nevertheless, it is investment and consumption decisions which are the positive or active forces in determining the level of savings and not vice versa. Saving can be regarded as a residual which must be equal to investment. It should be emphasised that this definition of saving says nothing about whether the saver, having saved part of his income, decides to invest it (i.e. to spend his income on buying factories, plant, machinery, etc.), to hoard it as cash or to lend it, by buying securities or in other ways. All that we are concerned with is the fact that part of income is not consumed. Savings is the difference between income and consumption.

The key problem, which we must now emphasise, is this fact that investment and saving decisions are often separate in the modern economy. The people who decide to build factories are rarely the people who have saved to pay for them. Decisions to consume (i.e. not to save) are taken by people—consumers—who are usually quite separate from those who decide to invest—entrepreneurs. It is important to stress this because we saw that in the 'Crusoe' type of barter economy Crusoe decides at one and the same time to refrain from consuming and to invest. There is no such automatic or direct link between savings and investment in a monetary economy. A study of the people who make savings decisions tells one nothing about the decisions which entrepreneurs are making about investment. Yet, despite this, savings must equal investment.

(a) A first
approximation

How can this happen? Let us consider, as a first approximation, a situation where we temporarily ignore the multiplier. Consumption is fixed and investment variable. If investment increases, income must rise by the same amount as investment. Otherwise, payments to employers $(C+I)$ would differ from payments made by employers to factors of production $(C+S)$, which are then spent or saved. This would be an odd state of affairs indeed. While savings must equal investment, both before and after the change in investment, they do not do so because of any deliberate act on the part of savers. Savings are equal to investment because income is now greater, but consumption is fixed. The members of the community have received larger incomes, whether they expected to or not; since consumption has not risen, savings must have done so. The equality of savings and investment has come about, not through a deliberate decision to save more out of a given income: it has come about because income has increased. Because consumption is constant, savings rise by exactly the same amount as investment. Similarly, if consumption were constant and investment fell, savings would fall by exactly the same absolute amount as investment had fallen.

The illustration is, of course, over-simplified. The multiplier ensures that consumption does not remain constant when income rises. This does not alter the principle, which ensures the *ex-post* equality of savings and investment. If consumption and investment both change, there will be a consequent change in savings. If nothing at all out of an increase in income is consumed, someone must have saved an amount equal to the absolute difference between the increase in income and the (zero) increase in consumption. This must equal the increase in the volume of investment. But, as we have stressed all along, the increase in investment is the dominant factor. Savings are brought into equality with the changed investment through a change in the level of income. 'The act of investment in itself cannot help causing the residual or margin, which we call saving, to increase by a corresponding amount.'[1]

9.3 'Involuntary' savings and investment

The above analysis was more realistic, but still over-simplified. We assumed that changes in investment were always the result of deliberate decisions on the part of entrepreneurs. This overlooks the possibility that some or all of the increased investment will be 'involuntary'; that it will result not from a deliberate decision to purchase capital assets but from a rise in producers' stocks of finished goods. We have seen that stocks (inventories) are part of investment. They are not consumed, but are stored for future use. However, the increase in stocks need not be a result of deliberate decisions to increase them. It may result from a falling-off in demand. Consumers may buy fewer goods than entrepreneurs had expected them to buy when they planned their output. Consumers have saved more, and their increased savings are balanced by unintended investment in extra stocks of finished goods. It is perfectly possible for both investment and savings to diverge from what savers and investors respectively had intended that they should be. It is important, however, to

[1] Keynes, *op. cit.*, p. 64.

remember that it is realised saving which depends on realised investment and not vice versa. Investment never depends on saving, except in a roundabout way through changes in consumption, which in turn lead to changes in inventories of finished goods, raw materials and components, to changes in income, and so on. In a 'Crusoe' economy, a decision to save always implies a simultaneous decision to invest. Savings and investment are not merely equal; they are identical. In a money economy, there is no direct link between savings and investment at all. Money saved by one person can cause another to have difficulty in selling consumer goods. So inventories pile up and unintended 'investment' increases. In a monetary system *an individual* can 'save' without necessarily causing corresponding investment. Similarly, *an individual* can invest even though no one is deliberately 'saving' to finance that investment.

9.4 Ex-ante
and ex-post
equilibrium

*(a) Ex-ante
magnitudes*

Ex-post (or 'realised' or 'actual') savings and *ex-post* investment are always equal. Yet we now know that these *ex-post* magnitudes need not be equal to what people expected them to be beforehand (or *ex-ante*). There is no reason why what people expect to save should equal what they are actually able to save. *Ex-ante* savings need not equal *ex-post* savings. Even if all fixed investment is carried out as planned, inventories may increase or decrease by more or less than was expected.

We have been talking so far, where we have spoken of savings and investment as equal, of *ex-post* savings and *ex-post* investment. After all acts of consumption and investment during a period have been carried out, savings *must* equal investment. While 'anticipated', 'planned' or *ex-ante* savings and investment need not be equal, savings and investment must be equal *ex-post*. They will become equal through unintended changes in the level of income.

Table 20.1

	Ex-ante values	Ex-post values
Consumption	70	70
Savings	30	40
Investment	40	40
Income	100	110

Two examples will show this. Suppose that the position in an economy is as shown in Table 20.1. Suppose that, in a given year, consumers expect income to be 100. Out of this income, they intend to spend 70 and save 30. However, firms intend to invest 40 in new plant, etc. *Ex-ante* investment is greater than *ex-ante* savings. If both consumers and businesses carry out their plans, consumption will be 70 and investment 40. Income will therefore rise to 110. Since consumers carry out their plans to spend 70, this leaves savings of 40. Savings equal investment. As we have said, if *ex-ante* investment is greater than *ex-ante* savings, and planned consumption and investment are carried out, income will rise to equate *ex-post* savings and *ex-post* investment.

Table 20.2

	Ex-ante values	*Ex-post values*
Consumption	70	70
Savings	30	20
Investment	20	20
Income	100	90

Next, we consider the economy in Table 20.2. Here, income is again expected to be 100. With this income, *ex-ante* consumption is again 70 but *ex-ante* investment is only 20. *Ex-post*, therefore, we have incomes of only 90 (consumption of 70 and investment of 20). Since they are still determined to carry out their intentions, consumers spend 70. They therefore save 20. Again, savings equal investment but, because *ex-ante* savings are greater than *ex-ante* investment, income falls.

In practice, of course, plans for consumption and investment will not be made in advance for a whole year and held to whatever happens to income. There will be more continuous adjustment. Nevertheless, the principle we are enunciating still holds. If *ex-ante* investment is greater than *ex-ante* savings, income rises. If *ex-ante* investment is less than *ex-ante* savings, income will fall.

9.5 Summary

To sum up: if income is constant, and if everyone acts so as to keep it constant, *ex-ante* income equals *ex-post* income. Then, *ex-ante* consumption must equal *ex-post* consumption, and *ex-ante* investment must equal *ex-post* investment. *Ex-ante* savings will also equal *ex-post* savings, and *ex-ante* savings will equal *ex-ante* investment. But if *ex-ante* investment exceeds *ex-ante* savings, income will rise. Savings out of the increased income will raise *ex-post* savings to equal *ex-post* investment. On the other hand, if *ex-ante* savings are greater than *ex-ante* investment, income will fall. *Ex-post* savings and investment will still be equal, but only because the community is now too poor to save as much as it had hoped. This is the reason why economists sometimes talk of inequalities between savings and investment. *Ex-ante* differences are quite likely but *ex-post* savings and investment must be equal. Incomes will always change so that the community as a whole is just rich enough or poor enough to save exactly the same amount of money as is being invested.

Suggested reading

KEYNES, J. M.   *General Theory*, London, 1936, chapters 8, 9 and 10.

ACKLEY, GARDNER   *Macro-economic Theory*, New York, 1961, chapters 10, 11 and 12.

FERBER, R.   'Research on Household Behaviour', *Surveys of Economic Theory*, published by the American Economic Association and the Royal Economic Society, London and New York, 1966, p. 114.

21

Investment

We have shown what determines the volume of consumption expenditure in any economy at any time. We now turn to the second component of aggregate demand and see what determines the volume of investment. We know that investment is an important means of creating employment both directly, and indirectly through multiplier effects. In this chapter we shall first discuss the factors which determine the volume of investment which is undertaken in any year by firms and individuals in the private sector of a capitalist economy. We then consider 'investment' in houses and consumer durables. We go on to look at government investment.

1. Private investment

1.1 What we mean by investment

Our first concern is to show how private businesses decide how much investment to undertake. It is important to point out at this stage that by investment we do not mean the purchase of existing paper securities—bonds, debentures, equities—or indeed the *existing* physical assets lying behind them. Such transactions merely represent a change in the ownership of assets that already exist. They do not create income and employment. What we are interested in is the purchase of *new* factories, plant, machines and so on—investment in steel, concrete and glass. Only if assets are newly-constructed can their purchase give employment to men who build them. We shall describe a transaction by which the ownership of *existing* capital goods changes hands when securities are bought or sold—what is often referred to in ordinary speech as 'investment'—as a 'purchase (or sale) of securities'. Nevertheless, new investment by a firm will normally be financed by the issue of *new* equities, or *new* debentures.

1.2 The 'cost' of investment

We begin with the 'pure' Keynesian model of investment and proceed to complicate it. The basic point about private business investment is that it is undertaken only if it is expected to yield a return to the investor. Moreover, anyone who has liquid resources available for investment will usually have one important alternative to investing his money in new capital equipment. He can earn interest by putting his money into fixed-interest securities of some kind, instead of taking a risk by building a factory or buying a machine in the hope that it will be profitable. It follows that if private business investment is to be undertaken in an economy, not only must the investor expect to earn a money return from it. That money return must itself be somewhat greater than the return the investor could obtain if he were to buy existing bonds. At the very least, the return must slightly exceed the rate of interest on fixed-interest securities.

(a) Opportunity cost

In other words, there is an 'opportunity cost' if one uses one's own money to buy a capital asset. One foregoes the return one *could* have earned from investing these funds in the next-best alternative. To simplify his analysis in writing the *General Theory*, Keynes assumed that the *only* alternative to investing in one's business was the purchase of fixed-interest bonds. We shall follow Keynes in using this simplifying assumption for the present.

(b) Interest cost

Of course, the businessman may not be using his own money to undertake investment. It will then be necessary, at the very least, for the interest he has to pay on borrowed money to be covered by expected returns. This leads to the same result. Whether one invests one's own funds, or borrowed money, the relevant cost to be compared with the return on the investment is the rate of interest on bonds.

1.3 The inducement to invest

We can therefore assume that entrepreneurs borrow to finance their investment by issuing commercial debentures bearing a fixed rate of interest. This means that the yield expected from acquiring one more new unit of capital, *the marginal efficiency of capital* as Keynes calls it, must never fall below the current rate of interest on bonds if that unit of investment is to be worthwhile. In Keynesian theory, the inducement to invest depends on the return from assets—the marginal efficiency of capital—on the one hand, and the rate of interest on the other. We must now study these two factors more closely.

2. The marginal efficiency of capital

2.1 Prospective yield

We turn first to the marginal efficiency of capital. This represents the demand function for new investment goods. An entrepreneur who decides to build a new factory or buy a new machine first considers the prospective yield of the asset, as we saw in Chapter 14. In evaluating a new asset, he looks at the series of prospective returns he can obtain from selling the output produced by that asset during its life. He then has to deduct from this series of expected future returns the running costs (and the costs of cooperating factors) which he thinks he will incur in obtaining output during the life of the asset. This leaves him with a series of 'net' returns which he will expect to accrue to him over the years as the owner of the asset. It is the sum-total of this series of net returns (or 'annuities')[1] which we defined in Chapter 14 (following Keynes) as the *prospective yield* of the asset.

2.2 Supply price

But, as we also saw in Chapter 14, the prospective yield of an asset is not the only thing which an investor has to consider when he is acquiring a new asset. He will have to pay whatever it costs to have the asset produced. This amount is known as its *supply price*. It is important to reiterate that the supply price of any kind of asset is not the price of any *existing* asset of that kind. It is the cost of producing a brand new one.

2.3 The marginal efficiency of capital defined

With these two concepts, prospective yield and supply price (or replacement cost), we can now give a precise definition of the *marginal efficiency of capital*. The marginal efficiency of *a particular kind* of capital asset, for example, for a particular machine tool, can be calculated by relating the prospective yield of a new machine of that kind to its supply price. The marginal efficiency of any asset shows what an entrepreneur expects to be able to earn from acquiring one more asset of that kind, as compared with what he has to pay to buy it. Keynes's definition is this. 'I define the marginal efficiency of capital as being equal to that rate of discount which would make the present value of the series of annuities given by the returns expected from the capital-asset during its life just equal to its supply price.'[2] In other words, the marginal efficiency of *a particular type* of capital asset is the rate at which the prospective yield expected from one additional unit of that particular asset must be discounted if it is just to equal the (replacement) cost of the asset. It is the *internal rate of return* on that asset.

[1] If the returns accrue once per annum they are known as 'annuities'.
[2] *General Theory*, p. 135.

2.4 The marginal efficiency of capital in general

This explains what is meant by the marginal efficiency of *a particular type* of capital asset. But the concept of the marginal efficiency of capital *in general* is also needed in macro-economic theory. In any given situation, this will be the marginal efficiency of the next unit of that particular asset which it is most worthwhile for the community to produce another unit. In other words, the marginal efficiency of capital in general is the highest of all the individual marginal efficiencies of the various assets which could be produced but have not yet been produced. It will show, in any situation, what the highest internal rate of return to the community could be if one more capital asset (of the most worthwhile kind) were to be produced.

It is always possible to calculate the marginal efficiency of any particular type of asset, beginning from the existing stock of that asset. It is also possible to construct a schedule showing what the marginal efficiency of any asset would be when the existing stock of the asset was at all possible levels. The only generalisation one can make about the shape of such a marginal efficiency of capital schedule is this. In any given period of time, the marginal efficiency of every type of asset will diminish, as investment in it increases. The main reason for this is that the prospective yield of any type of asset will fall as more units of it are produced. Second, the supply price of the asset may rise. If more assets of a given type are produced, the more fully will firms be able to meet the demand for the product(s) which they make. The price(s) of the product(s) they make will fall. The need for more similar assets will be less urgent. It is also possible, but not certain, that the supply price of the asset will rise as increasing demand for it increases its cost.

2.5 The marginal efficiency of capital curve

Since we can construct schedules showing the marginal efficiency of each individual type of asset, we can do the same for the marginal efficiency of capital in general. This gives us Fig. 21.1. Here, the rate of interest is measured up by the y-axis and the amount of investment undertaken in a particular period of time along the x-axis. The curve

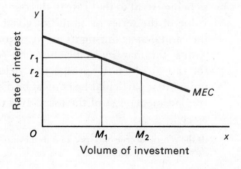

Fig. 21.1

MEC (representing the schedule of the marginal efficiency of capital in general) shows the volumes of investment which would be undertaken, in a given period, at different rates of interest. For example, if the rate of interest is Or_1, OM_1 investment will be undertaken in the period under consideration. If the rate of interest falls to Or_2, the volume of investment will be OM_2.

As we saw in Chapter 14, one can expect businessmen who wish to maximise their profits to invest in new capital assets up to the point where the internal rate of return is just equal to the rate of interest. Entrepreneurs will equate the marginal efficiency of each asset with the rate of interest. We now begin to see the relationship between investment and the rate of interest in this 'pure' Keynesian model. It is clear from Fig. 21.1 that, given the marginal efficiency of capital schedule, the rate of interest must fall if there is to be an increase in the volume of investment in an economy. If the rate of interest is Or_1, the volume of investment is OM_1. If the rate of interest falls to Or_2, investment rises to OM_2.

2.6 Business expectations

This is moving too far ahead. For the moment, we are concerned with what determines the prospective yield on capital goods. What determines entrepreneurs' views on the prospective yield of assets? Production conditions are likely to be fairly stable in the short run, so that the supply prices of assets, one determinant of the marginal efficiency of capital, will usually be fairly stable too. Entrepreneurs' estimates of the prospective yields of assets, the other determinant of the marginal efficiency of capital, will be the important factor in the short run. By their stability or instability, they will determine whether the demand for capital goods is stable or changeable. Businessmen's expectations do change at intervals, and this is an important factor influencing the level of investment activity.

2.7 Two points to emphasise

(a) Prospective and not retrospective yields

Before we turn to a more complete discussion of the factors determining businessmens' expectations, two points about the marginal efficiency of capital must be emphasised. First, the marginal efficiency of any type of asset has nothing at all to do with what the yield on that asset actually turns out to have been, looked at historically, when the asset has worn out. The marginal efficiency of an asset shows the return which is expected from investing in a brand-new unit, not the return that was actually obtained from an existing unit up to the point where it became valueless.

(b) Prospective yield covers the 'whole' life of the asset

Second, it is important to stress once more that the prospective yield on which the marginal efficiency of an asset depends is composed of the total returns expected from the asset during the *whole* of its life (after deducting the costs incurred in maintaining it and the costs of the other factors of production that cooperate with it in producing the product). It is dangerous to assume that *all* the prospective annual returns from an asset will be equal. The later revenues from an asset can be the same as the earlier one only if the economy remains in static or 'stationary' equilibrium with prices, output and population always constant. And even if the revenues were the same, the cost of running the machine would probably be higher in the later years of its life as it became less efficient physically. More expenditure would be incurred in maintaining it.

3. Long-term expectation

The importance of the marginal efficiency of capital is that it emphasises the important role that business expectations play in determining the level of investment and so of GNP. It is a concept which gives business expectations an important position in macroeconomic theory. We must therefore now discuss the way in which a businessman's estimate of the yield from any individual asset is linked to the more general phenomenon of business confidence. Keynes, in particular, emphasised the link between estimates of the prospective yield of assets and expectations about the future as these reveal themselves in Stock Exchange prices.

3.1 The state of short-term expectation

Keynes felt that expectations about the prospective yields of capital assets were based on 'partly existing facts which we can assume to be more or less known for certain, and partly future events which can only be forecasted with more or less confidence'.[1] Among the former set of facts, Keynes listed the size of the existing stock of capital assets and the strength of consumer demand for goods which require considerable amounts of those assets for their production. These facts determine the *state of short-term expectation*.

3.2 The state of long-term expectation

Among the latter sets of facts, Keynes included expectations about future changes in the size of the stock of capital assets; and about changes in the level of aggregate demand during the future life of the assets whose prospective yields are being considered. Keynes defined

[1]*Op. cit.*, p. 147.

the state of expectations dependent on these later considerations as the *state of long-term expectation.*

Investors acquiring new assets are obviously more concerned with long-run forces than with short-run ones. Moreover, as the above list shows, the factors upon which long-term expectation depends are very uncertain. The result is that when businessmen invest they are forced to put undue weight on those factors about which they feel most confident. The facts of the existing situation, and those future events which seem most likely to occur, enter with disproportionate weight into decisions to invest. The state of long-term expectation thus depends not only upon what firms expect to happen, but also on how certain they are that it *will* happen—on the confidence which firms have when they forecast the future. It depends in part on how far firms think that their estimates are more likely to be right or wrong. This, in turn, will usually depend on how many certain facts there are, as compared with those about which businessmen feel vague and unsure.

(a) The state of confidence

Keynes therefore held that *the state of confidence* was important. It was a factor which earlier economists had either ignored or treated in very general terms. Indeed, economists writing since Keynes have also had relatively little to say about it. Keynes thought it was important to be more explicit than his predecessors had been about this 'state of confidence' but that it would be dangerous to make arbitrary *a priori* assumptions about it. He therefore spent some time in the *General Theory* explaining what he thought to be the determinants of business expectations and, especially, in analysing behaviour on the Stock Exchange. Keynes was, of course, an active investor himself, and this is doubtless one reason why he put so much emphasis on Stock Exchange behaviour. Another reason must have been the shattering effect of the crash on Wall Street in 1929, and the influence this had both on Stock Exchange sentiment and on business opinion generally during the period between 1929 and the time when the *General Theory* was written.

3.3 Stock Exchange valuation

Let us proceed by assuming that the rate of interest is given and see why fluctuations in the expected earnings of particular types of investment, or of particular firms, can then occur. If the rate of interest is given, changes in the capital values of particular investments must be due solely to changes in their prospective yields, as forecast by those dealing on the Stock Exchange.

Keynes maintained that in this context: 'The outstanding fact is the extreme precariousness of the basis of knowledge on which our estimates of prospective yield have to be made ... If we speak frankly, we have to admit that our basis of knowledge for estimating the yield ten years hence of a railway, a copper mine, a textile factory, the goodwill of a patent medicine, an Atlantic liner, a building in the City of London, amounts to little and sometimes to nothing; or even five years hence'.[1] This means that, since most capital assets last for at least five or ten years before wearing out, considerable risks have to be taken when a great deal of business investment is carried out. It would be surprising if the actual results of acquiring capital assets bore a very close relationship to the expected results.

(a) Irrevocable decisions

Keynes argued that in earlier periods, for example in the nineteenth century, decisions to invest once made were usually made irrevocably, both by the community and by the individual entrepreneur. This was so, even though no-one could make a precise calculation of prospective profits. Indeed, had such investment been based on accurate knowledge of prospective returns, it is doubtful whether much would have taken place at all. It seems likely that throughout history the realised results of overall investment activity have been rather less favourable than those who invested thought they would be. As Keynes put it: 'If human nature felt no temptation to take a chance, no satisfaction (profit apart) in constructing a factory, a railway, a mine, or a farm, there might not be much investment merely as a result of cold calculation.'[2]

(b) Elements of instability

In the past, then, when the private entrepreneur invested his money it was irretrievably sunk. Keynes felt that the divorce between ownership and control in modern industry, and above all the development of an organised Stock Exchange, had brought a danger of instability into the economic system. On the Stock Exchange the prospects of many investments are reconsidered and reviewed daily—even hourly. More than this, it is now possible to 'invest' money one day and to 'disinvest' it the next. 'It is as though a farmer, having tapped his barometer after breakfast, could decide to remove his capital from the farming business between 10 and 11 in the morning and reconsider whether he should return to it later in the week.'[3]

[1] *Op. cit.*, pp. 149–50. The whole of the chapter from which this quotation is taken (*General Theory*, chapter 12, 'Long-Term Expectation') is well worth reading in the original.
[2] *Op. cit.*, p. 150.
[3] *Op. cit.*, p. 151.

*(c) The link
with investment*

The revaluations of investments which the Stock Exchange makes are primarily made to allow securities which represent titles to *existing* assets to be bought and sold. Their exchange has no direct effect in creating employment. Yet, inevitably, these transactions exert an indirect effect on new investment. When investment is being carried out by making new issues through the capital market, the ease with which they can be floated will depend on the Stock Exchange values of similar investments, rather than on any individual's estimate of the true prospects of such investments. 'A high quotation (on the Stock Exchange) for existing equities involves an increase in the marginal efficiency of the corresponding type of capital, and therefore has the same effect (since investment depends on a comparison between the marginal efficiency of capital and the rate of interest) as a fall in the rate of interest.'[1]

*(d) How
'investors' behave*

Of course, the fact that when the price of a company's existing shares are high makes it easier for the firm to borrow is not necessarily a bad thing in itself. If the ease with which money for investment in physical assets can be raised depends on Stock Exchange values, and if Stock Exchange values are based on accurate forecasts of the prospects of the various companies whose shares are quoted, the effects will be beneficial. Unfortunately, in revaluing assets so frequently, the Stock Exchange has made it possible for large numbers of people to make their revaluations at the same time. Most of these people are usually just as ignorant as each other of the true values of the assets being valued. Keynes therefore argued that investors fall back on the convention of expecting 'that the existing state of affairs will continue indefinitely, except in so far as we have specific reasons to expect a change.'[2] This is not important so long as the existing state of affairs does continue. The trouble begins when conditions change. The inevitable result of such a mass valuation is that when views on the prospects of a particular firm's investments alter, they often alter quite suddenly and in the same direction. As a result, it seems to be an inherent feature of the modern Stock Exchange that alternating waves of optimism and pessimism (sometimes small, sometimes somewhat excessive) are inevitable.

*(e) The
professionals*

It was not only the ignorant investor who was subjected to Keynes's criticism. Even the professional dealer was not exempt. Keynes saw the professional dealer as more concerned with earning a living than

[1]Keynes, *op. cit.*, p. 151, footnote.
[2]*Op. cit.*, p. 152.

with giving a correct valuation to investments irrespective of the effect on his income. The professional is seen as making little attempt to find out what the value of an asset will be in ten or twenty years' time, but as guessing how the market will value it in a few days' or a few weeks' time. He does this in order to live on the capital profits which he makes by guessing correctly. As Keynes said: 'It is not sensible to pay 25 for an investment of which you believe the prospective yield to justify a value of 30, if you also believe that the market will value it at 20 three months hence.'[1] The result, according to Keynes, was that instead of providing a mechanism for giving accurate estimates of the prospective long-term yields of investments, the Stock Exchange provided estimates of how mass opinion would value those investments in a few days' or weeks' time.

(f) Non-economic factors

Nor did he see this as the only important feature of the Stock Exchange. He thought it likely that any valuation which was made would have little economic basis. For mass psychology is prone to over estimate the importance of non-economic factors. One particularly good example of this occurred in Britain early in 1946. One morning, financial newspaper headlines ran roughly as follows: 'Share prices rise as Russian troops leave Persia.' 'Severe fall later when favourite fails to win Grand National.' Now it is probable that political moves, such as the Russian withdrawal from Persia, do have important effects on the prospective yield of investments. But it is most unlikely that any difference is made whichever horse wins an important race.

(g) How volatile is the Stock Exchange?

It would be wrong to exaggerate Keynes's view of the volatility of Stock Exchange opinion. In the first place, we have seen that Keynes was writing very much under the shock of the 1929 crash on Wall Street. Since 1929 there has fortunately not been another catastrophic collapse in share prices, though there have certainly been some substantial ones. In the second place, we must not suggest that professional Stock Exchange investors frequently and deliberately distort the values of investments, thereby making realistic estimates of their prospective yields impossible. Since there can never be accurate foreknowledge of future events, it is inevitable that all estimates of prospective yields, whoever makes them, depend to some extent on whim, sentiment or chance. However, it is important to realise that, in most modern economies, estimates of the value of

[1] *Op. cit.,* p. 155.

existing investment—and therefore estimates of the prospective yields of similar projected investments—are influenced in this way by the prevailing opinions of those who buy and sell shares on the Stock Exchange, by convention and by institutional arrangements.

We can now see, in outline, the reason why the fact that the prospective yields—and hence the marginal efficiencies of various assets—depend on expectations about the future, introduces an element of instability into the demand for investment goods. Investment tends to be sensitive to changes in stock market prices, and these prices are themselves likely to fluctuate to a smaller or greater extent in sympathy with fluctuating business optimism and pessimism.

4. Investment by consumers

A similar 'pure' Keynesian analysis can be applied to consumer purchases of long-lived assets, though Keynes himself did not do so explicitly. As we have explained, investment decisions by consumers are normally concerned with buying houses, so we shall concentrate on them here.

4.1 House purchase

It may seem less credible that a consumer should make careful calculations about house purchase than it is that businessmen should make careful calculations about buying factories, machinery, vehicles, etc. Nevertheless, it will be useful to look at what would happen if all house-purchase decisions were taken in a technically-correct way, and relax this assumption later.

Ideally, what the consumer should do is to begin by calculating the money value of the benefits which he will derive from owning a house, in each future year. He will then discount these, using whatever seems the appropriate discount rate. This will usually be the rate of interest at which money can be borrowed for house purchase. This will give a present value for the stream of benefits to be derived from owning the house. If this present value is greater than the (current) price of the house it will be bought, or a more expensive one considered. It follows that where all consumers behave in this 'ideal' way, there will again be a demand curve for houses which will slope downwards from left to right. The lower the rate of interest, the more houses will be bought.

4.2 Non-durable consumer goods

It will be helpful at this stage to return for a moment to the theory of consumer demand outlined in Chapters 2, 3 and 4. We shall not attempt to integrate this discussion into the macro-economics analysis of Part Two, but it is important to dwell on it briefly because it is likely that changes which we foreshadowed in Chapter 20 will alter this branch of economic theory in the future.

In Chapters 2 to 4, we assumed that the consumer was buying non-durable goods which he would actually consume soon after purchase. In practice, a fair proportion of most consumers' income, especially in developed countries, is spent on durable consumer goods. Indeed, the national income statistics for the United States distinguish between consumer expenditure on durable and non-durable consumer goods, even in summary tables that deal with national income only at the aggregate level. In other countries, one usually has to look at the more-detailed statistics to find this information.

It follows that a fair proportion of consumer-spending decisions are actually capital-investment decisions. Most people will make a smallish number of major investment decisions during their lives—when they buy cars, houses, etc. They will also make a very large number of smaller investment decisions when buying less-expensive consumer durables. Very few consumers will consistently make the kind of choice we have described above when we discussed buying a house by explicitly taking into account a discount rate, when they buy less-expensive durable consumer goods. But they may well allow for the time-value of money in an intuitive way. For, of course, many purchases of consumer durables do have an explicit interest cost; money has to be borrowed from a hire purchase company. Even if this is not the case, there will usually be an opportunity cost, because money used to buy a car or television set is thereby prevented from earning interest by being lent to a bank or hire purchase company or invested on the Stock Exchange.

We shall not pursue this discussion here, but it is important to realise that a significant part of consumers' expenditure in developed economies is more like investment expenditure than consumption expenditure.

5. The 'pure' Keynesian theory of investment

We must now sum up the argument of this chapter so far. The volume of investment undertaken in any period depends on the relationship between the rate of interest and the marginal efficiency of capital. The schedule of the marginal efficiency of capital—the demand curve for investment goods as a function of the rate of interest—slopes downwards to the right. The shape and position of this demand curve for investment goods depends in large degree on individuals' and firms' expectations of future earnings from capital assets. We have seen that such expectations are likely to be uncertain, so that the demand for investment goods may well be uncertain too. We are trying to discover enough of the important determinants of the level of income and employment to be able to build up an elementary theory of macro-economics. It is therefore undesirable to include expectations. First, they are very difficult to allow for, as we have seen. Second, it is possible to blame almost any event on some peculiarity of expectations. It is dangerous to put too much emphasis on them in a simple analysis like this.

Fortunately, this does not destroy our macro-economic theory. As we have seen, entrepreneurs tend to base their expectations largely on existing facts—hoping that everything will continue in the future as it is at present. The most important fact of the existing situation which will influence entrepreneurs in making investment decisions is the level of consumption. As we saw in Part One, the demand for investment goods is a derived demand, which depends ultimately on current expenditure on consumption. If consumption expenditure is high, investment will be high too; if consumption expenditure is low, investment will also be low. We shall therefore make the simplifying assumption throughout the rest of Part Two that current investment depends on current consumption. The existence of expectations will mean that in the real world the dependence is more complicated, but in our simple theory we may overlook this.

We shall assume that the demand for investment goods is a function of the rate of interest on the one hand, and of the level of consumption expenditure on the other. Relationships of this kind are shown in Figs. 21.2a and 21.2b. In Fig. 21.2a, investment is measured along

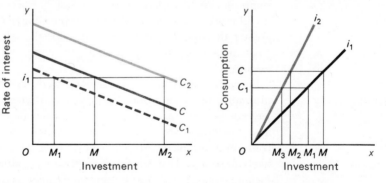

Fig. 21.2 a | b

the x-axis and the rate of interest up the y-axis. Assuming that consumption is at given level, say C, then the amount of investment undertaken at various rates of interest is shown on the marginal efficiency of capital curve, C. With different levels of consumption, investment at each rate of interest will differ. When consumption is C_2 (higher than C) investment is greater at each rate of interest than when consumption is either C or C_1. So, for example, when the rate of interest is i_1, investment is greater (at OM_2) when consumption is

C_2 than when it is C. (Investment is then OM.) When consumption is low (at C_1) investment is also low, at OM_1.

Figure 21.2b gives an alternative snapshot of the picture shown in Fig. 21.2a. Here, investment is still measured along the x-axis but consumption is now measured up the y-axis instead of the rate of interest. At the rate of interest i_1, the marginal efficiency of capital curve, i_1, shows the volume of investment (on the x-axis) undertaken at each level of consumption. Investment (OM) is greater when consumption is higher (at OC) and lower (OM_1) when it is lower (at OC_1). On the curve i_2, the rate of interest has risen to i_2. Investment at each level of consumption is now lower than when the rate of interest was i_1. These diagrams show, on our simplified assumptions about expectations, the dependence of investment on consumption, on the one hand, and on the rate of interest, on the other.

There are one or two differences between consumption and investment which it is useful to bear in mind. First, while the demand for consumption goods (especially non-durables) is likely to be fairly stable over time, the demand for investment goods is not. Because the inducement to invest depends so largely on expectations about the future, the demand for investment goods can change considerably even when consumption remains relatively stable. By ignoring expectations, we have been able to show investment as a simple function of consumption.

However, in Fig. 21.2a, if investors become pessimistic the curve showing investment of any rate of interest (for a given level of consumption, say C) will move to the left; if they become more confident, it will move to the right. The bigger the change in expectations, the greater the shift of the curve. While for the sake of simplicity it is convenient to ignore expectations, their importance must never be forgotten.

Second, it must always be remembered that investment depends ultimately on consumption; if no one consumes, no one will invest. Investment can thus be expressed as a function of income instead of as a function of consumption. For income (by definition) equals consumption plus investment and we have seen that consumption is likely to be a fairly stable function of income. However, the fact that income equals consumption plus investment, means that this would make investment partially dependent on itself. To avoid this complication, we shall assume that investment depends on consumption rather than on income.

In this 'pure' Keynesian model, then, the current demand for investment goods depends ultimately on estimates of current consumption expenditure, modified to allow for future changes in firms' and individuals' expectations. The demand for investment goods is given by the schedule of the marginal efficiency of capital.

6. Keynesian theory modified

This 'pure' Keynesian theory needs some modification. As it stands, it implies that all investment responds to the same influences. Since Keynes wrote, it has increasingly come to be agreed that there are two main elements in investment.

6.1 Autonomous investment

First, there is what economists call *autonomous investment*. This is 'long-range' investment in houses, roads, public buildings and other parts of the 'infrastructure'; it also includes 'long-range' investment intended to bring in major innovations. Autonomous investment probably depends more on population growth and technical progress than on anything else, though it may be somewhat affected by changes in the level of income. For a higher income makes it possible to provide, for example, more or better houses, roads, etc., for the community and once this happens the community may wish to provide them.

Autonomous investment is a major element in investment in most economies. For our purposes in this chapter, we need not worry over the fact that autonomous investment depends more on population growth or technical progress than on changes in the rate of interest. Like Keynes, when he wrote the *General Theory*, we are here concerned with short-run issues; with questions like what determines the level of GNP in a given year. We can therefore leave aside a deeper study of the role of autonomous investment. This is more appropriate in the context of the kind of theory of economic growth which we shall outline in Part Three.

6.2 Induced investment

The other kind of investment is described by economists as *induced investment*. This is investment both in fixed assets and in the stocks (inventories) that are required if the economy is to be able to produce a bigger output as aggregate demand rises. The 'pure' Keynesian theory is defective, as indeed Keynes feared it was when he wrote the *General Theory* in the 1930s, because the empirical evidence suggests that induced investment depends more on income than on the rate of interest. This resurrects one of Keynes's fears; that monetary policy working through the rate of interest will have little influence on the level of investment. The marginal efficiency of capital curve, at any given level of income, may be very steep; it may be interest-inelastic. Direct government investment, or other measures like investment grants or investment subsidies, may therefore be needed if a country wishes to increase its level of investment. We shall look at one rather mechanical model relating induced investment to consumption (or income) in the next section (7). What is important here is that we should understand that in practice investment is divided into an autonomous and an induced part and that the influence of the rate of interest on either is probably limited.

6.3 Government investment

Government investment is determined in similar ways to government current expenditure. Political factors will help to determine the amount of investment carried out in the public sector. This may be large if a great deal is spent on investment in housing and, say, in industries providing coal, steel, power and transport. However, political influences will determine whether such investment is public or private. In the UK, the central government invests little but the local authorities build large numbers of houses and the nationalised industries invest heavily.

As this implies, government investment usually concentrates on the infrastructure: roads, public buildings, hospitals, schools, etc., and may include investment in houses and in the transport, fuel and power industries. In other words a great deal of government investment is autonomous; it depends mainly on changes in population and on the public's view of the kind of investment that is appropriate. Consequently, as we shall see in more detail in Chapter 23, government investment can be, and often is, undertaken without too much attention being paid to the commercial value of the investment. This can be good or bad according to the circumstances.

6.4 Consumer durables

While we have seen that investment in houses by private individuals is included in investment, we have not included expenditure on consumer durables. Nevertheless, we saw in Chapter 20 and in section 4 of this chapter that perhaps we should separate expenditure on non-durable consumer goods from expenditure on durable consumer goods. The latter is much more akin to investment expenditure. We conform to current practice in including expenditure on durable consumer goods in consumption, while wondering whether it will continue for much longer to be seen as reasonable to do so.

7. The accelerator

We have seen that the multiplier shows how a small change in investment can exert a magnified effect on consumption and hence on income and employment. Another concept considers the relationship between income and investment. Indeed, it has a rather longer history than the multiplier. It is known as the principle of acceleration of derived demand.

Quite simply, the *acceleration principle* (often called the *accelerator*) says this. If the demand for any consumption good increases, this will raise the 'derived' demand for the factor of production, perhaps a machine, which makes it. But this investment in machines will rise proportionately even faster than the demand for the product has risen. The term *accelerator* is thus a metaphor, and in a sense it is incomplete. The accelerator in economics is not the same as the accelerator on a motor car. The idea embodied in the accelerator is not so much one of ever-increasing demand as one of a functional relationship between the demand for consumption goods and the demand for the machines which make them. It makes the level of investment a function not of the level of consumption, but of the *rate of change* of consumption.

7.1 The accelerator and the multiplier

There is therefore some sort of parallel between the acceleration principle and the multiplier. The multiplier shows the effect on income (and on consumption) of a change in investment. The accelerator shows the effect on investment of a change in income (and consumption). The two concepts might be confused, so the reader should keep them clearly distinct in his mind.

There is one rather important difference between the two concepts. The multiplier depends ultimately on psychology; it depends on the propensity to consume, which is a behaviour relationship determined by consumers' tastes and habits. The accelerator depends on a narrow, technical fact. It depends on the fact that a given amount of capital is required to produce a given amount of final output. The accelerator is based on technology.

7.2 What the accelerator explains and does not explain

The acceleration principle dates back to 1914 and beyond. The idea was popularised mainly by J. M. Clark, with whose name it is usually associated.[1] The basis on which it was constructed was the knowledge that fluctuations in employment, output, etc., in the investment goods industries are greater than those in the consumption goods industries. Nevertheless, the accelerator does not pretend to be able to explain all fluctuations of this kind. For example, the prices of raw materials tend to fluctuate rather more than do the prices of capital goods. The acceleration principle is unnecessary to explain this fact.

[1] See 'Business Acceleration and the Law of Demand', *Journal of Political Economy*, March, 1917, p. 217.

(a) Fluctuations in primary product prices

The reason lies in the fact that the supply of raw materials—agricultural products or minerals—is more inelastic in response to demand changes than is the supply of manufactured goods. The way in which an industrial economy meets falling prices is to reduce output very sharply following small falls in price, allowing unemployment to increase. With an agricultural commodity, the amount of unemployment caused by falling prices is often small. Because an individual farmer is a 'price taker' who cannot influence the price he gets, whether or not this is affected by government intervention, it pays him to produce as much as he can and sell it for what it fetches. During the 1930s, in particular, commodity prices had to fall very sharply if this same supply was to be disposed of when demand had fallen off. Largely because of this, modern governments often intervene to prevent prices fluctuating in this way. They buy up agricultural products when there is an excess supply of them, thus maintaining the price; they hope to sell them off at times when there is excess demand. The reasons for fluctuations in agricultural prices can therefore be shown quite simply, using the kind of analysis set out in Chapter 7.

(b) Why does investment fluctuate more than output?

The problem which the accelerator seeks to solve is more difficult. It is this. Why are fluctuations in employment in the investment goods industries greater than those in consumer goods industries? By analogy, why are fluctuations in durable consumer goods industries greater than those in industries making non-durable consumer goods? It does not require great thought to see that the relationship between changes in the demand for house room and subsequent events in the building industry must be very similar to the relationship between changed demand for consumer goods and subsequent events in the industry producing machines to make them. The essential fact, upon which the accelerator depends, is that machines are durable goods. The accelerator operates only where the investment goods concerned are durable and its importance stems from that durability.

7.3 The accelerator at work

(a) Our assumptions

Let us, then, outline the theory of the 'accelerator'. We begin by studying a situation where the demand for a part of 'final output'—a particular consumer good—has been stable for a considerable length of time. To simplify this discussion we assume that all prices in the economy are constant. This means that there is a stable derived demand for the machines making these consumer goods, the size of which will depend on the number of machines required to make a given quantity of consumer goods. Let us assume that the situation is that each machine costs £25 000. This amount has to be invested in a machine to obtain an output of, say, £5 000 worth of consumer goods. The capital-output ratio is five. In equilibrium, the value of the stock of machines will therefore be five times the value of the annual output of consumer goods.

Let us also assume that 10 per cent of the machines are replaced each year. The annual output of the machine-making industry will be equal to just one-tenth of the stock of these particular machines. So long as the demand for the consumer goods is constant, the demand for machines will be a constant 'replacement' demand. There will be no 'net' investment at all, after production to make good depreciation has been allowed for. 'Gross' investment will be positive, and will equal 10 per cent of the total stock of machines.

Let us assume that, in our hypothetical economy, the stock of machines is making an output of the consumer goods which sells for £1m per annum. The capital stock of 200 machines required to produce this output is therefore worth £5m. The capital-output ratio is five. If the life of each machine is 10 years and the economy has settled down in equilibrium, the output of the investment goods industry will be 20 machines per annum, costing £500 000. If we suppose that all replacement machines for any year are ordered on 1 January of that year, we have a very simple model.

(b) A change in demand for consumer goods

Let us now suppose that the demand for consumer goods increases by 10 per cent, to £1·1m. If the industry wants to make all these additional consumer goods, it will need another 20 machines. On 1 January next, therefore, new machines costing £500 000 will be ordered, while the replacement demand of £500 000 for 20 machines will continue as before. The demand for machines will thus rise from 20 to 40 and expenditure will increase from £500 000 to £1m (an increase of 100 per cent) in order to deal with an increase of only 10 per cent of the demand for consumer goods. The amount of output required for the machine-making industry has doubled and employment has increased too. We assume that the industry has excess capacity and does not itself need to invest. If it does have to invest, the accelerator will be even bigger.

(c) The accelerator defined

Here, then, we have an explanation of fluctuations in employment and investment in the machine-making industries. This is the accelerator at work. The operation of the accelerator can be explained in this way. In the whole economy, the stock of capital required (in physical terms) will depend on the rate of demand for final output (also in physical terms). Any change in the level of final output will call for a change in the size of the stock of capital. This change will be equal to v times the change in output. Here, v is the amount of capital required to produce £1 worth of output; it is the capital-output ratio. It is also the accelerator. If, in any economy, an increment of final output is denoted by δY, and the amount of investment required to produce this extra output is denoted by δI, then $\delta I = v \delta Y$.

Whether the demand for machines in any year will actually double, as the result of a rise of 10 per cent in the demand for consumer goods, will depend on the length of life of the machines required to make them. This will determine the level of the replacement demand for machines, as well as the amount of capacity required in the machine-making industry to produce these machines. If a machine lasts for more than 10 years, the *proportionate* effect on the amount of capital required in the machine-making industry will be even greater. If machines last less than ten years, the *proportional* effect will be smaller. The accelerator is not concerned with this, but with the size of the capital-output ratio. This is the link between δY and δI. The length of life of machines determines only the proportionate change in the size of demand for the machine-making industry's product.

A general statement of the acceleration principle is this. If the demand for consumption goods rises, and if producers try to satisfy this demand fully from the earliest possible moment, there will be a change in the amount of investment required. This is equal to δY multiplied by the accelerator (v).

(d) Subsequent events

Let us return to our model. Let us suppose that the initial increase in the demand for consumer goods has already taken place. Having increased by 10 per cent and led to a demand for 40 machines in one year, the demand now remains stable. There will now be no accelerator effect at all in the demand for machines in the following year. The 20 new machines having been made, the demand for machines will return to the old level of 20 per annum for replacements. It can begin to exceed 20 only when some machines have worn out. This is likely to take 10 years. After a time, when long-run equilibrium has been reached, 22 machines a year will be demanded instead of the original 20—if no new change has intervened. However, this is such a long period that a change is bound to have occurred.

Although the increased demand for consumer goods has turned out to be permanent, the effect on the machine-making industry is disappointing. Even in the long run, when replacement demand has risen to 22 machines per annum, 18 fewer machines will be ordered than in the first year after the increase of 10 per cent in demand. In this simple model, if one wants to avoid fluctuations in activity in the machine industry, one must ensure either that the demand for consumption goods remains permanently constant, or else that it increases at a constant rate. If the demand for consumer goods is constant for ever, the demand for machines will be constant for ever too. Similarly, there could be a constant increase in employment and capital employed in the machine-making industry if there were a constant increase from year to year in the demand for consumer goods. The expression $\delta I = v\delta Y$ would then always be positive. It is the *falling off* in the rate of increase of consumption, and *not* a decline in the *absolute level* of consumption, which causes the contraction in the demand for machines. In practice, of course, one need not go quite to this extreme. If one merely wanted to ensure that employment in the machine industry would not fall, one could take into account the fact that when consumption had increased for several years, the demand for 'replacements' would grow. The rate of increase in consumption could then slacken off, without a fall in employment in the machine-making industry.

To give an example, if in the first year the demand for consumer goods rises by 10 per cent, 20 new machines are ordered, raising the demand for machines from 20 to 40. Once some of these machines wear out, the output of the machine industry can be held steady so long as demand continues to increase, even though it may do so at a slower and slower rate. When long-run equilibrium has been reached, the replacement demand alone will be sufficient to keep the investment industry at work. But consumption would have had to double — quite an achievement. It follows, therefore, that on our assumptions in this simple model, unless there is a continual though not necessarily constant growth of demand, the effect of a single increase in the demand for consumer goods will be first to expand, and then to contract, the demand for machines.

7.4 Limitations of the accelerator

There are a number of points at which it is difficult to accept this extremely simplified model, on which we have so far based our discussion of the accelerator. If anything, the explanation of fluctuations in the capital goods industry provided by the accelerator is too good to be realistic; our assumption about the industry has been too rigid. If an increase in demand always resulted in a much more than proportionate increase in the output of machines, fluctuations in the investment goods industries would be even larger than they are.

Like many economic models, this model of the accelerator is too simple. However, the reason why it is too simple is that we are making assumptions about technology rather than economics. In particular, we have assumed great inflexibility of output in the consumer goods industry and great flexibility in the investment goods industry.

(a) The amount of excess capacity

In our model we have made the following assumptions. So far as the consumption goods industry was concerned, we assumed that there was no excess capacity at all. We assumed that no machines were idle and that expedients like shiftworking were out of the question. If excess capacity did exist, then an increase in consumer demand could be met with the existing equipment and the accelerator would not work.

In the investment goods industry, we assumed exactly the opposite —that there *was* surplus capacity. If there were no excess capacity in the machine-making industry, an increase in the derived demand for machines could not result in an increased supply of machines. The strict working of the accelerator depends on the ability of the machine-making industry to produce greatly increased numbers of machines quickly, without anyone investing large amounts of capital in order to do so. It depends on the existence of excess capacity in the investment industry. The actual situation will be much less rigid. Once this is recognised we can see that, in practice, we shall not be dealing with a technological relationship after all; it will be an economic one.

(b) Flexibility of output

Even if the machine-making firms are working to capacity when the rise in demand for consumer goods leads to a rise in demand for machines, the increased demand for machines can probably be met, at least temporarily. It can be met by reducing stocks of finished machines, by working the extra shifts we have assumed to be impossible, and so on. However, stocks cannot be reduced below zero, and working double shifts or using other expedients is expensive. If the increase in demand is expected to last long enough to make it worthwhile, new capital will be invested in the machine-making industry. On the other hand, if the rise in business is expected to be only temporary, the additional demand will be met by expedients like those we have mentioned. This is very much the situation we discussed at the end of Chapter 9 when discussing Fixprice markets. Only if the rise in demand is expected to be permanent is a profit-maximising entrepreneur in the machine-making industry likely to install much additional equipment.

(c) Economic calculations

Obviously, this view of the accelerator is more realistic but it shows that the size of the accelerator (v) will not remain constant over time. In particular, its value is likely to be affected by what businessmen calculate to be the profits they will earn over the life of the new capital assets required to make more machines, if they install them. The accelerator theory, in its strict form, asks the entrepreneur to assume, as he installs any amount of capital, that the demand for machines will remain adequate in future. He is asked to do this despite the fact that it is a sudden increase in demand that has led him to consider the investment at all. In practice, the entrepreneur will have to make his own economic calculations: about the future demand for the final product made by the machine; about the future demand for machines themselves; about the costs and availability of machines; about interest rates; and so on. We are then well into a very complicated theory of investment. We shall return to some of these issues in discussing the problems of economic growth in Part Three. For the moment, this is as far as it is convenient to go. Readers who wish to pursue this matter further are referred to the suggested reading at the end of the chapter.

7.5 The usefulness of the accelerator

In the light of this discussion, we may well ask whether the accelerator is so restricted in its application that it should be ignored in any realistic discussions of what affects income and employment. The fact that it has held its own since 1914 as a useful tool of economic analysis may seem to give the lie to this view. Yet it is significant that Keynes entirely ignored the acceleration principle when writing the *General Theory*. He did not mention the accelerator, which is a technical concept, but stressed psychological concepts like the multiplier and the marginal efficiency of capital. Keynes seems to have believed that the volatile nature of business expectations were more important in determining the volume of investment, and hence employment, than the accelerator.

7.6 The multiplier and accelerator combined

Despite these difficulties, some economists have used the acceleration principle in formal, mathematical models to show the way the economy would react if it were initially in equilibrium and then there was a sudden increase in demand for output. Not surprisingly, in the light of our analysis, it turns out that on many assumptions about the size of both the accelerator and the multiplier, a change in the demand for final output will lead to oscillations in the economy. These may be damped, so that they ultimately fade away. However, on quite reasonable assumptions about the size of the multiplier and accelerator, the oscillations will be explosive. They will stop increasing only because of some constraint in the economy, like a full-employment ceiling, which damps the fluctuations down. There is too little space to go into detail about this here. In any case, a satisfactory analysis requires the use of difference equations, which many readers will not yet have met. The paper by Professor Samuelson quoted in the selected reading at the end of this chapter, and mentioned in Chapter 25, gives a good introduction to the subject. The book *A Contribution to the Theory of the Trade Cycle*, by Sir John Hicks, provides a more extensive discussion. Both these works were extremely influential when they first appeared.

7.7 Static assumptions

The assumptions made about expectations in the theory of the accelerator are rarely made explicit, but they are important. They are 'static'. That is to say, it is assumed that if conditions alter the response of consumers and entrepreneurs to these changes is to believe that they will be permanent. If entrepreneurs expected that the change in demand would be only temporary, they would not buy the extra machines. If they expected further, or greater, increases they would not content themselves with relatively modest increases in investment. It is therefore important always to remember that every theory of employment makes some assumptions about expectations, even if they are only implicit ones.

Suggested reading

KEYNES, J. M.	*General Theory*, London, 1936, chapters 11 and 12.
CLARK, J. M.	'Business Acceleration and the Law of Demand', *Journal of Political Economy*, March, 1917, p. 217.
ACKLEY, GARDNER	*Macroeconomics*, New York, 1961, chapter 17.
SAMUELSON, P. A.	'Interactions between the Multiplier Analysis and the Principle of Acceleration', *Review of Economics and Statistics*, May, 1939, p. 75. Reprinted in *Readings in Business Cycle Theory*, Blakiston Series, 1944.

22

The rate of interest

1. The rate of interest defined

In Keynesian macro-economics, the rate of interest is the second important determinant of the volume of investment undertaken in any period, the marginal efficiency of capital being the first. The rate of interest is the price at which loans of money are made; it is the price of money in terms of bonds. As we have seen, Keynes's theory assumed that the alternative to holding money was to hold bonds. For the present, we shall continue to make this assumption. The rate of interest equates the desirability of holding bonds with the desirability of holding money.

To begin with, we shall concentrate on the rate of interest on bonds. We shall look especially at the long-term rate of interest on undated government bonds. We have already seen one British example—4 per cent Consolidated Stock. A purchaser of 4 per cent Consols is entitled to a continuing *annual* payment of £4 on every bond with a face value of £100, whatever he has paid for the bond. Thus, if the market price of a £100 bond falls to £50, the current rate of interest must be 8 per cent. If it rises to £200, the current rate of interest must be 2 per cent.

In the first part of this chapter, we shall be concerned primarily with the long-term rate of interest on irredeemable government stock but, except in the early part of the chapter, we are not concerned *only* with the gilt-edged rate. Nor are we solely concerned with long-term rates of interest. We take Keynes's view that, 'In general discussion, as distinct from specific problems where the period of the debt is expressly specified, it is convenient to mean by the rate of interest the complex of the various rates of interest current for different periods of time.'[1] Since all interest rates, short and long, are interrelated we can use the phrase 'the rate of interest' to include them all.

Since the rate of interest is the price of money loans, it is not surprising that it should be determined by supply and demand. On the one hand, the rate of interest depends on the supply of money available to the community. On the other hand, it depends on the

[1] *General Theory*, p. 167, footnote.

demand for that money—on liquidity preference. What determines these? The supply of money—the size of the money stock—is something which we can assume for the moment to be given. As we saw in Chapter 18, the size of the money supply is determined by the actions of the monetary authorities, working on the banking system. To be able to consider one thing at a time, we shall assume for the present that the money supply is fixed. We shall also ignore the complications arising from the fact that monetary policy often alters the asset structure of the banking system, rather than the money supply alone.

2. Liquidity preference

The demand for money, the community's liquidity preference, is an independent variable in Keynes's system just as the supply of money is. Liquidity preference—the demand for money—depends ultimately on the psychology of the community, just as the supply of money depends on the banking system. We have seen (pp. 408–411) that the demand for money can be split up into three parts. Money is held: (a) to satisfy the transactions motive; (b) to satisfy the precautionary motive; and (c) to satisfy the speculative motive. We shall assume, for the present, that the demand for money under the transactions and precautionary motives depends *only* on the level of income and that the demand for money under the speculative motive depends *only* on the rate of interest.

We can then divide liquidity preference into two parts, which we shall label L_1 and L_2. L_1 is that part of liquidity preference which arises from the transactions and precautionary motives. L_2 is the part which arises from the speculative motive. If we denote the amount of money held under L_1 as M_1, and that held under L_2 as M_2, M_1 will be a function only of income (Y) and M_2 a function only of the rate of interest (i). Symbolically: $M = M_1 + M_2$; $M_1 = L_1$ (Y) and $M_2 \times L_2(i)$.

2.1 The liquidity preference schedule

We have seen how important it is to avoid confusion about the meaning of the demand for money. All money is created by the banking system and all has to be held by someone. Consequently, the total supply of money, M, must equal the total amount held. While the amount of money actually demanded in any situation is always equal to the amount actually supplied, different amounts would have been demanded had the rate of interest, or the level of income, been different. Liquidity preference is therefore not a constant amount of money in all circumstances. There is a schedule of the demand for money—a schedule of liquidity preference. This shows how much money the community would wish to hold at various levels of income and of the rate of interest. Two ways of depicting liquidity preference schedules are given in Fig. 22.1.

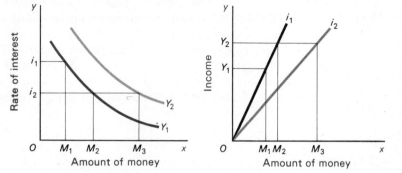

Fig. 22.1 a | b

(a) Two diagrams for liquidity preference

Both parts of Fig. 22.1 show the relationship between three variables: the amount of money (M), the rate of interest (i), and income (Y). In Fig. 22.1a, the curve Y_1 shows liquidity preference at various rates of interest when income is Y_1. It shows how much money is demanded at each interest rate when income is Y_1. Similarly, the curve Y_2 shows liquidity preference at these rates of interest when income is Y_2. Y_2 is greater than Y_1, so that the second curve is above the first. Other curves could be drawn showing liquidity preference at other levels of income. In Fig. 22.1b, instead of drawing each curve for a particular level of income, the rate of interest is taken as given instead. Thus the curve i_1 shows how much money will be demanded when income is at various levels and the rate of interest is i_1. Similarly, the curve i_2 shows liquidity preference at these same levels of income when the rate of interest is lower—at i_2.

From Fig. 22.1a the following conclusions can be drawn: (1) The community will hold more money at lower rates of interest than at higher ones, if income is constant. For example, when income is Y_1 and the rate of interest is i_1, the amount of money OM_1 is held. When the rate of interest falls to i_2, the amount of money demanded rises to OM_2 though income is constant at Y_1. (2) At a given rate of interest, more money is held when income is higher. For example, when the rate of interest is i_2 and income is Y_1, OM_2 of money is demanded. If the rate of interest remains at i_2 but income rises to Y_2, liquidity preference rises to OM_3.

Figure 22.1b gives the same information. One can again see that: (1) If the rate of interest is given, people hold more money when their incomes are higher. When the rate of interest is i_1 and income is OY_1, the amount of money demanded is OM_1. When income rises to OY_2, the amount of money demanded rises to OM_2. This diagram emphasises that liquidity preference depends on the level of income as well as on the rate of interest. The fact that the liquidity preference schedules are here drawn as straight lines implies that the amount of money demanded rises in exact proportion with income. This need not be the case, though it may be. (2) Given the level of income, more money will be held if the rate of interest falls. For instance in Fig. 22.1b, where income is OY_2 and the rate of interest is i_1, the amount of money held is OM_2. When the rate of interest falls to i_2, with income still OY_2, the amount of money demanded rises to OM_3.

3. Liquidity preference and the rate of interest

3.1 The cost of holding money

(a) The transactions motive

So far, we have assumed that the demand for money under the transactions and precautionary motives (L_1) depends only on the level of income, and that under the speculative motive (L_2) only on the rate of interest. We must now relax these assumptions. In practice, even the demand for money under L_1 is unlikely to be completely independent of the rate of interest. Since we are assuming that bonds are the only substitute for money, holding *any* money under L_1 represents a sacrifice of interest; it has an opportunity cost. Money that is *not* held can be used to buy bonds and earn interest. It is therefore likely that, in the long run, if the rate of interest is high people will try to hold less money under L_1. Similarly, if the rate of interest is low, the opportunity cost of holding money will be smaller. Consequently, people will not be so careful to keep down the amount of money they hold under L_1. In recent years, economists have drawn attention to the fact that money held represents a kind of inventory. As with other kinds of inventory, there is a cost to holding it. With money, the cost is the rate of interest paid (or sacrificed) on money held in cash. While it may take individuals, or indeed firms, some time to adjust to higher interest rates, over longish periods less money will be held to satisfy L_1 if the rate of interest is high than is held if it is low. In the short run, this is less certain. In any case, for most of the time increases in the amount of money held under L_1 will be more strongly affected by changes in the level of incomes than by changes in the rate of interest. Where money is treated as an 'inventory' in this way, work on optimal inventory policy by business economists and operational researchers suggests that the demand for money under the transactions motive will be a function not of income but more probably of the square root of income.[1]

[1] For a fuller explanation of this see H. G. Johnson, *Essays in Monetary Economics*, London, 1967, chapter 5.

(b) The speculative motive

It is equally true that holding money to satisfy the speculative motive (L_2) again involves a cost. People who hold money under L_2 in order to speculate on changes in the rate of interest (in bond prices) also have to sacrifice interest which they could otherwise have earned. The higher the rate of interest, the greater the sacrifice incurred in order to hold this *masse de manoeuvre*. So, it may also be that a high rate of interest could have some effect in reducing the amount of money held under L_2. Macro-economic theory is therefore moving towards treating all money held, whether under L_1 or L_2, as influenced both by the rate of interest and by the level of income. We shall look at this in more detail later.

3.2 Expectations

For the moment, we must turn to consider Keynes's view that the demand for money to satisfy the speculative motive depends less on the current rate of interest than on *expectations of changes* in the rate of interest, with the capital gains that they make possible. We can then link expectations about future interest rates to the current rate of interest. We can establish a connection between the facts of the existing situation, the current rate of interest and the demand for money under L_2, a demand which largely depends on expectations about future interest rates. Why is it that people hold money to satisfy L_2? Why, when income is constant, do people hold more or less money at different times because of changes in their expectations about the future rate of interest?

(a) About commodity prices

Those economists who wrote before Keynes did recognise the dependence of the demand for money on expectations, but they did not recognise that it was expectations about *changes in the rate of interest* which were important. The view of earlier economists was that the only close substitutes for money were commodities. They thought that 'speculators' were interested in the future prices of commodities because they could move their resources out of money into goods if goods were expected to become dearer. They could then make profits by selling when prices had risen. On the other hand, if people expected commodity prices to fall, it would pay them to hold money rather than commodities. This money could be used to buy larger amounts of commodities when they had become cheaper. This was the generally-accepted theory of earlier economists and the one which Keynes challenged.

If people expect commodity prices to fall, this is clearly a good reason for refusing to hold commodities. However, it is not, in itself, enough to induce people to hold money instead. It is just as reasonable to think that people will sell goods in order to hold bonds as to think that they will sell goods in order to hold money. If people expect the money prices of goods to fall, but think that the rate of interest will remain constant, they have no reason to switch to holding money. If anyone feels quite certain that the rate of interest will remain constant, then he can back his expectations about commodity prices just as easily (and more profitably) by buying bonds rather than by acquiring cash. If he does not expect the rate of interest to change, he can expect to sell his bonds for cash, without loss, at any moment. If the rate of interest is constant, he can both store his wealth safely and earn interest on it. There is also the practical point that speculating on changes in commodity prices requires more expertise than speculating on changes in the rate of interest. Uncertain expectations about the future of *commodity prices alone* are therefore insufficient to explain the desire to hold money under the speculative motive. For the reasons we have given, the important factor determining the desire to hold money for speculative purposes is expectations of changes in bond prices. The size of L_2 depends on expectations of changes in the rate of interest.

(b) About the rate of interest

Let us now look in detail at the way in which we can connect expectations about the future rate of interest with the current rate of interest. In that way we can link the present and the future. If the rate of interest is high at any moment, people are likely to expect it to fall in the future. A high rate of interest means low bond prices. The lower bond prices are at present, compared with the 'normal' level, the more likely it will seem that a future recovery is going to take place. At the same time, a high rate of interest guarantees a high reward in the form of interest, as a partial offset to fears of a further *fall* in bond prices. It will seem sensible to hold bonds rather than money. A high current rate of interest will therefore lead to expectations of a fall in the future, so that little money will be held for speculative purposes.

If the rate of interest is low compared with the 'normal' rate, the argument is reversed. There will then be an inducement to hold fairly large amounts of money. The fact that the rate of interest is low will mean that people expect it to rise in the future. Bond prices will be expected to fall and it will be foolish to hold bonds, especially as the yield on bonds will be low and the sacrifice of interest, if cash is held instead, correspondingly small.

This is how the present rate of interest is connected with the future rate. However, the term 'normal' rate of interest perhaps needs explaining. At any moment of time, every individual who deals in bonds, and the total number of people who do, will have a view of what is a 'normal' rate of interest. This will be derived from experience of the past. It is divergences from this 'normal' rate which lead those who trade in bonds to buy or sell them. It is these divergences which lead to changes in liquidity preference.

4. The determination of the rate of interest

We can now go on to discuss more fully how the rate of interest is determined. To begin, we shall simplify the analysis by assuming that liquidity preference (the demand for money) depends *only* on the rate of interest and that the level of income remains constant. It is important to bear this temporary assumption in mind.

We can then say that the demand for money depends on the rate of interest, just as we can say that the amount of any commodity which is demanded depends on its price. The amount of money held depends on what the rate of interest is, just as the amount of any goods which are actually exchanged in the market depends on what their market prices are. However, this tells only half the story, since price is a dependent variable. Just as the equilibrium price of a good is fixed by the demand and supply conditions for it, so the rate of interest is determined by the demand for and supply of money. When it has been thus determined, the rate of interest shows how much money will be held.

4.1 A simple model

To see the way in which the demand and supply of money determine the rate of interest, we begin with the simplest possible case. Let us assume that the supply of money is fixed and is shown by the black, vertical supply curve *MM* in Fig. 22.2. We suppose that the demand for money at each interest rate is shown by the brown liquidity preference schedule (*LP*) in Fig. 22.2. The rate of interest will be *Oi*,

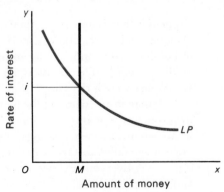

Fig. 22.2

where the supply of money is OM. This is the only rate of interest at which the total money supply will *all* be held by someone.

Let us now suppose there is a spontaneous change of 'tastes' which shifts the liquidity preference schedule. We can now trace the effect of this change on the rate of interest. Let us assume that the liquidity preference schedule shifts to the right. This means that at the existing price of bonds—at the current rate of interest—some people are more eager than they were to hold money instead of bonds. Indeed, this is true at every interest rate.

This does not necessarily mean that anyone actually buys or sells bonds. For example, suppose we assume that demand increases equally all over the market—that everyone's demand for money changes to exactly the same extent. In this the first model, there will be no buying or selling of bonds. No one will acquire more money; nor will anyone sell any bonds. Yet the price of bonds will fall. What

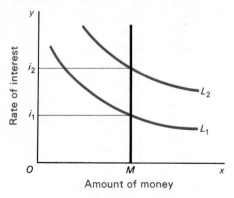

Fig. 22.3

happens is that people revise their views of the relative attractiveness of money and bonds, taking a more pessimistic view of the desirability of holding bonds and a more optimistic view of the desirability of holding money. The result is an immediate fall in bond prices. Everyone's view is the same—that bond prices must fall.

A change in the demand for money therefore need not cause any turnover in the market for bonds at all. There need be no change whatever in anyone's holdings of bonds or of money. Once bond prices have fallen to take account of the change in views, everyone is inactive. Everyone's views of the future level of both interest rates and bond prices has changed to exactly the same extent. The rate of interest rises correspondingly; bond prices fall, but no bonds are traded. This can be seen from Fig. 22.3.

Here, rates of interest are measured up the y-axis and amounts of money along the x-axis. The curve L_1 shows how much money is demanded initially at each rate of interest. The initial rate of interest must therefore be i_1, if all the (fixed) supply of money (OM) is to be held. Now let us suppose that everyone wants to hold more money at each rate of interest. The liquidity preference schedule moves to the right, so that the new equilibrium position is on the curve L_2. If the supply of money remains fixed at OM, the only rate of interest at which all this money (OM) will be held is i_2. The rate of interest thus rises to i_2. Bond prices fall proportionately, in order to allow it to happen.

(b) Increased trading of bonds

The first model is too simple since it allows for no sale or purchase of bonds at all. In practice, there will always be some buying and selling of bonds going on all the time, whatever the rate of interest is. The real question to ask therefore is: Does that amount change? Does a change in views about bond prices lead to an increase in Stock Exchange dealing in bonds? We could alter the model discussed above to show that an identical change of view by everyone would lead to *no change* in the amount of trading that was occurring. However, a more interesting second model would be where one group of people changed their views about bond prices, becoming more anxious to hold money and less anxious to hold bonds, but no one else's views changed at all. In this case, there would be a change in one part of the market that was not paralleled in other parts. In this situation, there would have to be increased exchange of bonds. The people whose views had changed would wish to sell bonds; other people would therefore have to be induced to buy them. This would cause increased trading in bonds, a fall in bond prices and a rise in the rate of interest.

(c) Spontaneous and induced changes in liquidity preference

The third and real model will be still more complicated. When bond prices change, there will usually have been a spontaneous change in the views of some people about bond prices. Associated with this there will probably be induced changes in the views of other people.

For example, if a group of people suddenly decided that bond prices were likely to fall, and became more anxious to hold money, they would sell bonds. Bond prices would fall to the extent required if the sales were to be achieved. However, this would lead other bond holders to realise that some people were selling bonds. They might well decide to change their own views too, but they need not change them at the same time or to the same extent. They need not even all change in the same direction. A good deal would depend on what financial journalists and other experts, to whom investors listen, had to say about the future of interest rates. Because of these changes in views, some people might become very anxious to sell bonds and hold cash; others not quite so anxious to hold cash; and so on. Some people might even decide that bond prices were going to *rise* and not fall, so that they actually became *more* anxious to hold bonds—they wanted to buy bonds for cash.

Whether bond prices fall or rise will therefore depend on whether those who expect a fall in bond prices, and want to sell bonds, are trying to sell more bonds than those who expect a rise in bond prices want to buy. If the former group is predominant, bond prices will rise and interest rates fall, and vice versa. In either case, an increase in number of bond market transactions is likely.

This seems to be a more realistic picture of what actually happens. If it is, then the result of changed views about bond prices will be a rise in interest rates if the net effect is that those who take a more dismal view of bond prices predominate in the market, and vice versa. If the effect on balance is that the pessimists predominate, then, in our simple model where the choice is between cash and bonds the liquidity preference schedule will shift to the right. More money will be demanded and the rate of interest will rise. If the net effect is to reduce liquidity preference at each rate of interest, then the interest rate will fall.

We have so far assumed that whether or not all views change simultaneously, or to the same extent, the size of the money supply is constant. The result is that although on balance people want to hold more money, they are unable to do so. The additional money is not there to be held. They can hold more money only if more is supplied. Since more is *not* supplied, something else in the system has to give way. It is bond prices and interest rates which change. Bond prices alter so that the existing supply of money and the new demand for money become consistent with each other. This leads to a new rate of interest. After the change, the total supply of money is again held by people who are content to hold it at the new rate of interest, while the supply of bonds is also again held by people who are content to hold them at their new prices. But, because the amount of money is unchanged, interest rates have to rise if the demand for it is to be satisfied; bond prices have to fall.

Where there is a sharp and sudden change in bond prices and thus in the rate of interest, an increase in purchases and sales of bonds over and above the existing rate is very likely. The fact that there has been a sharp movement away from the existing state of affairs means that people's preconceived ideas have suddenly been shattered. The chances are that they will be more uncertain than usual about what the future holds in store, so that individual views about the future of bond prices change differently. This third model is the most realistic one.

4.3 Changes in monetary policy

However, we have to go even farther. We must see how the central bank, or the government, can use monetary policy to alter the rate of interest.

(a) A change in the money supply

Let us first assume that the supply of money is changed but that the liquidity preference does not alter. We have seen that the supply of money is controlled by the central bank working on the monetary system through devices like open-market operations or changes in primary or secondary reserve ratios. In order to simplify the analysis, let us ignore the complications caused by the fact that any open-market purchase of securities is multiplied in its effect on the system as a whole because of the cash-deposit ratio, as modified by the 'drain of cash'. Let us also ignore the fact that there may be a time-lag before the full effect of a change in monetary policy, in expanding bank credit, has worked itself out. We shall assume that the central bank can alter the deposits of joint-stock banks immediately by a given amount.

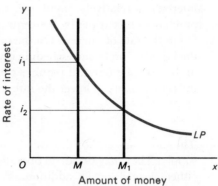

Fig. 22.4

If the central bank increases the supply of money, but liquidity preference is unchanged, the rate of interest must fall. This can be seen from Fig. 22.4. The community's (given) liquidity preference schedule is the curve *LP*. The amount of money originally in existence is OM and the rate of interest is initially i_1. The central bank now increases the supply of money from OM to OM_1. As a result, the interest rate falls to i_2. One way of explaining what happens when the central bank enters the bond market in this way is to say that all other lenders take the same view of the relative attractiveness of money and bonds, but the central bank changes its attitude. It becomes more anxious to hold bonds relatively to cash. In order to acquire these, it must bid up bond prices far enough to persuade some individuals to sell them. It creates money for these individuals to hold. The rate of interest falls and the community is induced to hold all the money which is now available. The rate of interest is the one where the demand for money again equals the supply, but the amount of money held is bigger.

If anyone becomes more anxious to hold bonds and no one becomes less keen, the price of bonds rises. If the central bank increases the money supply by open-market operations, we may say that the central bank has become more anxious to hold bonds rather than cash. The price of bonds will therefore rise. However, it may rise a little or a great deal, depending on how reluctant people are to disgorge bonds and hold money instead. Someone *must* be persuaded to sell bonds if open-market operations are to succeed, but the extent of the persuasion needed will differ from occasion to occasion. If bond-holders are reluctant to sell, even though the central bank is bidding up the price of bonds considerably, liquidity preference will increase very little as the rate of interest falls. Since we are assuming that cash and bonds are the only alternative assets which can be held, a slow increase in the demand for money as interest rates fall implies a corresponding reluctance by bond holders to sell bonds. The demand for liquidity is not very 'elastic' in response to changes in the rate of interest; a relatively small effort, in the shape of open-market purchases of securities by the central bank, will cause a considerable fall in the rate of interest. On the other hand, where the elasticity of the liquidity preference schedule is very great in response to changes in the rate of interest, it requires considerable purchases of bonds by the central bank to lower the rate of interest.[1]

(b) Influencing liquidity preference

The monetary authorities are not restricted to acting on the money supply. They may decide to operate directly on liquidity preference, either instead or in addition. For example, the Chancellor of the Exchequer or Finance Minister may announce that it is govern-

[1] This discussion has assumed, for simplicity, that when the central bank increases the supply of money by open-market operations it always buys long-term securities. In practice, many central banks pay as much, if not more, attention to the market for short-term securities, e.g. treasury bills. The results will be much the same in either case.

ment policy that interest rates should fall. Since the monetary authorities have the power, if they wish to use it, to force interest rates down, it is likely that what he says will be believed. People's views of what is a 'normal' interest rate will therefore alter. If they now regard the existing interest rates as rather high, the liquidity preference curve may move downwards, from, say, the curve L_1 in Fig. 22.5 to the curve L_2. The rate of interest will fall from i_1 to i_2

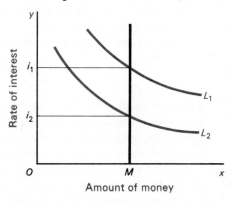

Fig. 22.5

without there being any change in the money supply (M). In some countries, it may well be that attempts to change liquidity preference, and so the rate of interest, will be more indirect. For example, in the UK, changes in bank rate[1] often seem intended to give signals of this kind to the bond market.

Alternatively, the government may leave the financial community to derive clues about its intentions from the nature of government activities in the short-term and long-term money markets. So long as the message is understood, and liquidity preference is affected in the desired direction, interest rates can be raised or lowered. The only qualification to this, as we shall see later, appears to be where interest rates have reached such a low level that no one thinks it possible for them to fall further. It was this kind of resistance which seems to have prevented the British Chancellor of the Exchequer, in 1947, from reducing long-term interest rates below about $2\frac{3}{4}$ per cent.

5. The rate of interest and investment

We have here the essence of the Keynesian theory of the rate of interest, but we must introduce some more complications. We have so far assumed that liquidity preference depends only on the rate of

[1] Technically, the bank rate is the rate of interest at which the Bank of England will discount (buy) treasury bills. However, the bank rate is more important than this, because many other interest rates charged and offered by banks, hire purchase companies, insurance companies, etc., have been tied by convention to the bank rate. However, these links are weaker since the changes of September 1971.

interest. Though this is a useful simplification, it is not a very realistic one. Liquidity preference also depends on the level of income. A change either in liquidity preference or in the money supply will alter the rate of interest. This will affect the level of incomes by altering the volume of investment activity. The change in incomes will in turn effect liquidity preference. We must now analyse the nature of this effect on liquidity preference. It may be felt through the transactions motive, the precautionary motive or the speculative motive. What one has to do is to try to discover which part of liquidity preference is likely to be most affected.

5.1 *The direct effect*

In order to proceed, let us assume that the liquidity preference schedule is given and go on to trace the indirect effects of a fall in the rate of interest caused by a rise in the quantity of money. The main secondary effect will be on investment. The normal result of a fall in the rate of interest, with a given schedule of the marginal efficiency of capital, is for investment to increase. We saw this earlier. The result will be an increase in income, whose amount will depend on the size of the multiplier.

As income rises, so does the amount of money held under L_1. The transactions motive, in particular, will absorb a larger amount of money as income rises, so that not all of the increased demand for money resulting from a fall in the rate of interest will be due to a change in demand under the speculative motive. The transactions motive will also play its part.

In macro-economics, one cannot ignore these indirect repercussions of a change in any variable. The indirect results of a change in the rate of interest may be just as important as the direct ones. The variables in a macro-economic system are rather like the balls a juggler uses. If he is to keep them all in the air at once, he can neglect any one of them for more than a split second only at his peril. So, with general equilibrium analysis of this kind, to neglect one variable may result in giving a wrong answer. The effect of a change in the amount of money in the system is not merely that the rate of interest falls; as a result, income and employment rise. Nevertheless, in Keynesian economics the fall in the rate of interest is the vital link in the chain by which an increase in the supply of money is seen to raise the level of employment. It is the mechanism by which an increase in the money supply is introduced into the economy. Even so, the efficacy of a fall in the rate of interest in creating employment will depend on whether this fall causes a large or small increase in investment. This, in turn, depends on businessmen's expectations. Both individuals and firms are at some times more in the mood for expanding investment in response to a fall in the rate of interest than at others.

One can, however, legitimately expect that the effect of a fall in the rate of interest on investment will be in the right direction—that it is unlikely to reduce investment. In the 1930s it was argued by some economists that entrepreneurs might be alarmed by government interference with the rate of interest, so that they might invest less rather than more. Their alarm at the government's 'cheap money' policy might lower the marginal efficiency of capital schedule so much that the fall in the rate of interest was more than outweighed. Experience since then certainly does not suggest that this is likely. A much more real danger is that, while it will not shift to the left, the marginal efficiency of capital schedule may be inelastic to changes in the rate of interest. The marginal efficiency of capital may diminish rapidly as investment increases, so that this will be the weak link in the chain connecting a fall in the rate of interest with an increase in GNP.

5.2 Keynesian theory in a nutshell

Here, in its essentials, we have the Keynesian remedy for unemployment. The government is in a position to tell the central bank to increase the money supply either by buying securities or in some other way, and so to lower the rate of interest. This 'cheap money' policy makes investment less expensive to finance. Provided that the marginal efficiency of capital schedule is relatively elastic and does not shift to the left as a result of the government's policy measures, investment and incomes will rise. If the marginal efficiency schedule does shift, perhaps because of changed business expectations, it may be necessary to reinforce the lowering of the rate of interest by more direct methods. If entrepreneurs fail to invest when they can do so cheaply, government investment may have to be increased instead. This would raise incomes directly and might well encourage private investment. Similarly, government intervention might be necessary if the marginal efficiency schedule were inelastic to reductions in the rate of interest. However, the risk is now that the balance of investment will be wrong. Unless there are a number of nationalised manufacturing industries, too much investment may go into the infrastructure—into housing, roads, the social services and government buildings—and too little into manufacturing. Even if there *are* nationalised industries to invest more, the balance of public and private investment may be 'wrong'.

**6.
Commercial
risk and
interest rates**

There are two other points to note. First, we have explained that the rate of interest is the rate at which entrepreneurs can borrow to finance investment. In other words, we are mainly concerned with the rate of interest on long-term loans issued by firms—on debentures. In this chapter, we have discussed only the rate of interest on short- or long-term government securities. In many countries, not least the UK, the central bank does not deal in commercial debentures, only in government securities. It is thus important to understand what is the link between the rate of interest on treasury bills, on government bonds and on commercial debentures.

First, the rate of interest on debentures will almost always be higher than on government bonds. Commercial bonds involve a greater risk than do government bonds, certainly in developed countries. Government securities are the 'safest' possible securities; the danger of repudiation is, for all practical purposes, non-existent in developed countries. Commercial enterprises, however, do sometimes find it impossible to meet their liabilities. No firm, however reputable, can guarantee that changes, for example, in consumers tastes, or in the costs of research and development will not affect its profits. British readers will think of firms like Rolls-Royce. The greater risk incurred by those who invest in commercial bonds means that they normally demand an appropriate return. The more risky the firm, the higher the return demanded will be.

If we describe the rate of interest on government bonds as the 'pure' or 'riskless' rate of interest, the rate of interest on commercial debentures will exceed this 'pure' rate by a 'risk premium'. There will be a relatively stable differential between the rate of interest on government bonds and that on commercial bonds. At the same time, the rate of interest on the debentures of particular firms will differ according to the presumed 'risk', in this case of the failure of the particular firm issuing them. The rate of interest on government bonds and on industrial debentures will, however, fall and rise in unison. Government bonds and commercial bonds are close substitutes. Central bank action which lowers the rate of interest on government bonds will lower rates on industrial debentures too.

This does not mean any serious qualification to the theory. When we discussed liquidity preference, we assumed that people could choose between holding money or one sort of bond. We assumed that there were no other close substitutes for money and bonds, and ignored what would happen if there were. Our admission that there are various kinds of bonds means that the demand for money is a slightly more complicated phenomenon than we have made it appear. Nevertheless, if we assume a close link between interest rates on government bonds and on commercial debentures, we can see that a fall in the rate of interest on government securities will affect interest rates on commercial debentures, which are an important influence on business investment. Indeed, we can go further and suppose that *all* interest rates will rise and fall together. By acting on prices of government bonds, the central bank can change the rate of interest at which firms can borrow when they issue debentures. Indeed, it can also alter the rate of interest that individuals have to pay if they borrow money to buy houses, cars and so on.

7. Why money interest rates are positive

7.1 The liquidity trap

The other point is very important. Indeed, it is the distinguishing characteristic of the Keynesian theory of the rate of interest. We have already seen that the size of the increase in the money supply which the central bank has to bring about in order to cause a given fall in the rate of interest will depend on the 'elasticity' of the liquidity preference schedule. The steeper (the less interest-elastic) the liquidity preference schedule, the larger the fall in the rate of interest obtained from a given increase of the money supply. However, it is important to realise that interest-elasticity may well be different at different rates of interest. If the central bank wants to lower the rate of interest from 6 to 5 per cent, it is likely that it will be able to do so much more easily than if it wants to lower it from 3 to 2 per cent. This is partly because the proportionate change is greater. It is also because the lower the rate of interest, the more likely people are to think that it will rise again in the near future, with the consequent danger of capital losses for bond holders. The lower the interest rate is, the harder it will be to persuade those who deal in bonds, whether professionals or not, that high bond prices are likely to persist. This is because, in order to reduce the rate of interest to any level, the central bank has to buy up all the bonds owned by anyone who thinks that the existing price of bonds is too high to last. The lower the rate of interest is, the more people will think that this is the case and the more bonds the central bank will have to buy.

One can go further even than this. Keynes put great emphasis on his belief that there were strong forces preventing the rate of interest falling below a certain level, which he thought was probably between 2 and 4 per cent. Once the rate of interest fell to this level, he thought that *everyone* would become convinced that it could not fall further, and that it might well rise again. The central bank would be unable to bid up the price of securities farther even if it bought up all the securities in existence. In other words, at this point liquidity preference would have become absolute, or infinite. All the extra money which the central bank created would be absorbed by the community without inducing any fall in the rate of interest.

Keynes therefore held that the liquidity preference schedule was asymmetrical as one moved downwards along it. Beyond a certain point, he thought that it became horizontal; that liquidity preference became absolute. This is shown in Fig. 22.6. Here, when the rate of interest falls to 2 per cent the liquidity preference schedule becomes infinitely elastic—it becomes a horizontal straight line. The rate of interest is so low that no further rise in bond prices can occur. The

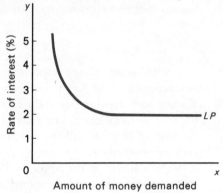

Fig. 22.6

lower the rate of interest, the greater the risk of capital losses if it rises again, and the smaller the likelihood that a further fall will bring about capital gains. In addition, the gains in the hope of which these capital losses are risked are very small. A man may be willing to risk a capital loss on a security which brings him £10 a year in interest, but he will not be so keen to do so if it brings in only £2. Yet when the rate is 2 per cent, the risk (and the potential size) of such a capital loss is much greater than when it is 10 per cent.

7.2 Transactions costs

It may be wondered why it is that at such rates of interest everyone feels that 'rock bottom' has been reached. Indeed, it is likely that *no one* would be prepared to hold securities at such low rates of interest, even if they were expected to persist. One reason is that there is always some trouble and expense to be incurred in turning a security into money. Yet money can always be spent at a moment's notice; it is perfectly liquid. It is therefore necessary to offer everyone who buys securities some small inducement if he is to be persuaded to put his money into illiquid assets. He has to be compensated for their 'imperfect moneyness'. It follows that the rate of interest cannot fall to zero; money and securities can never be perfect substitutes. Indeed, it should be remembered that any argument like this which talks of the individuals switching their resources from one asset to another has to take account of the cost of the necessary transaction. Though this has usually not been stated explicitly in this chapter up to this point, it should always be remembered.

7.3 Commercial risk

This argument holds for government securities. They always earn a positive rate of interest, partly because they are imperfect substitutes for money but mainly because, when interest rates are very low, most people feel that they are bound to rise in the future. Turning to commercial bonds, we have seen that there is an additional reason why interest rates cannot fall very low. The rate of interest on such bonds has to be high enough to cover the risk of default by the borrower. The rate of interest which borrowers have to pay will remain substantial even if the 'pure' rate of interest, where no such risk of default exists, falls to a negligible figure.

7.4 Influences counteracting the liquidity trap

Economists often describe the situation where the liquidity preference schedule becomes horizontal, as the 'liquidity trap'. Any attempt to reduce the rate of interest further fails because all extra money created by the central bank is caught in this 'trap'.

(a) Stamped money

The conclusion Keynes drew was that the prospects for increasing investment by lowering the rate of interest were not very bright in situations where the rate of interest on commercial debentures would have to fall below 3 to 4 per cent in order to increase investment. Ingenious solutions to this problem have been put forward. One suggestion was that governments might introduce 'stamped' money; that the holders of money might have to put a postage stamp on every bank note at intervals, thus introducing a cost for holding money. Presumably charges would also be levied on bank deposits in proportion to their size. This would mean that bonds, which would not be 'stamped', would be able to bear a very low rate of interest— perhaps even a negative one. The aim would be to stimulate investment.

(b) Inflation

We have perhaps achieved similar results through inflation since Keynes's time. Since 1945 *real* rates of interest on bonds (after allowing for the effect of inflation on interest payments) have become very low. At times, in many countries, they have been negative. By accident rather than design, we *have* achieved this result for short periods. Perhaps this has encouraged investment. In theory, it should have done, so long as inflation did not reduce prospective yields in proportion.

8. Some post-Keynesian ideas on interest

Perhaps the most important development in interest-rate theory since Keynes wrote has been the integration of the three motives for holding money. Modern economic theorists explicitly reject the idea that the transactions demand for money bears a simple, proportional relationship to the level of transactions in the economy. As we have seen, they accept that money holdings simply represent a different kind of inventory and that the size of the inventory of money held for transactions purposes will be smaller when the rate of interest is higher, and vice versa. However, they argue that the amount of money held will continue also to be a function (probably a complex one) of income. This means that economists now see the whole demand for money as determined both by the level of income and by the rate of interest.

8.1 The role of wealth

More than this, a good deal of the discussion of the rate of interest since Keynes wrote has cast doubt on the importance of short-term speculation on changes in the rate of interest as a major cause of changes in the demand for money. It has also emphasised that wealth (as well as income) is a factor determining the size of the demand for money. This has interesting results because the value of individual and collective wealth depends, in turn, on the rate of interest. As we have seen, the lower the rate of interest, the greater the capital value of bonds. This applies to other assets too. Since the capital value of any asset is the (discounted) value of its future earnings, a lower rate of interest increases the value of *all* capital assets; it raises total wealth. Similarly, a rise in the rate of interest will raise the discount rate which has to be applied to the future earnings of assets and so will lower their present value. This means that if the government uses economic policy measures (for example, tax changes) that have a smaller (or less-easily calculated) effect on the rate of interest they will also have less effect on total wealth and so, perhaps, on the demand for money.

8.2 The choice of a portfolio of assets

Perhaps the most important post-Keynesian development has been the abandonment of Keynes's simple distinction between money and bonds as the only assets between which individuals have to choose. A number of writers, especially Tobin, have emphasised that both individuals and institutions are concerned with building up *portfolios* of assets, in which money, short-term securities, long-term securities and physical assets of various kinds all find their place. The result is that anyone who holds financial assets will have to behave in the way we saw, in Chapter 18, that banks have to behave. He has to balance liquidity against profitability. He has to ensure that he has sufficient assets that are less liquid but more profitable to balance the assets which are less profitable but more liquid. The percentage which liquid assets bear to total assets will depend on the likelihood that the individual will need cash quickly. And, in post-Keynesian analysis, cash need not mean bank notes or non-interest-bearing bank deposits. Cash can be defined to suit the purposes of the theorist (or the econometrician) considering a particular problem. It can include deposits in savings banks, hire-purchase companies, building societies and so on.

Perhaps the most important development is an insistence on the fact that professionals dealing on the Stock Exchange, as well as banks and insurance companies and other institutions, who have sold long-run bonds because they fear a rise in the rate of interest will not actually switch into cash. They will switch from long-term to short-term securities. For the individual the choice may again be not to hold actual cash but to put funds temporarily into a building society, a savings bank or a hire-purchase company. Again, he may be seen as investing in a short-term security in the sense of one that can be redeemed without capital loss, though some economists would again argue that, despite earning interest, he can still be seen as holding 'cash'.

8.3 'Shortening' the portfolio

Expectations still enter in, of course, as in Keynes's original theory. Anyone who thinks that the rate of interest is going to rise can switch some or all of his long-term holdings into shorter ones. He can preserve the capital value of his assets without needing to sacrifice interest by holding actual cash. The expectation of a rise in the rate of interest will therefore still *reduce* the average length of life of the assets which individuals wish to hold. It will 'shorten' their portfolios. Similarly, the expectation of a fall in the rate of interest will *lengthen* the average life of the assets which people want to hold. Keynes saw the 'shortening' of a portfolio as a switch from one asset (bonds) into the only other one he recognised (cash). The more general theory of liquidity preference now favoured by economists looks at portfolios which contain assets of various kinds, not simply cash and bonds.

What then happens can be seen by considering Fig. 22.7. An individual is here confronted with the kind of choice that individuals *do* face. He has to choose what proportions of his assets to hold in cash, in short-term securities, in long-term securities and in physical assets. An expectation of a rise in the rate of interest will lead the investor to shorten the average length of life of the assets he holds. He will move towards the left-hand end of the spectrum in Fig. 22.7. He may well not choose to hold more actual cash, but he will certainly hold more short-term and fewer long-term securities.

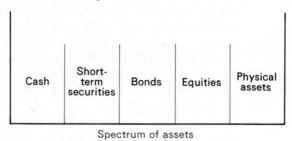

Spectrum of assets

Fig. 22.7

(a) The effect on interest rates

If everyone does this, the result is likely to be that expectations are borne out. Long-term interest rates will rise, though short-term interest rates may fall somewhat as some funds move from long-term securities to shorter ones. What if *all* holders of long-term securities decided, at a particular moment, to sell these and reinvest in short-term securities?

The analysis earlier in this chapter shows why this would not happen. If *all* investors tried to sell long-term securities because they thought their price was too high, the price of these securities would fall at once, or very quickly, to that level which investors as a whole thought could be sustained. The increase in the rate of interest on long-term securities would take place before enough of them had been sold to make many funds available for moving into shorter ones. The process by which a change in views about the future of the rate of interest alters people's relative holdings of different kinds of asset is therefore more complex than the simple Keynesian model makes it appear.

(b) The effect on investment

Of course, if the desired portfolio of assets for individuals and firms shifts to the left along the spectrum in Fig. 22.7, this will mean a relative loss of desire to hold long-term assets of all kinds, including buildings, machinery and other capital assets. Another way of putting what we said in Chapter 21 is therefore that, if the preference of individuals and organisations shifts toward short-term and away from long-term assets, this will reduce the willingness of the community to hold (or indeed to build) physical assets like factories and machines, most of which have longish lives; and, in the case of buildings, very long lives. This will reduce investment in new physical assets. In Chapter 21, we depicted this as the result of an increase in the rate of interest. Here, we look at the problem in a more sophisticated way, and link it to a 'shortening' of the total portfolio of different kinds of asset that the community wishes to hold at any moment of time.

8.4 The role of the monetary authorities

In all of this we have ignored the role of the monetary authorities— the central bank and the government. If the monetary authorities want to lower the rate of interest, the preceding analysis shows that it may be possible to do this without necessarily increasing the money supply as much as Section 22.4 implied. What the monetary authorities have to do is to buy long-term securities and to obtain the funds required by selling short-term securities.

(a) Switching

Such a process is known as 'switching'. It will lower the long-term rate of interest, though possibly at the expense of raising the short-term rate somewhat. This may be acceptable if the fall in the long-term rate increases investment. If it does not, then the monetary authorities will have to increase the size either of the commercial banks' deposits with the central bank or of their holdings of short-term government securities, for example, treasury bills. This is likely to increase the money supply either directly, because the commercial bank's deposits with the central bank have increased, or indirectly, because the increasing supply of treasury bills increases the liquidity of the banks and allows them to lend more freely to public and private industry. If the monetary authorities operate in this way to reduce the supply of long-term securities and to increase that of short-term securities they will, of course, be altering the structure of the national debt. They will be shortening the average maturity of the national debt; and increasing the proportion of short-term to long-term securities in it. This extends what was said about banks in Chapter 18; much monetary policy is concerned with altering the structure of assets and liabilities. We are now extending our view to the whole community. We are looking at alterations in the relationship between the assets and liabilities of individuals, banks and the government itself. However, the *ownership* of these assets is important. Altering the asset structures of the banks may well alter the size of the money supply; operating on the assets of the non-bank public can not.

(b) Funding

The opposite process can, of course, be undertaken as well. The monetary authorities may engage in 'funding'. They may sell long-term securities to the public, thus raising the long-term rate of interest. They may then use the funds so acquired to reduce the supply of short-term securities. As with 'switching', 'funding' can have different combinations of effects on the rate of interest and on the money supply. If a small amount of selling of long-term bonds by the central bank increases the long-term rate of interest substantially, there will be little effect on the quantity of short-term securities and therefore on the banks' cash and liquidity. On the other hand, if sales of long-term bonds have little effect on the long-term rate of interest, the central bank will have to sell large amounts of bonds to have much effect on the interest rate. This will cause a large reduction in the public's cash and other relatively liquid assets, especially treasury bills. The fact that monetary policy can affect the rate of interest and/or the quantity of money is important. We have already emphasised this, but have not so far made clear the complexity of the real-world process. One is concerned not merely with money and bonds, but with the whole spectrum of assets, financial and physical.

8.5 Some general equilibrium complications

This complexity arises partly because of the fact that we are dealing with a general-equilibrium problem. For example, while central banks will normally deal only in short- or long-term government securities, individuals may well deal in equities too.

(a) A complication

There is a complication here. At a given moment of time, a rise in the rate of interest is likely to reduce the values both of bonds and equities; a higher rate of discount will have to be used (with given prospective yields) to estimate the present value of any equity. However, if the rise in the rate of interest reduces investment, it will probably also reduce GNP and so business profits. This in turn is likely to lead to a greater fall in equity prices than in bond prices, because the interest payment on bonds is a fixed and guaranteed sum of money. The difficulty in bringing equity prices into the discussion is therefore that they depend not only on the rate of interest but also on the marginal efficiency of capital. On the other hand, bond prices depend only on the rate of interest. The result is that if we bring equities into the discussion we are dealing with supply factors (in the shape of the rate of interest) and demand factors (in the form of the marginal efficiency of capital) simultaneously. This is obviously one reason why Keynes's original analysis found it easier to deal with money and bonds as the only two alternative assets. Keynes reduced the complexity of the analysis, but at the expense of some loss of realism because the problem he was tackling was really a general equilibrium one.

9. Empirical evidence on the demand for money

9.1 Does the liquidity trap exist?

There has been a great deal of econometric work in recent years, aimed at discovering whether or not the Keynesian 'liquidity trap' exists. Work, soon after World War II, by Tobin attempted to isolate 'idle' cash balances from those required for transactions purposes. His analysis suggested that there was a hyperbolic relationship between idle balances and interest rates. This implied that there *was* a liquidity trap, because the demand curve for idle balances approached the horizontal as the rate of interest fell. This study was published in 1947, but recent work has failed to identify a similar relationship. It is thought that the major reason for this is that Tobin did not allow for the influence of total wealth on liquidity preference. More recently, a major study by Bronfenbrenner and Meyer has attempted to relate the demand for 'idle' money to three variables: to the short-term interest rate, to wealth and to 'idle' balances held in the previous year. Their conclusion was that the demand for idle balances was interest-inelastic, with no tendency for interest-elasticity to increase as the interest rate fell. They naturally saw this as evidence against the existence of the liquidity trap. At about the same time, around 1960, results of other studies were published by Friedman and by Latané. Using the permanent-income hypothesis, Friedman produced a demand function for money which was not interest-elastic. On the other hand, Latané found that the ratio of money to income *was* a function of the long-term interest rate. Again, Meltzer, relating the demand for money to wealth rather than income, found a substantial interest-elasticity of demand for money.

9.2 Some empirical evidence

The evidence is obviously inconclusive, and it is tempting to say that one should cling to the idea of the liquidity trap because this is essential to the Keynesian approach to macro-economics. Without going so far, our view is that the idea that there will be some low positive rate of interest at which the demand for money become infinite is very appealing. Certainly, British experience around 1947 when the Chancellor of the Exchequer, Dr Dalton, attempted to reduce the long-term interest rate to $2\frac{1}{2}$ per cent, suggests that a liquidity trap does sometimes operate. Dalton's effort to reduce the long-term interest rate had to be abandoned in face of the fact that no one was prepared to take the bonds the government was trying to issue at such low interest rates. Against this, however, is the fact, already mentioned, that 'real' as distinct from money interest rates were negative in many major countries during parts of 1970 and 1971. In the UK, with prices rising by about 10 per cent between 1970 and 1971, rates of interest on long-term government securities of between 8 and 10 per cent meant zero or negative 'real' rates of return. While there may be some low, positive *money* rate of interest at which the demand for money becomes infinite, it seems that the real rate of interest at which this happens, if it happens at all, will at times be a negative one. The issue, which unfortunately is a very important one, remains in doubt. One can only hope that further econometric work will resolve it one way or the other before too long.

Suggested reading

KEYNES, J. M.　*General Theory*, London, 1936, chapters 13 and 15.

HICKS, J. R.　*Value and Capital*, Oxford, 1946, chapters 11, 12, 13 and 19.

OHLIN, BERTIL　'Some Notes on the Stockholm Theory of Savings and Investment, *Economic Journal*, 1937, Part I, p. 53; Part II, p. 221.

KEYNES, J. M.　'Alternative Theories of the Rate of Interest', *Economic Journal*, 1937, p. 241.

KEYNES, J. M.　'The "Ex-Ante" Theory of the Rate of Interest', *Economic Journal*, 1937, p. 663.

ROBERTSON, D. H.　'Mr Keynes and Finance', *Economic Journal*, 1938, p. 314. Keynes's comments on this note, ibid., p. 318.

LERNER, A. P.　'Alternative Formulations of the Theory of Interest', *Economic Journal*, 1938, p. 211.

JOHNSON, H. G.　'Monetary Theory and Policy', *American Economic Review*, 1962, pp. 335–84. This paper is reprinted as chapter 1 in H. G. Johnson, *Essays in Monetary Economics*, London, 1969. There is an extensive bibliography at the end of Professor Johnson's paper, and readers are encouraged to study from it at least the papers mentioned in this chapter.

23

The macro-economic system

1. The determinants of employment

Moving towards a complete understanding of macro-economic theory is rather like building a house. One has to learn about the meaning and importance of the various bits and pieces before one can put them together and see the whole building in its entirety. We have now reached a stage where we can start the building operation and see what kind of explanation of the way a modern economy operates and what kind of solution to its problems macro-economic theory offers. We have been able to give a number of hints about the way in which the different parts of the system behave, but we have not yet shown how they all fit together.

We shall do this in three stages. First, we shall give a brief, verbal outline of the way a macro-economic system works. Finally, we shall look at it diagrammatically.

2. A verbal description

As we saw at the beginning of our analysis of macro-economic theory, we can safely assume that employment is a function of income. When a community has a large income it has high employment; when its income is small, employment is low. But looking at a country's income means only looking in another way at the sum of expenditure on both consumption and investment goods by individuals, firms and the government. In order to explain why income or employment is high or low, we must consider the size of these three items—consumption, investment (public and private) and government expenditure on current account. These are the items of expenditure on which income depends.

As we have seen, consumption, investment and government expenditure on current account depend in turn on various other factors, which are therefore the ultimate determinants of the level of activity. The relationship between these variables stated in Keynes's original theory is shown in Table 23.1. This gives, in a rather crude form, the relationship between the important variables in the macro-economic system. The first equation simply states that the GNP, or income (Y), is made up of consumption, investment and government expenditure on current account. The remainder of Table 23.1 shows how these components of income are determined.

Table 23.1

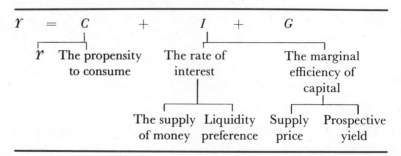

Consumption depends more than anything else on the level of income (Y) and the community's consumption function, though it is also somewhat affected by the quantity of assets owned by members of the community. As we saw, the average propensity to consume decreases in the short run as income rises, though it appears to be roughly constant in the long run. In the pure Keynesian analysis, investment depends on the marginal efficiency of capital on the one hand, and the rate of interest on the other. Again, the marginal efficiency of capital depends on prospective yield and supply price, while the rate of interest depends on the demand for money—liquidity preference—and the supply of money. Going beyond the original Keynesian analysis, we saw in Chapter 21 that while a good deal of investment will be autonomous, or long-range, most investment by firms will be 'induced' by changes in the level of income. Investment by the government is likely to depend mainly on forces like the rate of growth of population and society's view of what amount and kind of investment it is desirable for the government to carry out. Similarly, government expenditure on current account is not much influenced by economic factors, except perhaps in the sense that a higher level of income will allow the community to choose, if it wishes, for the government to carry out more higher-quality activities now that the higher level of income makes this possible. Government expenditure, both on goods and services and on capital assets, depends very much on the policy of the government of the day, the mood of society and the influence of pressure groups.

2.1 How can income and employment be increased?   In Table 23.1 we see in a simple form the shape of a macro-economic system of the kind we have been discussing in Part Two. On the basis of this table we can trace the effects of a change in one variable through the economic system. More important, we can ask questions like: How can unemployment be reduced?

First, we know that employment depends on income, so that an increase in employment can only come from an increase in income. From the equation $Y=C+I+G$ we see that an increase in income requires an increase in C, I or G. How can this be brought about?

(a) How to increase consumption

Consumption depends on income itself and on the consumption function. Since income is a dependent variable, it can be altered only by altering the independent variables in the system. However, it may be possible to modify the consumption function. If the consumption function can be raised—if people can be induced to spend a greater proportion of disposable income on consumption—income will rise. As we saw in Chapter 20, the consumption function depends on the psychology of consumers. Unless consumers can be persuaded to change their behaviour, consumption cannot increase. It is reasonable to think that consumers' behaviour would be difficult to alter and that consumers would resent interference with their habits. There are, however, some possibilities.

First, the rich tend to have a lower propensity to consume than the poor. If one takes income away from the rich (for example, in taxation) and gives it to the poor (for example, in welfare benefits), one can increase consumption. In this way, the propensity to consume for the community as a whole can be raised. Consumption and income will both rise with it. This may sound a somewhat drastic procedure; it has not been used very much. This is so despite the fact that, in the 1930s, partly under the influence of Keynes, it was often argued that redistribution of income from rich to poor would be an effective way of raising effective demand and so increasing employment.

Keynes himself was not particularly attracted to this line of action. He thought that those who advocated an attempt to increase consumption as the real solution to the problem of unemployment laid 'a little too much emphasis on increased consumption at a time when there is still much social advantage to be gained from increased investment',[1] adding: 'I am myself impressed by the great social advantages of increasing the stock of capital until it ceases to be scarce.'[2] Nevertheless, Keynes felt that the wisest course, in the end, might be 'to advance on both fronts at once'.[3] It is not surprising, therefore, that Keynes should have laid more stress on ways of

[1] *General Theory*, p. 325.
[2] *ibid.*
[3] *ibid.*

increasing investment than raising consumption. It is one of the minor ironies of our time that capital is *still* scarce, despite Keynes's confidence that the problem of capital scarcity would soon vanish. Moreover, there have been few serious attempts to alter the distribution of income in most countries. What re-distribution has taken place has been concerned less with reducing unemployment than with achieving other political and social objectives like greater equality of incomes.

(b) How to increase investment

If it is difficult to alter consumption in order to increase the level of activity, what about investment? We have seen that autonomous investment tends to be relatively unaffected by economic factors, though it is true that governments can speed-up or delay investment which is carried out in the public sector. Investment by private firms depends on the schedule of the marginal efficiency of capital, and on the rate of interest. The schedule of the marginal efficiency of capital slopes downwards to the right. With a given marginal efficiency of capital schedule, more investment will be forthcoming only if money to carry it out can be borrowed more cheaply. At a given rate of interest, there will be more investment only if the marginal efficiency of capital schedule can be moved to the right. The aim of any community which seeks to create investment must therefore be either to raise the marginal efficiency of capital or to lower the rate of interest.

The marginal efficiency of capital can be increased only if the prospective yield of assets rises, or if their supply prices fall. The supply price of assets is not likely to respond much to deliberate attempts to lower it. It is not possible to do much in the short run to alter physical conditions of production. The prospective yield of investment in general is probably easier to alter, though, as we shall see, it is easier to alter downwards than upwards. One popular method of altering prospective yield is to give firms investment grants, or to allow them to write-off (depreciate) assets against taxation more quickly. This is a way of making the purchase of capital assets more profitable. For, if the asset is not bought, the investment grant is not paid; accelerated depreciation of it is not possible. Government encouragement to investment of this kind will increase the internal rate of return on all investment projects. It therefore moves the marginal efficiency of capital curve to the right. However, even here, it is probably easier for a government to create business pessimism than to make businessmen optimistic. Tough speeches by government ministers, predicting bad economic conditions in the future; an increase in taxes on profits and therefore on the fruits of investment;

or cuts in investment grants will reduce investment fairly quickly. Attempts to work in the opposite direction may do little to stimulate investment, unless GNP is already increasing. It is much harder to make businessmen optimistic than to alarm them. The only way in which businessmen can be persuaded to invest more is if they genuinely believe that the demand for the output of the assets will be there when they have been acquired. Certainly, experience in the UK in the 1960s and 1970s suggests that businessmen have to be unusually impressed by government exhortation if they are to be persuaded to invest in capital assets ahead of the actual appearance of increased demand. Consequently, the best way of increasing prospective yield is to increase demand either by increasing consumption or by increasing government expenditure.

At first sight, the rate of interest may seem to provide a rather more attractive target for would-be employment creators. Depending as it does on the demand and supply of money, the rate of interest is likely to be responsive to judicious intervention. Liquidity preference, being another psychological phenomenon, may well be best left alone. If it can be altered at all by government action, it is probably easier to increase than reduce. It is usually easier for governments to frighten bond-holders than to make them confident by exhortation alone. The amount of money, being under the control of the monetary authorities, seems much more suited to government action. By increasing the supply of money, with a given liquidity preference schedule, the rate of interest can be reduced and investment increased. Even here, there are snags. We have already seen that Keynes believed in the existence of a liquidity trap, where liquidity preference became absolute at a positive rate of interest, and it was impossible to reduce the rate of interest further. Keynes's great fear was certainly that the simultaneous existence of a liquidity trap, and of a (steep) marginal efficiency of capital schedule that was inelastic to changes in the rate of interest, would prevent monetary policy having much effect on the level of investment. However, we must not be too pessimistic. As we shall see in Chapter 24, changes in the money supply do appear to lead to significant changes in the level of activity. Keynes may have been too pessimistic.

(c) Changes in government expenditure

Nevertheless, it is likely that increasing government expenditure will be the most effective way of increasing the level of activity quickly. So far, we have largely ignored it. The reason is that government expenditure does not depend closely on independent economic variables like the rate of interest or the consumption function. As we have already seen, it is under the control of politicians and is relatively little affected by economic forces. It is precisely for this reason that increasing government expenditure is a particularly effective way of increasing employment. Alone of all the elements of the GNP, looked at from the expenditure side, it can be controlled at will by government.

The government can therefore influence the level of activity in two ways. First, it can use fiscal or monetary policy, as outlined in the preceding paragraphs. Second, it can spend money, either on current account or on capital goods, and so increase the GNP directly. Where the aim is to increase investment, the state can undertake whatever investment projects appear desirable, without too close a calculation of their prospective yield. Keynes, in particular, suggested that the government could offset the vagaries of the marginal efficiency of capital in this way. This, then, is how government action can increase the level of activity.

2.2 How can demand pressure be reduced

Similarly, government policy can reduce aggregate demand and so reduce inflationary pressure. Macro-economic theory really is a 'general' method of analysis. It can explain the problems of inflation and over-employment just as easily as those of unemployment. In the same way as unemployment results from a deficiency of aggregate demand, so inflation occurs when aggregate demand is higher than that required to buy the full-employment output at the current level of prices.

(a) Increasing productivity

This raises one important point. When there is unemployment, macro-economic analysis can ignore aggregate supply. It then seems foolish to try to increase aggregate supply (at constant prices), for example, by raising the efficiency of labour. It seems more sensible to try to ensure that all unemployed labour is at work before trying to make men and machines produce more. When full employment has been reached, this objection vanishes. The cause of inflation is that the aggregate demand price exceeds the aggregate supply price at full employment. One way in which equilibrium could be reached would be if the aggregate supply price could somehow be raised. When there is full employment, this cannot be done by putting more men to work and hence raising the aggregate output of the community. There are no more men to employ. Yet the aggregate supply price *must* rise to equal the aggregate demand price. If the economy is one with relatively free markets, the only way in which the aggregate supply price can be increased is through a rise in the prices of goods and of factors of production—through inflation. The full-employment output will then be sold for an amount of money equal to the aggregate demand price; output will not have increased, but the value of aggregate supply will have risen to equal the value of aggregate demand because of price increases.

Of course, there is now the possibility that increased output may come, not from taking on more men, since they are all employed, but from enabling each to produce more efficiently. It may be possible to devise new production methods and better ways of organising activity, or to invent new machinery. Certainly, if there is an excess of aggregate demand over aggregate supply at the full employment level of activity, everything possible should be done to increase output. One needs an upward shift of the aggregate supply schedule. In so far as the aggregate supply price can be increased through more goods of all kinds being produced by the same number of men, and *not* through prices being increased, this is all to the good. Nevertheless, the extent to which this can be done quickly is often exaggerated in public discussion. In the short run, productive efficiency cannot be increased very much; a reduction in aggregate demand is the only way to avoid inflation. In the long run, everything must obviously be done to obtain increased output from the same labour force by improving industrial efficiency. Only to the extent that this can be done will there be an improvement in the standard of living. This is one of the issues we shall look at in Part Three. However, it is important to realise that there is likely to be relatively little scope for increasing aggregate supply by improving efficiency in the short term. In most developed economies, it is difficult to increase output per man by more than 3 to 4 per cent per annum, however strenuous an effort is made. If inflation is proceeding at a rate higher than this, a reduction of aggregate demand is the only way to avoid price rises. It should be noted here, that if this were an *open* economy, increases in domestic prices could be avoided by allowing the excess of aggregate demand over aggregate supply to be taken up by an increase in imports and/or a reduction in exports. Enough extra goods and services would be available to the community for there to be no excess demand for home produce. If the balance of payments were not sufficiently strong, this would then lead to a balance of payments problem. But at least it *would* eliminate the inflationary pressure and keep down domestic prices. A reduction in the balance of payments surplus (an increase in imports relatively to exports) is *deflationary*.

(b) Reducing consumption

If none of these courses of action are acceptable and the objective is still to reduce aggregate demand, the government must operate on consumption, on investment or on its own expenditure. Again, because consumption depends on income and on the consumption function, consumption can be reduced only if the propensity to consume can be altered, perhaps by people being persuaded to save more at each level of income. In times of economic crisis, or of war, it is sometimes possible to reduce or eliminate an excess of aggregate demand by persuading people to save more for patriotic reasons. It is doubtful whether very much can be hoped for in this direction in normal times, though it is possible that raising rates of interest may do something to increase savings, particularly if backed up by exhortation. It is much more likely that taxation will have to be used to reduce aggregate demand. Here again, as we saw in Chapter 19, the remedy will not work if the increased taxes are paid out of income that would otherwise have been saved. A major difficulty is that times of inflation are times when people are likely to be saving less, not more. Since prices are rising, people want to keep up their spending in order to maintain their existing standards of living. Again, the fact that prices are rising means that a rational consumer will wish to buy goods now rather than in the future; if he waits, prices will have risen further.

Reversing the argument used about unemployment, one solution might be to redistribute incomes from those with a high propensity to consume (the poor) to those with a low propensity to consume (the rich). However effective it might be economically, it will be politically difficult to pursue such a policy very far in most countries.

(c) Reducing investment

It is much more likely that investment will be the element in expenditure that has to be reduced. Investment by business can be reduced either by lowering the prospective yield or by raising the rate of interest. Governments may reduce the prospective yield, for example, by withdrawing grants to investment that were already being made, by increasing taxation from profits or simply by pronouncements that make businessmen more pessimistic about the future. Similarly, the rate of interest will often rise automatically in times of high employment, because the demand for money for transactions purposes will increase with increasing activity and rising prices. Unless the supply of money is also increased, this will raise the rate of interest. If this automatic rise in interest rates is not sufficient, it will be possible to raise interest rates further by reducing the money supply. How far this will reduce investment will depend on the elasticity of the marginal efficiency of capital schedule. We have seen that Keynes thought this would be rather inelastic. It is more likely to be altered by the overall effect of a restrictive policy beginning to reduce consumption and government expenditure so that the (downward) operation of the accelerator will reduce investment.

(d) Timing policy measures

This leads to an important point. Experience suggests that it is only too easy to pursue this kind of restrictive policy for too long. Restrictions on consumption, or government expenditure on current account, or uninvestment will be accentuated by the multiplier. A recession may well develop. Partly because civil servants and politicians will be reluctant to reverse their policies quickly, and partly because the lags in a modern economy are often considerable, it is only too easy for reflationary measures to be taken too late. Then, the business community as a whole may well revise its estimates of prospective yields on investment downwards, perhaps drastically. The effect will be to lower the marginal efficiency of capital, and to reduce the level of economic activity far too far for comfort. A restrictive economic policy introduced in the time of prosperity, if it is not reversed in time, may well cause excessive pessimism to replace the excessive optimism of the boom period. While it may not bring about serious deflation, this can cause a very unpleasant recession. Once again, it is the unstable nature of business expectations which is at the root of the difficulty.

(e) Lags and government economic policy

Consequently, while we do not nowadays seem likely to see a serious depression like that of the 1930s, business expectations do change rather more drastically than one would like. In times of high activity, businessmen tend to be too optimistic; in times of recession, they tend to become too pessimistic. These swings of business opinion tend to be reflected in lags in the economy. If the government takes action to increase activity during a recession, this action may well take several months to show any results. Particularly if the preceding restrictions have been kept on for too long, the government may then begin to panic and bring in new reflationary measures before the earlier ones have been allowed to show whether they are working or not. One result is then likely to be that the recession is followed by a more violent recovery than the government intended. Again the fluctuations are exaggerated. Lags may well occur with consumer expenditure, but they are likely to be much longer with investment. The institution of a system of investment grants may not increase investment for two or three years. It takes as long as that to plan and build a modern plant. Moreover, even though businessmen may be making plans to increase investment quite soon after the investment grants are introduced, it is not easy in a complex market economy to know exactly what they are planning, though surveys of business intentions are now giving useful information about this in many countries.

The way that lags make government economic policy more difficult should never be overlooked. Indeed, as we shall see later in another context, it is sometimes argued by the 'Chicago School' of economists, in the United States, that the lags that occur in modern economies are such that the timing of most economic policy measures is bound to be misjudged. The Chicago School therefore argues that the best economic policy is one which intervenes as little as possible in the economy. They would advocate, for example, an economic policy which confined itself to increasing the supply of money by a percentage equal to the rate of growth of the productive capacity of the economy. Thus, for example, the money supply might be allowed to increase at 4 per cent per annum, with no other economic policy-making at all.

What we have been saying is that while reducing aggregate demand is the best way to reduce inflation, it may not happen quickly enough to remove the temptation to overdo the deflationary measures. This is particularly true when a government is attempting to reduce inflation by reducing its own investment. Where governments are engaged in the construction of roads, or, indirectly through nationalised industries, of power stations or gas grids, it will not be feasible to cut down such activity immediately. The result may well be that reductions can only be made after a year or two has elapsed; by the time they occur the reduction in government expenditure will probably accentuate a recession already caused by a fall in private consumption and investment. Considerable lags may still occur even if it is its own current expenditure which the government cuts in order to reduce inflation. Few governments will be prepared, quickly, to cut the numbers of civil servants, members of the armed forces, etc. There is therefore every reason for fearing, with the Chicago School, that detailed intervention in the economy will make matters worse rather than better.

The timing of economic policy measures, certainly in the UK during the last twenty years, has been far from outstanding. It is true that if changes in government expenditure are the method chosen for deflating or reflating the economy, they can be decided on precisely and carried out exactly. But this is of little help if they are badly timed. Though this type of expenditure often bears the brunt of any attack on inflation, it is far from the ideal method. One cannot avoid a sneaking sympathy for the Chicago School in its belief that a 'flexible' economic policy often makes matters worse rather than better.

3. Equations   We now move on to summarise macro-economic theory using equations. While there is the disadvantage that one cannot now discuss the working of a macro-economic system with the subtleties and nuances that verbal analysis allows, an algebraic statement does have the opposite virtue of precision. It allows us to make the structure of a macro-economic system quite explicit. As we have seen, the first model of a macro-economic system to obtain general acceptance in most countries was the 'Keynesian' one from the *General Theory*. Keynes himself clearly had such a complete system in his mind, although he rarely presented his mathematical functions explicitly. However, it was not long after the *General Theory* had been published that other economists gave their own summaries of what it was about. A useful mathematical formulation was published in an article by Dr Oscar Lange in 1938. We shall base our algebraic summary on that article.

3.1 The liquidity preference function   Dr Lange argued that the whole of the *General Theory* could be summed up in four fundamental equations, linking the main variables in the system. First, there is the liquidity preference function, linking the amount of money and the rate of interest:

$$M = L\,(i,\,Y) \qquad . \qquad . \qquad . \qquad . \qquad . \quad (1)$$

This equation shows that the amount of money (M) which people hold is a function of the rate of interest and the level of income. In the original Keynesian statement, the amount of money which people held under the speculative motive was considered to depend entirely on the rate of interest; that held under the transactions and precautionary motive was seen to depend wholly on the level of income. We explained in Chapter 22 that economists now see the total demand for money as depending both on the rate of interest and the level of income. The functional relationship between M and i is therefore such that as i increases M falls and vice versa. With high interest rates, less money is held because it is worthwhile to speculate on a fall in interest rates in the near future. At the same time, it is also worthwhile to economise on cash held for transactions purposes. On the other hand, Y and M both rise and fall together. The functional relationship, L, between M and i and Y is the liquidity-preference function.

3.2 The consumption function   The second equation is:

$$C = \emptyset(Y,\,i) \qquad . \qquad . \qquad . \qquad . \qquad . \quad (2)$$

This equation shows that consumption depends on the level of income and on the rate of interest. As we have seen, Keynes felt that the most important relationship between these variables was between Y and C. As Y rises, C rises; as Y falls, C falls. He was less certain about the way in which, with a given income, consumption would respond to a change in the rate of interest. He felt that any effect, in whichever direction, would be very small. Many contemporary economists would agree that the rate of interest is not an important variable in this equation, though they would probably now wish to bring in a term representing the consumer's wealth. The functional relationship, ø, in Lange's second equation is the consumption function.

3.3 The investment function

Third, there is the investment function showing what determines the level of investment:

$$I = F\,(i,\,C) \qquad . \qquad . \qquad . \qquad . \qquad . \qquad (3)$$

We see here that investment depends on the rate of interest and on consumption. Investment depends on the rate of interest because, given the marginal efficiency of capital, investment will be greater if the rate of interest is lower, and smaller if the rate of interest is higher. The marginal efficiency of capital, on the other hand, depends, in any giyen state of expectations, on consumption. The greater the amount of consumption, the greater will be the marginal efficiency of capital: given the rate of interest, the greater investment will be. Investment depends on consumption as well as on the rate of interest. Contemporary economists would still accept this though they would wish to emphasise that the interest-elasticity of investment may be low. Moreover, many economists today would wish to distinguish between autonomous and induced investment, as we did in Chapter 21. This would make the theory much more complicated, and we have tried to keep it simple. Because autonomous investment would be a function of time, its introduction would lead to the sort of dynamic analysis we shall study in Part Three. For the moment, we shall confine ourselves to a static analysis and retain Lange's original equation (3). Here, F is the marginal efficiency of capital function.

3.4 An identity

Fourth, there is an equation showing that income is identical with consumption plus investment:

$$Y = C + I. \qquad . \qquad . \qquad . \qquad . \qquad . \qquad (4)$$

3.5 Equations and unknowns

In these four equations, there are five unknowns, M, Y, C, I and i. But since equation (4) is an identity, Y is given once we know C and I. This means that we can reduce the unknowns to four (excluding Y), and the equations to three (ignoring equation (4)). We have only three significant equations. It follows that if we are to work out the values of the unknowns from the equations we must reduce the unknowns from four to three. Any system of simultaneous equations must have an equal number of equations and unknowns. Since there are only three effective equations in this system, we must have only three unknowns to be able to solve them. One of the four unknowns must be given. The system is determinate only if we know the size of consumption, investment, the rate of interest or the money supply. Once we know the value of one unknown, we can discover the values of the other three from equations (1), (2) and (3).

It is usual to take M, the amount of money, as given, since this is the variable which is completely under the control of the monetary authorities. We then know M, L, ø and F, and can thus determine the values of C, Y, I and i. Provided that the four equations are mutually consistent, the system will be in equilibrium. If they are not consistent, changes in the variables in the system will have to occur to bring about the equilibrium of the whole system.

4. A system of diagrams

In order to make sure that we have completely understood the meaning of these equations, it will be useful to put them in the form of four diagrams, as we have done in Fig. 23.1. In Fig. 23.1a, we have the liquidity preference schedule (or function) showing what the rate of interest is when various amounts of money are held. Let us assume that the economy shown in Fig. 23.1 is originally in equilibrium with an income of Y_0 (£6000). An amount of money of M_0 (£3000) is at that time in existence; this means that the rate of interest will be i_0 (6 per cent), as can be seen in Fig. 23.1a. With the rate of interest at i_0 (6 per cent), Fig. 23.1b shows that the consumption function is such that, out of the income Y_0 (£6000), C_0 (£4000) will be spent on consumption.[1] Similarly, Fig. 23.1c shows that with a rate of interest of i_0 (6 per cent) and consumption of C_0 (£4000), investment will be I_0 (£2000). Finally, Fig. 23.1d shows that when consumption plus investment is £6000 income is £6000 (Y_0). The 45° line shows that $C+I$ always equals Y. Since income is £6000, as in the original situation, it follows that the amount of money, M_0, and all the other variables are compatible with equilibrium at the current level of income. There will be no change in the system. It is in equilibrium.

[1] The assumption here is that the marginal propensity to consume is a constant, whatever the level of income. This enables us to draw the curves as straight lines.

If this were not the case and if, for example, consumption and investment had equalled, say, £8000, income would rise to £8000. We should then have to consider equilibrium with different values of the variables, for this would mean that the system was not in equilibrium. Income would have risen, which would have changed the position of the liquidity preference schedule; that would have affected the rate of interest and so on. The effect of the various changes would have to be traced through the complete system.

Fig. 23.1 a | b
c | d

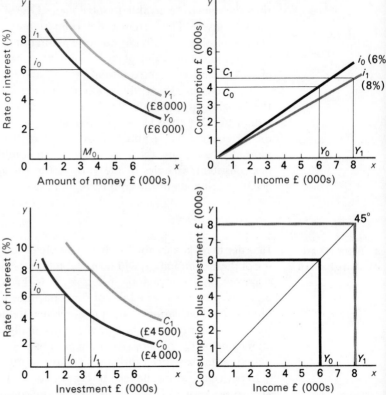

Still using Fig. 23.1, we can trace what would happen if income did rise to £8000 with money worth £3000 still in existence. The liquidity preference schedule would rise to Y_1; the demand for money under the transactions motive would have increased now that income had risen from Y_0 to Y_1—from £6000 to £8000. Assuming M to be fixed at £3000, the rate of interest would rise to i_1, (8 per cent, as shown in Fig. 23.1a). With i_1 at 8 per cent and with an income of £8000, consumption rises to £4500 (C_1 in Fig. 23.1b). The consumption function moves slightly to the right as the rate of interest rises—people save slightly more. Investment, with i_1 at 8 per cent and C_1 at £4500, is £3500 (Fig. 23.1c). From Fig. 23.1d we can see that income which is equal to $C+I$ ($£4\,500+£3\,500$) is now $£8\,000$. Since this is equal to the new and higher income of $£8\,000$ (Y_1) the system is in equilibrium at this new level of income.

The set of diagrams is thus able to show whether or not the system is in equilibrium just as the equations did. Provided one knows the shape of the four functions and the value of any one of the dependent variables (M, C, I and i), one can work out changes in the whole system which will follow on a change in any one variable.

5. The Hicks-Hansen diagram

Before concluding this chapter, we shall look at an alternative method which puts the whole position in one diagram. While less revealing, because it conceals what is happening 'behind the scenes', there is an attractive simplicity to being able to show everything in one diagram. This is known as the Hicks-Hansen diagram which is shown in Fig. 23.2. This shows that the economy is an equilibrium

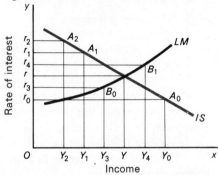

Fig. 23.2

with the rate of interest of r and a level of income of Y. Before we can explain what this means we must show how the IS and LM curves are derived.[1]

The IS curve shows all those combinations of the rate of interest and the level of income at which savings and investment would be equal. Given that macro-economic equilibrium requires savings to equal investment, it shows all those combinations of the rate of interest and the level of income where the savings/investment side of the economy will be in equilibrium.

5.1 Deriving the IS curve

We show what this means in Fig. 23.3. In Fig. 23.3a, we show a 'Keynesian' situation, where investment depends on the rate of

[1]We may note that this device was the outcome of an article by J. R. (now Sir John) Hicks, entitled 'Mr Keynes and the Classics' (*Econometrica*, 1937, p. 461). It was developed by the American economist Alvin H. Hansen (see, for example, his *Monetary Theory and Fiscal Policy*, chapter 5).

*(a) A
'Keynesian'
situation*

interest and the level of income. For simplicity, we show only two (brown) curves, relating investment to income, out of all the possible ones there are; we show one for each of two rates of interest. With the lower rate of interest (r_0), where the curve is I_0, investment is greater at each level of income than with the higher rate of interest (r_1) and the curve I_1.

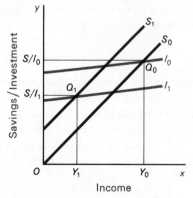 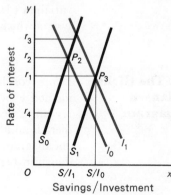

Fig. 23.3 a | b

In Fig. 23.3a, we also show two black curves representing savings at each level of income, for two different rates of interest. With the lower rate of interest (r_0) we have a savings function of S_0.[1] Since this is a 'Keynesian' analysis, we assume that the rate of interest has little effect on savings, but that savings do increase slightly as the rate of interest rises. The curve S_1, with a higher rate of interest (r_1), is therefore a little higher than the curve S_0.

What we are interested in is in points like Q_0 and Q_1. Q_0 shows that with the rate of interest, r_0, savings are equal to investment when income is Y_0. In this situation, savings are S/I_0. The next stage is to show this equilibrium position on the Hicks-Hansen diagram. We cannot show Q_0, since the axes show different variables from those in Fig. 23.3a. We can show what the point Q_0 means only by introducing point A_0 into the Hicks-Hansen diagram (Fig. 23.2). This shows that with the rate of interest of r_0, savings are equal to investment when income is at the level Y_0. Similarly, the point A_1 tells us that (as Q_1 in Fig. 23.3a shows) with the higher rate of interest (r_1), savings (S/I_1) are equal to investment at the (lower) income of Y_1.

*(b) A 'classical'
diagram*

The *IS* curve is therefore drawn through all points like A_0 and A_1 which show the levels of income where savings are equal to invest-

---

[1]Readers will appreciate that rates of interest cannot be shown along either axis in Fig. 23.3a. Where the subscript $_0$ is used, we refer to income, savings, investment etc., with the rate of interest, r_0, and so on.

ment, at the various rate of interest shown on the y-axis in the Hicks-Hansen diagram. One advantage of this diagram is that if we prefer the 'classical' assumption that savings vary strongly with the rate of interest, we can show this too. Thus, in Fig. 23.3b, we show two (brown) curves relating investment to the rate of interest. At the lower level of income (Y_1) investment (I_0) is lower at each rate of interest than at the higher level of income (Y_2).[1] Then, investment is shown by the curve I_1. Similarly, the black curves $(S_0$ and $S_1)$ show that at any level of the rate of interest the higher the income the greater the level of saving. In addition, because we are making the 'classical' assumption that savings respond strongly to changes in the rate of interest, the savings curves are not very steep. With an income of Y_1, saving (on the x-axis) is much greater if the rate of interest is higher, at r_3, than when it is r_4. Hence, the points where savings are equal to investment on Fig. 23.3b are P_2 and P_3. Because savings respond strongly to increases in the level of income, P_3 represents a higher level of investment and a lower rate of interest than P_2. If we want to do so, we can transfer this information to the Hicks-Hansen diagram in Fig. 23.2. For example, point A_2 shows what point P_2 shows in Fig. 23.3b. With an income of Y_2 savings and investment are equal at the rate of interest r_2. In Fig. 23.3b, point P_3, *not* transferred to Fig. 23.2, shows that at the rate of interest r_1, savings and investment are equal at S/I_0.

5.2 Deriving the LM curve

We have now seen how to construct the IS curve. How do we construct the LM curve? In fact, the LM curve is rather easier to construct. Let us take any level of income along the horizontal x-axis of the Hicks-Hansen diagram in Fig. 23.2. Now, we know that at each of these levels of income there will be a transactions demand for money.[2] Consider the level of income Y_3. If we denote the total money supply by M and the transactions demand for money at the level of income Y_3 by M_1, the amount of money remaining to satisfy the speculation motive will be:

$$M_2 = M - M_1$$

In order to discover where the LM curve lies, what we have to do is to discover what the rate of interest would *have* to be for the amount of money left over $(M_2$ in the above equation) to be just equal to the speculative demand for money. What point B_0 on the Hicks-Hansen diagram (Fig. 23.2) shows is, therefore, that with a level of

[1] Here, one cannot show income directly on the diagram, so that the subscript $_0$ refers to the situation where income is Y_0, and so on.
[2] For simplicity, we include the precautionary motive in with the transactions motive.

income Y_3, the rate of interest will have to be r_3 if the total money supply is to be held. Again, point B_1 shows that if income were Y_4, then the rate of interest would have to be r_4 if all money available for speculative purposes were just to be held. (It should be intuitively obvious that we are here assuming that the demand for money for transactions purposes depends solely on the level of income and not on the rate of interest. This is a reasonable simplification for our present purposes.)

The LM curve can therefore be constructed quite simply. At each level of income, we simply discover what the transactions demand for money is; we then deduct this from the total amount of money available. This tells us what level of the rate of interest *has* to be if all this money is to be held for speculative purposes.

*5.3
Manipulating
the Hicks-
Hansen diagram*

This is how the *IS* curve and the *LM* curve are constructed. Let us now see what they teach us. Let us consider the Hicks-Hansen diagram in Fig. 23.4. Suppose that the original *IS* and *LM* curves are IS_0 and LM_0. Equilibrium will then occur when the rate of interest

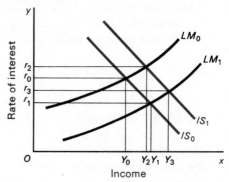

Fig. 23.4

is r_0 and the level of income is Y_0. Only in this position will the economy be in equilibrium with savings equal to investment, and the money supply fully used in satisfying the transactions and speculative demands. This demonstrates, in a different diagram, the kind of equilibrium which we showed with equations and diagrams in sections 3 and 4 of this chapter.

*(a) A change in
the money supply*

Let us now see what happens if there is a change in data. First, let us see what happens if there is an increase in the supply of money. It should be obvious from what we did in constructing the original *LM* curve that, if the supply of money increases, the *LM* curve will move to the right. At any level of income, the rate of interest will have to be lower if all the money available for speculative purposes is to be held. At any level of the rate of interest, the level of income will have to be greater if all the money available for transactions purposes is to be absorbed. Thus, if the money supply is increased, if the IS curve is unchanged and if the LM curve in Fig. 23.4 moves from LM_0 to LM_1, the rate of interest falls to r_1. Savings and investment are still equal, but the level of income is now Y_1.

(b) A shift in the IS curve Similarly, if the propensity to consume increases, the IS curve will move to the right. Let us suppose that the curve is now IS_1. With the original curve, LM_0, this means that the economy is in equilibrium with an income of Y_2 and a rate of interest of r_2.

(c) Shifts in both curves Now suppose that there is not only an increase in the money supply which moves the LM curve to LM_1, but also an increase in the propensity to consume. This raises the level of income at which savings and investment are equal at each different level of the rate of interest. This is again shown by the curve IS_1. In these circumstances, the economy will now be in equilibrium at the level of income Y_3 and the rate of interest r_3.

6. Conclusion What we have done in this chapter is to show three different ways in which the equilibrium of a macro-economic system can be depicted. We now go on to look at some outstanding problems about Keynes's approach.

Suggested reading

KEYNES, J. M.	*General Theory*, London, 1936, chapters 7 and 18.
LANGE, OSCAR	'The Rate of Interest and the Optimum Propensity to Consume', *Economica*, 1938, p. 12. This has been reprinted in *Readings in Business Cycle Theory*, Blakiston Press, Philadelphia, 1944, p. 169.
ACKLEY, GARDNER	*Macroeconomic Theory*, Macmillan, New York, 1961, chapter 24.

24

Keynes and the 'classical' economists

In this chapter, we look at three areas of macro-economics where there is still conflict between Keynesian and 'classical' ideas. These areas are: (1) the relationship between the money supply and the level of output and prices; (2) the precise significance of Keynes's assumption that money wages are inflexible; and (3) whether or not money is 'neutral'. That is, whether changes in the supply of money will leave relative prices (including the rate of interest) unchanged so that the 'real' factors in the economy are unaffected by changes in the money supply.

1. The equation of exchange

We begin with the differences between the Keynesian and 'classical' ideas about the role of money in the economy. We are concerned with the way changes in the money supply affect the level of income, the price level and so on. The views of the 'classical' economists about the relationship between the quantity of money and the general level of prices are summed up in what is known as the 'quantity theory of money'. Attention is focused on the connection between the price level and the supply of money. There is no single quantity theory of money which can be accepted as authoritative. Almost all economists writing before Keynes put some stress on the relationship between the quantity of money in an economy and the level of prices, but their pronouncements were made with differing emphases and degrees of precision. Indeed, a great deal of pre-Keynesian writing about the role of money in the economy had little or nothing to say about what was cause and what effect in the relationship between the money supply and the level of national income. In particular, a good deal of emphasis was put on two equations which looked at the relationship between the money supply and the price level, without directly implying anything at all about causality.

First, there was the 'equation of exchange' or the 'Fisher equation', so called because it was formulated by the American economist

Professor Irving Fisher. The equation of exchange states that if M is the amount of money; if V is the velocity of circulation (or the number of times that each unit of money is spent during a given period); if P is the price level; and if T is the volume of trade (or the quantity of goods exchanged against money during the period), then $MV = PT$. In words, the quantity of money multiplied by the number of times that each unit of this money is used during any period of time, equals the price level of output multiplied by the quantity of output bought during the same period.

It is often said nowadays that the quantity of theory of money is a 'truism': that it is self-evident. Keynes himself says that 'the quantity theory is a truism which holds in all circumstances, though without significance'.[1] Indeed, where the equation of exchange is concerned one can go even further. It is not merely a truism; it is a tautology. It is true by definition and asserts nothing at all about causal relationships in the real world. It cannot say what is the cause of any change and what the effect: it cannot show which is the independent and which the dependent variable.

Since it is a tautology, the equation of exchange makes no assertion about happenings in the real world. It is not a theory showing the effect of, say, a change in the amount of money on prices. If we denote the expenditure of the community in a given period by E, the equation of exchange can be written as $E = E$; it is true by definition. The equation $MV = PT$ merely splits up expenditure in two different ways. From the point of view of the community as spenders, total spending is equal to the money they hold (M) multiplied by the number of times (V) which each unit of that money is used during any period—say, a year. From the point of view of the community as producers, the expenditure of the community in the same period is the volume of trade (T) (the quantity of goods and services exchanged) multiplied by the price (P) at which these transactions take place.

Rewriting the equation $E = E$ as $MV = PT$ merely means that, from the point of view of a set of individuals as consumers, expenditure can be summed up as $M \times V$. For the same people as producers, expenditure on buying their output is $P \times T$. The equation $MV = PT$ is true by definition. It is therefore desirable to use the term quantity theory only when one is referring to statements which describe some causal result of a change in the amount of money on prices. The equation $MV = PT$ is not a theory about the behaviour of P in response to a change in M. It merely states an identity.

Nevertheless, the Fisher equation, the equation of exchange, does have some value. It does look at the expenditure of the community as spenders on the one hand, and as producers on the other. It also

[1]*General Theory*, p. 209.

U

distinguishes what are the significant parts of expenditure looked at from these viewpoints. This is important, since one cannot fully analyse the 'rigid' and 'less rigid' versions of the quantity theory without separating the relevant variables in the way that the Fisher equation does.

2. The Cambridge equation

The other equation is known as the 'Cambridge equation'. This refines the relationships in the equation of exchange. In the Fisher equation, P stands for the average price at which all transactions in the economy have been carried out. It is therefore neither a whole-sale nor a retail price index as we know them today. For example, it will include the values of bonds or equities traded during the relevant period of time. More than this, as we saw in our discussion of elementary national income accounts, it is important not to 'double-count' and this is what the Fisher equation does. It includes both, say, expenditure by final consumers on cars and motor manufacturers' expenditure on wages, components, etc. The Cambridge equation is intended to remedy this defect. It is concerned only with final purchases of goods and services. The right-hand side of the equation is therefore not PT; it is P_1R, where R represents the final output of all goods and services included in the GNP, after eliminating all double counting. P_1 represents the prices at which these goods and services are traded. Having altered the right-hand side of the equation of exchange in this way, we have to alter the left-hand side to match this. Instead of V, we write V_1. We are now concerned not with the velocity of circulation for *all* transactions, but only for those transactions which represent the purchase of final commodities. The Cambridge equation is therefore:

$$MV_1 = P_1R.$$

This equation is again a tautology; it merely states the obvious. However, the Cambridge equation has often been stated in an alternative form, which begins to bring economic behaviour into the analysis. This other equation is:

$$M = KP_1R.$$

In the form in which we stated it above, the Cambridge equation was concerned with the 'income velocity' of circulation (V_1). We wanted to know how many times each piece of money changed hands during any year, in purchasing final output. We ignored all other uses of money. Those who developed the Cambridge equation wanted also to look at things in a slightly different way. Instead of emphasising the number of times each piece of money changed hands, they wanted to look at the money stock as a proportion of income or expenditure during the year. As we now know, P_1R denotes the total value of final output—it represents the total national expenditure, or the total national income. The symbol K, therefore, denotes the fraction which the money supply represents of that total national income. Indeed, the reason R is used in the Cambridge equation is that those who developed it wanted to emphasise that it is *real income* which concerns us. We are concerned with the goods and services which people buy with their income, to consume or use in other ways, and not with intermediate products or paper securities, which are bought in order to make final goods or to yield a money profit.

Perhaps this will become clearer if we consider an example. Let us imagine a small, hypothetical economy. In this economy, there is a money supply of £100. The GNP in this economy (that is, P_1R) is £400. It is immediately obvious that, if we use V_1 to represent income-velocity of cirulation, then V_1 is 4. However, it is also immediately obvious that the total money supply is equal to one-quarter of the annual income. Symbolically:

$$V_1 = \frac{1}{K}.$$

The difference between V_1 and K is simply that when we look at income-velocity, we are concerned with the speed with which money changes hands within the economy. On the other hand, when we calculate K, we are interested in money not as a medium of exchange that moves round; we are looking at money as a stock to be held. A good deal of emphasis was put by the 'classical' economists on what they described as 'the demand for real balances'. They saw the community as choosing how big a proportion of its annual real income it wished to hold in the form of cash. In this sense, we can justifiably say that the Cambridge equation moves us on from the tautology represented by the equation of exchange to a study of economic behaviour. As we shall see later, the contemporary version of the quantity theory of money emphasises that people will choose how big a proportion of their incomes they want to hold in the form of cash. The quantity theory, nowadays, sees people as increasing their spending when their money balances are above the level that they feel they need; it sees them as reducing their spending when they feel that these money balances are below that level.

Nevertheless, while the Cambridge equation began to bring economic behaviour into the study of the quantity theory, it was concerned only with stating variables in an economic system. It did not state a theory, in the sense of a statement that implied cause and effect.

3. The quantity theory of money

To see what 'classical' economists had to say about causality we have to move on to the quantity theory proper. The strictest version of this, and the one with which we shall be mainly concerned in this chapter, is what we may call the 'rigid' version. This states that prices always change *in exact proportion* with changes in the quantity of money. If the amount of money is doubled, prices are doubled. If the amount of money is halved, prices are halved. So, if M represents the amount of money and P represents the price level, this version of the quantity theory of money can be expressed as $M=kP$, where k is a constant.

We may go on to note that some economists have held to a 'less rigid' version of the quantity theory, abandoning the idea that prices bear a proportional relationship to the quantity of money. This version of the quantity theory states that if the amount of money (M) increases, prices will rise; and if M decreases, prices will fall. But there is no attempt to say *by how much* prices will alter as M alters. This is the 'unrigorous' version of the quantity theory. It is obviously so unrigorous that it cannot be tested. For our purposes in this chapter, it will be much more valuable if we keep to the rigid quantity theory.

We have seen that the rigid quantity theory assumes a proportional relationship between changes in the money supply and changes in the price level. This means that it implicitly assumes the velocity of circulation and the volume of trade to be constant. Theoretically, one could assume that both V and T *were* variable, but that any change in one was exactly cancelled out by a change in the opposite direction by the other. The likelihood that this will happen is so remote that we can safely interpret the rigid quantity theory as assuming that both V and T are constant.

This rigid quantity theory is obviously most likely to hold when there is full employment. With full employment, T cannot alter, because all resources are employed; changes in M can exert an effect only on P. Of course, it is possible that V may alter, and so offset or magnify changes in M. Nevertheless, so long as any increase in M, and any consequent increase in prices, is relatively small, V could well be constant and the rigid quantity theory could hold. However, if the rate of price rise becomes high, money will become progressively more and more valueless. People are likely to spend money more and more quickly in order to avoid being left holding money which is depreciating rapidly. In these circumstances, V is likely to rise. If it does, the strict version of the quantity theory will fail to explain the situation. It follows that the situation in which the rigid quantity theory is most likely to hold is where there is full employment with moderate, but not rapid, rates of price increase.

We can therefore conclude that the rigid quantity theory is likely to give a fairly realistic picture of what happens where there is full employment, but moderate rates of price increase. What is much more difficult to explain is what happens when there is less than full employment. At one extreme, one could conceive of a situation where as M increased, T rose in proportion, so that both V and P remained constant. This is not a situation which can be explained at all in terms of the rigid quantity theory. The link here is between money supply and output, not between money supply and prices. Indeed, dissatisfaction with the quantity theory dates back to the 1930s, when Keynes was writing. At that time, it was seen that the important connection was between money supply, output and employment rather than between money supply and prices. Of course, the difficulty is that although this extreme case is possible it *is* an extreme case. Even if V remains constant, T will not necessarily rise in proportion with M. Costs may be increasing as output increases, perhaps because firms' cost curves slope upwards even with constant costs of factors, or perhaps because factors of production are able to obtain higher incomes as output increases. While it is difficult to be more explicit than this, it will be helpful if we look in detail at one or two possible relationships between changes in money supply and changes in prices and output.

4. Two models for defining inflation and full employment

Before doing this, however, we must note the difficulty of providing a satisfactory formal definition of inflation. The 'classical' theorists, as we have seen, assumed that full employment always existed, so that any increase in the amount of money would always raise prices. *Any* increase in the supply of money was inflationary. However, where there is not full employment the effects of an increase in the money supply are likely to be divided in some proportion between raising prices and raising output. In general, it seems that an increase in the money supply will be more likely to raise output rather than prices the more unemployment there is. With high unemployment, an increase in the supply of money can scarcely be described as inflationary. Yet prices may rise slightly, perhaps because industry is producing under conditions of diminishing returns. Is this slight price rise inflationary? The problem of definition: Are all price rises inflationary? When is full employment reached? Where do 'acceptable' price increases associated with increasing output end? Where does inflation start?—will be more easily settled, in so far as they can be settled at all, after we have discussed the behaviour of output and prices in conditions both of unemployment and of full employment.

Let us, then, consider a hypothetical economy with a good deal of unemployment. As we shall see later, one of the differences between the 'classical' and 'Keynesian' view of these matters, is over the precise way in which an increase in the money supply works through the economy to increase output and/or prices. For the moment, let us assume that the 'Keynesian' process, described in Chapter 23 is the relevant one. The amount of money (M) in a hypothetical economy is increased by open-market operations. We then assume that the economy is one where it is always possible for such an increase in the supply of money to raise employment by lowering the rate of interest, and hence increasing investment, so long as full employment has not been reached.

<table>
<tr><td>4.1 A simple
model</td><td>We shall assume, as a first approximation, that all factors of production are in infinitely elastic supply so long as there is any unemployment and that they are homogeneous and perfectly divisible. We also assume that effective demand and the quantity of money always increase and decrease together in exactly the same proportions (i.e. that V is constant). On these assumptions, so long as there is any unemployment, a sufficient increase in M can always bring about full employment. Industry is producing under constant returns, so that prices neither rise nor fall as output increases.</td></tr>
</table>

In this model, once full employment is reached, output ceases to respond *at all* to changes in the supply of money and so in effective demand. The elasticity of supply of output in response to changes in the supply of money, which was infinite as long as there was unemployment, falls to zero. The entire effect of changes in the supply of money is exerted on prices, which rise in exact proportion with the increase in effective demand. On the very simplified assumptions we are so far making, we can conclude, with Keynes, that 'so long as there is unemployment, *employment* will change in the same proportion as the quantity of money; and when there is full employment *prices* will change in the same proportion as the quantity of money'.[1]

This situation is shown diagrammatically in Fig. 24.1a and 24.1b. Figure 24.1a shows the relationship between changes in the supply of money and changes in output. As the amount of money rises from zero to £OQ, physical output rises in proportion and the output curve, showing output as a function of the amount of money, is a rising straight line passing through the origin. The slope will depend on production conditions and on the scales on the two axes. Once the amount of money rises to £OQ, the full employment output ON is being produced. No further rise in M can now cause any rise in output above ON, so that the output curve becomes vertical at that

[1]*Op. cit.*, p. 296.

output. Figure 24.1b shows the relationship between prices and the supply of money. So long as the supply of money is less than that which brings about full employment (i.e. £OQ), prices are constant at the level OR. Once the money supply exceeds £OQ, any further

Fig. 24.1 a | b

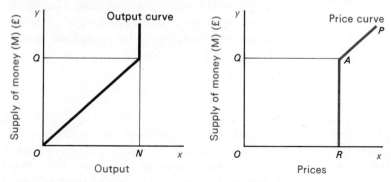

rise in M increases prices in exact proportion with the rise in M. The price curve (RP) becomes a rising straight line. In Fig. 24.1b, this happens beyond point A; AP produced would pass through the origin. In this model, then, inflation begins as soon as the amount of money exceeds £OQ. But so long as M is less than £OQ, no price rise occurs as M is increased.

4.2 Complicating the model

(a) The relationship between money and aggregate demand

These assumptions are much too simple. We must now complicate the analysis by making them more realistic. The least realistic assumption is that aggregate demand always changes in exactly the same proportion as the amount of money. In the Keynesian model, the link between a rise in M and the consequent increase in effective demand is a change in investment. The increase in M causes a fall in the rate of interest, and investment rises. As the interest rate falls and the rise in investment leads to a rise in the GNP, there will be an increase in the demand for money for both transactions and speculative purposes. However, there is no particular reason why the increase in liquidity preference should just be in proportion to the increase in the money supply. In other words, V may rise or fall as the process continues. Similarly, even though one can expect a fall in the rate of interest to stimulate investment and, through the multiplier, lead to a rise in aggregate demand, there is no reason why the increase in liquidity preference that results should be the same, for the same absolute increase in M, at different levels of the GNP. Again, the precise way in which the increased GNP is shared between sections of the community that have different marginal propensities to consume will affect the size of the multiplier, and so the impact of the increased investment on the GNP. The connection between a change in M and the resulting change in output will be nothing like so simple as we have assumed.

The only generalisation one can make with certainty is that an increase in M is very unlikely to cause a *fall* in effective demand (or income). Changes in M and in Y are likely to be in the same direction. But one can make no useful predictions about the nature of the relationship between them.

(b) The lack of homogeneity of factors of production

We must also abandon the assumption of homogeneous factors of production. This again is not realistic. In the real world there will be both increasing and decreasing returns to scale. It seems probable that, over those ranges of output which are important in practice, if returns to scale are not constant they are more likely to diminish than increase, though this need not happen. What it does seem reasonable to assume is that costs, and hence prices, will begin to rise a little before full employment is reached.

(c) Bottlenecks

There are two main reasons why this is likely to happen. First, prices of finished goods are likely to rise when employment reaches high levels, because some factors of production will be in inelastic supply. Some specialised factors may be in short supply while others, which are unfortunately not interchangeable with them, are still unemployed. This will cause firms to bid up the prices of the 'bottleneck' factors and will lead to price increases in some sectors of the economy while there is still unemployment elsewhere. Some factor (and commodity) prices may rise quite sharply before full employment has been reached.

(d) Trade union pressures

The second reason is that trade unions are likely to press for higher wages, at least in the most prosperous parts of the economy, long before unemployment has vanished. Again, one cannot generalise about what trade unions will do when there is high unemployment. However, even if they aggresively seek and obtain higher wages, it is likely that the effect of spending these wages will feed through into rising output rather than rising prices. As full employment is approached, the rate of increase in wage awards is likely to be greater, and it may well be that this will cause prices to rise somewhat. Of course, once full employment is reached, any further increase in money wages is bound to push up prices because supply cannot increase any more. Indeed, one may well have a 'spiral' of inflation, with increased wages leading to higher prices; higher prices leading to even bigger increases in wages; and so on.

(e) A summary   To sum up: the simplified assumptions with which we set out in order to contrast the behaviour of output, prices and the supply of money in conditions of unemployment and full employment need complicating in four ways. If this is done we shall have a more realistic theoretical framework, and also a more satisfactory basis for discussing the nature of inflation. The four complications are: (1) changes in aggregate demand will not normally be in exact proportion to changes in the supply of money; (2) while it is difficult to say whether returns to scale will diminish or increase as output rises from very low levels to the full employment level, returns are unlikely to be constant over the whole range of output and may well diminish towards the full employment level; (3) that 'bottlenecks' will often occur while some resources are still unemployed; and (4) that money wages will usually rise more than in proportion with output, at some stage before full employment is reached.

5. The definition of full employment

These factors lead to the curves shown in Fig. 24.2, rather than those in Fig. 24.1. In Fig. 24.2a, as the quantity of money supplied rises above zero, output at first rises proportionately. Once returns begin to diminish, however, output rises more slowly. When the full

Fig. 24.2 a | b

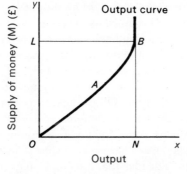

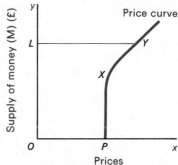

employment output (ON) is neared, bottlenecks occur and money wages rise so that the rate of growth of output slackens off considerably. When £OL of money has been pumped into the economy, full employment is reached and output ceases to increase at all as M rises further. The whole effect of the increasing money supply is then to raise factor and commodity prices. In Fig. 24.2b, prices remain constant to begin with, as output increases, but soon start to rise under the influence of diminishing returns. Towards the level of full employment, prices rise more quickly. Once full employment is reached (where $M=\pounds OL$), the elasticity of supply of output falls to zero and prices rise in proportion with the supply of money.

We may now return to the conundrums from section 4 of this chapter. When does inflation begin? Is it when prices begin to rise? Or is it when elasticity of supply of output in response to changes in the supply of money is zero? And when is full employment reached?

5.1 The simple model

In our first, simple model the answers are easy. So long as any factors of production remain unemployed, the elasticity of supply of output in response to changes in M (which we shall denote as e_0) $=1$. A given proportionate change in M calls forth exactly the same proportionate change in output. Once all factors are in use, e_0 falls to zero and employment is full. Again, when there is unemployment the elasticity of prices in response to changes in M (which we can denote by e_p) $=0$. When employment is full, $e_p=1$. Prices rise in proportion with M and inflation has begun.

5.2 The more complex model

In the case portrayed in Fig. 24.2, however, the problem is more complicated. In Fig. 24.2a, below point A on the output curve (showing the effect of changes in M on output), $e_0=1$. Above point B, $e_0=0$. B may here be defined as the point where full employment is reached. Employment is full at every point beyond B: that is when M is greater than $\pounds OL$. We may therefore define full employment, theoretically, as occurring when the elasticity of supply of output in response to increases in the supply of money (or alternatively in aggregate demand) is zero. One difficulty is that, in practice, it rarely proves possible for an economy to reach the point where $e_0=0$. There is always some frictional unemployment; some men are always changing jobs. There may well be structural or voluntary unemployment too. The idea that full employment occurs only when 100 per cent of the labour force is employed, so that $e_0=0$, is useless in practice. Nevertheless, it seems desirable to have an unambiguous theoretical definition of full employment. Everyone would agree (to refer again to Fig. 24.2a) that full employment would occur at a point much nearer to B than to A.

6. The definition of inflation

Just as it is difficult to define full employment, there is a similar difficulty in defining inflation. Nevertheless, when there is full employment, a rise in the supply of money is always accompanied by a rise in prices. If there is full employment, one may justifiably call a situation inflationary when either prices or the supply of money are rising, because in practice both will rise together. Referring again to Fig. 24.2b it is clear that, in the situation shown there, no one could describe the increase in M as inflationary below point X on the price curve. Nor could there be doubt that the situation is inflationary above point Y. It is the range between X and Y which causes us trouble. As we have seen, the existence of bottlenecks and the fact that money spent begins to rise more rapidly than output before full employment is reached means that there is here modified inflation. It may aptly be called a 'cost inflation', because costs are rising. 'True inflation', as Keynes called it, begins only when the elasticity of supply of output in response to changes in M (e_0) has fallen to zero.

We see, then, that in practice there is no clear dichotomy between conditions of price stability and of inflation, as there is in the simplified model we used earlier. Conditions are unambiguously inflationary when output is completely unresponsive to changes in money supply. Below this level, even if prices are rising, price increases cannot be seen as entirely harmful, even though they would be if they were unaccompanied by increases in output. In this situation, rising prices are the penalty paid by society for an increase in output; prices must rise if extra output is to be obtained.

This analysis confirms the fact that where there is full employment, conditions will be unambiguously inflationary if there is an increase in the supply of money. However, this discussion also confirms that, below the full employment level, inflation is much more difficult to define. Now that we no longer assume with the 'classical' economists that employment is always full, those who prefer the quantity theory approach nevertheless have to see part of the increase in the money supply as feeding through into increases in the GNP, and only part of it into increases in prices.

7. Keynes and the quantity theorists

This leaves open the major issue which still separates Keynesian economists from the quantity theorists. The latter group is large. For our purposes in discussing this issue we shall concentrate on the ideas of Professor Milton Friedman of the University of Chicago.

7.1 The Keynesian mechanism

As we have seen, the 'pure' Keynesian view of the way monetary policy works to expand any economy is this. With a given liquidity preference schedule, an increase in M will reduce the rate of interest. With a given marginal efficiency of capital curve, the fall in the rate of interest will increase investment. With a given consumption function, this increase in investment will, through the multiplier, lead to a multiple effect on the GNP. The neo-Keynesian view would be that the change in the rate of interest would not merely effect investment but would also alter consumption. However, this is an unimportant point. The basic conflict is between the Keynesians and the quantity theorists, not between the Keynesians themselves.

7.2 Friedman's view

Milton Friedman's analysis would concentrate attention on money balances, in the way we have already described when discussing the Cambridge equation. A decrease in M would be seen as decreasing money balances below the required level, relative to real income. Because money balances had fallen below the desired level, perhaps because money supply had been reduced by the monetary authorities, members of the community would reduce their spending. The aim would be to bring money balances back to the required proportion of real income. What is left unclear, in this description, is the way in which increased or decreased spending works through the economy. The Keynesian view was that changes in the interest rate would affect investment and perhaps consumption. The Friedmanite view is that monetary policy alters the pattern of assets that people want to hold. However, the Friedmanites would argue that tracing through the effects of changes in the supply of money to different interest rates, and so to different categories of spending, is too complicated. One is much better occupied in relating changes in the quantity of money directly to changes in the level of the GNP, though it is admitted that there will be lags in this relationship.

7.3 The points at issue

We are back, in other words, to the quantity theory. It is obvious that the quantity theorists will find analysis and explanation simplest if they can postulate a stable relationship between the GNP and the money supply. Unlike the Keynesians, they will find that their theory will be 'proved' if empirical research shows that the demand for money does not alter significantly in response to changes in the rate of interest. While Keynesians, especially those seeking evidence for the liquidity trap, are seeking empirical evidence showing that the interest-elasticity of demand for money is infinite, the Friedmanites are seeking empirical evidence to show that interest-elasticity is zero, or nearly so. They can then claim that the rigid quantity theory holds. In other words, what the Friedmanites are doing is to treat the economy as a 'black box'. They believe that it is too difficult to show precisely what processes within the economy connect changes in M to changes in the GNP. They therefore postulate that, whatever these processes are, they are likely to be accompanied by a low (or better still zero) interest-elasticity of demand for money.

7.4 The findings of empirical research

There has recently been a good deal of empirical research seeking to resolve these issues. In particular Friedman and Meiselman, in a study covering the period 1897–1958, showed that the quantity of money was a better predictor of consumption than investment was. They found that the quantity of money provided a better explanation of the GNP than the multiplier did, except during the 1930s. This gave some comfort to the Keynesians, who were able to argue that the 1930s was precisely the period which Keynes's theory was intended to explain. In this sense, the Keynesian revolution was vindicated. However, empirical work is still continuing and no firm conclusions have been reached.

What one can say is that the contemporary quantity theorists do seem to have shown that there is a broad association between the GNP, consumption and money supply, though this relationship holds more satisfactorily in some periods than in others. However, while this view sees the money supply as the main factor leading to fluctuations in income, it accepts that the causal influences are slow and variable in acting. This leads the contemporary quantity theorists to the view that monetary policy should not be used for the 'fine tuning' of the economy when one is trying to deal with short-term fluctuations in economic activity.

7.5 Money and capital

It is perhaps worth emphasising that the views of Milton Friedman on these issues are closely associated with his concept of 'permanent income'. For example, Friedman takes the view that since money is a capital good, the demand for money is a problem in capital theory. Unlike the Keynesians, however, Friedman links the demand for money to the total wealth of the individual, including human capital. He ends with a demand for money which is a function of the price level and its rate of change, bond and equity yields, income and the ratio of non-human to human wealth. Indeed, Friedman's demand function for money has become difficult to distinguish from the modern Keynesian one. Nevertheless, the similarity should not be over-emphasised because Keynesian theory did not put as much emphasis on the importance of capital as Friedman does. Moreover, Friedman's 'income' is not that measured in national income accounts like those in Chapter 19. It is income treated as the return on a stock of wealth; or wealth measured by the income it yields.

Friedman's work is important because it brings monetary theory closer to the basic principal of capital theory—to the view that income is the yield on capital, and capital the present value of future income. Once again, as we have frequently found in this book, economic theorists are discovering that an increasing range of problems can be treated as aspects of capital theory. In addition, of course, Friedman emphasises the importance of human capital. This is another field of economics which will almost certainly be developed considerably in the near future.

7.6 Views on inflation

Before leaving this discussion of the differences between the Keynesians and quantity theorists, it will be useful to say a little more about the problems of inflation. We have seen that it is not always easy to decide whether conditions are inflationary, since one will frequently find output and prices going up simultaneously. It will be difficult to be sure, in practice, when full employment is reached. Since World War II, most countries have been prepared to accept annual rates of price increase of around 3 or 4 per cent per annum without displaying much concern. Indeed, especially in the UK since 1945, it has been the effects of a high level of aggregate demand on the balance of payments rather than on the domestic price level that have most frequently led to action to restrain demand.

A major problem is the one discussed in the last section. In the immediate post-war period, economists were impressed with how successfully Keynesian methods of analysis had enabled them to diagnose, if not to cure, the inflationary problems of World War II. In particular, the Keynesian model had drawn attention to the relationship between savings and investment. Inflation was seen as the result of an excess of investment over savings. It was therefore suggested that investment should be reduced: for example, by direct cuts in government investment, by increases in interest rates or by reductions in tax allowances to reduce private investment. At the same time, increased taxation on consumers was seen as a way of taking away income that would have been spent by consumers, diverting this into a 'budget surplus'. This was to be used by the government to reduce debt and/or the money supply; it would not be spent on current account.

The attraction of the Keynesian analysis was that, unlike the quantity theory, it did get inside the 'black box' and did suggest ways of intervening directly on consumption, savings or investment rather than relying on cuts in the supply of money, working through to the GNP because of a fixed, or stable, velocity of circulation. Another attraction of the Keynesian analysis, emphasised by Professor Harry Johnson, is that Keynes did not provide a theory of what determined money wages. This enabled economists when they applied Keynesian theory to a full employment situation, to make whatever assumptions they wished about the determination of money wages. There was an advantage because economists were then free to assume that wages were determined in whatever way they found most convenient: by negotiations; by the interaction of supply and demand; or by a struggle to maintain, or improve, the share of wages in the GNP.

(a) The Phillips curve

Perhaps the most generally-used assumption has been that underlying what is known as the 'Phillips curve'. Phillips emphasised a link between the level of unemployment and the rate of wage increase. As we have seen, Keynes's analysis in the *General Theory* suggested that, along with bottlenecks in various markets, trade unions would

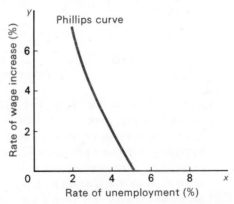

Fig. 24.3

be likely to raise wages more rapidly when unemployment rates were low. What Phillips did was to study the relationship between unemployment and changes in money wages in the UK over the period 1862–1957.[1] This study appeared to identify a relationship, which had remained stable over the whole period, between the rate of wage increase and the percentage of unemployment. Such a relationship is shown in the Phillips curve, an example of which is

[1] A. W. Phillips, 'The Relation Between Unemployment and the Rate of Change in Money Wages in the United Kingdom, 1862–1957,' *Economica*, 1958, p. 283.

given in Fig. 24.3. This curve shows that in a hypothetical economy, when unemployment is 4 per cent, wages rise at 2 per cent per annum. When unemployment is 5 per cent wages do not rise at all. Although there are doubts about the realism of the Phillips curve, it has been widely accepted as a useful concept. Certainly, the idea that when there is more unemployment there is more competition for jobs, and so less pressure for higher wages, sounds plausible.

The problem, of course, is to discover what the *actual* relationship is at any point of time. For example, in the UK in the early 1970s, there was some consternation over the fact that the Phillips curve appeared to have shifted bodily to the right. This is what has happened to the hypothetical curve in Fig. 24.4. The dark-brown curve is the

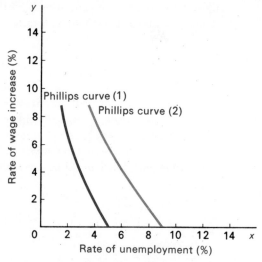

Fig. 24.4

same as that in Fig. 24.3. The light-brown curve, shows that if unemployment were 4 per cent, instead of wages increasing at 2 per cent per annum as with the dark-brown curve, they will now increase at 8 per cent per annum. Similarly where, as with the original curve, 5 per cent unemployment would have been required to ensure no increase in wages at all, with the light-brown curve wage increases would fall to zero only with 9 per cent unemployment.

It is true that in this way Phillips introduced an empirically-measurable relationship between the rate of wage increase and the rate of unemployment into economic theory. On the other hand, it is far from easy to discover precisely where the Phillips curve lies for any economy. Only if the relationship remains stable can the rate of wage increase accompanying a given level of unemployment be predicted. Indeed, this problem, accompanied by doubts over whether the Phillips curve actually exists at all, make it very difficult to use as the basis of economic policy.

(b) Demand-pull and cost-push

Another notion which has been widely used during the post-war period, is the distinction between cost-push and demand-pull inflation. In various countries at various times since the war, economists have argued over whether inflation was the result of a push from costs or a pull from demand. These debates were keen—for example, in the USA, in the late 1950s especially, and in the UK during much of the post-war period (at times when the economy was not actually in recession). A major consequence of this distinction, has been that at times when inflation seemed to be of the demand-pull variety, a preference for deflation of demand as a solution to the current inflationary difficulties was expressed by many people. At times when cost-push inflation seemed to be the problem, the preference was for an incomes policy, or some other way of reducing increases in wages. For example, when wages were increasing at more than 10 per cent per annum in the UK in late 1970, most people saw the problem as one of cost-push. Many economists drew the conclusion that some kind of incomes policy was necessary, if only it could be successfully introduced.

In practice, it is extremely difficult to show by empirical tests whether inflation is demand-pull or cost-push. The result is that many suggestions for policy measures, even by leading economists, are often based only on partial and sketchy empirical evidence. Another problem is that a 'pure' demand-pull or a 'pure' cost-push inflation is rarely found. What is more common is a mixture of the two. At the same time, while it would be generally agreed that demand-pull inflation could not persist without a continuing increase in the money supply, the same would be true of cost-push inflation. Any increase in the velocity of circulation which was possible in practice, would be relatively limited. Any 'pure' cost-push inflation would be brought to an end relatively quickly, unless the monetary authorities were prepared to increase the supply of money. What has happened in practice, for example, in both the UK and the USA in the early 1970s, is that both governments were unwilling to allow unemployment to rise to the levels which would have been implied, given the apparent position of the Phillips curve, if a restrictive monetary policy had been used to reduce the rate of wage increase.

Whatever their initial causes, most inflations in most countries contain an element of both cost-push and demand-pull. The result is that, particularly since it is extremely difficult to show econometrically what the role of each type of inflation is in any economy at any moment, the distinction has been more useful in theory than in practice.

(c) Other empirical findings

This difficulty in discovering precisely how any inflationary process is working itself out has strengthened the hands of the quantity theorists. This was especially true in the late 1960s. We have already outlined their argument. They hold that since the process by which changes in the money supply work through to increase the level either of the real GNP or of money GNP, it is better to look at the observed effect of changes in the money supply on changes in the real or money GNP.

Empirical evidence suggests that, certainly over longish periods of time, changes in the money supply appear to have more effect on the level of the GNP than does direct intervention to alter consumption or investment. The modern quantity theorists therefore argue that anti-inflationary policies should concentrate on maintaining careful control over the money supply. This procedure avoids difficulties over whether the inflation being tackled is of the cost-push or demand-pull variety. The strictest form of the quantity theorists' argument is one put forward by the Chicago School in the USA. This holds that if one wants a long-run increase in the GNP of, say, 4 per cent, one should allow the money supply to increase by 4 per cent per annum. One should then leave this increase in the money supply to work through to the GNP and not attempt any 'fine tuning' of the economy through changes in fiscal policy.

As we saw earlier in this chapter, empirical studies have not resolved the dispute between the 'Keynesians' and the 'Friedmanites' over this issue. One possible practical 'test' was abandoned. Attempts to control inflation through control of the money supply during the early 1970s were ended by both the British and American governments because unemployment in each country had reached intolerable levels before inflation was reduced to an acceptable rate.

It therefore seems that both discussion and empirical testing of the respective merits of Keynesian and Friedmanite ideas will continue for some time.

7.7 Hyper-inflation

Before leaving the problem, it will be worth saying something about situations where inflation becomes very serious. Extreme inflation has never occurred recently in Britain or the USA but did happen in some central European countries during the 1920s and the 1940s.

The main feature of hyper-inflation is that money loses almost all of its value. Prices rise to fantastic levels, and the velocity of circulation becomes enormous. Money loses value so rapidly that people are unwilling to hold it for more than a few moments. One of the chief dangers of such inflation lies in a failure to appreciate its power. For the strict quantity theory overlooks the part which changes in V can exert, wherever the increase in the supply of money is considerable. If the amount of money doubles, it is possible that prices will double; that V will remain constant so that only the direct effect of M on P need be considered. A much larger increase in M, such as occurs in hyper-inflation, will certainly raise V. This in turn will raise prices more than in proportion to the intial rise in M. If the supply of money is increased to a hundred times its original amount, prices are unlikely to become only a hundred times as high. They may well rise to a thousand or even a hundred-thousand times the old level. The velocity of circulation will become very large.

Put into Keynesian language, what has happened is this. The velocity of circulation is the obverse of liquidity preference. If the demand for money is high, then money circulates slowly, V is low; and vice versa. Changes in V are, so to speak, the external manifestation of changes in liquidity preference. It is therefore possible to explain the rise in V, induced by a large increase in M, in terms of liquidity preference. The explanation is familiar. When prices rise beyond a certain point, people speculate on the likelihood of a continuing price rise. This is not important in normal times, for liquidity preference is then unresponsive to changes in commodity prices. A change in the rate of interest will affect the demand for money; if rising prices of goods and services do affect it at all, they will increase it through a rise in the transactions motive. More expensive goods and services will require more money to purchase them. If commodity prices rise sharply and at an increasing rate however, people will realise that the only possible result must be that money will become quite valueless. Liquidity preference therefore falls off sharply.

As soon as they see signs of runaway inflation, people make a deliberate attempt to spend as much cash as they can and to buy goods instead. Instead of holding bank notes and deposits, they will buy real estate and art treasures. Explaining this in terms of the conventional motives for liquidity, we may say that bonds are normally a close substitute for money. With very rapid inflation, bonds become just as useless as money. Since they bear interest fixed in terms of money, and since they are only redeemable in terms of money, bonds and money both become valueless. As a result, no one bothers to hold money for speculation in bonds on the Stock Exchange. Nor may they feel that equities reflect the real values of assets. Instead, everyone buys 'real' assets of kinds which they think will best retain their value after the inflation is over. Since to hold either money or bonds is to risk loss, the speculative and precautionary motives for holding money vanish. Everyone holds goods.

The transactions motive is likely to survive rather longer in hyper-inflation. While it is now foolish to use money as a store of value, it can still be used as a medium of exchange. The inconvenience of barter makes people use money as a medium of exchange for as long as possible. Nevertheless, even though money is still used as a medium of exchange, the amount of money held under the transactions motive will increase much less than in proportion to rises in prices. Even those who are paid weekly will spend all their earnings immediately they receive them. If they keep money for a day, or even an hour, prices will have risen. The effect may even be that they demand to be paid daily instead of weekly. So may those paid monthly. Even the demand for money to satisfy the transactions motive will then fall off sharply.

The concept of liquidity preference is therefore able to explain hyper-inflation as satisfactorily as it can explain normal monetary conditions. However, in these conditions, unless there is a sharp reversal of monetary policy and liquidity preference is increased considerably, it is certain that the existing type of money will be unable to maintain its position as money for much longer.

In concluding this discussion of hyper-inflation, we should perhaps point out that many people imagine that once inflation exceeds some rate, say 10 per cent, it must gradually accelerate into hyper-inflation. Evidence, particularly from Latin America, shows that countries can maintain very rapid inflation for long periods of time without it accelerating. It seems that acceleration will take place only if the *rate of increase* of the money supply accelerates. To this extent at least, the quantity theorists appear to be vindicated.

8. Money wages and employment

The next problem we must consider is the relationship between money wages and employment. We saw in Chapter 17 that one of the main points at issue between Keynes and the 'classical' economists was whether a cut in money wages would increase employment. We saw that workers will strongly resist any suggestion that money wages should be cut, though they will often be prepared to accept cuts in 'real' wages caused by rising prices, providing these cuts are not too large. What we must now do is to discover whether those economists who maintain that a cut in money wages will increase employment are *theoretically* right. The suggestion that money wages should be cut is so objectionable that a wage cut can rarely be put into practice. Nevertheless, it is important to discover whether there is *theoretical* justification for the view that wage cuts can increase employment. If Keynes was merely saying that the best assumption one can make is that money wages are rigid, because trade unions will not accept money-wage cuts, this leads to important conclusions. However, it does not alter the earlier theory, which held that if trade unions *would* accept a cut in money wages, employment would increase. The important point is therefore to discover what the Keynesian analysis argues about an economy where everyone *is* prepared to accept a cut in money wages. Would this nevertheless be an economy where full employment was impossible?

8.1 The 'classical' view

The reason why we have had to postpone a discussion of the 'classical' idea that a reduction in money wages will increase employment to this stage in this book is that the analysis of the effects of a cut in money wages is more complicated than one might suppose. The indirect effects, which 'classical' theory ignored, are very important.

The 'classical' explanation of the effect of wage cuts was relatively simple. It argued that if wages fell, the prices of the products made by labour fell too. This increased output to an extent depending on the rate at which the marginal revenue productivity of labour was diminishing—on the elasticity of demand for labour. It is possible to interpret such a statement as meaning that if money wages are cut, the demand for the output of labour as a whole is unaffected. Arguing from the fact that the cut in money wages in a single industry will increase employment, some economists have therefore argued that a cut in wages in all industries will increase employment in all industries. While in particular-equilibrium analysis one is justified in taking the demand for the product of the individual industry as given, there is no such justification when one considers all industries together. The demand for the product of one industry depends largely on the wages paid to, and amounts of money spent by, workers in other industries. A general-equilibrium analysis of wage cuts is futile unless it pays attention to the problem of whether aggregate demand will rise or fall as wages are reduced. The question we must answer is: Will aggregate demand in terms of money remain constant? Or, if it comes to the worst, will it fall less than in proportion to the cut in money wages? If the answer is yes, employment will rise when wages are cut; if it is no, employment will fall.

The 'classical' economists, by neglecting the role of effective demand in their analysis of changes in money wages, seemed to assume that there was a direct link between wages and rising employment. However, in Keynesian macro-economic analysis one has to consider the effect on employment of any change in the economy by seeing what happens to the three main determinants of income and employment: (1) the propensity to consume; (2) the rate of interest; and (3) the marginal efficiency of capital. The Keynesian argument is that the main repercussions will be as follows.

First, a reduction in money wages will reduce money prices, the extent of the reduction depending on the nature of supply conditions, and especially on the ratio of wages to total production costs. This will result in some redistribution of real income from wage earners to those in the community whose money incomes have not been reduced. Keynes thought that the net effect would probably be to reduce the propensity to consume. For wage earners are likely to consume more out of their incomes than other (probably richer) sections of the community.

Second, a great deal depends on whether entrepreneurs believe that although money wages have fallen at the present moment, they will rise again in the future. If they do, this will be favourable to employment. For if entrepreneurs believe that wages will rise, they will feel more optimistic about future economic prospects and the marginal efficiency of capital will rise. Again, the fact that money wages, and therefore prices, are expected to rise in the future will make it desirable to buy consumer goods now rather than later; this may temporarily raise the propensity to consume. On the other hand, if the fact that wages have fallen already is taken as an indication that they will fall even further in the near future, this will tend to reduce employment. The marginal efficiency of capital will be depressed; entrepreneurs will regard future prospects for selling consumption goods as less rosy. Consumers will also postpone consumption until further wage reductions have reduced prices.

Third, the fact that the wage bill has fallen and that prices, and perhaps some other incomes, have fallen, will mean a reduction in liquidity preference. The demand for money under the transactions motive will fall. What we are saying is that the 'real' value of the money supply has risen. Each unit of money will buy more goods; its purchasing power has increased. The result of the fall in liquidity preference is that the rate of interest will fall unless the money supply is reduced; investment will be stimulated. If it is expected that wages and prices will continue to fall, this may lead to expectations of further falls in the rate of interest and so will tend to reduce the demand for money for speculative purposes.

Fourth, the effect of falling prices on the burden of debt may be unfavourable. If prices fall far enough, entrepreneurs may be unable to pay debenture holders their interest, and firms may fall into the hands of receivers. Again, the burden of the National Debt—largely made up of fixed interest-bearing securities—will become important. High taxation will sap business confidence. The effect of both these factors will be to reduce investment.

Finally, we must point out that we are concerned in this book with a 'closed system'. In practice, the main favourable effects of a reduction in money wages are likely to come from its effect on the exporting industries, which can now sell their goods more cheaply as compared with foreigners.

If we confine our attention to a 'closed economy', we see that the main hope of increased investment lies either in a rise in the marginal efficiency of capital or in a fall in the rate of interest. Let us consider these possibilities more carefully. There is a hope that if wages are thought to have fallen to 'rock bottom', the effect may be to raise the marginal efficiency of capital or to lead to a fall in the rate of interest. Entrepreneurs will look forward to a time of rising prices and activity, and current consumption will be stimulated because people hope to forestall the expected price rises by buying now. The worst possible situation is where wages and prices are expected to continue a slow but steady slide downwards.

There remains the rate of interest. What can one hope for here? If the amount of money falls as money wages fall, one can hope for little. If the quantity of money can be kept stable while the level of wages falls, the fact that the demand for money under the transactions motive (and perhaps the speculative motive) will also fall, will reduce the rate of interest. The rise in the 'real' quantity of money will have a beneficial effect. Keynes therefore concluded that it would be possible to reduce the rate of interest by lowering money wages but keeping the supply of money constant.

The problem, as we have already seen, is that two factors may still prevent the economy from moving towards full employment. First, although to begin with there may be a fall in the demand for money under both the transactions and speculative motives, once the rate of interest reaches a very low level a 'liquidity trap' may operate. The demand for money under the speculative motive may increase, because people cannot believe that it is safe to hold bonds at such low interest rates. They will expect interest rates to rise and bond prices to fall. Second, even if the rate of interest can be reduced substantially, the slope of the marginal efficiency of capital schedule may be so steep that even a substantial reduction in the rate of interest will have little effect on investment, or indeed consumption. We know that there is some doubt whether these constraints, and particularly the liquidity trap, exist. Nevertheless, they represent Keynes's reply to the suggestion that, provided money wages can be cut far enough, under-employment equilibrium is impossible.

8.3 The rejoinder

The response to this argument has come particularly from those who adhere to the quantity theory of money. They have concentrated on the point, which indeed Keynes admitted, that the reduction in money prices, resulting from a cut in money wages, would increase in 'real' value of money balances. However, we know that the Keynesian view is that the way in which an increase in money supply is transmitted through the economy is through a fall in the rate of interest, while the modern quantity theorists regard the transmission process as so complex that it is best ignored. They therefore argue that the important result of the fall in prices is to increase the real value of money balances above what the community regards as necessary. Because, in this sense, people have become wealthier, they will increase their spending and this will raise the GNP. There may or may not be a fall in the interest rate.

(a) The Pigou effect

The process by which an increase in the real value of money balances leads to economic expansion is usually described as the 'Pigou effect', after the late Professor Pigou, or 'the real-balance effect'. While many economists doubt whether the real-balance effect will be strong enough to bring an economy back to full employment, this is a theoretical possibility. The tendency is therefore to concentrate on the practical rather than the theoretical implications of Keynes's assumption of rigid money wages.

It seems to be generally agreed that the best explanation of what Keynes was doing is that he agreed that, given time, it might be possible to reduce money wages sufficiently to bring about full employment. However, he was emphasising that any such process worked so slowly that it could not be treated as a practical possibility. It is safer to assume that wages are rigid than to assume that they are flexible enough to allow the working of the Pigou effect to bring about full employment.

The crucial point is that one is likely to achieve much less success in attempting to lower the rate of interest, and hence increase investment, by reducing the level of money wages than by increasing the supply of money. There are three substantial practical objections to following a 'flexible wage policy' as an alternative to an open-market 'flexible money policy'. These are as follows.

(b) The possibility of wage flexibility

First, as we have suggested, it is quite unreasonable to expect that trade unions will (or should) accept all-round reductions in money wages of equal size for every class of labour. In democratic states, the accepted system of collective bargaining between individual unions and employers' associations means that any wage reductions would be piecemeal. Workers in the worst bargaining position would suffer most seriously and most quickly. In a democratic society, it is much easier to affect interest rates by open-market operations than by cuts in money wages. A dictatorship might succeed, a democracy never would.

Second, for reasons of social justice it is unreasonable to expect workers alone to accept cuts in money wages. Such cuts must inevitably decrease their standard of living relatively to that of other sections of the community. Since some classes in the community have their incomes fixed in terms of money, social justice requires that all classes should have their incomes fixed in the same way. A policy of increasing the supply of money in a depression is preferable to cutting wages.

Finally, a cut in money wages would increase the burden of debt, while a policy of increasing the supply of money would reduce it. An increased burden of debt in most communities would place an intolerable burden on debtors; and most of the biggest debtors are businesses.

In a closed system, it is certain that best short-run policy is to keep money wages as stable as possible. Stable wages and prices will prevent the expectations of entrepreneurs becoming unduly optimistic or pessimistic. The effect will be to reduce the extent of fluctuations in employment, even though they cannot be prevented entirely. In the long run, when production is likely to rise steadily, one can choose between constant wage levels and slowly-falling prices; or constant prices and slowly-rising money wages. In practice, however, long-run problems tend to be less important than short-run ones.

8.4 Summing up   How, then, can one sum up the debate between Keynes and the 'classical' economists on the relationship between cuts in money wages and the level of employment? On the theoretical plane, the difference of opinion seems to have narrowed down to whether or not the Pigou effect will be strong enough to bring about full employment. Some economists apparently think that it is, though there are many doubters. In practice, this disagreement is unimportant since cuts in money wages seem to be ruled out in most circumstances. On the other hand, cuts in 'real' wages can be, and are, brought about by prices rising faster than money wages. While it is doubtful whether Keynes has produced a significantly different *theory* of the effects of cuts in money wages from that of the earlier 'classical' economists, his practical conclusions are very different and are almost universally accepted. In practice, cuts in money wages are unlikely to be brought about quickly enough to make them a practical way of achieving full employment.

9. Money in a near-barter economy

In conclusion, we return to the question whether a monetary economy is significantly different from a barter economy. Keynes's economy was *very* different from a barter economy. He was concerned with an economy where variables like income and employment were likely to alter, so that peoples' expectations about the future were important. In particular, he saw the holding (indeed hoarding) of money as an important part of the mechanism linking present and future. In his theory, the fact that people could alter their money holdings in this way affected the rate of interest and so the amount of investment and of income. Keynes's economy was very different from the barter economy. It must be added, however, that a good deal of recent discussion has been concerned with an economy which is as much like a barter economy as possible, except that it uses money.

A major question is whether, in such an economy, money is 'neutral'? Would a rise in the money supply raise all prices (including the rate of interest) in the same proportion? If it did, money would be neutral; a mere 'veil' as Pigou called it, which concealed the 'real' operation of the economy without actually altering it. The discussion has revolved around the significance of the real-balance effect. Don Patinkin, in particular, has emphasised its role.[1] If the quantity of money in a near-barter economy is doubled and all prices double, real balances will be unaltered. Nothing 'real' will change. However, an accidental increase in prices will reduce real balances below the desired level. This will reduce spending, in the way we have seen already, and prices will fall. The existence of real balances ensures price stability.

This leads to a difficulty. The fact that real balances are brought into the analysis, for example by Patinkin, means that money is *not* a veil. One cannot discuss relative prices in this model without bringing in money supply. Nevertheless, in one sense, the 'classical' view is unscathed; *relative* prices are not affected by the supply of money. The discussion has therefore moved on to the question whether one needs to retain the (monetary) real-balance effect in the 'real' analysis of relative prices.

In the excellent review article given in the suggested reading, Harry Johnson concludes that the real balance effect can be ignored so long as one is dealing with equilibrium situations, where all money prices change simultaneously, and in the same proportion as money balances. Here, real balances will not alter if the price level changes. Real balances are needed only to ensure an equilibrium between the supply and the demand for money. If these are equal, one can go on to ignore money and to look at relative prices alone.

---

[1] Don Patinkin, *Money, Interest and Prices*, Evanston, 1956.

Suggested reading

ROBERTSON, SIR DENNIS	*Lectures on Economic Principles,* London, 1963, Part 3, chapter 1.
KEYNES, J. M.	*General Theory,* London, 1936, chapters 19, 20 and 21.
KEYNES, J. M.	'Relative Movements of Real Wages and Output', *Economic Journal,* 1939, p. 34.
FRIEDMAN, MILTON and HELLER, WALTER W.	*Monetary versus Fiscal Policy: A Dialogue,* New York, 1969.
JOHNSON, H. G.	*Essays in Monetary Economics,* London, 1967, chapters 2 and 3.

Part 3

The theory of growth

25

Some basic concepts

1. Statics and dynamics

So far, this book has been concerned either with statics or comparative statics. Static analysis discusses the question of how, for example, an equilibrium price is arrived at in a market where the demand and supply curves are known and remain unchanged. Static analysis enables us to analyse a situation where consumers, firms, industries and whole economies are in stable, or static, equilibrium at certain levels of prices, output, income and employment. However, while much of the discussion up to this point has been static in this sense, we have occasionally dealt in an elementary way with the results of once-for-all changes in demand conditions. Allowing for the effects of the passage of time on prices and output in a growing economy is one of the most difficult tasks that economic theory faces. Until the late 1930s the only real step in this direction had been Marshall's important distinction between the long and the short run. As we saw in Chapter 7, the main way in which Marshall used this tool of analysis was to compare the short- and long-run effects of a once-for-all change in the demand for its product on the equilibrium price and output of a competitive industry. Similarly, the discussion in Chapter 20 showed how big a change in national income would result from a given alteration in investment spending, when all the multiplier effects of that alteration had been allowed to work themselves out completely. In both these cases we were concerned with what economists call comparative statics. We compared the sizes of particular variables before and after a given change in conditions had exerted its full influence on them. We were comparing two different, static levels of activity, one before a change and one after the effects of that change had been fully worked out. The term 'comparative statics' is therefore an obvious one to use when describing such a situation.

Though the economic problems that can be dealt with in this way are interesting, they are limited ones and exclude many important and pressing problems. In particular, much more advanced methods of analysis are needed to explain and analyse the problems of economic fluctuations—booms and slumps—and the causes of economic growth. These are questions which have rightly attracted much of the attention and analysis of economists in recent years, but they cannot be dealt with adequately by the kind of economic theory used so far in this book.

2. The beginnings

The first steps towards developing the theories of economic fluctuations and economic growth, which are now widely accepted, were taken in the 1930s and early 1940s. Neither Marshall, Keynes or their contemporaries did more than make a few suggestive asides. During the 1930s the work of Frisch[1], Kalecki[2] and Samuelson[3] paved the way for mathematical analyses of economic fluctuations based on the interaction of the multiplier and the accelerator.[4] These analyses are still too mechanical to explain reality fully. They cannot allow convincingly for changes in the expectations that consumers and businessmen hold about the future, or for changes in the degree of excess capacity in an economy. Nevertheless, they have made it possible to throw a good deal of light on what exactly are the main causes of economic fluctuations.

In the 1930s, too, the foundations of a theory of steady economic growth which abstracted from fluctuations were being laid by Sir Roy Harrod (as he now is) in England and Evsey D. Domar in the USA. Indeed, it is remarkable how many of the more recent developments in growth theory were accurately foreshadowed by Sir Roy Harrod in a path-breaking series of lectures which he delivered in London in 1947.[5]

One major problem which will face us throughout Part Three is that it is very difficult to isolate fluctuations in a growing economy from the trend growth rate around which those fluctuations take place. There is no doubt that economic growth can, and usually does, give rise to short-term fluctuations in the economy, though there is much dispute over how far the fluctuations themselves help or hinder growth. In Part Three we shall largely ignore fluctuations. The problems of economic growth are so important and so complex that it will be well worthwhile spending most of our time in Part

---

[1]Ragnar Frisch, 'Propagation and Impulse Problems', in *Economic Essays in Honour of G. Cassel,* London, 1933.

[2]M. Kalecki, *Essays in the Theory of Economic Fluctuations,* London, 1939, and other writings.

[3]P. A. Samuelson, 'Interactions between the Multiplier Analysis and the Principle of Acceleration', *Review of Economics and Statistics,* May, 1939, p. 75. Reprinted in *Readings in Business Cycle Theory,* Blakiston Series, 1944.

[4]See, for example, J. R. Hicks, *A Contribution to the Theory of the Trade Cycle,* Oxford, 1950.

[5]R. F. Harrod, *Towards a Dynamic Economics,* London, 1948.

Three studying the factors in any economy which determine the trend-rate of growth. It is around this that fluctuations can, and will, take place. The study of economic fluctuations is, in any case, a substantial subject in its own right.

The analysis of steady growth in Part Three will therefore provide readers with a starting point from which they can proceed to study original writings, not only on theories of long-run growth themselves but also on theories of shorter-run economic fluctuations.

**3.
Comparative
statics
revisited**

The first requirement in passing from analysis using statics and comparative statics to a study of economic growth is to become accustomed to looking, not at rates of output per period of time, but at *rates of change* in the rate of output *between* periods of time. This difference can be illustrated by looking again, in slightly different terms, at the working of the multiplier, which was discussed in Chapter 20.

In Fig. 25.1 we measure the level of national income up the y-axis and time (in months) along the x-axis. We suppose, as multiplier

Fig. 25.1

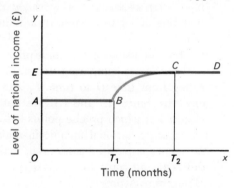

analysis does, that the economy is initially in an under-employment equilibrium; national income, at $£OA$ $(=BT_1)$, is assumed to be well below the full employment level. Between time O and time T_1, the level of the national income is constant at the level of $£OA$—its rate of growth is zero. To anticipate the terminology we shall use later, we shall denote the rate of growth of national income by the symbol G_y. We may then say that, in this initial situation, $G_y=0$.

At the point of time T_1, the government institutes a public investment programme, increasing the level of investment by $£I$ in each succeeding period of time, in our particular example each month. This brings the multiplier into operation. For several months there is a rise in national income. Then at time T_2 national income finally reaches the new, stable equilibrium level of $£OE$ $(=CT_2)$. Here, the

v

Some basic concepts

rate of growth of income, having been positive since T_1, approaches zero asymptotically. The rise in national income between T_1 and T_2 is $£AE$ (or CT_2-OA), where $AE=I\dfrac{1}{1-c}$. All we have done is to sum a convergent series. Where I is the extra investment per period of time and c the marginal propensity to consume this series is:

$$I+cI+c^2I+c^3I \quad . \qquad . \qquad . \qquad . \qquad . \quad c^nI$$

We know from the discussion in Chapter 22 that this series sums to $I\dfrac{1}{1-c}$, where $\dfrac{1}{1-c}$ $(=k)$ is the income, or investment multiplier. (As in Chapter 20, we are assuming that *no* extra private investment outlays are induced by the operation of the public investment programme.)

It is important to note that, for this conclusion to hold, the extra government investment spending of $£I$ must be repeated in each period of time after T_1. If the government were merely to spend a single extra amount of $£1$ in month T_1, national income would rise somewhat initially, but would soon relapse again to the original level. Though this fact is not always completely understood, multiplier analysis assumes a *permanent* rise in the level of investment spending of a given, constant amount in each succeeding period of time.

This discussion of the multiplier is an example of comparative statics. We are comparing two static levels of income, the one, OA, ruling from time O to time T_1 and the other, OE, from time T_2 onwards. Since AB and CD are both straight lines, it is quite immaterial at which precise points between O and T_1 and beyond T_2 we measure national income in making the comparison. The simplicity of comparative statics is its main attraction. One is comparing different, but constant, levels of output; one is not tracing the path of output over time.

4. Dynamic economics

In dynamic economics we do just this. For example, in Fig. 25.1 the dotted line BC traces out the path along which income grows between T_1 and T_2. It shows the way in which the multiplier effects of the extra government investment operate, as time passes, to raise national income from OA to OE. In order to study this movement of the economy from B to C one has to use more powerful tools of analysis than those of comparative statics; one has to embark on economic dynamics. The question becomes one of analysing rates of growth of income, G_y, where these rates of growth are now positive, and no longer zero. Nor, as Fig. 25.1 shows clearly, need the rates of growth of income be constant. Between B and C, the *rate* of growth of income begins by being high, as the steep slope of BC shows. It then diminishes until, at C, it has fallen to zero. In yet other situations, the rate at which income is growing may be an increasing one, starting at, say, 2 per cent and rising to, say, 6 per cent per annum. Indeed, one could quite well have alternating periods of increasing, decreasing and constant rates of growth of income.

Let us sum up the argument so far. In static economics we take certain basic elements in the economy to be given and known—for example, the size and ability of the population, the quantity of natural resources, the tastes of consumers and so on. These basic factors determine the levels of output of the various goods, their prices and the incomes of the factors of production which make them. In dynamic economics, some or all of these basic elements are supposed to be changing, so that our task is to determine the *rates* at which output is altering.

The discussion so far has been in terms of national income (or output) and it is clear that income (output) must be one of the most important variables for us to study in dynamic economics. The ultimate aim of any economic system is to satisfy the material needs and wants of its members by providing them with a supply of goods and services to consume. The faster this supply grows, the more affluent the economy is. However, we shall also be interested in the changes which occur in other elements in the system. National income depends on a number of underlying factors, so that growth theory concentrates on three major variables besides national income (or output). One is the rate of change of population, or, more usually, of the actual work force. The second is the rate of growth of the community's stock of capital goods—the rate of capital accumulation. Finally, there is what is the most vital but perhaps least-understood element lying behind growth—technical progress. This is a somewhat obscure phenomenon. Its rate is determined not only by the introduction of improved methods of production based on past inventions, what the economists call 'innovation'. It is also determined by the rate at which new inventions capable of forming the basis for future innovations are being made. We must consider both invention and innovation in our theory of growth. Technical progress will also depend, in part, on the extent to which resources are being devoted to the task of educating and developing the inventors, innovators, workers and managers of the future. This, too, we must consider.

In strict logic, any theory of growth which claims to be truly comprehensive ought to allow for and analyse continuous and outright decline in an economy. However, we shall ignore the possibility of a steady decline in income; not least because outright decline does not appear to be characteristic of modern economies. Our task is to consider the conditions which must be fulfilled if various steady rates of growth are to be achieved. In order to simplify the analysis, we shall make the assumption that all rates of growth, whether high or low, are constant ones. We shall be concerned with 'steady-state' growth, with the economy in a condition of steady, overall growth. If we can discover the factors underlying constant rates of growth, we can discover how growth rates are determined. This should also give us some insight into how they can be increased or reduced.

5. The determinants of economic growth

Modern growth theory begins from the obvious starting-point that to produce goods one must employ labour, on the one hand, and capital goods, on the other. It goes on to take the view that, while the employment of both capital and labour is essential if the economy is to produce at all, economic growth is especially the result of capital accumulation. What kind of reasoning lies behind this view?

5.1 The accumulation of capital

The answer can be seen if one considers an economy with a constant labour force, where no increase in output can come from putting more people to work. However, we are oversimplifying a complex situation, so that our explanation is only provisional. Although there is no change in the number of people actually at work in this hypothetical economy, production will be increasing as time passes. There are two reasons for this. One is that the accumulation of capital will be continuing. With the labour force constant, even if more efficient capital assets are not being introduced (even if there is no innovation) the accumulation of capital will be going on. With the labour force constant, it follows by simple arithmetic that the amount of capital per man—what economists call the capital-labour ratio—will be rising. The fact is that each man will work with more capital. Hence he can produce more. Because both output and capital stock can increase in this way, when the labour force is constant, and, indeed, even when it is declining, growth is closely linked with capital accumulation.

A major reason for this basic tendency for capital per man to rise is that capital assets are mostly long-lived things. With a population, and hence with a labour force, even a very high birth rate can be associated with a constant population, provided only that the death rate is equally high. However, capital assets can scarcely fail to accumulate in a modern economy, since one cannot conceive of any government allowing a situation to persist where depreciation is so high that the annual net increase in the total stock of capital goods (*net* investment) is negative, or even zero. Unless conditions in the economy are quite catastrophic, there will always be some gross investment, some construction of new capital goods. We can be confident that obsolescence and wear-and-tear are unlikely to cancel out the whole of this gross investment. While a significant part of gross investment will always be taken up in making good the continuous depreciation of the community's total stock of capital, there will usually be something left over each year to provide a net addition to that stock of capital. Only in the kind of calamitous depression that the USA suffered in the early 1930s can there be no *net* accumulation of capital during any given year.

5.2 Technical progress

The second reason why growth of national income will occur even in an economy with a static population is because there will be technical progress. It will be possible to equip the constant population with progressively more efficient and more productive machines as time passes.

This explains why capital and growth are intimately linked. First, even if there is no technical progress in the economy, it will often be possible to increase output per man by equipping each man with more capital, given the existing technology. Second, all contemporary economies will be experiencing technical progress. And this technical progress will be introduced into the economy mainly through investment in new capital assets, embodying improved production methods. It is only where there is a significant rate of investment in new assets that technical progress will be able to have a rapid effect on the economy.

Growth theory therefore accepts the fact that, with or without technical progress, more capital goods will be required if there is to be growth. It goes on to acknowledge that these capital goods can be produced only if people save, thereby freeing resources from consumption and devoting them to increasing the stock of capital goods.

As we saw in Part Two, Keynesian employment theory was originally based on the all-too-obvious proposition (for the years he was writing about) that there were already sufficient resources available to produce substantially more than the current output. Keynes's aim was to show that, in these conditions, a rise in the level of spending would be desirable since it would bring some unused resources into employment. However, although Keynes was able to overlook them in his short-run analysis, there were serious long-run contradictions in it.

The fact that increased outlay on investment made up part of the extra spending that Keynes wanted to see encouraged, meant that the employment policy he advocated was in a sense a self-defeating one. Because his was fundamentally a short-run analysis, Keynes could legitimately concentrate on the fact that an increase in spending would increase employment, and thereby allow the existing capital assets and labour force to be more fully employed. However, a long-run analysis, and above all a theory of growth, cannot do this. Simply because there *is* investment, the quantity of capital assets available to a community will be growing all the time. The more successful the policy of curing unemployment by increasing investment in any year is, the more extra spending of all kinds will be needed in the following year to keep the newly-enlarged capital stock fully used. In this sense, Keynesian employment policy can be described as self-defeating. The more investment is undertaken in order to maintain income in a given period of time, the more extra income has to be created in the future in order to keep those new investment goods fully at work. Certainly, any acceptable theory of growth has to regard a continuous rise in the size of the stock of capital assets as both inevitable and desirable. Only by using more and more capital assets relatively to labour can a society raise its living standards. As we have seen, this is the way in which technical progress, embodied in new machinery, etc., is introduced into the economy.

5.3 Population increase

We have now looked at the role of capital and technical progress in economic growth. As for population, its effect on economic growth is mixed. If one is concerned only with the growth of aggregate income, then rising population helps to increase aggregate income by increasing the labour force. If one is concerned with the income per head, there is no unambiguous answer. All will depend on whether conditions are such as to raise income more or less than the population is rising. We shall return to this issue later.

To put all this in another way, the essential point is that one has to look both at the aggregate spending of the community and at the resources available to it. In Part One, we took for granted the sufficiency of overall aggregate demand and concentrated on the way in which an economy uses its resources to supply goods to meet this demand. In Part Two we took the adequacy of the volume of productive resources available to the economy as axiomatic and concentrated on the way in which sufficient demand could be generated to keep them occupied. Now, in Part Three, we must look at both aggregate supply simultaneously in order to see how the economy will grow if the two are kept in balance. The need for such balance is therefore stressed in growth theory, which is, indeed, often concerned with 'balanced growth' equilibrium.

6. The fundamental growth equation

Having explained briefly what economic growth is, we shall now set out the elements of the basic model we shall use to study the problems of economic growth. Between any two successive periods of time in any economy there will be a certain rise in income (output). We denote this as ΔY.[1] Now, the absolute increase in income (ΔY) between any two points of time, is obviously identical with the increase in the stock capital between those two points of time (ΔK) multiplied by the extra amount of output which has actually been produced during that period of time. Assuming that both the extra capital stock and the output it yields are measured in money, we can write this as $\dfrac{\Delta Y}{\Delta K}$. Symbolically, we may therefore write:

$$\Delta Y = K \times \frac{\Delta Y}{\Delta K}.$$

It is usually found most convenient to proceed in terms of *rates of growth* of income and capital. We can do this if we divide both sides of the equation by Y. This gives us:

$$\frac{\Delta Y}{Y} = \frac{\Delta K}{Y} \times \frac{\Delta Y}{\Delta K}.$$

For simplicity, we have already decided to use the symbol G_y to represent $\dfrac{\Delta Y}{Y}$; the proportionate increase in income. Since ΔK is merely investment (I) during the time period in question, we can also rewrite the right-hand side of the equation. We arrive at the expression:

$$G_y = \frac{I}{Y} \times \frac{\Delta Y}{\Delta K} \quad . \qquad . \qquad . \qquad . \qquad . \quad (1)$$

The essence of balanced growth is that the economy should advance at a steady rate, with savings (S) equal to investment (I). This means that, since we shall be concerned with balanced growth, we may rewrite $\dfrac{I}{Y}$ as $\dfrac{S}{Y}$. $\dfrac{S}{Y}$ in turn is often written as s, and represents the savings ratio—the fraction of income saved. Equation (1) then becomes:

$$G_y = s \times \frac{\Delta Y}{\Delta K} \quad . \qquad . \qquad . \qquad . \qquad . \quad (2)$$

[1] This follows the established mathematical practice of using the Greek capital letter delta to stand for a small, but finite, increment in any variable, in this case Y.

Growth theory puts considerable emphasis on the role of what is known as the capital-output ratio. We have already noted that production will be higher in any economy if more output is obtained from each unit of the (given) capital stock which the economy possesses. Output will be much higher if a machine costing £3 000 produces enough output to sell for £1 000 each year than if the machine's output sells for only £100 (with given product prices). As a convenient, shorthand way of introducing the productivity of capital into growth theory, economists use the concept of the capital-output ratio. This relates the value of a particular piece of capital equipment, or the value of the total capital stock of a country, to the output which it produces in a given time period—usually a year. So, if the machine mentioned above is bought for £3 000 and produces goods worth £1 000 in a given year, the machine's capital-output ratio for any year is obviously $\dfrac{£3\,000}{£1\,000}$ or three. Similarly, if the total capital of any country is worth £10 000 million and it produces goods worth £2 500 million in any year, the nation's capital-output ratio in that year is four. It should be clear that the capital-output ratio is simply the inverse of the annual rate of return on (productivity of) capital. If, as in this second example, the capital-output ratio is four, the productivity of capital is 25 per cent per annum; if the productivity of capital is 10 per cent per annum, the capital-output ratio is ten, and so on. Economists normally denote the capital-output ratio by the symbol v.

It follows from this that the expression $\dfrac{\Delta Y}{\Delta K}$, in equation (1) above, is the inverse of the *marginal* capital-output ratio. It shows the *marginal* increment of income which is obtained from a *marginal* addition to the national capital stock. We can therefore replace $\dfrac{\Delta Y}{\Delta K}$ in equation (1) by the expression $\dfrac{1}{v}$.

Equation (1) now becomes $G_y = s \times \dfrac{1}{v}$ or

$$G_y = \frac{s}{v} \qquad . \qquad . \qquad . \qquad . \qquad . \qquad . \qquad (3)$$

(In Part Three we shall normally assume that the average capital-output ratio—that between the whole national capital stock and the national income—is constant and so is always equal to the *marginal* capital-output ratio. As explained above, we shall also (unless otherwise stated) assume that the savings-ratio $\dfrac{S}{Y}$ (or s) is constant.

Equation (3) is a tautology in the sense that it is always true by definition, though we shall later put constraints on it by assuming that s and v are both constant. Equation (3) states the self-evident truth that the increase in output during any period must always be exactly equal to the extra units of capital goods installed in that period multiplied by the output *actually obtained* from each of those extra units of capital stock. However, there are other similar growth equations which are not tautologies, and we shall discover that a study of the relationships between these various equations and between the variables in them can teach us a great deal about economic growth.

7. The warranted rate of growth

The fundamental growth equation, in the tautological sense in which we have so far used it, merely states what *has* happened in a given period of time. It says nothing about whether the rate of growth it represents—the rate of growth which actually has been achieved—is satisfactory or not, in the sense of whether it will provide the basis for a steady advance of the economy. The form of the fundamental equation which sets out the requirements which must be met if steady growth is to be satisfactory to entrepreneurs may be written:

$$G_{\mathrm{w}} = \frac{s}{v_{\mathrm{r}}} \quad . \qquad . \qquad . \qquad . \qquad . \qquad . \qquad (4)$$

G_{w} is what Sir Roy Harrod christened the 'warranted' rate of growth. It is that rate of growth which leaves producers as a whole just satisfied with the growth that has actually taken place and therefore just prepared to repeat it. Although output is almost certain to be rising more rapidly in some 'growth' sectors of the economy than in others, and although there may be outright declines in some trades, these movements are compatible with the overall growth of the economy at a certain rate. Similarly, within a whole industry, some firms may feel the need to increase their own rates of growth, while others may be impelled to reduce them. On balance, these individual decisions cancel out in the sense that, for the whole economy, a certain rate of growth will leave entrepreneurs just satisfied with that rate of growth and just ready to repeat it. This rate of growth is the 'warranted' rate.

This explains why we have written v_{r} instead of v in equation (4). Because equation (3) was a tautology, v represented the *actual* marginal capital-output ratio. It showed the extra amount of capital installed during the period, divided by the extra output produced during that period. It showed what had happened, but not whether producers were satisfied with what had happened. The size of v in equation (3) is therefore somewhat accidental. If there is a boom in the economy, and the extra capital installed is fully used, the marginal capital-output ratio will be lower than it would be if there had been a slump and there was only enough work to keep the economy's capital goods partly occupied.

v_r is different. It represents a relationship which is given by the state of science and technology. It shows the extra amount of capital which is required, in the existing state of technical knowledge and technical practice, to sustain an annual rise in output of one unit. It shows this in a situation where the extra capital is just fully-employed in the sense in which the firms themselves define that term. If a rise in output of £1 in any year needs an extra investment of just £4 to make it optimally profitable, the marginal capital-output ratio, v_r, is four. £16000 worth of capital must be installed in order to allow output to rise by £4000 per annum with the capital optimally employed. In other words, the equation for the warranted rate of growth derives from the notion that if the initial capital stock is just sufficient to produce a given output, then any extra output can be obtained only by installing extra capital on a scale which is technically determined. The size of v_r depends solely on the size of the capital-output ratio which currently-accepted production methods (and notions of what is an acceptable rate of profit) require.

8. The natural rate of growth

The warranted rate of growth, then, is one which, if attained, would allow producers as a whole to be just satisfied with the way the economy was growing. It is an equilibrium rate of growth in the sense that it will perpetuate itself. Yet this rate of growth will not necessarily be compatible with physical and human conditions in the economy. These cannot simply be ignored. In order to show what rate of growth can be justified by physical production conditions, we have to introduce the concept of the 'natural' rate of growth, G_n. This also may be stated in the form of an equation, namely one showing what rate of growth is possible in the physical conditions prevailing in the economy.

Economic theory holds that the two factors determining the size of G_n are the rate of population increase and the rate of technical progress. We shall assume throughout this discussion that there is no 'involuntary' or 'Keynesian' unemployment. Because there is no unemployed labour which can be put to work, it follows that the only way in which more people can be employed will be if there is an increase in population. The second source of increased output will be technical progress. This will increase output per man. It follows that economists define technical progress to mean the same thing, in this context, as the increase in productivity. They are concerned entirely with increases in output per man. For the economist, 'productivity' means output per unit of input. If the word 'productivity' is not qualified, it is safe to assume that it is the productivity of labour, i.e. output per man employed, that is meant.

It follows that, so far as the labour force is concerned, we are assuming that there is no possibility of increasing it by drawing on a 'pool' of unemployed. We are also ruling out increases in 'participation rates'; that is, bringing more of the existing population into work by, say, increasing the number of married women at work, raising the retirement age or lowering the school-leaving age. We are also assuming that there is no scope for increasing output significantly by raising the efficiency with which *existing* labour and capital assets are being used by firms or employers, bringing efficiency in all firms closer to the standards reached by the best. In practice both these things are likely to be possible, but their distinguishing feature is that, even if something could be done in such ways to raise output per head of population, it would inevitably be a once-for-all process. Once all the available married women, old-age pensioners and so on had been given jobs, and once all firms had (miraculously!) become as efficient as the best, there would be no more scope at all for using these ways of raising output per man. They can offer short-run but not long-run growth. They are not to be scorned, but they are not relevant to a theory of long-run growth.

To sustain long-run growth, one is forced back to the opportunities provided by population increase or by technical progress. Hence, if we denote the rate of population growth by l and the rate of technical progress—or the rate of increase of productivity—by t, we may define the natural rate of growth as:

$$G_n = l + t. \qquad . \qquad . \qquad . \qquad . \qquad . \quad (5)$$

Strictly, the right-hand side of this equation should read $l + t + lt$. The letter t relates to the effect of technical progress in increasing the productivity of the existing population. The symbols lt denote the increase in output obtained by applying new technology to the (small) increase in the labour force. Since lt will be very small, it can reasonably be ignored.

9. The Harrod-Domar equation

Equation (3), our fundamental growth equation ($G_y = \dfrac{s}{v}$), is often described as the 'Harrod-Domar equation', but though similar equations were discovered at about the same time by these two economists, they are not identical. Domar wanted to answer the question: how much will output have to rise in a growing economy

if all the additional productive capacity which capital accumulation
provides is to be fully used? For reasons which will be considered in
detail in the next chapter, but which should be intuitively obvious,
Domar discovered that investment would have to rise quickly
enough to absorb all the savings which rising incomes made available.
This gave him the equation:

$$\frac{\Delta I}{I} = sa \quad . \qquad . \qquad . \qquad . \qquad . \qquad . \quad (6)$$

This equation states that the rate of growth of investment $(\frac{\Delta I}{I})$
must, for full employment, be equal to the proportion of income
saved, s, multiplied by the output-capital ratio, a. It will be obvious
that the right-hand side of equation (6) gives exactly the same result
as the right-hand side of Harrod's equation (3). Domar was multiplying s by the output-capital ratio; Harrod was dividing s by the
capital-output ratio.

Domar had only one equation, which showed what the rate of
growth of investment (and therefore, with a constant capital-output
ratio, the rate of growth of income) would *have* to be in order to yield
full employment. He was describing what may be called an equilibrium growth path. Harrod, on the other hand, as we have seen, was
concerned with three different growth equations. The one which
comes nearest to the Domar equation was that for the warranted
rate of growth. In fact, Harrod's original equation differed in actual
notation from the version we gave above in equation (3). It read
$G_w C_r = s$. Harrod was saying that the rate of growth, G_w, which
would just leave businessmen content and would therefore encourage
them to maintain that rate of growth, would depend on the savings
ratio and the required capital-output ratio. He wrote the latter as C_r
instead of our v_r and he multiplied G_w by it instead of dividing s by it.
Consequently, even this 'Harrod equation' did not describe a full-
employment growth path, but only one which would persuade
entrepreneurs to continue the existing growth rate.

It is obvious that there is no guarantee whatever that the 'warranted' rate of growth will be a full employment rate of growth.
Indeed, it is precisely because this is so that Harrod brings in the
natural rate of growth, in order to show what the growth rate would
need to be to sustain full employment of labour. Nor will full employment for labour necessarily ensure full employment of capital assets.
Domar, on the other hand, assumed, by implication, that full
employment of labour *and* capital occurred simultaneously. Domar's
was one important growth equation; Harrod's equation was one of
a series which between them set out a complete theory of growth.

We must now use Harrod's three different rates of growth: the actual rate of growth, G_y; the warranted rate of growth, G_w; and the natural rate of growth, G_n, to explain in outline the way in which an economy grows.

Suggested reading

DOMAR, E. D.   *Essays in the Theory of Economic Growth*, Oxford, 1957, especially 'Expansion and Employment' and 'The Problem of Capital Accumulation'.

HARROD, R. F.   *Towards a Dynamic Economics*, London, 1948, chapters i and iii.

SAMUELSON, P. A.   'Fiscal Policy and Income Determination', *Quarterly Journal of Economics*, 1941–2, p. 575.

26

A simple growth model

1. Balanced-growth equilibrium

Many of the recent theoretical studies of economic growth have been based on Harrod's three growth equations, set out in Chapter 25. It goes almost without saying that the only situation where there will be no problems in economic growth will be where all three rates of growth are equal. The actual rate of growth will be the same as the warranted rate, so that the business community will be perfectly content to perpetuate the existing rate of growth. At the same time, these two rates will both equal the natural rate; the economy will be growing as fast as is possible with the existing rates of population growth and of productivity increase (technical progress). It is possible that, even in this situation, the community may feel that the rate of growth is too slow in the sense that it would prefer a faster one. However, in order to bring about such an increase, it would be necessary to make fundamental changes in the structure of the economy—for example, by speeding-up the rate of growth of population or the rate of technical progress.

1.1 The 'golden age'

Nevertheless, the equality of the three rates guarantees that the economy is in equilibrium and represents a very satisfactory situation. Indeed, by describing the situation where the three rates are equal as a 'golden age', Professor Joan Robinson has emphasised that 'it represents a mythical state of affairs not likely to obtain in any actual economy'.[1] For the warranted rate of growth is determined by the value of s, the savings ratio, and of v_r, the required capital-output ratio, in the equation $G_w = \dfrac{s}{v_r}$. At the same time the natural rate of growth is determined by the rate of population increase (l) and the rate of technical progress (t). The happy situation where $G_y = G_w = G_n$ will occur only when the four variables, s, v, l and t have the right values, and this seems likely to occur only by chance.

[1]Joan Robinson, *The Accumulation of Capital*, London, 1956, p. 99.

Consequently, the Harrod-Domar discussion of growth assumed that the four key variables were all set quite independently of each other. Other economists argue that at least some of the variables are connected. Professor Kaldor, in particular, has taken the view that there are links between the rate of population increase and the rate of technical progress on the one side and the savings ratio on the other. For the present, we shall assume that s, v, l and t are all known, constant over time and determined independently of each other. We shall also assume that, despite this, a 'golden age' has been reached where $G_y = G_w = G_n$. What kind of balanced-growth equilibrium will one then have?

1.2 Balanced growth examined

We shall concentrate our analysis on the three basic variables: Y, the national income; K, the stock of capital assets; and L, the labour force. In balanced-growth equilibrium, with $G_y = G_w = G_n$, the national income will be growing at the rate of G_y—say, at 2, 3 or 4 per cent per annum as the case may be. Since we are assuming that the capital-output ratio is constant, it follows that the stock of capital must be growing at exactly the same rate as income. Since we are assuming that the actual rate of growth equals the warranted rate, so that any extra capital goods are just fully employed, any other result would mean that the capital-output ratio is altering. This leads to a first, and rather obvious conclusion. Given a constant capital-output ratio (v), balanced-growth equilibrium requires the national income and the capital stock to grow at the same rate as each other. Otherwise, one will either have capital growing faster than output, with excess capacity developing as some or all capital assets become underemployed; or one will have too few capital assets to produce the output that is being demanded. There would be a shortage of capacity. In either case the balanced-growth equilibrium would disappear.

(a) Without technical progress

Although at first sight this seems a rather trivial point, it will be worth going into a little further. For the moment, let us assume that all growth in output depends on an increase in the size of the population and that there is no contribution at all to growth from technical progress. The equation for the natural rate of growth, $G_n = l + t$, then becomes $G_n = l$; all growth results from increases in population. For balanced-growth equilibrium in these circumstances, national income and the capital stock will both have to grow at the same rate as the labour force. It follows that $\dfrac{K}{L}$ (the amount of capital per head),

$\frac{K}{Y}$ (the capital-output ratio) and $\frac{Y}{L}$ (income per head) will all remain constant as aggregate national income increases. Although the total stock of capital is growing, capital *per head* is constant; although aggregate income is growing, income *per head* remains unchanged. Existing techniques are being extended to employ more people, each of whom uses exactly the same production methods, and hence exactly the same amount of capital, as each member of the original labour force. There is what economists call *capital widening*. There is no rise either in capital per man or in capital per unit of output, as growth proceeds. The capital-intensity of production, whether measured in terms of capital per unit of output or of capital per man, remains unaltered.

(b) With technical progress

If we now allow for the existence of technical progress, t becomes positive. If we further assume that l remains at the same level as in the previous paragraph, the effect of technical progress will be to increase the rate of growth that is compatible with physical production conditions; it will raise G_n. However, we are continuing to assume that there is balanced growth, with $G_y = G_n = G_k$. Technical progress therefore makes possible a rise in the rate of growth of income. Since the rate of growth of capital and income must remain equal in balanced-growth equilibrium, this calls, in turn, for an equal rise in the rate of growth of the capital stock as compared with its rate of growth when population alone was changing, and there was no technical progress. This may seem a little paradoxical at first sight, since one can easily become accustomed to the notion that technical progress, like manna, drops from heaven as a free food. We shall need to look at this assumption in more detail later. For the moment, we merely need to stress the fact that the requirement of a more rapid rise in the capital stock follows automatically from our assumption that v is constant. We take it for granted that technical progress is 'embodied' by spending money on installing extra capital goods or, equally important, by spending it on applying new ideas resulting from research and/or education.

1.3 Capital widening versus capital deepening

The simplest way of looking at the question is to regard the increase in the rate of growth of income—of productivity per man—as the result of the increase in capital per head, whether this is brought about through the installation of more machinery or by the application of increased knowledge. This increase in capital per head will manifest itself in a rise of income per head, at the rate of t. In other words, part of the growth of both income and capital is required to keep income per head from falling. In our notation, this will be l. This part of growth maintains income per head by permitting capital widening; it keeps capital per man constant as the labour force rises. The remainder of the rise in income per head, in this case t, represents a rise in income per head achieved by increasing the amount of capital per man—by what economists call *capital deepening*. It will be remembered that strictly the equation for the natural rate of growth is $G_n = l + t + lt$. The new techniques must be provided for the *additional* members of the labour force as well as the original ones, and this will require a growth of investment by lt. However, we are ignoring lt because it will be very small.

In this simple model $\dfrac{Y}{L}$ rises as $\dfrac{K}{L}$ rises, but $\dfrac{K}{Y}$ remains unchanged; technical progress comes to exactly the same thing as a rise in capital per man, with income per head increasing only to the extent that there *is* technical progress. Production becomes more capital-intensive in the sense that there is more capital per man, but there is no change in the amount of capital relatively to output. $\dfrac{K}{Y}$ (or v) remains constant.

One reason for this, of course, is that we are assuming that there are constant returns to scale as the amount of labour and capital increases. An extra man, equipped with the currently-accepted amount of capital per worker is assumed to produce exactly the same output as each existing man. An extra pound's worth of capital, whether it equips a new worker or adds to the average amount of capital used by each existing worker, always leads to exactly the same increase in the level of output. Each unit of capital always has the same productivity. This follows obviously enough from the assumption of a constant capital-output ratio, since the capital-output ratio is simply the inverse of the productivity of capital.

This discussion obviously raises the question whether the aim of economic policy should be to increase aggregate national income, or income *per head*. There is clearly no single or simple answer to this question which is basically not an economic one at all.

2. The next stages in the analysis

To continue this outline of a simple theory of growth we shall concentrate on the supply side. We have seen that, so far as demand is concerned, the emphasis is on the warranted rate of growth. The need is for a rate of growth which leaves businessmen just content to perpetuate it and also induces the community to provide just enough savings to finance the amount of investment which it implies. It is the rate of profit which they earn that determines whether or not businessmen *will* be satisfied with the existing rate of growth. For balanced growth, the rate of growth which just provides a satisfactory balance between savings, investment and consumption for the community must also provide a satisfactory level of profit for entrepreneurs. We already know that this is not an easy requirement to satisfy, but even if it is satisfied this is not the end of the story. The supply side, in the shape of the natural rate of growth, also has to be considered. Only if all three growth rates—natural, warranted and actual—are equal is balanced-growth equilibrium possible.

The two elements in our equation for the natural rate of growth are the rate of population increase and the rate of technical progress. Technical progress is a very complex phenomenon and we shall find it desirable to devote the next chapter almost entirely to it. At this stage we shall ignore technical progress. We shall assume that the natural rate of growth equals the rate of growth of the labour supply $(G_y = l)$.

We have already noted that the characterisitc feature of the Harrod-Domar growth model is that there are three important, fixed elements. First, there is a constant rate of growth of population, l. Second, both the amount of capital $\dfrac{K}{Y}$ and the amount of labour $\dfrac{L}{Y}$ needed to produce a unit of output are constant. Third, the proportion of income devoted to savings (s) is constant. We have also seen that only by chance can there be a 'golden-age' equilibrium, with the values of g, s, v and l consistent with each other. We shall now go on to see how far it is possible for there to be growth equilibrium even if some of the variables are out of line with the others. We begin with labour.

3. Adjusting to the labour supply: (1) A variable capital-output ratio

So long as we are assuming that there is no technical progress, the process of economic growth consists in equipping the labour force as adequately as possible with capital equipment appropriate to the existing state of technical and managerial knowledge. Exactly what happens to the economy will therefore depend on the relative rates of growth of the population and of the capital stock. Let us assume that the capital-output ratio and the capital-labour ratio are both determined by the existing state of technology, and that, since we are assuming that there is no technical progress, both $\dfrac{K}{Y}$ and $\dfrac{K}{L}$ remain unchanged.

Let us further suppose that the existing population has already been completely equipped with machines appropriate to the current state of technique.[1] In order that the newest members of the growing labour force may be similarly equipped with machines, it is clear that the rates of growth of the capital stock and of the labour force will have to be equal. (We are continuing to make the assumption that the labour force represents a constant proportion of the population.) Provided that luck or clever government policy keeps the actual and warranted rates of growth in line, the ideal situation will, of course, be the one where $G_y = G_w = G_n = G_k$. The rate of growth of the labour force will be just equal to the rate of growth of income and therefore, with a constant capital-output ratio, also just equal to the rate of growth of the capital stock. As soon as they join the labour force, new workers will be equipped with exactly the same machinery as is being used by the existing members of the labour force.

This is clearly asking a good deal. The amount of capital per man is determined by the existing state of technique, and this will fix the amount of net investment required in any year. For example, if the state of technology requires each man to use a machine worth £100, and if the labour force is rising by 100000 men per year, new machines worth a total of £10 million will have to be constructed each year. On the other hand, the amount of net saving carried out by the members of the community during the year will depend on the level of income and the propensity to save. It cannot be taken for granted that the state of technique, the rate of growth of the population and the propensity to save will bear exactly the right relationship to each other, though we shall later consider Kaldor's suggestion that there are links between population growth and saving. We must consider what will happen if balanced growth does not occur.

Since a constant amount of labour is required to produce each unit of output, income cannot permanently grow faster than population. Income might be able to do this if the capital stock was growing more quickly than the population, but such a situation can continue only for limited periods. Indeed, it can occur at all only if there is initially a surplus of unemployed workers waiting to be given jobs. With the given constant capital-output ratio which we are assuming and with a rate of growth of the capital stock which is greater than the rate of growth of the labour force, men to man all the new machines that were being installed could be found only if there were a 'pool' of unemployed to draw on. Otherwise some of the machines being built would have no-one to operate them.

[1] Readers will, of course, appreciate that it is not only machines but buildings, vehicles, and indeed stocks of raw materials and finished goods as well as work in progress, that must be provided in order to enable output to rise without running into capital shortage. It will save space if we use the word 'machines' in this discussion to cover all capital employed in production.

Once the pool of unemployed has been exhausted, there may well be a crisis. Indeed, Marx predicted that exactly this kind of crisis would occur. He contended that the disappearance of the pool of unemployed would mean that capitalists would be forced to compete with each other for labour and would therefore bid up wages in order to obtain workers. This would eliminate profits. Capital accumulation would cease, there would be industrial depression and the 'reserve army' of unemployed would be recreated. As a result, wages would fall, profits would reappear, and the process of capital accumulation would begin again.

Even if one does not take quite as gloomy a view as Marx did, it is obvious that the rate of capital accumulation cannot outpace the rate of growth of the labour supply for very long. Only the existence of a very large number of unemployed workers can prevent the fairly rapid emergence of idle capacity and the onset of depression—so long, of course, as we assume that the capital-labour ratio cannot be altered.

For growth equilibrium, rather than short-term growth in income, we cannot replace the Harrod-Domar condition $G_y = G_n$ by the inequality $G_y \geqslant G_n$. Growth of income can be as high as the rate of growth of population, or it can be less. It cannot be more. The condition must be $G_y \leqslant G_n$.

In purely technical economic terms, $G_y < G_n$ is an acceptable solution. No constraint is imposed on growth by a shortage of labour. What happens instead is that there is continuing growth in unemployment and this is unlikely to be acceptable politically. The public will call for action to improve the situation. The government will be pressed to alter s or v in order to reduce unemployment.

3.1 The neo-classical production function

There are a number of growth models where the capital-output ratio is variable, especially those of Samuelson, Solow and Swan. These are known as neo-classical growth models because they postulate a continuous production function, with a changing capital-output ratio, and not the fixed capital-output ratio of the Harrod-Domar model.

If the existing rate of growth of income is so low that unemployment rises continually, one solution would be to raise the capital-labour ratio and to support each man with more expensive machinery. In a sense this would be wasteful, since the alternative would be for the community to consume more, and economists have always assumed that the ultimate end of any economy is to make possible consumption and not the accumulation of capital goods. Nevertheless, regarded purely as a way of restoring balanced-growth equilibrium, a rise in the capital-labour ratio is certainly a way out.

Since we are continuing to assume, as we did throughout Part One, that there is diminishing marginal productivity to a single variable factor of production (see pp. 261-269), there will be diminishing returns as the ratio of capital to labour is raised. Output per man will rise, though not by so much as the capital-labour ratio has risen. This will mean that while the rise in $\frac{K}{L}$ will make full employment of labour possible, and will also raise *aggregate* national income, it will lead to a fall in the *rate of growth* in income as compared with the rate before the pool of unemployed was exhausted. Even so, this expedient may be better than allowing unemployment to go on rising. It will certainly be better for those who would otherwise have been unemployed. Judged in terms of the level of income, the position is less clear but this is a valuable reminder that in the theory of growth one has to take account both of absolute levels of income and of rates of growth of income.

(a) Varying the capital output ratio

Let us look at the problem in more detail. We are now postulating a continuous production function linking output to the inputs of capital and labour. We keep our other assumptions. There are constant returns to scale and there is no technological progress. We also return to the assumption that $G_y = G_n$. We now have to see how an alteration in the capital-output ratio can allow the rate of growth to rise to the level required by population growth. If the economy is to be in equilibrium at full employment, we must have $G_n = \frac{s}{v}$. Because we are assuming, for the present, that there is no technical progress, the rate of increase in the labour force equals the natural rate of growth. So, $l = \frac{s}{v}$, or $v = \frac{s}{l}$.

Since we assume that s and l are given and constant, we need to know what level of v is consistent with this level of $\frac{s}{l}$.

We construct Fig. 26.1. On the y-axis we show output (income) per man and on the x-axis we show capital per man. The production function is the brown line OF. It shows what income per head will be at all levels of capital per head. With no capital, income is zero. As capital per head is increased, the increase in income per head obtained from the same marginal increase in the amount of capital per head declines. Finally, with a capital per head of OX, income (output) per head is OY. This is the maximum income per head obtainable with the existing technology; beyond F, the production function is horizontal.

Let us now draw in the black line OR. The slope of this line shows output per head divided by capital per head. It shows the capital-output ratio required for G_w to equal G_n, given the (proportional) savings ratio of the community. Symbolically, it shows $\frac{Y}{L} \div \frac{K}{L} =$ $\frac{Y}{L} \times \frac{L}{K} = \frac{Y}{K}$. Now $\frac{Y}{K}$ is the inverse of the capital-output ratio. Since $v = \frac{s}{l}, \frac{1}{v} = \frac{l}{s}$. The slope of OR is therefore $\frac{l}{s} = \frac{1}{v}$. It will be remembered that, because we are assuming that there is no technical progress, l is the natural rate of growth and $\frac{s}{v}$ the warranted rate of growth. So we can see that the natural and warranted rates of growth are equal at point R. (If $\frac{l}{s} = \frac{1}{v}$, then $v = \frac{s}{l}$.) The slope of OR, in other words, is given by the proportion of income saved and the growth of the labour force.

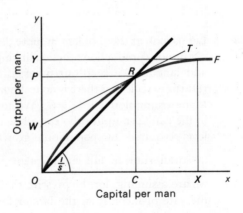

Fig. 26.1

(b) A continuous production function

We now move on to consider the production function. The slope of WT, the tangent at R to the production function OF, shows the marginal product of capital at R. In other words, it shows the rate of profit at R, which is required by the levels of s and l. It shows the extra income derived from a small increase in capital. If we continue the tangent at R back to the y-axis, the intercept WP shows the share of profit in income OP. It shows capital per head (OC) multiplied by the rate of profit (r). The remainder of income, namely OW, goes to wages. Wage per man is OW. r is also the marginal product of capital at R given by the slope of WT. R is a point where all the elements in the model are compatible ($G_n = \frac{s}{v} = G_y$).

(c) The significance of the neo-classical production function

If there is a continuous, smooth production function like *OF*, then there is bound to be some point, like *R*, where there is balanced-growth equilibrium. The neo-classical model, with its smooth, continuous production function can generate full employment at *some* rate of growth of income. This is why it is known as a neo-classical model. It shares the optimism of the 'classical' economists that full employment is attainable at *some* level of G_y. What the neo-classical model says is that if capital is growing faster than population, then the two can be brought back into equilibrium by increasing the capital-intensity of production. Similarly, if capital is increasing less rapidly than population, full employment equilibrium can be brought about by reducing the capital-intensity of production. Harrod-Domar, on the other hand, assumed a fixed, unalterable capital-output ratio. In Fig. 26.1, there is no reason why this capital-output ratio should leave the economy at a point like *R*. Balanced-growth equilibrium may not occur. In the Harrod-Domar model it cannot be brought about by a change in the capital-output ratio, since *v* is fixed.

The neo-classical model now occupies a central position in modern growth theory. It avoids the problem which arises in the Harrod-Domar model if the natural and warranted rates of growth diverge. It does this because it allows the warranted rate of growth to alter through changes in the capital-output ratio. However, this means that *s* is irrelevant to the rate of growth. Changes in the warranted rate of growth result from changes in *v*, not in *s*.

Suppose there are two economies where *l* is the same; population is growing equally rapidly; but saving is different in the two economies. For balanced-growth equilibrium, $\frac{s}{v}$ must equal *l*. So, the rate of growth in each economy must be the same. However, the capital-output ratio must then be higher in the economy with the higher savings. The level of income per head will also be higher in the economy with the higher capital-output ratio and the higher savings; the *rate of growth* of income would be the same.

We now move on to consider savings. We shall return to our initial assumption that the capital-output ratio is constant, but shall allow the savings ratio to vary. First, let us look more carefully at the mechanism by which savings and investment have to adjust to each other in a growing economy.

4. Savings, investment and balanced growth

The essential condition for balanced-growth equilibrium is that savings and investment, both *ex-ante* and *ex-post*, must always be equal. It will be useful to spell out the implications of this requirement in some detail. We shall do so by using Figs. 26.2a and 26.2b. First, however, we must now expand something that was said earlier.

We have so far treated capital accumulation as though it were an unambiguous concept. In fact, it is important to distinguish carefully between the role of net and gross investment in economic growth. Growth theory is concerned with increases in the national income, especially those achieved by increasing the national capital stock. If all gross investment were devoted simply to making good depreciation—to keeping the existing capital stock intact—there would be no net investment and no basis for economic growth. With a given capital-output ratio and a given, perpetually-maintained, capital stock (zero net investment) output would be constant too. Only in so far as the capital stock increases can there be growth. Our main concern will therefore be with net income and net investment—with the excess of gross investment over depreciation. It is net investment alone (unless the capital-output ratio is altering) that can lead to economic growth.

We may now return to the main argument. The economy considered in Figs. 26.2a and 26.2b is in balanced-growth equilibrium.

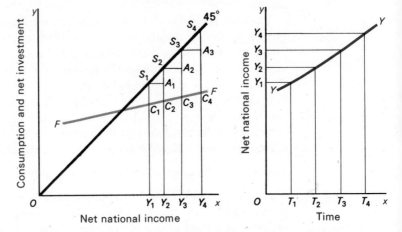

Fig. 26.2 a | b

We assume that in each period of time a certain amount of net investment is undertaken, that all of the additional capital installed is available to raise production in the following period and that it is indeed used to do so. The growth process has been going on for some time, but we begin to study it at time T_1; income at this stage is OY_1. The line FF is a long-term consumption function. This consumption function shows that with an income of OY_1 consumption will be C_1Y_1 and savings C_1S_1. (While FF is a consumption function or propensity to consume, it differs from the kind discussed on pp. 460-467 in that it is assumed to hold good over a long period of time and not at a particular moment of time.)

For the economy to be in equilibrium, with savings equal to investment, C_1S_1 must be invested. Since we are concerned only with net saving and net investment, this means that the capital stock has increased by C_1S_1. As a result, net output (net income) in the succeeding period of time can, and indeed for equilibrium in the economy must, exceed OY_1 by an amount equal to C_1S_1 divided by what we have already described (in equation (4), Chapter 25 p. 595) as the required capital-output ratio. Let us suppose that this required capital-output ratio is two. The extra output obtained from the additional investment of C_1S_1 will then be $\frac{1}{2}C_1S_1$. We therefore draw A_1S_1 equal to $\frac{1}{2}C_1S_1$ and parallel to the x-axis. If we now construct the perpendicular S_2Y_2 to pass through A_1, we obtain the equilibrium output for the period T_2. For, since the line OS_4 is drawn at $45°$ to the x-axis, A_1S_1 is equal to A_1S_2. If an output of S_2Y_2 is produced, there will just be full employment of both the existing and the newly-produced capital goods. The warranted and actual rates of growth will be equal. It will be appreciated that since OS_4 is at $45°$ to the x-axis S_2Y_2 equals OY_2, S_3Y_3 equals OY_3 and so on.

Out of this income (output) of S_2Y_2, C_2Y_2 will be consumed and C_2S_2 invested. With our assumed marginal capital-output ratio of two, this will mean that, in period T_3, output can rise by half of C_2S_2. We may therefore draw A_2S_2 equal to half the length of C_2S_2 and parallel to the x-axis. So we can draw the line S_3Y_3 through A_2. The preceding analysis can then be applied again. Full employment output in period T_3 will be S_3Y_3, of which C_3S_3 will be invested. This will increase the full employment output in period T_4 to S_4Y_4. The process will continue in the same way so long as there is no divergence between savings and investment. The way in which net income is changing over time is shown by the YY curve in Fig. 26.2b, where time is measured on the horizontal axis and income on the vertical axis.

It follows from what has been said above that, for a steady rate of growth, savings and investment must always remain equal to each other, and businessmen must be continually satisfied with the resultant levels of activity. This is clearly not a realistic situation. In the first place, our assumption that all the investment carried out in any period gives rise to the appropriate amount of extra output in the next period is not plausible. Lags in bringing new plant into full production are likely to make the actual situation much less tidy, and leave much more scope for departures from equilibrium than Fig. 26.2 implies. Much more serious, however, the continued equality of savings and investment can result only from sheer chance in a world where a multitude of individuals decide quite independently of each other what to save and what to invest so that divergences between saving and investment are continually possible.

5. Adjusting to the labour supply: (2) A variable savings ratio

We can now move on to see how a change in the savings ratio may allow the economy to adjust to a slow rate of growth of population. If we abandon the simple Harrod-Domar assumption that a given proportion (s) of the GNP is saved, we find a number of alternative theories. We first consider a hypothesis that has been greatly used, especially by Joan Robinson and Nicholas Kaldor. They divide the community into two classes—wage-earners and profit-earners. The hypothesis is that the savings of both classes are a function of their incomes, but that the propensity to save of wage-earners is lower than that of profit-earners. The result is that the community's overall savings-ratio depends on the distribution of income.

5.1 The 'classical' savings function

A special case of this hypothesis is where the propensity to save out of wages is zero and the propensity to save out of profits is positive and constant. We shall describe this, following Hahn and Matthews, in their valuable review article, quoted in the 'Suggested reading' to this chapter, as the 'classical' savings function, though it has also been variously described as the Kaldorian, Cambridge, Marxian, etc. There is, indeed, an especially interesting category of this case: the extreme 'classical' savings function. Here, all wages are consumed and all profits are saved. This means that the savings ratio (s) is equal to the share of profits in the GNP, which has interesting consequences.

We have already seen that in balanced-growth equilibrium with the capital-output ratio constant, both income and the capital stock grow at exactly the same rates. If we denote the rate of growth of the capital stock by G_k, then equation (3) in Chapter 25—our fundamental growth equation—gives us a further equation:

$$G_k = \frac{s}{v} \qquad \qquad . \qquad . \qquad . \qquad . \qquad (7)$$

If we assume that all profits (which we shall denote by π) are saved and that all wages (w) are consumed, we may rewrite s, the savings ratio, as $\frac{\pi}{Y}$. Since $\frac{1}{v}$, the inverse of the capital-output ratio, equals $\frac{Y}{K}$, this means that we can rewrite equation (7) as $G_k = \frac{\pi}{Y} \times \frac{Y}{K}$. Cancelling out the Ys on the right-hand side of the equation, this leaves us with:

$$G_k = \frac{\pi}{K}.$$

That is to say, the rate of growth of the capital stock equals the rate of profit on capital. If we denote the rate of profit on capital by r, we have:

$$G_k = r \qquad . \qquad . \qquad . \qquad . \qquad . \qquad (8)$$

In words, the rate of growth of the capital stock (G_k), on these assumptions, is exactly equal to the *rate of profit* (r) on that aggregate capital stock.

5.2 Income distribution and savings

We may now return to the question whether variations in savings can equate the warranted and natural rates of growth. We assume that v is constant, that $\dfrac{W}{Y}$ is zero and that $\dfrac{\pi}{Y}$ is constant and positive. The equality of the warranted and natural rates of growth now becomes possible through the redistribution of income. If income is redistributed from capitalists to workers, the savings ratio will fall. If income is redistributed from workers to capitalists, the savings ratio will rise. There are, however, limits to this. The volume of savings required to equate the warranted and natural rates of growth must not be less than the propensity to save of workers (here assumed to be zero). Nor must it be greater than the propensity to save of capitalists (here assumed to be one). Balanced-growth equilibrium is impossible if it requires either smaller savings than would occur if all income went to workers, or larger savings than would occur if all income went to capitalists. On our assumptions, savings are variable between these extremes via income redistribution—but not outside them.

In fact, most of the economists who have used the classical savings function have assumed a variable capital-output ratio as well. This allows the warranted rate of growth to adjust to the natural rate both through a change in s and through one in v.

6. Adjusting to the labour supply: (3) A variable capital-output ratio and a variable savings ratio

Let us now relax both assumptions and allow both s and v to vary. Let us continue to denote profits by π, but use s_c to represent the savings of capitalists. With the classical savings function, savings can then be written as s_c. We can therefore rewrite $G_y = \dfrac{s}{v}$ as:

$$G_y = \frac{s_c}{Y} \times \frac{Y}{K} = \frac{s_c}{K}.$$

But $\dfrac{Y}{K}$ is the rate of profit on capital, which we have denoted by r.

The equation then becomes:

$$G_y = s_c r . \qquad \qquad \cdot \qquad \cdot \qquad \cdot \qquad \cdot \qquad \cdot \quad (9)$$

Equation (9) is merely a general statement of equation (8). G_y (or G_k in balanced-growth equilibrium) equals the rate of profit on capital multiplied by the savings ratio of capitalists. In equation (8) the savings ratio of capitalists is one, so that s_c can disappear. This conclusion is an interesting one which becomes very important in linear growth models of the kind developed by the mathematician Neuman, though there is not sufficient space to go into detail about them here.

6.1 The neo-classical view

Instead, we proceed to consider a situation where there is a smooth production function displaying a unique relationship between the distribution of income (and so the savings ratio) and the amount of capital per man (and so the capital-output ratio). This gives us Fig. 26.3, where we add the classical savings function to Fig. 26.1.

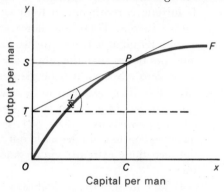

Fig. 26.3

Here, the dark-brown line OF again represents the production function. Balanced-growth equilibrium requires G_w to equal r. The marginal productivity of capital (r) at any capital-output ratio is given by the slope of OF at the appropriate point. In Fig. 26.1, the warranted rate of growth was given by $\dfrac{l}{s}$. So, because savings are made only out of profit, in Fig. 26.3 we have $G_w = \dfrac{l}{s_c}$. Equilibrium therefore occurs at point P where $r = \dfrac{l}{s_c}$. The line TP begins from T and not O, and has a different slope from the line OR in Fig. 26.1. The slope of TP differs from that of OR because it represents $\dfrac{l}{s_c}$ and not $\dfrac{l}{s}$. It begins at T, because savings come only from profits; and the distance OT represents wages.

In the balanced-growth equilibrium given by point P in Fig. 26.3, all factors receive an amount equal to their marginal productivity. The wage per man (OT) is the marginal productivity of labour; the rate of profit (r) is given by the slope of TP and is equal to the marginal productivity of capital. The total return to capital is TS. The fact that we have introduced a classical savings function allows the capital-output ratio and/or the savings ratio to alter in order to equate the warranted and natural rates of growth.

However, there are differences. In Fig. 26.1, with the proportionate savings function (giving the slope OR) the capital-output ratio did not depend on the shape of the production function. It depended on the (proportional) savings function. For balanced growth, the capital-output ratio had to be the one where OR cut the production function OF. The marginal productivity of capital (r) depended on the slope of the production function at the point (R) where OR cut it.

With a classical savings function in Fig. 26.3, the marginal productivity of capital (r) depends on the distribution of income, given the shape of the production function. The capital-output ratio now *does* depend on the shape of OF. The similarity is that, in both cases, the share of profits in income $(\frac{\pi}{Y}$ in Fig. 26.1 and $\frac{rK}{Y}$ in Fig. 26.3$)$ depends on the shape of the production function.

6.2 Professor Kaldor's view

Next, we consider Professor Kaldor's views. Kaldor is one of those economists who employ a classical savings function, but not a production function of the kind that we have used in this chapter. Instead, he has a technical-progress function. Kaldor also makes the capital-output ratio the result of an investment function, the precise nature of which has altered in the successive versions of his theory. Finally, Kaldor abandons the assumption of perfect competition. This means that the profit margin per unit of output at any given capital-output ratio can vary. It also means that there need be no link, as, for example, there is in Fig. 26.3, between the distribution of income and the marginal productivities of capital and labour.

6.3 Other savings functions

We shall look in a moment at the way in which Kaldor thinks that savings and population growth may be linked. Before doing so, we may note two other possible savings functions. First, one can alter the classical savings function to allow for the possibility that workers save as well as capitalists. This assumption has been used by Kaldor,

Pasinetti and others. Second, one can proceed from the other extreme, beginning from the neo-classical idea that investment somehow adjusts to the level of full-employment saving, to bring about the kind of equilibrium shown in Fig. 26.2. On this hypothesis, all saving is made by firms; they save exactly the amount needed to finance the investment they have decided on other grounds that they will carry out. Consequently, the savings function disappears from the growth model and an investment function replaces it. What then happens will depend on the nature of the investment function. This kind of assumption seems to lie behind Schumpeter's ideas on growth —some of which we shall outline in Chapter 27.

It is clear from this discussion that a large number of assumptions about savings are possible. As we saw in Chapter 20, there is a great deal of empirical evidence about savings. This evidence certainly suggests what the growth theorists who use a classical savings function require; namely that the proportion of profits saved should be clearly greater than the proportion of other income saved. To this extent, there is empirical support for the classical savings function.

7. Wages, savings and population growth

The final matter we must consider in this discussion of balanced-growth equilibrium is the possibility that there is a link between population growth and other elements in the system, especially savings. This would mean that if G_y and G_n diverged, the natural rate of growth could alter. Balanced-growth equilibrium could be maintained by an alteration in the natural rate of growth as well as, or instead of, an alteration in the warranted rate.

7.1 A Malthusian possibility

One possibility (a Malthusian one) is that the supply of labour might be infinitely elastic at the real wage which represented the subsistence level. This would mean that the wage rate was given but that the rate of growth of population became variable. Whenever the real wage rate rose above the subsistence level, the population would rise to the degree needed to bring it down to the subsistence level again. In these circumstances, the factor which would determine the rate of growth of population would be the level of savings. The higher the savings ratio (and in balanced-growth equilibrium the investment ratio too) the higher would be the rate of growth of aggregate GNP. However, this increase in income would not lead to an increase in income per head. Given our assumptions, population would increase at the same rate as income, leaving income per head constant. In other words, any rise in income would lead to a proportional rise in population, so that productivity per head $\dfrac{Y}{L}$ remained constant. Both output per head and income per head would be unaltered; population and aggregate income would rise at the same rate as each other. And this rate would be determined by the savings ratio.

7.2 Kaldor's theory

We have already seen that Professor Kaldor, the Cambridge economist, has suggested that there may be a link between savings and population growth which could help to prevent Marxian crises. Marx saw crises as inevitable whenever the rate of capital accumulation exceeded the rate of population growth.

(a) The assumptions

Let us look at the question simply in terms of the distribution of income between profits and wages. We shall assume that the warranted and actual rates of growth of income are equal so that entrepreneurs are just satisfied with the profits they are earning at the current rate of growth. We have seen that the rate of growth of the capital stock can exceed the rate of growth of population only if there is a 'pool' of unemployed to draw on. Let us once again assume that all profits are saved and that there are no savings from other incomes. The rate of profit on capital which keeps businessmen just content with the existing rate of growth will then be exactly the same as both the rate of growth of income and the rate of growth of the capital stock.

(b) Avoiding a Marxian crisis

If the supply of unemployed workers is now exhausted, and no change is made in the capital-labour ratio, the Marxian argument is that a crisis would be inevitable, with rising wages cutting profits and leading to depression. Kaldor suggests that there is no inherent reason why there should be such a crisis, or why the existence of a labour reserve is essential if capital accumulation is to continue. There may, instead, be a move to a new balanced-growth equilibrium, provided that a change in the distribution of income between profits and wages is possible.

Since there is no longer any unemployed labour to call upon, and since we are assuming that there is no change in the capital-labour ratio, balanced-growth equilibrium requires a fall in the rate of growth of the capital stock. This will bring the rate of growth of capital (and income) back into equality with the (slower) rate of growth of the labour force. In balanced-growth equilibrium, savings must equal investment. This means that, since there has been a fall in the rate of growth of the capital stock in the new situation, that is to say in investment, to equal the (slower) rate of growth of the labour force, there must have been a corresponding fall in savings. Since all savings are made out of profits and all profits are saved, there must also have been a fall in profits, bringing them into line with the (reduced) amount of investment.

This not only requires a fall in the ratio of profits to income—$\frac{\pi}{Y}$. It also requires a fall in the rate of profit on capital ($\frac{\pi}{K}$ or r). For balanced growth on our assumptions, r must always equal G_y, which must also equal G_k and l—the rate of growth of the population.

(c) A fall in profits

Provided that entrepreneurs are willing to accept this fall in the rate of profits, which is of course the major proviso, growth can continue. Aggregate wages (W) will rise. This will lower the share of profits (π) in income. As $\frac{\pi}{Y}$ falls, so will $\frac{S}{Y}, \frac{I}{Y}$ and therefore G_k. The result will be a new balanced-growth equilibrium—a new 'golden age'. The (identical) fall in the shares of profits, savings and investment in income will have reduced G_y and G_k to equality with l. Instead of the rate of growth of population adjusting to savings, savings adjust to population growth.

8. Growth and profits

This example gives an excellent illustration of the complexity of growth economics. One must always keep one's attention on a number of variables. These must be considered both as absolute quantities and in terms of their rates of growth. Equilibrium growth—a 'golden age'—requires all the variables to adjust to each other. Not least in this example, the rate of profit on capital must be sufficient to satisfy entrepreneurs. A satisfactory profit rate is as crucial an element in the theory of balanced-growth equilibrium as it was, in the shape of the marginal efficiency of capital, in static employment theory. In the real world, the problem of maintaining adequate profits is bound to be a major pre-occupation of governments committed to securing and maintaining steady growth. In the early 1960s, for example, American businessmen complained of 'profitless prosperity'. It should certainly not be thought to be axiomatic that entrepreneurs will always be satisfied with whatever rate of profit the growth of the labour supply (or indeed the rate of technical progress) allows.

It should have been obvious all along that the rate of return on capital one gets from this model is very small. Where all savings come from profits, and where no profits are consumed, the rate of profit on capital is equal to the rate of growth of the capital stock. In balanced-growth equilibrium, this would be equal to the rate of population growth, which is unlikely to be very high. While these low rates of profit are no doubt partly the result of using oversimple assumptions, they ought not to be entirely surprising. In this kind of balanced-growth situation, with no technical progress, the economy is engaged solely in equipping new members of the labour force with capital equipment of exactly the same kind as that already being used by all existing members of the population. With the population growing at, say, 3 per cent per annum, the capital stock will be growing at just the same rate, but income *per head* will never alter. This will clearly not lead anyone to spend heavily on capital goods.

This simple theory, while it has enabled us to lay bare the essentials of the theory of economic growth, has thus far ignored the crucial element; we have ruled out technical progress. When we allow for technical progress, as we must now do, the role of investment changes. The possibility of profitable and large-scale capital accumulation becomes significantly greater. Capital accumulation ceases to mean merely equipping a growing labour force in accordance with time-honoured techniques. It becomes the vehicle by which new techniques and new products are brought into the economy. A completely fresh dimension is therefore given to economic growth.

9. Departures from balanced growth

We have so far concerned ourselves exclusively with balanced growth. This is clearly not a realistic procedure. Departure from balanced growth is continually possible. To put the analysis in perspective, therefore, we must spend a little time now looking at the difficulties that stand in the way of this actually happening. Let us concentrate for the moment on divergences between G_y and G_w.

It will be remembered that the equation for the actual rate of growth is $G_y = \dfrac{s}{v}$ and that for the warranted rate is $G_w = \dfrac{s}{v_r}$. The difference between the two equations is that in the latter we say what value the capital-output ratio *must* have to leave entrepreneurs just satisfied with past growth, while in the former equation we give the growth rate its actual value, which certainly need not be the same.

It is obvious that if G_y is above G_w, then v must be smaller than v_r. This follows immediately from a study of the two equations, since s is the same in both. If v is less than v_r, this means that businessmen

w

will find that the stock of capital goods (including, of course, stocks of raw materials, goods in progress and finished goods in warehouses and shops) is smaller than they feel to be necessary for efficient production. Entrepreneurs will therefore increase their orders for stocks and for fixed capital assets. This will raise the actual rate of growth even farther above the warranted rate, and will lower v even farther below v_r.

In a similar way, if G_y is less than G_w, v will be greater than v_r. The opposite situation will then result. Businessmen will find that the capital stock is too big for producing the current output and will try to run it down, though this will take time. The more entrepreneurs reduce investment, however, the farther will v rise above v_r. As a result, investment will be reduced still more.

This is the analysis by which Harrod demonstrates what he regards as the essential instability of a growing economy. Far from bringing the economy back into equilibrium, each movement away from equilibrium strengthens the forces leading to instability and moves the economy progressively farther away from the desired line of advance. The higher G_y rises above G_w, the bigger will be the orders placed for capital goods and the bigger will be the divergence between G_y and G_w. The actual rate of growth depends on the actions of millions of entrepreneurs and consumers who are proceeding by trial and error—on what Harrod has called the 'collective trials and errors of vast numbers of people'. It would therefore be very remarkable if they were to hit on precisely the value G_w for the actual rate of growth of the economy. Yet, if they do not, it is Harrod's pessimistic conclusion that their experience will lead them to drive the economy farther and farther away from G_w. This is why economists often describe Harrod's balanced growth as a 'knife-edge' equilibrium. The line traced out by G_w represents a distinctly unstable equilibrium path.

In practice, of course, movements away from this equilibrium path will not take the economy permanently upwards or downwards. On the upward side, a rise in income will sooner or later run into the ceiling imposed by the limited resources of the economy. The maximum possible growth rate will then be the natural rate of growth. The economy will either bump along the full-employment 'ceiling', or it may relapse into depression, when entrepreneurs find it impossible to continue the exhilarating upward movement of the national income at the high rate of G_y and are forced back to the slower rate of G_n.

9.1 The 'ceiling' and the 'floor'

The upward movement of the economy is therefore bound to be halted in the end by the full-employment ceiling. Some economists,

notably Professor Hicks, have suggested that fluctuations will therefore take place between this ceiling and a somewhat similar 'floor'.
There is some argument over what exactly determines the level of
the floor. Harrod argues fairly strictly in terms of the accelerator,
as we outlined it in Chapter 19. He is mainly concerned with what
economists call induced investment—investment which is 'induced'
by the need to install more capacity in order to produce a bigger
output. Other economists, including Hicks, have put more emphasis
than Harrod does on the importance of what they call 'autonomous'
investment—that part of investment which is of a long range character
and goes on all the time somewhat independently of short-run
changes in income. For them, autonomous investment includes
public investment, investment in direct response to inventions and
so on. While arguing that in the long run 'all capital outlay is justified
by the use to which it is put'[1] Harrod concedes that there will be
some autonomous investment in the short run 'which no one expects
to see justified or not justified within a fairly short period'.[2]

9.2
*Autonomous
investment and
the 'floor'*

If there is some autonomous investment, the level of the floor beyond
which any downward movement of the economy can never go will
depend on the size of these autonomous elements in investment and,
indeed, in consumption too. It will also depend on the amount of
income created because both autonomous consumption and autonomous investment have to be 'multiplied', because of the effect of the
multiplier. There will, for example, be a minimum amount below
which consumers will not allow their consumption expenditure to
fall, however severely depressed the economy is, even if they have to
draw on savings to do so. This will supplement autonomous investment in its effect on income. Because of this, even the kind of cumula-
tive downward movement of G_y away from G_w which Harrod
envisaged, will come to an end once the floor is reached, though there
is no guarantee that any subsequent recovery will end in a 'golden
age'.

**Suggested
reading**

HAHN, F. H. and MATTHEWS, R. C. O.	'The Theory of Economic Growth: A Survey', *Economic Journal*, 1964, p. 779, especially sections 1 and 2.
HARROD, R. F.	*Towards a Dynamic Economics*, London, 1948, chapter iii.
KALDOR, N.	'Capital Accumulation and Economic Growth', in F. A. Lutz and D. C. Hague, *The Theory of Capital*, London, 1961, especially sections i–vi.

[1] *Towards a Dynamic Economics*, p. 79.
[2] *Ibid.*

27

Technical progress and capital accumulation

1. The role of technical progress

For well over a century economists have accepted the fact that the accumulation of capital is one of the crucial elements in economic growth. However, despite the pioneering work of J. A. Schumpeter, beginning in the 1900s, it is only in the last ten or twenty years that the role of technical progress has been widely accepted by economists. It is now agreed that, on the one hand, it helps to make possible a steady rise in productivity, and, on the other, it sustains a continuing growth of demand.

The attitude of 'classical' economics can be broadly stated in the following way. The 'classical' economists usually assumed that technical knowledge was given and unchanging over time, and that there was a fixed amount of labour available to the economy. This assumption implies that, at any particular moment, the community's stock of capital is of a given size, and that there are a number of new investment projects which it would be profitable to initiate. It would be impossible to carry out all these investment projects during any given period of time without overloading the economy and so causing inflation. Nevertheless, provided that the community is making *net* savings, some of the new investment schemes will be undertaken with these savings.

Having looked at some aspects of the labour supply in Chapter 26, we shall assume throughout this chapter that the labour supply is constant. The discussion in the previous chapter may therefore lead one to wonder what form the new investment will take. For we have been mainly concerned so far with situations of balanced-growth equilibrium where investment was required in order to allow new workers to be equipped in accordance with existing techniques. Investment was consequently proceeding at exactly the same rate as the labour force was growing. In those circumstances, with no technical progress, a constant labour force would require no net investment at all. In this chapter, we first look at capital accumulation and at its links with technical progress in a situation where the labour force is constant, so that we can concentrate entirely on the effects of technical progress. We shall postulate that if no technical progress is occurring, any net investment will be concerned with bringing the amount of capital per member of the (constant) labour force up to the level that existing techniques require. Where technical progress *is* occurring, investment will, in addition or instead, be concerned with raising productivity by increasing capital per man, whenever new production techniques make this profitable.

1.1 A
'classical' model

Professor Hicks has put the 'classical' economists' position neatly in a diagram similar to Fig. 27.1.[1] The rate of return (r), which business-

Fig. 27.1

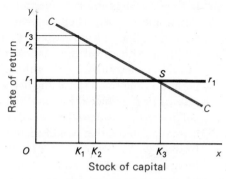

Stock of capital

men must expect on the investment they undertake, is measured up the *y*-axis. In the present context this need not be distinguished from the rate of interest, which the 'classical' economists regarded as the device which would regulate the investment undertaken in any period of time. Investment would be kept low enough to avoid overloading the economy, but high enough to maintain full employment.

In Fig. 27.1, the stock of capital is shown on the *x*-axis. If the stock of capital at any particular moment is K_1, the rate of return which businessmen can earn from new investment will be a little less than r_3. If the economy is to grow with full employment, the rate of interest must be rather lower than r_3, say, at r_2. It will then just pay businesses to borrow enough money (or use their own funds) to make a net addition of K_1K_2 to the capital stock during the present time period, say, a year. This will mean that the community ends the year with a capital stock of K_2. The dark brown CC curve therefore shows the rates of return that can be obtained from various aggregate capital stocks. In this it differs from the marginal efficiency of capital curves used in Part Two, which linked the rate of return to *levels of investment* and not to levels of the aggregate capital stock.

[1] J. R. Hicks, 'Thoughts on the Theory of Capital: The Corfu Conference', *Oxford Economic Papers* (New Series), 1960, p. 123.

Assuming that the supply of labour is constant and that there is no change in technical knowledge, the rate of return on net investment will have fallen somewhat below r_2 by the end of the year. If there are positive net savings, which is likely, the rate of interest will also have to fall below r_2 if investment is to be undertaken and full employment maintained in the next year.

1.2 The stationary state

The 'classical' economists believed that the rate of interest would gradually decline, continuously rationing investment to the amount possible without inflation, until it finally reached a level at which both net savings and net investment had fallen to zero. In Fig. 27.1, this would happen where the capital stock was K_3 and the rate of interest r_1. The economy would then have reached what economists like J. S. Mill called the 'stationary state'. So long as the stock of capital was less than K_3, the rate of return would be high enough to permit businessmen to use the net savings of the community to raise it towards K_3. Once the capital stock reached K_3, net savings would fall to zero, businessmen would refrain from net investment and capital accumulation would therefore come to an end. There would be some *gross* investment, but all of this would be devoted to keeping the existing stock of capital intact. Depreciation would equal gross investment; net investment would be zero and therefore equal to net savings. Incomes, population and the standard of living would be constant too. If, by some miscalculation, the capital stock did rise above K_3, net *dissaving* would occur, so that the capital stock would fall back again to K_3. In other words, point S in Fig. 27.1 represents a position of stable equilibrium—the 'classical' economists' stationary state.

To judge from their writings, the 'classical' economists appear to have thought that such a stationary state was far enough away to be regarded mainly as an academic curiosity. Although they never put their argument in graphical form, Professor Hicks suggests[1] that the 'classical' economists must have wished to imply that the CC curve in a diagram such as Fig. 27.1 was very elastic. Capital accumulation could therefore go on for a very long time before it reduced the rate of return to r_1. To put this another way, the 'classical' doctrine implied that, in Fig. 27.1, distances like K_1K_2 would be very small; the economy would move only by very small steps towards a distant stationary state. At the same time, the 'classical' economists' optimism about maintaining full employment implied that these steps would nevertheless be big enough to maintain a high level of employment and activity in the economy.

[1]*Loc. cit.*, p. 125.

By contrast, Keynes clearly regarded any curve like CC as being rather steep, even where there was technical progress. We saw on p. 538 that he felt one could reach a position where capital would cease to be scarce within a reasonably short period of time. Nor was this all. Quite apart from its implication that the CC curve was likely to be very steep, Keynesian economics cast doubts on the realism of drawing a horizontal r_1r_1 curve. An economy which has a larger stock of capital is bound (with a constant capital-output ratio) to produce a bigger income than one with less capital. Yet we saw in Chapter 20 that savings are likely to be quite closely correlated with income. A bigger income is likely to mean bigger savings. A horizontal line like r_1r_1, showing the rate of interest (or return) at which net savings are zero, then makes little or no sense.

1.3 Keynesian pessimism

Indeed, if one argues that such a curve can be drawn at all, it must slope downwards quite steeply to the right. Only a very sharp fall in the rate of interest can discourage savings sufficiently to reduce net savings to zero. Without this fall in the interest rate, members of the community will save so much that equilibrium between savings and investment will be impossible. Even if the rate of interest did fall sharply, the only situation where the static equilibrium of a *stationary state* could be reached might well be one where there was a *negative* rate of interest. Even with a zero interest rate, there would be an excess of *ex-ante* savings over *ex-ante* investment and the economy would suffer from the kind of under-employment that Keynes was so concerned about.

Indeed, the situation may well be worse even than this. We have seen that a zero rate of interest is not a practical possibility, since there is likely to be some minimum rate, say 2 or 3 per cent, below which even the most determined cheap money policy cannot hope to push interest rates. Liquidity preference will have become infinite in the way envisaged in Fig. 22.4. Instead of moving steadily towards a stationary state, the economy will suffer from persistent unemployment.

This kind of situation is clearly very far removed from the 'classical' one. It is much more pessimistic about the possibility of growth. The belief that the CC curve is steep implies that opportunities for profitable investment are limited; the fear that excessive savings may accumulate at all positive rates of interest implies that Keynesian unemployment is inevitable.

1.4 The effects of technical progress

Fortunately, we have not actually experienced such a distressing situation except, perhaps, during the great depression of the 1930s. A major reason why the conclusions of this discussion appear to be unduly pessimistic is that we have not so far removed our assumption that there is no technical progress. When we relax this extremely restrictive assumption the position becomes much more cheerful, as is shown in Fig. 27.2. So long as there is no technical progress, the

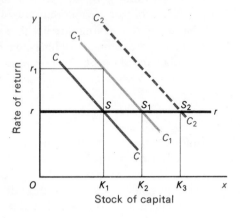

Fig. 27.2

situation is just as it was in Fig. 27.1. A stationary state is sooner or later reached at point S, with a capital stock of K_1. In the real world, however, we are likely to find continuing technical progress. What happens then?

The answer is that both capital accumulation and the growth of the national income can continue indefinitely. Technical progress therefore turns out to be even more essential to economic growth than capital accumulation. Where there is no technical progress, capital accumulation can lead to growth in income per head only so long as the labour force has not been fully equipped in accordance with the latest techniques, and so long as consumers have not been supplied with as much as they want of all existing goods, at the prices and in the quantities determined by existing production methods. Once that happens, growth comes to an end. It is technical progress alone which ensures that the stationary state is not merely very far off, but will *never* arrive so long as technical progress continues and so long as consumers can be given the opportunity to satisfy progressively more and more of their wants. Of course, even without technical progress, the *aggregate* GNP can rise if the population is increasing. However, we are taking the view that it is the rate of growth of income per head rather than the rate of growth of aggregate income that we mean when we talk about economic growth.

2. How technical progress works

Technical progress is of two main kinds. First, new products can be introduced. Second, new processes can be developed, which give more output per man—which raise productivity. The stimulus from new products will be felt mainly on the demand side. Their existence will encourage consumers to spend rather than save. We shall postpone a discussion of this aspect of technical progress for the moment since we are at present concentrating on the supply side.

2.1 Capital deepening

So far as supply is concerned, the main contribution of technical progress is that, as we have already seen on p. 597, it increases the natural rate of growth. It does so when the labour force is growing more slowly than output, because it allows more-capitalistic methods of production to be introduced which raise output per man through increases in capital per man—through capital deepening. So far in this chapter we have been assuming that the labour force is constant. Once the stationary state is reached, at point S in Fig. 27.2, net investment cannot then avoid coming to a halt. In the absence of technical progress, there is no way of altering the capital-labour ratio once the whole labour force, available when the economy is at point S, is fully equipped with capital assets appropriate to existing techniques. Once we allow for the existence of technical progress, however, businesses can invest in more capital-intensive production methods, supporting each worker with more equipment. This will shift the CC curve to the right. What happens then will depend on the precise circumstances.

2.2 Bursts of technical progress

To take the simplest case, let us begin where the economy depicted in Fig. 27.2, is in equilibrium at point S with the rate of return at r. A new technical advance is now made and it becomes profitable to invest in a wide range of new machinery designed to raise output per man. This shifts the CC curve to the right; it actually moves to C_1C_1. If no further technical progress takes place the economy will, in time, settle down in a new equilibrium position. There will again be a stationary state, at point S_1. When CC first shifts to C_1C_1, with the capital stock at its initial level of K_1 inherited from the original stationary state, there will be an initial rise in the rate of return to r_1. As the stock of capital rises towards K_2, and the whole labour force is equipped with machines appropriate to the new techniques, the rate of return will fall back towards r.

Similarly, if a second, discrete burst of technical progress takes place which raises the amount of capital which can be used with each man, the C_1C_1 curve shifts to C_2C_2. The stationary-state equilibrium situation associated with C_2C_2 will be at S_2, with a capital stock of K_3. One extreme model showing how economic growth was generated by technical progress would therefore be one where quite separate bursts of technical progress took place at intervals. The gap between the 'bursts' of innovation would, however, be long enough for the economy to be able on each occasion to move to a new stationary-state equilibrium position (as at S, S_1 and S_2) before a new burst of technical progress occurred.

At the other extreme, one could have a situation where technical progress went on continuously and steadily, with the CC curve moving a little to the right in each period of time by, say, the same percentage or the same absolute distance.

2.3 Other ways of adapting to technical progress

One could then postulate a number of possible situations. Capital accumulation might just keep pace with technical progress; it might lag further and further behind it; or it might even move ahead of it for part of the time. These situations can be studied in Fig. 27.3.

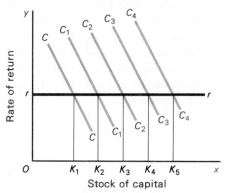

Fig. 27.3

This shows an economy where technical progress shifts the CC curve to the right by the same absolute distance in each period of time. We begin to study the economy in period one when it is in stationary-state equilibrium with a capital stock of K_1. By the end of period two, the CC curve has moved to C_1C_1. One situation, where capital accumulation just keeps pace with technical progress, would be where businessmen knew from past experience what would happen to the CC curve in each time period and where they therefore arranged to take advantage of all technical progress just as soon as it occurred. At the end of period two, businessmen would therefore have just kept up with the technical progress that had already taken place. The capital stock would be K_2 and, in the absence of further technical progress, there would now be a stationary state. However, during period three, there is a new shift of the CC curve to C_2C_2. The perfect foresight of businessmen enables them to predict this shift and to increase the capital stock to K_3 by the end of the period, again just taking advantage of technical progress as it occurs.

A variant of this would be where technical progress always ran slightly ahead of capital accumulation. For example, in Fig. 27.3 technical progress might, by the end of period two, have reached a point where it was appropriate to employ a capital stock of K_3 with the given labour force. However, capital accumulation might have raised the capital stock only to K_2. By the end of period three, when a capital stock of K_4 would be appropriate to the existing state of technical knowledge, the actual stock might be only K_3, and so on. A 'moving equilibrium' situation would then have been reached and could persist indefinitely.

Another possible situation would be where the appropriate capital stock rose from K_1 to K_2, from K_2 to K_3 and so on, but the actual capital stock fell further and further behind the appropriate one. Such an economy would be in no danger of ending up in a stationary state, since the number of possible (and profitable) investment projects would be growing steadily and continuously. But it would not be raising its standard of living (or the GNP if we were assuming that the population could change too) as fast as technical conditions would allow.

Finally, one could have a situation where capital accumulation temporarily ran ahead of technical progress. Thus, a capital stock of K_4 might have been accumulated at a time when one of K_2 was appropriate. The economy would then have to refrain from accumulation until technical progress caught up again. For example, if net investment were to remain at zero for two periods, the capital stock —at K_4—would once more have become appropriate to the state of demand. On the other hand, if there was some net disinvestment during these two time periods, the capital stock of a little below K_4 would become appropriate to the state of technical progress a little before the end of period three.

This particular example emphasises another major difficulty caused by the existence of technical progress. While the capital stock of K_4 would become appropriate at the end of period three, the fact that the economy (let us call it Economy A for the moment) had a capital stock of the right *size* would not guarantee that it was of the right *composition*. Part of Economy A's capital stock of K_4 would be somewhat out of date, having been accumulated at a time when it was not justified by the movement of the CC curve. A different economy, Economy B, which had developed in line with exactly the same technical progress and not ahead of it, would have been investing during periods two and three in machines based on the technical advances made during those periods. Only if, in Economy A, there had been sufficient replacement of worn-out machinery during periods two and three by new machinery based on developments during those periods could the economy in which investment had run ahead of technical progress have as productive a collection of capital assets as the one where development had been slower and steadier.

2.4 The age structure of capital

This raises two very important points. First, it makes clear how important it is for high productivity that the age structure of the community's stock of assets should be favourable. So long as there is technical progress, the lower is the average age of a community's capital assets, the higher will be its output per man. The second point is, that even if the size of the community's stock of capital assets were to remain completely unchanged, there could still be a rise in productivity caused by technical progress, because new and more productive machines had replaced older and less productive ones. Indeed, one of the ways in which technical progress leads to growth is by making entrepreneurs more willing to scrap old machines, because they can be replaced with much more productive new ones. Both aggregate demand and aggregate supply are therefore sustained. Investment (and income) rise, and so does productivity. (We must also note that in such a situation it is extremely difficult to be certain whether the size of the community's capital stock *is* unchanged. The fact of continuing technical progress makes the task of national income statisticians, who are trying to decide how far the depreciation of the nation's capital stock has been made good in a given period, virtually an impossible one. Worn-out machines are not replaced by identical ones, so that complicated calculations are needed in order to discover how many new machines just make good the loss of a given number of worn-out ones.)

We have now considered two extreme situations. One was where there were sudden, discontinuous bursts of technical progress; the other was where technical progress went on continuously. In reality, the situation will lie somewhere between these two extremes. Some technical progress appears to occur at all, or most, times. On the other hand, there also seem to be some periods when technical progress is extremely rapid. To take account of this, we shall later consider the views of Schumpeter, who put great emphasis on the 'bunching' of innovations.

2.5 Invention and innovation

This is perhaps a convenient point at which to repeat the economist's standard distinction between invention—the actual discovery of new products and processes—and innovation—the commercial production of these new products or the commercial application of these new processes. While our emphasis in this chapter has been on innovation, we must not forget that innovation could never have taken place at all if it were not for the inventions underlying it.

·3. The neutrality of innovations

Economists make considerable use of the notion of labour-saving and capital-saving innovations. It will therefore be useful to spend a little time defining what these are. A useful starting point is the situation where an innovation is neither capital-saving nor labour-saving. Economists then say that it is neutral. There are two commonly-used definitions of neutrality, the first by Hicks and the second by Harrod.

3.1 Hicks-neutral technical progress

Professor Hicks's definition was given in his *Theory of Wages*.[1] This definition is framed in terms of the kind of static economic theory discussed in Part One. Hicks defines a neutral innovation as one where, if certain quantities of two factors of production are being used to produce a given output, the effect of the innovation is to increase the marginal productivity of each in exactly the same

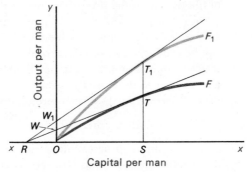

Fig. 27.4

Capital per man

proportion. For example, let us suppose that a particular output of a product is produced by 10 units of capital and 100 units of labour. Initially, the marginal productivity of capital is, say, 10 units of the product in question, and the marginal productivity of labour is 1 unit of it. A neutral innovation will raise these productivities in the same proportion. It may raise the marginal product of labour from, say, 1·0 unit to 1·2 units, and that of capital from 10 to 12 units.

The meaning of Hicks-neutral technical progress is shown by Fig. 27.4. As in Figs. 26.1 and 26.3, we show capital per man to the

[1] London, 1932, pp. 121–2.

right of O along the x-axis and output per man up the y-axis. To the left of O, along the x-axis, we show OR, the ratio between the marginal products of labour and capital, as we shall see.

Initially, there is an equilibrium at point T on the production function, OF. We know from Fig. 26.1 that OW shows the wage (marginal product of labour) and the slope of WT the marginal product of capital, at point R. Let us now discover what OR measures. Consider the triangle OWR. Since the slope of RW gives the marginal product of capital (r), we can write:

$$r = \frac{OW}{OR}.$$

Manipulating this equation, we have:

$$OR = \frac{OW}{r}.$$

In other words, OR measures the ratio between the marginal product of labour and the marginal product of capital in this equilibrium situation.

Hicks-neutral technical progress requires the ratio, OR, between the marginal product of labour and the marginal product of capital, to remain constant for any given value of the capital-labour ratio. In Fig. 27.4, therefore, Hicks-neutral technical progress requires that if technical progress moves OF upwards (say to OF_1) the ratios of the two marginal products must be the same at all points on any vertical line from the x-axis, like the line ST_1. Because OF_1 is above OF, technical progress has increased the amount of output which can be produced at every level of the capital-labour ratio. However, if this technical progress is to be Hicks-neutral, the tangent to T_1 at OF_1 must pass through R, as the line RT_1 does. Only then will the ratio between the marginal productivities of labour and capital $\frac{OW_1}{r_1}$ equal the original ratio $\frac{OW}{r}$. We therefore have Hicks-neutral technical progress along the vertical line ST_1 with the production functions OF and OF_1. For Hicks-neutral technical progress *all* tangents to production functions along a vertical line like ST_1 must pass through the same point, like R.

It is possible, of course, that we could have Hicks-neutral technical progress for this value of the capital-labour ratio, but not for others. The definition of Hicks-neutral technical progress is therefore usually the stricter one that the ratio of the marginal products of the factors are constant, as OF moves upwards, at *every* value of the capital-labour ratio. That is, technical progress is Hicks-neutral only if the ratio between the marginal products of the two factors is equal at each point along *any* vertical line from the x-axis in a diagram like Fig. 27.4.

Definitions of capital-saving and labour-saving innovations follow from this. A capital-saving innovation is one where, with a given input of the two factors, the innovation raises the marginal productivity of labour relatively to the marginal product of capital. One can then produce the given output with less capital relatively to labour. If the most profitable way of producing the firm's output now requires an absolute fall in the input of capital, but this is compensated by an increase in the amount of labour employed, then it is said that the innovation is absolutely labour-using and capital-saving. If, however, there is a reduction in the amounts of both factors, the innovation will be described as relatively capital-saving. Although less of each factor is being used, the input of labour has fallen less than has the input of capital.

On Hicks's definition, a firm will, in all save the most exceptional circumstances, react to a capital-saving innovation by reducing its input of capital relatively to that of labour. The precise way in which the relative and absolute amounts of the factors used will change as the result of the innovation will depend on various elasticities. It will depend on the elasticities of substitution between capital and labour in the economy, for these will help to determine what effects the innovation has on the prices of the two factors. It will also depend on the elasticities of demand for the products of the various industries that make up the economy.

What has been said above holds similarly for a labour-saving innovation. This will be one where, at the original output and with a given input of the two factors, the marginal productivity of capital is raised relatively to the marginal productivity of labour. Since the same output can now be produced with a smaller total amount of the two factors, the input of at least one of them will fall. The amount of labour used may be reduced absolutely and that of capital may rise; the innovation will then be absolutely labour-saving and capital-using. Or the amount of both factors used may fall, with the input of labour falling proportionately more than the input of capital. The innovation will then be relatively labour-saving. Once again, however, the exact amounts of the two factors used will depend on the various elasticities of demand and substitution, as Hicks has explained.[1]

3.2 Harrod-neutral technical progress The dependence of Hicks's definition of neutral technical progress on these elasticities makes it a rather complicated analytical tool to use. It has also been criticised, especially by Harrod, because it makes neutrality depend on circumstances 'quite unrelated to the intrinsic character of the innovation itself', such as the elasticities of demand

[1] *Theory of Wages*, pp. 121–7.

for factors of production and for products. It is also a concept framed in accordance with the traditions of static economics. For all these reasons, the economics of growth makes a good deal of use of an alternative definition which Harrod put forward in *Towards a Dynamic Economics*.

It will be remembered that Hicks's definition of neutral technical progress looks at the ratio between the marginal products of the factors when the capital-labour ratio is constant. Harrod's definition is in terms of a relationship between the rate of profit and the capital-output ratio. Harrod-neutral technical progress requires *both* that the marginal product of capital (assumed to be equal to the rate of profit, r) is constant *and* that the capital-output ratio is constant too. If there is technical progress, and r remains constant, then that technical progress is Harrod-neutral if the capital-output ratio is also constant. However, if r is unchanged after technical progress but the capital-output ratio *rises*, then that technical progress is labour-saving; if the constant r is associated with a *fall* in the capital-output ratio, then the technical progress is capital-saving. It follows that in perfect competition a constant r means that Harrod-neutral technical progress leaves the distribution of income between profits and wages unaltered.

We saw that the strict definition of Hicks-neutral technical progress required that the ratio between the marginal products of capital and labour must be unchanged by technical progress at *each* level of the capital-labour ratio. Similarly, the strict definition of Harrod-neutral technical progress requires that the rate of profit must remain constant with technical progress so long as the capital-output ratio is constant as well. This holds *whatever* the level of the capital-output ratio.

We can show Harrod-neutral technical progress diagrammatically in Fig. 27.5. The production function is originally OF and the economy is at P with an output (income) per man of OY_1. The capital-output ratio is $\dfrac{OK_1}{OY_1}$. The line OR is a straight line passing through P. This means that the capital-output ratio at point R $\dfrac{OK_2}{OY_2}$ is the same as at P $\dfrac{OK_1}{OY_1}$.

Suppose that there is technical progress, that this raises the production function from OF to OF_1 and that the economy is now in equilibrium at R. Harrod-neutral technical progress requires that the marginal productivity of capital (r), the rate of profit, is constant as one moves along a line (here OR) with a given level of v, where $\dfrac{OY_1}{OK_1} = \dfrac{OY_2}{OK_2}$. This, in turn, requires that the slope of OF at P must be equal to that of OF_1 at R. That is, the tangents at P and R must have the same slope. For these tangents, *AB* and *CD*, measure the marginal product of capital at *P* and *R* respectively. This is the case in Fig. 27.5. We may describe this relationship between *OF* and *OF*$_1$ by saying that *OF*$_1$ is a 'radial projection' of *OF*. At any point along any ray like *OR*, the slope of the production function (the rate of profit) is constant. The strict definition of Harrod-neutrality requires

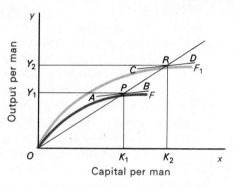

Fig. 27.5

that this shall be so generally, and that the relationship shall not hold simply along *one* ray like *OR*.

In terms of older concepts, this means that Harrod-neutral technical progress leaves the length of the production process unaltered. It does not make production more 'roundabout'. Harrod's definition has the attraction that it is framed in terms of the central concept of the theory of growth—the capital-output ratio—and that it can be used to consider either an innovation in an individual firm or industry or one affecting the economy as a whole. On the other hand, labour does not enter directly into Harrod's definition of a neutral innovation, which is entirely in terms of the relationship between capital and output.

One reason for this is that the concept is intended to apply to a dynamic and not a static situation. In a static economics, one can legitimately classify innovations in terms of their effects on the productivity of given, constant amounts of factors of production. In dynamic theory this would be quite inappropriate. The essence of the theory of growth is that it must be able to deal with situations where the supply of factors of production is *not* constant. Since the growth theory we are considering assumes constant returns to scale, changes in the relationship between capital and output can come about only through innovation. Yet changes may well occur in the relationship between output and labour on the one hand, and capital and labour on the other, that have nothing whatever to do with innovation.

For example, let us consider an economy where income and capital are both growing at exactly the same rate, but the labour force is growing more rapidly. If full employment of labour is maintained, capital per man must be falling; the growth process itself will be, in a sense, capital-saving and labour-using. If an innovation were to occur in this situation, one would want to separate out the labour-saving or labour-using characteristics of the innovation itself from the 'labour-using' growth situation into which the innovation came.

This is what Harrod's definition is intended to do. Provided that it leaves the capital-output ratio constant, a neutral innovation will not *itself* affect the relationship between labour and capital. Output per 'machine' will rise by the same proportion as output per man. However, each machine can now produce more output. Therefore, provided that the price of the product remains unchanged, the *value* of a machine in terms of output will have risen in exactly the same proportion as the value of the machine's product has risen. The capital-output ratio will be unchanged. Harrod's way of putting this is to say that a neutral innovation is one which, roughly speaking, raises the productivity of the labour that is engaged in making machines by the same percentage as it raises the productivity of the remaining labour—the labour employed in operating these machines. With a Harrod-neutral innovation, the productivity of all labour rises in exactly the same proportion however near to or far from the production of final output it may be working.

We have already seen that Harrod's definition of neutrality means that, provided the rate of interest remains constant, a neutral innovation leaves the distribution of the national income between wages and profits unchanged. Let us look a little more closely at why this is so. At the end of the last chapter we saw that, on certain simplifying assumptions, a constant capital-output ratio will leave the relative share of wages and profits in national income unchanged as balanced growth proceeds. The essential point to grasp is how, to continue to talk in terms of our simple model, when there are only the two factors of production—labour and capital—growth will raise the incomes of both workers and capitalists. While the *rate* of wages per man employed will rise, the *rate* of profit per pound's-worth of capital employed will not. The worker's standard of living will rise because his wage has risen. The capitalist's standard of living will rise too, but it will do so because he gets much the same rate of return on each pound's-worth of a bigger stock of capital assets.

An entrepreneur investing £100 in a new machine today will probably aim at roughly the same *rate* of return as he would have done a century ago, but his factory, machinery, etc., will be worth much more, even allowing for price changes. The Industrial Revolution has raised the size and value of the British capital stock, not the *rate* of return on each unit of it. Once this point is understood, the relationship of growth to income distribution becomes much clearer.

Let us then apply Harrod's definition of a neutral innovation to a situation where the capital stock is growing at the same rate as the labour force; $(G_k=l)$. Output (and income) per man will also be growing at the same rate, because we assume that the capital-output ratio is constant. So long as the rate of interest (rate of return) is also constant, the incomes of capitalists will grow just as fast as the incomes of workers. The capital stock and the wages of labour will be growing at the same speed. The constant rate of return that the capitalist gets on his growing capital stock will therefore enable the income he earns from it just to keep pace with the rising wage earned by each worker. We can go on to say what will happen where innovation is labour- or capital-saving in Harrod's sense. If there is a capital-saving innovation, with a constant rate of interest, this will increase the share of the national income going to labour; a labour-saving one will reduce it.

3.3 Hicks-neutral versus Harrod-neutral technical progress

We can, of course, express both Hicks-neutral and Harrod-neutral technical progress mathematically. For both, technical progress is an exogenous function of time (t) so that the production function can be written:

$$Y=f(K, N, t).$$

Where technical progress is Hicks-neutral, then the production function will be of the particular form:

$$Y=A(t)f(K, N).$$

Where $A(t)$ is some increasing function of t. With Harrod-neutral technical progress, however, the production function takes the particular form:

$$Y=f(K, A(t)N).$$

While still an increasing function of time, $A(t)$ is linked to labour and not to $f(K, L)$. With Hicks-neutral technical progress, the passage of time raises the productivity of both capital and labour in the same proportion. With Harrod-neutral technical progress, it is the efficiency of the labour force which is altered.

3.4 The Robinson-Uzawa theorem

This is why Joan Robinson and Uzawa have been able to show that Harrod-neutral technical progress is very similar to what economists often describe as 'labour-augmenting' technical change. Population growth increases the labour force, L, at the rate of growth l. Harrod-neutral technical progress increases the labour force measured in efficiency units, $A(t)N$. With population growth, there is an increase in the number of men at work; Harrod-neutral technical progress increases the amount of work each man can do. The result is that, both with population growth and with Harrod-neutral technical progress, the GNP rises at a given rate. The difference is that, with Harrod-neutral technical progress, income per head (real wage per head) increases; with population growth it remains the same. As Joan Robinson and Uzawa have shown, on the strict definition, Harrod-neutral technical progress raises income at the same rate whatever the (constant) level of the capital-output ratio. It is this rate which measures technical progress.

It is perhaps worth noting, finally, that it *is* possible for technical progress to be *both* Hicks-neutral *and* Harrod-neutral. This can only happen if the elasticity of substitution between capital and labour is one. The only production function with this characteristic is known as the Cobb-Douglas production function. This is why it is freely used in growth models, for example, by Solow and Swan in their neo-classical models. Its attraction is its unambiguous neutrality together with its ease of mathematical manipulation.

Where Q is output, and x_1 and x_2 the inputs of two factors, the Cobb-Douglas function is:

$$Q = A x_1{}^a x_2{}^{1-a}$$

a must be positive but less than one.

4. The measurement of capital

It will have become clear that we are measuring the capital-output ratio for the purpose of these definitions in terms of the value of output. A neutral innovation raises the output of a certain product by a given percentage. If the price of that product remains constant, this will not only raise the value of output by the given percentage; it will also raise the value (in terms of the product) of a 'machine' which makes that product by exactly the same proportion.

This raises the major question of how capital should be valued. In our simple illustrations, there has been no problem. For example, we have been implying that all machines become more productive by exactly the same proportion when an innovation occurs. In practice, this will not happen. Only the newest machines will offer the full benefits of the innovation. This means that if one tries to calculate the value of a country's or an industry's capital stock, one must somehow compare the values of old and new machines. With substantial technical progress, a 1960 machine is virtually impossible to compare with a 1970 machine. There is a problem of 'vintages'.

One cannot legitimately measure capital in physical units at all; an old machine is quite different from a new one. The index number problems which statisticians meet in trying to compare the relative 'values' of such 'new' and 'old' machines are virtually insoluble. Indeed, some economists, particularly Joan Robinson, go so far as to hold that it is not really possible to talk of 'quantities' of capital at all; capital cannot be measured. This very important difficulty besetting all theories of capital or growth should never be forgotten, though it has not prevented us learning a great deal from these simple models of economic growth.

Our discussion makes it clear that in a growing economy, the introduction of a labour-saving innovation need not lead to unemployment. Provided that the growth of the capital stock is proceeding rapidly enough, it may be possible to continue to keep labour fully employed. Certainly, since the eighteenth century, the Industrial Revolution has dramatically improved rather than worsened the living standard of the ordinary worker in North America and Western Europe. So long as the growth of income and capital can be kept in line with the growth of the labour force, labour-saving innovations will raise average living standards because they make labour more productive. There is, however, one important qualification to be noted. Our use of averages and aggregates hides the individual problems that growth can cause.

5. Regional employment and technological change

While it may not be too difficult to keep the whole labour force reasonably fully employed, this will rarely be true of each and every part of it, particularly if there are obstacles to the easy movement of labour between different parts of the country or between different trades and occupations. Suppose that the traditional trades in one long-established industrial area decline, but that the industries that inherit their joint share of consumer spending are located in other parts of the country. There may well be unemployment in the old, declining area, *even if* the workers there could do the jobs in the new industries without difficulty, and *even if* labour is very scarce in the expanding industries. This will happen if workers and their families in the old area are unwilling or unable to move away to the new areas, whether for personal, social or economic reasons. There will then be *structural* unemployment of the kind described on p. 433. One should never forget that the hypothesis of complete freedom of movement for factors of production, frequently made in this book, is a simplifying assumption only.

The introduction of labour-saving innovations may also lead to unemployment for workers in particular industries. If one industry introduces very strongly labour-saving machinery, this is bound to lead to a fall in employment there, unless the price of its product can be reduced very sharply and demand is sufficiently elastic to allow the industry's output to rise a great deal. In practice, it is likely that unemployment will develop, and those unemployed may find it difficult to get new jobs if their skills are very specialised—very specific. Even if the skills required are not very specific, there will still be unemployment if workers or employers in other growing industries erect barriers against men from the industry where 'automation' has taken place. Unemployment caused in this way by strongly labour-saving innovations is known as *technological* unemployment. It may well be concentrated in a rather small area if the industry which has been 'automated' is localised. The human and social problems associated with structural unemployment will then arise as well.

If large-scale structural or technological employment emerges, it is likely that nothing short of intervention by the government will be sufficient to prevent it persisting for long periods. Redundancy payments, retraining schemes, financial support for workers who move to new areas and efforts to move new firms and industries to areas where there is structural or technological unemployment are likely to be the only answer.

There will also be problems in firms for which capital-saving innovations have made old machinery obsolete. The main question, in a world where technical progress is continuous and substantial, will be whether it will pay to install more modern machines in place of older ones.

6. When to replace assets

It cannot be said too often that there is no economic reason for scrapping a machine simply because it is old. What matters are its costs of production and its productivity (profitability), not its age. Let us suppose that a new machine has been developed and that a firm is deciding whether or not to replace an existing machine with it. Subject to one proviso, the change will be worth while so long as the *total* costs of production on the new machine are less than the *variable* costs of continuing to operate the old one. The proviso is that the rate of return on the new capital which has to be invested in order to install the more modern machine must be an acceptable one. In other words, the machine must offer a rate of return on the capital invested at least equal to the rate which the firm would obtain from any alternative investment—including investment in government securities or industrial debentures. It must offer a rate of return on the capital invested at least equal to its opportunity cost; to the most profitable opportunity that the firm would have to sacrifice if it invested in the new machine.

For example, let us suppose that the existing machine is worth literally nothing as scrap. It might require running repairs (user cost) of £300 a year if it were kept going, and all the cooperating factors of production might cost another £2 000 a year. Let us further suppose that the new machine and the old one each produce exactly the same volume of output. (One could allow for differences in these outputs by bringing the total receipts from selling the outputs of each of the two machines into the calculation.) The total variable costs of the new machine in a year might be £750 (including user cost). If the new machine is expected to last for ten years, and if it costs £7 500, the depreciation cost each year for the new machine will be £750 (£7 500 divided by ten). The *total* annual cost of using the new machine will then be £1 500, made up of £750 for variable costs and £750 for depreciation. At £1 500, the total annual cost of running the new machine is therefore £800 less than the annual cost of £2 300 incurred in running the old machine. The only remaining issue is whether this expected saving of £800 a year represents an acceptable rate of return over ten years on the £7 500 which will have to be spent to install the new machine. If it is, the firm should install it.

The main defect of this particular model is that we have assumed that there is only one new machine to be considered. We have assumed that no complications are introduced by the fact that technical progress is always occurring and that it might therefore pay to wait a little longer for an even better new machine. One could amend our calculation to allow for this by altering the assumed length of life of the new machine when calculating depreciation charges on it. We have estimated that the new machine will last for ten years; but this must be a reasonable assessment of its *economic* and not its technical life. It must not be an engineer's guess at the length of time before the machine ceases to work; it must be a businessman's guess at the length of time that will elapse before the machine has become obsolete, through the development of new ones, and must be replaced. But it *will* be a guess. This kind of calculation can never be precise.

In times of rapid technical progress entrepreneurs have to make decisions on replacing machinery as best they can in a world where the future is always uncertain. They have to steer a middle course between two equally ridiculous extremes. They will not try to be completely equipped all the time with only the very latest machines, buildings and so on. To attempt to do so in any industry where technical progress was even moderately rapid would lead to bankruptcy through exceptionally heavy investment, and the consequent burden of a huge capital charge. Nor will they continually put off replacement in the hope (or fear) that a radically-improved machine is always just round the corner. Investment in new capital assets will be made in the light of a sober assessment of the likelihood of further technical progress on the one hand, and of the need to keep the firm efficient and profitable on the other. As a result, even firms for which technical progress is fairly rapid are likely to bring only a certain, proportion of their plant and machinery fully up to date every year. This will always keep them reasonably well abreast of technical progress.

7. Schumpeter and 'creative destruction'

We have so far concentrated on the currently-accepted theory of economic growth, and this has a strongly mathematical flavour. Before we leave growth theory, we must consider a much less narrowly economic view of growth. It is one which, while no one has yet succeeded in expressing it in simple, mathematical terms, goes to the very heart of the phenomenon of economic development in a capitalist economy. This theory has been advanced by Joseph A. Schumpeter (1870–1950). He was the leading Austrian economist of his day, though he spent the last part of his life in the USA. Strictly speaking, we are here abandoning our resolve to consider growth separately from fluctuations, since Schumpeter regarded fluctuations as an integral part of growth and, indeed, essential to it.

Schumpeter conceived the essence of his theory at an early age, stating it in his *Theory of Economic Development* in 1909. The novel contribution of this book was the great emphasis it laid on the role of the innovator in fostering economic growth. Towards the end of the 1930s, Schumpeter's *Business Cycles* developed and elaborated his views, but still in a rather narrowly economic framework. However, within a few years, *Capitalism, Socialism and Democracy* had appeared. This is one of the pioneering works of our time—an attempt to link economic, political and sociological analysis and thereby obtain a convincing picture of the working of capitalism. From a purely technical economic point of view, it might perhaps be better to concentrate on Schumpeter's earlier books, but it is only in *Capitalism, Socialism and Democracy* that the wider implications of his views are clearly seen. We shall therefore summarise its argument here.

To Schumpeter, there are two essential features of economic development under capitalism. First, the introduction of new products is an essential part of the process of growth. We have already said a good deal about the introduction of new production methods, but we must now give equal emphasis to this other aspect of innovation. For Schumpeter, the essential characteristic of innovation was that it implied alterations in combinations of factors of production which could not be achieved by the kind of infinitesimal changes considered in traditional price theory. Neither small increments or decrements in the amounts of the factors of production already used, nor the substitution of new factors at the margin, could yield major changes in supply.

Innovation, however, implied radical alterations in production methods, in management and in organisation. It meant the introduction of new products and the exploitation of new markets or sources of raw materials. Of these, it is the introduction of new products that we have studiously ignored so far. Yet it is radically new products which give an extra dimension to growth, and indeed make it very difficult to measure the rise in satisfactions which consumers get from spending their growing incomes as time goes on.

In modern societies, economic growth does not mean merely an increase in the physical output of homogeneous commodities, though we have so far discussed it in precisely these terms. Growth means the introduction of completely new products and the continual improvement of existing ones. One cannot realistically compare the satisfactions derived from a 'T' model Ford with those given by a modern Ford car fitted with automatic transmission. To talk of the price or the benefits obtained from 'a car', or to measure output simply by allowing for changes in 'car' prices, is unrealistic. This means, incidentally, that the price increases, shown in official price indices are often exaggerated. They do not allow sufficiently for product improvement. Again, how can one compare the standard of living of a working class family owning a television set with that of a similar family in the days before television had been even dreamed of? The introduction of new methods of production, or of more scientific management, may increase the *quantity* of output dramatically, in ways that we have already outlined. But the advent of new products transforms the whole of human life in a way that perhaps makes it necessary to use quite different terminology. Perhaps one should speak here of economic development rather than of economic growth.

The second point is that, over the past century, the benefits derived from economic development of this kind have gone to those with lower rather than those with higher incomes. The essence of capitalist development has been that, as Schumpeter put it, 'mass production means production for the masses'. Only if he can sell to the masses can the innovator reap the economies and rewards of large-scale and highly-mechanised production. 'The capitalist achievement does not typically consist in providing more silk stockings for queens but in bringing them within the reach of factory girls in return for steadily decreasing amounts of effort.'[1]

For Schumpeter, economic growth meant an increase in the quantity of output but also a revolution in its quality and composition. In addition, there was always, inevitably, fluctuation as well as growth. In particular, Schumpeter maintained in the face of all the sceptics a firm belief in the existence of the 'long wave' in economic activity, often called the Kondratieff after its discoverer. Schumpeter believed, with Kondratieff, that over a period of fifty or sixty years one could find evidence of a long, general upswing in the economy, followed by a similar decline. For example, he believed that the upswing of a 'long wave' began in the 1840s, reached a peak about 1855 and was then followed by a decline which ended about 1897.

It was Schumpeter's view that each of these long-wave upswings consisted of a miniature industrial revolution, followed by the absorption of its effects by the economy during the long-wave downswing. Each period of upswing brought new production methods, new forms of economic organisation, new products and new markets. All forms of innovation were present. There was a large and permanent increase in the goods available to the community, though once the upswing ended there was the halt to expansion during the decline. The economy then adjusted itself to the new situation and consolidated the ground that had been gained.

Schumpeter described this process as one of 'creative destruction'. He saw certain parts of the economic structure being destroyed from within, with new structures being created in their place. This process was going on incessantly. Though innovations would be introduced mainly during upswings, the economy would be engaged for the remainder of the time in absorbing the effects of these revolutionary innovations. It is for this reason that, from his very earliest writings, Schumpeter stressed the importance of the innovator for economic development. Schumpeter's innovator is the forceful pioneer, the entrepreneur *par excellence,* who presses on the process of creative destruction by exploiting commercially new products and processes, most of which were actually invented by other people. Nor is the innovator content to satisfy the demand for existing products more effectively, either by installing new production methods or by satisfying old wants with new goods. He is concerned with creating entirely new demands. It is the producer who, as a rule, initiates economic change and who 'educates' consumers if necessary. They are brought to want new things.

Because he held these views, Schumpeter was much more tolerant than many earlier (and later) economists had been of inefficient, often monopolistic, businesses. He did not think that what mattered was that, in keen competition, inefficient producers would be driven

[1]*Capitalism, Socialism and Democracy* (3rd English edition), London, 1949, p. 67.

out of business because their prices were undercut by their more efficient rivals. He was not particularly concerned whether all firms were producing in reasonably competitive industries or not. Schumpeter contended that in both competitive industries and in monopoly, the most important types of competition were quite different.

> In capitalist reality, as distinguished from its textbook picture, it is not that kind of competition which counts, but the competition from the new commodity, the new technology, the new source of supply, the new type of organisation (the largest-scale unit of control, for instance)—competition which commands a decisive cost or quality advantage and which strikes not at the margins of the profits and the outputs of existing firms, but at their foundations and their very lives. This kind of competition is as much more effective than the other as a bombardment is in comparison with forcing a door.[1]

The activities of the innovator, therefore, not only make economic growth and progress possible; they transform the whole nature and role of competition itself.

In a nutshell, Schumpeter's theory is that at intervals a number of innovators will begin to apply new ideas commercially on a fairly large scale, thereby creating a burst of investment activity. Through the action of the multiplier, and the accelerator too, this will lead to a boom in the economy. However, innovation may be imitated, and what may well have begun with a few pioneers leading the way will build up into a wave of innovating investment as others follow suit. This long upswing will be followed by the downswing, while the economy, so to speak, digests the innovations. In particular, inefficient producers will be driven out of business.

One interesting point arises here. While it is essential to Schumpeter's theory that there should be 'bunching' of innovations, there is no suggestion that *inventions* need to be, or are, bunched in the same way. It is arguable that inventions occur in a relatively random manner whether the economy is booming or depressed. It is the conditions in which innovators are willing to exploit these inventions commercially which, according to Schumpeter's theory, will occur mainly during the upswing of the 'long wave'. Although he was never very explicit about this, Schumpeter seems to have held the view that invention went on steadily all the time.

What is quite clear is that in advancing this theory of growth, Schumpeter was concerned to propagate a theory which would fit one particular historical situation. He wanted to explain the process of growth in contemporary capitalism. While this is understandable

[1]Schumpeter, *op. cit.*, p. 84.

enough, it nevertheless gives point to a valuable warning from Professor Hicks.

It is all very well for us to have *theories* of economic phenomena which constantly repeat themselves—like the formation of prices, the balancing of international payments, even the rise and decline of particular industries. But the long-run growth of an economy is not a thing that repeats itself; it does not repeat itself in different nations; their growth is all part of a single world story. One cannot argue from what did happen in the United States in a certain period so as to establish laws of economic development. All we ought to hope to get from our analysis is a better understanding of what did happen in the United States at that time. It is worth our while to construct theoretical models in order to improve our understanding of such phenomena. But the theorist, as such, is only a toolmaker; the explanation of what happened is the historian's business not his.[1]

8. Investment in human capital

The discussion in this chapter makes it clear that economists now understand the roles both of innovation and of capital accumulation in fostering economic growth reasonably well. However, their attention has been concentrated almost exclusively on investment in tangible capital assets like buildings, machinery and vehicles. The role of investment in the education and training of human beings is only beginning to be fully understood, and more research into and analysis of the question is needed. Nevertheless, there are some rather obvious principles which we may enunciate.

The influence of accumulated human skill and knowledge on economic growth can be seen very clearly if one considers what has happened in countries that have been devastated by war. Within ten years, countries like Germany and Japan were virtually rebuilt. The process of physical renewal goes ahead amazingly fast. Yet if the accumulated knowledge and skill of the German and Japanese people could somehow have been destroyed, and it had been impossible to import similar knowledge and skill from abroad, the process of rebuilding would have taken centuries. The whole history of scientific and technological discovery and learning would have had to be repeated. This illustration shows in a very striking way how, over the centuries, investment in the education and training of human beings has brought us to a position where the accumulated capital stock that it represents is our most valuable possession. So long as this

[1] J. R. Hicks, 'Thoughts on the Theory of Capital: The Corfu Conference', *loc. cit.* p. 132.

knowledge remains, even the most devastating destruction can be made good. It is vitally important for economic growth that we should always seek to get the best possible return from our investment in human skill and knowledge.

The process of investment in people has three main elements. First, each new generation must be given the appropriate parts of the knowledge already accumulated by previous generations. Not all such knowledge will be relevant to contemporary living, and the effectiveness of the educational system will depend on the success with which teachers decide which particular pieces of knowledge are relevant to modern living and are able to teach them. Nor can anyone hope to accumulate *all* the knowledge that now exists. Some specialisation, though certainly not complete specialisation, is essential. And, even on their own special subjects, it is more important that students should know *where* knowledge can be found rather than that they should attempt to hold it all in their minds.

Having been taught where to find this knowledge, students need also to be taught how to understand and to apply it. They must learn how to learn. This is the second element in education for growth. The modern citizen must learn how to use existing knowledge effectively to operate existing machinery and processes and to run existing factories, offices and organisations. He must also learn how to improve the efficiency of the various component parts of the economy. Only in this way can there be rapid technical progress in the use of machinery and the organisation of work. As a British businessman has put it, efficient management in the twentieth century consists not so much in the application of tools to materials as in the application of logic to work. An effective educational system must teach each new generation to see how existing knowledge can be used to develop new products, to introduce new processes and production methods and to improve the efficiency of organisation in business, government and the social services. In other words, education must help innovators to see how to apply existing knowledge in new ways.

This leads to the third element in education for economic growth. People must not learn merely how to apply old ideas in new ways; they must be encouraged to develop entirely new ideas, products and processes as well. This is where the help that education can give is limited. Education can provide the innovators and inventors of the future with the technical and social understanding that they need in order to understand the world they live and work in and what it currently offers. It cannot, except by vague hints and clues, show where new ideas, new products and new processes are necessary, and how they can be developed and introduced. All education can do is to give innovators the best possible knowledge and understanding of the world as it is, and to encourage them to use energy, initiative and imagination in changing it.

It follows from what we have said that a decision to spend money on education, whether taken by a child, his parents or the government, is an investment decision in just the same way as is an entrepreneur's decision to build or buy a new machine. It is doubtful whether education is looked on in this light by many individuals or families; there is surprisingly little evidence that governments which provide 'free' education look on it as an important investment in economic growth. Quite often, there is merely a vague feeling that education is 'a good thing'. Yet every time, for the individual at least, a decision to spend money on education is an investment decision of a most difficult kind. With a child of ten or fifteen, one is trying to look a full fifty-five or sixty years ahead when deciding if a particular training for him would be worthwhile. Even if the child or his family is prepared to look at this question of spending on education as a purely rational economic decision, the various elements in that decision are not always capable of being put into money terms. Nevertheless, both individuals and governments should try to do just that.

Let us look briefly at the kind of issues involved. Suppose that a boy of fifteen is deciding whether to leave school now or to spend another two years there, followed by three at a university. Let us further suppose that the child's parents would get no government support through scholarships if the boy stayed on at school.

If the child were to leave school at once, he might expect to earn, say, £2000 a year, on the average, over his lifetime. If the retiring age is sixty-five, this means that he will earn a total of £100000 over the fifty years of his working life. To continue with his education for another five years might cost, say, a total of £6000 on fees, books, board and lodging and so on. As a graduate, the boy might expect to earn an average of £3000 a year over his working life of forty-five years. He will have had to pay more for his education, and he will have had his working life shortened by the five extra years he spends at school and university. But he will get a higher annual salary as a result. It must be stressed that this is a matter of expectations, not of certainties. Otherwise, this would not be an investment decision at all. Every investment decision involves uncertainty since one is looking into the future. The decision has to be taken on the best estimates that one can make.

In this particular example, the extra spending on education is likely to be profitable. The boy 'invests' £6000 in education, and sacrifices five years of income. However, over his remaining working

life of forty-five years he will now earn a total of £135000. This is
£35000 more than the £100000 which he would have earned had
he started work at fifteen. An initial investment of £6000 has brought
in an extra £35000 over the next forty-five years. If a reasonable
proportion of the extra income would be earned before he was
forty, the boy's decision is reasonably clear to anyone whose time
horizon is not abnormally short. If necessary, it would pay the family
to borrow money at quite a substantial rate of interest in order to
pay for the education. In practice, this is unlikely to be necessary,
because the national or local government may be willing to pay.

Let us look in more detail at this. Let us, not quite realistically,
suppose that the £6000 is borrowed after five years. If the boy's extra
income were spread evenly over his life, then borrowing £6000 at
10 per cent would give a net present value at the age of twenty (after
deducting the initial investment of £6000) of about £4000. (The
reason interest is relevant is that either the £6000 has to be borrowed
at interest, or else the boy has to meet an opportunity cost: to invest
his own money and thereby sacrifice interest or other satisfactions.)
If most of the extra income came *after* the boy was forty, which is
quite possible, the decision would be less clear. One would have to
estimate the time profile of the extra earnings and discount them.

If *all* the extra earnings came after the boy was forty were evenly
spread, and if the discount rate were 10 per cent, the net present
value of this investment at the age of twenty would be only about
£1900 even before allowing for the investment of £6000 at the age
of twenty. Coming only after the boy was forty, these returns would
have to be heavily discounted. A *substantially* greater increase in
income after forty would be required in order to make the decision
to stay on at school and university worthwhile.

*9.2 For the
nation*

There is, however, one important qualification to our argument so
far when we look at this matter from the national viewpoint. Our
example assumed that the £6000 that the boy had to spend on his
education represented its full cost. If his fees covered the whole cost
of board and lodging, teacher's salaries, school and university
buildings and so on, this would be true. If not, then the state's
calculation would differ from the individual's. The individual should
not allow the fact that his education is being subsidised by the state
to enter into his decision. He should decide what to do in the light of
the payments he actually has to make, not what these would be if he
paid the full costs of education. If he is being subsidised, it is only
sensible that he should accept the subsidy.

The state cannot calculate in this way. The cost of the subsidy has to be allowed for when the nation's position is being considered. As a result, it might turn out that the total cost to the nation was not £6000 over the five years but, say, £12 000. This would obviously make the investment much less attractive. With a discount rate of 10 per cent, the net present value would be —£3 000 after allowing for the initial investment of £12 000, provided that the extra earnings were spread evenly over the boy's life. The investment would not necessarily be ruled out. The situation would depend on the present value of alternative ways of spending the £12 000, and on the way in which the extra income earned by the graduate was spread over his life.

This is only a hypothetical example of the benefits to be derived from education, but it is perhaps too pessimistic for a country like Britain. Economists think that the annual return on investment in education in developed countries is actually around 10 per cent. Provided that the extra income earned by a university graduate during his life is a realistic measure of his extra value to society, it is in both the individual and the national interest that he should spend longer being educated. From the national point of view, expenditure on education, whether at school, college or university, should, in principle, be increased until the return at the margin is just equal to the return from other investment elsewhere in the economy.

To summarise, our example shows the way in which a rational calculation of the costs and benefits of investment in education might be made. This chapter has left us in no doubt that technical progress plays a central role in increasing economic growth; we have also seen that education and training are crucial for technical progress. Any country which puts rapid economic growth high in its list of national aims must make this kind of calculation so as to plan investment in education rationally. There may, of course, be a strong case for giving some education to everyone for its own sake, and that would be a wholly reasonable thing to do. Yet, looking at education purely in economic terms, one cannot avoid the conclusion that most countries need a much more careful study of ways of increasing both its scale and its effectiveness. In many cases, this would be the best contribution that a country could make towards fostering rapid economic growth within its borders.

Suggested reading

HAHN, F. H. and MATTHEWS, R. C. O.	'The Theory of Economic Growth: A Survey', *Economic Journal*, 1964, p. 779, especially section 2.
HARROD, R. F.	*Towards a Dynamic Economics,* London, 1948.
HICKS, J. R.	'Thoughts on the Theory of Capital: The Corfu Conference', *Oxford Economic Papers* (New Series), 1960, p. 123.
KALDOR, NICHOLAS	'Capital Accumulation and Economic Growth', in F. A. Lutz and D. C. Hague, *The Theory of Capital,* London, 1961, p. 177.
SCHUMPETER, J. A.	*Capitalism, Socialism and Democracy,* London, 1949, especially chapters v–x.

x

Conclusion

1. The economics of scarcity

We can now make some general comments on what we have tried to do in this book. One way of summing up the difference between the analysis of Part One and that of Part Two is to say that the former was concerned with the economics of scarcity, the latter with the economics of waste. In Part One we assumed that all resources in the community were fully employed, and that to set more resources to producing one commodity inevitably meant that less of another commodity would be made. We were concerned with scarcity.

2. The economics of waste

In Part Two, we were concerned with what can be described as the economics of waste. We showed that an economy can be in equilibrium and yet have substantial unemployed resources in men, machines and buildings. They could have been usefully employed in producing goods and services, but are left idle because the level of activity is not high enough to keep them all at work. While this distinction is clearly an over-simplification, to describe Part One as studying scarcity and Part Two as studying waste is to make a useful distinction.

3. The economics of promise

Similarly, Part Three is concerned with what we may call the economics of promise, in the sense that it points the way to the conquest of both scarcity and waste. While we saw that in every modern economy production is limited by the scarcity of resources, a dynamic theory of economics can teach us a great deal about how to get the best out of these limited resources by combining full employment with balanced growth. However, there is more than this to the economics of promise.

(a) Technical progress

We also saw in Part Three that any realistic theory of growth must allow for technical progress. It is here that an important hope for the future lies. By taking advantage of what technical progress has to offer, we may find that scarcity can be significantly reduced in the future. The economics of promise looks to a world where the problems of both scarcity and waste have been overcome.

(b) Problems of population growth

However, this optimism must be tempered. One need only look around the world to see that economic growth is not without its own problems. First, population increase means that a rise in the GNP need not mean a similar rise in GNP per head. If population growth is rapid it may offset or more than offset the effects of technical progress. Especially in under-developed countries, rising GNP is then accompanied by much slower increases in GNP per head. While developed countries are less likely to suffer from this problem, increases in their own populations lead to competition for food and raw materials with under-developed countries, as the latter attempt to increase their own growth rates.

(c) Problems of measuring growth in the real GNP

Second, although it is standard practice for economists to equate rises in GNP per head with rises in standards of living, this is not as straightforward a matter as it seems. Some things that go to make up the standard of living are not included in the GNP. Leisure (and the satisfactions derived from leisure) is the most important example. A fall in the GNP may not mean a fall in the standard of living if it is accompanied by a rise in the amount of leisure that the population is enjoying.

(d) Problems of pollution

In addition, the problems of pollution mean that an increasing output of goods and services is often accompanied by damage to the environment. For example, a rise in the output of petroleum and chemical products may lead to more pollution. An observed 'increase' in the real GNP is then accompanied by a reduction in the satisfactions that the community derives from its surroundings, which cancels out some part of the satisfactions derived from the increase in the GNP. Indeed, the situation can be quite a paradoxical one. An increase in the production of, say, plastic packs and containers may have to be accompanied by increased expenditure on destroying them. The GNP then will not only include the incomes of those paid to produce the plastic packs initially; it will also include the incomes of those who have to be paid to destroy them after use. A part, at least, of every country's GNP represents payments to those employed to eliminate the ill effects of the activities of the rest of the community. This has always been the case; for example, with the refuse collector. It is now more generally true. To that extent, using the GNP as an index for economic performance is misleading.

In the future, communities may decide to forego part of economic growth by refusing to produce some new products that will damage the environment. Even if they do not, the rising cost of offsetting the ill effects of increasing output will mean that the actual increase in the GNP is less than the apparent one. While the economics of promise is a good shorthand description of the analysis in Part Three, the difficulties associated with economic growth cannot be ignored.

4. Comments on Part One

(a) Partial equilibrium

We now look in rather more detail at the three parts of the book. In the price theory of Part One we spent most of our time discussing particular equilibrium and our theory was, therefore, Marshallian in the sense of being partial-equilibrium analysis. We usually confined our analysis to one market at a time and tried only briefly, at the end, to connect up these individual markets in a general-equilibrium system. The reason why we spent so much time discussing this kind of economics, which pervades Marshall's *Principles of Economics*, is that while the *Principles* is not now widely-read, Marshall's book remains a central one in Anglo-Saxon micro-economics. We have, of course, said a great deal about ideas to be found in more recent writing, especially those of Joan Robinson and Professor Chamberlin, but all this kind of analysis is Marshallian in a broad sense. It is all particular-equilibrium analysis. Moreover, very few significant advances have been made in this field since the 1930s, almost all of them concerned with oligopoly. The main developments have been in macro-economic and growth theory.

(b) General equilibrium

Apart from Walras, whose work we described briefly, Pareto[1] was also an enthusiastic writer on general equilibrium. Today, Hicks's *Value and Capital* still gives a good, standard treatment of general-equilibrium analysis. But in English (and American) economics particular-equilibrium analysis has always held pride of place. Only the European tradition has put the emphasis on general-equilibrium analysis. And the fact remains that, both in its theoretical contribu-

[1]See his *Manuel d'Economie Politique Pure*, Paris, 1909.

tions and in its practical applications, particular-equilibrium analysis has been the more successful.

5. Comments on Part Two

(a) Keynes as a theorist

Part Two was concerned with macro-economic theory. This branch of economics is at least as strongly overshadowed by Keynes as is particular-equilibrium analysis by Marshall. The ideas that Keynes originally put forward in the *General Theory* have been refined, extended and indeed criticised by other economists, especially Duesenberry, Patinkin, Tobin, Modigliani, Kaldor and Joan Robinson. However, the initial Keynesian statement remains something that cannot be ignored, though it now has to be elaborated and sometimes corrected. The name of Keynes still dominates this area of economics in the way that Marshall's dominates particular-equilibrium analysis.

The differences are, first, that because Keynes was the originator of macro-economic theory there have been more basic challenges to what he wrote than with Marshall. Although Marshall was challenged by the newer theories of imperfect and monopolistic competition, these were essentially extending the Marshallian approach. Marshall was in a real sense summing up the end of a long debate, while Keynes's book was revolutionary in the sense that when it appeared it caused great consternation in academic circles. The second difference is that, especially during the 1960s, Keynesian theory was severely criticised, especially by the modern quantity theorists, not least Professor Friedman. Marshallian theory has escaped serious challenge. Its only challenger, imperfect competition theory, was itself basically Marshallian. Not only have the quantity theorists challenged some of Keynes's theoretical analysis. They have also doubted whether the 'fine tuning' of the economy through fiscal measures is possible in the way that Keynes, and more especially his followers, have suggested.

(b) Other contributors

We have tried to give credit to the main contributors to modern macro-economic theory. We have at each stage stated the original Keynesian view and then explained how this has been modified by later writing and research.

(c) Keynes as a practical man

Nevertheless, with all the amendments and challenges to the *General Theory*, Keynes's influence on public affairs was during his lifetime, and still is, greater than that of any other twentieth-century economist. The importance of Keynes's analysis for the history of economic doctrines lies especially in the fact that his theory was so readily applicable to the problems of the 1930s and 1940s. In particular, the analysis put forward in the *General Theory*—an analysis which had been intended to provide an explanation of the mass unemployment of the 1930s—was destined to play a vital part in enabling Great Britain to overcome the inflationary stresses of the Second World War. To a smaller degree it has underlain post-war fiscal policy. Readers who are interested in Keynes's influence on practical affairs are referred to Sir Roy Harrod's exhaustive biography *The Life of John Maynard Keynes*.[1]

6. Comments on Part Three

The writings on which Part Three was based are also diverse. However, in growth economics no single writer has yet come to dominate the subject in the way that Marshall dominated (and, indeed, still dominates) price theory. Nor is there any one author whose influence underlies the whole of the theory of growth in the way that Keynes's writings still permeate macro-economic theory. Keynes's own influence even on the theory of growth is far from negligible. Static, Keynesian employment theory provided the starting point for growth theory, and Keynesian concepts like aggregate demand and supply, savings and investment have an important place in it. Schumpeter's contribution to growth theory was also an important one.

Nevertheless, with the subject matter and tools of analysis of growth theory still being developed and extended, the names of contemporary economists predominate. One can find no single author or work that covers more than a very small part of the field. Nor is it clear who, if anyone, will become *the* growth theorist. Sir Roy Harrod will surely be regarded as the founder of growth economics after pointing the way ahead so clearly and with such genius in 1947. Nevertheless, as we have seen in Part Three, Domar, Hicks, Joan Robinson, Kaldor and Schumpeter have all made their own important contributions. Nor should one forget the work of other economists like Chapernowne and Meade in England, Samuelson and Solow in the USA or Swan in Australia.

7. The role of economic theory

We pointed out in the Introduction that the value of economic theory lies in providing a framework of analysis which can be used by applied economists in interpreting facts about the real world. It will

[1]London, 1951.

probably be useful to say something now about the usefulness of economic theory, of the kind we have outlined, in helping to analyse such practical problems.

(a) Rationality and consumers

It will be remembered that our main underlying assumption has been that of 'rationality'. We have assumed, in particular, that consumers always strive to obtain the greatest possible satisfaction from spending their incomes, and that businessmen always try to make the biggest profits they can. Some economists have criticised this concept of rationality and have suggested that it is not a useful hypothesis about the real world. So far as consumers are concerned, one's views naturally depend to some extent on one's beliefs about human psychology. But there must be few people who would claim that the great majority of consumers attempt to derive *as little* satisfaction as they can from spending their limited incomes. Admittedly, some consumers may not know what is best for themselves, and may spend their money on goods which actually harm them. Others may buy goods which they expect will give them satisfaction, but which do not. In general, however, the assumption we have made seems a sensible one.

(b) Rationality and businessmen

The assumption of rationality in the theory of the firm has been much more severely criticised. It has been suggested that to claim that all businessmen want to maximise profits is ridiculous. Critics of marginal analysis concentrate their attacks on two main lines. On the one hand, it is suggested that entrepreneurs do not wish to make as much money as possible—that businessmen are not greedy calculating machines. On the other hand, it has been suggested that, since businessmen can never be quite sure about demand conditions for their products, even if they know what cost conditions are, they will only be producing an output which they *think* maximises profits. This need not be the output which actually does maximise profits.

The first criticism is quite justifiable. It is possible that many businessmen do not wish to maximise profits, but the assumption of 'rationality' amongst businessmen seems the most reasonable one to make until empirical research provides a better hypothesis. So far it has failed to do so. In any case, where competition is keen, firms have little choice. To survive, they must maximise profit. The second criticism is rather more difficult to deal with. If businessmen are not sure what the demand and cost conditions for their product really are, they may well go on for a considerable length of time producing outputs which do not maximise profits. Yet since they are not certain what line of action really would maximise profits there is very little they can do to improve matters. This kind of situation is especially likely to occur where there is monopoly or oligopoly. It probably accounts for the belief, current amongst economists, that in such situations entrepreneurs are content to go on charging existing prices for their products, so long as profits are reasonable. They may fear that any change will be for the worse.

A further type of hypothesis about the real world which applied economists will have to test more thoroughly before making confident generalisations is Keynes's view that there is a 'liquidity trap'. As we have seen, the empirical evidence is inconclusive. Keynes's view may be wrong and it is the job of the applied economists and/or econometricians to go on putting this kind of hypothesis to the test, by comparing it with real-world experience.

8. The value of economic theory

(a) In pricing problems

Whatever they think about the actual assumptions made in current economic theory, however, applied economists will generally find it useful in discussing problems of the pricing of basic raw materials or foodstuffs. It is impossible to produce sensible generalisations without analysing these problems in terms of demand and supply, and the elasticity of demand and supply. Similarly, economists considering the effects of changes in government expenditure will have to use the concept of the multiplier. They will have to try to provide a fairly precise measurement of its size.

Lastly, we may consider the usefulness of economic theory in helping in the formulation of economic policy. It might be thought that, since in the post-war period market conditions have often been abnormal with inflation persisting in most parts of the world in greater or smaller degree, price theory of the kind outlined in Part One would be useless. It is true that conditions since 1945 have been very different from those in the 1930s. The fact remains that ordinary price theory (suitably handled) can deal with all the main pricing problems, even in inflation.

(b) In macro-economic policy problems

Macro-economic theory is intended to handle other problems which arise in both unemployment and inflation. Since 1945 the problem of waste, in the sense of general unemployment, has been rather less important. For over a decade, employment was full, or more than full, in most countries. While unemployment has been greater in recent years, the level of activity in the world has still been much higher than in the inter-war period. At the same time, inflation is a continuing problem. But macro-economic theory is perfectly capable of analysing the problems of inflation. Indeed, its ability to handle both inflation and recession is its great strength. It may also be that the relatively high level of activity maintained in the post-war world has itself been partly the result of the fact that Keynes's own influence on practical affairs was so strong. Some (at least) of his theories have been put into practice as policy-makers have attempted to avoid the evils of excessive demand and inflation on the one hand and excessive deflation and unemployment on the other.

(c) In problems of growth

There is little criticism of the relevance of the theory of growth. It goes only too obviously to the root of current economic problems the world over. Those whose responsibility it is in any country to pursue rapid economic expansion while avoiding both inflation and unemployment, must note the analysis of balanced growth. For balanced growth is their aim. Even here there are problems. As we have seen, these include the problems of rapid population growth and pollution of the environment.

9. Some unsolved problems

Unfortunately, our knowledge of growth economics remains incomplete. Unlike the theories of price and employment, where most of the basic analytical issues are settled, the theory of growth is still undergoing quite radical changes. As policy-makers strive to improve the performance of the economy, so growth theorists strive to improve their explanations of how growth occurs and how it can be accelerated. We are here at the very frontiers of knowledge. This is not the realm of the textbook or the teacher, but that of the researcher. No one can tell how the theory of economic growth will develop in the next ten or twenty years. All one can say is that as each new theoretical development occurs the policy-maker will be watching anxiously to see what lessons he can learn from it. And it will be surprising if the problems of the environment—population growth and pollution—do not remain important.

10. Building one's own models

We have shown in this book that in order to analyse economic problems one must first build models of economic systems which approximate to reality, without being unnecessarily complicated. One must attempt to make general assumptions which lay bare the essentials of these systems. The models which we have used here are not necessarily those which are the most appropriate to any particular economic system. It is possible that our assumptions, even though they are widely used, do not apply to the real world of today. But this does not mean that a study of the models themselves is not sensible. What we have tried to do is to give readers a general picture of the way in which economic models can be constructed, and of the kinds of assumption which have to underlie them. The reader who has mastered the analysis of this book will have seen how such models can be constructed and handled. He will therefore be able to construct his own hypothetical economies for himself. He can then use his own models to solve the problems in which he is most interested, making those assumptions which in his view come closest to reality.

Readers who wish to continue their study of economic theory will find it helpful to read the books given on page 661.

Parts of some of them have already been recommended in reading lists to individual chapters.

Further reading

ALLEN, R. G. D.	*Mathematical Analysis for Economists*, London, 1938.
ALLEN, R. G. D.	*Mathematical Economics* (2nd edition, London, 1959.
DORFMAN, R., SAMUELSON, P. A. and SOLOW, R. M.	*Linear Programming and Economic Analysis*, New York, 1958.
DUESENBERRY, J. S.	*Income, Saving and the Theory of Consumer Behaviour*, Cambridge, Mass., 1949.
FELLNER, WILLIAM	*Competition among the Few*, New York, 1949.
FRIEDMAN, MILTON	*A Theory of the Consumption Function*, Princeton, N. J., 1957.
HANSEN, BENT	*A Study in the Theory of Inflation*, London, 1951.
HICKS, J. R.	*Value and Capital* (2nd edition), Oxford, 1946.
HICKS, J. R.	*A Contribution to the Theory of the Trade Cycle*, Oxford, 1950.
HICKS, J. R.	*Capital and Growth*, Oxford University Press, 1965.
JOHNSON, H. G.	*Essays in Monetary Economics*, London, George Allen and Unwin, 1967.
LANGE, OSCAR	*Price Flexibility and Employment*, Bloomington, Ind., 1944.
LERNER, A. P.	*The Economics of Control*, New York, 1946.
LUTZ, F. A. and HAGUE, D. C.	*The Theory of Capital*, London, 1961.
PATINKIN, DON	*Money, Interest and Prices*, Evanston, Ill., 1956.
ROBINSON, JOAN	*The Accumulation of Capital*, London, 1956.
SAMUELSON, P. A.	*The Foundations of Economic Analysis*, Cambridge, Mass., 1947.
SCHUMPETER, J. A.	*Capitalism, Socialism and Democracy* (3rd English edition), London, 1949.
SCHUMPETER, J. A.	*History of Economic Analysis*, London, 1954.
SCHUMPETER, J. A.	*The Theory of Economic Development*, New York, 1934.

Index